RECONSTRUCTING GENDER

RECONSTRUCTING GENDER
A Multicultural Anthology

Fourth Edition

Estelle Disch
University of Massachusetts Boston

Boston   Burr Ridge, IL   Dubuque, IA   Madison, WI   New York
San Francisco   St. Louis   Bangkok   Bogotá   Caracas   Kuala Lumpur
Lisbon   London   Madrid   Mexico City   Milan   Montreal   New Delhi
Santiago   Seoul   Singapore   Sydney   Taipei   Toronto

McGraw-Hill Higher Education $\&$

A Division of The **McGraw-Hill** Companies

RECONSTRUCTING GENDER: A MULTICULTURAL ANTHOLOGY
Published by McGraw-Hill, a business unit of The McGraw-Hill Companies, Inc., 1221 Avenue of the Americas, New York, NY, 10020. Copyright © 2006, 2003, 2000, 1997 by The McGraw-Hill Companies, Inc. All rights reserved. No part of this publication may be reproduced or distributed in any form or by any means, or stored in a database or retrieval system, without the prior written consent of The McGraw-Hill Companies, Inc., including, but not limited to, in any network or other electronic storage or transmission, or broadcast for distance learning. Some ancillaries, including electronic and print components, may not be available to customers outside the United States.

This book is printed on acid-free paper.

2 3 4 5 6 7 8 9 0 FGR/FGR 0 9 8 7 6

ISBN-13: 978-0-07-299742-2
ISBN-10: 0-07-299742-7

Publisher: *Phillip A. Butcher*
Sponsoring Editor: *Sherith H. Pankratz*
Senior Marketing Manager: *Daniel M. Loch*
Senior Project Manager: *Christina Thornton-Villagomez*
Associate Designer, Cover and Interior: *Marianna Kinigakis*
Senior Photo Research Coordinator: *Alexandra Ambrose*
Cover Credit: *Conversaciones* by Luz Inéz Mercier/Praxis International Art, Lima, Peru: praxis@chavin.rcp.net.pe
Senior Media Project Manager: *Nancy Garcia*
Senior Production Supervisor: *Carol A. Bielski*
Permissions Editor: *Frederick T. Courtright, The Permissions Company*
Compositor: *ElectraGraphics, Inc.*
Printer: *Quebecor World Fairfield Inc.*

Library of Congress Cataloging-in-Publication Data

Disch, Estelle
Reconstructing gender : a multicultural anthology / [edited by] Estelle Disch. —4th ed.
  p. cm.
Includes bibliographical references and index.
ISBN 0-07-299742-7 (softcover : acid-free paper)
1. Sex role. 2. Masculinity. 3. Femininity. 4. Women—Psychology. 5. Socialization. I. Disch, Estelle.

HQ1075.R43 2006
305.3—dc22

2005041597

The Internet addresses listed in the text were accurate at the time of publication. The inclusion of a Web site does not indicate an endorsement by the authors of McGraw-Hill, and McGraw-Hill does not guarantee the accuracy of the information presented at these sites.

www.mhhe.com

About the Editor

Estelle Disch is professor of sociology at the University of Massachusetts Boston where she has been active in curricular transformation, general education reform, and faculty development. She has written extensively on pedagogical issues in diverse classrooms. Her research focuses on the effects of sexual abuse by professionals and on assessing learning in university courses. She has served as a consultant and trainer related to creating more open and accepting campus climates and has run many workshops for professionals related to maintaining appropriate professional boundaries.

Contents

PART IV: COMMUNICATION   212

PART V: SEXUALITY   257

PART VI: FAMILIES   299

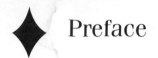 # Preface

About a decade ago in my undergraduate Sociology of Gender course,[1] I asked the class to sit in small groups and identify gender-related problems that each student was currently facing and that were not too personal to discuss in the class. I then asked the students to assess to what extent their problems were personal troubles, that is, specific to themselves as individuals, or public issues, reflective of wider issues in the social order and experienced by many people.[2] When the groups reported back, two men responded, "We were raised never to hit girls, and now with the women's movement, we want to know whether or not that's OK." Their question was serious, and the class exploded. Many women in the room became very upset and started yelling at the two men. (I later learned that at least a third of the women in the room had been raped.) I was caught off guard and realized that the course was not designed to effectively address the various issues embedded in the men's question. I did not have nearly enough material on men's socialization and behavior. I was particularly concerned about providing students with enough information to help them begin to make sense of the high rates of men's violence toward women and toward each other.

In my search for better materials about men's socialization, I found a growing literature in men's studies to accompany the already huge literature in women's studies and the sociology of gender. But my favorite articles were scattered in a wide range of sources. Although some excellent anthologies were available about and by women and men separately, no one volume available at that time and appropriate for use in a social science course gave substantial attention to both genders. Although the choice of texts has grown considerably since 1996, I have chosen to revise this one three times in order to keep it current. Thus, this book is designed to meet the needs of faculty who want to teach about both women and men from a multicultural perspective but who want to use one anthology instead of two. I define multicultural broadly to include the perspectives and experiences of a wide range of people within the context of power and inequality.

The creation of this book has been made possible by the explosion of work by and about people of color, people of various ethnicities, gay men, lesbians, bisexuals, transgendered people, people with disabilities, and working-class people. Most of the readings included here are ones that colleagues and I have used in classrooms with success. By success, I mean that many students have become engaged with the material in various ways: becoming excited or angered by the ideas expressed, talking with friends and family about the material, making sense of their own experience in relation to the authors' experiences, feeling excited to learn more about a particular issue, or becoming politically involved in response to what they are learning. I teach in a way that encourages interaction among students,[3] and I am particularly committed to using articles that stimulate discussion. I welcome readers' feedback about what works in classrooms and what doesn't.

This book also emerges, in part, from questions and concerns that I've experienced in my own life, especially my own experience growing up in a sexist, racist, anti-Semitic, white, economically privileged, Protestant family. With three older brothers and a sports-oriented father who was a physician, I often felt like I was immersed in a male club. This club demanded rigid gender conformity of my brothers. My least-athletic brother was brutally teased and called a sissy because of his lack of athletic ability, his pain while watching my father and my other brothers shoot ducks, his interest in music, his ability to cry, and his chubby body. I watched my father rage when my aunt bought that particular brother a pink shirt. My survival strategy in this system was to attempt to fit into the male club. By about age seven I had learned to shoot frogs with a .22 rifle, to clean fish, to brace myself against the pain I felt watching a duck thrash in the water after being shot, to enjoy watching baseball games (or to pretend that I did), and to be otherwise tough and strong.

I also learned about racist and anti-Semitic attitudes in my family. I can remember my grandmother expressing disapproval that my best friend was Jewish and my father telling me an anti-Semitic "joke" that I repeated to my best friend, who didn't find it funny. Unfortunately, we had no skills at age 10 or so to discuss what was wrong with the "joke." And I can remember my father complaining about the presence of Black baseball players, actors, and newscasters on TV—"That man's got a white man's job." Luckily, my mother provided a contrast to my father's views. She did not participate in his racist and anti-Semitic discussions, spoke freely about her poverty-stricken origins, and left me with the opportunity to question his values.

I am impressed to this day at the contradictions embedded in what my father expected of boys and men. On the one hand, he seemed at his happiest in the all-male hunting and fishing cultures in which he spent as much free time as he could. When these men went hunting, they slept in close quarters, spent days together in tiny gunning boats or hiding in duck blinds, cooked elaborate meals at the end of the day, and kept house—all with no women present. (I begged to go on these trips but was barred.) On the other hand, his homophobia was always there, levying disrespect at any boy or man who might be "too feminine," who might acknowledge his love for a man, or who might choose to make a life with men doing much of what my father, his friends, and my brothers did on hunting trips.

Another personal interest that informs my selections for this anthology is my knowledge about male violence and sexual abuse toward boys, girls, women, and men. I continue to be baffled at our inability to effectively prevent that abuse. I am not so much shocked by the facts (I have accepted them after years of awareness) but by the entrenched system of violence and domination that teaches new generations of people, especially men, how to be violent and oppressive. For 12 years, I worked with survivors of sexual abuse committed by health care and mental health care providers and clergy and have been struck by the fact that the vast majority of offenders—against both men and women—are men.[4] Although offenses of this type are brutally damaging when perpetrated by members of either gender, the overwhelming imbalance toward male perpetrators has led me to wonder what has caused so many of them to be so exploitative or violent. I am reminded of a very disturbing photo essay of men who had attended a residential religious school in which male clergy physically and sexually abused many of the boys.[5] One of the men shown tells of the abuse he suffered as a child and reports that when he learned that his younger brother was about to be put in the same school, he killed his brother to save him from the abuse. It appears that the only way he had learned to address brutal situations was to be brutal himself.

I am also informed here by 25 years of working collectively with others: 10 years working with white, mostly middle-class almost exclusively heterosexual women and men in alternative mental health centers; 10 years in a feminist therapy collective where a group of mixed-class white heterosexual women and lesbians learned to work closely together; and in working groups at the University of Massachusetts Boston, where faculty, students, and staff built a multicultural, broad-based coalition to win the passage of a diversity requirement for undergraduate students.[6] I have learned that diverse women and men can work together using decision-making processes in which conflict is discussed, compromises are negotiated, and leadership and rewards are shared. If people are committed to communicating and working together and working on their prejudices, then differences of gender, race, culture, class, sexual orientation, disability, and age can be addressed and dealt with in order to accomplish common goals.

I am also concerned in this anthology with the entrenchment of privilege. I have observed how much time and attention it has taken me to unravel my own prejudices and become aware of my privileges, and I wonder how we will ever construct a humane social order when it is so difficult for those with privilege to see how caught we are in its cushioned web. Even with an education that communicated democratic values, a mother who worked full time and talked extensively about growing up poor, an older brother who mentored me into liberal/radical views, and a feminist movement and support system that has especially supported my anti-racist and multicultural activism, I still find it difficult to stay fully conscious of some of the oppressive attitudes I have learned. Although I have analyzed enough of my socialization to feel fully capable of working on my attitudes and am able to openly apologize for any lingering insensitivities, I believe that I will be working on this for the rest of my life. I hope the readings that follow will help those with more privilege become clear about what that means for them, that those with less privilege will find inspiration for empowerment, and that both groups will find ways to work toward a more egalitarian social order—one in which all people will have an opportunity to work with others in shared ways, in which real community can evolve from positions of equal respect, and in which all people enjoy basic human rights free of poverty, violence, preventable illness, and discrimination.

I have chosen to include increasingly more material on international issues with each revision of this book, always centering on issues with a direct connection to the United States. The events of September 11, 2001 followed by the wars in Afghanistan and Iraq, led me to include essays aimed at helping readers understand some of the issues surrounding those events.

Many people have helped with this book. Serina Beauparlant, my former editor at Mayfield Publishing, approached this project with enthusiasm and support throughout its birth and development and saw the book through two editions. My editors at McGraw-Hill—Sally Constable, Jill Gordon, and Sherith Pankratz—energetically embraced the third and fourth editions and moved the projects to completion. Becky Thompson (Simmons College) convinced me that I should do the book in the first place and has provided ongoing support, feedback, and creative suggestions for all four editions. Our ongoing discussions about racism and teaching over the years have contributed to my thinking in many ways. Reviewers were also very helpful as I grappled with major changes in this edition:

Kathleen R. Martin, Florida International University

Sara L. Spurgeon, University of Arizona

Robert B. Jenkot, Southern Illinois University

Vivyan C. Adair, Hamilton College

Jan AbuShakrah, Portland Community College

Janine Minkler, Northern Arizona University

Heather Dillaway, Wayne State University

Don Sabo, D'Youville College

Other friends, family, colleagues, and students provided direct or indirect support for this edition, such as suggestions for readings or helpful conversations. They include: Pat Aron, Elsa Auerbach, Larry Blum, Peggy Barett, Chris Bobel, Caroline Brown, Jorge Capetillo-Ponce, Connie Chan, Robert Disch, Linda Dittmar, Cynthia Enloe, Susan Gore, Jean Hardisty,

Kathleen Kelley, Esther Kingston-Mann, Winston Langley, Elaine Morse, Siamak Movahedi, Emmett Schaefer, Russell Schutt, Tim Sieber, Mariamne Whatley, Nancy Worcester, Raul Ybarra, and Vivian Zamel. Allan Enario provided essential office assistance. The production staff at McGraw-Hill—Christina Thornton-Villagomez, Project Manager—kept the project moving smoothly and on schedule. My compañera and intellectual colleague Rita Arditti talked with me extensively about all four editions of the book as they evolved, helped me to clarify my thoughts, suggested many new articles and references for me to consider, and lent me numerous books from her library on feminist and multicultural studies. Finally, thanks go to my best teachers—the terrific students at the University of Massachusetts Boston, who frequently challenge and always engage me.

Supplements

Instructor's Manual/Test Bank

For each reading and part introduction, there are multiple choice, true/false, and short answer/essay questions. There are also questions for classroom discussion, journal reading, and take home exams.

Race/Class/Gender/Sexuality SuperSite

This companion Web site provides information about the book, including an overview, summaries of key features and what's new in the fourth edition, information about the authors, and Practice Test Questions.

Non-text-specific content on this site includes an annotated list of Web links to useful sites; a list of professional resources (e.g., professional journals); links to Web sites offering Census 2000 information; a glossary; flashcards; and a comprehensive list (annotated and listed by category) of films and videos in the areas of race, class, gender, ethnicity, and sexuality.

Visit the SuperSite by going to www.mhhe.com/raceclassgender.

NOTES

1. This was a course at the University of Massachusetts Boston, a public urban university with about 12,000 students, all of whom commute.
2. The class had read an excerpt from C. Wright Mills, *The Sociological Imagination* (New York: Oxford University Press, 1959), in which Mills discusses personal troubles and public issues.
3. This teaching method is described in Estelle Disch, "Encouraging Participation in the Classroom," in Sara Davis et al., eds., *Coming Into Her Own: Educational Success for Girls and Women* (Jossey-Bass, 1999); Becky Thompson and Estelle Disch, "Feminist, Anti-Racist, Anti-Oppression Teaching: Two White Women's Experience," *Radical Teacher* 41 (Spring 1992), pp. 4–10.
4. In a study of survivors of sexual professional abuse, in which I am the principal investigator, 88 percent of the women and 94 percent of the men were abused by men.

5. Photo essay by E. Jan Mundy, "Wounded Boys, Courageous Men," displayed at the Linkup Conference, Chicago, September 1–4, 1995.

6. I have documented this work in an essay entitled, "The Politics of Curricular Change: Establishing a Diversity Requirement at the University of Massachusetts at Boston," in Becky W. Thompson and Sangeeta Tyagi, eds., *Beyond a Dream Deferred: Multicultural Education and the Politics of Excellence* (Minneapolis: University of Minnesota Press, 1993), pp. 195–213.

General Introduction

. . . the system of patriarchy . . . seems to have nearly run its course — it no longer serves the needs of men or women and in its inextricable linkage to militarism, hierarchy, and racism it threatens the very existence of life on earth.

GERDA LERNER[1]

As a Black lesbian feminist comfortable with the many different ingredients of my identity, and a woman committed to racial and sexual freedom from oppression, I find I am constantly being encouraged to pluck out some one aspect of myself and present this as a meaningful whole, eclipsing or denying the other parts of self. But this is a destructive and fragmenting way to live.

AUDRE LORDE[2]

No one is simply a man or a woman. Each of us embodies intersecting statuses and identities, empowered and disempowered, including physical and demographic traits, chosen and unchosen. In any discussion of gender, serious students of the social order need to be prepared to ask, Which men? Which women? If students of gender studies choose to be conscious of the complexity of human life, much of the literature on human nature and gender needs to be read carefully, and any generalizations made with extreme caution. Sometimes findings about men are generalized to describe people in general. Sometimes data from racially mixed populations are combined and analyzed as a whole, leaving out the details and differences between groups. And sometimes when there are only small numbers of, say, women or people of color in a study, those respondents are excluded from analysis for lack of a large enough group. In any of these cases, the voices of the few are obscured by those of the many. Unless we focus on the few alongside the many, we not only lose the voices of the few, but we also lose any meaningful understanding of the relationship between the few and the many, particularly in terms of power, privilege, disempowerment, and empowerment. The readings in this book invite you to hear the perspectives of many women and men whose voices have been ignored, marginalized, or silenced in the past.

This collection of readings focuses on power, addressing the conditions under which the gender system intersects with other factors to create various kinds of power and powerlessness. The readings also address how people empower themselves, both personally and collectively. This book is grounded in several important intellectual perspectives that support the acquisition of inclusive knowledge as a prerequisite to empowerment. These perspectives are based on the assumption that we need to understand the complexity of human experience in order to develop effective strategies for humane, inclusive social change.

1

Gender in Historical Perspective— Using a Sociological Imagination

An important sociological knowledge seeker, C. Wright Mills, argued in 1959 that it is possible to understand human lives only if we can understand the connections between those lives and the social and historical contexts in which they are lived. He further argued that people need to understand the sources of their problems in order to fully understand why their lives are difficult. Thus, he encouraged people to distinguish between problems that affect only themselves and perhaps a few others from those problems experienced by large numbers of people and that have their cause in social structures beyond particular individuals or families. He referred to the former as "personal troubles" and to the latter as "public issues." He urged people to develop a "sociological imagination" so that they could place themselves in social context and identify how public issues affect them at the personal level, arguing that people need to know the source of their difficulties in order to make sense of their lives.[3] Understanding the source of one's difficulties opens the possibility of shifting the blame off of oneself and onto the social order, when appropriate. It also opens the possibility of working with others to change aspects of the social order that create difficulties for many individuals. Thus, our mental health and our effective resistance to social structures that we find oppressive depend upon our possession of a sociological imagination.

The second wave of the feminist movement in the United States, which started in the mid-1960s, incorporated a sociological imagination when it adopted the phrase "the personal is political." Arguing that larger political realities were felt at the personal level, women were encouraged to look beyond themselves for the sources of their problems in order to feel less alone and less to blame for the difficulties they faced. Analysis of the real sources of problems allowed women both to understand their personal situations better and to devise individual and collective means of resistance. In many situations, women have used the link between the political and the personal to help each other understand sexism as it is played out in the political structure, the community, the workplace, schools, families, and bedrooms. In response to this awareness, women have established a national network of services for women such as shelters for battered women, rape crisis centers, and health centers, and have worked for legal changes to help end discrimination on the basis of sex or gender.[4]

A sociological imagination is essential for helping us to understand both ongoing realities—such as gender discrimination—and events such as the attacks on the World Trade Center and the Pentagon on September 11, 2001 and the subsequent U.S.-initiated wars in Afghanistan and Iraq. Without an understanding of the historical context, the September 11 attacks might be comprehensible only in terms of individual psychopathology. A look at other factors, however, offers both plausible explanations and suggestions for how future attacks might be rendered less likely. The history of U.S. policy toward Saudi Arabia, the Gulf War, the Israeli-Palestinian conflict, religious fundamentalism, and recent history in Afghanistan all help to set the stage for making sense of the attacks and their gendered nature. People caught up in these events or their aftermaths are finding their personal lives deeply affected. Apart from the horrendous grief and turmoil in families who lost loved ones in the September 11 attacks and the wars that followed, the personal implications are wide ranging. Consider, for example, the effects of the U.S. counterattack on the people of Afghanistan, most of whom had nothing to do with the conflict but were caught in the cross fire, often forced to flee for their lives. Consider women in Afghanistan, free of Taliban rule but now living under a government controlled by a regime that has its own record of violence. Consider U.S. soldiers mobilized for war, pulled out of school or careers and away from their loved ones in response to government mandates, possibly coming home disabled or dead. Consider the partners of the men and women called to combat, worrying about their loved ones and coping at home without the support of their partners. Consider Arab American men, targeted now for racial profiling because men from Arab countries perpetrated the attacks on September 11. Consider innocent dark-skinned men from any cultural group, ordered off of planes because they "look Arabic." Consider men detained under the new anti-terrorism legislation without the ordinary due process of law that U.S. citizens and residents have come to expect. Consider a U.S. citizen who criticizes the U.S. government's response to September 11 and finds his or her job threatened because of the criticism. Consider the rise in Christian white supremacist hate group activity following September 11. Or consider the costs to social programs when a huge proportion for the federal budget is spent on war.

A sociological imagination helps us see that the personal problems that evolve from the events of September 11 are by no means personal troubles in Mills's use of that term. They are public issues, shared by many others, reflective of realities that go way beyond individual motivation or control, and that stretch, in fact, into the highly complex realms of international trade, foreign policy, the quest for oil, and religious values; these problems cannot be addressed by individuals alone. Some of the readings in this book will attempt to put September 11 and the current war in Iraq in perspective. A major goal of this book generally is to help readers explore many of the social realities and events that surround and explain individual experiences.

The material in this book was written primarily in the United States in the late twentieth and early twenty-first centuries, a period in which many gender-related trends and events were occurring. This period of history has seen growing scholarship and activism among women, especially women of color. This period of history also saw conflict among white women, including writings and activism by those who object to feminism and by those who critique what mainstream feminism has stood for.[5] This time in history also saw an increase in research and writing by pro-feminist men, especially those working for changes in men's usual roles, often working for a cessation of violence against women.[6] During this period, other groups of men also became increasingly public about their various disenchantments with either their own roles or those of women. A men's rights movement emerged to protest the kinds of power its members perceived women to have. A Christian men's movement emerged calling for men to take back the power they had lost as women began to develop more public power. A "mythopoetic" men's movement began to hold men-only retreats at which primarily white, middle-class men attempted to contact their "essential masculinity." The Million Man March in 1995 provided an empowering experience for many Black men, highlighted some of the tensions and conflicts over men's roles and responsibilities in the Black community, and elicited a range of responses from Black women and men.[7]

Increased attention to the situations of boys emerged in the 1990s, matching to some extent the attention to girls that had been going on since the 1980s. Some authors attended to boys in general, looking at everyday violence and school failure, calling for more careful attention to boys' emotional and educational needs.[8] Others addressed the needs of boys in urban contexts, considering the impact of poverty and racism.[9] Others decried the lack of attention to boys in the context of criticizing the feminist-driven attention to girls.[10]

A series of school shootings, such as the one at Columbine High School in Littleton, Colorado, brought particular attention to the potential for violence of seemingly normal white, middle-class boys.[11] Sociologist Michael Kimmel, critical of the media discussion of "youth violence," emphasized that what had occurred was male, rather than youth, violence, encouraging a discussion of masculinity: "In a way, Eric Harris and Dylan Klebold weren't deviants, but over-conformists to norms of masculinity that prescribe violence as a solution. Like real men, they didn't just get mad, they got even."[12] Standard masculinity, many authors argue, can be detrimental. Embedded in the attention to boys is a concern by some authors that expected standards of behavior do not fit boys and men and that we might, in fact, be attempting to impose on males the standards of expression of feeling, open communication, and "good behavior" that are more likely to be found in girls and women.[13] The lesson from this is that boys as well as girls need serious attention, within the various contexts in which they attempt to live satisfying lives.

The nineties also brought increased attention to men, particularly white men who felt left out of major trends in the wider society. Some felt left out of the economic boom in the nineties; others felt alienated by the increase in attention to women; some felt troubled by the increasing diversification of U.S. society; and some continue to feel troubled by one or more of these.[14]

Another trend that characterizes this time in history is growing public awareness of transgender issues. Media and scholarly attention to this issue has grown substantially in the nine years since I assembled the first edition of this book. The literature includes writings by scholars documenting third and fourth genders in Native American and other cultures[15] as well as writings by people interested in stretching gender boundaries and challenging the two-gender system as it is currently constructed in mainstream U.S. culture.[16] Leslie Feinberg, a central spokesperson for what she calls "Trans liberation," describes the participants in this movement:

> We are masculine females and feminine males, cross-dressers, transsexual men and women, intersexuals born on the anatomical sweep between female and male, gender blenders, many other sex and gender-variant people, and our significant others. All told, we expand understanding of how many ways there are to be a human being.[17]

The Utne Reader brought attention to this issue on a recent cover: "It's 2 AM. Do you know what sex you are? Does Anybody?" Even Cosmopolitan ran a story in November 1998 entitled "The man I married was really a woman."[18] The editors of Utne Reader summed up the issue this way:

> Queer theorists call gender a social construct, saying that when we engage in traditional behaviors and sexual practices, we are nothing but actors playing ancient, empty roles. Others suggest that gender is performance, a collection of masks we can take on and off at will. So are we witnessing the birth of thrilling new freedoms, or the disintegration of values and behaviors that bind us together? Will we encounter new opportunities for self-realization, or hopeless confusion? Whatever the answers, agreeing that our destinies aren't preordained will launch a search that will profoundly affect society, and will eventually engage us all. (p. 45)

In an unusual twist, a same-gendered couple in Texas was allowed to marry because one of them was transgendered and was genetically male.[19] How transgender issues will intersect with other issues of oppression is yet to be defined, although Leslie Feinberg is deeply committed to seeing Trans liberation in the context of other social justice struggles and is herself actively engaged in social justice struggles for all oppressed people.

The writings in this book have also emerged in a virulent political era in which attacks on feminists, people of color, poor people, Jewish people, and gay men, lesbians, and transgendered people have been and continue to be common. The hate murders of James Earl Byrd, Jr., a Black man in Texas, and Matthew Shepard, a gay man in Wyoming, are recent examples.[20] Even more recently, Sakia Gunn, a 15-year-old lesbian in Newark, New Jersey, was stabbed to death in May 2003 after telling her assailant that she was a lesbian. In October 2002, Gwen Araujo, a transgendered 17-year-old, was beaten and strangled to death by a group of men. Fred Martinez, a two-spirit Native American teen was murdered in 2001 in Colorado. In 2002, two black transgendered girls, Ukea Davis and Stephanie Thomas, were shot in Washington,

D.C. And in 2003, Nikki Nicholas, a black trans teen was beaten and shot near Detroit. The National Coalition of Anti-Violence Programs reports a 16 percent increase in violence against black queers in 2003.[21] Hate-crime figures for 2003 were about the same as they were for 2002. They reflected particular targeting based on race (52%), especially of blacks. Hate crimes based on religion and sexual orientation each accounted for 16 percent of the total 7,489 incidents.[22] Reports of bias against Muslims are up since September 11, 2001, in a context laden with fear and hostility.[23] Issues of affirmative action remain on the table as universities struggle with how to legally address the need for a diverse student body. Assaults on people with disabilities, including sexual assaults on over 75 percent of mentally disabled women according to some studies, continue seemingly unchecked.[24] Also on the disability front, the Supreme Court struck a serious blow to the 1990 Americans with Disabilities Act in February 2001 by supporting a state's right to not provide reasonable accommodations in a case in Alabama in which a man with asthma was not assured a smoke-free environment and a woman with breast cancer was demoted.[25]

This period of history has also been characterized by an increase in poverty in the United States. Changes in welfare policy in 1996 created major challenges for poor women.[26] Wealth is increasingly concentrating in the hands of a small number of individuals[27] while many families struggle to pay their essential bills, often causing adults to work more than one job. (See Rubin, Part VI and Hays, Part VIII for more information about poverty and families.)

Another recent trend that sets the stage for an analysis of gender is increased awareness of globalization. Major shifts in the world's economy that favor industrialized nations over developing ones have provoked international protests against the World Trade Organization, the World Bank, the G-8 nations (the world's most economically powerful countries), and the International Monetary Fund. Growing awareness of structural adjustment policies that increasingly impoverish developing nations has provoked these protests, such as those in Seattle, Montreal, and Genoa, as people (many of them young) attempt to right the wrongs they see occurring. As U.S. corporations establish factories overseas in order to take advantage of inexpensive labor, women have begun to organize for better wages and working conditions (see Enloe, Part VIII). Understanding of the workings of Mexican border factories (maquiladoras) where the products of U.S. corporations are assembled or built, primarily by women, has provoked outrage due to the poor working conditions and sweatshop wages. And sweatshop conditions within the United States persist, in part because workers are afraid that corporations will move the factories to other countries if they fight too hard for better wages or working conditions.[28]

Increased attention to human rights is another trend that characterizes the current era. A world-wide movement is attempting to bring a human rights perspective into people's everyday consciousness. Rights to such essential things as food, shelter, education, health care, and physical safety are frequently ignored in many places in both the United States and the rest of the world. The recruitment of children — primarily boys — into militias is a major breach of children's rights. The use of child labor and the selling of children into slavery are gaining worldwide attention.[29] An effort to demonstrate the link between women's rights and human rights is happening in many countries. The United Nations' Convention on the Elimination of All Forms of Discrimination Against Women (CEDAW), accepted by 179 countries, serves as a basis for examining women's rights as human rights. Efforts to establish CEDAW at the local level in the United States are under way since the United States as a country has not signed CEDAW (see Arditti, Part XI). An early definition of feminism in the contemporary women's movement connects to this issue: feminism is the radical notion that women are human. There remains a lot of work to do to convince both women and men of this fact.

Since George W. Bush took office in 2001, several major issues have emerged against the backdrop of what I have just described. These include the war against terrorism in Afghanistan, Iraq, and the United States; the eroding of women's reproductive rights; the backlash against same-sex marriage; and the merging of church and state. All of these have deep implications for the gendered aspects of people's lives.

The aftermath of September 11, 2001 has drawn thousands of U.S. citizens, primarily men who are disproportionately poor and working class, into combat or preparation for combat. At home, the Patriot Act and its accompanying subversion of civil liberties has primarily affected dark-skinned men and women who wear head scarves. Racial profiling, a long-standing problem in law enforcement that has been subject to periodic reviews, has attracted much recent attention.[30] A spokesperson for Amnesty International concluded that "Racial profiling is to the 21st century what Jim Crow laws were to the last, turning entire groups of people into second-class citizens and denying them the rights to which we are all due.[31] Accompanying the war in Iraq and other terrorism battles are the costs of these efforts — both direct costs in terms of dollars and indirect costs in terms of potential negative effects, often called "blowback." The direct costs have increased the federal deficit to record levels, leaving less money available for public services such as education, affordable housing, and health care. The attacks on September 11 were one example of blowback — retaliation for the United States policy in the Middle East. Time will tell what else is in store for the United States as we forge ahead without a lot of international support in the seemingly interminable war in Iraq, and against terrorism more generally.

Related to any discussion of the war on terrorism is our understanding of what security means. National security — the attempt to protect the United States from future attacks — needs to be distinguished from human security — protection of the human individual from breaches of their human rights. Human rights activist Charlotte Bunche argues ". . . it is imperative to maintain focus on human rights as a crucial component of human security." She emphasizes that the right to bodily integrity, reproductive rights, and freedom from violence are essential components of security for women.[32]

Women's reproductive rights have been under attack since President Bush took office. A bill banning so-called partial birth abortion was passed by Congress and signed by President Bush. Although lower courts have found the law unacceptably vague and have thrown it out, Michigan has passed its own version of the law.[33] Its constitutionality is likely to be decided by the Supreme Court. Related to the Supreme Court, the politics of future appointees is on many people's minds, since President Bush has already nominated anti-choice judges in lower courts.[34] President Bush also imposed the "Global Gag Rule," blocking funds to the United Nations Population Fund because the money might possibly go to clinics that make referrals for abortions. An effect of his decision has been a worldwide cutback of health services to women and children. In response to policies like these, in April 2004 more than a million people, representing a broad coalition of groups, gathered in Washington D.C. in support of reproductive rights in what was most likely the largest women's rights demonstration in history.

There is substantial backlash to efforts to institute gay marriage in the United States, as evidenced by voters' rejection of same-sex marriage by large margins on referendums in 11 states in the 2004 election. In fact, the high turnout of those opposed to gay marriage may have helped President Bush win the election.[35] Resistance to same-sex marriage is part of the larger issue of the relationship between church and state. The idea of civil rights for same-sex couples conflicts with the religious "sanctity" of marriage in many peoples' minds, leading some advocates of same-sex rights to advocate for the establishment of civil unions for *all* couples while eliminating civil marriage and leaving marriage to religious institutions. That option would provide legal equality for all committed couples without requiring marriage of anyone, although the likelihood of doing this is not high, given the general blurring of the boundaries between church and state under President Bush.

Although a majority of people in the United States object to allowing same-sex couples to marry, rejecting the 2003 decision of the Massachusetts Supreme Court in favor of same-sex marriage, a majority supports some sort of legal recognition such as civil unions.[36] Marriage has been legalized in several countries (The Netherlands, Belgium, and Canada), and legal arrangements that provide some of marriage's benefits are available in many others. (See an essay by E. J. Graff in Part VI for more details about this). Here in the United States, Vermont approved civil unions in 2000 and Connecticut did so in 2005. Lesbian and gay parents in the United States who want to co-adopt each other's children may do so in many states. The American Academy of Pediatrics has recommended legalizing same-sex adoption, arguing that children ". . . deserve the security of two legally recognized parents."[37] Various court rulings have acknowledged the legitimacy of same-sex couples related to child support, visitation, etc.[38]

The struggle for lesbian, gay, bisexual, and transgender rights exists in a complex social and political climate. Even President George W. Bush and former Secretary of State Colin Powell have been accused of being too pro-gay because of allowing gay men to serve the current administration in various ways.[39] Following the Supreme Court's support in June 2000 of the Boy Scouts' policy of barring gays as scout leaders and members, objection to the policy began to grow not only in the ranks of scout members and leaders (with membership reportedly down 4.5 percent in 2001), but also in the institutions in which scouts tend to recruit new members—in schools and other public settings—making recruitment more difficult. A Boston-area Boy Scout council voted to adopt a "don't ask, don't tell" policy so that gay leaders and members could remain in the Scouts without technically breaching the national ban on gays.[40] The National Education Association recently adopted a plan to make schools more respectful, and hopefully safer, for lesbian, gay, bisexual, and transgendered students and school employees.[41] And in Japan, a youth center was found guilty of discrimination when it banned a gay youth group from using the center. The discrimination occurred in 1990, and the Tokyo High Court handed down its decision seven and a half years later.[42]

Resistance to same-sex marriage is part of the larger issue of the relationship between church and state. Other church-state issues that are currently being debated are abortion rights as mentioned above and federally funded faith-based initiatives. The latter become especially controversial when, based on religious principles, institutions receiving federal funds are allowed to discriminate in hiring, violating various anti-discrimination laws. The debate about the separation of church and state takes place in a wider context as well, as we watch France grapple with the fallout of its policy to not allow children to wear head coverings or other ostensible religious symbols in public schools.[43] Although Muslim women interviewed in France have wide ranging attitudes about headscarves, the public association of headscarves with fundamentalists has overshadowed their voices.[44]

These changes are occurring in a context in which it appears to some observers that many people in the United States are increasingly less likely to engage with each other in mutually supportive ways, leading to what sociologist Robert Putnam calls a decline in "social capital," which in turn seems to lead to less safety, declining health, and less civic engagement.[45] Writers and activists, however, continue to promote and to engage in progressive social change. A large and growing anti-war movement objects to the wars in Iraq and Afghanistan. Young feminists have established magazines to address girls' and young women's needs. *Teen Voices, New Moon* (for girls 8 to 14), *Bitch, Bust,* and *Fabula* join an array of books by "third wave" feminists.[46] Membership in the Third Wave Foundation stood at about 5,000 members in 2004.[47] How all this activism will evolve is unpredictable, but I am heartened by this clarity of thought and continuing struggle for justice in an era of war, racial profiling, hate crimes, backlash, and economic conservatism. People committed to democracy and pluralism will especially need the knowledge that inclusive scholarship provides, both now and in the future, as people formerly silenced make themselves heard and suffer the anger and violence of those who would prefer them to be invisible or at least silent. For example, as the U.S. population became more multicultural and less white, white supremacist and militia activity increased. As gay, lesbian, bisexual, and transgendered people have increasingly refused to be labeled and closeted, more resistance to freedom of sexual and affectional expression has been mounted. Continued resistance to the same-sex marriage movement in spite of small gains provides a powerful example. And as the wealth in the United States has been moving increasingly into the hands of a small proportion of very rich people, poor women and children, especially those on public assistance (or removed from public assistance because of time limits imposed by the new Temporary Aid to Needy Families program), continue to suffer. Even though the cost of the now-defunct AFDC (Aid to Families with Dependent Children) constituted less than 1 percent of the federal budget, welfare under the Clinton presidency was treated as if it were a major cause of the national deficit, and few voices were calling for a more family-friendly policy.[48]

Dissident Voices

Hearing from a wide range of men and women across many disciplines is crucial to an effective understanding of what is going on about gender. Sociology; women's studies; men's studies; African American studies; Asian American studies; Latin American studies; Native American studies; gay, lesbian, bisexual, transgender, and queer studies; disability studies; studies of aging; and American studies have welcomed the voices and experiences of previously silenced people into scholarly discourse. The expansion of work by people in these fields has provided a rich, exciting base of new information that continues to grow. This book includes research, essays, and autobiographical material from this literature.[49]

By including men's studies in this book, I do not mean to imply that the situations of men are equivalent to those of women. Although women are almost all oppressed in one way or another by some men and by patriarchal structures, the reverse is not true. Thus, while men might suffer from detrimental aspects of male socialization such as participation in war, premature death, increased exposure to violence, and higher rates of suicide, it is generally not women who control the outcome of men's lives. Male-dominated institutions and individual powerful men control both women and less-empowered men. And powerful men reap great benefits from our male-dominant structure even if they do tend to die younger than women and suffer other difficulties related to being male.

Many of the writers in men's studies are dissatisfied with male-dominated society, having personally experienced the painful aspects of male socialization. This perspective puts these writers in a good position to analyze masculinities from within. Their voices are dissident within the ranks of powerful men, and many would not be particularly welcome in boardrooms, locker rooms, or faculty meetings. They are outsiders as they critique the bastions of hegemonic masculinity — the dominant, white, heterosexual, patriarchal, privileged masculinity that still controls many aspects of people's lives. Hegemonic masculinity, which promotes the tough, take-charge, don't-feel image of men, frequently dominates the socialization process in spite of increasing efforts to develop other masculinities and femininities.[50] The writers referred to earlier who are concerned with the fate of boys are particularly attuned to the damage that hegemonic masculinity can do.

An examination of masculinity in male-dominated society is a crucial aspect of both women's studies and men's studies, especially if we try to understand how to work toward a social order in which there is less violence. A look at the literature on men violently abused as children, for example, suggests that about a third of them grow up to violently abuse others.[51] An understanding of adult male abusers leads us to examine how children are socialized and helps us to understand the process by which many baby boys grow into violent or controlling men. Another perspective suggests that circumstances at any point in life can contribute to violent responses, lending support to the sociological perspective that propensity to violence is socialized rather than inherent (e.g., citizens become soldiers when a country is involved in war, as is currently the case in the United States). Many of the men included in this book critique the gender system and are committed to working to end a social system that teaches men to be violent and that leaves boys and men frequently victimized and revictimized by other violent men.

It is useful here to mention some potential conflicts between women's studies and men's studies. One basic question concerns the extent to which men can effectively criticize a system in which they have experienced various amounts of privilege. Another question is the issue of crossover — can men effectively study women or women effectively study men?[52] The study of women by men raises the larger question of whether it is possible for someone from a more-empowered group to study, effectively understand, and analyze the experiences of people from a less-empowered group. Certainly there is a long history of "scholarship" by men distorting or ignoring the lives of women and by white people distorting or ignoring the lives of people of color. A third area of conflict is the use of the term "feminist" when applied to men. Both sides of this question have passionate proponents, including those who claim that the term "feminist man" is an inherent contradiction and others who claim that it isn't.[53] Finally, limited resources in academia are an issue. The development of gender studies and men's studies poses a potential threat to women's studies on some campuses, just as multicultural studies can pose a threat to Black or Africana studies in some situations. These threats include both possible cutbacks in resources and the potential of these programs being placed in a larger structure controlled by someone from another discipline. Philosopher and Men's Studies professor

Harry Brod concludes that the men's studies field is a necessary addition to academe but that resources for the development of this relatively new field should not come from women's studies.[54]

Intersecting Identities

Another recent effort at truth seeking is the attention now paid to the complex combination of identities held by each individual.[55] The readings included here address the concerns of Patricia Hill Collins, Audre Lorde, Gloria Anzaldúa, James Baldwin, W. E. B. Du Bois, Suzanne Pharr, and others who ask us to acknowledge such complexities. Sociologist W. E. B. Du Bois, writing in 1903, called for awareness of what he named the "double-consciousness" of African Americans—the awareness that they can't simply be Americans, working toward whatever goals they might have; rather, they are simultaneously forced to deal with racism, seeing themselves through the eyes of hateful others. Thus, Du Bois says, African American men and women can never experience themselves as simply men or women because they are constantly hated or pitied.[56]

The importance of acknowledging multiple aspects of identity is also powerfully stated by Patricia Hill Collins, who addresses the complex combination of oppression and privilege held by each individual. She argues that individuals can simultaneously be members of both privileged and oppressed groups, citing the example of white women who are "penalized by their gender but privileged by their race."[57] Collins also argues that there is a matrix of domination, compelling us to look at the intersecting aspects of oppression in individuals and groups. She names race, class, and gender as the three axes of oppression that typically characterize Black women's experiences, and she lists other axes of oppression as well that may or may not affect particular individuals such as sexual orientation, religion, and age. Collins further argues that domination occurs at several levels including personal biography, group-community interaction, and social institutions.[58] The readings in this volume have been chosen to reflect experience in and analysis of oppression, privilege, or both at all three levels, as well as reflecting people's empowerment struggles at these various levels.

Naming and Owning Privilege

This book is also grounded in the tradition of scholars and activists who struggle to bring privilege into focus.[59] In her well-known essay on white privilege, women's studies scholar Peggy McIntosh names her professional white privilege and heterosexual privilege and discusses how difficult it was to hold onto her awareness of her privileges as she worked on the essay; ideas about how she was privileged kept slipping away unless she wrote them down.[60] Sociologist Michael S. Kimmel tells about his difficulty in naming and owning his race and gender. Before attending a seminar on feminist theory in which race and gender were discussed, when he looked in the mirror, Kimmel saw "... a human being ... universally generalizable ... the generic person." As a middle-class, white man, he had difficulty identifying how gender and race had affected his experience.[61] Anti-violence and anti-racist activist Paul Kivel, in a recent guide for white people who want to work for racial justice, provides a "white benefits checklist" that addresses the intersections of class and race. He also provides a checklist of the "costs of racism for white people."[62]

Similar to the matrix of domination argued for by Patricia Hill Collins, we might also conceive of a matrix of privilege. Assuming that most people and groups possess some degree of privilege, however limited, we can frequently examine oppression and privilege together. We can identify where privilege lies and analyze how it smoothes the way for those who possess it and simultaneously makes life more difficult for those who don't. The issue here, however, is not simply to identify privilege. Rather, as the late writer Audre Lorde said, we should make it available for wider use. Thus, a white person who opposes racism might use his or her contacts with groups of white people as opportunities to educate them about racism. A man who opposes sexism might use his contacts with other men to educate them about sexism.

Privilege is a difficult concept for many of those who have it because it is frequently unnamed in wider U.S. society. In a social order whose mainstream values include individual achievement and competition, many people with privilege are supported to assume that they deserve the "luck" or "normalcy" they experience, whereas those who lack privilege are encouraged to blame themselves.[63] Thus, an able-bodied person might experience the ability to walk up a flight of stairs as simply a normal thing to do, rather than seeing the expectation that all people walk as part of a system that treats stair climbing as normal and thus fails to build ramps for those on wheels. A white person might assume that white is "normal," might feel lucky to be white, and might fail to see that the alleged superiority of whiteness is a piece of a racist system that keeps people of color from moving freely in the social order. A person born wealthy is likely to be taught that he or she deserves the wealth rather than to be taught how wealth is related to poverty in U.S. society. Although people with less privilege are usually astute analysts of how privilege works, those who enjoy it are frequently less conscious of its impact.[64] Thus, a challenge for progressive people with privilege, especially for those with substantial privilege, is to become aware of the nuances of privilege and to learn how to use it in ways that raise consciousness about oppression and promote fairness.

Another possibility for those with privilege is to identify some of the liabilities that accompany privilege and to use that awareness to work toward changing the system. For example, many white professional men lead highly stressful, dissatisfying lives with restricted access to their feelings and a limited capacity for intimacy. Writer Mark Gerzon, a white professional man, convincingly criticizes the roles and role models available to men like himself and calls for new roles to replace them. After describing what he believes are archetypal roles for men, he asks men to reject these roles in exchange for more democratic and humane ones. Instead of frontiersmen, he wants men to be healers—of both people and the earth; instead of breadwinners, men should be companions; instead of soldiers, mediators; instead of experts, colleagues; and instead of lords, nurturers. Gerzon's work emerged from his dissatisfaction with being male in spite of his race and class privilege.[65]

A denial of privilege can greatly limit our understanding of how our worlds work and how losing that privilege might affect us. White people who are not conscious of their white privilege, or who simply accept the system around them without question, spend their lives in what I think of as powerful denial—knowing at some unconscious level that they do not deserve and did not earn the skin-color privilege they enjoy, yet pretending at some level that they deserve it. Many temporarily able-bodied people are thrown into deep shock when they become disabled because they have structured their lives in ways that avoided people with disabilities and that allowed them to pretend that disability would never affect them. They therefore have no framework in which to combine personhood and disability and have suddenly become something that they have previously despised. I have heard many of my students, especially male students, say that they'd rather be dead than physically disabled.

The Reconstruction of Knowledge

Based on the kinds of truth telling identified thus far—the importance of a sociological imagination and the need to hear marginalized voices, acknowledge intersecting identities, and name privilege—numerous scholars have called for the reconstruction of knowledge.[66] Philosopher Elizabeth Minnich, for example, argues convincingly that four basic errors in knowledge need to be corrected as we move toward more inclusive knowing.[67] The first error is overgeneralization based on information gathered from small sectors of the population throughout history—primarily empowered male writers and the people they chose to acknowledge in their writing. Philosopher Harry Brod argues assertively that the study of men as men, in all the nuances of their experiences with masculinity, is crucial to the study of human beings. He asserts that to generalize from male experience to human experience not only distorts what human experience is, but also distorts what is specifically male.[68] Historian Gerda Lerner calls for a restructuring of thought and for an analysis that acknowledges that half the people in the world are women. She argues that all generalizations about human beings need to acknowledge this fact.[69] The selections in this book should help readers challenge inaccurate generalizations about men and women and develop new, more limited generalizations.

A second error in knowledge identified by Elizabeth Minnich is circular reasoning, which justifies traditional knowledge based on the standards embedded in that knowledge. In sociology, for example, for many years certain topics were not studied at all, particularly women's experiences. Students, especially women students, who couldn't relate to the material presented were seen as inadequate. Ultimately, women sociologists began studying gender, and the field of sociology was forced to become more inclusive. Joyce Ladner, for example, in *Tomorrow's Tomorrow,* not only studied Black adolescent girls, but also refused to accept the standard sociological definition of their lives as "deviant." Rather, she identified some of the ways in which her respondents found empowerment in an economically limited, racist context.[70] Ladner studied and redefined a population that usually had no direct voice in the sociological literature.

The third knowledge error identified by Minnich is our attachment to mystified concepts. When we let go of these concepts, new questions and new avenues for research emerge. Masculinity and femininity are two mystified concepts that are frequently used but seldom accurately defined in everyday discourse. Yet as we examine the literature in women's studies and men's studies, for example, we find that many men and women do not conform to the dominant Anglo ideals of femininity and masculinity. Many men, for instance, do not fit the strong, tough, take-charge mode; do not enjoy fighting; and would like more freedom to express their feelings. And, in fact, many men do express themselves openly.[71] Martín Espada (Part I), Tommi Avicolli (Part II), Phil Petrie (Part IV), and Don Sabo (Part V) all provide examples of men breaking ranks with the masculine norms presented in mainstream U.S. culture. Many women also do not fit the stereotypical visions of women presented in mainstream culture, especially in the media. Christy Haubegger (Part III), Martha Coventry (Part III), bell hooks (Part VII), and Melanie Kaye/Kantrowitz (Part IX), among others, provide examples of women who refuse narrow and limited ideas about gender.

Gender itself is a mystified concept for the many people who see it as biologically determined. Recent scholars in gender studies argue convincingly, however, that there is nothing necessary or predictable about gender. In fact, it is becoming more commonly known that human bodies do not come in just two sexes but rather fall along a continuum between female and male.[72] Gender, then, rather than being dictated by body types, is socially determined, or "constructed" in various contexts. Sociologist Judith Lorber, in her recent book Paradoxes of Gender, encourages us to "challenge the validity, permanence, and necessity of gender."[73]

Heterosexuality is another mystified concept related to masculinity and femininity that has proven hard to even question. So "normal" is heterosexuality that it is difficult to imagine a world without this expectation.[74] The "sissy" and "lezzie" insults levied at boys and girls who do not conform to heterosexist expectations have a lot to teach us about how charged and compelling the heterosexual mandate is. In spite of fashion trends toward androgynous clothing in the mainstream media at times, individuals who choose to express themselves through androgynous presentations risk ridicule and ostracism in many circles. Some of the ridicule stems from standards of masculinity and femininity; some of it relates more directly to homophobia.[75] Those who love someone of the same sex know at deeply painful levels the costs of breaking with the heterosexual ideal. This ideal is also tightly bound up with the requirement to match gender with sex. For example, an ironic twist of fate occurred in a tragic atrocity; the man who massacred thirteen women in Montreal because they were studying engineering spared one of the women present because he perceived her to be a man.[76]

Many new questions emerge if we examine the heterosexual ideal: What would life be like without the insults and labels aimed at boys who are gentle, at girls who are athletes, at women who study engineering, or at men who study nursing? What explains the discomfort of the majority of us who want or need people to fit into gender categories? How does this affect the lives of girls, boys, men, and women who express love for someone of the same sex or live their lives in the gender to which they have not been assigned? How does it affect the social order when bisexual women and men who could choose to relate sexually/affectionally to members of the opposite gender choose to do so with the same gender instead? We cannot begin to address these questions without careful attention to the heterosexual ideal and its accompanying homophobia. I often ask myself how gender roles might look without homophobia. Would there even be gender roles as we know them?

Finally, the fourth knowledge error identified by Minnich is our inability, without new knowledge systems, to discard or correct prior ones. If, however, we can embrace new models of knowledge, we can discard or adapt the old ones. Sociologist Charles Lemert's edited volume, *Social Theory: The Multicultural and Classic Readings,* provides an excellent example of this. By expanding the definition of who is considered a social theorist, Lemert allows new voices to enter sociological discourse and invites readers to consider a wide range of contemporary thinkers not usually included in texts on sociological theory.[77] Ronald Takaki's *A Different Mirror: A History of Multicultural America* provides another very good example of a new knowledge system. Takaki focuses on the lives of ordinary people, including those in various racial and ethnic groups, rather than on the lives of politicians and other famous people. He examines class and gender within the groups he studies.[78] We have the opportunity at this time in history to explore sources of news outside the mainstream media in order to raise and address unpopular questions in this time of war and curtailment of civil liberties.[79]

Empowerment—Challenging the Patriarchal System

The need for inclusive knowledge has broad implications for empowerment at the interpersonal, community, and policy levels. Without inclusive knowledge, we cannot develop comprehensive empowerment strategies or inclusive social policy. Without seeing the complexity of human experience and the complexity of human oppression, we cannot begin to address the real needs of human beings caught in systematically oppressive social structures. Marilyn Frye makes this point effectively and graphically with the metaphor of the bird cage in her essay "Oppression."[80] She argues that when someone is caged, or oppressed, it is crucial to examine all the bars of the cage to get a full understanding of the inability to escape; close, myopic examination of just one bar will not give a full understanding of why the person is trapped. For example, if we look at gender discrimination on the job, we might wonder why women can't just overcome the prejudice and discrimination they experience and get on with their lives, even if they make less money, are passed over for promotions, and can support their families only marginally. But if we simultaneously look at other factors, such as sexual harassment within the workplace, racism, fatphobia, heterosexism, ableism, and violence against women and children, we will come to a clearer understanding of how certain people and groups are caught in a web that they often can't escape; barriers, the bars of the cage, are erected everywhere they turn.

Another metaphor I find useful in making sense of oppression and privilege in order to frame social change is the idea of being tied down. If a person is tied by one oppression rope, say, sexual harassment, it's likely that she or he has some movement, is able to see how the knots are tied, and may be able to maneuver to untie the knots, slide under the rope, or move in and out of the rope at different times, depending on the context. If a rope is light, she or he might even break it. But if someone is tied by several ropes, such that she or he cannot move enough to clearly see the sizes and quality of the ropes or the configurations of the knots, there is little possibility for escape. If we imagine that each oppression is a different rope and that the power of oppressions might vary, creating light ropes and heavy ones, a person could be tied down by an almost infinite combination of ropes of different sizes and strengths. And occasionally there will be people tied by no ropes at all at various moments, such as wealthy, white, Anglo-Saxon, Protestant, heterosexual, married, able-bodied, muscular, normal-weight, physically attractive, tall (but not too tall) men in their middle years who are in good health and are seen as mentally stable.

The presence or absence of ropes is a public, not a private, matter. The vast majority of people do not tie themselves down; they are born with limitations due to the structure of the socioeconomic system in which they are situated. German social theorist Max Weber called this system of possibilities "life chances," referring to the array of opportunities, however limited or plentiful, with which a person is born.[81] Although we live in an alleged democracy that offers the potential for upward mobility for anyone, the probability of that happening is severely limited, especially for those born under multiple ropes. Equal access to wealth and other privileges is not structurally guaranteed, even for white, able-bodied men; and many white people in the middle class are currently experiencing downward mobility.[82]

There is no systematic training for untying or breaking the ropes of oppression. Those held by fewer ropes are usually not encouraged to share their privilege by helping others to escape their ropes. Those tied down often learn survival, resilience, resistance, and liberation skills from their families, cultures, and communities but are offered little systematic support from the wider social order. Instead, those tied by many ropes are likely to attend poor schools in which race, class, gender, disability, and sexual orientation interact to produce high rates of failure or marginal functioning.

The oppressive social structure surrounding many people sets in place some probabilities for success or failure. It is important to acknowledge, however, how groups and individuals blocked from success in the privileged, wealthy centers of power find ways to empower themselves, solve problems, and survive against very difficult odds. They do, at times, escape from multiple ropes. For example, some people from highly dysfunctional families have grown up to establish healthy relationships for themselves. The strength and resilience found in poor communities, especially in communities of color, also portray empowerment within otherwise very trying circumstances.[83] Many of the readings in this book report on resilience and personal agency in response to various oppressions.

A look at the web of ropes that surrounds us or the structure of the cages we are in can help us understand how our lives are limited and how to develop institutional, community, and individual strategies for empowerment. An understanding of multiple oppressions helps us see how people can resist oppression at both individual and collective levels and helps us understand why people don't usually escape from multiple ropes. This understanding is especially important in a patriarchal social order in which virtually every woman is tied down by some variety of gender oppression.

Patriarchy, defined in various ways by various theorists, has as its core male control of women. The pervasiveness of the effects of gender oppression and gender socialization has led sociologist Judith Lorber to call gender a social institution (see Part II of this book). Feminist historian Gerda Lerner names an array of ways in which women are socialized, indoctrinated, and coerced into cooperation with patriarchal systems. For example, women are prevented from fully participating in such empowering activities as education (including learning women's history), politics, and the use of economic resources. Lerner names several dynamics particular to women that make this cooperation with patriarchy especially difficult to resist or subvert. First, she argues, women have internalized the idea of their own inferiority. Second, historically, wives and daughters have lived under male domain where they exchange submission for protection and unpaid labor for economic maintenance. Third, women with substantial class privilege have a more difficult time seeing themselves as deprived and subordinated, thus making it especially hard for women of different classes to work together. Fourth, women are separated by their differences in sexual expression and sexual activities.[84] When we add race, age, and ability differences to these class and sexual divisions, the likelihood of women uniting against patriarchy becomes even less probable.

In spite of these extremely powerful structures that conspire to limit the roles and options of both genders and render those who are multiply oppressed close to powerless at times, there is a long history of resistance to patriarchy.[85] Although a unified revolt against patriarchy will probably not occur in the forseeable future, people are fighting back in various ways and struggling to change the systems that support inequality. Many of the writers in this book have struggled for empowerment of one sort or another and provide hopeful exceptions to this often-oppressive picture. The pages that follow contain examples of people finding their voices, telling unpopular truths, taking charge of their own needs, offering concrete advice for improving the lives of women and men, and organizing for change. Don Sabo, for example, critiques male sports culture (Part V); Christy Haubegger embraces her round body (Part III); and Robert Allen works to prevent male violence (Part IX).

I define power broadly to include a range of personal and collective actions. At a personal level, empowerment includes the ability to name and assert one's identity in all its complexity, including the naming of one's privilege and oppression. Related to this is the refusal to accept someone else's definition of who one is. Possessing a sociological imagination is another form of personal power; this allows us to know where we fit historically in the world, to know what our options are likely to be, and to know how to determine whether our pain stems from a personal trouble or from a public issue felt at the personal level. A sociological imagination contributes to the ability to challenge dominant ideas and to develop a healthy skepticism about how the world works. Based on informed analyses of what is wrong with the social order, people can use the power of knowledge to determine what kinds of social changes to work toward. Finally, people can empower themselves by taking political action, both individually and collectively.

Empowerment develops in stages. The first stage is awareness that something is not right. In order to conceptualize what's wrong, people need inclusive knowledge to develop a case for what feminist writer Elizabeth Janeway calls "disbelief," a piece of which is the refusal to accept the definition of oneself that is put forward by those with more power.[86] Janeway argues that in order to mistrust or disbelieve the messages of those in power, validation from others is necessary. Speaking of women, she argues, "the frightening experience of doubting society's directives and then doubting one's right to doubt them is still very recent."[87] Thus, if one's mistrust of the system is not solid, the presence of other disbelievers is likely to strengthen one's position. The role of Black churches in validating this mistrust has been well documented; congregants name how the racist power structure perpetuates itself, and they support each other to work to lessen its onslaught.[88] Women's consciousness-raising groups have also served this purpose.[89] The civil rights movement served to do this for its members in the 1960s as organizations like the National Association for the Advancement of Colored People and the Student Nonviolent Coordinating Committee supported their members to define the system of racism as unacceptable and to fight against it as they registered voters, engaged in sit-ins and boycotts, and integrated formerly white establishments and institutions in the face of virulent opposition.

Once people are convinced that something is wrong or unfair in their lives, they can consider taking steps toward making it right at several levels. At the individual level, people can practice personal acts of passive resistance, direct confrontation, or other actions such as telling the truth about how they really feel; challenging someone who said something hurtful or insulting; leaving an abusive relationship; insisting on not always being in a particular role in a relationship; avoiding contact with people whose attitudes are disrespectful, including refusing to frequent certain places; and making a public statement. On a collective level, people can resist oppressive arrangements by joining forces. This might happen in small or large ways, including movements for social change in communities, institutions, legislative bodies, other governmental structures, and international forums. All of these levels of resistance to oppressive structures and relationships are necessary if we are to create, in Gerda Lerner's words, ". . . a world free of dominance and hierarchy, a world that is truly human."[90]

• • •

Regarding Language

A white student from a university other than my own e-mailed me to complain that I had capitalized Black but not white in the previous edition of this text. I considered various alternatives, including capitalizing both White and Black, putting the word black in lowercase, or varying the capitalization — using black as an adjective (e.g., black individuals) and Black as a noun when referring to a group (e.g., Blacks in the United States). I examined how various other writers handled this issue and discovered that some capitalize Black and others do not. Out of respect, especially, for Black writers who choose to capitalize Black, and with awareness that the nature of racism confers a version of ethnic status on all people who appear to be of African descent even though they belong to a wide range of ethnicities, I have chosen to continue to capitalize the word Black and leave white in lowercase except when referring to white ethnic groups (e.g., French, Italian, etc.).

The term *race* is itself so problematic that many scholars regularly put the word in quotation marks in order to remind readers that it is a social construction rather than a valid biological category. Genetically, there is currently no such thing as "race" and the category makes little or no sense from a scientific standpoint.[91] What is essential, of course, is the meaning that people in various cultural contexts attribute to differences in skin color or other physical characteristics. Thus, when a study of women with breast cancer reveals that although white women have higher rates of breast cancer, Black women are 34 percent more likely than white women to die of the disease, it is important to be cautious in attributing the differences to alleged "racial" differences of a biological nature as if the differences were genetically determined. In fact, studies of people living in polluted environments show that chromosomal aberrations caused by pollution can make people more vulnerable to illnesses, including cancer. When being Black correlates with being exposed to higher levels of pollution, the environmental question needs to be addressed before conclusions about causes of high death rates are attributed to "race."[92]

I have chosen not to put the word race in quotation marks but I encourage readers to keep in mind that when I or other authors in this book discuss race, we are addressing the sociocultural aspects of skin color, including some of the ways in which various social groups are privileged and/or oppressed in various social contexts. We do not intend to imply that differences between groups are genetic, immutable, or innate. In fact, if we were to imagine a world without prejudice and discrimination, we might begin to imagine a world in which skin color made little or no difference.

NOTES

1. Gerda Lerner, *The Creation of Patriarchy* (New York: Oxford, 1986), pp. 228–29.
2. Audre Lorde, "Age, Race, Class, and Sex: Women Defining Difference," in *Sister Outsider* (Freedom, CA: Crossing Press, 1984), p. 120.
3. C. Wright Mills, *The Sociological Imagination* (New York: Oxford University Press, 1959).
4. For a review of legal changes and challenges ahead, see Jo Freeman, "The Revolution for Women in Law and Public Policy," in Jo Freeman, ed., *Woman: A Feminist Perspective*, 5th ed. (Mountain View, CA: Mayfield, 1995), pp. 365–404.
5. For objections to feminism, see writings by Beverly LaHaye (Concerned Women for America) and Phyllis Schlafly; for critiques of mainstream feminism, see Camille Paglia, *Sexual Personae: Art and Decadence from Nefertiti to Emily Dickinson* (London: Penguin, 1990); Christina Sommers, *Who Stole Feminism?* (New York: Simon & Schuster, 1994); Katie Roiphe, *The Morning After: Sex, Fear, and Feminism* (London: H. Hamilton, 1994).
6. For a summary of the development of the contemporary women's movement, including a review of women's activism from the nineteenth century to the present, see Margaret Andersen, *Thinking about Women: Sociological Perspectives on Sex and Gender*, 5th ed. (New York: Macmillan, 2000). For a representative look at the scholarship of pro-feminist men, see Michael S. Kimmel and Michael A. Messner, eds., *Men's Lives*, 5th ed. (Boston: Allyn & Bacon, 2001). See also Stephen J. Ducat, *The Wimp Factor: Gender Gaps, Holy Wars, & the Politics of Anxious Masculinity* (Boston: Beacon Press, 2004).
7. For an overview of public masculinity movements and politics, see Michael A. Messner, *Politics of Masculinities: Men in Movements* (Thousand Oaks, CA: Sage, 1998). For a critique of the mythopoetic men's movement, see Michael S. Kimmel and Michael Kaufman, "The New Men's Movement: Retreat and Regression with America's Weekend Warriors," *Feminist Issues* (fall 1993), pp. 3–21. For a look inside Promise Keepers, one of the large evangelical men's organizations, from the perspective of a feminist woman observer, see Donna Minkowitz, "In the Name of the Father" *Ms.* (November/December 1995), pp. 64–71. For a

discussion of the Million Man March and the O. J. Simpson case, see Henry Louis Gates, Jr., "Thirteen Ways of Looking at a Black Man," *The New Yorker* (October 23, 1995), p. 56ff. For a presentation of various men's movement positions not represented in this book, see Robert Bly, *Iron John* (New York: Random House, 1990); Stephen B. Boyd, *The Men We Long to Be: Beyond Domination to a New Christian Understanding of Manhood* (New York: HarperCollins, 1995); Warren Farrell, *The Myth of Male Power: Why Men Are the Disposable Sex* (New York: Berkeley Books, 1993); Sam Keen, *Fire in the Belly: On Being a Man* (New York: Bantam, 1991); Keith Thompson, ed., *To Be a Man: In Search of the Deep Masculine* (New York: Putnam, 1991).

8. William Pollock, *Real Boys: Rescuing Our Sons from the Myths of Boyhood* (New York: Random House, 1998); Daniel Kindlon and Michael Thompson, *Raising Cain: Protecting the Emotional Life of Boys* (New York: Ballantine Books, 1999, 2000).

9. Geoffrey Canada, *Reaching Up for Manhood: Transforming the Lives of Boys in America* (Boston: Beacon Press, 1998); Ann Arnett Ferguson, *Bad Boys: Public Schools and the Making of Black Masculinity* (Ann Arbor; University of Michigan Press, 2000); James Garbarino, *Lost Boys: Why Our Sons Turn Violent and How We Can Save Them* (New York: Free Press, 1999, 2000).

10. Christina Hoff Sommers, *The War Against Boys: How Misguided Feminism Is Harming Our Young Men* (New York: Simon & Schuster, 2000).

11. James Garbarino, "Some Kids Are Orchids," *Time* 154, no. 25 (1999), p. 51.

12. Michael S. Kimmel, *The Gendered Society* (New York: Oxford University Press, 2000).

13. Kimmel, *The Gendered Society*; William Pollock, *Real Boys.*

14. Susan Faludi, *Stiffed: The Betrayal of Modern Man* (New York: Harper Collins, 1999); Michelle Fine, Lois Weis, Judi Addelston, and Julia Marusza, "(In) Secure Times: Constructing White Working-Class Masculinities in the Late 20th Century," in Theodore F. Cohen, ed., *Men and Masculinity: A Text Reader* (Belmont, CA: Wadsworth, 2001), pp. 422–435; Sally Robinson, *Marked Men: White Masculinity in Crisis* (New York: Columbia University Press, 2000).

15. Sabine Lang, *Men as Women, Women as Men: Changing Gender in Native American Cultures* (Austin, TX: University of Texas Press, 1998); Stephen O. Murray and Will Roscoe, *Boy-Wives and Female Husbands: Studies in African Homosexualities* (New York: St. Martin's Press, 1998); Will Roscoe, *Changing Ones: Third and Fourth Genders in Native North America* (New York: St. Martin's Press, 1998).

16. Phyllis Burke, *Gender Shock* (New York: Anchor/Doubleday, 1996); Cheryl Chase, "Hermaphrodites with Attitude: Mapping the Emergence of Intersex Political Activism," *GLQ* 4, no. 2 (1998), pp. 189–211; Martha Coventry, "The Tyranny of the Esthetic: Surgery's Most Intimate Violation," *On the Issues*, VII, no. 3 (Summer 1998), pp. 16ff; Leslie Feinberg, *Transgender Warriors: Making History from Joan of Arc to Ru Paul* (Boston: Beacon Press, 1996); Leslie Feinberg, *Trans Liberation: Beyond Pink or Blue* (Boston: Beacon Press, 1998).

17. Feinberg, *Trans Liberation*, p. 5

18. *UTNE Reader* (September–October 1998); "The Man I Married Was Really a Woman," as told to James Oliver Cury, *Cosmopolitan* (November 1998), pp. 176ff.

19. Michelle Koidin, "Transsexual Union Sanctioned: Chromosomes Key as Couple Is Granted Texas Marriage License." *The Boston Globe* (September 7, 2000), p. A18.

20. For ongoing lists of bias-related murders, assaults, arson attacks, bombings, threats, cross burnings, harassment, intimidation, and vandalism, see *Klanwatch Intelligence Report*, published by the Southern Poverty Law Center, Montgomery,

AL. For reports on right-wing political activity in general, see *The Public Eye*, published by Political Research Associates, Somerville, MA. For examples of anti-abortion violence, see *Ms.* (May/June 1995). See also Patricia Wong Hall and Victor M Hwang, *Anti-Asian Violence in North America* (Lanham, MD: Rowman & Littlefield, 2001); Helen Zia, *Asian American Dreams: The Emergence of an American People* (New York: Farrar, Straus and Giroux, 2000).

21. Daisy Hernández, "Young and Out: Anything but Safe," *ColorLines* (Winter 2004), pp. 26–29.

22. www.fbi.gov/page2/nov01/hatestats112204.htm.

23. Diane E. Lewis, "Workplace Bias Claims Jump after Sept. 11," *The Boston Globe*, 260, no. 145 (November 22, 2001), p. B1.

24. David Crary, "Assaults on Disabled People Called Epidemic, 'Invisible,'" *The Boston Globe* (Tuesday December 26, 2000), pp. A20, A21.

25. Derrick Z. Jackson, "High Court Makes a Case for Discrimination," *The Boston Globe* (Wednesday February 28, 2001), p. A19.

26. Sharon Hays, *Flat Broke with Children: Women in the Age of Welfare Reform.* New York: Oxford University Press, 2003.

27. John Iceland, *Poverty in America: A handbook.* (Berkeley, CA: University of California Press, 2003).

28. Altha J. Cravy, *Women and Work in Mexico's Maquiladoras* (Lanham, MD: Rowman & Littlefield Publishers, Inc., 1998); Miriam Ching Yoon Louie, *Sweatshop Warriors: Immigrant Women Workers Take on the Global Factory* (Cambridge, MA: South End Press, 2001); Crista Wichterich, *The Globalized Woman: Reports from a Future of Inequality* (New York: Zed Books, 2000).

29. Videorecording "Stolen Childhoods" (Vineyard Haven, MA: Galen Films, 2003).

30. Nancy Murray et al., *Mass Impact: the Domestic War Against Terrorism – Are We on the Right Track?* (American Civil Liberties Union of Massachusetts, 2004).

31. Benjamin Jealous, "Profiles of the Profiled," *Amnesty International*, no. 4 (Winter 2004), p. 18.

32. Charlotte Bunche, "A Feminist Human Rights Lens on Human Security," Center for Women's Global Leadership, Rutgers University, p. 4, web version.

33. "Yet Another Abortion Ban," *Women's eNews* (June 12, 2004), on-line version.

34. Frances A. McMorris, "Bush Successful in Appointing Activist Judges," *Women's eNews* (June 25, 2004), on-line version.

35. Scott S. Greenberger, "Gay-Marriage Ruling Pushed Voters: Mobilized Bush, Left Kerry Wary" *The Boston Globe* 266, no. 130 (Nov. 7, 2004), p. B1.

36. David W. Moore and Joseph Carroll, "Support for Gay Marriage/Civil Unions Edges Upward" Gallup News Service (May 17, 2004), web version.

37. American Academy of Pediatrics Press Release [no author], "AAP Supports Adoption by Same-Sex Parents" (February 4, 2002), www.aap.org/advocacy/releases/febsamesex.htm.

38. Randall Chase, "Estranged Lesbian Partner Is Told to Pay Child Support," *The Boston Globe* (March 18, 2002), p. A3.

39. See, for example, "Jobs and Money: A Small Step Forward for Same-Sex Couples," *The Guardian* (London), (April 7, 2001), p. 7; Ben White, "Conservatives Rip Bush as Soft on Gays," *The Boston Globe* 260, no. 93 (2001), p. B2.

40. Catherine Holahan, "Mass. Scout Unit Allows Gay Leaders," *The Boston Globe* 260, no. 32 (Wednesday August 1, 2001), pp. A1, A15; Claudia Kolker, "Scouts Divided: A Fixture under Seige," *The Boston Globe* (November 26, 2000), p. A25.

41. National Education Association [news release, no author], NEA Board Adopts Plan to Make Schools Safer" (February 8, 2002), www.nea.org/nr/nr020208.html.

42. Barbara Summerhawk, Cheiron McMahill, and Darren McDonald, trans. eds., *Queer Japan: Personal Stories of Japanese Lesbians, Gays, Bisexuals and Transsexuals* (Norwich, VT: New Victoria Publishers, 1998).

43. Jane Kramer, "Taking the Veil: How France's Public Schools Became the Battleground in a Culture War," *The New Yorker* (November 22, 2004), p. 58ff.

44. Caitlin Killian, "The Other Side of the Veil: North African Women in France Respond to the Headscarf Affair," *Gender & Society* 17, no. 4 (August 2003), pp. 567–590.

45. Robert D. Putnam, *Bowling Alone: The Collapse and Revival of American Community* (New York: Simon & Schuster, 2000).

46. Jennifer Baumgardner and Amy Richards, *Manifesta: Young Women, Feminism, and the Future* (New York: Farrar, Straus and Giroux, 2000); Barbara Findlen, ed., *Listen Up: Voices from the Next Feminist Generation* (Seattle, WA: Seal Press, 2001); Rebecca Walker, ed., *To Be Real: Telling the Truth and Changing the Face of Feminism* (New York: Anchor Books, 1995); Uphira Edut, ed., *Body Outlaws: Young Women Write about Body Image and Identity* (Seattle, WA: Seal Press, 1998 and 2000).

47. Anastasia Higginbotham, "Alive and Kicking," *The Women's Review of Books* XVIII, no. 1 (October 2000), pp. 1ff. Personal communication with Third Wave Foundation staff, November 2004.

48. Randy Albelda and Chris Tilly, "It's a Family Affair: Women, Poverty, and Welfare" in Diane Dujon and Ann Withorn, eds., *For Crying Out Loud: Women's Poverty in the United States* (Boston: South End Press, 1996), p. 79. (Reprinted in Part VIII of this book.)

49. For a look at some of the voluminous literature available, consider some of the following. For an extensive bibliography on the sociology of women and women's studies, see Margaret L. Andersen, *Thinking about Women* (Boston: Allyn and Bacon, 2000), pp. 353–87. For an extensive bibliography on the sociology of gender, with references to other disciplines as well, see Claire M. Renzetti and Daniel J. Curran, *Women, Men, and Society* (Boston: Allyn & Bacon, 1995), pp. 525–85. For books and journal articles related to African American men, see Don Belton, ed., *Speak My Name: Black Men on Masculinity and the American Dream* (Boston: Beacon Press, 1995); Richard G. Majors and Jacob U. Gordon, eds., *The American Black Male: His Present Status and His Future* (Chicago: Nelson-Hall Publishers, 1994); and Herb Boyd and Robert L. Allen, eds., *Brotherman: The Odyssey of Black Men in America—An Anthology* (New York: Ballantine, 1995). For references to gay, lesbian, bisexual, and queer studies, see Henry Abelove, Michele Aina Barale, and David M. Halperin, eds., *The Lesbian and Gay Studies Reader* (New York: Routledge, 1993); Christie Balka and Andy Rose, eds., *Twice Blessed: On Being Lesbian or Gay and Jewish* (Boston: Beacon Press, 1989); Monica Dorenkamp and Richard Henke, *Negotiating Lesbian and Gay Subjects* (New York: Routledge, 1995); Thomas Geller, ed., *Bisexuality: A Reader and Sourcebook* (Ojai, CA: Times Change Press, 1990); Karla Jay, ed., *Dyke Life: A Celebration of the Lesbian Experience* (New York: Basic Books, 1995); Kobena Mercer, *Welcome to the Jungle: New Positions in Black Cultural Studies* (New York: Routledge, 1994); Michael Warner, ed., *Fear of a Queer Planet* (Minneapolis: University of Minnesota Press, 1993). For information on gender, aging, and other intersections, see especially Eleanor Palo Stoller and Rose Campbell Gibson, eds., *Worlds of Difference: Inequality in the Aging Experience* (Thousand Oaks, CA: Pine Forge, 1994); and James S. Jackson, Linda M. Chatters, and Robert Joseph Taylor, eds., *Aging in Black America* (Newbury Park, CA: Sage, 1993). For recent writing about Jewish women and men, see Aviva Cantor, *Jewish Women/Jewish Men: The Legacy of Patri-*

archy in Jewish Life (San Francisco: HarperSanFrancisco, 1995); Lynn Davidman and Shelly Tenenbaum, eds. *Feminist Perspectives on Jewish Studies* (New Haven: Yale University Press, 1994); T. M. Rudavsky, *Gender and Judaism: The Transformation of Tradition* (New York: New York University Press, 1995); Rachel Josefowitz Siegel and Ellen Cole, eds., *Celebrating the Lives of Jewish Women: Patterns in a Feminist Sampler* (New York: The Harrington Park Press, 1997). A recent anthology of writings by people with disabilities is Kenny Fries, ed., *Staring Back: The Disability Experience from the Inside Out* (New York: Plume, 1997).

50. For a discussion of hegemonic masculinity, see R. W. Connell, *Gender and Power* (Palo Alto: Stanford University Press, 1987) and Sharon R. Bird, "Welcome to the Men's Club: Homosociality and the Maintenance of Hegemonic Masculinity," *Gender & Society* 10, no. 2 (April 1996), pp. 120–32.

51. Bella English, "Looking Horror in the Eye," *The Boston Globe* 259 (July 27, 2000), p. F1. For related work see Paul Miller and David Lisak, "Associations between Childhood Abuse and Personality Disorder Symptoms in College Males," *Journal of Interpersonal Violence* 14, no. 6 (1999), p. 642(1); for a look at men and women who do not repeat destructive patterns from their families, see Steven J. Wolin and Sybil Wolin, *The Resilient Self: How Survivors of Troubled Families Rise above Adversity* (New York: Villard Books, 1994).

52. For examples of recent crossover research, see Todd W. Crosset, *Outsiders in the Clubhouse: The World of Women's Professional Golf* (Albany: State University of New York Press, 1995); the late Elliot Liebow, *Tell Them Who I Am: The Lives of Homeless Women* (New York: Penguin, 1993); Lillian Rubin, *Families on the Fault Line* (New York: Harper, 1994); Kathleen Gerson, *No Man's Land: Men's Changing Commitments to Family and Work* (New York: Basic Books, 1993); and Christine L. Williams, *Still a Man's World: Men Who Do "Women's Work"* (Berkeley: University of California Press, 1995); Ronald Takaki, *A Different Mirror: A History of Multicultural America* (Boston: Little, Brown, 1993).

53. See Renate Duelli Klein, "The 'Men-Problem' in Women's Studies: The Expert, the Ignoramus and the Poor Dear," *Women's Studies International Forum* 6, no. 4 (1983), pp. 413–21; Michael Awkward, "A Black Man's Place(s) in Black Feminist Criticism," in Marcellus Blount and George P. Cunningham, eds., *Representing Black Men* (New York: Routledge, 1996), pp. 3–26.

54. Harry Brod, "Scholarly Studies of Men: The New Field Is an Essential Complement to Women's Studies," *The Chronicle of Higher Education* (36, N. 27), p. B2. See also, Harry Brod, *The Making of Masculinities: The New Men's Studies* (Boston: Allen & Unwin, 1987).

55. Gloria Anzaldúa, *Borderlands/La Frontera: The New Mestiza* (San Francisco: Spinsters/Aunt Lute, 1987); Gloria Anzaldúa, ed., *Making Face, Making Soul/Haciendo Caras: Creative and Critical Perspectives by Women of Color* (San Francisco: Aunt Lute, 1987); Patricia Hill Collins, *Black Feminist Thought: Knowledge, Consciousness, and the Politics of Empowerment* (New York: Routledge, 1990); Patricia Hill Collins, *Fighting Words: Black Women and the Search for Justice* (Minneapolis: University of Minnesota Press, 1998); Audre Lorde, *Sister Outsider* (Freedom, CA: Crossing Press, 1984); Audre Lorde, *A Burst of Light* (Ithaca, NY: Firebrand Books, 1988); Cherríe Moraga and Gloria Anzaldúa, eds., *This Bridge Called My Back: Writings by Radical Women of Color* (Watertown, MA: Persephone Press, 1981); Rebecca Walker, ed., *To Be Real: Telling the Truth and Changing the Face of Feminism* (New York: Anchor Books, 1995). See also W. E. B. Du Bois, *The Souls of Black Folk* (New York: Penguin, 1989).

56. Du Bois, *Souls*, p. 5.

57. Collins, *Black Feminist Thought*, p. 225.

58. Collins, *Black Feminist Thought*, p. 227.

59. See for example Elly Bulkin, Minnie Bruce-Pratt, and Barbara Smith, *Yours in Struggle: Three Perspectives on Anti-Semitism and Racism* (Ithaca, NY: Firebrand Books, 1984); Judith Katz, *White Awareness: Handbook for Anti-Racist Trainings* (Norman, OK: Oklahoma University Press, 1978); Jane Lazarre, *Beyond the Whiteness of Whiteness: Memoir of a White Mother of Black Sons* (Durham, NC: Duke University Press, 1996); Peggy McIntosh, "White Privilege and Male Privilege: A Personal Account of Coming to See Correspondences through Work in Women's Studies," in Margaret L. Andersen and Patricia Hill Collins, *Race, Class, and Gender, An Anthology* (Belmont, CA: Wadsworth, 1995), pp. 76–87; Ruth Frankenberg, *White Women, Race Matters: The Social Construction of Whiteness* (Minneapolis: University of Minnesota Press, 1993).

60. McIntosh, "White Privilege."

61. Michael S. Kimmel, "Invisible Masculinity," *Society* 30, no. 6 (September/October 1993), pp. 29–30.

62. Paul Kivel, *Uprooting Racism: How White People Can Work for Racial Justice* (Philadelphia: New Society Publishers, 1996), pp. 30–32 and 37–39.

63. For a critique of competition, see Alfie Kohn, *No Contest: The Case against Competition* (Boston: Houghton Mifflin, 1986).

64. In the 1970s, I had difficulty teaching the concept of social class to students at an elite private college, whereas the working class and poor students I taught at a nearby public college grasped this concept with ease. For a discussion of people with less power as astute observers of those with more power, see Jean Baker Miller, *Toward a New Psychology of Women* (Boston: Beacon Press, 1977).

65. Mark Gerzon, *A Choice of Heroes: The Changing Face of American Manhood* (Boston: Houghton Mifflin, 1992), pp. 235–62.

66. Harry Brod, ed., *The Making of Masculinities: The New Men's Studies* (Boston: Allen & Unwin, 1987); Patricia Hill Collins, *Black Feminist Thought: Knowledge, Consciousness, and the Politics of Empowerment* (New York: Routledge, 1990); Patricia Hill Collins, *Fighting Words: Black Women and the Search for Social Justice* (Minneapolis, University of Minnesota Press, 1998); Sandra Harding, *The Science Question in Feminism* (Ithaca, NY: Cornell University Press, 1986); bell hooks, *Feminist Theory from Margin to Center* (Boston: South End Press, 1984); Evelyn Fox Keller, *Reflections on Gender and Science* (New Haven, CT: Yale University Press, 1985); Kimmel and Messner, *Men's Lives*; Lerner, *The Creation of Patriarchy* (New York: Oxford University Press, 1986); Elizabeth Kamarck Minnich, *Transforming Knowledge* (Philadelphia, PA: Temple University Press, 1990); Joseph H. Pleck and Jack Sawyer, eds., *Men and Masculinity* (Englewood Cliffs, NJ: Prentice Hall, 1974); Ronald Takaki, *A Different Mirror: A History of Multicultural America* (Boston: Little, Brown, 1993).

67. Minnich, *Transforming Knowledge*, pp. 185–87.

68. Harry Brod, "Scholarly Studies of Men: The New Field Is an Essential Complement to Women's Studies," *The Chronicle of Higher Education* (March 1990). Reprinted in Karin Bergstrom Costello, ed., *Gendered Voices: Readings from the American Experience* (New York: Harcourt Brace, 1996), pp. 333–36.

69. Lerner, *The Creation of Patriarchy*, p. 220.

70. For some early work on gender by women sociologists, see Jessie Bernard, *Women, Wives, Mothers: Values and Options* (Chicago: Aldine, 1975); Joyce Ladner, *Tomorrow's Tomorrow* (Garden City, NY: Doubleday, 1995); Marcia Millman and Rosabeth Moss Kanter, eds., *Another Voice* (Garden City, NY: Doubleday, 1975);

Alice Rossi, ed., *Essays on Sex Equality* (Chicago: University of Chicago Press, 1970); Alice Rossi, ed., *The Feminist Papers* (New York: Columbia University Press, 1973); Anne Oakley, *The Sociology of Housework* (London: Mertin Robertson, 1974).

71. For a discussion of research on this issue, see Joseph H. Pleck, "The Gender Role Strain Paradigm: An Update" in Ronald F. Levant and William S. Pollack, eds., *A New Psychology of Men* (New York: Basic Books, 1995), pp. 11–32.

72. Anne Fausto-Sterling, "The Five Sexes: Why Male and Female Are Not Enough," in Karen E. Rosenblum and Toni-Michelle C. Travis, eds., *The Meaning of Difference: American Constructions of Race, Sex and Gender, Social Class, and Sexual Orientation* (New York: McGraw-Hill, 1996), pp. 68–73.

73. Judith Lorber, *Paradoxes of Gender* (New Haven: Yale University Press, 1994), p. 5.

74. Suzanne Pharr, *Homophobia: A Weapon of Sexism* (Chardon Press, Inverness, CA 1988); Adrienne Rich, "Compulsory Heterosexuality and Lesbian Existence," *Signs* 5 (Summer 1980), pp. 631–60.

75. Jennifer Reid Maxcy Myhre talks about reactions she receives as a woman with a crew cut: "'Daddy, is that a boy or a girl?' I hear the six-year-old girl whisper the question as I pass by. I smile at her; she articulates aloud what the adults around her are thinking. Her question does not offend me in the way that the 'What are you, some kinda monk?' from the burly man in the fast food restaurant, or the 'Hey, is that a fag?' shouted at me from behind as I walk hand-in-hand with a man down the street, offends me." "One Bad Hair Day Too Many or the Hairstory of an Androgynous Young Feminist," in Barbara Findlen, ed., *Listen Up: Voices from the Next Feminist Generation* (Seattle, WA: Seal Press, 1995), p. 132.

    I am reminded also of a talk I heard by the former director of a lobbying group for women's issues in Massachusetts. She reported that it was highly unacceptable for women to wear slacks in the Massachusetts State House if they expected to have any influence. She herself had decided to make the concession of wearing skirts and dresses in order to be more effective in her work.

76. Minnie Bruce Pratt, *S/HE* (Ithaca, NY: Firebrand Books, 1995), p. 186.

77. Charles Lemert, *Social Theory: The Multicultural and Classic Readings* (Boulder, CO: Westview Press, 1993). Lemert includes Audre Lorde, Gloria Anzaldúa, Cornell West, and Virginia Woolf, among many others.

78. Ronald Takaki, *A Different Mirror: A History of Multicultural America* (Boston: Little, Brown, 1993).

79. Democracy Now (www.democracynow.org); Independent Media (www.indymedia.org); Free Speech Radio News (www.fsrn.org); Women's International News Gathering Service (www.wings.org); Between the Lines (www.btlonline.org); and Women's eNews (www.womensenews.org).

80. Marilyn Frye, "Oppression," in *The Politics of Reality: Essays in Feminist Theory* (Freedom, CA: The Crossing Press, 1983), pp. 1–16.

81. Max Weber, "Class, Status, Party," in S. M. Miller, ed., *Max Weber: Selections from His Work* (New York: Crowell, 1963), p. 43.

82. See Katherine S. Newman, *Falling from Grace: The Experience of Downward Mobility in the American Middle Class* (New York: Free Press, 1988) and *Declining Fortunes: The Withering of the American Dream* (New York: Basic Books, 1993).

83. For discussions of individual survival after painful childhoods, see Linda T. Sanford, *Strong at the Broken Places: Overcoming the Trauma of Childhood Abuse* (New York: Random House, 1990) and Stephen J. Wolin and Sybil Wolin, *The Resilient Self: How Survivors of Troubled Families Rise above Adversity* (New York: Villard Books, 1994). For a review of past and current literature on strategies for coping with poverty and racism as well as some new qualitative data documenting

creative responses to poverty among single African American women on AFDC, see Robin L. Jarrett, "Living Poor: Family Life among Single Parent, African-American Women," in *Social Problems* 41, no. 1 (February 1994), pp. 30–49.

84. Lerner, *The Creation of Patriarchy*, pp. 217–19.

85. Sandra Morgen and Ann Bookman, "Rethinking Women and Politics: An Introductory Essay," in Ann Bookman and Sandra Morgen, eds., *Women and the Politics of Empowerment* (Philadelphia: Temple University Press, 1988), p. 4.

86. Elizabeth Janeway, *Powers of the Weak* (New York: Knopf, 1980), p. 167.

87. Janeway, *Powers of the Weak*, p. 168.

88. James Blackwell, *The Black Community: Diversity and Unity* (New York: Harper-Collins, 1991).

89. Hester Eisenstein, *Contemporary Feminist Thought* (Boston: G. K. Hall, 1983) cited in Andersen, *Thinking about Women*.

90. Lerner, *The Creation of Patriarchy*, p. 229.

91. Audrey Smedley and Brian D. Smedley, "Race as Biology Is Fiction, Racism as a Social Problem Is Real: Anthropological and Historical Perspectives on the Social Construction of Race," *The American Psychologist* 60 1, (January 2005), p. 16(ff); Gerda Lerner, *Why History Matters: Life and Thought* (New York: Oxford University Press, 1997), p. viii.

92. Rita Arditti, "Breast Cancer Rates Differ by Race," *BCA Newsletter* # 84 (December 2004/January 2005), p. 3ff. www.bcaction.org; Frederica Perera et al. "DNA Damage from Polycyclic Aromatic Hydrocarbons (PAHs) in Mothers and Newborns from Northern Manhattan, the World Trade Center area, Poland, and China," *Cancer Epidemiology, Biomarkers & Prevention* 14(3), (March 2005).

PART I

It's Not Just about Gender

The gender system is socially constructed. Political, educational, occupational, and religious institutions, along with the family, create and enforce expectations for how women and men should behave in all known societies. Although the gender rules vary from one cultural setting to another, all settings have such rules, and most of these rules are rooted in patriarchy—the control or dominance of women by men, and the control of less-empowered men by men with more power. Within these institutions, people are systematically socialized to become women or men via complex processes of learning and are frequently bombarded with gender rules from many sources simultaneously.

Although individuals can break or stretch the rules without changing the structures surrounding human lives, individual change will not have much impact on the structures. For example, many individual women in the United States are committed to holding jobs requiring high levels of responsibility and competence but are blocked from promotion for such reasons as sexism, racism, ageism, and homophobia. Men who want to be involved in their children's lives often find it difficult. For some, the need to hold more than one job in order to make ends meet severely limits their time at home. For those with more economic privilege, work demands often require long, inflexible hours at the office. Men who are unemployed and might have more time to spend with their children frequently find their inability to provide economic support to their families humiliating and thus stay away. And men who do find the time to get involved are often met with disbelief and disapproval from health care and educational systems accustomed to dealing only with mothers. Thus, even when individuals are motivated to stretch the boundaries of gender, social structures often impede them.

How we express our maleness or femaleness varies widely from one social context to another. Sociologists, anthropologists, biologists, and others argue convincingly that it is not reproductive biology alone that determines how a person develops. Rather, there is an interaction between one's genetic, biological makeup, usually referred to as sex, and the expectations for male and female behavior in the social contexts in which a person lives, usually referred to as gender.[1] In an interesting example of nonconformity, David Beuchner, a famous concert pianist, decided to change his gender and become Sara Beuchner. As Sara, she had a much more difficult time finding work and booking agents, and university hiring committees were unprepared and unaccepting of the gender switch, even though her skills at the piano remained unchanged.

Expectations for what constitutes femininity and masculinity along with the options available to different women and men are deeply affected by sexism, poverty, racism, homophobia, heterosexism, and other cultural constraints and expectations. Thus, in order to understand people's identities and opportunities, we need to understand the privilege or oppression that they experience, the historical times and the circumstances in which they are currently living, the structural arrangements that surround their lives, and the possibilities for empowerment that they encounter or create.

This part of the book includes seven essays that address the experiences of people from various groups: African American (Patricia Hill Collins), Asian American (Helen Zia), Latino (Martín Espada), Native American (Paula Gunn Allen), Jewish (Ruth Atkin and Adrienne Rich), Muslim (Farida Shaheed) and white heterosexual (Peggy McIntosh). Though prejudice, marginality, overt discrimination, or hatred is described in all of these essays, it is experienced somewhat differently by members of each group. And the historical contexts, including such issues as broken treaties, immigration history, the structure of various societies, and attitudes and prejudices, vary enough to create different kinds of men and women in each of these groups. The final three essays look at the larger structural picture. First, Maxine Baca Zinn and Bonnie Thornton Dill provide a conceptual framework that helps us understand the complexities of how race and gender intersect. Zinn and Dill encourage us to let go of notions about imagined common experiences of "all women" or "all men" and to acknowledge the infinite diversity that we will encounter when we take a closer look not only at various groups but at individuals within those groups. Next, Allan Johnson discusses the system of patriarchy. Finally, Rosalind Petchesky looks at curtailment of various human rights in the context of war.

The authors in Part I identify intersecting oppressions in various combinations and encourage us to think in more complex ways about how people become who they are. They help us to look at what ties people down and what provides unearned privilege. These writers ask for a humane world in which economic and social injustice would not exist. You might want to reflect on how what these authors say affects you: Do the issues presented ring true to your own experience? Have you observed or directly experienced any of the oppressive situations or privileges described by these authors? Have you thought about patriarchy as a system? How have you been affected by the war against terrorism?

NOTE

1. For more about this issue, see Margaret Andersen, *Thinking about Women: Sociological Perspectives on Sex and Gender,* 3rd ed. (New York: Macmillan, 1993), chapter 2, pp. 21–51; Marion Lowe and Ruth Hubbard, eds., *Woman's Nature* (New York: Pergamon Press, 1983); Anne Fausto-Sterling, *Myths of Gender* (New York: Basic Books, 1985); Ruth Hubbard, M. S. Henifin, and B. Fried, eds., *Women Look at Biology Looking at Women* (Cambridge, MA: Schenckman, 1979).

1

THE PUERTO RICAN DUMMY
AND THE MERCIFUL SON

MARTÍN ESPADA

Martín Espada has published his fifth book of poems, *Imagine the Angels of Bread* (W. W. Norton), which won an American Book Award and was a finalist for the National Book Critics' Circle Award. A former tenant lawyer, Espada currently teaches in the English Department at the University of Massachusetts, Amherst.

I have a four-year-old son named Clemente. He is not named for Roberto Clemente, the baseball player, as many people are quick to guess, but rather for a Puerto Rican poet. His name, in translation, means "merciful." Like the cheetah, he can reach speeds of up to sixty miles an hour. He is also, demographically speaking, a Latino male, a "macho" for the twenty-first century.

Two years ago, we were watching television together when a ventriloquist appeared with his dummy. The ventriloquist was Anglo; the dummy was a Latino male, Puerto Rican, in fact, like me, like my son. Complete with pencil mustache, greased hair, and jawbreaking Spanish accent, the dummy acted out an Anglo fantasy for an Anglo crowd that roared its approval. My son was transfixed; he did not recognize the character onscreen because he knows no one who fits that description, but he sensed my discomfort. Too late, I changed the channel. The next morning, my son watched Luis and María on *Sesame Street*, but this is inadequate compensation. *Sesame Street* is the only barrio on television, the only neighborhood where Latino families live and work, but the comedians are everywhere, with that frat-boy sneer, and so are the crowds.

However, I cannot simply switch off the comedians, or explain them (how do you explain to a preschooler that a crowd of strangers is angrily laughing at the idea of *him?*). We live in western Massachusetts, not far from Springfield and Holyoke, hardscrabble small cities that, in the last generation, have witnessed a huge influx of Puerto Ricans, now constituting some of the poorest Puerto Rican communities in the country. The evening news from Springfield features what I call the "Puerto Rican minute." This is the one minute of the newscast where we see the faces of Puerto Rican men, the mug shot or the arraignment in court or witnesses pointing to the blood-stained sidewalk, while the newscaster solemnly intones the mantra of gangs, drugs, jail. The notion of spending the Puerto Rican minute on a teacher or a health care worker or an artist in the community never occurs to the television journalists who produce this programming.

The Latino male is the bogeyman of the Pioneer Valley, which includes the area where we live. Recently, there was a rumor circulating in the atmosphere that Latino gangs would be prowling the streets on Halloween, shooting anyone in costume. My wife, Katherine, reports that one Anglo gentleman at the local swimming pool took responsibility for warning everyone, a veritable Paul Revere in swim trunks wailing that "The Latinos are going to kill kids on Halloween!" Note how 1) Latino gangs became "Latinos" and 2) Latinos and "kids" became mutually exclusive categories. My wife wondered if this warning contemplated the Latino males in her life, if this racially paranoid imagination included visions of her professor husband and his toddling offspring as gunslingers in full macho swagger, hunting for "gringos" in Halloween costumes. The rumor, needless to say, was unfounded.

Then there is the national political climate. In 1995, we saw the spectacle of a politician, California Governor Pete Wilson, being seriously considered for the presidency on the strength of his support for Proposition 187, the most blatantly anti-Latino initiative in recent memory. There is no guarantee, as my son grows older, that this political pendulum will swing back to the left; if anything, the pendulum may well swing farther to the right. That means more fear and fury and bitter laughter.

Into this world enters Clemente, which raises certain questions: How do I think of my son as a Latino male? How do I teach him to disappoint and disorient the bigots everywhere around him, all of whom have bought tickets to see the macho pantomime? At the same time, how do I teach him to inoculate himself against the very real diseases of violence and sexism and homophobia infecting our community? How do I teach Clemente to be Clemente?

My son's identity as a Puerto Rican male has already been reinforced by a number of experiences I did not have at so early an age. At age four, he has already spent time in Puerto Rico, whereas I did not visit the island until I was ten years old. From the time he was a few months old, he has witnessed his Puerto Rican father engaged in the decidedly nonstereotypical business of giving poetry readings. We savor new Spanish words together the same way we devour mangoes together, knowing the same tartness and succulence.

And yet, that same identity will be shaped by negative as well as positive experiences. The ventriloquist and his Puerto Rican dummy offered Clemente a glimpse of his inevitable future: not only bigotry, but his growing awareness of that bigotry, his realization that some people have contempt for him because he is Puerto Rican. Here his sense of maleness will come into play, because he must learn to deal with his own rage, his inability to extinguish the source of his torment.

My father has good reason for rage. A brown-skinned man, he learned rage when he was arrested in Biloxi, Mississippi, in 1950, and spent a week in jail for refusing to go to the back of the bus. He learned rage when he was denied a college education and instead struggled for years working for an electrical contractor, hating his work and yearning for so much more. He learned rage as the political triumphs of the 1960s he helped to achieve were attacked from without and betrayed from within. My father externalized his rage. He raged at his enemies and he raged at us. A tremendous ethical and cultural influence for us nonetheless, he must have considered himself a failure by the male career-obsessed standards of the decade into which I was born: the 1950s.

By adolescence, I had learned to internalize my rage. I learned to do this, not so much in response to my father, but more in response to my own growing awareness of bigotry. Having left my Brooklyn birthplace for the town of Valley Stream, Long Island, I was dubbed a spic in an endless torrent of taunting, bullying, and brawling. To defend myself against a few people would have been feasible; to defend myself against dozens and dozens of people deeply in love with their own racism was a practical impossibility. So I told no one, no parent or counselor or teacher or friend, about the constant racial hostility. Instead, I punched a lamp, not once but twice, and watched the blood ooze between my knuckles as if somehow I could leech the poison from my body. My evolving manhood was defined by how well I could take punishment, and paradoxically I punished myself for not being man enough to end my own humiliation. Later in life, I would emulate my father and rage openly. Rarely, however, was the real enemy within earshot, or even visible.

Someday, my son will be called a spic for the first time; this is as much a part of the Puerto Rican experience as the music he gleefully dances to. I hope he will tell me. I hope that I can help him handle the glowing toxic waste of his rage. I hope that I can explain clearly why there are those waiting for him to explode, to confirm their stereotypes of the hot-blooded, bad-tempered Latino male who has, without provocation, injured the Anglo innocents. His anger — and that anger must come — has to be controlled, directed, creatively channeled, articulated — but not all-consuming, neither destructive nor self-destructive. I keep it between the covers of the books I write.

The anger will continue to manifest itself as he matures and discovers the utter resourcefulness of bigotry, the ability of racism to change shape and survive all attempts to snuff it out. "Spic" is a crude expression of certain sentiments that become subtle and sophisticated and insidious at other levels. Speaking of crudity, I am reminded of a group organized by white ethnics in New York during the 1960s under the acronym of SPONGE: The Society for the Prevention of the Niggers Getting Everything. When affirmative action is criticized today by Anglo politicians and pundits with exquisite diction and erudite vocabulary, that is still SPONGE. When and if my son is admitted to school or obtains a job by way of affirmative action, and is resented for it by his colleagues, that will be SPONGE, too.

Violence is the first cousin to rage. If learning to confront rage is an important element of developing Latino manhood, then the question of violence must be addressed with equal urgency. Violence is terribly seductive; all of us, especially males, are trained to gaze upon violence until it becomes beautiful. Beautiful violence is not only the way to victory for armies and football teams; this becomes the solution to everyday problems as well. For many characters on the movie or television screen, problems are solved by *shooting* them. This is certainly the most emphatic way to win an argument.

Katherine and I try to minimize the seductiveness of violence for Clemente. No guns, no soldiers, and so on. But his dinosaurs still eat each other with great relish. His trains still crash, to their delight. He is experimenting with power and control, with action and reaction, which brings him to an imitation of violence. Needless to say, there is a vast difference between stegosaurs and Desert Storm.

Again, all I can do is call upon my own experience as an example. I not only found violence seductive; at some point, I found myself enjoying it. I remember one brawl in Valley Stream when I snatched a chain away from an assailant, knocked him down, and needlessly lashed the chain across his knees as he lay sobbing in the street. That I was now the assailant with the chain did not occur to me.

I also remember the day I stopped enjoying the act of fistfighting. I was working as a bouncer in a bar, and found myself struggling with a man who was so drunk that he appeared numb to the blows bouncing off his cranium. Suddenly, I heard my fist echo: *thok.* I was sickened by the sound. Later, I learned that I had broken my right ring finger with that punch, but all I could recall was the headache I must have caused him. I never had a fistfight again. Parenthetically, that job ended another romance: the one with alcohol. Too much of my job consisted of ministering to people who had passed out at the bar, finding their hats and coats, calling a cab, dragging them in their stupor down the stairs. Years later, I channeled those instincts cultivated as a bouncer into my work as a legal services lawyer, representing Latino tenants, finding landlords who forgot to heat buildings in winter or exterminate rats to be more deserving targets of my wrath. Eventually, I even left the law.

Will I urge my son to be a pacifist, thereby gutting one of the foundations of traditional manhood, the pleasure taken in violence and the power derived from it? That is an ideal state. I hope that he lives a life that permits him pacifism. I hope that the world around him evolves in such a way that pacifism is a viable choice. Still, I would not deny him the option of physical self-defense. I would not deny him, on philosophical grounds, the right to resistance in any form that resistance must take to be effective. Nor would I have him deny that right to others, with the luxury of distance. Too many people in this world still need a revolution.

When he is old enough, Clemente and I will talk about matters of justification, which must be carefully and narrowly defined. He must understand that abstractions like "respect" and "honor" are not reasons to fight in the street, and abstractions like "patriotism" and "country" are not reasons to fight on the battlefield. He must understand that violence against women is not acceptable, a message which will have to be somehow repeated every time another movie trailer blazes the art of misogyny across his subconscious mind. Rather than sloganizing, however, the best way I can communicate that message is by the way I treat his mother. How else will he know that jealousy is not love, that a lover is not property?

Knowing Katherine introduced me to a new awareness of many things: compassion and intimacy, domestic violence and recovery. Her history of savage physical abuse as a child—in a Connecticut farming community—compelled me to consider what it means to heal another human being, or to help that human being heal herself. What small gestures begin to restore humanity?

WHEN THE LEATHER IS A WHIP

At night,
with my wife
sitting on the bed,
I turn from her
to unbuckle
my belt
so she won't see
her father
unbuckling
his belt

Clemente was born on December 28, 1991. This was a difficult birth. Katherine's coccyx, or tailbone, broken in childhood, would break again during delivery. Yet only with the birth could we move from gesture to fulfillment, from generous moments to real giving. The extraordinary healing that took place was not only physical but emotional and spiritual as well. After years of constant pain, her coccyx bone set properly, as if a living metaphor for the new opportunity represented by the birth of this child.

WHITE BIRCH

Two decades ago rye whiskey
scaled your father's throat,
stinking from the mouth
as he stamped his shoe
in the groove between your hips,
dizzy flailing cartwheel down the stairs.

The tail of your spine split,
became a scraping hook.
For twenty years a fire raced
across the boughs of your bones,
his drunken mouth a movie
flashing with every stabbed gesture.

Now the white room of birth is throbbing:
the numbers palpitating red on the screen of machinery
tentacled to your arm; the oxygen mask wedged
in a wheeze on your face; the numbing medication
injected through the spine.
The boy was snagged on that spiraling bone.

Medical fingers prodded your raw pink center
while you stared at a horizon of water
no one else could see, creatures leaping silver
with tails that slashed the air
like your agonized tongue.

You were born in the river valley,
hard green checkerboard of farms,
a town of white birches
and a churchyard from the workhorse time,
weathered headstones naming women
drained of blood with infants coiled inside
the caging hips, hymns swaying
as if lanterns over the mounded earth.

Then the white birch of your bones,
resilient and yielding, yielded again,
root snapped as the boy spilled out of you
into hands burst open by beckoning
and voices pouring praise like water,
two beings tangled in exhaustion,
blood-painted, but full of breath.
After a generation of burning
the hook unfurled in your body,
the crack in the bone dissolved:
One day you stood, expected again
the branch of nerves
fanning across your back to flame,
and felt only the grace of birches.

Obviously, my wife and son had changed me, had even changed my poetry. This might be the first Puerto Rican poem swaying with white birch trees
instead of coconut palms. On the other hand, Katherine and I immediately set
about making this a Puerto Rican baby. I danced him to sleep with blaring

salsa. Katherine painted *coquís* — tiny Puerto Rican frogs — on his pajamas. We spoon-fed him rice and beans. He met his great-grandmother in Puerto Rico.

The behavior we collectively refer to as "macho" has deep historical roots, but the trigger is often a profound insecurity, a sense of being threatened. Clemente will be as secure as possible, and that security will stem in large part from self-knowledge. He will know the meaning of his name.

Clemente Solo Vélez was a great Puerto Rican poet, a fighter for the independence of Puerto Rico who spent years in a prison as a result. He was also our good friend. The two Clementes met once, when the elder Clemente was eighty-seven years old and the younger Clemente was nine months. Fittingly, it was Columbus Day, 1992, the five-hundredth anniversary of the conquest. We passed the day with a man who devoted his life and his art to battling the very colonialism personified by Columbus. The two Clementes traced the topography of one another's faces. Even from his sickbed, the elder Clemente was gentle and generous. We took photographs, signed books. Clemente Solo Vélez died the following spring, and eventually my family and I visited the grave in the mountains of Puerto Rico. We found the grave unmarked but for a stick with a number and letter, so we bought a gravestone and gave the poet his name back. My son still asks to see the framed photograph of the two Clementes, still asks about the man with the long white hair who gave him *his* name. This will be family legend, family ritual, the origins of the name explained in greater and greater detail as the years pass, a source of knowledge and power as meaningful as the Book of Genesis.

Thankfully, Clemente also has a literal meaning: "merciful." Every time my son asks about his name, an opportunity presents itself to teach the power of mercy, the power of compassion. When Clemente, in later years, consciously acts out these qualities, he does so knowing that he is doing what his very name expects of him. His name gives him the beginnings of a moral code, a goal to which he can aspire. "Merciful": Not the first word scrawled on the mental blackboard next to the phrase "Puerto Rican male." Yet how appropriate, given that, for Katherine and me, the act of mercy has become an expression of gratitude for Clemente's existence.

BECAUSE CLEMENTE MEANS MERCIFUL
— for Clemente Gilbert-Espada
    February 1992

At three AM, we watched
the emergency room doctor
press a thumb against your cheekbone
to bleach your eye with light.
The spinal fluid was clear, drained
from the hole in your back,
but the X ray film
grew a stain on the lung,

explained the seizing cough,
the wailing heat of fever:
pneumonia at the age
of six weeks, a bedside vigil.
Your mother slept beside you,
the stitches of birth still burning.
When I asked, "Will he be OK?"
no one would answer: "Yes."
I closed my eyes and dreamed
my father dead, naked on a steel table
as I turned away. In the dream,
when I looked again,
my father had become my son.

So the hospital kept us: the oxygen mask,
a frayed wire taped to your toe
for reading the blood,
the medication forgotten from shift to shift,
a doctor bickering with radiology over the film,
the bald girl with a cancerous rib removed,
the pediatrician who never called, the yawning intern,
the hospital roommate's father
from Guatemala, ignored by the doctors
as if he had picked their morning coffee,
the checkmarks and initials at five AM,
the pages of forms flipping like a deck of cards,
recordkeeping for the records office,
the lawyers and the morgue.

One day, while the laundry
in the basement hissed white sheets,
and sheets of paper documented dwindling breath,
you spat mucus, gulped air, and lived.
We listened to the bassoon of your lungs,
the cadenza of the next century, resonate.
The Guatemalan father
did not need a stethoscope to hear
the breathing, and he grinned.
I grinned too, and because Clemente
means merciful, stood beside the Guatemalteco,
repeating in Spanish everything
that was not said to him.

I know someday you'll stand beside
the Guatemalan fathers,
speak in the tongue
of all the shunned faces,
breathe in a music

we have never heard, and live
by the meaning of your name.

Inevitably, we try to envision the next century. Will there be a men's movement in twenty years, when my son is an adult? Will it someday alienate and exclude Clemente, the way it has alienated and excluded me? The counterculture can be as exclusive and elitist as the mainstream; to be kept out of both is a supreme frustration. I sincerely do not expect the men's movement to address its own racism. The self-congratulatory tone of that movement drowns out any significant self-criticism. I only wish that the men's movement wouldn't be so *proud* of its own ignorance. The blatant expropriation of Native American symbols and rituals by certain factions of the movement leaves me with a twitch in my face. What should Puerto Rican men do in response to this colonizing definition of maleness, particularly considering the presence of our indigenous Taíno blood?

I remember watching one such men's movement ritual, on public television, I believe, and becoming infuriated because the drummer couldn't keep a beat. I imagined myself cloistered in a tent with some Anglo accountant from the suburbs of New Jersey, stripped to the waist and whacking a drum with no regard for rhythm, the difference being that I could hear Mongo Santamaría in my head, and he couldn't. I am torn between hoping that the men's movement reforms itself by the time my son reaches adulthood, or that it disappears altogether, its language going the way of Esperanto.

Another habit of language that I hope is extinct by the time Clemente reaches adulthood is the Anglo use of the term "macho." Before this term came into use to define sexism and violence, no particular ethnic or racial group was implicated by language itself. "Macho," as employed by Anglos, is a Spanish word that particularly seems to identify Latino male behavior as the very standard of sexism and violence. This connection, made by Anglos both intuitively and explicitly, then justifies a host of repressive measures against Latino males, as our presence on the honor roll of many a jail and prison will attest. In nearby Holyoke, police officers routinely round up Puerto Rican men drinking beer on the stoop, ostensibly for violating that city's "open container" ordinance, but also as a means of controlling the perceived threat of macho volatility on the street. Sometimes, of course, that perception turns deadly. I remember, at age fifteen, hearing about a friend of my father's, Martín "Tito" Pérez, who was "suicided" in a New York City jail cell. A grand jury determined that it is possible for a man to hang himself with his hands cuffed behind him.

While Latino male behavior is, indeed, all too often sexist and violent, Latino males in this country are in fact no worse in that regard than their Anglo counterparts. Arguably, European and European-American males have set the world standard for violence in the twentieth century, from the Holocaust to Hiroshima to Vietnam.

Yet, any assertiveness on the part of Latino males, especially any form of resistance to Anglo authority, is labeled macho and instantly discredited. I can recall one occasion, working for an "alternative" radio station in Wisconsin, when I became involved in a protest over the station's refusal to air a Spanish-language program for the local Chicano community. When a meeting was held to debate the issue, the protesters, myself included, became frustrated and staged a walkout. The meeting went on without us, and we later learned we were *defended,* ironically enough, by someone who saw us as acting macho. "It's their culture," this person explained apologetically to the gathered liberal intelligentsia. We got the program on the air.

I return, ultimately, to that ventriloquist and his Puerto Rican dummy, and I return, too, to the simple fact that my example as a father will have much to do with whether Clemente frustrates the worshippers of stereotype. To begin with, my very *presence* — as an attentive father and husband — contradicts the stereotype. However, too many times in my life, I have been that Puerto Rican dummy, with someone else's voice coming out of my mouth, someone else's hand in my back making me flail my arms. I have read aloud a script of cruelty or rage, and swung wildly at imagined or distant enemies. I have satisfied audiences who expected the macho brute, who were thrilled when my shouting verified all their anthropological theories about my species. I served the purposes of those who would see the Puerto Rican species self-destruct, become as rare as the parrots of our own rain forest.

But in recent years, I have betrayed my puppeteers and disappointed the crowd. When my new sister-in-law met me, she pouted that I did not look Puerto Rican. I was not as "scary" as she expected me to be; I did not roar or flail. When a teacher at a suburban school invited me to read there, and openly expressed the usual unspoken expectations, the following incident occurred, proving that sometimes a belly laugh is infinitely more revolutionary than the howl of outrage that would have left me pegged, yet again, as a snarling, stubborn macho.

MY NATIVE COSTUME

When you come to visit,
said a teacher
from the suburban school,

don't forget to wear
your native costume.

But I'm a lawyer,
I said.
My native costume
is a pinstriped suit.

You know, the teacher said,
a Puerto Rican costume.

Like a guayabera?
The shirt? I said.
But it's February.

The children want to see
a native costume,
the teacher said.

So I went
to the suburban school,
embroidered guayabera
short sleeved shirt
over a turtleneck,
and said, Look kids
cultural adaptation.

The Puerto Rican dummy brought his own poems to read today. *Claro que sí.* His son is always watching.

2

FROM NOTHING, A CONSCIOUSNESS

HELEN ZIA

Helen Zia, the daughter of Chinese immigrants, grew up in the fifties when there were only 150,000 Chinese Americans in the entire country. An award-winning journalist, Zia has covered Asian American communities and social and political movements for more than twenty years. She lives in the San Francisco Bay Area.

Despite my deference to traditional Chinese behavior, the day finally came when I had to disobey my father. I had received several offers of full scholarships to attend college. Like the Chinese who lined up for the imperial civil service examinations in hopes of a new life, I viewed college as my means of escape from the narrow life of making flower shop baby novelties in our dull New Jersey town.

Though my father was proud of my educational achievement, he didn't want me to leave for college. He had already stated his desire for me to attend the closest school to home. When the time came for him to sign the college registration forms, he refused. "The proper place for an unmarried daughter is at home with her parents," he insisted. He wanted to keep me out of trouble until I found a husband to do the overseeing.

I could see the doors to my future slamming shut. At age seventeen, I had never knowingly disobeyed my father. I policed myself, turning down dates, invitations to parties, and even educational opportunities away from home, because I thought Dad would disapprove. I was caught between two conflicting Asian ideals. The Three Obediences* demanded subservience from females, but the primacy of education taught me to seek advancement through study. My American side told me to heed my own call.

Somehow I mustered the courage to shout, "No! I'm going to college." I don't know who was more surprised by my outburst, my father or me. He said nothing more about the subject, and I continued my preparations to leave. I also finally learned that the world wouldn't end if I challenged authority, a lesson I would take with me to college.

My father was right on one account—I intended to look for trouble in the campus political and social movements that appeared on the news each night. The call for civil rights was all around me, beginning in my own high school. Women's liberation offered an alternative to the Three Obediences. Then there was the war in Vietnam, involving yet another Asian enemy. My father was against the war because he saw U.S. involvement in Southeast Asia as a continuation of American domination over the people of Asia. At the dinner table my father lectured us about the immorality of the war; the next day I'd go to school and sit through government propaganda films and civics teachers condemning the Communist scourge and extolling the importance of the war effort to democracy.

For an Asian American kid, the worst part about the Vietnam War was watching the carnage on the news every night, with people who looked like my mom and dad machine-gunned from U.S. helicopters, scorched by American-made napalm, executed at point-blank range, igniting themselves with gasoline in protest, being massacred in their homes and ridiculed on TV shows. It seemed that we had killed the entire population of Vietnam many times over for all the dead who were reported in the body counts each night.

The constant barrage aimed at stirring up patriotic zeal against the Vietnamese enemy took its toll on Asian Americans, in the same way that the previous hostilities with Japan, China, and North Korea had. Many kids in my school had relatives fighting—and dying—in Vietnam. One classmate could barely look at me because I reminded her of the war that killed her older brother. Encountering her in gym class was awkward and sad. At the dry cleaner's and the doughnut shop where I worked in the summers, plenty of GIs would stop in, and some would have to comment. "They're everywhere, aren't they?" a soldier customer said to his buddy as I handed

---

*[The daughter obeys the father, the wife obeys the husband, and, eventually, the widow obeys the son.]

him his laundered and starched fatigues. I had become the local personification of a war nearly ten thousand miles away. Since I looked like the enemy, I must be the enemy.

At the same time, there was no place for me in the debates over national issues like the war or racial equality. People like me were absent from everything that was considered to be "American" — from TV, movies, newspapers, history, and everyday discussions that took place in the school yard. It was hard to feel American when I wasn't treated like one. Yet I didn't feel Asian, either: I couldn't speak Chinese and I hardly knew Chinatown, let alone China. The void left me with many questions.

In the spring of my senior year in high school, the small group of Asian American undergraduates at Princeton University invited me to an orientation meeting. My incoming first-year class had the largest number of Asian Americans ever — sixteen men and four women, nearly as many as the three upper classes combined. I was excited to be part of this tiny but growing Asian student body, coming to Princeton on a full scholarship, part of the wave that drove the university to open its doors to women for the first time in more than two hundred years. In the decades before my arrival, Princeton and the other Ivy League schools accepted only a few Asian students a year, most likely from Asia, not American-born Asians. Though I graduated from high school at the top of my class, I knew that I never would have been admitted to Princeton were it not for the civil rights movement. I was eager to find this movement, as soon as I could escape the watchful eyes of my parents.

The day of my orientation program happened to coincide with a massive student protest and strike at Princeton. The common areas were a sea of young people with placards, banners, and peace signs. Some were locked in earnest debate; others were simply playing Frisbee in the sun. Excited to have found my element, I headed to the Little Hall dormitory to meet the Asian American students.

When I and the handful of other visiting high school seniors knocked on the door that afternoon, we were shocked to find that our hosts were still asleep. About a half-dozen or so Asian American undergraduates were sprawled in various parts of the dorm suite. Strewn around them were beer cans, liquor bottles, ashtrays full of cigarette butts, and other paraphernalia. I was glad that my non-smoking, teetotaler parents had not come along, or I might never have made it to college after all. Our student mentors had been up all night, protesting, partying, debating the role that Asian American students should play in the Third World liberation movement and antiwar student strikes. They regaled us with tales of their lives as Asian American student protesters. I was on the road to discovering my own identity as an Asian American.

I wasn't alone in my quest. The Asian American baby boomers were all approaching college age. For the first time in American history, we were being admitted into colleges and universities in visible numbers as racial barriers began to come down. Some students were from immigrant families like mine, while others were multi-generation Americans.

The foreign-born Chinese students called us American-born types "jock sings," or "hollow bamboo" — Chinese on the outside, but empty inside. The kids from Hawaii were so much more secure in both their Asianness and their Americanness, having grown up in an Asian American majority; they called Japanese Americans from the mainland "katonks" — empty coconuts. The Chinatown kids seemed streetwise and hip, while students from places such as Phoenix, Buffalo, and Columbus were more like me, having grown up without seeing many faces like our own. Some Asian Americans I met called for Yellow Power, in the same spirit as Black Power advocates; others were so assimilated that they were called "bananas."

For the first time in my life, I heard about the internment of 120,000 Japanese Americans from third-generation—Sansei—Japanese American students. The experience of being incarcerated for presumed disloyalty was so painful that many of their parents refused to discuss it with them. I heard about Chinese "paper sons" who were "adopted" by Chinese men living in the United States after all immigration records were destroyed in the San Francisco earthquake of 1906. And about the Filipino "manongs" — old uncles—who worked the farms of California and the West, moving from harvest to harvest. We taught ourselves much of this information, using dog-eared mimeographed course syllabi gathered from Asian American courses in California and elsewhere like a new Holy Grail.

I began to make the connections between past history and my own life, understanding, for example, how the effort to deport my father in the early 1950s was linked to Chinese Americans of the 1800s. When the Immigration and Naturalization Service debated whether to permit my underemployed father to stay in the United States, the fact that he was the sole breadwinner for two infant U.S. citizens by birth swayed their decision. Henry and I were Americans thanks to an 1898 Supreme Court decision in response to a lawsuit by Wong Kim Ark.

I imagined people with Asian faces taking part in American life in a way that I had never before dreamed possible. A new generation of Asian Americans was injecting itself into national debates on civil rights, equality for women, poverty, workplace and labor issues, South African apartheid—we didn't limit the breadth of our vision. Just like the other baby boomers of all races in that 1960s and 1970s era, we knew we were making history. The excitement of that historical sweep added an element of grandeur to our activities; we weren't afraid to think big.

In the spring of 1971, a joint committee of the black, Latino, and Asian American students decided it was time to make the university address the racial inequities on campus. Princeton had very few students of color then, about a hundred in an undergraduate student body of nearly four thousand.

We agreed that life at Princeton for students of color was akin to being stuck in a vast snowdrift, and it was time to thaw the university out. Our small numbers didn't deter us.

The leadership wanted to make a bold, definitive statement, so they decided that our loose grouping of minority students—Third World students— should seize and occupy Firestone Library and call for a massive rally at the University Chapel. We would denounce racism at Princeton and the racist war in Vietnam. We would demand an end to the war, as well as the creation of programs, courses, and a center for Third World students. To a first-year student from a sheltered Confucian home in New Jersey, this was the big time.

Princeton in 1971 was almost entirely male, having admitted its first women undergraduates in 1969. I was one of the half-dozen Asian American women students on campus, and the only one involved in this grandiose plan. Until then I assisted the guys by taking on useful "female" chores like learning to run a mimeograph machine. But this ambitious library plan caught us shorthanded, and somehow I was assigned the task of handling security for the takeover.

Firestone Library is bigger than most castles—and built like one. In my one previous attempt at security, I had installed a padlock on my bedroom door so my brothers wouldn't trash my room; that failed when they screwed the latch off the door. But I took my job very seriously and ran through all of Firestone, getting a good aerobic workout. Our little band of Third World men and a few women entered Firestone one afternoon and refused to come out. We secured the building and declared it occupied. I missed the main action, if there was any, because I was so busy running around and checking all the doors and windows.

The next day, we marched out of Firestone and declared victory before a huge rally at the chapel. My brush with student activism changed my life. Not just because of my successful tenure as security czar, during which I protected our sit-in from Princeton's wild squirrels, but because of the rally that followed. In the days leading up to our library takeover, it was somehow decided that several Asian Americans should speak about the racism of the Vietnam War. This was an important moment, because, as relative political newcomers, we would often defer to the more numerous black and Latino students. But we had a lot to say about racism and the war, and our Asian faces would make a powerful statement. It was also decided that an Asian woman should be among the speakers.

This idea posed a certain logistical problem, since there were so few Asian American female undergraduates. None of us would do it. I had never spoken to a group larger than my fifth-grade class, and the very idea made my stomach churn. Yet the thought that no one would talk about women of Vietnam and the war seemed terribly wrong. In the course of my patrol runs through Firestone the night before the rally, I decided that someone had to do it, even if it had to be me.

During our triumphant march out of the library and into the crowded chapel, packed with a thousand or more people, I fought nausea and panic. I had never met a Vietnamese woman, and what did I know about war? But my mother's stories rescued me: stories of the war that she had witnessed from her childhood spent fleeing Japanese soldiers, of the terrible brutality, of rape, torture, mutilation, and murder, and of the tremendous will to survive. I managed to walk through the long chapel without stumbling, and to speak of my mother's experiences and the inhumanity of this war.

After the rally, an undergraduate student from Vietnam thanked me. Marius Jansen, one of my professors and a distinguished scholar of Japanese history, gave me a puzzled look and told me I didn't sound like myself at all. His comment made me pause to think, for the first time, about the images I must project as an Asian American woman, and the images that might be projected back on me. Most of all, I was relieved and astonished that I, who a year earlier couldn't correct my teacher's pronunciation of my name, had spoken out loud. This Asian American movement was transforming me in a way such that I might transform others. Through it, I began to find my voice.

Finding my voice didn't always mean that my words were welcome, even among my Asian American pals. One day early in my second year, I was walking across campus with my classmate Alan, a street-smart Chinatown boy from California. We were headed to the newly established Third World Center—the prize from our student strike and occupation of the library. On the way, we argued over the relative importance of race and gender. "The revolution must fight racism first," Alan said to me. "Race is primary. Only after we eliminate racism can we fight sexism. Women will have to wait." It was like being at home with my brothers. I called Alan a male chauvinist; a pig, even.

Furious at such attitudes from our "revolutionary" Asian American brothers, the Asian American women at Princeton organized a seminar on Asian American women. Our numbers had grown enough to establish the first course on this topic on the East Coast, perhaps in the country. We didn't ask the men *not* to participate, but they didn't anyway. In our own space, we explored the social, historical, and political context of our mothers' and grandmothers' lives in Asia, their journeys to America, their experiences in sweatshops, on plantations, at home. We discussed our lives as Asian American women. I began to understand the Confucian hierarchy that forced women and girls into perpetual subordination. We, on the other hand, vowed never to accept being less than equal to our brothers.

But our class on Asian American women didn't explore the silences that our newly created Asian American "family" imposed on us. We didn't talk about sexual harassment or date rape within our own community. The language and the concepts didn't quite exist yet. But the incidents did. My academic adviser, a distinguished Chinese professor, gave unsolicited advice—

about sex—to his female students during their faculty consultations. When the professor added such tidbits to the discussion of my thesis, my newly discovered voice failed me. I had run headlong into the quandary common to women of color and others from beleaguered communities: if we air our dirty laundry, we bring shame on ourselves and our community. With the status of Asian Americans so fragile, why drag down one of the few respected Asian American professors? Years later, I learned that another female student, a European American, had filed a report with the university. The esteemed professor had been disgraced—but, at least, not by one of "his own."

Women's liberation didn't offer much help at the time. I felt alienated after my visits to the campus women's center. The women I met were more interested in personal consciousness raising than social consciousness raising. I wanted to do both, but their lives as white women were so removed from mine, which was entwined with my life as an Asian American. Yet this distance didn't prove that race was primary, either. Other experiences made that clear, such as the time I met Gus Hall, a perennial candidate for president, on the ticket of the American Communist Party. He was speaking at Princeton with his running mate, Herbert Aptheker. Some Third World students were invited to a small luncheon for them; Alan and I went as representatives of the newly formed Asian American Students Association. Throughout the entire reception and luncheon, Hall and Aptheker, who were both white, spoke primarily to the African American students, pointedly ignoring Alan and me. To these American Communists, Asian Americans had no political currency; in their eyes, we didn't exist, or perhaps they assumed from our Asian faces that we were predisposed to support China, a bitter foe of the Soviets. It was the first time I witnessed such a blatant race ploy by political "progressives," but it wouldn't be the last.

A whole generation of Asian Americans was getting an education about our identity. We couldn't wait to leave the safe confines of our campuses, to share our lessons and our pride in this newfound heritage. Many of us went into Asian American enclaves as community organizers, intent on making changes there. Our campus experiences made it abundantly clear that if Asian Americans were to take our rightful place in American society, we would have to scratch and dig and blast our way in, much as the railroad workers had through the Rockies one hundred years earlier.

Few in America, or even in our own communities, paid much attention to these young Asian Americans. Among the separate—and expanding—Asian immigrant groups, the vision of pan-Asian unity was not compelling; survival was their main focus.

Still, a dynamic process was set in motion: we were reclaiming our stake in a land and a history that excluded us, transforming a community that was still in the process of becoming. We were following our destinies as Asian Americans.

3

THE PAST IS EVER PRESENT
Recognizing the New Racism

PATRICIA HILL COLLINS

Patricia Hill Collins is Charles Phelps Taft Distinguished Professor of Sociology within the Department of African American Studies at the University of Cincinnati. She is the author of *Black Feminist Thought: Knowledge, Consciousness, and the Politics of Empowerment* (Routledge), winner of the Jesse Bernard Award of the American Sociological Association and the C. Wright Mills Award of the Society for the Study of Social Problems. She is also the author of *Fighting Words: Black Women and the Search for Justice* and co-editor of *Race, Class, and Gender: An Anthology.* She lectures widely in the United States and abroad.

> *It's just me against the world, baby, me against the world.*
> *I got nothin' to lose — it's just me against the world.*
>
> — *TUPAC SHAKUR*

Black youth born after the great social movements of the 1950s and 1960s should have faced a bright future. Social movements of the past fifty years celebrated victories over historical forms of racism, perhaps naively believing that they were creating a new foundation for this new generation. The end of colonialism and dismantling of racial apartheid within the United States and in South Africa signaled the possibilities for antiracist, democratic societies in which Blackness would no longer serve as a badge of inferiority. Yet the actual social conditions that confront this global cohort and their responses to it have turned out to be quite different. When it comes to Black youth, poor housing, inferior education, precarious health status, and dwindling job prospects reoccur across diverse societies. Whether in newly democratic nation-states such as South Africa, African nation-states that have had formal independence for over thirty years, advanced industrial societies such as the United States, Great Britain, France, and Germany, or historically independent states of the Caribbean and Latin America, youth who are noticeably of African descent fare worse than their lighter-skinned counterparts. For many, Tupac Shakur's words, "I got nothin' to lose — it's just me against the world," ring true.

Victory over one form of racism has not, apparently, ensured triumph over others. How is it that social conditions can change so dramatically yet still relegate Black youth to the bottom of the social hierarchy?[1] As hip-hop social critic Bakari Kitwana points out, "now more than ever . . . divided generations must begin to understand the ways that the new Black youth culture both empowers and undermines Black America. As brilliant a moment in history as the civil rights and Black power eras were, the older generation must realize they cannot claim any real victory if the hip-hop generation cannot build significantly on those gains."[2] The emergence of new Black youth culture in the United States that simultaneously empowers and undermines African American progress signals a new phase in the contours of racism itself as well as antiracist initiatives that will be needed to counter it.

What's new about this new racism? First, new patterns of corporate organization have made for an increasingly global economy. In particular, the concentration of capital in a few corporations has enabled them to shape many aspects of the global economy. One outcome is that, on a global scale, wealth and poverty continue to be racialized, with people of African descent disproportionately poor.[3] Second, local, regional, and national governmental bodies no longer yield the degree of power that they once did in shaping racial policies. The new racism is transnational.[4] One can now have racial inequality that does not appear to be regulated by the state to the same degree. For example, the legal support given racial segregation in the United States has been abandoned yet African Americans remain disproportionately at the bottom of the social hierarchy. Third, the new racism relies more heavily on the manipulation of ideas within mass media. These new techniques present hegemonic ideologies that claim that racism is over. They work to obscure the racism that does exist, and they undercut antiracist protest.[5] Globalization, transnationalism, and the growth of hegemonic ideologies within mass media provide the context for a new racism that has catalyzed changes within African, Black American, and African-Diasporic societies. From one society to the next, Black youth are at risk, and, in many places, they have become identified as problems to their nation, to their local environments, to Black communities, and to themselves.[6]

This new racism reflects the juxtaposition of old and new, in some cases a continuation of long-standing practices of racial rule and, in other cases, the development of something original. In the United States, the persistence of poor housing, poor health, illiteracy, unemployment, family upheaval, and social problems associated with poverty and powerlessness all constitute new variations of the negative effects of colonialism, slavery, and traditional forms of racial rule. The new racism reflects sedimented or past-in-present racial formations from prior historical periods.[7] Some elements of prior racial formations persist virtually unchanged, and others are transformed in response to globalization, transnationalism, and the proliferation of mass media. Each racial formation reflects distinctive links among characteristic forms of economic and political exploitation, gender-specific ideologies developed to justify Black exploitation, and African American men's and women's reactions both to the political economy and to one another. Each also generated distinctive African American political responses that aimed to provide a better life for each generation of Black youth.

• • •

The Closing Door: The Post-Civil Rights Era

Many accounts of the vanishing color line make little room for the Tupac Shakurs among contemporary Black youth. Instead, they celebrate a new multicultural America that seems bent on sweeping Tupac's nihilism under the rug and relegating racism to the dustbins of the past. For example, in *Love's Revolution,* Maria Root points to increased rates of interracial marriage, especially for Black men, as evidence of a "revolution" in values that is ushering in a new nonracial America.[8] Identifying the growth of a new Black middle class as evidence of racial uplift, well-respected social scientist William Julius Wilson argues that racism diminishes the further up the economic ladder African Americans climb.[9] In this regard, he joins other scholars who view the racial ideologies and practices of Latin American nations where "money whitens" as applicable for American race relations. All of these factors matter — mass media, marital rates, and a changing social class structure all indicate that former patterns of racial segregation have given way to something new. But what?

For all Americans, the political, economic, and social reorganization of American society that began in the 1970s and took shape during the 1980s and 1990s suggested that a more democratic, multicultural America was at hand. Politically, much changed in the United States. Social movements by Blacks, Latinos, women, and gays and lesbians, among others, catalyzed a changing legal climate in the United States. In a span of less than twenty-five years, legal reforms set the stage for the erosion of a wide array of mechanisms for reproducing social inequality in American society. In addition to the 1954 *Brown v. Board of Education* Supreme Court decision, in the decades that followed, the Civil Rights Act of 1964 prohibited discrimination on the basis of race, color, religion, sex, age, ethnicity, or national origin; the Fair Housing Law of 1968 prohibited discrimination against people seeking housing on the basis of race, color, religion, or national origin; and the Voting Rights Act of 1965 repealed local discriminatory practices against African American voters, an act amended in 1975 and 1982 to include linguistic minorities. The Immigration Act of 1965 removed barriers to immigration for people from primarily non-White nations. The 1967 *Loving v. Virginia* Supreme Court decision removed all legal barriers to interracial marriage. In 2003, in *Lawrence and Garner v. Texas,* the Supreme Court struck down an antisodomy law that made it illegal for same sex partners to engage in sexual conduct that was allowed for different sex partners. In essence, the court ruled that the sexual practices of LGBT people were covered under privacy laws. Collectively, this new legal infrastructure provided a legal context for challenging deep-seated customs across virtually all segments of American society.

In contrast to the victories in the legal system, the changing contours of residential racial segregation during the twenty-year period from 1980 to 2000 suggested that, for many African Americans, this new multicultural America would remain elusive. In 1999, African Americans (55.1 percent) were far more likely than non-Hispanic Whites (21.7 percent) to live inside the central city boundaries of metropolitan areas.[10] This overarching framework of disproportionately Black central cities and disproportionately White greater metropolitan areas produced new patterns of residential racial segregation. While residential racial segregation declined overall, for large segments of the Black population, especially poor and working-class African Americans, residential racial resegregation within urban areas persisted.[11] The concentration of poor and working-class Black people in racially segregated neighborhoods has been so severe in metropolitan areas with large Black populations, that it is often described as "hypersegregation."[12]

By the 2000 census, the African American population numbered 36.4 million people and was characterized by clear social class differences that took geographic form within patterns of racial segregation.[13] For middle-class African Americans and for those working-class African Americans who were able to move into the middle class, the Black political movements of the 1960s and 1970s delivered tangible, albeit tenuous, gains. The proportion of African Americans in the middle class clearly grew in this new legal climate, spurred by new opportunities that allowed many African Americans to join the middle class for the first time.[14] Women and men who acquired jobs as managers in corporations and government agencies, as well as certain staff and line positions in these sectors, benefited from the changed political climate. African American physicians, lawyers, teachers, university professors, engineers, journalists, and other professionals typically procured sufficient job security, job autonomy, decision-making power, and good salaries and benefits that enabled them to move into or up within a growing Black middle class.[15]

An increasingly heterogeneous Black middle class emerged, based in part on the paths that they followed to get there.[16] Some well-off African Americans were positioned to take advantage of the opportunities created by the civil rights movement. Their families had been middle-class for generations, had participated in Black community politics, and had functioned as a Black bourgeoisie or leadership class.[17] Far more African Americans arrived via the route of individual social mobility from the working class. This upward mobility typically required access to higher education; the protections provided by strong antidiscrimination and affirmative action programs in education and employment; the assimilation of White norms and values, including those concerning gender and sexuality; as well as the social skills needed to handle increasing contact with White people as colleagues and friends. No matter how they arrived in the Black middle class, many well-off Blacks engaged in yet another migration, this time out of African American inner-city neighborhoods into racially integrated urban and suburban neighborhoods. The Census Bureau reports that from 1980 to 2000 residential racial segregation declined for African Americans (although it was still higher than any other group).[18] Although these communities routinely re-segregated and often became all-Black enclaves, they did provide better housing, schools, and facilities for African American children.[19]

Ideally, African American children growing up in middle-class neighborhoods would retain the class benefits provided by their parents. There is some evidence that passing on middle-class economic gains in the post–civil rights era may be far more difficult than originally thought, in part, due to the proximity of Black middle-class neighborhoods to working-class and poor Black communities. Mary Patillo-McCoy's study of the difficulties faced by Black youth in the fictional Chicago neighborhood of Groveland illustrates the pressures facing middle-class Black youth. For one, they are often mistaken for delinquents by security guards and other officials because they mimic the dress, walk, and talk of working-class Black youth. In this way, stylistic choices often have tangible material consequences. For another, in a community in which the influences of ghetto life permeate everyday life, embracing ghetto styles takes on different meaning than for youth who are in predominantly White middle-class neighborhoods: "sometimes, when you dress like a gangsta, talk like a gangsta, and rap like a gangsta, soon enough you *are* a gangsta."[20]

Many poor and working-class African Americans need not assume the trappings of gangstas—the lack of economic options in their neighborhoods pressures them to become gangstas. For Black youth who feel they have "nothin' to lose" because they lack access to the housing, education, health care, and jobs needed for upward social mobility, the political victories of the civil rights and Black power movements failed to produce the promised economic development envisioned by civil rights activists. The hope was that the opportunities for Black working-class children would continue after the victories of the civil rights and Black power movements. But four back-to-back recessions in the 1970s, a growing White backlash against equal opportunity, and the ascendancy of conservative Republican administrations under Ronald Reagan (1980–1988) and George Bush (1988–1992) as well as the election of George W. Bush to the presidency in 2000 combined to shatter this expectation. In the 1980s, Republican administrations set about dismantling enforcement efforts for equal opportunity, cutting funding for urban programs, incarcerating growing numbers of African Americans in the burgeoning prison industry, shrinking the social welfare budget through punitive measures, and endorsing historical labor market patterns.[21] Fearful of losing conservative White voters who had traditionally supported the Democratic Party, party leaders shifted the party to the right. For example, in 1996, Democratic president Bill Clinton signed the Personal Responsibility and Work Opportunity Reconciliation Act, a law that, despite its lofty title, effectively shifted social welfare programs back to the states and signaled a retrenchment from federal social welfare programs.[22]

Participants in civil rights and Black Nationalist struggles saw their activism as providing opportunities for the next generation of Black youth to live better lives. They reasonably expected that, as did earlier generations of African Americans, Black youth living in inner-city areas might use routes for upward social mobility to better themselves. Instead, as the music of Tupac Shakur and other hip-hop artists reminds us, the door of economic opportunity closed and routes for upward social mobility seem distant memories. For far too many Black youth, inner-city neighborhoods have become dumping grounds, as one observer describes it, "jobless, crime-ridden ghettos [that] have become glorified, modern-day concentration camps."[23] Within inner-city neighborhoods, public schools are dilapidated, teachers are underpaid and overwhelmed, guns and the informal drug economy have made African American neighborhoods dangerous, and jobs have vanished.[24] Gone are the sports programs, music, debate clubs, and other elements of public school education that helped poor and working-class youth stay in school.

Poor and working-class Black youth who grew up in the 1980s and 1990s, often within racially segregated, inner-city neighborhoods, encountered markedly different economic, political, and social conditions than those that faced their parents or those provided to middle-class youth of all races. Despite coming of age during a time of unprecedented social change, regardless of gender, opportunities for poor Black youth eroded. For example, for children under age eighteen the poverty rate is consistently three times higher for Black children than for White children—in 1998, it was 37 percent for Black children versus 11 percent for non-Hispanic White children.[25] When it comes to poverty among Black children, gender did not make a significant difference. Black males under age eighteen had a poverty rate of 36 percent and Black females a rate of 37.3 percent.[26] With over one-third of all Black youth living in poverty, mainly in inner-city, racially segregated neighborhoods, young Black men and women *both* face limited prospects for quality education, well-paid employment, and stable family life. At the same time, poor and working-class Black youth also face gender-specific challenges in two main areas: (1) eroding work and family structures within urban Black working-class neighborhoods; and (2) the changing contours of Black working-class culture assaulted by drugs, crime, and guns.

The most noteworthy structural changes within African American working-class neighborhoods in the post–World War II period concern work and family.[27] Joblessness fosters family disruption for both men and women, and the effects on each have taken gender-specific forms. In this regard, the rapid growth of a criminal justice system that ensnares large numbers of young, working-class, urban African American men has separated them from their families and left many with slim prospects for stable family life.

There appears to be no place for young Black men in urban labor markets, but there is one in jails and prisons. Since 1980, whatever measures are used — rates of arrest, conviction, jail time, parole, or types of crime — African American men are more likely than White American men to encounter the criminal justice system. For example, in 1990, the non-profit Washington, D.C. based Sentencing Project released a survey suggesting that, on an average day in the United States, one in every four African American men aged 20–29 was either in prison, jail, or on probation/parole.[28] Incarcerating young Black men is profitable. The privatized prison industry capitalizes on the growth of prisons. This industry consists of a network of private corporations that provide every service imaginable to prisons and inmates, from prison construction and operation to telecommunications services, food, clothing, and medicine. Corporations also capitalize on cheap prison labor.[29] Jobless Blacks collecting unemployment insurance are unprofitable. In contrast, "the inroads that have been made in privatizing the prison industry have created a profit motive for keeping young Blacks locked up."[30]

In this context, women are left to head families, a structural change with great implications for African American youth and for Black working-class neighborhoods. By 1999, less than one-half (47 percent) of all Black families were married-couple families, 45 percent were maintained by women with no spouses present, while only 8 percent were maintained by men with no spouses present.[31] Families maintained by Black women are not inherently worse than those maintained by married couples but a sizeable majority of Black families that are maintained by women live in poverty.[32] Family income, however, is greatly affected by having a male earner in the household, primarily because men on average earn far more than women when they are able to find work. Family composition affects family income. For example, in 1998, 20.8 percent of Black families maintained by married couples had incomes less than $25,000. The corresponding percentage for Black families maintained by men with no spouse present was 43.1 percent and by Black women with no spouse present was 66.8 percent.[33] The lowest percentage of families with income under $25,000 was found among married couple families (20.8), the highest among families headed by single mothers (66.8), and the middle by single fathers heading families (43.1).

These structural changes in work and family affected the quality of life in Black urban neighborhoods, and they catalyzed changes within Black working-class culture. During the onslaught of drugs and guns in the 1980s, Black working-class neighborhoods simply became more dangerous. Residents of working-class, urban Black communities increasingly beset by drugs and crime used the terms "decent" and "street" families to distinguish stable yet vulnerable working-class families from working-class families in crisis.[34] In this context, the "decent" families, those where members had some connection to traditional jobs in the formal blue-collar labor market or the secondary labor markets, struggled to get by. Plagued by chronic unemployment, these families confronted uncertain industrial jobs, underpaid clerical work, and low-paid service work. Such families may move in and out of the social welfare system and individuals within these "decent" families may have difficulties with the police. In contrast, "street" families, those who have largely fallen out of the formal labor market and whose fate is linked to the informal economy of the global drug industry, have more tenuous connections to school, employment, and other markers of citizenship. They too may move in and out of the social welfare and penal systems, but they hold little hope of ever being "decent' or even wanting to become "decent."

Gender matters in this working-class variation of the tension between Black respectability and Black authenticity, between being "decent" and "street." The growth of the prison culture in the 1980s greatly influenced African American social organization, especially for young African American men. In particular, the arrest and imprisonment of Black street gangs in the 1970s and 1980s fostered more pronounced and organized gang structures within prisons that became conduits for hierarchies of masculinity. Prison gangs inevitably became connected to their street gang counterparts (in fact, many join gangs while in prison, primarily for protection). As the line between street gangs and prison gangs blurred, so did the distinctions between prison culture, street culture, and some aspects of Black youth culture. More important, this growing interconnectedness of prison, street, and youth culture, with the importance given to hierarchies of masculinity, affects African American neighborhoods and families. The valorization of thug life within Black youth culture, the growing misogyny within heterosexual love relationships, and the increased visibility (and some would say the increased virulence) of homophobic violence targeted to gay, lesbian, and bisexual African Americans all seem to be casualties of the incarceration of African American men and the ceaseless need to prove one's "manhood."[35]

Black women have often found themselves on the front line in dealing with issues that affect Black men. As girlfriends and wives, Black women are often the ones who bear the brunt of Black men's anger at a racism that has and continues to operate so thoroughly through gendered practices and ideologies. Reflecting the realities of street culture, some forms of rap music may serve the purpose of political expression concerning racism, but they also now operate as an important site for the spread of sexism and homophobia. Male artists who refer to Black girls and women as "bitches," "hos," "freaks," "skeezers," "gold diggers," and "chickenheads" malign Black women, "decent" and "street" alike. Protesting this misogyny in rap, Johnnetta Cole and Beverly Guy-Sheftall contend: "We are concerned because we believe that hip-hop is more misogynist and disrespectful of Black girls and women than other popular music genres. The casual references to rape and other forms of violence and the soft-porn visuals and messages of many rap music videos are seared into the consciousness of young Black boys and girls at an early age."[36]

Despite the misogyny that takes the form of Black women-blaming that permeates American culture, Black mothers who struggle to retain "decent" families remain justifiably worried about the effects of "street culture" on their sons. Black daughters often misunderstand this concern until they become mothers. Several African American autobiographies, especially those written by Black women, identify this theme of Black mothers who treat their sons differently from their daughters. For example, in her memoir *An American Story,* journalist Debra Dickerson describes her childhood as one of five siblings, four girls and one boy. Despite her academic achievements, her mother ignored her whereas her brother, who routinely did poorly, was repeatedly forgiven for his misdeeds.[37] In her aptly titled volume, *Mama's Girl,* Veronica Chambers reports similar differential treatment: "my brother . . . was the only person I ever met who almost flunked kindergarten. He was smart—eventually he would test better in math than I did—but he was badly behaved. As he got older, his behavior got worse, until it reached the point where he was always talking back to the teachers and never bothered to do any of the work."[38] Chambers's mother was so worried about her son that his actions formed the subject of many conversations with her women friends. Chambers felt neglected: "there was never any talk about me or what I needed. I was just a quick rest stop in their marathon conversations."[39]

Dickerson and Chambers viewed their mothers' behavior through the lens of childhood, and they came to the conclusion that a certain inequality stemmed from this differential treatment. But Black mothers who worry about the fate of their sons because they are single parents living in dangerous neighborhoods may also be reacting to bona fide threats to their sons' well-being. African American women are often particularly afraid for their sons, fearing that their son's race and size might get them killed for no reason. Marita Golden captures this fear for her son Michael growing up in Washington, D.C.:

> My son careened into adolescence. I heard the deepening of
> Michael's voice, witnessed the growth spurts that propelled him to
> a height that echoed his father's, saw the sudden appearance of
> muscles. . . . I was flushed with trepidation. Soon Michael would
> inhabit that narrow, corrupt crawl space in the minds of whites
> and some black people too, a space reserved for criminals,
> outcasts, misfits, and black men. Soon he would become a
> permanent suspect.[40]

Golden knew that her son must leave boyhood behind, but she sees all too clearly the costs of doing so. She does not want to join the legions of Black women who attend funerals, burying children who are far younger than they are.

These new social relations that disrupt Black families, incarcerate young men, leave Black women as single mothers, and foster new forms of Black working-class culture constitute yet another racial formation that builds upon and changes those of the past. Chattel slavery as a distinct form of bondage, the labor exploitation of rural Southern agriculture, and urban industrialization and the racial segregation of Black populations through ghettoization have all left their mark on today. These three racial formations may have peaked during specific periods of African American history, but now they overlap, draw strength from one another, and continue to contribute to the new racism. For example, reflecting this past-in-present racism, pockets of rural poverty in the contemporary American South are a direct consequence of sharecropping and other agricultural policies and technologies of the postemancipation South. Similarly, African American hyper-ghettos in Baltimore, Philadelphia, Detroit, Chicago, and other large metropolitan areas as well as urban/suburban housing patterns that make many cities *de facto* Black ghettos, are direct descendents of policies of *de facto* racial segregation developed during the height of urban industrialization. Even slavery persists, but not in the form of chattel slavery experienced by enslaved Africans in the American South. If one defines slavery as "the total control of one person by another for the purpose of economic exploitation,"[41] children and young women and men involved in prostitution and the situation of illegal immigrants held in debt bondage to pay off the cost of their passage constitute reworked versions of slavery.

Just as emerging structures of the new racism constitute a reformulation of former racial formations, the closing door of racial opportunity of the post–civil rights era also invokes ideas and practices about class, gender, and sexuality associated with those prior periods. All three past-in-present racial formations have effects that endure into the present and are likely to persist, regardless of changes in ideology. In *The Debt,* African American social critic Randall Robinson describes the legacy of these prior racial formations: "No nation can enslave a race of people for hundreds of years, set them free bedraggled and penniless, pit them, without assistance in a hostile environment, against privileged victimizers, and then reasonably expect the gap between the heirs of the two groups to narrow. Lines, begun parallel and left alone, can never touch."[42]

The contemporary closing door of opportunity must be judged in the context of prior racial formations dedicated to maintaining the "parallel lines" of separate and unequal opportunities and outcomes. Legal changes are necessary, but they are far from sufficient in responding to a new seemingly color-blind racism where the past is ever present. Contemporary ideas about race, gender, and sexuality did not drop from the sky. In this context, neither Black men nor women can win an oppression contest, because both face different challenges raised by the new racism. Both suffer from different expressions of the disappearing hope that the closing door of opportunity represents.

NOTES

1. For a comprehensive analysis of this same theme as it applies to African American women, see my discussion of the new politics of containment in chapter 2 of *Fighting Words* (Collins 1998, 11–43).
2. Kitwana 2002, 23.

3. For discussions of various aspects of globalization, race, and inequality, see Bales 1999; Lusane 1997; Bauman 1998; Mohanty 1997.

4. For a general overview of how race operates in a transnational framework, see Winant 2001. The framework of transnationalism is less often applied to African American experiences than those of Latinos.

5. For representative works on new racist ideologies, see Crenshaw 1997; Guinier and Torres 2002; Bonilla-Silva 2001; and Goldberg 1993. For race and media, see Entman and Rojecki 2000. For representative works in the field of Black cultural studies, consult Kelley 1994; Kelley 1997; Gates 1992; Neal 2002; Dent 1992b; Hall 1992; Dyson 1996.

6. For example, much attention has been given to the important issue of the poor school performance of African American youth (Fordham 1996), and Black males in particular (Arnett Ferguson 2000). Afro-Caribbean immigrants to the United Kingdom express similar concerns with their children's performance. This theme of Black youth being denied access to education and/or receiving differential treatment by schools run by dominant groups reappears across societies. Despite similar disadvantages among Black youth worldwide, a transnational discourse addressing issues peculiar to Black youth has not yet surfaced.

7. For a comprehensive treatment of racial formation theory, see Omi and Winant 1994.

8. Root 2001.

9. Wilson 1978.

10. McKinnon and Humes 2000, 2.

11. Five measures of racial residential segregation are typically used. Evenness measures the differential distribution of the population. Exposure measures potential contact among racial groups. Concentration refers to the relative amount of physical space occupied by a racial group. Centralization indicates the degree to which a racial group is located near the center of an urban area. Clustering measures the degree to which racial groups live disproportionately in contiguous areas (Iceland, Weinberg, and Steinmetz 2002, 7–10). The literature reports declines in residential racial segregation for African Americans across all five measures. However, the largest metropolitan areas (1 million or more population) had higher residential segregation than the middle-sized ones (500,000 to 999,999), which in turn had higher rates than smaller ones. The size of the metropolitan area and the size of the Black population within it seem to matter. Three of the five indexes showed a pattern of higher segregation in places with a higher percentage of Blacks in 2000, while two showed the reverse. In particular, as the percentage of the population that is Black increased, Blacks were (1) less likely to be evenly spread across the metropolitan area; (2) less likely to share common neighborhoods with Whites (isolation index); and (3) more likely to live near other Blacks (spatial proximity index) (Iceland, Weinberg, and Steinmetz 2002, 63).

12. For an analysis of racial segregation, see Massey and Denton 1993. Also, see Oliver and Shapiro 1995, 15–23. In 2000, the five most segregated metropolitan areas for Black people were Milwaukee, Detroit, Cleveland, St. Louis, and Newark. Cincinnati, Buffalo, and New York were roughly tied for sixth place, and the top ten was rounded out by Chicago and Philadelphia (although Philadelphia was roughly tied with Kansas City, New Orleans, and Indianapolis) (Iceland, Weinberg, and Steinmetz 2002, 68). By 2000, African Americans constituted a sizeable percentage of the populations of large American cities. Of the ten largest areas in the United States, Detroit had the largest proportion of Black people (83 percent), followed by Philadelphia (44 percent), and Chicago (38 percent). Two places — New York and Chicago — together accounted for nine percent

of the total Black population. The ten largest places for Blacks accounted for 20 percent of the total Black population (McKinnon 2001, 7).

13. McKinnon 2001.

14. The criteria used to define social class, for example, educational attainment, occupational level, and income, affect estimates of the size of the Black middle class. Here I emphasize occupational characteristics because these demonstrate race/gender patterns that are central to the arguments in this book.

15. Race and gender differences characterize this movement of African Americans into professional and managerial jobs. In 1999, the proportion of employed non-Hispanic White men (32 percent) in managerial and professional occupations was almost twice that of Black men (17 percent). Non-Hispanic White women (35 percent) were more likely than Black women (24 percent) to be in these positions. In this regard, White men and women were far closer in occupational status (32 and 35 percent) than Black men and women (17 and 24 percent) (McKinnon and Humes 2000).

16. This heterogeneity within the Black middle class should not obscure the major differences between middle-class Blacks and Whites. For an analysis of these differences in income and wealth, see Oliver and Shapiro 1995, 91–125.

17. Graham 2000.

18. Iceland, Weinberg, and Steinmetz 2002, 3–4.

19. Patillo-McCoy 1999.

20. Patillo-McCoy 1999, 123.

21. Race and gender also influenced the continued concentration of Black men and women in less desirable jobs. For example, Black men (17 percent) are more than twice as likely as White men (8 percent) to work in service occupations and almost twice as likely (31 percent compared to 17 percent) to be operators, fabricators, and laborers. Black women (27 percent) were more likely than non-Hispanic White women (15 percent) to be employed in service occupations (McKinnon and Humes 2000, 4). In essence, gender-segmented jobs of laborers and service work continued to characterize the occupational experiences of poor and working-class African Americans.

22. Much has been written about the PRWOR Act. For a discussion of how this act fits into a frame of "welfare racism," see Neubeck and Cazenave 2001, 115–144.

23. Kitwana 2002, 48.

24. Squires 1994.

25. McKinnon and Humes 2000, 5.

26. McKinnon and Humes 2000, 6.

27. Franklin 1997, 153–214.

28. Miller 1996, 1–9.

29. Kitwana 2002, 71–76.

30. Kitwana 2002, 76.

31. McKinnon and Humes 2000, 2.

32. Definitions of poverty seem to matter greatly in who gets counted as poor. In 1998, the official poverty threshold for a family of four was $16,600, leaving a sizeable gap between the $25,000 income threshold reported here and official poverty. Whatever the family composition, Black families are poorer than White ones, with families headed by Black women with no spouse present poorer than all. In 1998, poverty was highest in families maintained by women with no spouse present: 41 percent for Blacks compared to 21 percent for non-Hispanic Whites (McKinnon and Humes 2000, 6).

33. Varying explanations have been given for these patterns. William Julius Wilson's research links patterns of family organization to the changing contours of economic opportunities in Black urban neighborhoods (Wilson 1996; Wilson 1987). Wilson's research highlights how growing joblessness among African American men in the 1960s and 1970s correlates with (but does not necessarily cause) increasing rates of African American mother-child families. His work documents how the emergence of mother-child families among working-class African Americans can be attributed, in part, to a changing political economy that disadvantaged U.S. Blacks. Others criticize capitalist development itself (Squires 1994).

34. Anderson 1999.

35. The crisis within contemporary gender politics sparked Cole and Guy-Sheftall to write their book: "Now is a particularly critical time for *Gender Talk* because of what we perceive to be an embattled Black, mostly male leadership, a deepening crisis in Black male-female relationships, an embrace of patriarchal family values, and a backlash against feminism and Black feminists" (Cole and Guy-Sheftall 2003, xxxii).

36. Cole and Guy-Sheftall 2003, 186.

37. Dickerson 2000.

38. Chambers 1996, 44.

39. Chambers 1996, 46.

40. Golden 1995, 68.

41. Bales 1999, 6.

42. Robinson 2000, 74.

REFERENCES

Anderson, Elijah. 1999. *Code of the Street: Decency, Violence and the Moral Life of the Inner City.* New York: W. W. Norton.

Arnett Ferguson, Ann. 2000. *Bad Boys: Public Schools in the Making of Black Masculinity.* Ann Arbor: University of Michigan Press.

Bales, Kevin. 1999. *Disposable Slavery: New Slavery in the Global Economy.* Berkeley: University of California Press.

Bauman, Zygmunt. 1998. *Globalization: The Human Consequences.* New York: Columbia University Press.

Bonilla-Silva, Eduardo. 1996. "Rethinking Racism: Toward a Structural Interpretation." *American Sociological Review* 62 (June): 465–480.

Chambers, Veronica. 1996. *Mama's Girl.* New York: Riverhead Books.

Cole, Johnnetta Betsch, and Beverly Guy-Sheftall. 2003. *Gender Talk: The Struggle for Women's Equality in African American Communities.* New York: Ballantine.

Collins, Patricia Hill. 1998. *Fighting Words: Black Women and the Search for Justice.* Minneapolis: University of Minnesota Press.

Crenshaw, Kimberlé Williams. 1997. "Color Blindness, History, and the Law." *The House That Race Built.* Ed. Wahneema Lubiano, 280–288. New York: Pantheon.

Dent, Gina, ed. 1992b. *Black Popular Culture.* Seattle: Bay Press.

Dickerson, Debra J. 2000. *An American Story.* New York: Anchor.

Dyson, Michael. 1996. *Between God and Gangsta Rap: Bearing Witness to Black Culture.* New York: Oxford University Press.

Entman, Robert M., and Rojecki Andrew. 2000. *The Black Image in the White Mind: Media and Race in America.* Chicago: University of Chicago Press.

Fordham, Signithia. 1996. *Blacked Out: Dilemmas of Race, Identity, and Success at Capital High.* Chicago: University of Chicago Press.

Franklin, Donna L. 1997. *Ensuring Inequality: The Structural Transformation of the African-American Family.* New York: Oxford University Press.

Gates, Henry Louis. 1992. *Loose Canons: Notes on the Culture Wars.* New York: Oxford University Press.

Goldberg, David Theo. 1993. *Racist Culture: Philosophy and the Politics of Meaning.* Cambridge, Mass.: Blackwell.

Golden, Marita. 1995. *Saving Our Sons: Raising Black Children in a Turbulent World.* New York: Doubleday.

Graham, Lawrence Otis. 2000. *Our Kind of People: Inside America's Black Upper Class.* New York: HarperPerennial.

Guinier, Lani, and Gerald Torres. 2002. *The Miner's Canary: Enlisting Race, Resisting Power, Transforming Democracy.* Cambridge, Mass.: Harvard University Press.

Hall, Stuart. 1992. "What Is This 'Black' in Black Popular Culture?" *Black Popular Culture.* Ed. Gina Dent, 21–33. Seattle: Bay Press.

Iceland, John, Daniel H. Weinberg, and Erika Steinmetz. 2002. *Racial and Ethnic Residential Segregation in the United States: 1980–2000,* U.S. Census Bureau, Series CENSR-3. Washington, D.C.: U.S. Government Printing Office.

Kelley, Robin D. G. 1994. *Race Rebels: Culture, Politics, and the Black Working Class.* New York: Free Press.

———. 1997. *Yo' Mama's DisFUNKtional!: Fighting the Culture Wars in Urban America.* Boston: Beacon Press.

Kitwana, Bakari. 2002. *The Hip Hop Generation: Young Blacks and the Crisis in African-American Culture.* New York: Basic Books.

Lusane, Clarence. 1997. *Race in the Global Era: African Americans at the Millennium.* Boston: South End Press.

Massey, Douglas S., and Nancy A. Denton. 1993. *American Apartheid: Segregation and the Making of the Underclass.* Cambridge, Mass.: Harvard University Press.

McKinnon, Jesse. 2001. *The Black Population: 2000.* Vol. C2KBR/01–5. U.S. Census Bureau. Washington, D.C.: U.S. Government Printing Office.

McKinnon, Jesse, and Karen Humes. 2000. *The Black Population in the United States: March 1999.* Current Population Reports, Series P20–530. U.S. Census Bureau. Washington, D.C.: U.S. Government Printing Office.

Miller, Jerome G. 1996. *Search and Destroy: African-American Males in the Criminal Justice System.* New York: Cambridge University Press.

Mohanty, Chandra Talpade. 1997. "Women Workers and Capitalist Scripts: Ideologies of Domination, Common Interests, and the Politics of Solidarity." *Feminist Genealogies, Colonial Legacies, Democratic Futures.* Ed. M. Jacqui Mohanty Chandra and Talpade Alexander, 3–29. New York: Routledge.

Neal, Mark Anthony. 2002. *Soul Babies: Black Popular Culture and the Post-Soul Aesthetic.* New York: Routledge.

Neubeck, Kenneth J., and Noel A. Cazenave. 2001. *Welfare Racism: Playing the Race Card against America's Poor.* New York: Routledge.

Oliver, Melvin L., and Thomas M. Shapiro. 1995. *Black Wealth/White Wealth: A New Perspective on Racial Inequality.* New York: Routledge.

Omi, Michael, and Howard Winant. 1994. *Racial Formation in the United States: From the 1960s to the 1990s.* New York: Routledge.

Patillo-McCoy, Mary. 1999. *Black Picket Fences: Privilege and Peril among the Black Middle Class.* Chicago: University of Chicago Press.

Robinson, Randall. 2000. *The Debt: What America Owes to Blacks.* New York: Plume.

Root, Maria P. P. 2001. *Love's Revolution: Interracial Marriage.* Philadelphia: Temple University Press.

Squires, Gregory D. 1994. *Capital and Communities in Black and White: The Intersections of Race, Class, and Uneven Development.* Albany: State University of New York Press.

Wilson, William Julius. 1978. *The Declining Significance of Race.* Chicago: University of Chicago Press.

———. 1987. *The Truly Disadvantaged: The Inner City, the Underclass, and Public Policy.* Chicago: University of Chicago Press.

———. 1996. *When Work Disappears: The World of the New Urban Poor.* New York: Knopf.

Winant, Howard. 2001. *The World Is a Ghetto: Race and Democracy since World War II.* New York: Basic Books.

4

ANGRY WOMEN ARE BUILDING
Issues and Struggles Facing American Indian Women Today

PAULA GUNN ALLEN

Paula Gunn Allen is professor of English at UCLA. She was awarded the Native American Prize for Literature in 1990. That same year her anthology of short stories, *Spider Woman's Granddaughters,* was awarded the American Book Award, sponsored by the Before Columbus Foundation, and the Susan Koppleman Award. A major Native American poet, writer, and scholar, she has published seven volumes of poetry, a novel, a collection of essays, and two anthologies. Her prose and poetry appear widely in anthologies, journals, and scholarly publications.

The central issue that confronts American Indian women throughout the hemisphere is survival, *literal survival,* both on a cultural and biological level. According to the 1980 census, the population of American Indians is just over one million. This figure, which is disputed by some American Indians, is probably a fair estimate, and it carries certain implications.

Some researchers put our pre-contact population at more than 45 million, while others put it around 20 million. The U.S. government long put it at 450,000—a comforting if imaginary figure, though at one point it was put around 270,000. If our current population is around one million; if, as some researchers estimate, around 25 percent of Indian women and 10 percent of Indian men in the United States have been sterilized without informed consent; if our average life expectancy is, as the best informed research presently says, 55 years; if our infant mortality rate continues at well above national standards; if our average unemployment for all segments of our population—male, female, young, adult, and middle-aged—is between 60 and 90 percent; if the U.S. government continues its policy of termination, relocation, removal, and assimilation along with the destruction of wilderness, reservation land, and its resources, and severe curtailment of hunting, fishing, timber harvesting, and water-use rights—then existing tribes are facing the threat of extinction, which for several hundred tribal groups has already become fact in the past five hundred years.

In this nation of more than 200 million, the Indian people constitute less than one-half of one percent of the population. In a nation that offers refuge, sympathy, and billions of dollars in aid from federal and private sources in the form of food to the hungry, medicine to the sick, and comfort to the dying, the indigenous subject population goes hungry, homeless, impoverished, cut out of the American deal, new, old, and in between. Americans are daily made aware of the worldwide slaughter of native peoples such as the Cambodians, the Palestinians, the Armenians, the Jews—who constitute only a few groups faced with genocide in this century. We are horrified by South African apartheid and the removal of millions of indigenous African black natives to what is there called "homelands"—but this is simply a re-play of nineteenth-century U.S. government removal of American Indians to reservations. Nor do many even notice the parallel or fight South African apartheid by demanding an end to its counterpart within the border of the United States. The American Indian people are in a situation comparable to the imminent genocide in many parts of the world today. The plight of our people north and south of us is no better; to the south it is considerably worse. Consciously or unconsciously, deliberately as a matter of national policy, or accidentally as a matter of "fate," *every single government,* right, left, or centrist, in the western hemisphere is consciously or subconsciously ded-icated to the extinction of those tribal people who live within its borders.

Within this geopolitical charnel house, American Indian women strug-gle on every front for the survival of our children, our people, our self-respect, our value systems, and our way of life. The past five hundred years testify to our skill at waging this struggle: for all the varied weapons of ex-tinction pointed at our hands, we endure.

We survive war and conquest; we survive colonization, acculturation, assimilation; we survive beating, rape, starvation, mutilation, sterilization, abandonment, neglect, death of our children, our loved ones, destruction of our land, our homes, our past, and our future. We survive, and we do more than just survive. We bond, we care, we fight, we teach, we nurse, we bear, we feed, we earn, we laugh, we love, we hang in there, no matter what.

Of course, some, many of us, just give up. Many are alcoholics, many are addicts. Many abandon children, the old ones. Many commit suicide. Many become violent, go insane. Many go "white" and are never seen or heard from again. But enough hold on to their traditions and their ways so that even after almost five hundred brutal years, we endure. And we even write songs and poems, make paintings and drawings that say "We walk in beauty. Let us continue."

Currently our struggles are on two fronts: physical survival and cultural survival. For women this means fighting alcoholism and drug abuse (our own and that of our husbands, lovers, parents, children);[1] poverty; afflu-ence—a destroyer of people who are not traditionally socialized to deal with large sums of money; rape, incest, battering by Indian men; assaults on fer-tility and other health matters by the Indian Health Service and the Public

Health Service; high infant mortality due to substandard medical care, nutrition, and health information; poor educational opportunities or education that takes us away from our traditions, language, and communities; suicide, homicide, or similar expressions of self-hatred; lack of economic opportunities; substandard housing; sometimes violent and always virulent racist attitudes and behavior directed against us by an entertainment and education system that wants only one thing from Indians: our silence, our invisibility, and our collective death.

A headline in the *Navajo Times* in the fall of 1979 reported that rape was the number one crime on the Navajo reservation. In a professional mental health journal of the Indian Health Services, Phyllis Old Dog Cross reported that incest and rape are common among Indian women seeking services and that their incidence is increasing. "It is believed that at least 80 percent of the Native Women seen at the regional psychiatric service center (5 state area) have experienced some sort of sexual assault."[2] Among the forms of abuse being suffered by Native American women, Old Dog Cross cites a recent phenomenon, something called "training." This form of gang rape is "a punitive act of a group of males who band together and get even or take revenge on a selected woman."[3]

These and other cases of violence against women are powerful evidence that the status of women within the tribes has suffered grievous decline since contact, and the decline has increased in intensity in recent years. The amount of violence against women, alcoholism, and violence, abuse, and neglect by women against their children and their aged relatives have all increased. These social ills were virtually unheard of among most tribes fifty years ago, popular American opinion to the contrary. As Old Dog Cross remarks:

> Rapid, unstable and irrational change was required of the Indian people if they were to survive. Incredible loss of all that had meaning was the norm. Inhuman treatment, murder, death, and punishment was a typical experience for all the tribal groups and some didn't survive.
>
> The dominant society devoted its efforts to the attempt to change the Indian into a white-Indian. No inhuman pressure to effect this change was overlooked. These pressures included starvation, incarceration, and enforced education. Religious and healing customs were banished.
>
> In spite of the years of oppression, the Indian and the Indian spirit survived. Not, however, without adverse effect. One of the major effects was the loss of cultured values and the concomitant loss of personal identity. . . . The Indian was taught to be ashamed of being Indian and to emulate the non-Indian. In short, "white was right." For the Indian male, the only route to be successful, to be good, to be right, and to have an identity was to be as much like the white man as he could.[4]

Often it is said that the increase of violence against women is a result of various sociological facts such as oppression, racism, poverty, hopelessness, emasculation of men, and loss of male self-esteem as their own place within traditional society has been systematically destroyed by increasing urbanization, industrialization, and institutionalization, but seldom do we notice that for the past forty to fifty years, American popular media have depicted American Indian men as bloodthirsty savages devoted to treating women cruelly. While traditional Indian men seldom did any such thing—and in fact among most tribes abuse of women was simply unthinkable, as was abuse of children or the aged—the lie about "usual" male Indian behavior seems to have taken root and now bears its brutal and bitter fruit.

Image casting and image control constitute the central process that American Indian women must come to terms with, for on that control rests our sense of self, our claim to a past and to a future that we define and that we build. Images of Indians in media and education materials profoundly influence how we act, how we relate to the world and to each other, and how we value ourselves. They also determine to a large extent how our men act toward us, toward our children, and toward each other. The popular American media image of Indian people as savages with no conscience, no compassion, and no sense of the value of human life and human dignity was hardly true of the tribes—however true it was of the invaders. But as Adolf Hitler noted a little over fifty years ago, if you tell a lie big enough and often enough, it will be believed. Evidently, while Americans and people all over the world have been led into a deep and unquestioned belief that American Indians are cruel savages, a number of American Indian men have been equally deluded into internalizing that image and acting on it. Media images, literary images, and artistic images, particularly those embedded in popular culture, must be changed before Indian women will see much relief from the violence that destroys so many lives.

To survive culturally, American Indian women must often fight the United States government, the tribal governments, women and men of their tribe or their urban community who are virulently misogynist or who are threatened by attempts to change the images foisted on us over the centuries by whites. The colonizers' revisions of our lives, values, and histories have devastated us at the most critical level of all—that of our minds, our own sense of who we are.

Many women express strong opposition to those who would alter our life supports, steal our tribal lands, colonize our cultures and cultural expressions, and revise our very identities. We must strive to maintain tribal status; we must make certain that the tribes continue to be legally recognized entities, sovereign nations within the larger United States, and we must wage this struggle in many ways—political, educational, literary, artistic, individual, and communal. We are doing all we can: as mothers and grandmothers; as family members and tribal members; as professionals, workers, artists, shamans, leaders, chiefs, speakers, writers, and organizers, we daily demonstrate that we have no intention of disappearing, of being silent, or of quietly acquiescing in our extinction.

NOTES

1. It is likely, say some researchers, that fetal alcohol syndrome, which is serious among many Indian groups, will be so serious among the White Mountain Apache and the Pine Ridge Sioux that if present trends continue, by the year 2000 some people estimate that almost one-half of all children born on those reservations will in some way be affected by FAS. (Michael Dorris, Native American Studies, Dartmouth College, private conversation. Dorris has done extensive research into the syndrome as it affects native populations in the United States as well as in New Zealand.)

2. Phyllis Old Dog Cross, "Sexual Abuse, A New Threat to the Native American Woman: An Overview," *Listening Post: A Periodical of the Mental Health Programs of Indian Health Services*, vol. 6, no. 2 (April 1982) p. 18.

3. Old Dog Cross, p. 18.

4. Old Dog Cross, p. 20.

5

"J.A.P."-SLAPPING
The Politics of Scapegoating

RUTH ATKIN • ADRIENNE RICH

Ruth Atkin is a middle-class, Ashkenazi Jewish feminist activist born in the Midwest. She has been involved in progressive Jewish publishing since 1979 and is a founding and current editor of *Gesher's* successor, *Bridges: A Journal for Jewish Feminists and Our Friends*. On weekdays Ruth works as a medical social worker in an outpatient clinic serving veterans.

Adrienne Rich, the daughter of a Jewish father and a non-Jewish mother, is a poet and nonfiction writer and an activist. She worked for eight years in New Jewish Agenda, a national organization for progressive Jews, and was a founding editor of *Bridges: A Journal for Jewish Feminists and Our Friends*. Her most recent books are *What Is Found There: Notebooks on Poetry and Politics and Dark Fields of the Republic: Poems 1991–1995*. She lives in California.

Those who remember World War II may well recall the racist imagery and language levelled at Japanese people. The Japanese, formerly idealized as giving us exquisite art, magical paper toys, flower arranging, swiftly became the "Japs," to be "slapped" by American military force: yellow,

---

Ruth Atkin and Adrienne Rich, "'J.A.P.'-Slapping: The Politics of Scapegoating" from *Gesher* (January 1988). Reprinted with the permission of the authors.[1]

toothy torturers with a genetic flair for cruelty, the dastardly bombers of Pearl Harbor: the people who would deserve the genocidal bombings of Hiroshima and Nagasaki. The word "Jap" held its own in the monosyllabic language of "kike," "wop," "spic," "chink," "bitch," "slut" — short, brutal sounds like the impact of a fist. "Slap That Jap" was a familiar wartime slogan.

These memories of the 1940s are part of the background some of us bring to the recent explosion of "Jewish-American Princess" stereotypes on Eastern college campuses. The Jewish feminist magazine *Lilith* first reported the phenomenon in its Fall 1987 issue (#17); since then, articles have appeared in the *New York Times* and the Jewish press. A column, "No Laughing Matter," by Suzanne Messing, appeared in the feminist paper *New Directions for Women*. On December 9, [1987], National Public Radio broadcast a segment on the spread of "J.A.P.-baiting," interviewing Evelyn Torton Beck, Professor of Women's Studies at the University of Maryland and editor of *Nice Jewish Girls: A Lesbian Anthology*.

"J.A.P."-baiting has taken a range of forms: novels by post–World War II American Jewish writers such as Herman Wouk's *Marjorie Morningstar*; the routines of Jewish comedians; negative stereotyping of middle-class Jewish women in greeting cards, jewelry, T-shirts, graffiti; and ritualized verbal assaults on Jewish women on college campuses. The Jewish woman is stereotyped as rich, spoiled, avidly materialistic, and solely out for herself. Most of the negative attributes are, of course, familiar anti-Jewish stereotypes: here they are pushed onto the Jewish woman. *Lilith* reported that at Syracuse University basketball games, the pep band would point at certain women who stood up and chant "JAP, JAP, JAP." On other campuses have appeared such graffiti as: "I tolerate JAPS for sex"; "All JAPS are sluts"; "Solution to the JAP question: when they go for their nose jobs, tie their tubes as well." (This last graffito is packed with implications: the "J.A.P." is trying to assimilate, to pass; Jewish women should be sterilized [as thousands were under Hitler]. It implies a knowledge of Nazi vocabulary and practice that belies the theory of "J.A.P"-baiting as ignorant fun and games.)

A different kind of hostility identifies the "J.A.P." not as a "slut" but as a "frigid" woman, unwilling to "put out" sexually. Messing quotes a greeting card (published by Noble Press, New York): "Why do JAPS close their eyes while having sex? So they can pretend they're shopping." National Public Radio reports a fun-fair booth: "Make Her Prove She's Not a JAP — Make Her Swallow."

"J.A.P." imagery has been acceptable in the Jewish community and continues to be. According to the Chicago *Jewish Sentinel*, the National Federation of Temple Sisterhoods adopted a resolution at their national convention this fall condemning "J.A.P." jokes and images, since what began as an object of sexist humor has now become a tool of the anti-Semite. The resolution called on member sisterhoods to discontinue the sale of "J.A.P. items" in their Judaica shops. But if the sisterhoods had challenged the stereotyping of Jewish women from the first, it might have stood less chance to become the tool of the anti-Semite, and within the Jewish community "JAP items" would not have received the endorsement of the National Federation. The issue is sometimes trivialized as a matter of humor ("we can laugh at ourselves"), or on the grounds that the negative stereotypes contain a "kernel of truth." We need to examine these responses.

The semiotics, or signifying power, of the "J.A.P." stereotype is complex. A clear feminist perception is needed to decipher the scapegoating of the **women** within a historically scapegoated group. Within the Jewish community, scapegoating and negative labeling of Jewish women may reflect tensions over gender roles and conflicts specific to the group. They also reveal how Jews participate in the sexism of the society at large.

"Kaleidoscopic" is Susan Schnur's term (in *Lilith*) for the "JAP theme." Rarely have two forms of social hatred—misogyny and anti-Semitism—been so explicitly joined: the "materialistic, pushy" Jew and the "princess," the selfish, privileged rich woman. Conflate these two identities and you have an easy target in a time when the presence of women on campuses is threatening to men, when jobs after college are at a premium, and any woman can be perceived by any man as a competitor for his future job. In fact, "J.A.P." is a conflation of three hated identities: Jew, woman, and those people who are seen, in a society of vast inequalities and injustice, as having "made it."

But to understand the "J.A.P."-baiting phenomenon fully we need an understanding of how the mechanisms of anti-Jewish thought operate. The "Jewish Mother" stereotype—of a too-assertive, domineering woman, devouring the lives of her children—a leftover of the community-building, survival orientation of immigrant culture, is followed by the "Jewish American Princess." The next generation of epithets directed at Jewish women reflects the assimilation of the daughters into American society. As with any stereotype, a complex social pattern is crudely and simplistically caricatured. Young Jewish women are scapegoated for the material "success" of their parents' (usually their fathers') earning power. Scapegoating young Jewish women fits into the historic cyclical pattern of Jewish oppression, whereby some Jews have been allowed a limited access to power (as tax-collectors, money-lenders, etc.), creating the illusion of Jews overall having power. Every period of toleration of Jews in host countries has been followed by periods of economic and social unrest when ruling interests have withdrawn "protection" and support of Jews, and have encouraged the general population to direct their resentments against Jews. This phase has been brutal in the extreme: Eastern European pogroms; the Nazi camps.

Increasing numbers of people in America today are without basic necessities and comforts. The current atmosphere of growing resentment of material success is fully justified. But its historic precedents, for Jews, are troubling. As the economic situation in the U.S. widens the gap between rich and poor, we need to be on the alert for expressions of anger and frustration which divert attention from the real sources of economic hardship—the prioritizing of death over life, of profit over the basic needs of people. This hardship is shared by many Jews, especially older Jewish women. It is not a coincidence that "J.A.P."-baiting is occurring on college campuses, perceived as places of privilege.

Jews have been perceived, and to a certain extent correctly, as a "successful" minority group in America. Writing in *Lilith*, Francine Klagsbrun asks: "Isn't it odd that the term JAP, referring to a spoiled, self-indulgent woman, should be so widely used at a time when women are working outside their homes in unprecedented numbers, struggling to balance their home lives and their work lives, to give as much of themselves as they can to everybody — their husbands, their kids, their bosses?" In the same issue, Susan Schnur notes that "the characterizations of JAPs and Yuppies are often identical." She sees the label of Yuppies as "neutral or even positive," but many a bitter, long-stored anti-Yuppie joke was heard when Wall Street crashed last October. And it is perhaps not coincidental that the acronym "JAP" fits so neatly into a growing anti-Asian racism that has accompanied the increased perception of Asians as a "successful" minority. Insofar as a fraternity house booth inviting passers-by to "Slap a JAP" echoes the "Slap That Jap: Buy War Bonds" posters of World War II, it legitimizes anti-Semitism, misogyny, and anti-Asian racism simultaneously.

As the U.S. economy wavers, as American national identity itself wavers, anti-Semitism is one time-honored escape from critical thinking and political responsibility. Young Jewish women on college campuses may have received little in their education to help them interpret this double assault — especially since the "JAP" label can be applied to non-Jews as well. Some older Jewish women, too, as articles in both *Lilith* and *New Directions for Women* indicate, have reacted by accepting stereotyping, by suggesting that "We should be able to laugh at ourselves." Both Jewish men and women tell "J.A.P." jokes. But, according to Messing, "No one refers to herself as a JAP." Francine Klagsbrun observes, "When we put down other Jewish women, that is a form of self-hatred."

And yes, we do need to laugh at ourselves. But our humor cannot — for our own health — be founded on self-hatred. When we delight in ourselves as women, delight in ourselves as Jews, we can laugh out of the fullness of recognizing ourselves as necessarily flawed and sometimes ridiculous human beings. Our humor need not come out of the arsenal of those who would deny us our humanity.

NOTE

1. Thanks to Lilith: *The Jewish Women's Magazine*, 250 W. 57th Street, New York, NY 10107; *New Directions for Women*, 108 Palisade Ave., Englewood, NJ 07631; the Chicago *Jewish Sentinel*, 323 S. Franklin St., Rm. 501, Chicago, IL 60606.

6

WHITE PRIVILEGE
Unpacking the Invisible Knapsack

PEGGY MCINTOSH

Peggy McIntosh, associate director of the Wellesley College Center for Research on Women, is founder and co-director of the United States S.E.E.D. Project on Inclusive Curriculum (Seeking Educational Equity and Diversity). She is best known for her work on curricular revision, privilege systems, and feelings of fraudulence.

I was taught to see racism only in individual acts of meanness, not in invisible systems conferring dominance on my group.

Through work to bring materials from Women's Studies into the rest of the curriculum, I have often noticed men's unwillingness to grant that they are overprivileged, even though they may grant that women are disadvantaged. They may say they will work to improve women's status, in the society, the university, or the curriculum, but they can't or won't support the idea of lessening men's. Denials which amount to taboos surround the subject of advantages which men gain from women's disadvantages. These denials protect male privilege from being fully acknowledged, lessened or ended.

Thinking through unacknowledged male privilege as a phenomenon, I realized that since hierarchies in our society are interlocking, there was most likely a phenomenon of white privilege which was similarly denied and protected. As a white person, I realized I had been taught about racism as something which puts others at a disadvantage, but had been taught not to see one of its corollary aspects, white privilege, which puts me at an advantage.

I think whites are carefully taught not to recognize white privilege, as males are taught not to recognize male privilege. So I have begun in an untutored way to ask what it is like to have white privilege. I have come to see white privilege as an invisible package of unearned assets which I can count on cashing in each day, but about which I was 'meant' to remain oblivious. White privilege is like an invisible weightless knapsack of special provisions, maps, passports, codebooks, visas, clothes, tools, and blank checks.

Describing white privilege makes one newly accountable. As we in Women's Studies work to reveal male privilege and ask men to give up some of their power, so one who writes about having white privilege must ask, "Having described it, what will I do to lessen or end it?"

After I realized the extent to which men work from a base of unacknowledged privilege, I understood that much of their oppressiveness was unconscious. Then I remembered the frequent charges from women of color that white women whom they encounter are oppressive. I began to understand why we are justly seen as oppressive, even when we don't see ourselves that way. I began to count the ways in which I enjoy unearned skin privilege and have been conditioned into oblivion about its existence.

My schooling gave me no training in seeing myself as an oppressor, as an unfairly advantaged person, or as a participant in a damaged culture. I was taught to see myself as an individual whose moral state depended on her individual moral will. My schooling followed the pattern my colleague Elizabeth Minnich has pointed out: whites are taught to think of their lives as morally neutral, normative, and average, and also ideal, so that when we work to benefit others, this is seen as work which will allow "them" to be more like "us."

I decided to try to work on myself at least by identifying some of the daily effects of white privilege in my life. I have chosen those conditions which I think in my case *attach somewhat more to skin-color privilege* than to class, religion, ethnic status, or geographical location, though of course all these other factors are intricately intertwined. As far as I can see, my African American coworkers, friends and acquaintances with whom I come into daily or frequent contact in this particular time, place, and line of work cannot count on most of these conditions.

1. I can if I wish arrange to be in the company of people of my race most of the time.
2. If I should need to move, I can be pretty sure of renting or purchasing housing in an area which I can afford and in which I would want to live.
3. I can be pretty sure that my neighbors in such a location will be neutral or pleasant to me.
4. I can go shopping alone most of the time, pretty well assured that I will not be followed or harassed.
5. I can turn on the television or open to the front page of the paper and see people of my race widely represented.
6. When I am told about our national heritage or about "civilization," I am shown that people of my color made it what it is.
7. I can be sure that my children will be given curricular materials that testify to the existence of their race.
8. If I want to, I can be pretty sure of finding a publisher for this piece on white privilege.

9. I can go into a music shop and count on finding the music of my race represented, into a supermarket and find the staple foods which fit with my cultural traditions, into a hairdresser's shop and find someone who can cut my hair.

10. Whether I use checks, credit cards, or cash, I can count on my skin color not to work against the appearance of financial reliability.

11. I can arrange to protect my children most of the time from people who might not like them.

12. I can swear, or dress in second hand clothes, or not answer letters, without having people attribute these choices to the bad morals, the poverty, or the illiteracy of my race.

13. I can speak in public to a powerful male group without putting my race on trial.

14. I can do well in a challenging situation without being called a credit to my race.

15. I am never asked to speak for all the people of my racial group.

16. I can remain oblivious of the language and customs of persons of color who constitute the world's majority without feeling in my culture any penalty for such oblivion.

17. I can criticize our government and talk about how much I fear its policies and behavior without being seen as a cultural outsider.

18. I can be pretty sure that if I ask to talk to "the person in charge," I will be facing a person of my race.

19. If a traffic cop pulls me over or if the IRS audits my tax return, I can be sure I haven't been singled out because of my race.

20. I can easily buy posters, postcards, picture books, greeting cards, dolls, toys, and children's magazines featuring people of my race.

21. I can go home from most meetings of organizations I belong to feeling somewhat tied in, rather than isolated, out-of-place, outnumbered, unheard, held at a distance, or feared.

22. I can take a job with an affirmative action employer without having coworkers on the job suspect that I got it because of race.

23. I can choose public accommodation without fearing that people of my race cannot get in or will be mistreated in the places I have chosen.

24. I can be sure that if I need legal or medical help, my race will not work against me.

25. If my day, week, or year is going badly, I need not ask of each negative episode or situation whether it has racial overtones.

26. I can choose blemish cover or bandages in "flesh" color and have them more or less match my skin.

I repeatedly forgot each of the realizations on this list until I wrote it down. For me white privilege has turned out to be an elusive and fugitive subject. The pressure to avoid it is great, for in facing it I must give up the myth of meritocracy. If these things are true, this is not such a free country;

one's life is not what one makes it; many doors open for certain people through no virtues of their own.

In unpacking this invisible knapsack of white privilege, I have listed conditions of daily experience which I once took for granted. Nor did I think of any of these perquisites as bad for the holder. I now think that we need a more finely differentiated taxonomy of privilege, for some of these varieties are only what one would want for everyone in a just society, and others give license to be ignorant, oblivious, arrogant and destructive.

I see a pattern running through the matrix of white privilege, a pattern of assumptions which were passed on to me as a white person. There was one main piece of cultural turf; it was my own turf, and I was among those who could control the turf. *My skin color was an asset for any move I was educated to want to make.* I could think of myself as belonging in major ways, and of making social systems work for me. I could freely disparage, fear, neglect, or be oblivious to anything outside of the dominant cultural forms. Being of the main culture, I could also criticize it fairly freely.

In proportion as my racial group was being made confident, comfortable, and oblivious, other groups were likely being made inconfident, uncomfortable, and alienated. Whiteness protected me from many kinds of hostility, distress, and violence, which I was being subtly trained to visit in turn upon people of color.

For this reason, the word "privilege" now seems to me misleading. We usually think of privilege as being a favored state, whether earned or conferred by birth or luck. Yet some of the conditions I have described here work to systematically overempower certain groups. Such privilege simply *confers dominance* because of one's race or sex.

I want, then, to distinguish between earned strength and unearned power conferred systematically. Power from unearned privilege can look like strength when it is in fact permission to escape or to dominate. But not all of the privileges on my list are inevitably damaging. Some, like the expectation that neighbors will be decent to you, or that your race will not count against you in court, should be the norm in a just society. Others, like the privilege to ignore less powerful people, distort the humanity of the holders as well as the ignored groups.

We might at least start by distinguishing between positive advantages which we can work to spread, and negative types of advantages which unless rejected will always reinforce our present hierarchies. For example, the feeling that one belongs within the human circle, as Native Americans say, should not be seen as privilege for a few. Ideally it is an *unearned entitlement.* At present, since only a few have it, it is an *unearned advantage* for them. This paper results from a process of coming to see that some of the power which I originally saw as attendant on being a human being in the U.S. consisted in *unearned advantage* and *conferred dominance.*

I have met very few men who are truly distressed about systemic, unearned male advantage and conferred dominance. And so one question for me and others like me is whether we will be like them, or whether we will get truly distressed, even outraged, about unearned race advantage and conferred dominance and if so, what we will do to lessen them. In any case, we need to do more work in identifying how they actually affect our daily lives. Many, perhaps most, of our white students in the U.S. think that racism doesn't affect them because they are not people of color; they do not see "whiteness" as a racial identity. In addition, since race and sex are not the only advantaging systems at work, we need similarly to examine the daily experience of having age advantage, or ethnic advantage, or physical ability, or advantage related to nationality, religion, or sexual orientation.

Difficulties and dangers surrounding the task of finding parallels are many. Since racism, sexism, and heterosexism are not the same, the advantaging associated with them should not be seen as the same. In addition, it is hard to disentangle aspects of unearned advantage which rest more on social class, economic class, race, religion, sex and ethnic identity than on other factors. Still, all of the oppressions are interlocking, as the Combahee River Collective Statement of 1977 continues to remind us eloquently.

One factor seems clear about all of the interlocking oppressions. They take both active forms which we can see and embedded forms which as a member of the dominant group one is taught not to see. In my class and place, I did not see myself as a racist because I was taught to recognize racism only in individual acts of meanness by members of my group, never in invisible systems conferring unsought racial dominance on my group from birth.

Disapproving of the systems won't be enough to change them. I was taught to think that racism could end if white individuals changed their attitudes. [But] a "white" skin in the United States opens many doors for whites whether or not we approve of the way dominance has been conferred on us. Individual acts can palliate, but cannot end, these problems.

To redesign social systems we need first to acknowledge their colossal unseen dimensions. The silences and denials surrounding privilege are the key political tool here. They keep the thinking about equality or equity incomplete, protecting unearned advantage and conferred dominance by making these taboo subjects. Most talk by whites about equal opportunity seems to me now to be about equal opportunity to try to get into a position of dominance while denying that *systems* of dominance exist.

It seems to me that obliviousness about white advantage, like obliviousness about male advantage, is kept strongly inculturated in the United States so as to maintain the myth of meritocracy, the myth that democratic choice is equally available to all. Keeping most people unaware that freedom of confident action is there for just a small number of people props up those in power, and serves to keep power in the hands of the same groups that have most of it already.

Though systemic change takes many decades, there are pressing questions for me and I imagine for some others like me if we raise our daily consciousness on the perquisites of being light-skinned. What will we do with such knowledge? As we know from watching men, it is an open question whether we will choose to use unearned advantage to weaken hidden systems of advantage, and whether we will use any of our arbitrarily-awarded power to try to reconstruct power systems on a broader base.

7

CONTROLLED OR AUTONOMOUS: IDENTITY AND THE EXPERIENCE OF THE NETWORK, WOMEN LIVING UNDER MUSLIM LAWS

FARIDA SHAHEED

Farida Shaheed is a sociologist and activist who works with Shirkat Gah—Women's Resource Centre in Lahore, Pakistan and the Women Living Under Muslim Laws (WLUML) International Solidarity Network.

The International network Women Living under Muslim Laws (WLUML) was initially formed in response to several incidents urgently requiring action in 1984, all of which related to Islam, laws, and women. In Algeria, three feminists were arrested and jailed without trial, then kept incommunicado for seven months. Their crime was having discussed with other women the government's proposal to introduce a new set of laws on the family (Code de la Famille) that severely reduced women's rights in this field. In India, a Muslim woman filed a petition to the Supreme Court arguing that the application of religious minority law denied her rights otherwise guaranteed all citizens under the Constitution of India. In Abu Dhabi, for the alleged crime of adultery a pregnant woman was sentenced to be stoned to death two months after giving birth. In Europe, the Mothers of Algiers (a group formed by women divorced from Algerian men) were seeking access to or custody of their children.[1] Excepting the condemned woman, on whose behalf others initiated action, those concerned in each incident asked for international support. Starting as an action committee, WLUML coalesced into a network between 1984 and 1986, when it formulated its first Plan of Action.

Geographically scattered, these first incidents were symptomatic of the much wider problem confronting women in the Muslim world, who increasingly find that, in the tussle for political pre-eminence, political forces (in and out of office) are increasingly formulating legal, social, or administrative measures justified by reference to Islam that militate against women's autonomy and self-actualization.

To understand the logic underpinning WLUML's creation and in order to assess the possible impact of its actions and strategies, it is essential to first locate women in the complex web of Islam, law, and society in the Muslim world and to clarify some basic issues in this respect. First, the essential components of patriarchal structure in Muslim societies do not differ from those enumerated by non-Muslim feminists, and, like elsewhere, women's subordination occurs at multiple levels (kinship structures, state-building projects, anti-imperialist and populist ideologies, and national and international policies). Nor should women be viewed as passive victims, as "they are fully fledged social actors, bearing the full set of contradictions implied by their class, racial, and ethnic locations as well as gender" (Kandiyoti 1989, 8)[2]—all being factors that in turn moderate women's interaction with both the state and religion.

Second, the idea of one homogeneous Muslim world is an illusion and, in fact (as Deniz Kandiyoti puts it),

> So-called Islamic societies embody widely differing histories of state and class formation. The relationships between state and religion have correspondingly varied as they have evolved. . . . [But] all have had to grapple with the problems of establishing "modern" nation-states. This meant forging of citizenship, and finding new legitimizing ideologies and power bases. . . . Most Muslim states have failed to generate ideologies capable of coping realistically with social change. This and their histories of dependence vis-à-vis the West have led them to rely on Islam not only as the sole coherent ideology at their disposal but also as a symbol of their cultural identity and integrity. [1989, 5]

Third, when identity is transformed into a set of beliefs and behavioral patterns ordering community life, existing socioeconomic and political structures play a major role in shaping the transformation. Consequently, while it is frequently claimed that any given state, society, or community is Islamic, it is in fact not *Islamic* (i.e., that which is ordained) but *Muslim* (i.e., of those who adhere to Islam) and reflects the assimilation of Islam into prevailing structures, systems, and practices—hence the many significantly different varieties of Muslim societies that exist today. And, finally, the diversity of Muslim societies and the differing realities of women within them have produced a plethora of feminist responses in the political arena that range from the exclusively secular to the exclusively theological, with many permutations in between.

[. . .]

Formation of the Network

It is against this backdrop that the network Women Living under Muslim Laws was created to break women's isolation and to provide linkages and support to all women whose lives may be affected by Muslim laws.

[. . .]

The formulation of the network's name is an acknowledgment of both the complexity and diversity of women's realities in the Muslim world. A less obvious concern that went into the choice of name is that women affected by Muslim laws may not be Muslim, either by virtue of having a different religion or by virtue of having chosen another marker of political or personal identity. The emphasis in the title and in the group is therefore on the women themselves and their situations and not on the specific politicoreligious option they may exercise. As a network, WLUML therefore extends to women living in countries where Islam is the state religion as well as those from Muslim communities ruled by religious minority laws, to women in secular states where a rapidly expanding political presence of Islam increasingly provokes a demand for minority religious law, as well as to women in migrant Muslim communities in Europe, the Americas, and Australasia, and further includes non-Muslim women who may have Muslim laws applied to them directly or through their children.

Propelled by concrete, on-the-ground issues rather than the outcome of merely theoretical discourse, WLUML's objectives are to create and reinforce linkages between women and women's groups within Muslim communities, to increase their knowledge about both their common and diverse situations, and to strengthen their struggles by creating the means and channels needed to support their efforts internationally from within and outside the Muslim world. In essence, the purpose of WLUML is to increase the autonomy of women affected by Muslim laws by encouraging them to analyze and reformulate the identity imposed on them through the application of Muslim laws, and by so doing to assume greater control over their lives. The WLUML aims to achieve this by building a network of mutual solidarity and information flow; by facilitating interaction and contact between women from Muslim countries and communities, on the one hand, and between them and progressive and feminist groups at large, on the other; by promoting the exposure of women from one geographical area to another in and outside the Muslim world; and by undertaking common projects identified by and executed through network participants. The WLUML's initial Plan of Action clearly states that "its purpose is simply to facilitate access to information and to each other. Its existence therefore depends on our links and not on the specific activities undertaken or positions held by any group or individual involved in this process" (1986, 1).

Women Living under Muslim Laws believes that the seeming helplessness of a majority of women in the Muslim world in effectively mobilizing against and overcoming adverse laws and customs stems not only from their being economically and politically less powerful but also from their erroneous belief that the only existence possible for a Muslim woman that allows her to maintain her identity—however that may be defined—is the one delineated for her in her own national context. In fact, the common presumption both within and outside the Muslim world that there exists one homogeneous Muslim world is fallacy. Interaction between women from different Muslim societies proves that, while some similarities may stretch across cultures, classes, sects, schools, and continents, the diversities are at least equally striking. The different realities of women living under Muslim laws, according to WLUML, "range from being strictly closeted, isolated and voiceless within four walls, subjected to public floggings and condemned to death for presumed adultery (which is considered a crime against the state) and forcibly given in marriage as a child, to situations where women have a far greater degree of freedom of movement and interaction, the right to work, to participate in public affairs and also exercise a far greater control over their own lives" (1986, 5).

Dreaming of an alternative reality is not simply a matter of inspiration but, to a large extent, depends on accessing information on the sources of law and *customary practices* and on the political and social forces that determine women's current reality. Beyond this is the need to belong to a social collectivity. As mentioned above, the fear of being cut off from one's collective identity militates against women challenging "Muslim laws." Therefore, taking initiative against such laws is facilitated if women can be sure of the support of another collectivity that functions as an alternative reference group and, by so doing, may also help women redefine the parameters of their current reference group(s). In this, contacts and links with women from other parts of the Muslim world—whose very existence speaks of the multiplicity of women's realities within the Muslim context—provide an important source of inspiration. Likewise, information on the diversity of existing laws within the Muslim world gives material shape to alternatives. Both encourage women to dream of different realities—the first step in changing the present one.

In contrast, an inability to unravel the various strands of an apparently inseparable but actually composite identity presented in the name of Islam serves to silence and immobilize women. This silence is deepened by women's isolation in specific environments and their lack of knowledge about their official legal rights—both in terms of Muslim personal laws and/or civil codes and of the source of these laws. Most women remain ignorant of even the basic disparities between customary laws applied to them and the official version of Muslim laws. Action is likewise impeded by women's negligible access to information enabling them to challenge the validity of either type of law, including information about the strategies and struggles of other women in the Muslim world and the discussions and debates that flow from these.

Then there is the political use of Islam. In most of the Muslim world Islam has been used by those in power and those out of it, more often by right-wing elements than progressive forces but inevitably in a bid for political power: for consolidating support or legitimizing force (Mumtaz and Shaheed 1987, 1). This practice is so widespread as to provoke one feminist to conclude that "not only have the sacred texts always been manipulated, but manipulation of them is a structural characteristic of the practice of power in Muslim societies" (Mernissi 1992, 8–9). For women living under Muslim laws, one of the dangers is that politicoreligious groups find it convenient to cite so-called Islamic laws already being applied in different Muslim countries in support of their own demands for more stringent, essentially undemocratic or discriminatory "Islamic" laws. For their part, when women can cite examples of positive legislation or their demands are supported from within the Muslim world (though not necessarily from within a religious framework), their effectiveness is strengthened.

Women Living under Muslim Laws posits that it is only when women start assuming the right to define for themselves the parameters of their own identity and stop accepting unconditionally and without question what is presented to them as the "correct" religion, the "correct" culture, or the "correct" national identity that they will be able effectively to challenge the corpus of laws imposed on them. The WLUML is convinced that while controlling women through identity has multiple ramifications—in which religion, nationality, ethnicity, and class all come into play—"depriving [women] of even dreaming of a different reality is one of the most debilitating forms of oppression [they] face" (WLUML 1986, 7). It is the vision of a different reality that propels the reformulation of the present one, and it is here, in opening the doors to a multiplicity of possible alternatives, that the WLUML network hopes to make its most important contribution.

REFERENCES

Kandiyoti, Deniz. (1989). "Women and Islam: What Are the Missing Terms?" *Dossier 5/6* (Grabels), December 1988/May 1989, 5–9.

Mernissi, Fatima. (1992). *The Veil and the Male Elite: A Feminist Interpretation of Women's Rights in Islam*, Mary Jo Lakeland, trans. New York: Addison-Wesley.

Mumtaz, Khawar, and Farida Shaheed. (1987). *Two Steps Forward, One Step Back? Women of Pakistan*. London: Zed Books.

Shaheed, Farida. (1986). "The Cultural Articulation of Patriarchy: Legal Systems, Islam and the Women in Pakistan." *South Asia Bulletin* 6(1): 38–44.

WLUML. (1986). *Plan of Action (Aramon)*.

NOTES

1. In Algeria, the three feminists were released; however, the new Family Code was enacted in 1984, negatively affecting women. In India, the Muslim Women (Pro-

tection of the Rights on Divorce) Act 1986 allowed Muslim minority law to super-
sede the Constitutional provisions, depriving Muslim women of rights enjoyed by
others. In Abu Dhabi, after a strong international campaign of numerous groups,
the woman was repatriated to her own country, Sri Lanka. After several years, the
governments of Algeria and France signed a treaty providing for visiting rights to
divorced mothers of Algerian children.

2. For a more complete discussion on the subject of the cultural articulation of patriarchy, see Shaheed 1986; on the complexities of the situation, see Kandiyoti 1989.

8

THEORIZING DIFFERENCE
FROM MULTIRACIAL FEMINISM

MAXINE BACA ZINN • BONNIE THORNTON DILL

Maxine Baca Zinn teaches in the Department of Sociology at Michigan State University. She has written widely in the area of family relations, Chicano studies, and gender studies, including (most recently) *Women of Color in U.S. Society* (with Bonnie
Thornton Dill), *Diversity in Families* (with Stanley Eitzen), and *The Reshaping of America*.

Bonnie Thornton Dill earned her Ph.D. at New York University after working for a
number of years in anti-poverty and open-admissions programs in New York. She
is currently Professor of Women's Studies at the University of Maryland, College
Park, and was the founding director of the Center for Research on Women at Mem-
phis State University. She has contributed articles to such journals as *Signs, Journal
of Family History,* and *Feminist Studies* and is co-editor with Maxine Baca Zinn of the
book *Women of Color in American Society* for Temple University Press. She is also
conducting research on single mothers, race, and poverty in the rural South with a
grant from the Aspen Institute and the Ford Foundation.

Women of color have long challenged the hegemony of feminisms
constructed primarily around the lives of white middle-class
women. Since the late 1960s, U.S. women of color have taken issue
with unitary theories of gender. Our critiques grew out of the widespread
concern about the exclusion of women of color from feminist scholarship

Maxine Baca Zinn and Bonnie Thornton, "Theorizing Difference from Multiracial
Feminism," *Feminist Studies* 22, No. 2 (Summer 1996): 321–331. Reprinted with the
permission of the publisher, Feminist Studies, Inc.

and the misinterpretation of our experiences,[1] and ultimately "out of the very discourses, denying, permitting, and producing difference."[2] Speaking simultaneously from "within and against" *both* women's liberation *and* antiracist movements, we have insisted on the need to challenge systems of domination,[3] not merely as gendered subjects but as women whose lives are affected by our location in multiple hierarchies.

Recently, and largely in response to these challenges, work that links gender to other forms of domination is increasing. In this article, we examine this connection further as well as the ways in which difference and diversity infuse contemporary feminist studies. Our analysis draws on a conceptual framework that we refer to as "multiracial feminism."[4] This perspective is an attempt to go beyond a mere recognition of diversity and difference among women to examine structures of domination, specifically the importance of race in understanding the social construction of gender. Despite the varied concerns and multiple intellectual stances which characterize the feminisms of women of color, they share an emphasis on race as a primary force situating genders differently. It is the centrality of race, of institutionalized racism, and of struggles against racial oppression that link the various feminist perspectives within this framework. Together, they demonstrate that racial meanings offer new theoretical directions for feminist thought.

Tensions in Contemporary Difference Feminism

Objections to the false universalism embedded in the concept "woman" emerged within other discourses as well as those of women of color.[5] Lesbian feminists and postmodern feminists put forth their own versions of what Susan Bordo has called "gender skepticism."[6]

Many thinkers within mainstream feminism have responded to these critiques with efforts to contextualize gender. The search for women's "universal" or "essential" characteristics is being abandoned. By examining gender in the context of other social divisions and perspectives, difference has gradually become important—even problematizing the universal categories of "women" and "men." Sandra Harding expresses the shift best in her claim that "there are no gender relations *per se*, but only gender relations as constructed by and between classes, races, and cultures."[7]

Many feminists now contend that difference occupies center stage as *the* project of women studies today.[8] According to one scholar, "difference has replaced equality as the central concern of feminist theory."[9] Many have welcomed the change, hailing it as a major revitalizing force in U.S. feminist theory.[10] But if *some* priorities within mainstream feminist thought have been refocused by attention to difference, there remains an "uneasy alliance"[11] between women of color and other feminists.

If difference has helped revitalize academic feminisms, it has also "upset the apple cart" and introduced new conflicts into feminist studies.[12] For example, in a recent and widely discussed essay, Jane Rowland Martin argues that the current preoccupation with difference is leading feminism into dangerous traps. She fears that in giving privileged status to a predetermined set of analytic categories (race, ethnicity, and class), "we affirm the existence of nothing but difference." She asks, "How do we know that for us, difference does not turn on being fat, or religious, or in an abusive relationship?"[13]

We, too, see pitfalls in some strands of the difference project. However, our perspectives take their bearings from social relations. Race and class differences are crucial, we argue, not as individual characteristics (such as being fat) but insofar as they are primary organizing principles of a society which locates and positions groups within that society's opportunity structures.

Despite the much-heralded diversity trend within feminist studies, difference is often reduced to mere pluralism: a "live and let live" approach where principles of relativism generate a long list of diversities which begin with gender, class, and race and continue through a range of social structures as well as personal characteristics.[14] Another disturbing pattern, which bell hooks refers to as "the commodification of difference," is the representation of diversity as a form of exotica, "a spice, seasoning that livens up the dull dish that is mainstream white culture."[15] The major limitation of these approaches is the failure to attend to the power relations that accompany difference. Moreover, these approaches ignore the inequalities that cause some characteristics to be seen as "normal" while others are seen as "different" and thus, deviant.

Maria C. Lugones expresses irritation at those feminists who see only the *problem* of difference without recognizing *difference*.[16] Increasingly, we find that difference is recognized. But this in no way means that difference occupies a "privileged" theoretical status. Instead of using difference to rethink the category of women, difference is often a euphemism for women who differ from the traditional norm. Even in purporting to accept difference, feminist pluralism often creates a social reality that reverts to universalizing women:

> So much feminist scholarship assumes that when we cut through all
> of the diversity among women created by differences of racial
> classification, ethnicity, social class, and sexual orientation, a
> "universal truth" concerning women and gender lies buried
> beneath. But if we can face the scary possibility that no such
> certainty exists and that persisting in such a search will always
> distort or omit someone's experiences, with what do we replace this
> old way of thinking? Gender differences and gender politics begin
> to look very different if there is no essential woman at the core.[17]

What Is Multiracial Feminism?

A new set of feminist theories has emerged from the challenges put forth by women of color. Multiracial feminism is an evolving body of theory and practice informed by wide-ranging intellectual traditions. This framework does not offer a singular or unified feminism but a body of knowledge situating women and men in multiple systems of domination. U.S. multiracial feminism encompasses several emergent perspectives developed primarily by women of color: African Americans, Latinas, Asian Americans, and Native Americans, women whose analyses are shaped by their unique perspectives as "outsiders within"—marginal intellectuals whose social locations provide them with a particular perspective on self and society.[18] Although U.S. women of color represent many races and ethnic backgrounds—with different histories and cultures—our feminisms cohere in their treatment of race as basic social division, a structure of power, a focus of political struggle, and hence a fundamental force in shaping women's and men's lives.

This evolving intellectual and political perspective uses several controversial terms. While we adopt the label "multiracial," other terms have been used to describe this broad framework. For example, Chela Sandoval refers to "U.S. Third World feminisms,"[19] while other scholars refer to "indigenous feminisms." In their theory text-reader, Alison M. Jagger and Paula S. Rothenberg adopt the label "multicultural feminism."[20]

We use "multiracial" rather than "multicultural" as a way of underscoring race as a power system that interacts with other structured inequalities to shape genders. Within the U.S. context, race, and the system of meanings and ideologies which accompany it, is a fundamental organizing principle of social relationships.[21] Race affects all women and men, although in different ways. Even cultural and group differences among women are produced through interaction within a racially stratified social order. Therefore, although we do not discount the importance of culture, we caution that cultural analytic frameworks that ignore race tend to view women's differences as the product of group-specific values and practices that often result in the marginalization of cultural groups which are then perceived as exotic expressions of a normative center. Our focus on race stresses the social construction of differently situated social groups and their varying degrees of advantage and power. Additionally, this emphasis on race takes on increasing political importance in an era where discourse about race is governed by color-evasive language[22] and a preference for individual rather than group remedies for social inequalities. Our analyses insist upon the primary and pervasive nature of race in contemporary U.S. society while at the same time acknowledging how race both shapes and is shaped by a variety of other social relations.

In the social sciences, multiracial feminism grew out of socialist feminist thinking. Theories about how political economic forces shape women's lives were influential as we began to uncover the social causes of racial ethnic women's subordination. But socialist feminism's concept of capitalist patriarchy, with its focus on women's unpaid (reproductive) labor in the home, failed to address racial differences in the organization of reproductive labor. As feminists of color have argued, "reproductive labor has divided along racial as well as gender lines, and the specific characteristics have varied regionally and changed over time as capitalism has reorganized."[23] Despite the limitations of socialist feminism, this body of literature has been especially useful in pursuing questions about the interconnections among systems of domination.[24]

Race and ethnic studies was the other major social scientific source of multiracial feminism. It provided a basis for comparative analyses of groups that are socially and legally subordinated and remain culturally distinct within U.S. society. This includes the systematic discrimination of socially constructed racial groups and their distinctive cultural arrangements. Historically, the categories of African American, Latino, Asian American, and Native American were constructed as both racially and culturally distinct. Each group has a distinctive culture, shares a common heritage, and has developed a common identity within a larger society that subordinates them.[25]

We recognize, of course, certain problems inherent in an uncritical use of the multiracial label. First, the perspective can be hampered by a biracial model in which only African Americans and whites are seen as racial categories and all other groups are viewed through the prism of cultural differences. Latinos and Asians have always occupied distinctive places within the racial hierarchy, and current shifts in the composition of the U.S. population are racializing these groups anew.[26]

A second problem lies in treating multiracial feminism as a single analytical framework, and its principal architects, women of color, as an undifferentiated category. The concepts "multiracial feminism," "racial ethnic women," and "women of color" "homogenize quite different experiences and can falsely universalize experiences across race, ethnicity, sexual orientation, and age."[27] The feminisms created by women of color exhibit a plurality of intellectual and political positions. We speak in many voices, with inconsistencies that are born of our different social locations. Multiracial feminism embodies this plurality and richness. Our intent is not to falsely universalize women of color. Nor do we wish to promote a new racial essentialism in place of the old gender essentialism. Instead, we use these concepts to examine the structures and experiences produced by intersecting forms of race and gender.

It is also essential to acknowledge that race is a shifting and contested category whose meanings construct definitions of all aspects of social life.[28] In the United States it helped define citizenship by excluding everyone who was not a white, male property owner. It defined labor as slave or free, coolie or contract, and family as available only to those men whose marriages were recognized or whose wives could immigrate with them. Additionally, racial meanings are contested both within groups and between them.[29]

Although definitions of race are at once historically and geographically specific, they are also transnational, encompassing diasporic groups and crossing traditional geographic boundaries. Thus, while U.S. multiracial feminism calls attention to the fundamental importance of race, it must also locate the meaning of race within specific national traditions.

The Distinguishing Features of Multiracial Feminism

By attending to these problems, multiracial feminism offers a set of analytic premises for thinking about and theorizing gender. The following themes distinguish this branch of feminist inquiry.

First, multiracial feminism asserts that gender is constructed by a range of interlocking inequalities, what Patricia Hill Collins calls a "matrix of domination."[30] The idea of a matrix is that several fundamental systems work with and through each other. People experience race, class, gender, and sexuality differently depending upon their social location in the structures of race, class, gender, and sexuality. For example, people of the same race will experience race differently depending upon their location in the class structure as working class, professional managerial class, or unemployed; in the gender structure as female or male; and in structures of sexuality as heterosexual, homosexual, or bisexual.

Multiracial feminism also examines the simultaneity of systems in shaping women's experience and identity. Race, class, gender, and sexuality are not reducible to individual attributes to be measured and assessed for their separate contribution in explaining given social outcomes, an approach that Elizabeth Spelman calls "popbead metaphysics," where a woman's identity consists of the sum of parts neatly divisible from one another.[31] The matrix of domination seeks to account for the multiple ways that women experience themselves as gendered, raced, classed, and sexualized.

Second, multiracial feminism emphasizes the intersectional nature of hierarchies at all levels of social life. Class, race, gender, and sexuality are components of both social structure and social interaction. Women and men are differently embedded in locations created by these cross-cutting hierarchies. As a result, women and men throughout the social order experience different forms of privilege and subordination, depending on their race, class, gender, and sexuality. In other words, intersecting forms of domination produce *both* oppression *and* opportunity. At the same time that structures of race, class, and gender create disadvantages for women of color, they provide unacknowledged benefits for those who are at the top of these hierarchies — whites, members of the upper classes, and males. Therefore, multiracial feminism applies not only to racial ethnic women but also to women and men of all races, classes, and genders.

Third, multiracial feminism highlights the relational nature of dominance and subordination. Power is the cornerstone of women's differences.[32] This means that women's differences are *connected* in systematic ways.[33] Race is a vital element in the pattern of relations among minority and white women. As Linda Gordon argues, the very meanings of being a white woman in the United States have been affected by the existence of subordinated women of color: "They intersect in conflict and in occasional cooperation, but always in mutual influence."[34]

Fourth, multiracial feminism explores the interplay of social structure and women's agency. Within the constraints of race, class, and gender oppression, women create viable lives for themselves, their families, and their communities. Women of color have resisted and often undermined the forces of power that control them. From acts of quiet dignity and steadfast determination to involvement in revolt and rebellion, women struggle to shape their own lives. Racial oppression has been a common focus of the "dynamic of oppositional agency" of women of color. As Chandra Talpade Mohanty points out, it is the nature and organization of women's opposition which mediates and differentiates the impact of structures of domination.[35]

Fifth, multiracial feminism encompasses wide-ranging methodological approaches, and like other branches of feminist thought, relies on varied theoretical tools as well. Ruth Frankenberg and Lata Mani identify three guiding principles of inclusive feminist inquiry: "building complex analyses, avoiding erasure, specifying location."[36] In the last decade, the opening up of academic feminism has focused attention on the social location in the production of knowledge. Most basically, research by and about marginalized women has destabilized what used to be considered as universal categories of gender. Marginalized locations are well suited for grasping social relations that remained obscure from more privileged vantage points. Lived experience, in other words, creates alternative ways of understanding the social world and the experience of different groups of women within it. Racially informed standpoint epistemologies have provided new topics, fresh questions, and new understandings of women and men. Women of color have, as Norma Alarçon argues, asserted ourselves as subjects, using our voices to challenge dominant conceptions of truth.[37]

Sixth, multiracial feminism brings together understandings drawn from the lived experiences of diverse and continuously changing groups of women. Among Asian Americans, Native Americans, Latinas, and Blacks are many different national cultural and ethnic groups. Each one is engaged in the process of testing, refining, and reshaping these broader categories in its own image. Such internal differences heighten awareness of and sensitivity of both commonalities and differences, serving as a constant reminder of the importance of comparative study and maintaining a creative tension between diversity and universalization.

Difference and Transformation

Efforts to make women's studies less partial and less distorted have produced important changes in academic feminism. Inclusive thinking has provided a way to build multiplicity and difference into our analyses. This has led to the discovery that race matters for everyone. White women, too, must be reconceptualized as a category that is multiply defined by race, class, and other differences. As Ruth Frankenberg demonstrates in a study of whiteness among contemporary women, all kinds of social relations, even those that appear neutral, are, in fact, racialized. Frankenberg further complicates the very notion of a unified white identity by introducing issues of Jewish identity.[38] Therefore, the lives of women of color cannot be seen as a *variation* on a more general model of white American womanhood. The model of womanhood that feminist social science once held as "universal" is also a product of race and class.

When we analyze the power relations constituting all social arrangements and shaping women's lives in distinctive ways, we can begin to grapple with core feminist issues about how genders are socially constructed and constructed differently. Women's difference is built into our study of gender. Yet this perspective is quite far removed from the atheoretical pluralism implied in much contemporary thinking about gender.

Multiracial feminism, in our view, focuses not just on differences but also on the way in which differences and domination intersect and are historically and socially constituted. It challenges feminist scholars to go beyond the mere recognition and inclusion of difference to reshape the basic concepts and theories of our disciplines. By attending to women's social location based on race, class, and gender, multiracial feminism seeks to clarify the structural sources of diversity. Ultimately, multiracial feminism forces us to see privilege and subordination as interrelated and to pose such questions as: How do the existences and experiences of all people—men and women, different racial-ethnic groups, and different classes—shape the experiences of each other? How are those relationships defined and reinforced through social institutions that are the primary sites for negotiating power within society? How do these differences contribute to the construction of both individual and group identity? Once we acknowledge that all women are affected by the racial order of society, then it becomes clear that the insights of multiracial feminism provide an analytical framework, not solely for understanding the experiences of women of color but for understanding all women, and men, as well.

NOTES

1. Maxine Baca Zinn, Lynn Weber Cannon, Elizabeth Higginbotham, and Bonnie Thornton Dill, "The Costs of Exclusionary Practices in Women's Studies," *Signs* 11 (winter 1986): 290–303.
2. Chela Sandoval, "U.S. Third World Feminism: The Theory and Method of Oppositional Consciousness in the Postmodern World," *Genders* (spring 1991): 1–24.
3. Ruth Frankenberg and Lata Mani, "Cross Currents, Crosstalk: Race, 'Postcoloniality,' and the Politics of Location," *Cultural Studies* 7 (May 1993): 292–310.
4. We use the term "multiracial feminism" to convey the multiplicity of racial groups and feminist perspectives.
5. A growing body of work on difference in feminist thought now exists. Although we cannot cite all the current work, the following are representative: Michèle

Barrett, "The Concept of Difference," *Feminist Review* 26 (July 1987): 29–42; Christina Crosby, "Dealing with Difference," in *Feminists Theorize the Political*, ed. Judith Butler and Joan W. Scott (New York: Routledge, 1992), 130–43; Elizabeth Fox-Genovese, "Difference, Diversity, and Divisions in an Agenda for the Women's Movement," in *Color, Class, and Country: Experiences of Gender*, ed. Gay Young and Bette J. Dickerson (London: Zed Books, 1994), 232–48; Nancy A. Hewitt, "Compounding Differences," *Feminist Studies* 18 (summer 1992): 313–26; Maria C. Lugones, "On the Logic of Feminist Pluralism," in *Feminist Ethics*, ed. Claudia Card (Lawrence: University of Kansas Press, 1991), 35–44; Rita S. Gallin and Anne Ferguson, "The Plurality of Feminism: Rethinking 'Difference,'" in *The Woman and International Development Annual* (Boulder: Westview Press, 1993), 3: 1–16; and Linda Gordon, "On Difference," *Genders* 10 (spring 1991): 91–111.

6. Susan Bordo, "Feminism, Postmodernism, and Gender Skepticism," in *Feminism/Postmodernism*, ed. Linda J. Nicholson (London: Routledge, 1990), 133–56.

7. Sandra G. Harding, *Whose Science? Whose Knowledge? Thinking from Women's Lives* (Ithaca: Cornell University Press, 1991), 179.

8. Crosby, 131.

9. Fox-Genovese, 232.

10. Faye Ginsberg and Anna Lowenhaupt Tsing, Introduction to *Uncertain Terms: Negotiating Gender in American Culture*, ed. Faye Ginsburg and Anna Lowenhaupt Tsing (Boston: Beacon Press, 1990), 3.

11. Sandoval, 2.

12. Sandra Morgan, "Making Connections: Socialist-Feminist Challenges to Marxist Scholarship," in *Women and a New Academy: Gender and Cultural Contexts*, ed. Jean F. O'Barr (Madison: University of Wisconsin Press, 1989), 149.

13. Jane Rowland Martin, "Methodological Essentialism, False Difference, and Other Dangerous Traps," *Signs* 19 (spring 1994): 647.

14. Barrett, 32.

15. bell hooks, *Black Looks: Race and Representation* (Boston: South End Press, 1992), 21.

16. Lugones, 35–44.

17. Patricia Hill Collins, Foreword to *Women of Color in U.S. Society*, ed. Maxine Baca Zinn and Bonnie Thornton Dill (Philadelphia: Temple University Press, 1994), xv.

18. Patricia Hill Collins, "Learning from the Outsider Within: The Sociological Significance of Black Feminist Thought," *Social Problems* 33 (December 1986): 514–32.

19. Sandoval, 1.

20. Alison M. Jagger and Paula S. Rothenberg, *Feminist Frameworks: Alternative Theoretical Accounts of the Relations between Women and Men*, 3d ed. (New York: McGraw-Hill, 1993).

21. Michael Omi, and Howard Winant, *Racial Formation in the United States: From the 1960s to the 1980s*, 2d ed. (New York: Routledge, 1994).

22. Ruth Frankenberg, *The Social Construction of Whiteness: White Women, Race Matters* (Minneapolis: University of Minnesota Press, 1993).

23. Evelyn Nakano Glenn, "From Servitude to Service Work: Historical Continuities in the Racial Division of Paid Reproductive Labor," *Signs* 18 (autumn 1992): 3. See also Bonnie Thornton Dill, "Our Mothers' Grief: Racial-Ethnic Women and the Maintenance of Families," *Journal of Family History* 13, no. 4 (1988): 415–31.

24. Morgan, 146.

25. Maxine Baca Zinn and Bonnie Thornton Dill, "Difference and Domination," in *Women of Color in U.S. Society* (1994): 11–12.

26. See Omi and Winant, 53–76, for a discussion of racial formation.

27. Margaret L. Andersen and Patricia Hill Collins, *Race, Class, and Gender: An Anthology* (Belmont, Calif.: Wadsworth, 1992), xvi.

28. Omi and Winant.

29. Nazli Kibria, "Migration and Vietnamese American Women: Remaking Ethnicity," in *Women of Color in U.S. Society* (1994): 247–61.

30. Patricia Hill Collins, *Black Feminist Thought: Knowledge, Consciousness, and the Politics of Empowerment* (Boston: Unwin Hyman, 1990).

31. Elizabeth Spelman, *Inessential Women: Problems of Exclusion in Feminist Thought* (Boston: Beacon Press, 1988), 136.

32. Several discussions of difference make this point. See Baca Zinn and Dill, 10; Gordon, 106; and Lynn Weber, in the "Symposium on West and Fenstermaker's 'Doing Difference,'" *Gender & Society*, 9 (August 1995): 515–19.

33. Glenn, 10.

34. Gordon, 106.

35. Chandra Talpade Mohanty, "Cartographies of Struggle: Third World Women and the Politics of Feminism," in *Third World Women and the Politics of Feminism*, ed. Chandra Talpade Mohanty, Ann Russo, and Lourdes Torres (Bloomington: Indiana University Press, 1991), 13.

36. Frankenberg and Mani, 306.

37. Norma Alarçon, "The Theoretical Subject(s) of *This Bridge Called My Back* and Anglo-American Feminism," in *Making Face, Making Soul, Haciendo Caras: Creative and Critical Perspectives by Women of Color*, ed. Gloria Anzaldúa (San Francisco: Aunt Lute, 1990), 356.

38. Frankenberg. See also Evelyn Torton Beck, "The Politics of Jewish Invisibility," *NWSA Journal* (fall 1988): 93–102.

9
————————

PATRIARCHY, THE SYSTEM
An It, Not a He, a Them, or an Us

ALLAN G. JOHNSON

Allan G. Johnson has worked on issues of social inequality since receiving his Ph.D. in sociology from the University of Michigan in 1972. He has more than thirty years of teaching experience and is a frequent speaker on college and university campuses. His books include *Power, Privilege and Difference,* 2nd edition (2005), *The Gender Knot,* 2nd edition (2005), and *The Forest and the Trees: Sociology as Life, Practice, and Promise* (1997).

"**W**hen you say patriarchy," a man complained from the rear of the audience, "I know what you *really* mean—me!" A lot of people hear "men" whenever someone says "patriarchy," so that criticism of gender oppression is taken to mean that all men—each and every one of them—are oppressive people. Not surprisingly, many men take it personally if someone merely mentions patriarchy or the oppression of women, bristling at what they often see as a way to make them feel guilty. And some women feel free to blame individual men for patriarchy simply because they're men. Some of the time, men feel defensive because they identify with patriarchy and its values and don't want to face the consequences these produce or the prospect of giving up male privilege. But defensiveness more often reflects a common confusion about the difference between patriarchy as a kind of society and the people who participate in it. If we're ever going to work toward real change, it's a confusion we'll have to clear up.

To do this, we have to realize that we're stuck in a model of social life that views everything as beginning and ending with individuals. Looking at things in this way, we tend to think that if evil exists in the world, it's only because there are evil people who have entered into an evil conspiracy. Racism exists, for example, simply because white people are racist bigots who hate members of racial and ethnic minorities and want to do them harm. There is gender oppression because men want and like to dominate women and act out hostility toward them. There is poverty and class oppression because people in the upper classes are greedy, heartless, and cruel.

The flip side of this individualistic model of guilt and blame is that race, gender, and class oppression are actually not oppression at all, but merely the sum of individual failings on the part of blacks, women, and the poor, who lack the right stuff to compete successfully with whites, men, and others who know how to make something of themselves.

What this kind of thinking ignores is that we are all participating in something larger than ourselves or any collection of us. On some level, most people are familiar with the idea that social life involves us in something larger than ourselves, but few seem to know what to do with that idea. When Sam Keen laments that "THE SYSTEM is running us all,"[1] he strikes a deep chord in many people. But he also touches on a basic misunderstanding of social life, because having blamed "the system" (presumably society) for our problems, he doesn't take the next step to understand what that might mean. What exactly *is* a system, for example, and how could it run us? Do *we* have anything to do with shaping *it*, and if so, how? How, for example, do we participate in patriarchy, and how does that link us to the consequences it produces? How is what we think of as "normal" life related to male dominance, women's oppression, and the hierarchical, control-obsessed world in which they, and our lives, are embedded? . . .

. . . If we see patriarchy as nothing more than men's and women's individual personalities, motivations, and behavior, for example, then it probably won't even occur to us to ask about larger contexts—such as institutions like the family, religion, and the economy—and how people's lives are shaped in relation to them. From this kind of individualistic perspective, we might ask why a particular man raped, harassed, or beat a woman. We wouldn't ask, however, what kind of society would promote persistent *patterns* of such behavior in everyday life, from wife-beating jokes to the routine inclusion of sexual coercion and violence in mainstream movies. We are quick to explain rape and battery as the acts of sick or angry men; but we rarely take seriously the question of what kind of society would produce so much male anger and pathology or direct it toward sexual violence rather than something else. We rarely ask how gender violence might serve other more "normalized" ends such as male control and domination. . . .

. . . If the goal is to change the world, this won't help us. We need to see and deal with the social roots that generate and nurture the social problems that are reflected in the behavior of individuals. We can't do this without realizing that we all participate in something larger than ourselves, something we didn't create but that we have the power to affect through the choices we make about *how* to participate.

That something larger is patriarchy, which is more than a collection of individuals (such as "men"). It is a system, which means it can't be reduced to the people who participate in it. If you go to work in a corporation, for example, you know the minute you walk in the door that you've entered "something" that shapes your experience and behavior, something that isn't just you and the other people you work with. You can feel yourself stepping into a set of relationships and shared understandings about who's who and what's supposed to happen and why, and all of this limits you in many ways. And when you leave at the end of the day you can feel yourself released from the constraints imposed by your participation in that system; you can feel the expectations drop away and your focus shift to other systems such as family or a neighborhood bar that shape your experience in different ways. To understand a system like a corporation, we have to look at more than people like you, because all of you aren't the corporation, even though you make it run. If the corporation were just a collection of people, then whatever happened to the corporation would by definition also happen to them, and vice versa; but this clearly isn't so. A corporation can go bankrupt, for example, or cease to exist altogether without any of the people who work there going bankrupt or disappearing. Conversely, everyone who works for the corporation could quit, but that wouldn't necessarily mean the end of the corporation, only the arrival of a new set of participants. We can't understand a corporation, then, just by looking at the people who participate in it, for it is something larger and has to be understood as such.

So, too, with patriarchy, a kind of society that is more than a collection of women and men and can't be understood simply by understanding them. *We are not patriarchy,* no more than people who believe in Allah *are* Islam or Canadians *are* Canada. Patriarchy is a kind of society organized around certain kinds of social relationships and ideas. As individuals, we participate in it. Paradoxically, our participation both shapes our lives and gives us the opportunity to be part of changing or perpetuating it.[2] But *we are not it,* which means that patriarchy can exist without men having "oppressive personalities" or actively conspiring with one another to defend male privilege. To demonstrate that gender oppression exists, we don't have to show that men are villains, that women are good-hearted victims, that women don't participate in their own oppression, or that men never oppose it. If a society is oppressive, then people who grow up and live in it will tend to accept, identify with, and participate in it as "normal" and unremarkable life. That's the path of least resistance in any system. It's hard not to follow it, given how we depend on society and its rewards and punishments that hinge on going along with the status quo. When oppression is woven into the fabric of everyday life, we don't need to go out of our way to be overly oppressive in order for an oppressive system to produce oppressive consequences. As the saying goes, what evil requires is simply that ordinary people do nothing.

Patriarchy

The key to understanding any system is to identify its various parts and how they're arranged to form a whole. To understand a language, for example, we have to learn its alphabet, vocabulary, and rules for combining words into meaningful phrases and sentences. With a social system such as patriarchy, it's more complicated because there are many different kinds of parts, and it is often difficult to see just how they're connected. Patriarchy's defining elements are its male-dominated, male-identified, and male-centered character, but this is just the beginning. At its core, patriarchy is a set of symbols and ideas that make up a culture embodied by everything from the content of everyday conversation to literature and film. Patriarchal culture includes ideas about the nature of things, including men, women, and humanity, with manhood and masculinity most closely associated with being human and womanhood and femininity relegated to the marginal position of "other." It's about how social life is and how it's supposed to be; about what's expected of people and about how they feel. It's about standards of feminine beauty and masculine toughness, images of feminine vulnerability and masculine protectiveness, of older men coupled with young women, of elderly women alone. It's about defining women and men as opposites, about the "naturalness" of male aggression, competition, and dominance and of female caring, cooperation, and subordination. It's about the valuing of masculinity and maleness and the devaluing of femininity and femaleness. It's about the primary importance of a husband's career and the secondary status of a wife's, about child care as a priority in women's lives and its secondary importance in men's. It's about the social acceptability of anger, rage, and toughness in men but not in women, and of caring, tenderness, and vulnerability in women but not in men.

Above all, patriarchal culture is about the core value of control and domination in almost every area of human existence. From the expression of emotion to economics to the natural environment, gaining and exercising control is a continuing goal of great importance. Because of this, the concept of power takes on a narrow definition in terms of "power over"—the ability to control others, events, resources, or oneself in spite of resistance—rather than alternatives such as the ability to cooperate with others, to give freely of oneself, or to feel and act in harmony with nature.[3] To have power over and to be prepared to use it are defined culturally as good and desirable (and characteristically "masculine"), and to lack such power or to be reluctant to use it is seen as weak if not contemptible (and characteristically "feminine").

The main use of any culture is to provide symbols and ideas out of which people construct their sense of what is real. As such, language mirrors social reality in sometimes startling ways. In contemporary usage, for example, the words "crone," "witch," "bitch," and "virgin" describe women as threatening, evil, or heterosexually inexperienced and thus incomplete. In prepatriarchal times, however, these words evoked far different images.[4] The crone was the old woman whose life experience gave her insight, wisdom, respect, and the power to enrich people's lives. The witch was the wise-woman healer, the knower of herbs, the midwife, the link joining body, spirit, and Earth. The bitch was Artemis-Diana, goddess of the hunt, most often associated with the dogs who accompanied her. And the virgin was merely a woman who was unattached, unclaimed, and unowned by any man and therefore independent and autonomous. Notice how each word has been transformed from a positive cultural image of female power, independence, and dignity to an insult or a shadow of its former self so that few words remain to identify women in ways both positive and powerful.

Going deeper into patriarchal culture, we find a complex web of ideas that define reality and what's considered good and desirable. To see the world through patriarchal eyes is to believe that women and men are profoundly different in their basic natures, that hierarchy is the only alternative to chaos, and that men were made in the image of a masculine God with whom they enjoy a special relationship. It is to take as obvious the idea that there are two and only two distinct genders; that patriarchal heterosexuality is "natural" and same-sex attraction is not; that because men neither bear nor breast-feed children, they cannot feel a compelling bodily connection to them; that on some level every woman, whether heterosexual or lesbian, wants a "real man" who knows how to "take charge of things," including her; that females can't be trusted, especially when they're menstruating or accusing men of sexual misconduct. To embrace patriarchy is to believe that mothers should stay home and that fathers should work out of the home, regardless of men's and women's actual abilities or needs.[5] It is to buy into the notion that women are weak and men are strong, that women and children need men to support and protect them, all in spite of the fact that in many ways men are not the physically stronger sex, that women perform a huge share of hard physical labor in many societies (often larger than men's), that women's physical endurance tends to be greater than men's over the long haul, that women tend to be more capable of enduring pain and emotional stress.[6] And yet such evidence means little in the face of a patriarchal culture that dictates how things *ought* to be and, like all cultural mythology,

> will not be argued down by facts. It may seem to be making straightforward statements, but actually these conceal another mood, the imperative. Myth exists in a state of tension. It is not really describing a situation, but trying by means of this description to *bring about* what it declares to exist.[7]

To live in a patriarchal culture is to learn what's expected of us as men and women, the rules that regulate punishment and reward based on how we behave and appear. These rules range from laws that require men to fight in wars not of their own choosing to customary expectations that mothers will provide child care, or that when a woman shows sexual interest in a man or merely smiles or acts friendly, she gives up her right to say no and control her own body. And to live under patriarchy is to take into ourselves shared ways of feeling—the hostile contempt for femaleness that forms the core of misogyny and presumptions of male superiority, the ridicule men direct at other men who show signs of vulnerability or weakness, or the fear and insecurity that every woman must deal with when she exercises the right to move freely in the world, especially at night and by herself. . . .

The prominent place of misogyny in patriarchal culture, for example, doesn't mean that every man and woman consciously hates all things female. But it does mean that to the extent that we don't feel such hatred, it's *in spite of* paths of least resistance contained in our culture. Complete freedom from such feelings and judgments is all but impossible. It is certainly possible for heterosexual men to love women without mentally fragmenting them into breasts, buttocks, genitals, and other variously desirable parts. It is possible for women to feel good about their bodies, to not judge themselves as being too fat, to not abuse themselves to one degree or another in pursuit of impossible male-identified standards of beauty and sexual attractiveness. All of this is possible; but to live in patriarchy is to breathe in misogynist images of women as objectified sexual property valued primarily for their usefulness to men. This finds its way into everyone who grows up breathing and swimming in it, and once inside us it remains, however unaware of it we may be. So, when we hear or express sexist jokes and other forms of misogyny we may not recognize it, and even if we do, say nothing rather than risk other people thinking we're "too sensitive" or, especially in the case of men, "not one of the guys." In either case, we are involved, if only by our silence. . . .

To understand patriarchy, we have to identify its cultural elements and see how they are related to the structure of social life. We must see, for example, how cultural ideas that identify women primarily as mothers and men primarily as breadwinners support patterns in which women do most domestic work at home and are discriminated against in hiring, pay, and promotions at work. But to do anything with such an understanding, we also must see what patriarchy has to do with us as individuals—how it shapes us and how we, in choosing how to participate, shape *it.*

The System in Us in the System

One of the most difficult things to accept about patriarchy is that we're involved in it, which means we're also involved in its consequences. This is especially hard for men who refuse to believe they benefit from women's oppression, because they can't see how this could happen without their being personally oppressive in their intentions, feelings, and behavior. For many men, being told they're *involved* in oppression can only mean they *are* oppressive. . . .

. . . Societies don't exist without people participating in them, which means that we can't understand patriarchy unless we also ask how people are connected to it and how this connection varies, depending on social characteristics such as race, gender, ethnicity, age, and class. Capitalism, for example, didn't just happen on its own but emerged as an economic system in a patriarchal world dominated by men and their interests, especially white European men of the newly emerging merchant class. The same can be said of industrialization, which was bound up with the development of capital-ism in eighteenth- and nineteenth-century Europe. This line of thinking might seem to undermine the argument I've made about including systems in our thinking—"It really comes down to individuals after all"—but it's more complicated than that. The problem isn't society and it isn't us. It's the relationship between the two that we have to understand, the nature of the thing we participate in and how we choose to participate in it and how both are shaped in the process. In this sense, it's a mistake to equate patriarchy with men; but it's also wrong to act as though systems like patriarchy or cap-italism have nothing to do with gender and differences in power and inter-ests that distinguish and separate men and women. It's equally wrong to act as though all men or all women are the same, as though dynamics such as racism and class oppression don't affect how patriarchy operates and affects people's lives in different ways.

One way to see how people connect with systems is to think of us as oc-cupying social positions that locate us in relation to people in other positions. We connect to families, for example, through positions such as "mother," "daughter," and "cousin"; to economic systems through positions such as "vice president," "secretary," or "unemployed"; to political systems through positions such as "citizen," "registered voter," and "mayor"; to religious sys-tems through positions such as "believer" and "clergy." How we perceive the people who occupy such positions and what we expect of them depend on cultural ideas—such as the belief that mothers are naturally better than fa-thers at child care or the expectation that fathers will be the primary bread-winners. Such ideas are powerful because we use them to construct a sense of who we and other people are. When a woman marries, for example, how people (including her) perceive and think about her changes as cultural ideas about what it means to be a wife come into play—ideas about how wives feel about their husbands, for example, what's most important to wives, what's expected of them, and what they may expect of others. . . .

We can think of a society as a network of interconnected systems within systems, each made up of social positions and their relations to one another. To say, then, that I'm white, male, college educated, and a writer, sociologist, U.S. citizen, heterosexual, middle-aged, husband, father, brother, and son identifies me in relation to positions which are themselves related to posi-tions in various social systems, from the entire world to the family of my birth. In another sense, the day-to-day reality of a society only exists through what people actually do as they participate in it. Patriarchal culture, for ex-ample, places a high value on control and maleness. By themselves, these are just abstractions. But when men and women actually talk and men interrupt women more than women interrupt men, or men ignore topics introduced by women in favor of their own or in other ways control conversation,[8] or when men use their authority to sexually harass women in the workplace, then the reality of patriarchy as a kind of society and people's sense of them-selves as female and male within it actually happen in a concrete way.

In this sense, like all social systems, patriarchy exists only through people's lives. Through this, patriarchy's various aspects are there for us to see over and over again. This has two important implications for how we understand patriarchy. First, to some extent people experience patriarchy as external to them; but this doesn't mean that it's a distinct and separate thing, like a house in which we live. Instead, by participating in patriarchy we are of patriarchy and it is *of* us. Both exist *through* the other and neither can exist without the other. Second, patriarchy isn't static; it's an ongoing *process* that's continuously shaped and reshaped. Since the thing we're participating in is patriarchal, we tend to behave in ways that create a patriarchal world from one moment to the next. But we have some freedom to break the rules and construct everyday life in different ways, which means that the paths we choose to follow can do as much to change patriarchy as they can to perpetuate it.

We're involved in patriarchy and its consequences because we occupy social positions in it, which is all it takes. Since gender oppression is, by definition, a system of inequality organized around gender categories, we can no more avoid being involved in it than we can avoid being female or male. *All* men and *all* women are therefore involved in this oppressive system, and none of us can control *whether* we participate, only *how*. . . .

NOTES

1. Sam Keen, *Fire in the Belly: On Being a Man* (New York: Bantam, 1991), 207.
2. This is one of the major differences between organisms like the human body and social systems. Cells and nerves cannot "rebel" against the body and try to change it into something else.
3. For a thorough discussion of this distinction, see Marilyn French, *Beyond Power: On Men, Women, and Morals* (New York: Summit Books, 1985).
4. For discussions of language and gender, see Jane Caputi, *Gossips, Gorgons, and Crones* (Santa Fe: Bear and Company, 1993); Mary Daly, *Gyn/Ecology: The Metaethics of Radical Feminism* (Boston: Beacon Press, 1978); Dale Spender, *Man Made Language* (London: Pandora, 1980); Barbara G. Walker, *The Woman's Encyclopedia of Myths and Secrets* (San Francisco: Harper and Row, 1983): idem, *The Woman's Dictionary of Symbols and Sacred Objects* (San Francisco: Harper and Row, 1988). For a very different slant on gender and language, see Mary Daly (in cahoots with Jane Caputi), *Webster's First New Intergalactic Wickedary of the English Language* (Boston: Beacon Press, 1987).
5. See Arlie Hochschild (with Anne Machung), *The Second Shift* (New York: Avon Books, 1989).
6. See, for example, Rosalyn Baxandall, Linda Gordon, and Susan Reverby, eds., *America's Working Women: A Documentary History – 1600 to the Present* (New York: Vintage Press, 1976); Ashley Montagu, *The Natural Superiority of Women* (New York: Collier, 1974); Robin Morgan, ed., *Sisterhood Is Global* (New York: Anchor, 1990); and Marilyn Waring, *If Women Counted: A New Feminist Economics* (San Francisco: HarperCollins, 1988).
7. Elizabeth Janeway, *Man's World, Woman's Place: A Study in Social Mythology* (New York: Dell, 1971), 37.

8. See, for example, P. Kollock, P. Blumstein, and P. Schwartz, "Sex and Power in Interaction," *American Sociological Review* 50, no. 1 (1985): 34–46; N. Henley, M. Hamilton, and B. Thorne, "Womanspeak and Manspeak: Sex Differences and Sexism in Communication," in *Beyond Sex Roles,* ed. A. G. Sargent (New York: West, 1985), 168–185; and L. Smith-Lovin and C. Brody, "Interruptions in Group Discussions: The Effect of Gender and Group Composition," *American Sociological Review* 51, no. 3 (1989): 424–435.

10

REFLECTIONS ON GLOBAL GOVERNANCE AND TRANSNATIONAL FEMINIST MOVEMENTS IN AN ERA OF INFINITE WAR

ROSALIND POLLACK PETCHESKY

Rosalind Pollack Petchesky is Distinguished Professor of Political Science, Hunter College and the Graduate Center, City University of New York. Co-author of *Negotiating Reproductive Rights: Women's Perspectives across Countries and Cultures,* she is the founder and past international co-ordinator of the International Reproductive Rights Research Action Group (IRRRAG) and a MacArthur Fellow. Her recent response to 9/11, "Phantom Towers," has had an extraordinary impact, being published in a larger number of print and media sites in the U.S., Europe, Latin America and India. Professor Petchesky has long been active in women's, social justice, and peace efforts and is a board member of the Women's Environment and Development Organization and the international journal, *Reproductive Health Matters.*

A few years ago . . . it seemed as if there was a real promise of hope for the poor — both black and white — through the Poverty Program. There were experiments, hopes, new beginnings. Then came the buildup in Vietnam and I watched the program broken and eviscerated as if it were some idle political plaything of a society gone mad on war, and I knew that America would never invest the necessary funds or energies in rehabilitation of its poor so long as adventures like Vietnam continued to draw men and skills and money like some demonic destructive suction tube. So I was increasingly compelled to see the war as an enemy of the poor and to attack it as such.

(REV. MARTIN LUTHER KING, JR., 1967)

What is emerging is the need for globalization as an economic process to be subject to moral and ethical considerations and to respect international legal standards and principles.

(MARY ROBINSON, 2002)

Prologue

My purpose . . . has been twofold: first, to explore the manifold ways in which reproductive and sexual rights intersect with, and are embraced within, a wide range of health, human rights, human development and social and gender justice issues; and, second, to use this inquiry to rethink the complex political dynamics in which transnational women's NGOs [nongovernmental organizations] find themselves, as they manoeuvre within a globalizing yet deeply divided and grossly inequitable world. In the 1990s and early 2000s, transnational women's NGOs continued to play a central role in the creation and implementation of international norms and agreements related to reproductive and sexual rights. Feminist groups in the 1990s had a major impact at both international and national levels in shifting dominant discourses about reproduction, population and sexuality in a direction that puts the ends of women's health and empowerment above that of reducing population growth and that links sexual and reproductive rights to macroeconomic transformation and human development. This is a major historical achievement and a mark of the power of transnational women's NGOs and feminist ideas.

Yet in the new millennium an increasingly hostile economic, cultural and political climate has severely limited the translation of this discursive shift into effective policies and programmes. In the circumscribed world of UN conferences, women's groups have found themselves on the defensive even to retain the language achieved in the 1990s regarding sexual and reproductive health rights, much less to obtain the necessary accountability mechanisms and resources to make good on the promises. At the UN Special Session on Children in 2002, they managed—with extraordinary difficulty and skill—to defeat the agenda of conservative religious groups, led by the Bush administration, for "abstinence-only" sex education, reproductive health services that explicitly preclude abortion, family planning without contraceptives, and a definition of "the family" solely as marriage between a man and a woman. But the result was a mere two paragraphs on "sexual and reproductive health" that basically cross-reference the previous conference documents and give most emphasis to the important but uncontroversial goal of reducing maternal and neonatal morbidity and mortality (Girard 2002). At the Millennium Summit in 2000 and the Financing for Development Conference in 2002 women's health groups were powerless to prevent the holistic vision of Cairo and Beijing being replaced by a handful of "feasible," quantifiable, and presumably cost-effective targets. And in Johannesburg, at the World Summit on Sustainable Development in September 2002, the US-led conservative faction once again tried to subvert health, as a human right by making it conditional upon "national laws and cultural and religious values" and replacing every reference to human rights in the final Declaration with the nebulous phrase "human dignity."[1]

Meanwhile, women's and all progressive social justice groups have watched the UN itself—a political arena where it seemed to matter in the 1990s that we make "women's voices" heard—become increasingly ineffectual and subservient to global corporate, military and fundamentalist forces. These forces, despite their patent moral and ethical corruption, wield institutional and material power far greater than any that feminist groups could possibly attain at this moment—especially after 11 September 2001.

Shortly after the horrific attacks on the World Trade Center and the Pentagon, George W. Bush launched a "war against terrorism" that would have no end in time or space. Deploying a classic imperialist manipulation of feminism, its rationale was not only to avenge and protect America but also to "rescue" the women of Afghanistan, if not the entire Gulf and Central Asian regions. As I was revising this manuscript for publication, the US government was spending $2 billion a month to wage its "war against terrorism"—a total of $37 billion one year after the 11 September attacks and projected to multiply by tenfold over the ensuing decade (Stevenson 2002). Its search-and-destroy missions in the mountains of Afghanistan, its relentless bombings there that killed more innocent civilians than all those lost in the World Trade Center, and its efforts to fortify "homeland security" within the US had not succeeded in capturing Osama bin Laden or destroying the Al Qaeda network or making Afghanistan and Afghan women more secure or free from warlord violence.[2] Yet the Bush administration was proposing a $48 billion increase in its military spending for 2003, the largest increase in a generation (Dao 2002). It concluded a treaty on nuclear weapons with Russia that essentially abandoned the mutual protections of the old ABM treaty and preserved thousands of nuclear missiles for imminent use (Plesch 2002; Arkin 2002). And it proclaimed a new strategic doctrine of unprecedented bellicosity that would give the Imperial United States a unilateral right of pre-emptive attack and "permanent military supremacy" over "*any* imaginable adversary at *any* point in time" (Klare 2002: 12; Sanger 2002).[3] It thus prepared the way for a preemptive invasion of Iraq—against the opposition of the United Nations and most of the world, with only a single ally-in-arms, Britain—and the perpetuation of the bloody mimetic saga of Jihad vs. Crusade.

Why was this happening? What was it all about? Some astute observers of US foreign policy surmised that the Great Game this time—the ultimate stakes over which some lives become valued much more than others — is not very different from what it was through most of the last two centuries: land, water and, above all, oil. A former member of Tony Blair's Cabinet writes in the *Guardian* that the movement of massive numbers of US troops, tanks and fighter planes back into the Gulf region under cover of ousting the evil Saddam Hussein has more to do with instability in neighbouring Saudi Arabia and the goal of seizing control over "the world's largest oil reserves" before they fall "into the hands of an anti-American, militant Islamist government" than it does with "fighting the war on terrorism." With an overwhelming military presence in the region, "no longer would the US have to depend on [and protect] a corrupt and unpopular royal family to keep it supplied with cheap oil" (Mowlam 2002). *Corporate tribalism* — the allegiance to the oil, gas and military hardware industries based in the south-western and western US states — bears certain resemblances to ethnic and warlord tribalism. The Bush government, mirroring its jihadist enemies, thrives on war, a permanent state of war. But the war it seeks is not only against terrorism but for Unocal, the Carlyle Group, Aramco, Halliburton, cheap crude, unimpeded pipelines, unlimited SUVs, and a President whose image is manly (see Petchesky 2001/2002).

Amidst this grotesque explosion of masculinist militarism, feminist visions for social and gender justice embodied in UN documents come to seem utopian and futile, and the regime of international law and the UN agencies responsible for global health and conflict resolution are consigned to irrelevance. Human rights, multilateralism and international cooperation get buried beneath the wings of the phoenix superpower that issues ultimatums in return for rubber-stamp approvals. And lesser powers (Israel, India, Russia, China, Zimbabwe) follow the lead, declaring their own "wars against terrorism" to justify repressive policies. In such a climate, ideas like "health security," "human security" and "social security" become shadowy relics in the face of the prerogatives of "national security" (or oil security); the welfare state and the democratic state become ghosts in the citadel of the total security state. Of course, the US, which can boast 40 per cent of the world's military spending, already has sufficient high-tech military power to overwhelm any and all countries (if not terrorists with box-cutters). But its unrivalled imperial might is not gaining Americans more actual security in everyday life, any more than it is Afghanis or Israelis or Europeans. The world has never been more dangerous.

Women's human rights groups have been at the forefront of efforts to seek non-violent, multilateral solutions to conflicts through international law. The new International Criminal Court's founding statute makes rape, sexual slavery, enforced pregnancy and other forms of sexual violence war crimes and crimes against humanity. Resolution 1325, adopted unanimously by the UN Security Council in October 2000, calls attention to the gender dimensions of armed conflict and ensures women's equal participation in peacekeeping and peace-building efforts (Rome Statute 1998; Hague Appeal *et al.* 2000). These are historic achievements that women's peace groups can claim: without their efforts none would have come about. But the US, having "unsigned" the ICC treaty, threatens to subvert it; and Resolution 1325 remains a noble sentiment, unenforced in Afghanistan, the Middle East or anywhere else. "National sovereignty," now enfolded within a US imperial order, is alive and well, as much a patriarchal construct as ever. The "war against terror" becomes a pretext for power that claims immunity from international accountability, democracy and human rights.

A year before the fatal 11 September, leaders of 191 nations, including the US under Bush's watch, agreed to the following targets to be reached by 2015, as part of the Millennium Development Goals (MDGs): cut in half the proportion of people living in poverty and suffering from hunger; reduce by two-thirds the under-five mortality rate; reduce by three-quarters the maternal mortality ratio; halt and begin to reverse the spread of HIV/AIDS as well as the incidence of malaria and other major diseases; cut in half the proportion of people in the world without access to sustainable drinking water (then numbering over 1 billion but expected to reach 3 billion, or 40 per cent of the world's population, by 2015).[4] How sobering that only a year and a half later—in the shadow of the "war on terrorism" and the perpetual security state—this agenda, which seemed paltry and reductive to many of us at the time, now seems a veritable utopia.

Even Americans, in the heartland of imperial power, suffer a social and health toll exacted by militarism and the boundless "war on terrorism." Ironically, the anthrax scare and the perceived threat of bioterrorism that rattled the United States in the fall and winter of 2001 exposed the gaping inadequacies in the US public health system, after 15 years of budgetary cutbacks and privatization. For a brief moment, US health advocates thought the bioterrorism threat might be a wake-up call that would result in restoring decent funding for public health in the US. Yet the $11 billion the Bush administration budgeted to defend America against bioterrorism turned out to be for expanded stockpiles of vaccines and antibiotics, construction of containment laboratories, research into new drugs and biodetectors—in other words, a new bioterrorism industry, not more public hospitals, clinics or sexual and reproductive health or primary health care services for the poor (Stolberg 2001, 2002). In fact, Bush's budget would *reduce* Medicaid payments to public hospitals in at least 31 states and clamp down on other mechanisms states have found to finance health care for the poor and disabled (Pear 2002a). It would do little or nothing to address the escalating costs of prescription drugs for the elderly—far be it from the capital of global capitalism to regulate drug prices as most European countries and Canada do. And it would do absolutely nothing for the 41.2 million men, women and children without health insurance in the country—unless they happen to be victims of a bioterrorist attack, or foetuses. The Bush administration cynically offers pre-natal care to "unborn children," not to pregnant women, under the Children's Health Insurance Program—a cheap toss to right-wing anti-abortionists in the US but degrading to low-income women (Toner 2002; Pear 2002b). Losing one's job in America means losing health insurance; being uninsured in America is a low-grade, daily kind of terror.

This grim scenario brought me to a pessimistic train of questions that re-called Martin Luther King's ominous words in the midst of the Vietnam War, over thirty-five years ago. Can war — particularly a globalized state of perma-nent war and ubiquitous police surveillance — ever be compatible with the goal of assuring equity and justice in access to health care and a healthy life for all? Is the "war against terrorism" ultimately a war against health and all forms of social justice — an "enemy of the poor" and especially women? Will we allow human rights and women's empowerment to get buried in the ashes of 11 Sep-tember? I believe a worse danger than terrorism now is that all the resources that might have been channeled toward reducing misery; eliminating maternal mortality; treating, preventing and curing AIDS; and promoting equality will be diverted into the waging and deflecting of violence. As the US military-corporate establishment careens from Iraq towards new adventures in North Korea, Syria, the Philippines, Uzbekistan, Kyrgyzstan, Yemen and Iran; as our borders become more patrolled and fortified and Muslim, Arab and South Asian immigrants increasingly become the targets of unconstitutional deten-tions and racist harassment, I have to wonder whether this endless war and all its ancillary security production will sap the energies and budgets for health, education, and racial and gender justice for years to come — meanwhile in-flaming the global hostility and terror it was supposed to curtail.[5]

And yet . . . never was the need greater for those "international legal standards and principles" Mary Robinson calls for, to challenge the violence of global capitalism and global militarism and subject them to an effective system of democratic and participatory governance.

.   .   .

At the end of this project, the state of the world leaves me teetering between pessimism of the intellect and optimism of the will. Earlier in my thinking I had reservations about the fitness of the language of empire, yet today I find myself unavoidably reverting to it all the time. The Bush government's de-signs on the Middle East, Central Asia and Africa, on the replacement of regimes and the redrawing of maps; its pronouncements of not only mani-fest destiny but also absolute, uncontestable dominion over all other coun-tries and international organizations, have all the markings of classic impe-rialist behaviour (Armstrong 2002; Hardt and Negri 2000). As a citizen of this country, I will now have to work with many others to mobilize a huge mass movement at home to oppose this juggernaut that our government has be-come, and this will consume much of our energies and many (how many?) years, as it did in the days of Vietnam. We'll put on hold the battles for health, gender equality, racial equality and human rights.

Earlier I thought it accurate to designate only certain governments in the rest of the world as imperial lackeys and copycats, assuming that some would still exercise their veto in the Security Council and their power in other UN forums to counter US domination and hubris. Today I wonder if there will be any objectors left (besides Cuba, and perhaps Brazil under the new government of Lula) after all fall in line behind the scramble for markets and investments and the relentless march towards armaments and war in Iraq and beyond. Will this become a failed test of the UN's "relevance" as the Bush administration clearly wants? A whole world of lackeys and copycats.

Another scenario: on the last day of writing this book, there was a bomb scare in the famous Jewish delicatessen on the ground floor of the building where I live — where I have lived for the past eighteen years. As I left the building, suspended between fear and disbelief (probably it's all just a hoax), I remembered one thing I knew on 11 September a year ago: "As an American, a woman, a feminist and a Jew, I have to recognize that the bin Ladens of the world hate me and would like me dead" (Petchesky 2001/2002). But I also remembered what every moment since that day has confirmed: Bush's America not only will not but cannot "rescue" me, since its wealth and power and the hubris they generate do so much to foment the angers and hatreds that terrorists thrive upon. Why should I or any Americans have a privileged haven from the dangers and risks that menace the daily lives of so many others elsewhere?

Yet scattered among the grim and militaristic features of the post-9/11 world are also some hopeful signs, nourishing my optimism. In the wake of the corporate corruption scandals and the church paedophilia and sexual abuse scandals that crowded the headlines in 2001–2, these centres of power have lost some of their veneer of invincibility and holiness. Perhaps many more people will join the popular uprisings in Latin America, the women protesters who shut down the oil companies in Nigeria, and gay and lesbian, feminist and social justice groups everywhere in voicing their doubts about global capitalism and global fundamentalism.

In China a catastrophic HIV/AIDS epidemic has prompted a new social movement, including a petition from rural patients demanding "that the government provide free medicine, or medicine we can afford, and [that it] . . . produce copies of Western medicines as quickly as possible." Although the Chinese government jailed the principal organizer of the Chinese AIDS Action Project for nearly a month, it released him to continue his work after an international outcry and in order to pursue a desperately needed grant from the Global Fund to Fight AIDS. And, notwithstanding its eagerness to join the WTO, it promised to "manufacture a full complement of AIDS drugs if Western patent holders did not lower prices within the next few months." A not insignificant aspect of this story is that the activist in question, Dr. Wan Yanhai, has been organizing around AIDS and gay and lesbian rights since the mid-1990s and is linked through the Internet and direct connections to gay and lesbian and treatment access groups in the US and around the world (Rosenthal 2002a, 2000b, 2000c).

This recent development in China represents yet another eruption of global movements and coalitions for health as a human right, in a society that has had little affinity with human rights strategies and concepts. It is one more among many, many indicators that transnational movements for social justice, health rights and gender and sexual equality are growing stronger and more effective all the time and will be the force that democratizes global governance and transforms global capitalism through local democratic participation. Inevitably, women's movements are playing a leading role in this transformative process. As Eisenstein (2004) writes, "although global capital, as such, is no friend to women and girls, it unsettles existing gender relations in ways it cannot simply control."[6] Likewise, fundamentalisms have spawned resistance, however quiet, among women and girls in Iran, Afghanistan, India, and Israel and within the Catholic Church. And global militarism too will create its own backlash, as resentment builds against US bullying and women's and peace and human rights groups throughout the world demand that the UN uphold the principles written in its own Charter.

I see this vision of global governance through civil society representation, women's empowerment and local participatory democracy. I see it in my mind's eye, though I hear, more loudly than ever, the drums of war.

NOTES

1. See United Nations, World Summit on Sustainable Development (WSSD), Plan of Implementation (September 2002), Chapter VI ("Health and Sustainable Development"), paragraph 47; and United Nations, WSSD, "The Johannesburg Declaration on Sustainable Development," A/conf.199/L.6/Rev.2 (4 September 2002). Many thanks to Joan Ross Frankson and June Zeitlin for information on the outcomes at WSSD.

2. At this writing, rival groups still contended for power in most of the country; only the capital city of Kabul was considered stable; a car bomb had killed 28 bystanders in Kandahar; an assassination attempt on the US-backed president, Hamid Karzai, had come within inches of succeeding; and the Bush administration was still hesitating to join the International Security Force set up to help stabilize the country.

3. President Bush signalled this new doctrine in the same State of the Union address of January 2002 in which he called Iraq, Iran, and North Korea an "axis of evil," when he announced: "America will do what is necessary to ensure our nation's security. . . . I will not wait on events while dangers gather. I will not stand by as peril draws closer and closer. The United States of America will not permit the world's most dangerous regimes to threaten us with the world's most destructive weapons" (*New York Times*, 30 January 2002, p. A22). For further background to the doctrine, see the excellent article by Armstrong (2002).

4. The World Summit on Sustainable Development in 2001 added to this list the goal of cutting in half by 2015 the number of people in the world without access to sanitation.

5. Klare (2002), in an excellent overview of "The New Bush Doctrine," makes a similar point.

6. Quoting Lisa Lowe, Naples (2002) makes a very similar point: "Ironically 'the very processes that produce a racialized feminized proletariat . . . displace traditional and national patriarchies,' thus generating 'new possibilities precisely because they have led to a breakdown and a reformulation of the categories of nation, race, class, and gender'" (p. 9).

REFERENCES

Arkin, W. (2002) "Secret Plan Outlines the Unthinkable," *Los Angeles Times*, 10 March.

Armstrong, D. (2002) "Dick Cheney's Song of America," *Harper's Magazine*, October.

Dao, J. (2002) "Bush Sees Big Rise in Military Budget for Next 5 Years," *New York Times*, 2 February.

Eisenstein, Z. (2004) *Feminisms Against Empire* (forthcoming), Zed Books, London.

Girard, F. (2002) "UN Special Session on Children: Bush Administration Continues Its Attacks on Sexual and Reproductive Health," *Reproductive Health Matters,* Vol. 10, No. 20, November.

Hague Appeal *et al.* (2000) *Women Count, At Last!* Hague Appeal for Peace, The Hague, Netherlands.

Hardt, M. and A. Negri (2000) *Empire,* Harvard University Press, Cambridge, MA.

King, Jr., M. L. (2000/1967) "To Atone for Our Sins and Errors in Vietnam," in M. Marable and L. Mullings (eds.), *Let Nobody Turn Us Around: Voices of Resistance, Reform, and Renewal,* Rowman and Littlefield Publishers, Lanham, MD.

Klare, M. (2002) "Endless Military Superiority," *The Nation,* 15 July.

Mowlam, M. (2002) "Comment," *Guardian,* 5 September.

Pear, R. (2002a) "Budget Would Cut Medicaid Payments," *New York Times,* 1 February.

_____. (2002b) "After Decline, the Number of Uninsured Rose in 2001," *New York Times,* 30 September.

Pear, R. and R. Toner (2002) "Amid Fiscal Crisis, Medicaid Is Facing Cuts from States," *New York Times,* 13 January.

Petchesky, R. (2001/2002) "Phantom Towers: Feminist Reflections on the Battle between Global Capitalism and Fundamentalist Terrorism," *The Women's Review of Books,* November 2001; *Economic and Political Weekly,* Vol. 36, No. 43, 27 October–2 November 2001; *Ms. Magazine,* December 2001. Reprinted in: S. Hawthorne and B. Winter (eds.), *September 11, 2001: Feminist Perspectives,* Spinifex Press, Australia (2002); K. Pollitt and B. Reed (eds.), *Nothing Sacred: Women Respond to Religious Fundamentalism and Terror,* Nation Books, New York (2002); R. Menon (ed.), *Feminist Perspectives on Peace and Terror,* Kali for Women, New Delhi (2002).

Plesch, D. (2002) "Why Bush's Deal with Putin Doesn't Make the World a Safer Place," *Observer* (London), 26 May.

Robinson, M. (2002) "Globalization Has to Take Human Rights into Account," *The Irish Times,* 22 January.

Rome Statute/United Nations (1998) *Rome Statute of the International Criminal Court,* adopted by the United Nations Diplomatic Conference of Plenipotentiaries on the Establishment of an International Criminal Court, A/CONF.183/9, 17 July (*http://www.un.org/icc/part1.htm*).

Rosenthal, E. (2002a) "China Now Set to Make Copies of AIDS Drugs," *New York Times,* 7 September.

_____. (2002b) "China Frees AIDS Activist After Month of Outcry," *New York Times,* 20 September.

_____. (2002c) "AIDS Scourge in Rural China Leaves Villages of Orphans," *New York Times,* 25 August.

Sanger, D. (2002) "Bush to Outline Doctrine of Striking Foes First," *New York Times,* 20 September.

Stevenson, R. (2002) "New Study on Antiwar Spending Is Fodder for Rival Camps," *New York Times,* 6 September.

Stolberg, S. (2001) "Some Experts Say US Is Vulnerable to a Germ Attack," *New York Times,* 29 September.

_____. (2002) "Buckets for Bioterrorism, but Less for Catalog of Ills," *New York Times,* 4 February.

Toner, R. (2002) "Administration Plans Care of Fetuses in Health Plan," *New York Times,* 31 January.

PART II
Gender Socialization

The gender system, embedded in other institutions, ensures its continuance through systematic socialization of children, adolescents, and adults. Even though there is substantial variation in how different cultural groups and families within the United States and throughout the world teach their children to be girls or boys, and even though men and women are more alike than they are different, the presence of gender training persists, and the larger institutional structures reinforce it. Sociologist Michael Messner, for example, in a telling account of white male socialization in childhood, describes the day he attended his first little league practice and was told by his father that he threw like a girl. A week later, after careful coaching by his father and intense fear of being thought a sissy, he had learned to throw like a man.[1] In a study of Black and white elementary school children, Jacqueline Jordan Irvine concluded that teachers systematically encouraged Black girls to act submissive and that by upper elementary school, both Black and white girls are rendered relatively invisible in classrooms, receiving significantly less attention from teachers than boys of both races receive.[2]

From the time we are born until we die, gender socialization is a constant part of our lives. Although the genes that determine sex come in several combinations (not just two), and although the hormonal makeup and physical characteristics of human beings fall along a continuum defined as masculine at one end and feminine at the other, allowing for many combinations and permutations that define one's biological sex, the social contexts in which infants are assigned a gender do not allow for more than two categories in mainstream U.S. society. Based on examination of its genitalia, an infant will almost always be defined as female or male, whatever its chromosomal and hormonal makeup. Within this powerful system of gender assignment, women and men work to define their individual identities. Because gender is a socialized aspect of life rather than a purely genetic/ biological one, and because it is largely "socially constructed" rather than instinctual, there is flexibility in how it is expressed.

In a distressing illustration of how girl and boy children are treated differently from very early in their lives, authors of a study of infants with abusive head trauma found that most of the infant victims were boys (60.3 percent). Both women and men tended to abuse boys more than girls in ways serious enough to inflict head injury via shaken baby syndrome or impact trauma. The majority of perpetrators were men in the infants' lives—most typically fathers, stepfathers, or the mother's partner. The authors of the study suggest that perhaps adults have different expectations of male and female infants. If the latter is the case, it could be that tolerance for crying in girl babies is higher than it is for boys. These authors and others call for better parenting training, especially focused on men and boys.[3] The resistance of parents to give dolls to boys seems to be one piece of the failure to teach boys to care for children. The fact that more women than ever before are involved in the paid work force means that more men and boys are spending time with children, either because the parents are working split shifts (see Rubin, Part VI), or because men and boys are serving as babysitters more often.

A push toward gender equality in recent years in some aspects of schooling has led to higher math scores and greater success in science among girls. It has also led to higher rates of smoking, drinking, and drug use according to a report sponsored by the National Council for Research on Women.[4]

The field of gender socialization is currently facing some redefinition related to the role of hormones and genitals in human development. Since 1972, many academics and medical professionals have been arguing that gender is primarily socialized, independent of genes and hormones—that infants are psychologically undifferentiated at birth. In short, they argue that any baby could be raised in either gender if the family and community gave the child consistent messages. This conclusion was based on a single case reported by psychologist John Money concerning a biological male whose penis was accidentally destroyed in a routine circumcision at seven months of age. The parents, following the advice of Money and his medical team, decided to raise the child as a girl a year or so later, and the child's testicles were surgically removed.[5] The early reports on this boy/girl's life claimed that "Joan" had made a successful adjustment as a girl. In 1997, however, psychologist Milton Diamond and psychiatrist Keith Sigmundson reported that Joan had rejected the sex reassignment treatments at age 14 and decided to live as a heterosexual male from then on. He eventually married a woman with children. Adamantly rejecting the notion that gender must be based on genital appearance, size, and function, he stated "If that's all they think of me, that they gotta justify my worth by what I have between my legs, then I gotta be a complete loser."[6] Diamond and Sigmundson concluded that the early gender reassignment had been a mistake and later the same year offered guidelines for how to address situations in which children had unusual or injured genitals.[7] Later journalist John Colapinto wrote a book about this case, describing in detail the experiences of David Reimer (his real name) and exposing what he believed were serious ethical breaches in Money's treatment of both Reimer and the readers of his publications.[8] Sadly, David Reimer committed suicide in 2004. This case suggests that the extent to which gender is hardwired to physical sex is still unclear and will require further study.

Sex reassignment seems most successful when chosen by the person him- or herself. The negative aspects of forced gender reassignment surgery have been made especially clear by members of the Intersex Society of North America who argue that forced sex and gender assignments that contradicted their bodily truths have been destructive. They recommend assigning a gender to an infant, avoiding any unnecessary surgery, and allowing the child to choose how to express itself once it is old enough to understand what version of intersexuality it has and how it might like to live within that particular bodily reality. An example from the Dominican Republic illustrates this point. Children in three villages inherited a syndrome that produced somewhat ambiguous genitalia at birth but that later became male genitalia at puberty. These children were raised as girls who knew that they might become boys at puberty. They received a third gender label, "male genitalia at 12." Of 18 children originally raised as girls, 16 successfully assumed male genders after their penises developed.[9] At least one chose to remain female, even though her body had masculinized, because she enjoyed living as a girl/woman. The potential for resocialization is also clearly illustrated by adults who become transsexuals or transgendered, making a choice to resocialize themselves, to varying degrees, into the gender in which they were not raised. This resocialization process is often accompanied by a new sexual orientation as well.[10]

Research literature on adult development suggests that expressions of gender shift in various ways throughout the life cycle.[11] Men and women frequently grow more similar in midlife. Socialization patterns and expectations for male and female behavior also change over time, related to the historical context. For example, many women were needed in factories during World War II but were sent home when men, returning from the war, were given priority in hiring; these women were then encouraged to be housewives and mothers, forced to resocialize themselves to match prior expectations. Those who had to work, however, ended up with lower-paying jobs since the best jobs were given to men returning from the war.

Socialization as soldiers or fighters, increasingly obvious to people in the United States as we grapple with the aftermath of September 11, 2001, affects millions of young men (especially) and women worldwide. Recruitment of boys and men into national armies or resistance movements affects not only the young men themselves, but also their families and communities.[12] Turning people into fighters takes an intensive socialization process for which state armies are famous. The effects of militarism on women as well are widespread and well documented.[13]

This part of the book looks at selected aspects of gender socialization. A recurring theme in the study of gender socialization is the presence of homophobia overtly expressed against boys and girls who don't fit gender stereotypes and internalized by gay men, lesbians, bisexuals, and transgendered people as fear of ostracism or as self-hatred. The essays included here address the social construction of gender and gender inequality (Lorber), pressures for gender conformity (Avicolli and Due), and gender socialization in varied cultural/racial/class contexts in the United States (Messner, Nelson, and Cofer).

These articles urge us to become more conscious of various aspects of gender socialization and to consider ways to change what limits people of both genders from being fully human in their own right. There are policy implications here regarding how we accept people who don't fit the norms of masculinity and femininity; regarding the negative effects of limited economic options for poor and working-class children; and regarding the intersections of racism, homophobia, elitism, and sexism as they affect people's lives.

As you read the articles in this section, you might find it interesting to ask yourself what your life might have been like if you had been born a different sex. Then make your imagined experience more complex by varying your cultural group or your social class or your sexual orientation or all of these. Explore both pros and cons of these imagined new experiences as your invented self.

NOTES

1. Michael A. Messner, "Ah, Ya Throw Like a Girl!" in Michael A. Messner and Donald F. Sabo, eds., *Sex, Violence and Power in Sports: Rethinking Masculinity* (Freedom, CA: Crossing Press, 1994), pp. 28–32. Messner also reports that this way of throwing is so unnatural and injurious to the shoulder that few pitchers in childhood survive as pitchers into adulthood, having permanently injured their shoulders.

2. Jacqueline Jordan Irvine, "Teacher Communication Patterns as Related to the Race and Sex of the Student," *Journal of Educational Research* 78, no. 6 (1985), pp. 338–45; Jacqueline Jordan Irvine, "Teacher-Student Interactions: Effects of Student Race, Sex, and Grade Level," *Journal of Educational Psychology* 78, no. 1 (1986), pp. 14–21. Reported in Hilary M. Lips, "Gender-Role Socialization: Lessons in Femininity," in Jo Freeman, ed., *Women: A Feminist Perspective*, 5th ed. (Mountain View, CA: Mayfield, 1995), pp. 128–48.

3. Suzanne P. Starling, James R. Holden, and Carole Jenny, "Abusive Head Trauma: The Relationship of Perpetrators to Their Victims." *Pediatrics* 95, no. 2 (February 1995), pp. 259ff; Alisa Valdés-Rodríguez, "Shaken Baby Deaths Typically Involve Fathers: Young Males Need Infant-Care Training, Abuse Prevention Activists, Doctors Say," *The Boston Globe* (September 22, 1998), pp. B1, B8.

4. Lynn Phillips, *The Girls Report: What We Know & Need to Know about Growing Up Female* (New York: National Council for Research on Women, 1998).

5. John Money and Anke A. Ehrhardt, *Man & Woman, Boy & Girl: The Differentiation and Dimorphism of Gender Identity from Conception to Maturity* (Baltimore: Johns Hopkins University Press, 1972).

6. Milton Diamond and H. Keith Sigmundson, "Sex Reassignment at Birth," *Archives of Pediatric and Adolescent Medicine,* 151, no. 3 (March, 1997), p. 301.

7. Milton Diamond and H. Keith Sigmundson, "Management of Intersexuality: Guidelines for Dealing with Persons with Ambiguous Genitalia," *Archives of Pediatric and Adolescent Medicine,* 151, no. 10 (October, 1997), pp. 1046–50.

8. John Colapinto, *As Nature Made Him: The Boy Who Was Raised as a Girl* (New York: Harper Collins, 2000).

9. Anne Fausto-Sterling, *Myths of Gender* (New York: Basic Books, 1985), pp. 86–87.

10. For discussions of the experiences of transsexuals and gender benders, see the new *Journal of Gay, Lesbian, and Bisexual Identity.* Also see Jennifer Finney Boylan, *She's Not There: A Life in Two Genders* (NY: Broadway Books, 2003); Paul Hewitt, *A Self-Made Man: The Diary of a Man Born in a Woman's Body* (London: Headline, 1995); Richard Ekins, *Blending Genders: Social Aspects of Cross-Dressing and Sex Changing* (New York: Routledge, 1995). For a critical look at solving gender confusion via transsexual surgery, see Janice Raymond, *The Transsexual Empire: The Making of the She-Male* (NY: Teachers College Press, 1994).

11. Margaret L. Andersen, *Thinking about Women: Sociological Perspectives on Sex and Gender,* 3rd ed. (New York: Macmillan, 1993), p. 44.

12. David Filipov, "Afghan Boys Take Up Rifles to Become Men," *Boston Sunday Globe* (October 28, 2001), p. A20.

13. Cynthia Enloe, *Manueuvers: The International Politics of Militarizing Women's Lives* (Berkeley, CA: University of California Press, 2000); Cynthia Enloe, *The Morning After: Sexual Politics at the End of the Cold War* (Berkeley, CA: University of California Press, 1993); Dafna N. Izraeli, "Paradoxes of Women's Service in the Israel Defense Forces," in Daniel Maman, Eyal Ben-Ari, and Zeev Rosenhek (eds.), *Military, State and Society in Israel* (New Brunswick, NJ: Transaction Publishers, 2001), pp. 203–38.

11

THE SOCIAL CONSTRUCTION OF GENDER

JUDITH LORBER

Judith Lorber is Professor Emerita of Sociology and Women's Studies at Brooklyn College and The Graduate School, City University of New York. Her most recent books are *Breaking the Bowls: Degendering and Feminist Change* (2005); *Gender Inequality: Feminist Theories and Politics, 2nd Edition* (2001); and *Gender and the Social Construction of Illness, 2nd Edition,* co-authored with Lisa Jean Moore (2002).

Talking about gender for most people is the equivalent of fish talking about water. Gender is so much the routine ground of everyday activities that questioning its taken-for-granted assumptions and presuppositions is like thinking about whether the sun will come up.[1] Gender is so pervasive that in our society we assume it is bred into our genes. Most people find it hard to believe that gender is constantly created and re-created out of human interaction, out of social life, and is the texture and order of that social life. Yet gender, like culture, is a human production that depends on everyone constantly "doing gender" (West and Zimmerman 1987).

And everyone "does gender" without thinking about it. Today, on the subway, I saw a well-dressed man with a year-old child in a stroller. Yesterday, on a bus, I saw a man with a tiny baby in a carrier on his chest. Seeing men taking care of small children in public is increasingly common—at least in New York City. But both men were quite obviously stared at—and smiled at, approvingly. Everyone was doing gender—the men who were changing the role of fathers and the other passengers, who were applauding them silently. But there was more gendering going on that probably fewer people noticed. The baby was wearing a white crocheted cap and white clothes. You couldn't tell if it was a boy or a girl. The child in the stroller was wearing a dark blue T-shirt and dark print pants. As they started to leave the train, the father put a Yankee baseball cap on the child's head. Ah, a boy, I thought. Then I noticed the gleam of tiny earrings in the child's ears, and as they got off, I saw the little flowered sneakers and lace-trimmed socks. Not a boy after all. Gender done.

Gender is such a familiar part of daily life that it usually takes a deliberate disruption of our expectations of how women and men are supposed to act to pay attention to how it is produced. Gender signs and signals are so

ubiquitous that we usually fail to note them—unless they are missing or ambiguous. Then we are uncomfortable until we have successfully placed the
other person in a gender status; otherwise, we feel socially dislocated. In our
society, in addition to man and woman, the status can be *transvestite* (a person who dresses in opposite-gender clothes) and *transsexual* (a person who
has had sex-change surgery). Transvestites and transsexuals construct their
gender status by dressing, speaking, walking, gesturing in the ways prescribed for women or men—whichever they want to be taken for—and so
does any "normal" person.

For the individual, gender construction starts with assignment to a sex
category on the basis of what the genitalia look like at birth.[2] Then babies are
dressed or adorned in a way that displays the category because parents don't
want to be constantly asked whether their baby is a girl or a boy. A sex category becomes a gender status through naming, dress, and the use of other
gender markers. Once a child's gender is evident, others treat those in one
gender differently from those in the other, and the children respond to the different treatment by feeling different and behaving differently. As soon as they
can talk, they start to refer to themselves as members of their gender. Sex
doesn't come into play again until puberty, but by that time, sexual feelings
and desires and practices have been shaped by gendered norms and expectations. Adolescent boys and girls approach and avoid each other in an elab-
orately scripted and gendered mating dance. Parenting is gendered, with different expectations for mothers and for fathers, and people of different
genders work at different kinds of jobs. The work adults do as mothers and
fathers and as low-level workers and high-level bosses, shapes women's and
men's life experiences, and these experiences produce different feelings, consciousness, relationships, skills—ways of being that we call feminine or masculine.[3] All of these processes constitute the social construction of gender.

Gendered roles change—today fathers are taking care of little children,
girls and boys are wearing unisex clothing and getting the same education,
women and men are working at the same jobs. Although many traditional
social groups are quite strict about maintaining gender differences, in other
social groups they seem to be blurring. Then why the one-year-old's earrings? Why is it still so important to mark a child as a girl or a boy, to make
sure she is not taken for a boy or he for a girl? What would happen if they
were? They would, quite literally, have changed places in their social world.

To explain why gendering is done from birth, constantly and by everyone, we have to look not only at the way individuals experience gender but
at gender as a social institution. As a social institution, gender is one of the
major ways that human beings organize their lives. Human society depends
on a predictable division of labor, a designated allocation of scarce goods, assigned responsibility for children and others who cannot care for themselves, common values and their systematic transmission to new members,
legitimate leadership, music, art, stories, games, and other symbolic productions. One way of choosing people for the different tasks of society is on the

basis of their talents, motivations, and competence—their demonstrated achievements. The other way is on the basis of gender, race, ethnicity—ascribed membership in a category of people. Although societies vary in the extent to which they use one or the other of these ways of allocating people to work and to carry out other responsibilities, every society uses gender and age grades. Every society classifies people as "girl and boy children," "girls and boys ready to be married," and "fully adult women and men," constructs similarities among them and differences between them, and assigns them to different roles and responsibilities. Personality characteristics, feelings, motivations, and ambitions flow from these different life experiences so that the members of these different groups become different kinds of people. The process of gendering and its outcome are legitimated by religion, law, science, and the society's entire set of values.

Gender as Process, Stratification, and Structure

As a social institution, gender is a process of creating distinguishable social statuses for the assignment of rights and responsibilities. As part of a stratification system that ranks these statuses unequally, gender is a major building block in the social structures built on these unequal statuses.

As a *process*, gender creates the social differences that define "woman" and "man." In social interaction throughout their lives, individuals learn what is expected, see what is expected, act and react in expected ways, and thus simultaneously construct and maintain the gender order: "The very injunction to be given gender takes place through discursive routes: to be a good mother, to be a heterosexually desirable object, to be a fit worker, in sum, to signify a multiplicity of guarantees in response to a variety of different demands all at once" (J. Butler 1990, 145). Members of a social group neither make up gender as they go along nor exactly replicate in rote fashion what was done before. In almost every encounter, human beings produce gender, behaving in the ways they learned were appropriate for their gender status, or resisting or rebelling against these norms. Resistance and rebellion have altered gender norms, but so far they have rarely eroded the statuses.

Gendered patterns of interaction acquire additional layers of gendered sexuality, parenting, and work behaviors in childhood, adolescence, and adulthood. Gendered norms and expectations are enforced through informal sanctions of gender-inappropriate behavior by peers and by formal punishment or threat of punishment by those in authority should behavior deviate too far from socially imposed standards for women and men.

Everyday gendered interactions build gender into the family, the work process, and other organizations and institutions, which in turn reinforce gender expectations for individuals.[4] Because gender is a process, there is room not only for modification and variation by individuals and small groups but also for institutionalized change (J. W. Scott 1988, 7).

As part of a *stratification* system, gender ranks men above women of the same race and class. Women and men could be different but equal. In practice, the process of creating difference depends to a great extent on differential evaluation. As Nancy Jay (1981) says: "That which is defined, separated out, isolated from all else is A and pure. Not-A is necessarily impure, a random catchall, to which nothing is external except A and the principle of order that separates it from Not-A" (45). From the individual's point of view, whichever gender is A, the other is Not-A; gender boundaries tell the individual who is like him or her, and all the rest are unlike. From society's point of view, however, one gender is usually the touchstone, the normal, the dominant, and the other is different, deviant, and subordinate. In Western society, "man" is A, "wo-man" is Not-A. (Consider what a society would be like where woman was A and man Not-A.)

The further dichotomization by race and class constructs the gradations of a heterogeneous society's stratification scheme. Thus, in the United States, white is A, African American is Not-A; middle class is A, working class is Not-A, and "African-American women occupy a position whereby the inferior half of a series of these dichotomies converge" (P. H. Collins 1989, 770). The dominant categories are the hegemonic ideals, taken so for granted as the way things should be that white is not ordinarily thought of as a race, middle class as a class, or men as a gender. The characteristics of these categories define the Other as that which lacks the valuable qualities the dominants exhibit.

In a gender-stratified society, what men do is usually valued more highly than what women do because men do it, even when their activities are very similar or the same. In different regions of southern India, for example, harvesting rice is men's work, shared work, or women's work: "Wherever a task is done by women it is considered easy, and where it is done by [men] it is considered difficult" (Mencher 1988, 104). A gathering and hunting society's survival usually depends on the nuts, grubs, and small animals brought in by the women's foraging trips, but when the men's hunt is successful, it is the occasion for a celebration. Conversely, because they are the superior group, white men do not have to do the "dirty work," such as housework; the most inferior group does it, usually poor women of color (Palmer 1989).

Freudian psychoanalytic theory claims that boys must reject their mothers and deny the feminine in themselves in order to become men: "For boys the major goal is the achievement of personal masculine identification with their father and sense of secure masculine self, achieved through superego formation and disparagement of women" (Chodorow 1978, 165). Masculinity may be the outcome of boys' intrapsychic struggles to separate their identity from that of their mothers, but the proofs of masculinity are culturally shaped and usually ritualistic and symbolic (Gilmore 1990).

The Marxist feminist explanation for gender inequality is that by demeaning women's abilities and keeping them from learning valuable technological skills, bosses preserve them as a cheap and exploitable reserve army of labor. Unionized men who could easily be replaced by women collude in this process because it allows them to monopolize the better-paid, more interesting, and more autonomous jobs: "Two factors emerge as helping men maintain their separation from women and their control of technological occupations. One is the active gendering of jobs and people. The second is the continual creation of sub-divisions in the work processes, and levels in work hierarchies, into which men can move in order to keep their distance from women" (Cockburn 1985, 13).

Societies vary in the extent of the inequality in social status of their women and men members, but where there is inequality, the status "woman" (and its attendant behavior and role allocations) is usually held in lesser esteem than the status "man." Since gender is also intertwined with a society's other constructed statuses of differential evaluation—race, religion, occupation, class, country of origin, and so on—men and women members of the favored groups command more power, more prestige, and more property than the members of the disfavored groups. Within many social groups, however, men are advantaged over women. The more economic resources, such as education and job opportunities, are available to a group, the more they tend to be monopolized by men. In poorer groups that have few resources (such as working-class African Americans in the United States), women and men are more nearly equal, and the women may even outstrip the men in education and occupational status (Almquist 1987).

As a *structure,* gender divides work in the home and in economic production, legitimates those in authority, and organizes sexuality and emotional life (Connell 1987, 91–142). As primary parents, women significantly influence children's psychological development and emotional attachments, in the process reproducing gender. Emergent sexuality is shaped by heterosexual, homosexual, bisexual, and sadomasochistic patterns that are gendered—different for girls and boys, and for women and men—so that sexual statuses reflect gender statuses.

When gender is a major component of structured inequality, the devalued genders have less power, prestige, and economic rewards than the valued genders. In countries that discourage gender discrimination, many major roles are still gendered; women still do most of the domestic labor and child rearing, even while doing full-time paid work; women and men are segregated on the job and each does work considered "appropriate"; women's work is usually paid less than men's work. Men dominate the positions of authority and leadership in government, the military, and the law; cultural productions, religions, and sports reflect men's interests.

In societies that create the greatest gender difference, such as Saudi Arabia, women are kept out of sight behind walls or veils, have no civil rights, and often create a cultural and emotional world of their own (Bernard 1981). But even in societies with less rigid gender boundaries, women and men spend much of their time with people of their own gender because of the way work and family are organized. This spatial separation of women and men reinforces gendered differences, identity, and ways of thinking and behaving (Coser 1986).

Gender inequality—the devaluation of "women" and the social domination of "men"—has social functions and social history. It is not the result of sex, procreation, physiology, anatomy, hormones, or genetic predispositions. It is produced and maintained by identifiable social processes and built into the general social structure and individual identities deliberately and purposefully. The social order as we know it in Western societies is organized around racial, ethnic, class, and gender inequality. I contend, therefore, that the continuing purpose of gender as a modern social institution is to construct women as a group to be the subordinates of men as a group.

The Paradox of Human Nature

To say that sex, sexuality, and gender are all socially constructed is not to minimize their social power. These categorical imperatives govern our lives in the most profound and pervasive ways, through the social experiences and social practices of what Dorothy Smith calls the "everday/evernight world" (1990, 31–57). The paradox of human nature is that it is *always* a manifestation of cultural meanings, social relationships, and power politics; "not biology, but culture, becomes destiny" (J. Butler 1990, 8). Gendered people emerge not from physiology or sexual orientations but from the exigencies of the social order, mostly, from the need for a reliable division of the work of food production and the social (not physical) reproduction of new members. The moral imperatives of religion and cultural representations guard the boundary lines among genders and ensure that what is demanded, what is permitted, and what is tabooed for the people in each gender is well known and followed by most (C. Davies 1982). Political power, control of scarce resources, and, if necessary, violence uphold the gendered social order in the face of resistance and rebellion. Most people, however, voluntarily go along with their society's prescriptions for those of their gender status, because the norms and expectations get built into their sense of worth and identity as [the way we] think, the way we see and hear and speak, the way we fantasy, and the way we feel.

There is no core or bedrock in human nature below these endlessly looping processes of the social production of sex and gender, self and other, identity and psyche, each of which is a "complex cultural construction" (J. Butler 1990, 36). *For humans, the social is the natural.* Therefore, "in its feminist senses, gender cannot mean simply the cultural appropriation of biological sexual difference. Sexual difference is itself a fundamental—and scientifically contested—construction. Both 'sex' and 'gender' are woven of multiple, asymmetrical strands of difference, charged with multifaceted dramatic narratives of domination and struggle" (Haraway 1990, 140).

NOTES

1. Gender is, in Erving Goffman's words, an aspect of *Felicity's Condition:* "any arrangement which leads us to judge an individual's . . . acts not to be a manifestation of strangeness. Behind Felicity's Condition is our sense of what it is to be sane" (1983:27). Also see Bem 1993; Frye 1983, 17–40; Goffman 1977.

2. In cases of ambiguity in countries with modern medicine, surgery is usually performed to make the genitalia more clearly male or female.

3. See J. Butler 1990 for an analysis of how doing gender is gender identity.

4. On the "logic of practice," or how the experience of gender is embedded in the norms of everyday interaction and the structure of formal organizations, see Acker 1990; Bourdieu [1980] 1990; Connell 1987; Smith 1987.

REFERENCES

Acker, Joan. 1990. "Hierarchies, jobs, and bodies: A theory of gendered organizations," *Gender & Society* 4:139–58.

Almquist, Elizabeth M. 1987. "Labor market gendered inequality in minority groups," *Gender & Society* 1:400–14.

Bem, Sandara Lipsitz. 1993. *The Lenses of Gender: Transforming the Debate on Sexual Inequality.* New Haven: Yale University Press.

Bernard, Jessie. 1981. *The Female World.* New York: Free Press.

Bourdieu, Pierre. [1980] 1990. *The Logic of Practice.* Stanford, Calif.: Stanford University Press.

Butler, Judith. 1990. *Gender Trouble: Feminism and the Subversion of Identity.* New York and London: Routledge.

Chodorow, Nancy. 1978. *The Reproduction of Mothering.* Berkeley: University of California Press.

Cockburn, Cynthia. 1985. *Machinery of Dominance: Women, Men and Technical Know-how.* London: Pluto Press.

Collins, Patricia Hill. 1989. "The social construction of black feminist thought," *Signs* 14:745–73.

Connell, R. [Robert] W. 1987. *Gender and Power: Society, the Person, and Sexual Politics.* Stanford, Calif.: Stanford University Press.

Coser, Rose Laub. 1986. "Cognitive structure and the use of social space," *Sociological Forum* 1:1–26.

Davies, Christie. 1982. "Sexual taboos and social boundaries," *American Journal of Sociology* 87:1032–63.

Dwyer, Daisy, & Judith Bruce (eds.). 1988. *A Home Divided: Women and Income in the Third World.* Palo Alto, Calif.: Stanford University Press.

Frye, Marilyn. 1983. *The Politics of Reality: Essays in Feminist Theory.* Trumansburg, N.Y.: Crossing Press.

Gilmore, David D. 1990. *Manhood in the Making: Cultural Concepts of Masculinity.* New Haven: Yale University Press.

Goffman, Erving. 1977. "The arrangement between the sexes," *Theory and Society* 4:301–33.

Goffman, Erving. 1983. Felicity's Condition. *American Journal of Sociology* 89:1–53.

Haraway, Donna. 1990. "Investment strategies for the evolving portfolio of primate females," in *Jacobus, Keller, and Shuttleworth.*

Jacobus, Mary, Evelyn Fox Keller, & Sally Shuttleworth (eds.). (1990). *Body/politics: Women and the Discourse of Science.* New York and London: Routledge.

Jay, Nancy. 1981. "Gender and dichotomy," *Feminist Studies* 7:38–56.

Mencher, Joan. 1988. "Women's work and poverty: Women's contribution to household maintenance in South India," In *Dwyer and Bruce.*

Palmer, Phyllis. 1989. *Domesticity and Dirt: Housewives and Domestic Servants in the United States, 1920–1945.* Philadelphia: Temple University Press.

Scott, Joan Wallach. 1988. *Gender and the Politics of History.* New York: Columbia University Press.

Smith, Dorothy. 1987. *The Everyday World as Problematic: A Feminist Sociology.* Toronto: University of Toronto Press.

_____. 1990. *The Conceptual Practices of Power: A Feminist Sociology of Knowledge.* Toronto: University of Toronto Press.

West, Candace, & Don Zimmerman. 1987. "Doing gender." *Gender & Society* 1:125–51.

12

BOYHOOD, ORGANIZED SPORTS, AND THE CONSTRUCTION OF MASCULINITIES

MICHAEL A. MESSNER

Michael A. Messner is a professor of sociology and gender studies at the University of Southern California. His most recent books are *Politics of Masculinities: Men in Movements* (1997), *Men's Lives* (2004, edited with Michael Kimmel); *Paradoxes of Youth and Sport* (2002, edited with Margaret Gatz and Sandra Rokeach), and *Taking the Field: Women, Men, and Sports* (2002). His articles have appeared in *Gender & Society, Theory & Society, Men and Masculinities,* and *Sociology of Sport Journal.*

The rapid expansion of feminist scholarship in the past two decades has led to fundamental reconceptualizations of the historical and contemporary meanings of organized sport. In the nineteenth and twentieth centuries, modernization and women's continued movement into public life created widespread "fears of social feminization," especially among middle-class men (Hantover, 1978; Kimmel, 1987). One result of these fears was the creation of organized sport as a homosocial sphere in which competition and (often violent) physicality was valued, while "the feminine" was devalued. As a result, organized sport has served to bolster a sagging ideology of male superiority, and has helped to reconstitute masculine hegemony (Bryson, 1987; Hall, 1988; Messner, 1988; Theberge, 1981).

Michael A. Messner, "Boyhood, Organized Sports and the Construction of Masculinities" from *Journal of Contemporary Ethnography* (January 1990). Copyright © 1990 by Sage Publications, Inc. Reprinted with the permission of Sage Publications, Inc.

The feminist critique has spawned a number of studies of the ways that women's sport has been marginalized and trivialized in the past (Greendorfer, 1977; Oglesby, 1978; Twin, 1978), in addition to illuminating the continued existence of structural and ideological barriers to gender equality within sport (Birrell, 1987). Only recently, however, have scholars begun to use feminist insights to examine men's experiences in sport (Kidd, 1987; Messner, 1987; Sabo, 1985). This article explores the relationship between the construction of masculine identity and boyhood participation in organized sports.

I view gender identity not as a "thing" that people "have," but rather as a *process of construction* that develops, comes into crisis, and changes as a person interacts with the social world. Through this perspective, it becomes possible to speak of "gendering" identities rather than "masculinity" or "femininity" as relatively fixed identities or statuses.

There is an agency in this construction; people are not passively shaped by their social environment. As recent feminist analyses of the construction of feminine gender identity have pointed out, girls and women are implicated in the construction of their own identities and personalities, both in terms of the ways that they participate in their own subordination and the ways that they resist subordination (Benjamin, 1988; Haug, 1987). Yet this self-construction is not a fully conscious process. There are also deeply woven, unconscious motivations, fears, and anxieties at work here. So, too, in the construction of masculinity. Levinson (1978) has argued that masculine identity is neither fully "formed" by the social context, nor is it "caused" by some internal dynamic put into place during infancy. Instead, it is shaped and constructed through the interaction between the internal and the social. The internal gendering identity may set developmental "tasks," may create thresholds of anxiety and ambivalence, yet it is only through a concrete examination of people's interactions with others within social institutions that we can begin to understand both the similarities and differences in the construction of gender identities.

In this study I explore and interpret the meanings that males themselves attribute to their boyhood participation in organized sport. In what ways do males construct masculine identities within the institution of organized sports? In what ways do class and racial differences mediate this relationship and perhaps lead to the construction of different meanings, and perhaps different masculinities? And what are some of the problems and contradictions within these constructions of masculinity?

Description of Research

Between 1983 and 1985, I conducted interviews with 30 male former athletes. Most of the men I interviewed had played the (U.S.) "major sports" — football, basketball, baseball, track. At the time of the interview, each had been retired from playing organized sports for at least five years. Their ages ranged from 21 to 48, with the median 33; 14 were black, 14 were white, and 2 were Hispanic; 15 of the 16 black and Hispanic men had come from poor or working-class families, while the majority (9 of 14) of the white men had come from middle-class or professional families. All had at some time in their lives based their identities largely on their roles as athletes and could therefore be said to have had "athletic careers." Twelve had played organized sports through high school, 11 through college, and 7 had been professional athletes. Though the sample was not randomly selected, an effort was made to see that the sample had a range of difference in terms of race and social class backgrounds, and that there was some variety in terms of age, types of sports played, and levels of success in athletic careers. Without exception, each man contacted agreed to be interviewed.

The tape-recorded interviews were semi-structured and took from one and one-half to six hours, with most taking about three hours. I asked each man to talk about four broad eras in his life: (1) his earliest experiences with sports in boyhood, (2) his athletic career, (3) retirement or disengagement from the athletic career, and (4) life after the athletic career. In each era, I focused the interview on the meanings of "success and failure," and on the boy's/man's relationships with family, with other males, with women, and with his own body.

In collecting what amounted to life histories of these men, my overarching purpose was to use feminist theories of masculine gender identity to explore how masculinity develops and changes as boys and men interact within the socially constructed world of organized sports. In addition to using the data to move toward some generalizations about the relationship between "masculinity and sport," I was also concerned with sorting out some of the variations among boys, based on class and racial inequalities, that led them to relate differently to athletic careers. I divided my sample into two comparison groups. The first group was made up of 10 men from higher-status backgrounds, primarily white, middle-class, and professional families. The second group was made up of 20 men from lower-status backgrounds, primarily minority, poor, and working-class families.

Boyhood and the Promise of Sports

Zane Grey once said, "All boys love baseball. If they don't they're not real boys" (as cited in Kimmel, 1990). This is, of course, an ideological statement; in fact, some boys do *not* love baseball, or any other sports, for that matter. There are millions of males who at an early age are rejected by, become alienated from, or lose interest in organized sports. Yet all boys are, to a greater or lesser extent, judged according to their ability, or lack of ability, in competitive sports (Eitzen, 1975; Sabo, 1985). In this study I focus on those males who did become athletes—males who eventually poured thousands of hours into the development of specific physical skills. It is in boyhood that we can discover the roots of their commitment to athletic careers.

How did organized sports come to play such a central role in these boys' lives? When asked to recall how and why they initially got into playing sports, many of the men interviewed for this study seemed a bit puzzled: after all, playing sports was "just the thing to do." A 42-year-old black man who had played college basketball put it this way:

> It was just what you did. It's kind of like, you went to school, you played athletics, and if you didn't, there was something wrong with you. It was just like brushing your teeth: it's just what you did. It's part of your existence.

Spending one's time playing sports with other boys seemed as natural as the cycle of the seasons: baseball in the spring and summer, football in the fall, basketball in the winter—and then it was time to get out the old baseball glove and begin again. As a black 35-year-old former professional football star said:

> I'd say when I wasn't in school, 95% of the time was spent in the park playing. It was the only thing to do. It just came as natural.

And a black, 34-year-old professional basketball player explained his early experiences in sports:

> My principal and teacher said, "Now if you work at this you might be pretty damned good." So it was more or less a community thing—everybody in the community said, "Boy, if you work hard and keep your nose clean, you gonna be good." Cause it was natural instinct.

"It was natural instinct." "I was a natural." Several athletes used words such as these to explain their early attraction to sports. But certainly there is nothing "natural" about throwing a ball through a hoop, hitting a ball with a bat, or jumping over hurdles. A boy, for instance, may have amazingly dexterous inborn hand-eye coordination, but this does not predispose him to a career of hitting baseballs any more than it predisposes him to life as a brain surgeon. When one listens closely to what these men said about their early experiences in sports, it becomes clear that their adoption of the self-definition of "natural athlete" was the result of what Connell (1990) has called "a collective practice" that constructs masculinities. The boyhood development of masculine identity and status—truly problematic in a society that offers no official rite of passage into adulthood—results from a process of interaction with people and social institutions. Thus, in discussing early motivations in sports, men commonly talk of the importance of relationships with family members, peers, and the broader community.

Family Influences

Though most of the men in this study spoke of their mothers with love, respect, even reverence, their descriptions of their earliest experiences in
sports are stories of an exclusively male world. The existence of older brothers or uncles who served as teachers and athletic role models—as well as
sources of competition for attention and status within the family—was very
common. An older brother, uncle, or even close friend of the family who was
a successful athlete appears to have acted as a sort of standard of achievement against whom to measure oneself. A 34-year-old black man who had
been a three-sport star in high school said:

> My uncles—my Uncle Harold went to the Detroit Tigers, played pro
> ball—all of 'em, everybody played sports, so I wanted to be better
> than anybody else. I knew that everybody in this town knew them—
> their names were something. I wanted my name to be just like theirs.

Similarly, a black 41-year-old former professional football player recalled:

> I was the younger of three brothers and everybody played sports,
> so consequently I was more or less forced into it. 'Cause one brother
> was always better than the next brother and then I came along and
> had to show them that I was just as good as them. My oldest
> brother was an all-city ballplayer, then my other brother comes
> along he's all-city and all-state, and then I have to come along.

For some, attempting to emulate or surpass the athletic accomplishments
of older male family members created pressures that were difficult to deal
with. A 33-year-old white man explained that he was a good athlete during
boyhood, but the constant awareness that his two older brothers had been better made it difficult for him to feel good about himself, or to have fun in sports:

> I had this sort of reputation that I followed from the playgrounds
> through grade school, and through high school. I followed these
> guys who were all-conference and all-state.

Most of these men, however, saw their relationships with their athletic
older brothers and uncles in a positive light; it was within these relationships
that they gained experience and developed motivations that gave them a
competitive "edge" within their same-aged peer group. As a 33-year-old
black man describes his earliest athletic experiences:

> My brothers were role models. I wanted to prove—especially to
> my brothers—that I had heart, you know, that I was a man.

When asked, "What did it mean to you to be 'a man' at that age?" he replied:

> Well, it meant that I didn't want to be a so-called scaredy-cat. You
> want to hit a guy even though he's bigger than you to show that,

you know, you've got this macho image. I remember that at that young an age, that feeling was exciting to me. And that carried over, and as I got older, I got better and I began to look around me and see, well hey! I'm competitive with these guys, even though I'm younger, you know? And then of course all the compliments come — and I began to notice a change, even in my parents — especially in my father — he was proud of that, and that was very important to me. He was extremely important . . . he showed me more affection, now that I think of it.

As this man's words suggest, if men talk of their older brothers and uncles mostly as role models, teachers, and "names" to emulate, their talk of their relationships with their fathers is more deeply layered and complex. Athletic skills and competition for status may often be learned from older brothers, but it is in boys' relationships with fathers that we find many of the keys to the emotional salience of sports in the development of masculine identity.

Relationships with Fathers

The fact that boys' introductions to organized sports are often made by fathers who might otherwise be absent or emotionally distant adds a powerful emotional charge to these early experiences (Osherson, 1986). Although playing organized sports eventually came to feel "natural" for all of the men interviewed in this study, many needed to be "exposed" to sports, or even gently "pushed" by their fathers to become involved in activities like Little League baseball. A white 33-year-old man explained:

I still remember it like it was yesterday — Dad and I driving up in his truck, and I had my glove and my hat and all that — and I said, "Dad, I don't want to do it." He says, "What?" I says, "I don't want to do it." I was nervous. That I might fail. And he says, "Don't be silly. Lookit: There's Joey and Petey and all your friends out there." And so Dad says, "You're gonna do it, come on." And in my memory he's never said that about anything else; he just knew I needed a little kick in the pants and I'd do it. And once you're out there and you see all the other kids making errors and stuff, and you know you're better than those guys, you know: Maybe I *do* belong here. As it turned out, Little League was a good experience.

Some who were similarly "pushed" by their fathers were not so successful as the aforementioned man had been in Little League baseball, and thus the experience was not altogether a joyous affair. One 34-year-old white man, for instance, said he "inherited" his interest in sports from his father, who started playing catch with him at the age of four. Once he got into Little

League, he felt pressured by his father, one of the coaches, who expected him to be the star of the team:

> I'd go 0-for-four sometimes, strike out three times in a Little League game, and I'd dread the ride home. I'd come home and he'd say, "Go in the bathroom and swing the bat in the mirror for an hour," to get my swing level. . . . It didn't help much, though, I'd go out and strike out three or four times again the next game too [laughs ironically].

When asked if he had been concerned with having his father's approval, he responded:

> Failure in his eyes? Yeah, I always thought that he wanted me to get some kind of [athletic] scholarship. I guess I was afraid of him when I was a kid. He didn't hit that much, but he had a rage about him — he'd rage, and that voice would just rattle you.

Similarly, a 24-year-old black man described his awe of his father's physical power and presence, and his sense of inadequacy in attempting to emulate him:

> My father had a voice that sounded like rolling thunder. Whether it was intentional on his part or not, I don't know, but my father gave me a sense, an image of him being the most powerful being on earth, and that no matter what I ever did I would never come close to him. . . . There were definite feelings of physical inadequacy that I couldn't work around.

It is interesting to note how these feelings of physical inadequacy relative to the father lived on as part of this young man's permanent internalized image. He eventually became a "feared" high school football player and broke school records in weight-lifting, yet

> As I grew older, my mother and friends told me that I had actually grown to be a larger man than my father. Even though in time I required larger clothes than he, which should have been a very concrete indication, neither my brother nor I could ever bring ourselves to say that I was bigger. We simply couldn't conceive of it.

Using sports activities as a means of identifying with and "living up to" the power and status of one's father was not always such a painful and difficult task for the men I interviewed. Most did not describe fathers who "pushed" them to become sports stars. The relationship between their athletic strivings and their identification with their fathers was more subtle. A 48-year-old black man, for instance, explained that he was not pushed into sports by his father, but was aware from an early age of the community status his father had gained through sports. He saw his own athletic accomplishments as a way to connect with and emulate his father:

I wanted to play baseball because my father had been quite a good baseball player in the Negro leagues before baseball was integrated, and so he was kind of a model for me. I remember, quite young, going to a baseball game he was in—this was before the war and all—I remember being in the stands with my mother and seeing him on first base, and being aware of the crowd. . . . I was aware of people's confidence in him as a serious baseball player. I don't think my father ever said anything to me like "play sports." . . . [But] I knew he would like it if I did well. His admiration was important . . . he mattered.

Similarly, a 24-year-old white man described his father as a somewhat distant "role model" whose approval mattered:

My father was more of an example . . . he definitely was very much in touch with and still had very fond memories of being an athlete and talked about it, bragged about it. . . . But he really didn't do that much to teach me skills, and he didn't always go to every game I played like some parents. But he approved and that was important, you know. That was important to get his approval. I always knew that playing sports was important to him, so I knew implicitly that it was good and there was definitely a value on it.

First experiences in sports might often come through relationships with brothers or older male relatives, and the early emotional salience of sports was often directly related to a boy's relationship with his father. The sense of commitment that these young boys eventually made to the development of athletic careers is best explained as a process of development of masculine gender identity and status in relation to same-sex peers.

Masculine Identity and Early Commitment to Sports

When many of the men in this study said that during childhood they played sports because "it's just what everybody did," they of course meant that is was just what *boys* did. They were introduced to organized sports by older brothers and fathers, and once involved, found themselves playing within an exclusively male world. Though the separate (and unequal) gendered worlds of boys and girls came to appear as "natural," they were in fact socially constructed. Thorne's observations of children's activities in schools indicated that rather than "naturally" constituting "separate gendered cultures," there is considerable interaction between boys and girls in classrooms and on playgrounds. When adults set up legitimate contact between boys and girls, Thorne observed, this usually results in "relaxed interactions." But when activities in the classroom or on the playground are presented to children as sex-segregated activities and gender is marked by teachers and other adults ("boys line up here, girls over there"), "gender boundaries are heightened, and mixed-sex interaction becomes an explicit arena of risk" (Thorne, 1986; 70). Thus sex-segregated activities such as organized sports as structured by adults, provide the context in which gendered identities and separate "gendered cultures" develop and come to appear natural. For the boys in this study, it became "natural" to equate masculinity with competition, physical strength, and skills. Girls simply did not (could not, it was believed) participate in these activities.

Yet it is not simply the separation of children, by adults, into separate activities that explains why many boys came to feel such strong connection with sports activities, while so few girls did. As I listened to men recall their earliest experiences in organized sports, I heard them talk of insecurity, loneliness, and especially a need to connect with other people as a primary motivation in their early sports strivings. As a 42-year-old white man stated, "The most important thing was just being out there with the rest of the guys—being friends." Another 32-year-old interviewee was born in Mexico and moved to the United States at a fairly young age. He never knew his father, and his mother died when he was only nine years old. Suddenly he felt rootless, and threw himself into sports. His initial motivations, however, do not appear to be based on a need to compete and win:

> Actually, what I think sports did for me is it brought me into kind
> of an instant family. By being on a Little League team, or even just
> playing with all kinds of different kids in the neighborhood, it
> brought what I really wanted, which was some kind of closeness. It
> was just being there, and being friends.

Clearly, what these boys needed and craved was that which was most problematic for them: connection and unity with other people. But why do these young males find *organized sports* such an attractive context in which to establish "a kind of closeness" with others? Comparative observations of young boys' and girls' game-playing behaviors yield important insights into this question. Piaget (1965) and Lever (1976) both observed that girls tend to have more "pragmatic" and "flexible" orientations to the rules of games; they are more prone to make exceptions and innovations in the middle of a game in order to make the game more "fair." Boys, on the other hand, tend to have a more firm, even [in]flexible orientation to the rules of a game; to them, the rules are what protects any fairness. This difference, according to Gilligan (1982), is based on the fact that early developmental experiences have yielded deeply rooted differences between males' and females' developmental tasks, needs, and moral reasoning. Girls, who tend to define themselves primarily through connection with others, experience highly competitive situations (whether in organized sports or in other hierarchical institutions) as threats to relationships, and thus to their identities. For boys, the development of gender identity involves the construction of positional identities, where a sense of self is solidified through separation from others

(Chodorow, 1978). Yet feminist psychoanalytic theory has tended to over-simplify the internal lives of men (Lichterman, 1986). Males do appear to develop positional identities, yet despite their fears of intimacy, they also retain a human need for closeness and unity with others. This ambivalence toward intimate relationships is a major thread running through masculine development throughout the life course. Here we can conceptualize what Craib (1987) calls the "elective affinity" between personality and social structure: For the boy who both seeks and fears attachment with others, the rule-bound structure of organized sports can promise to be a safe place in which to seek nonintimate attachment with others within a context that maintains clear boundaries, distance, and separation.

Competitive Structures and Conditional Self-Worth

Young boys may initially find that sports give them the opportunity to experience "some kind of closeness" with others, but the structure of sports and athletic careers often undermines the possibility of boys learning to transcend their fears of intimacy, thus becoming able to develop truly close and intimate relationships with others (Kidd, 1990; Messner, 1987). The sports world is extremely hierarchical, and an incredible amount of importance is placed on winning, on "being number one." For instance, a few years ago I observed a basketball camp put on for boys by a professional basketball coach and his staff. The youngest boys, about eight years old (who could barely reach the basket with their shots) played a brief scrimmage. Afterwards, the coaches lined them up in a row in front of the older boys who were sitting in the grandstands. One by one, the coach would stand behind each boy, put his hand on the boy's head (much in the manner of a priestly benediction), and the older boys in the stands would applaud and cheer, louder or softer, depending on how well or poorly the young boy was judged to have performed. The two or three boys who were clearly the exceptional players looked confident that they would receive the praise they were due. Most of the boys, though, had expressions ranging from puzzlement to thinly disguised terror on their faces as they awaited the judgments of the older boys.

This kind of experience teaches boys that it is not "just being out there with the guys—being friends" that ensures the kind of attention and connection that they crave; it is being *better* than the other guys—*beating* them—that is the key to acceptance. Most of the boys in this study did have some early successes in sports, and thus their ambivalent need for connection with others was met, at least for a time. But the institution of sport tends to encourage the development of what Schafer (1975) has called "conditional self-worth" in boys. As boys become aware that acceptance by others is contingent upon being good—a "winner"—narrow definitions of success, based upon performance and winning, become increasingly important to them. A 33-year-old black man said that by the time he was in his early teens:

It was expected of me to do well in all my contests—I mean by my coaches, my peers, and my family. So I in turn expected to do well, and if I didn't do well, then I'd be very disappointed.

The man from Mexico, discussed above, who said that he had sought "some kind of closeness" in his early sports experiences, began to notice in his early teens that if he played well, was a *winner,* he would get attention from others:

It got to the point where I started realizing, noticing that people were always there for me, backing me all the time—sports got to be really fun because I always had some people there backing me. Finally my oldest brother started going to all my games, even though I had never really seen who he was [laughs]—after the game, you know, we never really saw each other, but he was at all my baseball games, and it seemed like we shared a kind of closeness there, but only in those situations. Off the field, when I wasn't in uniform, he was never around.

By high school, he said, he felt "up against the wall." Sports hadn't delivered what he had hoped it would, but he thought if he just tried harder, won one more championship trophy, he would get the attention he truly craved. Despite his efforts, this attention was not forthcoming. And, sadly, the pressures he had put on himself to excel in sports had taken most of the fun out of playing.

For many of the men in this study, throughout boyhood and into adolescence, this conscious striving for successful achievement became the primary means through which they sought connection with other people (Messner, 1987). But it is important to recognize that young males' internalized ambivalences about intimacy do not fully determine the contours and directions of their lives. Masculinity continues to develop through interaction with the social world—and because boys from different backgrounds are interacting with substantially different familial, educational, and other institutions, these differences will lead them to make different choices and define situations in different ways. Next, I examine the differences in the ways that boys from higher- and lower-status families and communities related to organized sports.

Status Differences and Commitments to Sports

In discussing early attractions to sports, the experiences of boys from higher- and lower-status backgrounds are quite similar. Both groups indicate the importance of fathers and older brothers in introducing them to sports. Both groups speak of the joys of receiving attention and acceptance among family and peers for early successes in sports. Note the similarities, for instance, in the following descriptions of boyhood athletic experiences of two men. First, a man born in a white middle-class family:

> I loved playing sports so much from a very early age because of early exposure. A lot of the sports came easy at an early age, and because they did, and because you were successful at something, I think that you're inclined to strive for that gratification. It's like, if you're good, you like it, because it's instant gratification. I'm doing something that I'm good at and I'm gonna keep doing it.

Second, a black man from a poor family:

> Fortunately I had some athletic ability, and, quite naturally, once you start doing good in whatever it is—I don't care if it's jacks— you show off what you do. That's your ability, that's your blessing, so you show it off as much as you can.

For boys from both groups, early exposure to sports, the discovery that they had some "ability," shortly followed by some sort of family, peer, and community recognition, all eventually led to the commitment of hundreds and thousands of hours of playing, practicing, and dreaming of future stardom. Despite these similarities, there are also some identifiable differences that begin to explain the tendency of males from lower-status backgrounds to develop higher levels of commitment to sports careers. The most clear-cut difference was that while men from higher-status backgrounds are likely to describe their earliest athletic experiences and motivations almost exclusively in terms of immediate family, men from lower-status backgrounds more commonly describe the importance of a broader community context. For instance, a 46-year-old man who grew up in a "poor working class" black family in a small town in Arkansas explained:

> In that community, at the age of third or fourth grade, if you're a male, they expect you to show some kind of inclination, some kind of skill in football or basketball. It was an expected thing, you know? My mom and my dad, they didn't push at all. It was the general environment.

A 48-year-old man describes sports activities as a survival strategy in his poor black community:

> Sports protected me from having to compete in gang stuff, or having to be good with my fists. If you were an athlete and got into the fist world, that was your business, and that was okay—but you didn't have to if you didn't want to. People would generally defer to you, give you your space away from trouble.

A 35-year-old man who grew up in "a poor black ghetto" described his boyhood relationship to sports similarly:

Where I came from, either you were one of two things: you were in
sports or you were out on the streets being a drug addict, or
breaking into places. The guys who were in sports, we had it a
little easier, because we were accepted by both groups. . . . So it
worked out to my advantage, cause I didn't get into a lot of
trouble—some trouble, but not a lot.

The fact that boys in lower-status communities faced these kinds of realities gave salience to their developing athletic identities. In contrast, sports
were important to boys from higher-status backgrounds, yet the middle-
class environment seemed more secure, less threatening, and offered far
more options. By the time most of these boys got into junior high or high
school, many had made conscious decisions to shift their attentions away
from athletic careers to educational and (nonathletic) career goals. A 32-year-
old white college athletic director told me that he had seen his chance to pursue a pro baseball career as "pissing in the wind," and instead focused on education. Similarly, a 33-year-old white dentist who was a three-sport star in
high school, decided not to play sports in college, so he could focus on getting into dental school. As he put it,

I think I kind of downgraded the stardom thing. I thought it was
small potatoes. And sure, that's nice in high school and all that, but
on a broad scale, I didn't think it amounted to all that much.

This statement offers an important key to understanding the construction
of masculine identity within a middle-class context. The status that this boy
got through sports had been *very* important to him, yet he could see that "on
a broad scale," this sort of status was "small potatoes." This sort of early recognition is more than a result of the oft-noted middle-class tendency to raise
"future-oriented" children (Rubin, 1976; Sennett and Cobb, 1973). Perhaps
more important, it is that the *kinds* of future orientations developed by boys
from higher-status backgrounds are consistent with the middle-class context.
These men's descriptions of their boyhoods reveal that they grew up immersed in a wide range of institutional frameworks, of which organized sports
was just one. And—importantly—they could see that the status of adult males
around them was clearly linked to their positions within various professions,
public institutions, and bureaucratic organizations. It was clear that access to
this sort of institutional status came through educational achievement, not
athletic prowess. A 32-year-old black man who grew up in a professional-class
family recalled that he had idolized Wilt Chamberlain and dreamed of being
a pro basketball player, yet his father discouraged his athletic strivings:

He knew I liked the game. I *loved* the game. But basketball was not
recommended; my dad would say, "That's a stereotyped image for
black youth. . . . When your basketball is gone and finished, what
are you gonna do? One day, you might get injured. What are you
gonna look forward to?" He stressed education.

Similarly, a 32-year-old man who was raised in a white middle-class family had found in sports a key means of gaining acceptance and connection in his peer group. Yet he was simultaneously developing an image of himself as a "smart student," and becoming aware of a wide range of non-sports life options:

> My mother was constantly telling me how smart I was, how good I was, what a nice person I was, and giving me all sorts of positive strokes, and those positive strokes became a self-motivating kind of thing. I had this image of myself as smart, and I lived up to that image.

It is not that parents of boys in lower-status families did not also encourage their boys to work hard in school. Several reported that their parents "stressed books first, sports second." It's just that the broader social context — education, economy, and community — was more likely to *narrow* lower-status boys' perceptions of real-life options, while boys from higher-status backgrounds faced an expanding world of options. For instance, with a different socioeconomic background, one 35-year-old black man might have become a great musician instead of a star professional football running back. But he did not. When he was a child, he said, he was most interested in music:

> I wanted to be a drummer. But we couldn't afford drums. My dad couldn't go out and buy me a drum set or a guitar even — it was just one of those things; he was just trying to make ends meet.

But he *could* afford, as could so many in his socioeconomic condition, to spend countless hours at the local park, where he was told by the park supervisor

> that I was a natural — not only in gymnastics or baseball — whatever I did, I was a natural. He told me I shouldn't waste this talent, and so I immediately started watching the big guys then.

In retrospect, this man had potential to be a musician or any number of things, but his environment limited his options to sports, and he made the best of it. Even within sports, he, like most boys in the ghetto, was limited:

> We didn't have any tennis courts in the ghetto — we used to have a lot of tennis balls, but not racquets. I wonder today how good I might be in tennis if I had gotten a racquet in my hands at an early age.

It is within this limited structure of opportunity that many lower-status young boys found sports to be *the* place, rather than *a* place, within which to construct masculine identity, status, the relationships. A 36-year-old white man explained that his father left the family when he was very young and his mother faced a very difficult struggle to make ends meet. As his words suggest, the more limited a boy's options, and the more insecure his family situation, the more likely he is to make an early commitment to an athletic career:

I used to ride my bicycle to Little League practice—if I'd waited for someone to pick me up and take me to the ball park I'd have never played. I'd get to the ball park and all the other kids would have their dad bring them to practice or games. But I'd park my bike to the side and when it was over I'd get on it and go home. Sports was the way for me to move everything to the side—family problems, just all the embarrassments—and think about one thing, and that was sports. . . . In the third grade, when the teacher went around the classroom and asked everybody, "What do you want to be when you grow up?" I said, "I want to be a major league baseball player," and everybody laughed their heads off.

This man eventually did enjoy a major league baseball career. Most boys from lower-status backgrounds who make similar early commitments to athletic careers are not so successful. As stated earlier, the career structure of organized sports is highly competitive and hierarchical. In fact, the chances of attaining professional status in sports are approximately 4:100,000 for a white man, 2:100,000 for a black man, and 3:1 million for a Hispanic man in the United States (Leonard and Reyman, 1988). Nevertheless, the immediate rewards (fun, status, attention), along with the constricted (nonsports) structure of opportunity, attract disproportionately large numbers of boys from lower-status backgrounds to athletic careers as their major means of constructing a masculine identity. These are the boys who later, as young men, had to struggle with "conditional self-worth," and, more often than not, occupational dead ends. Boys from higher-status backgrounds, on the other hand, bolstered their boyhood, adolescent, and early adult status through their athletic accomplishments. Their wide range of experiences and life changes led to an early shift away from sports careers as the major basis of identity (Messner, 1989).

Conclusion

The conception of the masculinity-sports relationship developed here begins to illustrate the idea of an "elective affinity" between social structure and personality. Organized sports is a "gendered institution"—an institution constructed by gender relations. As such, its structure and values (rules, formal organization, sex composition, etc.) reflect dominant conceptions of masculinity and femininity. Organized sports is also a "gendering institution"—an institution that helps to construct the current gender order. Part of this construction of gender is accomplished through the "masculinizing" of male bodies and minds.

Yet boys do not come to their first experiences in organized sports as "blank slates," but arrive with already "gendering" identities due to early developmental experiences and previous socialization. I have suggested here that an important thread running through the development of masculine identity is males' ambivalence toward intimate unity with others. Those boys who experience early athletic successes find in the structure of organized sport an affinity with this masculine ambivalence toward intimacy: The rule-bound, competitive, hierarchical world of sport offers boys an attractive means of establishing an emotionally distant (and thus "safe") connection with others. Yet as boys begin to define themselves as "athletes," they learn that in order to be accepted (to have connection) through sports, they must be winners. And in order to be winners, they must construct relationships with others (and with themselves) that are consistent with the competitive and hierarchical values and structure of the sports world. As a result, they often develop a "conditional self-worth" that leads them to construct more instrumental relationships with themselves and others. This ultimately exacerbates their difficulties in constructing intimate relationships with others. In effect, the interaction between the young male's preexisting internalized ambivalence toward intimacy with the competitive hierarchical institution of sport has resulted in the construction of a masculine personality that is characterized by instrumental rationality, goal orientation, and difficulties with intimate connection and expression (Messner, 1987).

This theoretical line of inquiry invites us not simply to examine how social institutions "socialize" boys, but also to explore the ways that boys' already-gendering identities interact with social institutions (which, like organized sport, are themselves the product of gender relations). This study has also suggested that it is not some singular "masculinity" that is being constructed through athletic careers. It may be correct, from a psychoanalytic perspective, to suggest that all males bring ambivalences toward intimacy to their interactions with the world, but "the world" is a very different place for males from different racial and socioeconomic backgrounds. Because males have substantially different interactions with the world, based on class, race, and other differences and inequalities, we might expect the construction of masculinity to take on different meanings for boys and men from differing backgrounds (Messner, 1989). Indeed, this study has suggested that boys from higher-status backgrounds face a much broader range of options than do their lower-status counterparts. As a result, athletic careers take on different meanings for these boys. Lower-status boys are likely to see athletic careers as *the* institutional context for the construction of their masculine status and identities, while higher-status males make an early shift away from athletic careers toward other institutions (usually education and nonsports careers). A key line of inquiry for future studies might begin by exploring this irony of sports careers: Despite the fact that "the athlete" is currently an example of an exemplary form of masculinity in public ideology, the vast majority of boys who become most committed to athletic careers are never well rewarded for their efforts. The fact that class and racial dynamics lead boys from higher-status backgrounds, unlike their lower-status counterparts, to move into nonsports careers illustrates how the construction of different kinds of masculinities is a key component of the overall construction of the gender order.

REFERENCES

Birrell, S. (1987) "The woman athlete's college experience: knowns and unknowns." *J. of Sport and Social Issues* 11:82–96.

Benjamin, J. (1988) *The Bonds of Love: Psychoanalysis, Feminism, and the Problem of Domination.* New York: Pantheon.

Bryson, L. (1987) "Sport and the maintenance of masculine hegemony." *Women's Studies International Forum* 10:349–360.

Chodorow, N. (1978) *The Reproduction of Mothering.* Berkeley: Univ. of California Press.

Connell, R. W. (1990) "An iron man: the body and some contradictions of hegemonic masculinity," in M. A. Messner and D. F. Sabo (eds.) *Sport, Men and the Gender Order: Critical Feminist Perspectives.* Champaign, IL: Human Kinetics.

Craib, I. (1987) "Masculinity and male dominance." *Soc. Rev.* 38:721–743.

Eitzen, D. S. (1975) "Athletics in the status system of male adolescents: a replication of Coleman's *The Adolescent Society.*" *Adolescence* 10:268–276.

Gilligan, C. (1982) *In a Different Voice: Psychological Theory and Women's Development.* Cambridge, MA: Harvard Univ. Press.

Greendorfer, S. L. (1977) "The role of socializing agents in female sport involvement." *Research Q.* 48:304–310.

Hall, M. A. (1988) "The discourse on gender and sport: from femininity to feminism." *Sociology of Sport J.* 5:330–340.

Hantover, J. (1978) "The boy scouts and the validation of masculinity." *J. of Social Issues* 34:184–195.

Haug, F. (1987) *Female Sexualization.* London: Verso.

Kidd, B. (1987) "Sports and masculinity," pp. 250–265 in M. Kaufman (ed.) *Beyond Patriarchy: Essays by Men on Pleasure, Power, and Change.* Toronto: Oxford Univ. Press.

Kidd, B. (1990) "The men's cultural centre: sports and the dynamic of women's oppression/men's repression," in M. A. Messner and D. F. Sabo (eds.) *Sport, Men and the Gender Order: Critical Feminist Perspectives.* Champaign, IL: Human Kinetics.

Kimmel, M. S. (1987) "Men's responses to feminism at the turn of the century." *Gender and Society* 1:261–283.

Kimmel, M. S. (1990) "Baseball and the reconstitution of American masculinity: 1880–1920," in M. A. Messner and D. F. Sabo (eds.) *Sport, Men and the Gender Order: Critical Feminist Perspectives.* Champaign, IL: Human Kinetics.

Leonard, W. M. II and J. M. Reyman (1988) "The odds of attaining professional athlete status: refining the computations." *Sociology of Sport J.* 5:162–169.

Lever, J. (1976) "Sex differences in the games children play." *Social Problems* 23:478–487.

Levinson, D. J. et al. (1978) *The Seasons of a Man's Life.* New York: Ballantine.

Lichterman, P. (1986) "Chodorow's psychoanalytic sociology: a project half-completed." *California Sociologist* 9:147–166.

Messner, M. (1987) "The meaning of success: the athletic experience and the development of male identity," pp. 193–210 in H. Brod (ed.) *The Making of Masculinities: The New Men's Studies.* Boston: Allen & Unwin.

Messner, M. (1988) "Sports and male domination: the female athlete as contested ideological terrain." *Sociology of Sport J.* 5:197–211.

Messner, M. (1989) "Masculinities and athletic careers." *Gender and Society* 3:71–88.

Oglesby, C. A. (ed.) (1978) *Women and Sport: From Myth to Reality.* Philadelphia: Lea & Farber.

Osherson, S. (1986) *Finding our Fathers: How a Man's Life is Shaped by His Relationship with His Father.* New York: Fawcett Columbine.

Piaget, J. H. (1965) *The Moral Judgment of the Child.* New York: Free Press.

Rubin, L. B. (1976) *Worlds of Pain: Life in the Working Class Family.* New York: Basic Books.

Sabo, D. (1985) "Sport, patriarchy and male identity: new questions about men and sport." *Arena Rev.* 9:2.

Schafer, W. E. (1975) "Sport and male sex role socialization." *Sport Sociology Bull.* 4:47–54.

Sennett, R. and J. Cobb (1973) *The Hidden Injuries of Class.* New York: Random House.

Theberge, N. (1981) "A critique of critiques: radical and feminist writings on sport." *Social Forces* 60:2.

Thorne, B. (1986) "Girls and boys together . . . but mostly apart: gender arrangements in elementary schools," pp. 167–184 in W. W. Hartup and Z. Rubin (eds.) *Relationships and Development.* Hillsdale, NJ: Lawrence Erlbaum.

Twin, S. L. (ed.) (1978) *Out of the Bleachers: Writings on Women and Sport.* Old Westbury, NY: Feminist Press.

13

WHO'S THE FAIREST OF THEM ALL?

JILL NELSON

Jill Nelson's work has appeared in *Essence, The New York Times, The Nation, USA Weekend,* and *The Village Voice.* She is a columnist for *MSNBC Online* and a contributing editor for *USA Weekend.*

Nearly three decades after I turned eighteen in 1970, the issues that I struggled with as a girl and young woman coming of age still dominate, the trinity of hair, body, and complexion prevail. It is only their manifestations that have changed.

In a wonderful collection of essays called *Home,* published in 1966, Leroi Jones, now Amiri Baraka, commented about television that the best thing about it was that black people weren't on it. Nowadays, our faces are all over television. Most of the time we're being arrested, robbing, shooting, posturing on talk shows, writhing in music videos. Black women are most often seen in music videos, gyrating in sexually explicit pantomime, the close-up, more often than not, on our juggling butts, breasts, or open thighs, although you may see a yard or two of synthetic hair fly by now and then. I may have known the women on my parents' album covers only as singing heads without bodies, but at least I knew they had heads. What I know after an afternoon watching music videos is that black women's bodies can now be used to sell things too. What's in their heads is irrelevant. Sometimes I think that, overall, invisibility might have been better.

Aside from a brief period in the late 1950s and 60s when the "Afro" was in style, the natural texture of most black women's hair remains, as it has historically been, unacceptable. The apparently neverending popularity of a variety of straightening devices, from the hot comb to chemical straighteners—now euphemistically called "relaxers," as if the problem is that sister's hair is uptight and all we need to do is to get it to cool out—attests to this. The proliferation in the last decade of hair weaves and braided extensions is a manifestation of black women's desire for hair that is not only straight but long, the better to toss. To black women, the message sent by the culture of beauty remains the same, i.e., that we genetically lack a fundamental element of desirability. The difference is that now we have thousands of products marketed specifically to us, the vast majority of them produced by white companies. This has nothing to do with inclusion and everything to do with cash. Just as when I was growing up we all knew the answer to the refrain of the Clairol ads, "Is it true blondes have more fun?," today when the actress Cybill Shepherd, blonde, straight-haired, and hawking L'Oreal hair products, declares she uses them "Because I'm worth it," we all know the flip side is that those of us who don't are worth less.

Not much has changed. The infrequent times when black women are portrayed as objects of desire in popular culture, their hair is invariably long, their features usually more Caucasian than Negroid, their bodies, since most often they are models, skinny. Happy as I was to see the images of black models Naomi Sims, Pat Cleveland, Alva Chin, Iman, and Pat Johnson break onto the scene when I was a young woman, it was clear most black women did not—and could not—look like them with their narrow noses, high cheekbones, and long, silky manes. Thirty years later, the same can be said of Veronica Webb and Tyra Banks. Even the popularity of the dark-skinned, British-born Naomi Campbell, whose natural hair is often shrouded in wigs, represents merely an updated version of white beauty in blackface, but this time with a twist: the black woman as exotic, animalistic, sexualized dominatrix. Still, note Campbell's long hair and colored contact lenses, making it clear that she is not the loathed and dreaded authentic black woman.

Stephanie Berry is a brown-skinned woman in her early forties who has been acting for thirteen years, and has recently begun getting television roles. Berry looks more like Every Sister than a model. "I have never been the love interest," she says. "I am always a single mother. I am always the parent of a male black child and he is always a victim or perpetrator of violence. I usually don't have a husband, and if I do, he dies too. I am always grieving." Berry tells the story of a recent audition. "I knew I was a grieving mother. I walked in and said, 'Okay, what happened to my baby this time? What did my boy do?' I was trying to make light. They didn't find it funny. I did not get the part."

In the last thirty years there has been little real alteration of the beauty industry's marketing of whiteness as the norm, the standard to which all the rest of us should aspire. For black girls and women this journey is as psychically devastating as it is omnipresent. Even if we manage to get rid of our hips, breasts, waistlines, grow our hair, get a weave or extensions, even if we go blonde, we will never possess the fundamental ingredient for female beauty in America, and that is whiteness.

In this climate, we conveniently forget that for most black Americans light skin is the result of rape and sexual exploitation during slavery; we are only interested in the proffered rewards or favor we believe come with lighter skin color. It is a psychological given that all people feel most immediately comfortable with those who look like them. It is not coincidence that the primary image of African American women we see in popular culture, particularly television and print advertisements, are light-skinned. It's gotten to the point that I often have to see a commercial two or three times to figure out if the green-eyed, crinkly-haired woman selling cereal or soda is black. If she's dark-skinned, chances are she's selling something that's a drag to use, like toilet bowl cleanser or a laxative. What we are witnessing is the rise of the biracial as favored black woman, even though it's stretching the point to suggest any of us are preferred. At the millennium, the culture has taken their contempt and our erasure one step further. Two of the most visible and acceptable images of black women in the eyes of the dominant culture are those offered by RuPaul and, occasionally, the Chicago Bulls' Dennis Rodman, black men in drag.

Black Americans twist the fruit of our enslavement into a prized possession. As much as black people don't like to talk about or admit it, a color caste system remains a dominant aspect of our communities, particularly for women. Put a truly beautiful chocolate-colored woman side by side with an average-looking beige one and I guarantee you that most black people will declare the lighter-skinned one prettier. Look at black couples and notice how often the woman's complexion is lighter than the man's, evidence that we continue, consciously or not, to find light-skinned women, and the increased chance that they will produce lighter-skinned children, more valuable. This is our version of "marrying up." Listen even to the language we use when talking about color. Light-skinned people are described as "fair"; language as value judgment. People are often described as "dark, *but* beautiful," as if their complexion were something to overcome. Too often, we hold darker children to behavioral standards that lighter children are not required to meet, as if their complexion confers upon them a state of grace that excuses or mitigates misbehavior, instant entitlement based upon color that extends, especially for women, into adulthood. In describing newborns, what black people always tell you is about the baby's color and the texture of their hair, even when they cannot recall the infant's name. We have a plethora of myths and folk wisdom relating to hair and complexion: A bald head on a baby means the child will have "good" hair, a thick head of hair means naps will follow, an infant's adult complexion can be judged by the color of the palms of its hands or soles of its feet, a clothespin on the nose will keep it from spreading, becoming a wide, Negroid nose.

Flip through an issue of *Vogue, Elle, Mademoiselle,* or any other women's magazine (a misnomer, since they should more accurately be called men's magazines, since their focus is on how men want to configure women), and black women are largely absent. When we are present, it is as images that conform to white notions of black beauty. There is no doubt that some of these women are beautiful, but Naomi Campbell is not most of us, any more than Kate Moss is most white women. The difference is that above and beyond the destructive myths of beauty, white women have a whole white culture that confers on them, in whatever twisted ways, the myriad rewards of whiteness. She is at least viewed as a woman, in the sweepstakes, and visible.

Most women, white and black, are not comforted by the dominant myths of beauty. The difference for black women is that we do not feel simply ugly, but totally outside, irrelevant, invisible. The significant and continuing success of *Essence,* the only fashion and beauty magazine targeted toward black women, is due in large part to the visibility it gives to black women in all our diversity of color, hair, and body. Almost three decades after its debut in 1970, *Essence* remains the only magazine that consistently recognizes and embraces the true range of black beauty. In the pages of *Essence,* our beauty is not dependent on our degree of whiteness or the subtle and overt racist and sexist fantasies of male photographers and art directors of black women as exotic, animalistic, overly sexualized objects of domination, degradation, and desire. In these pages, black women's beauty is normal, not aberrant. As a black woman, I have been trying to figure out what is beautiful, and functional, and comfortable for me and my sisters for most of my life.

Over the last ten years I've been having my hair cut shorter and shorter. In the late summer of 1996, when I am forty-four, I have my hair shaved to the scalp with an electric razor. When I leave my head is covered with a faint memory of brown and silver peach fuzz, I am as close to bald as I can get without lathering up and using a straight razor. I do this because I am tired of everything about hair—having it, combing it, thinking about it, plain feeling it. So, to test my theory that for me hair has finally become obsolete, I got rid of it. I want to see how people react to me, and how I react to myself, hairless. After the first few days, when I wake up startled by my own reflection in the mirror, I come to love it. I like the way it looks, the way it feels bristly when I run my hand over it from any direction, the fact that after four decades I have achieved hair that requires no maintenance.

The response of others is profound. Most black men's eyes skip over me rapidly, distastefully, as if they do not care to see someone who looks like me. I catch pure disdain in the eyes of several. A few stare, look intrigued, and rap to me, although most of these are young enough to be my children. Black women in general—with the exception of the few who are also either bald or wearing short naturals or dreadlocks, who give me a solidarity smile or compliment me—look at me as if I am totally unattractive, insane, and vaguely threatening. It is as if in deciding to be bald I am challenging our collective obsession with hair. Maybe I am. White people, women and men, look surprised and stare at me as I go by. Many people, across race, particularly women, give me a sympathetic smile, assuming, perhaps, that I am a cancer patient undergoing chemotherapy. Whatever a specific individual's response, the most interesting thing about being bald is that I am no longer invisible. Like it or not, everyone sees me. It is a wonderful sensation. Maybe a giant step in black women gaining visibility would be if we all shaved our heads. We would be both immediately visible and connected.

Barring such drastic action, a possible first step would be in acknowledging the commonality of our experiences as black girls and women in a hostile and alien culture. Sometimes that affirmation comes from simply making eye contact. Or talking to girls about self-image. Or teaching young women how to look at popular culture critically. Or telling another woman that she looks nice. That is sisterhood.

Several days after I cut my hair I walk to the subway station. The woman rapidly climbing the steps ahead of me has dark brown skin, a slim frame. I cannot see how old she is. A teenage girl walks slightly behind her. One of the girl's hands casually touches the woman's dreadlocks as she talks. As I close the distance between us I hear the girl say, "Really, Mom, you could go to the hairdresser and they twist them up right, fix up your locks, they'd look nice. People would notice you, people would be looking from across the street."

The woman turns slightly to look back at her daughter. She is smiling. "Forget it. This ain't no hairstyle," she says as I pull alongside her. She is probably in her early thirties. I reach out my hand and we slap five, briefly clasp hands, laugh. It is a moment of unspoken understanding, communion, knowing that hair, and so much of what we thought mattered to the business of our being women, doesn't matter at all, or much, or certainly not enough for her to go to a beauty salon and have her low-maintenance dreadlocks styled. It is obsolete. That there is too much work to be done and that she with her non–salon selected locks and me with my damn near bald head, and all the other sisters struggling for loving self-definition, are bad as we wanna be. At the bottom of the steps her daughter peels off, heading downtown. We climb the last flight of steps in tandem, going in the same direction.

14

THE MYTH OF THE LATIN WOMAN
I Just Met a Girl Named María

JUDITH ORTIZ COFER

Judith Ortiz Cofer is the author of *A Love Story Beginning in Spanish: Poems; Call Me Maria; The Meaning of Consuelo; Woman in Front of the Sun: On Becoming a Writer; The Line of the Sun; Silent Dancing; Terms of Survival; Reaching for the Mainland;* and *The Latin Deli: Prose and Poetry.* Her work has appeared in *The Georgia Review, Kenyon Review, Southern Review, Glamour* and other journals. Her work has been included in numerous textbooks and anthologies.

On a bus trip to London from Oxford University, where I was earning some graduate credits one summer, a young man, obviously fresh from a pub, spotted me and as if struck by inspiration went down on his knees in the aisle. With both hands over his heart he broke into an Irish tenor's rendition of "María" from *West Side Story.* My politely amused fellow passengers gave his lovely voice the round of gentle applause it deserved. Though I was not quite as amused, I managed my version of an English smile: no show of teeth, no extreme contortions of the facial muscles—I was at this time of my life practicing reserve and cool. Oh, that British control, how I coveted it. But María had followed me to London, reminding me of a prime fact of my life: you can leave the Island, master the English language, and travel as far as you can, but if you are a Latina, especially one like me who so obviously belongs to Rita Moreno's gene pool, the Island travels with you.

This is sometimes a very good thing—it may win you that extra minute of someone's attention. But with some people, the same things can make *you* an island—not so much a tropical paradise as an Alcatraz, a place nobody wants to visit. As a Puerto Rican girl growing up in the United States and wanting like most children to "belong," I resented the stereotype that my Hispanic appearance called forth from many people I met.

Our family lived in a large urban center in New Jersey during the sixties, where life was designed as a microcosm of my parents' casas on the island. We spoke in Spanish, we ate Puerto Rican food bought at the bodega, and we practiced strict Catholicism complete with Saturday confession and Sunday mass at a church where our parents were accommodated into a one-hour Spanish mass slot, performed by a Chinese priest trained as a missionary for Latin America.

As a girl I was kept under strict surveillance, since virtue and modesty were, by cultural equation, the same as family honor. As a teenager I was instructed on how to behave as a proper señorita. But it was a conflicting message girls got, since the Puerto Rican mothers also encouraged their daughters to look and act like women and to dress in clothes our Anglo friends and their mothers found too "mature" for our age. It was, and is, cultural, yet I often felt humiliated when I appeared at an American friend's party wearing a dress more suitable to a semiformal than to a playroom birthday celebration. At Puerto Rican festivities, neither the music nor the colors we wore could be too loud. I still experience a vague sense of letdown when I'm invited to a "party" and it turns out to be a marathon conversation in hushed tones rather than a fiesta with salsa, laughter, and dancing—the kind of celebration I remember from my childhood.

I remember Career Day in our high school, when teachers told us to come dressed as if for a job interview. It quickly became obvious that to the barrio girls, "dressing up" sometimes meant wearing ornate jewelry and clothing that would be more appropriate (by mainstream standards) for the company Christmas party than as daily office attire. That morning I had agonized in front of my closet, trying to figure out what a "career girl" would wear because, essentially, except for Marlo Thomas on TV, I had no models on which to base my decision. I knew how to dress for school: at the Catholic school I attended we all wore uniforms; I knew how to dress for Sunday mass, and I knew what dresses to wear for parties at my relatives' homes. Though I do not recall the precise details of my Career Day outfit, it must have been a composite of the above choices. But I remember a comment my friend (an Italian-American) made in later years that coalesced my impressions of that day. She said that at the business school she was attending the Puerto Rican girls always stood out for wearing "everything at once." She meant, of course, too much jewelry, too many accessories. On that day at school, we were simply made the negative models by the nuns who were themselves not credible fashion experts to any of us. But it was painfully obvious to me that to the others, in their tailored skirts and silk blouses, we must have seemed "hopeless" and "vulgar." Though I now know that most adolescents feel out of step much of the time, I also know that for the Puerto Rican girls of my generation that sense was intensified. The way our teachers and classmates looked at us that day in school was just a taste of the culture clash that awaited us in the real world, where prospective employers and men on the street would often misinterpret our tight skirts and jingling bracelets as a come-on.

Mixed cultural signals have perpetuated certain stereotypes—for example, that of the Hispanic woman as the "Hot Tamale" or sexual firebrand. It is a one-dimensional view that the media have found easy to promote. In their special vocabulary, advertisers have designated "sizzling" and "smoldering" as the adjectives of choice for describing not only the foods but also the women of Latin America. From conversations in my house I recall hearing about the harassment that Puerto Rican women endured in factories where the "boss men" talked to them as if sexual innuendo was all they understood and, worse, often gave them the choice of submitting to advances or being fired.

It is custom, however, not chromosomes, that leads us to choose scarlet over pale pink. As young girls, we were influenced in our decisions about clothes and colors by the women—older sisters and mothers who had grown up on a tropical island where the natural environment was a riot of primary colors, where showing your skin was one way to keep cool as well as to look sexy. Most important of all, on the island, women perhaps felt freer to dress and move more provocatively, since, in most cases, they were protected by the traditions, mores, and laws of a Spanish/Catholic system of morality and machismo whose main rule was: *You may look at my sister, but if you touch her I will kill you.* The extended family and church structure could provide a young woman with a circle of safety in her small pueblo on the Island; if a man "wronged" a girl, everyone would close in to save her family honor.

This is what I have gleaned from my discussions as an adult with older Puerto Rican women. They have told me about dressing in their best party clothes on Saturday nights and going to the town's plaza to promenade with their girlfriends in front of the boys they liked. The males were thus given an opportunity to admire the women and to express their admiration in the form of piropos: erotically charged street poems they composed on the spot. I have been subjected to a few *piropos* while visiting the Island, and they can be outrageous, although custom dictates that they must never cross into obscenity. This ritual, as I understand it, also entails a show of studied indifference on the woman's part; if she is "decent," she must not acknowledge the man's impassioned words. So I do understand how things can be lost in translation. When a Puerto Rican girl dressed in her idea of what is attractive meets a man from the mainstream culture who has been trained to react to certain types of clothing as a sexual signal, a clash is likely to take place. The line I first heard based on this aspect of the myth happened when the boy who took me to my first formal dance leaned over to plant a sloppy overeager kiss painfully on my mouth, and when I didn't respond with sufficient passion said in a resentful tone: "I thought you Latin girls were supposed to mature early"—my first instance of being thought of as a fruit or vegetable—I was supposed to *ripen,* not just grow into womanhood like other girls.

It is surprising to some of my professional friends that some people, including those who should know better, still put others "in their place." Though rarer, these incidents are still commonplace in my life. It happened to me most recently during a stay at a very classy metropolitan hotel favored by young professional couples for their weddings. Late one evening after the theater, as I walked toward my room with my new colleague (a woman with whom I was coordinating an arts program), a middle-aged man in a tuxedo, a young girl in satin and lace on his arm, stepped directly into our path. With his champagne glass extended toward me, he exclaimed, "Evita!"

Our way blocked, my companion and I listened as the man half-recited, half-bellowed "Don't Cry for Me, Argentina." When he finished, the young girl said: "How about a round of applause for my daddy?" We complied, hoping this would bring the silly spectacle to a close. I was becoming aware that our little group was attracting the attention of the other guests. "Daddy" must have perceived this too, and he once more barred the way as we tried to walk past him. He began to shout-sing a ditty to the tune of "La Bamba"—except the lyrics were about a girl named María whose exploits all rhymed with her name and gonorrhea. The girl kept saying "Oh, Daddy" and looking at me with pleading eyes. She wanted me to laugh along with the others. My companion and I stood silently waiting for the man to end his offensive song. When he finished, I looked not at him but at his daughter. I advised her calmly never to ask her father what he had done in the army. Then I walked between them and to my room. My friend complimented me on my cool handling of the situation. I confessed to her that I really had wanted to push the jerk into the swimming pool. I knew that this same man—probably a corporate executive, well educated, even worldly by most standards—would not have been likely to regale a white woman with a dirty song in public. He would perhaps have checked his impulse by assuming that she could be somebody's wife or mother, or at least *somebody* who might take offense. But to him, I was just an Evita or a María: merely a character in his cartoon-populated universe.

Because of my education and my proficiency with the English language, I have acquired many mechanisms for dealing with the anger I experience. This was not true for my parents, nor is it true for the many Latin women working at menial jobs who must put up with stereotypes about our ethnic group such as: "They make good domestics." This is another facet of the myth of the Latin women in the United States. Its origin is simple to deduce. Work as domestics, waitressing, and factory jobs are all that's available to women with little English and few skills. The myth of the Hispanic menial has been sustained by the same media phenomenon that made "Mammy" from *Gone with the Wind* America's idea of the black woman for generations; María, the housemaid or counter girl, is now indelibly etched into the national psyche. The big and the little screens have presented us with the picture of the funny Hispanic maid, mispronouncing words and cooking up a spicy storm in a shiny California kitchen.

This media-engendered image of the Latina in the United States has been documented by feminist Hispanic scholars, who claim that such portrayals are partially responsible for the denial of opportunities for upward mobility among Latinas in the professions. I have a Chicana friend working on a Ph.D. in philosophy at a major university. She says her doctor still shakes his head in puzzled amazement at all the "big words" she uses. Since I do not wear my diplomas around my neck for all to see, I too have on occasion been sent to that "kitchen," where some think I obviously belong.

One such incident that has stayed with me, though I recognize it as a minor offense, happened on the day of my first public poetry reading. It took place in Miami in a boat-restaurant where we were having lunch before the event. I was nervous and excited as I walked in with my notebook in hand. An older woman motioned me to her table. Thinking (foolish me) that she wanted me to autograph a copy of my brand new slender volume of verse, I went over. She ordered a cup of coffee from me, assuming that I was the waitress. Easy enough to mistake my poems for menus, I suppose. I know that it wasn't an intentional act of cruelty, yet with all the good things that happened that day, I remember that scene most clearly, because it reminded me of what I had to overcome before anyone would take me seriously. In retrospect I understand that my anger gave my reading fire, that I have almost always taken doubts in my abilities as a challenge—and that the result is, most times, a feeling of satisfaction at having won a convert when I see the cold, appraising eyes warm to my words, the body language change, the smile that indicates that I have opened some avenue for communication. That day I read to that woman and her lowered eyes told me that she was embarrassed at her little faux pas, and when I willed her to look up to me, it was my victory, and she graciously allowed me to punish her with my full attention. We shook hands at the end of the reading, and I never saw her again. She has probably forgotten the whole thing but maybe not.

Yet I am one of the lucky ones. My parents made it possible for me to acquire a stronger footing in the mainstream culture by giving me the chance at an education. And books and art have saved me from the harsher forms of ethnic and racial prejudice that many of my Hispanic *compañeras* have had to endure. I travel a lot around the United States, reading from my books of poetry and my novel, and the reception I most often receive is one of positive interest by people who want to know more about my culture. There are, however, thousands of Latinas without the privilege of an education or the entrée into society that I have. For them life is a struggle against the misconceptions perpetuated by the myth of the Latina as whore, domestic, or criminal. We cannot change this by legislating the way people look at us. The transformation, as I see it, has to occur at a much more individual level. My personal goal in my public life is to try to replace the old pervasive stereotypes and myths about Latinas with a much more interesting set of realities. Every time I give a reading, I hope the stories I tell, the dreams and fears I examine in my work, can achieve some universal truth which will get my audience past the particulars of my skin color, my accent, or my clothes.

I once wrote a poem in which I called us Latinas "God's brown daughters." This poem is really a prayer of sorts, offered upward, but also, through the human-to-human channel of art, outward. It is a prayer for communication, and for respect. In it, Latin women pray "in Spanish to an Anglo God/with a Jewish heritage," and they are "fervently hoping/that if not omnipotent,/at least He be bilingual."

15

HE DEFIES YOU STILL
The Memoirs of a Sissy

TOMMI AVICOLLI

Tommi Avicolli has adopted his mother's maiden name and is now using the name Tommi Avicolli Mecca. He is a working-class, Southern Italian American, queer writer, activist, and performer living in San Francisco. He has recently written and performed *Il Disgraziato* ("The Shameful One"), a play about coming out gay.

> You're just a faggot
> No history faces you this morning
> A faggot's dreams are scarlet
> Bad blood bled from words that scarred[1]

Scene One

A homeroom in a Catholic high school in South Philadelphia. The boy sits quietly in the first aisle, third desk, reading a book. He does not look up, not even for a moment. He is hoping no one will remember he is sitting there. He wishes he were invisible. The teacher is not yet in the classroom so the other boys are talking and laughing loudly.

Suddenly, a voice from beside him:

"Hey, you're a faggot, ain't you?"

The boy does not answer. He goes on reading his book, or rather pretending he is reading his book. It is impossible to actually read the book now.

"Hey, I'm talking to you!"

The boy still does not look up. He is so scared his heart is thumping madly; it feels like it is leaping out of his chest and into his throat. But he can't look up.

"Faggot, I'm talking to you!"

To look up is to meet the eyes of the tormentor.

Suddenly, a sharpened pencil point is thrust into the boy's arm. He jolts, shaking off the pencil, aware that there is blood seeping from the wound.

"What did you do that for?" he asks timidly.

"Cause I hate faggots," the other boy says, laughing. Some other boys begin to laugh, too. A symphony of laughter. The boy feels as if he's going to cry. But he must not cry. Must not cry. So he holds back the tears and tries to read the book again. He must read the book. Read the book.

When the teacher arrives a few minutes later, the class quiets down. The boy does not tell the teacher what has happened. He spits on the wound to clean it, dabbing it with a tissue until the bleeding stops. For weeks he fears some dreadful infection from the lead in the pencil point.

Scene Two

The boy is walking home from school. A group of boys (two, maybe three, he is not certain) grab him from behind, drag him into an alley and beat him up. When he gets home, he races up to his room, refusing dinner ("I don't feel well," he tells his mother through the locked door) and spends the night alone in the dark wishing he would die. . . .

These are not fictitious accounts—I *was* that boy. Having been branded a sissy by neighborhood children because I preferred jump rope to baseball and dolls to playing soldiers, I was often taunted with "hey sissy" or "hey faggot" or "yoo hoo honey" (in a mocking voice) when I left the house.

To avoid harassment, I spent many summers alone in my room. I went out on rainy days when the street was empty.

I came to like being alone. I didn't need anyone, I told myself over and over again. I was an island. Contact with others meant pain. Alone, I was protected. I began writing poems, then short stories. There was no reason to go outside anymore. I had a world of my own.

> In the schoolyard today
> they'll single you out
> Their laughter will leave your ears ringing
> like the church bells
> which once awed you. . . .[2]

School was one of the more painful experiences of my youth. The neighborhood bullies could be avoided. The taunts of the children living in those endless repetitive row houses could be evaded by staying in my room. But school was something I had to face day after day for some two hundred mornings a year.

I had few friends in school. I was a pariah. Some kids would talk to me, but few wanted to be known as my close friend. Afraid of labels. If I was a sissy, then he had to be a sissy, too. I was condemned to loneliness.

Fortunately, a new boy moved into our neighborhood and befriended me; he wasn't afraid of the labels. He protected me when the other guys threatened to beat me up. He walked me home from school; he broke through the terrible loneliness. We were in third or fourth grade at the time.

We spent a summer or two together. Then his parents sent him to camp and I was once again confined to my room.

Scene Three

High school lunchroom. The boy sits at a table near the back of the room. Without warning, his lunch bag is grabbed and tossed to another table. Someone opens it and confiscates a package of Tastykakes; another boy takes the sandwich. The empty bag is tossed back to the boy who stares at it, dumbfounded. He should be used to this; it has happened before.

Someone screams, "faggot," laughing. There is always laughter. It does not annoy him anymore.

There is no teacher nearby. There is never a teacher around. And what would he say if there were? Could he report the crime? He would be jumped after school if he did. Besides, it would be his word against theirs. Teachers never noticed anything. They never heard the taunts. Never heard the word, "faggot." They were the great deaf mutes, pillars of indifference; a sissy's pain was not relevant to history and geography and God made me to love honor and obey him, amen.

Scene Four

High school Religion class. Someone has a copy of *Playboy*. Father N. is not in the room yet; he's late, as usual. Someone taps the boy roughly on the shoulder. He turns. A finger points to the centerfold model, pink fleshy body, thin and sleek. Almost painted. Not real. The other asks, mocking voice, "Hey, does she turn you on? Look at those tits!"

The boy smiles, nodding meekly; turns away.

The other jabs him harder on the shoulder, "Hey, whatsamatter, don't you like girls?"

Laughter. Thousands of mouths; unbearable din of laughter. In the Arena: thumbs down. Don't spare the queer.

"Wanna suck my dick? Huh? That turn you on, faggot!"

The laughter seems to go on forever . . .

> Behind you, the sound of their laughter
> echoes a million times
> in a soundless place
> They watch you walk/sit/stand/breathe. . . .[3]

What did being a sissy really mean? It was a way of walking (from the hips rather than the shoulders); it was a way of talking (often with a lisp or in a high-pitched voice); it was a way of relating to others (gently, not wanting to fight, or hurt anyone's feelings). It was being intelligent ("an egghead" they called it sometimes); getting good grades. It means not being interested in sports, not playing football in the street after school; not discussing teams and scores and playoffs. And it involved not showing fervent interest in girls, not talking about scoring with tits or *Playboy* centerfolds. Not concealing naked women in your history book; or porno books in your locker.

On the other hand, anyone could be a "faggot." It was a catch-all. If you did something that didn't conform to what was the acceptable behavior of the group, then you risked being called a faggot. If you didn't get along with the "in" crowd, you were a faggot. It was the most commonly used put-down. It kept guys in line. They became angry when somebody called them a faggot. More fights started over someone calling someone else a faggot than anything else. The word had power. It toppled the male ego, shattered his delicate facade, violated the image he projected. He was tough. Without feeling. Faggot cut through all this. It made him vulnerable. Feminine. And feminine was the worst thing he could possibly be. Girls were fine for fucking, but no boy in his right mind wanted to be like them. A boy was the opposite of a girl. He was not feminine. He was not feeling. He was not weak.

Just look at the gym teacher who growled like a dog; or the priest with the black belt who threw kids against the wall in rage when they didn't know their Latin. They were men, they got respect.

But not the physics teacher who preached pacifism during lectures on the nature of atoms. Everybody knew what he was—and why he believed in the anti-war movement.

My parents only knew that the neighborhood kids called me names. They begged me to act more like the other boys. My brothers were ashamed of me. They never said it, but I knew. Just as I knew that my parents were embarrassed by my behavior.

At times, they tried to get me to act differently. Once my father lectured me on how to walk right. I'm still not clear on what that means. Not from the hips, I guess, don't "swish" like faggots do.

A nun in elementary school told my mother at Open House that there was "something wrong with me." I had draped my sweater over my shoulders like a girl, she said. I was a smart kid, but I should know better than to wear my sweater like a girl!

My mother stood there, mute. I wanted her to say something, to chastise the nun; to defend me. But how could she? This was a nun talking—representative of Jesus, protector of all that was good and decent.

An uncle once told me I should start "acting like a boy" instead of like a girl. Everybody seemed ashamed of me. And I guess I was ashamed of myself, too. It was hard not to be.

Scene Five

Priest: Do you like girls, Mark?
           Mark: Uh-huh.
Priest: I mean *really* like them?
           Mark: Yeah—they're okay.
Priest: There's a role they play in your salvation. Do you understand it, Mark?
           Mark: Yeah.
Priest: You've got to like girls. Even if you should decide to enter the seminary, it's important to keep in mind God's plan for a man and a woman. . . .[4]

Catholicism of course condemned homosexuality. Effeminacy was toler-ated as long as the effeminate person did not admit to being gay. Thus, priests could be effeminate because they weren't gay.

As a sissy, I could count on no support from the church. A male's sole purpose in life was to father children—souls for the church to save. The only hope a homosexual had of attaining salvation was by remaining totally celi-bate. Don't even think of touching another boy. To think of a sin was a sin. And to sin was to put a mark upon the soul. Sin—if it was a serious offense against God—led to hell. There was no way around it. If you sinned, you were doomed.

Realizing I was gay was not an easy task. Although I knew I was at-tracted to boys by the time I was about eleven, I didn't connect this attrac-tion to homosexuality. I was not queer. Not I. I was merely appreciating a boy's good looks, his fine features, his proportions. It didn't seem to matter that I didn't appreciate a girl's looks in the same way. There was no twitch-ing in my thighs when I gazed upon a beautiful girl. But I wasn't queer.

I resisted that label—queer—for the longest time. Even when everything pointed to it, I refused to see it. I was certainly not queer. Not I.

We sat through endless English classes, and history courses about the wars between men who were not allowed to love each other. No gay history was ever taught. No history faces you this morning. You're just a faggot. Ho-mosexuals had never contributed to the human race. God destroyed the queers in Sodom and Gomorrah.

We learned about Michelangelo, Oscar Wilde, Gertrude Stein—but never that they were queer. They were not queer. Walt Whitman, the "father of Amer-ican poetry," was not queer. No one was queer. I was alone, totally unique. One of a kind. Were there others like me somewhere? Another planet, perhaps?

In school, they never talked of the queers. They did not exist. The only hint we got of this other species was in religion class. And even then it was clouded in mystery—never spelled out. It was sin. Like masturbation. Like looking at *Playboy* and getting a hard-on. A sin.

Once a progressive priest in senior year religion class actually mentioned homosexuals—he said the word—but was into Erich Fromm, into homosexuals as pathetic and sick. Fixated at some early stage; penis, anal, whatever. Only heterosexuals passed on to the nirvana of sexual development.

No other images from the halls of the Catholic high school except those the other boys knew: swishy faggot sucking cock in an alley somewhere, grabbing asses in the bathroom. Never mentioning how much straight boys craved blow jobs, it was part of the secret.

It was all a secret. You were not supposed to talk about the queers. Whisper maybe. Laugh about them, yes. But don't be open, honest; don't try to understand. Don't cite their accomplishments. No history faces you this morning. You're just a faggot   faggot   no history   just a faggot

Epilogue

The boy marching down the Parkway. Hundreds of queers. Signs proclaiming gay pride. Speakers. Tables with literature from gay groups. A miracle, he is thinking. Tears are coming loose now. Someone hugs him.

> You could not control
> the sissy in me
> nor could you exorcise him
> nor electrocute him
> You declared him illegal illegitimate
> insane and immature
> But he defies you still.[5]

NOTES

1. From the poem "Faggot" by Tommi Avicolli, published in *GPU News,* Sept. 1979.
2. Ibid.
3. Ibid.
4. From the play *Judgment of the Roaches* by Tommi Avicolli, produced in Philadelphia at the Gay Community Center, the Painted Bride Arts Center and the University of Pennsylvania; aired over WXPN-FM, in four parts; and presented at the Lesbian/Gay Conference in Norfolk, VA, July, 1980.
5. From the poem "Sissy Poem," published in *Magic Doesn't Live Here Anymore* (Philadelphia: Spruce Street Press, 1976).

16

GROWING UP HIDDEN

LINNEA DUE

Linnea Due is a writer and managing editor of *Express,* an alternative weekly in Berkeley, California, where she lives. She is the author of three novels, *High and Outside, Give Me Time,* and *Life Savings,* and she was the coeditor of the anthology *Dagger: On Butch Women.* In 1992, her series on gay and lesbian teenagers won an award as one of the top six underreported stories of the year from Media Alliance/Project Censored.

G rowing up hidden—coming of age not only invisible but embattled in that invisibility—is hard to describe to someone who has not experienced it. A phrase like "a wolf in sheep's clothing" takes on special meaning to a gay kid—at least it did for me. Was I hiding because I was bad? Why didn't I feel bad if I was so bad I had to hide? What I should have asked—why do I have to hide?—was too obvious to require an answer, and yet it turned out to be the real question.

I don't remember ever not knowing who I was. For a while I revealed myself, saying I wanted to be strong ("Girls don't need to be strong"), that when I got married, my wife and I would have a wonderful house ("You won't have a wife, you'll have a husband"). By the time I went to summer camp, at age seven, I was already trying to tone myself down: people told me I was too raucous, too wild, and I had to drop that damn fool idea about getting married to a woman. I decided to shut up—not that I'd changed my mind, but it was easier than trying to explain myself to people who'd never met a girl like me.

In the closing days of camp, we were supposed to say who we were going steady with. No one was actually going with anybody—we were all too young—but I was still thrown into a quandary. If I were going to pledge my troth, it certainly would be to Stacy, with whom I'd been sneaking off all summer to plan our life together. Ken snagged me after dinner one night, just before campfire. "Look," he said bluntly, "you want to go with Stacy and I want to go with Roger. So what we'll do is tell everybody you're going with me and she's going with Rog."

God, what a mind! Such duplicity would never have occurred to me. It made me feel a little funny—wasn't it like lying?—but it wasn't a long stretch from the silence I'd been cultivating for a time anyway. As I became older, I edited myself more and more, especially after I realized that it wasn't that people hadn't known about girls like me, but that those girls were so horrible no one wanted to ever talk about them.

By then, I knew what I was called. I'd been risking my life balancing on my father's office chair, snatching books off the uppermost shelf as I rolled by. Richard von Krafft-Ebing's *Psychopathia Sexualis*. Havelock Ellis's *Sexual Inversion*. Freud. Erikson. I'd also been haunting the paperback rack at my neighborhood grocery, ripping off the romances of the '50s—*Beebo Brinker*, Ann Bannon, *Women on the Edge of Twilight*. Krafft-Ebing made me popular on the playground—I was the Susie Bright of Hilltop Elementary School—but my knowledge was a mixed blessing. I was glad to know people like me existed, but I also knew from my dad that a psychopath was the worst thing you could be. Finding my sexuality among those who fucked chickens or corpses made me feel—well, a little queer.

Still, I figured I was hiding successfully until the day my Girl Scout troop leader threw me out for being "too masculine." My world fell apart. I had believed censoring my thoughts was enough; I hadn't realized my manner and my body—the very way I moved—were betraying me daily. Something drastic had to be done.

Something was. I dropped out of the athletics I loved, wore nylons and makeup, carried my books in front of me, shortened my stride. I developed an imperious persona to go along with my new look and pretended an interest in boys (a breach of ethics I tried to mitigate by not letting them come too close). It was like learning a foreign language—and not coincidentally, I began drinking to blackouts.

From seventh through twelfth grades, I functioned as another person, someone I became in the morning and shed in the evening when, safely in my room, I could pore over my romances and daydream about kissing my own raven-haired beauty. It never occurred to me to look for her; my dreams ranked alongside my classmates' fantasies of becoming famous actresses or politicians. That I was labeling illusory the most important stuff of life—my identity and my relationships—didn't seem odd. Staying undercover was job number one.

My life as a spy reached a pinnacle of the absurd during my first year at Sarah Lawrence. I received a visit from several of my elementary school friends; they had traveled from Smith, from Brandeis, from Boston University, certain that I, the amateur sexologist, could set their minds at ease. They were worried, they explained haltingly, about those sailor/whore games we had played at slumber parties. Wasn't it weird for thirteen-year-old girls to practice kissing each other? Was I concerned that we had lesbian tendencies? Not at all, I replied heartily, and proceeded to regale them with a lot of assurances they wanted to hear. They went back to Massachusetts much relieved, and I lay on my bed and stared at the ceiling, wondering who was the bigger fool. Two years later, I didn't lie when the college president asked if I was a lesbian, though it meant leaving the school I loved; I would never lie again—not about that anyway.

PART III

Embodiment

Our relationships to our bodies and our decisions about how we present ourselves to the world are heavily influenced by the historical and cultural contexts in which we live. In U.S. society, these contexts are determined to a large extent by the media. A brief look at the history of clothing and fashion or at the history of women in sports, for example, shows changes in the ideal female body image over time. Laced corsets, once very popular, are now used by few women. Sports such as track and field, once considered unacceptable for women, are now acceptable for women athletes, although female athletes are much more easily accepted if they appear to be feminine. Current media images of young women support sexualized, thin bodies with bare midriffs.[1] Many of the dominant messages about bodies are tied to images of gender, race, and class, mandating different expectations for various women and men.[2] For example, in a study of Asian American women and cosmetic surgery, Eugenia Kaw reports an increase in the number of people from racial and ethnic minority groups in the U.S. electing racially specific plastic surgery. Whereas white women tend to choose liposuction, breast augmentation, or reduction of wrinkles, Asian American women, for example, tend to choose eyelid surgery to make their eyes wider, and nasal surgery to make their noses more prominent. Kaw concludes that Asian American women do this in order to escape racial prejudice by looking more Anglo. She further concludes that Asian American women are heavily influenced by the "medicalization" of racial features; rather than seen as normal, their eyelids and noses are seen as something to be fixed by medical intervention.[3]

Physical appearance is often an obsession for people in U.S. society, especially for people privileged enough to have the time and money to attend to their bodies. The pressure to look "right" can be internalized as profound self-disapproval. It drives many people to spend long hours exercising and preening and many years dieting. Even for people who would be considered attractive within their own communities, the dominant culture's obsession with youth, muscles, whiteness, blondness, and thinness can undermine positive attitudes for many.[4] With rare exceptions, most of us will look seriously "wrong" at some point if we have the privilege of growing old. People whose bodies don't match dominant images of what is defined as normal suffer immense discrimination, especially on the basis of skin color, weight, looks, age, or disability.[5] In one study, low-income middle school African American girls suffered more from both depression and poor body image than did their male counterparts, although many of the boys, too, were concerned about their weight.[6]

Boys and men seem to be increasingly concerned with their looks. Muscles are a big issue, leading to obsessive weight lifting and/or steroid use.[7] Gay men, adopting the pressure to please men that is pervasive in mainstream heterosexual culture, also suffer from body image dissatisfaction, topping the dissatisfaction list in some studies (followed by heterosexual women). Heterosexual men and lesbians seem to feel the most accepting of their bodies when these various groups are compared.[8] The year 2003 saw wider use of a trendy new word—metrosexual—used to describe heterosexual urban men who attend carefully to their bodies and homes, stretching the gender boundaries that define hegemonic masculinity to include more typically-feminine aspects.

Plastic surgery grows in popularity in spite of its high cost.[9] A case in England illustrates the pressure on teenage girls to have "perfect" bodies. Intense debate ensued when parents gave their teenage daughter, Jenna Franklin, a gift of silicone breast implants for her sixteenth birthday. The parents run a plastic surgery clinic and were supportive of their daughter's decision to have implants (the news reports said that she had been wanting implants since age twelve). Critics worried that surgery on someone that young could cause psychological damage and be done for the wrong reasons, and even the surgeon that Franklin's parents chose refused to do the surgery until she was at least eighteen years old; he was apparently concerned about both psychological issues and doing surgery on immature breasts, so Franklin was made to wait.[10] The demand for inexpensive plastic surgery has apparently stimulated the growth of underground beauty treatments performed by unlicensed practitioners who typically inject liquid silicone into lips, faces, or breasts, frequently leaving a wide range of health problems in their wake.[11]

The pressure to maintain virginity until marriage provoked the development of hymen reconstruction surgery long ago, but the issue seems to be getting more attention lately. Women from cultures where virginity at marriage is particularly important can protect their "honor" by having the surgery done. A surgeon in Toronto reports that primarily Muslim women inquire about or have the surgery. In Brooklyn, NY, plastic surgery clinics advertise "reconstrucción del hymen" for Latina women.[12]

The pressure toward perfect male and female bodies is perhaps most powerfully expressed in the treatment of infants born neither male nor female but intersex. In cases where medical teams cannot tell whether the infant is a boy or a girl, which is estimated to occur in about 1 in 1,500 or 1 in 2,000 births, the child is assigned to one sex or the other based on visual appearance of the genitals.[13] Then, typically, a series of surgical and hormonal treatments is done in order to bring the child's body into conformity with the assigned gender. The lack of tolerance for a body that does not conform with gender appears to be most profound in medical settings. There is resistance to this pressure, however, on various fronts. The Intersex Society of North America (ISNA) (www.isna.org) has begun to organize and educate around this issue, arguing against surgical and hormonal intervention until the child is old enough to decide for her/himself. Occasionally parents have also resisted the pressure for sex reassignment, creating serious frustration for medical professionals at times.[14] And in some unusual cases, children are allowed to choose for themselves whether to change their bodies physically, though all seem to be assigned a gender at birth.[15] Some professionals in the United States and Canada are supporting the recommendation of ISNA on the heels of the outrage expressed by many intersex people whose lives have been fraught with identity confusion, emotional pain, and lack of sexual sensation as a result of medical treatment and as a result of the lies that frequently surround these cases.[16]

The need to convert bodies might not be so intense if third-gender options existed in mainstream U.S. society. Males who live as females in many societies (called berdaches, hijiras, or xaniths, and common in many Native American tribes) have a specific role that allows for a break from what is expected.[17] Other societies have female men—women who behave as men in terms of work, marriage, parenting, and possession of the economic resources to purchase a wife.[18] Societies that have these options might be better equipped to deal with intersex people since there are already more than two genders.

Sports-oriented culture intensifies the pressure for a perfect body. Sports themselves are also a problem for many athletes, because sports are highly competitive, few participants are able to make a career of sports (see Messner, Part II), sports injuries occur frequently, sexism pervades sports, and sports support heterosexism and homophobia. Homophobia is ever-present; male athletes are pressured to nurture their homophobia as they express their athletic masculinity in homoerotic contexts, and female athletes are pressured to be feminine, lest they look too much like men and challenge the division of the world into male and female.[19] The intersex issue plays a role here too. Genetic testing is sometimes required of athletes to assure that there are not any men competing as women or vice versa. Occasionally (perhaps as often as 1 in 500 tested athletes), someone who has lived her life, say, as a woman is informed that she has a Y chromosome and is actually, in a genetic sense, male and therefore disqualified. In one such case, a woman with a Y chromosome was disqualified from competition because she was genetically male but later gave birth to a child.[20]

Objectification pervades our understanding of gender. People are frequently seen not for who they are but for what they represent to both themselves and observers. People may become beauty objects, sex objects, racial objects, athletic objects, unattractive objects, disabled objects, or simply objects to abuse. The media feed this process by providing distorted messages about how people should look, what makes people happy, and how people spend their time: middle-class, white housewives excited over laundry detergent or toothpaste, white men buying cars and selling life insurance, Black men with muscular bodies playing sports, and so on. Few women believe they have acceptable bodies, and the media nurture this insecurity and self-hatred, pounding away at the expectation of perfection, leading people to see themselves as imperfect objects. Even men are now seeking plastic surgery in increasing numbers to mask the effects of aging or to lengthen or enlarge their penises.[21]

According to a recent television documentary, of 40,000 female applicants to a modeling agency, only four were selected as acceptable.[22] Despite the impossibility of ever looking like a model for the vast majority of women, the media message is so powerful that many women wish they did. Many will have face-lifts, get breast implants, or go on extreme diets in quest of the perfect body despite the health risks involved. According to a study by sociologists Diana Dull and Candace West, plastic surgery is a heavily gendered process. The plastic surgeons they interviewed readily supported plastic surgery to enhance a woman's appearance, but they did not support it to enhance a man's appearance.[23]

A few years ago, the National Institutes of Health recently lowered the point at which a person is defined as overweight, effectively affixing a stigmatizing label to an additional twenty-nine million people who were not defined as overweight before the change in definition. Many of these newly "overweight" people can expect to suffer weight discrimination, including lectures about weight from their doctors and increased difficulty getting health insurance.[24] Author and nurse Pat Lyons, director of Free at Last: The Women's Body Sovereignty Project, asks people to help diminish fat discrimination by doing such things as not commenting about weight, accepting bodies as they are, not telling "fat jokes," and supporting healthy lifestyles for people of all sizes.[25] Author Natalie Kusz, in a powerful personal narrative about what it is like to be fat, lists an array of insults that she has experienced, such as unsolicited advice about dieting, being told to walk when she is driving, being called "fatass," etc. She discusses the courage it takes simply to leave her home and face the public. On a positive note, Kusz changes her approach to her body. Rather than spending about 70% of her energy on food (calorie counts, etc.) she decided to give up her lifelong dieting and food obsession, eat when she wanted to, let her body become the size it needed to be, and free her energies for more productive pursuits such as parenting, writing, and caring for an ailing father.[26]

The authors in this section address various aspects of embodiment, including women's pursuit of the perfect body (Elayne Saltzberg and Joan Chrisler); eating troubles among women of color and white women (Becky Thompson); approaches to appearance and varieties of gender expression in Native American culture (Leslie Marmon Silko); the social cost of living in a Black male body (Brent Staples); the struggle for manhood in the face of disability (Leonard Kriegel); the experience of living with an aging body (Barbara MacDonald); embracing a round woman's body in a Latino context (Christy Haubegger); and dealing with the impact of genital surgery among intersexuals (Martha Coventry).

The authors in this chapter argue either directly or indirectly for a world in which people are seen for who they are as people, rather than as physical objects to be liked, ridiculed, abused, or ignored. I am reminded here of a day a few years ago when a person walked past my office. I couldn't tell whether the person was male or female, noticed only that the person was medium height, white, and solidly built with relatively short brown hair. I found myself thinking, "That person is in an interesting package." I have since then pondered the package image. In most circumstances, when given a package, our impulse is to open it to find out what's inside. In the case of bodies, however, the wrapping frequently has such an impact that we have no interest in opening the package—that is, finding out more about the person within it—simply because the person's packaging does not appeal to us for whatever reason. And, as a result of external responses, the person inside risks incorporating those responses into their personalities, frequently as internalized oppression. Many of the authors in this section would like to see a world in which the person inside was more important than the packaging and in which the packaging would not become a cause for hatred, physical harm, or blocked access to opportunities.

As you read these essays, you might want to reflect upon your own responses to various forms of embodiment. What are your gut reactions to various kinds of people? What helps you get past various physical presentations to find out who is home inside a body that you might find off-putting in some way? How do you feel about your own body? Can you name a few things that you like about it? Or that you don't like about it? Have you known any people who were sexually or physically abused? How did that affect their sense of their bodies? If you had been born into a different kind of body package, how might your life be different? Consider ability/disability, skin color, appearance, hair, size, height, etc.

NOTES

1. Frontline (Public Broadcasting System), *The Merchants of Cool*, video aired January 31, 2002.
2. On the history of fashion and clothing, see Saltzberg and Chrisler, this chapter. For a discussion of clothing and identity, see Mary Ellen Roach-Higgins, Joanne B. Eichner, and Kim K. P. Johnson, eds., *Dress and Identity* (New York: Fairchild Publishers, 1995). For a history of women in sports, see Susan K. Cahn, *Coming on Strong: Gender and Sexuality in Twentieth-Century Women's Sport* (Cambridge, MA: Harvard University Press, 1994). For perspectives on the influence of the media on gender, see Gail Dines and Jean M. Humez, eds., *Gender, Race and Class in Media: A Text-Reader* (Thousand Oaks, CA: Sage, 1995).
3. Eugenia Kaw, "Medicalization of Racial Features: Asian-American Women and Cosmetic Surgery" in Rose Weitz, ed., *The Politics of Women's Bodies: Sexuality, Appearance, and Behavior* (New York: Oxford, 1998), pp. 167–183.
4. For an interesting discussion of the use of blue contact lenses by people with brown eyes, including women of color, see Susan Bordo, "'Material Girl'—The Effacements of Postmodern Culture," in *Unbearable Weight: Feminism, Western Culture and the Body* (Berkeley, CA: University of California Press, 1993), pp. 245–249.
5. For discussions of the impact of looks, obesity, and various kinds of disabilities on employment and other aspects of life, see Susan E. Browne, Debra Connors, and Nanci Stern, eds., *With the Power of Each Breath* (Pittsburgh: Cleis Press, 1985);

Lisa Schoenfielder and Barbara Wieser, eds., *Shadow on a Tightrope* (Iowa City: Aunt Lute, 1983); Irving Kenneth Zola, *Missing Pieces: A Chronicle of Living with a Disability* (Philadelphia: Temple University Press, 1982); Gwyneth Matthews, *Voices from the Shadows: Women with Disabilities Speak Out* (Toronto: Women's Educational Press, 1983); Lucy Grealy, *Autobiography of a Face* (Boston: Houghton Mifflin, 1994); Kennie Fries, ed., *Staring Back: The Disability Experience from the Inside Out* (New York: Plume, 1997).

6. Kathryn Grant, Aoife Lyons, Dana Landis, Mi Hyon Cho, Maddalena Scudiero, Linda Reynolds, Julie Murphy, and Heather Bryant, "Gender, Body Image, and Depressive Symptoms among Low-Income African American Adolescents," *Journal of Social Issues* 55, no. 2 (1999), pp. 299–316.

7. Barbara Meltz, "Boys and Body Image," *The Boston Globe* (June 1, 2000), pp. F1ff; Alan M. Klein, "Life's Too Short to Die Small: Steroid Use Among Male Bodybuilders," in Donald F. Sabo and David Frederick Gordon, eds., *Men's Health and Illness: Gender, Power and the Body* (Thousand Oaks, CA: Sage, 1995), pp. 105–120.

8. Dawn Atkins, "Introduction: Looking Queer," in Dawn Atkins, ed., *Looking Queer: Body Image and Identity in Lesbian, Bisexual, Gay, and Transgender Communities* (New York: Haworth Press, 1998), pp. xxix–li.

9. For a discussion of cultural aspects of cosmetic surgery, see Kathy Davis, *Dubious Equalities and Embodied Differences: Cultural Studies on Cosmetic Surgery.* (Lanham, MD: Rowman and Littlefield, 2003).

10. Chris Holme, "'You've Got to Have Breasts to Be Successful. Every Other Person You See on TV Has Had Implants': Teenager Justifies Decision in Face of Outrage from Experts." *The Herald* (Glasgow) (January 5, 2001), p. 3.

11. Aime Parnes, "In Florida, Risky Shots at Being Beautiful," *The Boston Globe* (May 1, 2001), p. A1 ff.

12. Sylvana Paternostro, "Northern Ladies," in *In the Land of God and Man: A Latin Woman's Journey* (New York: Penguin Putnam, Inc., 1999), pp. 270–288; Susan Oh, "Just Like a Virgin? Surgeons Restore Hymens for Cultural Reasons and Tighten Vagina Walls for Better Sex," *Maclean's* 113, no. 24 (June 12, 2000), p. 44ff.

13. Phyllis Burke, *Gender Shock: Exploding the Myths of Male and Female* (New York: Anchor, 1966); Cheryl Chase, "Hermaphrodites with Attitude: Mapping the Emergence of Intersex Political Activism," *GLQ* 4, no. 2 (1998); Alice Domurat Dreger, "'Ambiguous' Sex—Or Ambivalent Medicine? Ethical Issues in the Treatment of Intersexuality," *The Hastings Center Report* 28, no. 3 (May–June 1998), pp. 24–35. The estimate of number of cases is from Dreger.

14. Katherine Rossiter and Shonna Diehl, "Gender Reassignment in Children: Ethical Conflicts in Surrogate Decision-Making," *Pediatric Nursing* 24 no. 1 (January–February 1998), pp. 59–62.

15. Froukje M. E. Slijper, Stenvert L. S. Drop, Jan C. Molenaar, and Sabine M. P. F. de Muinck Keizer-Schrama, "Long-Term Psychological Evaluation of Intersex Children," *Archives of Sexual Behavior* 27 no. 2 (April–May 1998), p. 125(20), p. 6, internet version. William George Reiner, "Case Study: Sex Reassignment in a Teenage Girl," *Journal of the American Academy of Child and Adolescent Psychiatry* 35, no. 6 (June 1996), p. 799(5). The latter article describes an intersex Hmong child who was raised as a girl and decided she wanted to be a boy at age 14. Her doctors supported her decision and provided relevant medical treatment to help her body become more male.

16. Milton Diamond and H. Keith Sigmundson, "Management of Intersexuality: Guidelines for Dealing with Persons with Ambiguous Genitals," *Archives of Pediatric and Adolescent Medicine* 151, no. 10 (October 1997), pp. 1046–1050.

17. Gary Mihalik, "More Than Two: Anthropological Perspectives on Gender," *Journal of Lesbian and Gay Psychotherapy* 1, no. 1 (1989), pp. 105–118. John C. Wood, *When Men Are Women: Manhood among Gabra Nomads of East Africa* (Madison: Wisconsin University Press, 1999).

18. Judith Lorber, *Paradoxes of Gender* (New Haven: Yale University Press, 1994), pp. 17–18. Antonia Young, *Women Who Become Men: Albanian Sworn Virgins.* (Oxford, UK: Berg, 2000).

19. For research and critical analysis of gender and sports, see Greta Cohen, ed., *Women in Sports: Issues and Controversies* (Newbury Park, CA: Sage, 1993); Susan K. Cahn, *Coming on Strong* (Toronto: Free Press, 1994); Pat Griffin, *Strong Women, Deep Closets: Lesbians and Homophobia in Sport* (Champaign, IL: Human Kinetics, 1998); Michael A. Messner, *Power at Play: Sports and the Problem of Masculinity* (Boston: Beacon Press, 1992); Michael A. Messner and Donald F. Sabo, *Sex, Violence and Power in Sport: Rethinking Masculinity* (Freedom, CA: Crossing Press, 1994).

20. Phyllis Burke, *Gender Shock* (New York: Anchor/Doubleday, 1996), p. 229.

21. Dale Koppel, "About Face: The Focus on Appearance Is Becoming a Male Obsession," *Your Health, The Boston Globe* (April 23, 1995), pp. 10, 23, 26. An ad in *The Boston Globe* announced plastic surgery for "male enhancement" in May 1995.

22. *The Famine Within,* Public Broadcasting System (winter 1995).

23. Diana Dull and Candace West, "Accounting for Cosmetic Surgery: The Accomplishment of Gender," *Social Problems* 38, no. 1 (February 1991), pp. 54–70.

24. Pat Lyons, "The Great Weight Debate: Where Have All the Feminists Gone?" *The Network News* 23, no. 5 (September–October 1998), pp. 1ff.

25. Lyons, p. 5.

26. Natalie Kusz, "The Fat Lady Sings" in Cathi Hanauer, Ed., *The Bitch in the House: 26 Women Tell the Truth about Sex, Solitude, Work, Motherhood, and Marriage* (New York: Harper, 2003), pp. 239 247.

17

BEAUTY IS THE BEAST
Psychological Effects of the Pursuit
of the Perfect Female Body

ELAYNE A. SALTZBERG • JOAN C. CHRISLER

Elayne A. Saltzberg Daniels is a Psychology Fellow at the Yale University School of Medicine, where, among other activities, she works at the Yale Psychiatric Institute with women who have eating disorders. She earned her doctorate in clinical psychology at Rhode Island University and her master's degree at Connecticut College. She has recently completed a research project on the impact of breast cancer surgery on women's body image and sexual functioning, and she has published several articles on body image, eating disorders, and women's pursuit of beauty.

Joan C. Chrisler is a professor of psychology at Connecticut College. She earned her doctorate in experimental psychology at Yeshiva University while working nights as a waitress and serving as a shop steward in the hotel and restaurant workers union. Dr. Chrisler has published extensively on the psychology of women and women's health issues, and is particularly known for her work on weight and eating behavior and on psychosocial aspects of the menstrual cycle. She is coeditor of four books: *Arming Athena: Career Strategies of Women in Academe, Lectures on the Psychology of Women, Variations on a Theme: Diversity and the Psychology of Women,* and *New Directions in Feminist Psychology.*

Ambrose Bierce (1958) once wrote, "To men a man is but a mind. Who cares what face he carries or what he wears? But woman's body is the woman." Despite the societal changes achieved since Bierce's time, his statement remains true. Since the height of the feminist movement in the early 1970s, women have spent more money than ever before on products and treatments designed to make them beautiful. Cosmetic sales have increased annually to reach $18 billion in 1987 (Ignoring the economy, 1989), sales of women's clothing averaged $103 billion per month in 1990 (personal communication, U.S. Bureau of Economic Analysis, 1992), dieting has become a $30-billion-per-year industry (Stoffel, 1989), and women spent $1.2 billion on cosmetic surgery in 1990 (personal communication, American

Elayne A. Saltzberg and Joan C. Chrisler, "Beauty Is the Beast: Psychological Effects of the Pursuit of the Perfect Female Body" from *Women: A Feminist Perspective,* edited by Jo Freeman. Reprinted with permission.

Society of Plastic and Reconstructive Surgeons, 1992). The importance of beauty has apparently increased even as women are reaching for personal freedoms and economic rights undreamed of by our grandmothers. The emphasis on beauty may be a way to hold on to a feminine image while shedding feminine roles.

Attractiveness is prerequisite for femininity but not for masculinity (Freedman, 1986). The word *beauty* always refers to the female body. Attractive male bodies are described as "handsome," a word derived from "hand" that refers as much to action as appearance (Freedman, 1986). Qualities of achievement and strength accompany the term *handsome*; such attributes are rarely employed in the description of attractive women and certainly do not accompany the term *beauty*, which refers only to a decorative quality. Men are instrumental; women are ornamental.

Beauty is a most elusive commodity. Ideas of what is beautiful vary across cultures and change over time (Fallon, 1990). Beauty cannot be quantified or objectively measured; it is the result of the judgments of others. The concept is difficult to define, as it is equated with different, sometimes contradictory, ideas. When people are asked to define beauty, they tend to mention abstract, personal qualities rather than external, quantifiable ones (Freedman, 1986; Hatfield & Sprecher, 1986). The beholder's perceptions and cognitions influence the degree of attractiveness at least as much as do the qualities of the beheld.

Because beauty is an ideal, an absolute, such as truth and goodness, the pursuit of it does not require justification (Herman & Polivy, 1983). An ideal, by definition, can be met by only a minority of those who strive for it. If too many women are able to meet the beauty standards of a particular time and place, then those standards must change in order to maintain their extraordinary nature. The value of beauty standards depends on their being special and unusual and is one of the reasons why the ideal changes over time. When images of beauty change, female bodies are expected to change, too. Different aspects of the female body and varying images of each body part are modified to meet the constantly fluctuating ideal (Freedman, 1986). The ideal is always that which is most difficult to achieve and most unnatural in a given time period. Because these ideals are nearly impossible to achieve, failure and disappointment are inevitable (Freedman, 1988).

Although people have been decorating their bodies since prehistoric times, the Chinese may have been the first to develop the concept that the female body can and should be altered from its natural state. The practice of foot binding clearly illustrates the objectification of parts of the female body as well as the demands placed on women to conform to beauty ideals. The custom called for the binding of the feet of five-year-old girls so that as they grew, their toes became permanently twisted under their arches and actually shrank in size. The big toe remained untouched. The more tightly bound the feet, the more petite they became and the more attractive they were considered to be (Freedman, 1986; Hatfield & Sprecher, 1986; Lakoff & Scherr,

1984). The painful custom of foot binding finally ended in the twentieth century after women had endured over one thousand years of torture for beauty's sake (Brain, 1979).

In the sixteenth century, European women bound themselves into corsets of whalebone and hardened canvas. A piece of metal or wood ran down the front to flatten the breasts and abdomen. This garment made it impossible to bend at the waist and difficult to breathe. A farthingale, which was typically worn over the corset, held women's skirts out from their bodies. It consisted of bent wood held together with tapes and made such simple activities as sitting nearly impossible. Queen Catherine of France introduced waist binding with a tortuous invention consisting of iron bands that minimized the size of the waist to the ideal measurement of thirteen inches (Baker, 1984). In the seventeenth century, the waist was still laced, but breasts were once again stylish, and fashions were designed to enhance them. Ample breasts, hips, and buttocks became the beauty ideal, perhaps paralleling a generally warmer attitude toward family life (Rosenblatt & Stencel, 1982). A white pallor was also popular at that time, probably as an indication that the woman was so affluent that she did not need to work outdoors, where the sun might darken her skin. Ceruse, a white lead-based paint now known to be toxic, was used to accentuate the pallor.

Tight corsets came back into vogue in Europe and North America in the mid-nineteenth century, and many women were willing to run the risk of developing serious health problems in order to wear them. The tight lacing often led to pulmonary disease and internal organ damage. American women disregarded the advice of their physicians, who spoke against the use of corsets because of their potential to displace internal organs. Fainting, or "the vapors," was the result of wearing such tightly laced clothing that normal breathing became impossible. Even the clergy sermonized against corsets; miscarriages were known to result in pregnant women who insisted on lacing themselves up too tightly. In the late nineteenth century, the beauty ideal required a tiny waist and full hips and bustline. Paradoxically, women would go on diets to gain weight while, at the same time, trying to achieve a smaller waistline. Some women were reported to have had their lower ribs removed so that their waists could be more tightly laced (Brain, 1979).

In the twentieth century, the ideal female body has changed several times, and American women have struggled to change along with it. In the 1920s, the ideal had slender legs and hips, small breasts, and bobbed hair and was physically and socially active. Women removed the stuffing from their bodices and bound their breasts[1] to appear young and boyish. In the 1940s and 1950s, the ideal returned to the hourglass shape. Marilyn Monroe was considered the epitome of the voluptuous and fleshy yet naive and childlike ideal. In the 1960s, the ideal had a youthful, thin, lean body and long, straight hair. American women dieted relentlessly in an attempt to emulate the tall, thin, teenage model Twiggy, who personified the 1960s' beauty ideal. Even pregnant women were on diets in response to their doctors' orders not to gain more than twenty pounds, advice physicians later rejected as unsafe (Fallon, 1990). Menopausal women begged their physicians to prescribe hormone replacement therapy, which was rumored to prevent wrinkles and keep the body youthful, and were willing to run any health risk to preserve their appearance (Chrisler, Torrey, & Matthes, 1989). In the 1970s, a thin, tan, sensuous look was "in." The 1980s' beauty ideal remained slim but required a more muscular, toned, and physically fit body. In recent decades the beauty ideal has combined such opposite traits as erotic sophistication with naive innocence, delicate grace with muscular athleticism (Freedman, 1988), and thin bodies with large breasts. The pressure to cope with such conflicting demands and to keep up with the continual changes in the ideal female body is highly stressful (Freedman, 1988) and has resulted in a large majority of American women with negative body images (Dworkin & Kerr, 1987; Rosen, Saltzberg, & Srebnik, 1989). Women's insecurity about their looks has made it easy to convince them that small breasts are a "disease" requiring surgical intervention. The sophisticated woman of the 1990s who is willing to accept the significant health risks of breast implants in order to mold her body to fit the beauty ideal has not progressed far beyond her sisters who bound their feet and waists.

The value of beauty depends in part on the high costs of achieving it. Such costs may be physical, temporal, economic, or psychological. Physical costs include the pain of ancient beauty rituals such as foot binding, tattooing, and nose and ear piercing as well as more modern rituals such as wearing pointy-toed, high-heeled shoes, tight jeans, and sleeping with one's hair in curlers. Side effects of beauty rituals have often been disastrous for women's health. Tattooing and ear piercing with unsanitary instruments have led to serious, sometimes fatal, infections. Many women have been poisoned by toxic chemicals in cosmetics (e.g., ceruse, arsenic, benzene, and petroleum) and have died from the use of unsafe diet products such as rainbow pills and liquid protein (Schwartz, 1986). The beauty-related disorders anorexia nervosa and bulimia have multiple negative health effects, and side effects of plastic surgery include hemorrhages, scars, and nerve damage. Silicone implants have resulted in breast cancer, autoimmune disease, and the formation of thick scar tissue.

Physical costs of dieting include a constant feeling of hunger that leads to emotional changes, such as irritability; in cases of very low caloric intake, dieters can experience difficulty concentrating, confusion, and even reduced cognitive capacity. The only growing group of smokers in the United States are young women, many of whom report that they smoke to curb their appetites (Sorensen & Pechacek, 1987). High heels cause lower back pain and lead to a variety of podiatric disorders. Furthermore, fashion trends have increased women's vulnerability in a variety of ways; long hair and dangling earrings have gotten caught in machinery and entangled in clothing and led to injury. High heels and tight skirts prevent women from running from danger. The *New York Times* fashion reporter Bernardine Morris was alarmed to

see in Pierre Cardin's 1988 summer fashion show tight wraps that prevented
the models from moving their arms (Morris, 1988).

Attaining the beauty ideal requires a lot of money. Expensive cosmetics
(e.g., makeup, moisturizers, and hair dyes and straighteners) are among the
most popular and are thought to be the most effective, even though their ingredients cost the same (and sometimes are the same) as those in less expensive products (Lakoff & Scherr, 1984). Health spas have become fashionable again as vacation spots for the rich and famous, and everyone wants to
wear expensive clothing with designer labels. Plastic surgery has become so
accepted and so common that, although it's quite expensive, surgeons advertise their services on television. Surgery is currently performed that can
reduce the size of lips, ear lobes, noses, buttocks, thighs, abdomens, and
breasts; rebuild a face; remove wrinkles; and add "padding" to almost any
body part. Not surprisingly, most plastic surgery patients are women (Hamburger, 1988).

Beauty rituals are time-consuming activities. Jokes about how long
women take to get ready for a date are based on the additional tasks women
do when getting dressed. It takes time to pluck eyebrows, shave legs, mani-
cure nails, apply makeup, and arrange hair. Women's clothing is more complicated than men's, and many more accessories are used. Although all
women know that the "transformation from female to feminine is artificial"
(Chapkis, 1986, p. 5), we conspire to hide the amount of time and effort it
takes, perhaps out of fear that other women don't need as much time as we
do to appear beautiful. A lot of work goes into looking like a "natural"
beauty, but that work is not acknowledged by popular culture, and the tools
of the trade are kept out of view. Men's grooming rituals are fewer, take less
time, and need not be hidden away. Scenes of men shaving have often been
seen on television and in movies and have even been painted by Norman
Rockwell. Wendy Chapkis (1986) challenges her readers to "imagine a similar cultural celebration of a woman plucking her eyebrows, shaving her
armpits, or waxing her upper lip" (p. 6). Such a scene would be shocking
and would remove the aura of mystery that surrounds beautiful women.

Psychological effects of the pursuit of the perfect female body include
unhappiness, confusion, misery, and insecurity. Women often believe that if
only they had perfect looks, their lives would be perfectly happy; they blame
their unhappiness on their bodies. American women have the most negative
body image of any culture studied by the Kinsey Institute (Faludi, 1991). Dissatisfaction with their bodies is very common among adolescent girls
(Adams & Crossman, 1978; Clifford, 1971; Freedman, 1984), and older
women believe that the only way to remain attractive is to prevent the development of any signs of aging. Obsessive concern about body shape and
weight have become so common among American women of all ages that
they now constitute the norm (Rodin, Silberstein, & Striegel-Moore, 1985).
The majority of women in the United States are dieting at any given time.
For them, being female means feeling fat and inadequate and living with

chronic low self-esteem (Rodin et al., 1985). Ask any woman what she would like to change about her body and she'll answer immediately. Ask her what she likes about her body and she'll have difficulty responding.

Those women who do succeed in matching the ideal thinness expected by modern beauty standards usually do so by exercising frenetically and compulsively, implementing severely restrictive and nutritionally deficient diets, developing bizarre eating habits, and using continuous self-degradation and self-denial. Dieting has become a "cultural requirement" for women (Herman & Polivy, 1983) because the ideal female body has become progressively thinner at the same time that the average female body has become progressively heavier. This cultural requirement remains in place despite the fact that physiology works against weight loss to such an extent that 98 percent of diets fail (Chrisler, 1989; Fitzgerald, 1981). In fact, it is more likely for someone to fully recover from cancer than for an obese person to lose a significant amount of weight and maintain that loss for five years (Brownell, 1982). Yet a recent study (Davies & Furnham, 1986) found that young women rate borderline anorexic bodies as very attractive. Thus, even the thinnest women find it nearly impossible to meet and maintain the beauty ideal.

The social pressure for thinness can be directly linked to the increasing incidence of anorexia nervosa and bulimia among women (Brumberg, 1988; Caskey, 1986). There are presently at least one million Americans with anorexia nervosa, and 95 percent of them are women. Between sixty thousand and 150,000 of them will die as a result of their obsession (Schwartz, 1986). Although cases of anorexia nervosa have been reported in the medical literature for hundreds of years (Bell, 1985), it was considered to be a rare disorder until the 1970s. Today's anorexics are also thinner than they were in the past (Brumberg, 1988). It is estimated that at least seven million American women will experience symptoms of bulimia at some point in their lives (Hatfield & Sprecher, 1986). A recent study (Hall & Cohn, 1988) found that 25 to 33 percent of female first-year college students were using vomiting after meals as a method of weight control. An accurate estimate of the number of women who are caught in the binge-purge cycle is difficult because women with bulimia are generally secretive about their behavior and the physical signs of bulimia are not nearly as obvious as those of anorexia nervosa.

Exercise has become for many women another manifestation of their body dissatisfaction. Studies have found that most men who exercise regularly do so to build body mass and to increase cardiovascular fitness; most women who exercise do so to lose weight and to change the shape of their bodies in order to increase their attractiveness (Garner, Rockert, Olmstead, Johnson, & Coscina, 1985; Saltzberg, 1990). Exercise has lost its status as a pleasurable activity and become yet another way for women to manipulate their bodies, another vehicle for narcissistic self-torture. Reports of the number of women exercising compulsively are increasing and may become as widespread as compulsive calorie counting and the compulsive eating habits of anorexics and bulimics.

Beauty ideals are created and maintained by society's elite. Racism, class prejudice, and rejection of the disabled are clearly reflected (Chapkis, 1986) in current American beauty standards. For example, women from lower socio-economic groups typically weigh more than women in higher socioeconomic groups (Moore, Stunkard, & Srole, 1962); they are thus excluded by popular agreement from being considered beautiful. The high costs of chic clothing, cosmetics, tanning salons, skin and hair treatments, weight loss programs, and plastic surgery prevent most American women from access to the tools necessary to approach the ideal. Furthermore, the beauty standard idealizes Caucasian features and devalues those of other races (Lewis, 1977; Miller, 1969). In recent years, Asian American and African American women have sought facial surgery in order to come closer to the beauty ideal (Faludi, 1991), and psychotherapists have noted increased reports from their black women clients of guilt, shame, anger, and resentment about skin color, hair texture, facial features, and body size and shape (Greene, 1992; Neal & Wilson, 1989; Okazawa-Rey, Robinson, & Ward, 1987). Obviously, women with visible disabilities will never be judged to have achieved "perfection." Whoopi Goldberg's routine about the black teenager who wrapped a towel around her head to pretend it was long, blonde hair and Alice Walker's (1990) essay about her psychological adjustment after the eye injury that resulted in the development of "hideous" scar tissue provide poignant examples of the pain women experience when they cannot meet beauty standards.

The inordinate emphasis on women's external selves makes it difficult for us to appreciate our own internal selves (Kano, 1985). The constant struggle to meet the beauty ideal leads to high stress and chronic anxiety. Failure to meet the beauty ideal leads to feelings of frustration, low self-worth, and inadequacy in women whose sense of self is based on their physical appearance. The intensity of the drive to increase attractiveness may also contribute to the high rate of depression among women.[2]

Insecurity is common even among beautiful women, and studies show that they are as likely as their plain sisters to be unhappy about their looks (Freedman, 1988). Beautiful women are all too aware of the fleeting nature of their beauty; the effects of aging must be constantly monitored, and these women worry that the beauty ideal they've tried so hard to match may change without warning. When such women lose their beauty due to illness or accidents, they often become depressed and are likely to have difficulty functioning in society and to believe that their entire identity has been threatened.

Given the high costs of striving to be beautiful, why do women attempt it? Attractiveness greatly affects first impressions and later interpersonal relationships. In a classic study titled "What Is Beautiful Is Good," psychologists Kenneth Dion, Ellen Berscheid, and Elaine Walster Hatfield (1972) asked college students to rate photographs of strangers on a variety of personal characteristics. Those who were judged to be attractive were also more likely to be rated intelligent, kind, happy, flexible, interesting, confident, sexy, assertive, strong, outgoing, friendly, poised, modest, candid, and successful than those judged unattractive. Teachers rate attractive children more highly on a variety of positive characteristics including IQ and sociability, and attractive babies are cuddled and kissed more often than unattractive babies (Berscheid & Walster, 1974). Attractive people receive more lenient punishment for social transgressions (Dion, 1972; Landy & Aronson, 1969), and attractive women are more often sought out in social situations (Walster, Aronson, Abrahams, & Rottman, 1966; Reis, Nezlek, & Wheeler, 1980).

Furthermore, because unattractive people are more harshly punished for social transgressions and are less often sought after as social partners, failure to work toward the beauty ideal can result in real consequences. Television newswoman Christine Craft made the news herself when she was fired for being too old and too unattractive. Street harassers put women "in their place" by commenting loudly on their beauty or lack of it. Beauty norms limit the opportunities of women who can't or won't meet them. Obese women, for example, have experienced discrimination in a number of instances including hiring and promotion (Larkin & Pines, 1979; Rothblum, Miller, & Gorbutt, 1988) and college admissions (Canning & Mayer, 1966). Obese people even have a harder time finding a place to live; Lambros Karris (1977) found that landlords are less likely to rent to obese people. Even physicians view their obese patients negatively (Maddox & Liederman, 1969).

There is considerable evidence that women's attractiveness is judged more harshly than men's. Christine Craft was fired, yet David Brinkley and Willard Scott continue to work on major television news shows; their abilities are not thought to be affected by age or attractiveness. Several studies (Adams & Huston, 1975; Berman, O'Nan, & Floyd, 1981; Deutsch, Zalenski, & Clark, 1986; Wernick & Manaster, 1984) that asked participants to rate the attractiveness of photographs of people of varying ages found that although attractiveness ratings of both men and women decline with age, the rate of decline for women was greater. In one study (Deutsch, Zalenski, & Clark, 1986), participants were asked to rate the photographs for femininity and masculinity as well as attractiveness. The researchers found that both the attractiveness and femininity ratings of the female photographs diminished with age; the masculinity ratings were unaffected by the age or attractiveness of the photographs. Women are acutely aware of the double standard of attractiveness. At all ages women are more concerned than men about weight and physical appearance and have lower appearance self-esteem; women who define themselves as feminine are the most concerned about their appearance and have the lowest self-esteem (Pliner, Chaiken, & Flett, 1990). In fact, women are so concerned about their body size that they typically overestimate it. Women who overestimate their size feel worse about themselves, whereas men's self-esteem is unrelated to their body size estimates (Thompson, 1986). In a review of research on the stigma of obesity, Esther Rothblum (1992) concluded that the dieting industry, combined with Western attitudes toward weight and attractiveness, causes more pain and problems for women than for men.

Thus, the emphasis on beauty has political as well as psychological consequences for women, as it results in oppression and disempowerment. It is important for women to examine the effects that the pursuit of the perfect female body has had on their lives, challenge their beliefs, and take a stand against continued enslavement to the elusive beauty ideal. Women would then be able to live life more freely and experience the world more genuinely. Each woman must decide for herself what beauty really is and the extent to which she is willing to go to look attractive. Only a more diverse view of beauty and a widespread rebellion against fashion extremes will save us from further physical and psychological tolls.

Imagine an American society where the quality and meaning of life for women are not dependent on the silence of bodily shame. Imagine a society where bodies are decorated for fun and to express creativity rather than for self-control and self-worth. Imagine what would happen if the world's women released and liberated all of the energy that had been absorbed in the beautification process. The result might be the positive, affirming, healthy version of a nuclear explosion!

NOTES

1. Bras were originally designed to hide breasts.
2. Statistics indicate that women are far more likely than men to be diagnosed as depressed. The ratio is at least 3:1 (Williams, 1985).

REFERENCES

Adams, Gerald R., & Crossman, Sharyn M. (1978). *Physical attractiveness: A cultural imperative.* New York: Libra.

Adams, Gerald R., & Huston, Ted L. (1975). Social perception of middle-aged persons varying in physical attractiveness. *Developmental Psychology, 11,* 657–58.

Baker, Nancy C. (1984). *The beauty trap: Exploring woman's greatest obsession.* New York: Franklin Watts.

Bell, Rudolph M. (1985). *Holy anorexia.* Chicago: University of Chicago Press.

Berman, Phyllis W., O'Nan, Barbara A., & Floyd, Wayne. (1981). The double standard of aging and the social situation: Judgments of attractiveness of the middle-aged woman. *Sex Roles, 7,* 87–96.

Berscheid, Ellen, & Walster, Elaine. (1974). Physical attractiveness. *Advances in Experimental Social Psychology, 7,* 158–215.

Bierce, Ambrose. (1958). *The devil's dictionary.* New York: Dover.

Brain, R. (1979). *The decorated body.* New York: Harper & Row.

Brownell, Kelly. (1982). Obesity: Understanding and treating a serious, prevalent, and refractory disorder. *Journal of Consulting and Clinical Psychology, 55,* 889–97.

Brumberg, Joan J. (1988). *Fasting girls.* Cambridge, MA: Harvard University Press.

Canning, H., & Mayer, J. (1966). Obesity: An influence on high school performance. *Journal of Clinical Nutrition, 20,* 352–54.

Caskey, Noelle. (1986). Interpreting anorexia nervosa. In Susan R. Suleiman (Ed.), *The female body in western culture* (pp. 175–89). Cambridge, MA: Harvard University Press.

Chapkis, Wendy. (1986). *Beauty secrets: Women and the politics of appearance.* Boston: South End Press.

Chrisler, Joan C. (1989). Should feminist therapists do weight loss counseling? *Women & Therapy, 8*(3), 31–37.

Chrisler, Joan C. , Torrey, Jane W., & Matthes, Michelle. (1989, June). *Brittle bones and sagging breasts, loss of femininity and loss of sanity: The media describe the menopause.* Paper presented at the meeting of the Society for Menstrual Cycle Research, Salt Lake City, UT.

Clifford, Edward. (1971). Body satisfaction in adolescence. *Perceptual and Motor Skills, 33,* 119–25.

Davies, Elizabeth, & Furnham, Adrian. (1986). The dieting and body shape concerns of adolescent females. *Child Psychology and Psychiatry, 27,* 417–28.

Deutsch, Francine M., Zalenski, Carla M., & Clark, Mary E. (1986). Is there a double standard of aging? *Journal of Applied Social Psychology, 16,* 771–85.

Dion, Kenneth K. (1972). Physical attractiveness and evaluation of children's transgressions. *Journal of Personality and Social Psychology, 24,* 207–13.

Dion, Kenneth, Berscheid, Ellen, & Walster [Hatfield], Elaine. (1972). What is beautiful is good. *Journal of Personality and Social Psychology, 24,* 285–90.

Dworkin, Sari H., & Kerr, Barbara A. (1987). Comparison of interventions for women experiencing body image problems. *Journal of Consulting and Clinical Psychology, 34,* 136–40.

Fallon, April. (1990). Culture in the mirror: Sociocultural determinants of body image. In Thomas Cash & Thomas Pruzinsky (Eds.), *Body images: Development, deviance, and change* (pp. 80–109). New York: Guilford Press.

Faludi, Susan. (1991). *Backlash: The undeclared war against American women.* New York: Crown Publishers.

Fitzgerald, Faith T. (1981). The problem of obesity. *Annual Review of Medicine, 32,* 221–31.

Freedman, Rita. (1984). Reflections on beauty as it relates to health in adolescent females. In Sharon Golub (Ed.), *Health care of the female adolescent* (pp. 29–45). New York: Haworth Press.

Freedman, Rita. (1986). *Beauty bound.* Lexington, MA: D. C. Heath.

Freedman, Rita. (1988). *Bodylove: Learning to like our looks — and ourselves.* New York: Harper & Row.

Garner, David M., Rockert, Wendy, Olmstead, Marion P., Johnson, C., & Coscina, D. V. (1985). Psychoeducational principles in the treatment of bulimia and anorexia nervosa. In David M. Garner & Paul E. Garfinkel (Eds.), *Handbook of psychotherapy for anorexia nervosa and bulimia* (pp. 513–62). New York: Guilford.

Greene, Beverly. (1992). Still here: A perspective on psychotherapy with African American women. In Joan C. Chrisler & Doris Howard (Eds.), *New directions in feminist psychology: Practice, theory, and research* (pp. 13–25). New York: Springer.

Hall, L., & Cohn, L. (1988). *Bulimia: A guide to recovery.* Carlsbad, CA: Gurze Books.

Hamburger, A. C. (1988, May). Beauty quest. *Psychology Today, 22,* 28–32.

Hatfield, Elaine, & Sprecher, Susan. (1986). *Mirror, mirror: The importance of looks in everyday life.* Albany: State University of New York Press.

Herman, Peter, & Polivy, Janet. (1983). *Breaking the diet habit.* New York: Basic Books.

Ignoring the economy, cosmetic firms look to growth. (1989, July 13). *Standard and Poor's Industry Surveys, 1,* 37–38.

Kano, Susan. (1985). *Making peace with food: A step-by-step guide to freedom from diet/weight conflict.* Danbury, CT: Amity.

Karris, Lambros. (1977). Prejudice against obese renters. *Journal of Social Psychology, 101,* 159–60.

Lakoff, Robin T., & Scherr, Raquel L. (1984). *Face value: The politics of beauty.* Boston: Routledge & Kegan Paul.

Landy, David, & Aronson, Elliot. (1969). The influence of the character of the criminal and his victim on the decisions of simulated jurors. *Journal of Experimental Social Psychology, 5,* 141–52.

Larkin, Judith, & Pines, Harvey. (1979). No fat person need apply. *Sociology of Work and Occupations, 6,* 312–27.

Lewis, Diane K. (1977). A response to inequality: Black women, racism, and sexism. *Signs,* 3(2), 339–61.

Maddox, G., & Liederman, V. (1969). Overweight as a social disability with medical implications. *Journal of Medical Education, 44,* 214–20.

Miller, E. (1969). Body image, physical beauty, and color among Jamaican adolescents. *Social and Economic Studies,* 18(1), 72–89.

Moore, M. E., Stunkard, Albert, & Srole, L. (1962). Obesity, social class, and mental illness. *Journal of the American Medical Association, 181,* 138–42.

Morris, Bernardine. (1988, July 26). Paris couture: Opulence lights a serious mood. *New York Times,* p. B8.

Neal, Angela, & Wilson, Midge. (1989). The role of skin color and features in the black community: Implications for black women and therapy. *Clinical Psychology Review, 9,* 323–33.

Okazawa-Rey, Margo, Robinson, Tracy, & Ward, Janie V. (1987). Black women and the politics of skin color and hair. *Women & Therapy,* 6(1/2), 89–102.

Pliner, Patricia, Chaiken, Shelly, & Flett, Gordon L. (1990). Gender differences in concern with body weight and physical appearance over the life span. *Personality and Social Psychology Bulletin, 16,* 263–73.

Reis, Harry T., Nezlek, John, & Wheeler, Ladd. (1980). Physical attractiveness in social interaction. *Journal of Personality and Social Psychology, 38,* 604–17.

Rodin, Judith, Silberstein, Lisa, & Striegel-Moore, Ruth. (1985). Women and weight: A normative discontent. In Theo B. Sonderegger (Ed.), *Nebraska symposium on motivation: Psychology and gender* (pp. 267–307). Lincoln: University of Nebraska Press.

Rosen, James C., Saltzberg, Elayne A., & Srebnik, Debra. (1989). Cognitive behavior therapy for negative body image. *Behavior Therapy, 20,* 393–404.

Rosenblatt, J., & Stencel, S. (1982). *Weight control: A natural obsession.* Washington, DC: Congressional Quarterly.

Rothblum, Esther D. (1992). The stigma of women's weight: Social and economic realities. *Feminism & Psychology,* 2(1), 61–73.

Rothblum, Esther D., Miller, Carol, & Gorbutt, Barbara. (1988). Stereotypes of obese female job applicants. *International Journal of Eating Disorders, 7,* 277–83.

Saltzberg, Elayne A. (1990). *Exercise participation and its correlates to body awareness and self-esteem.* Unpublished master's thesis, Connecticut College, New London, CT.

Schwartz, Hillel. (1986). *Never satisfied: A cultural history of diets, fantasies, and fat.* New York: Free Press.

Sorensen, Gloria, & Pechacek, Terry F. (1987). Attitudes toward smoking cessation among men and women. *Journal of Behavioral Medicine, 10,* 129–38.

Stoffel, Jennifer. (1989, November 26). What's new in weight control: A market mushrooms as motivations change. *New York Times,* p. C17.

Thompson, J. Kevin. (1986, April). Larger than life. *Psychology Today,* pp. 41–44.

Walker, Alice. (1990). Beauty: When the other dancer is the self. In Evelyn C. White (Ed.), *The black women's health book: Speaking for ourselves* (pp. 280–87). Seattle: Seal Press.

Walster, Elaine, Aronsen, Vera, Abrahams, Darcy, & Rottman, Leon. (1966). Importance of physical attractiveness in dating behavior. *Journal of Personality and Social Psychology, 4,* 508–16.

Wernick, Mark, & Manaster, Guy J. (1984). Age and the perception of age and attractiveness. *Gerontologist, 24,* 408–14.

Williams, Juanita H. (1985). *Psychology of women: Behavior in a biosocial context.* New York: Norton.

18

YELLOW WOMAN
AND A BEAUTY OF THE SPIRIT

LESLIE MARMON SILKO

Leslie Marmon Silko, a former professor of English and fiction writing, is the author of novels, short stories, essays, poetry, articles, and filmscripts. She has won prizes, fellowships, and grants from such sources as the National Endowment for the Arts and *The Boston Globe.* She was the youngest writer to be included in *The Norton Anthology of Women's Literature,* for her short story "Lullaby." Ms. Silko lives in Tucson, Arizona.

My great-grandmother was dark and handsome. Her expression in photographs is one of confidence and strength. I do not know if white people then or now would consider her beautiful. I do not know if the old-time Laguna Pueblo people considered her beautiful or if the old-time people even thought in those terms. To the Pueblo way of thinking, the act of comparing one living being with another was silly, because each being or thing is unique and therefore incomparably valuable because it is the only one of its kind. The old-time people thought it was crazy to attach such importance to a person's appearance. I understood very early that there were two distinct ways of interpreting the world. There was the white people's way and there was the Laguna way. In the Laguna way, it was bad manners to make comparisons that might hurt another person's feelings.

In everyday Pueblo life, not much attention was paid to one's physical appearance or clothing. Ceremonial clothing was quite elaborate but was used only for the sacred dances. The traditional Pueblo societies were communal and strictly egalitarian, which means that no matter how well or how poorly one might have dressed, there was no social ladder to fall from. All food and other resources were strictly shared so that no one person or group had more than another. I mention social status because it seems to me that most of the definitions of beauty in contemporary Western culture are really codes for determining social status. People no longer hide their face-lifts and they discuss their liposuctions because the point of the procedures isn't just cosmetic, it is social. It says to the world, "I have enough spare cash that I can afford surgery for cosmetic purposes."

In the old-time Pueblo world, beauty was manifested in behavior and in one's relationships with other living beings. Beauty was as much a feeling of harmony as it was a visual, aural, or sensual effect. The whole person had to be beautiful, not just the face or the body; faces and bodies could not be separated from hearts and souls. Health was foremost in achieving this sense of well-being and harmony; in the old-time Pueblo world, a person who did not look healthy inspired feelings of worry and anxiety, not feelings of well-being. A healthy person, of course, is in harmony with the world around her; she is at peace with herself too. Thus an unhappy person or spiteful person would not be considered beautiful.

In the old days, strong, sturdy women were most admired. One of my most vivid preschool memories is of the crew of Laguna women, in their forties and fifties, who came to cover our house with adobe plaster. They handled the ladders with great ease, and while two women ground the adobe mud on stones and added straw, another woman loaded the hod with mud and passed it up to the two women on ladders, who were smoothing the plaster on the wall with their hands. Since women owned the houses, they did the plastering. At Laguna, men did the basket making and the weaving of fine textiles; men helped a great deal with the child care too. Because the Creator is female, there is no stigma on being female; gender is not used to control behavior. No job was a man's job or a woman's job; the most able person did the work.

My Grandma Lily had been a Ford Model A mechanic when she was a teenager. I remember when I was young, she was always fixing broken lamps and appliances. She was small and wiry, but she could lift her weight in rolled roofing or boxes of nails. When she was seventy-five, she was still repairing washing machines in my uncle's coin-operated laundry.

The old-time people paid no attention to birthdays. When a person was ready to do something, she did it. When she no longer was able, she stopped. Thus the traditional Pueblo people did not worry about aging or about looking old because there were no social boundaries drawn by the passage of years. It was not remarkable for young men to marry women as old as their mothers. I never heard anyone talk about "women's work" until after I left Laguna for college. Work was there to be done by any able-bodied person who wanted to do it. At the same time, in the old-time Pueblo world, identity was acknowledged to be always in a flux; in the old stories, one minute Spider Woman is a little spider under a yucca plant, and the next instant she is a sprightly grandmother walking down the road.

When I was growing up, there was a young man from a nearby village who wore nail polish and women's blouses and permed his hair. People paid little attention to his appearance; he was always part of a group of other young men from his village. No one ever made fun of him. Pueblo communities were and still are very interdependent, but they also have to be tolerant of individual eccentricities because survival of the group means everyone has to cooperate.

In the old Pueblo world, differences were celebrated as signs of the Mother Creator's grace. Persons born with exceptional physical or sexual differences were highly respected and honored because their physical differences gave them special positions as mediators between this world and the spirit world. The great Navajo medicine man of the 1920s, the Crawler, had a hunchback and could not walk upright, but he was able to heal even the most difficult cases.

Before the arrival of Christian missionaries, a man could dress as a woman and work with the women and even marry a man without any fanfare. Likewise, a woman was free to dress like a man, to hunt and go to war with the men, and to marry a woman. In the old Pueblo worldview, we are all a mixture of male and female, and this sexual identity is changing constantly. Sexual inhibition did not begin until the Christian missionaries arrived. For the old-time people, marriage was about teamwork and social relationships, not about sexual excitement. In the days before the Puritans came, marriage did not mean an end to sex with people other than your spouse. Women were just as likely as men to have a *si'ash,* or lover.

New life was so precious that pregnancy was always appropriate, and pregnancy before marriage was celebrated as a good sign. Since the children belonged to the mother and her clan, and women owned and bequeathed the houses and farmland, the exact determination of paternity wasn't critical. Although fertility was prized, infertility was no problem because mothers with unplanned pregnancies gave their babies to childless couples within the clan in open adoption arrangements. Children called their mother's sisters "mother" as well, and a child became attached to a number of parent figures.

In the sacred kiva ceremonies, men mask and dress as women to pay homage and to be possessed by the female energies of the spirit beings. Because differences in physical appearance were so highly valued, surgery to change one's face and body to resemble a model's face and body would be unimaginable. To be different, to be unique was blessed and was best of all.

19

"A WAY OUTA NO WAY"
Eating Problems among African-American, Latina, and White Women

BECKY W. THOMPSON

Becky W. Thompson is the author of *A Hunger So Wide and So Deep: A Multiracial View of Women's Eating Problems* (1994), *A Promise and a Way of Life: White Anti-Racist Activism* (2001), and *Mothering Without a Compass: White Mother's Love, Black Son's Courage* (2000). She coedited, with Sangeeta Tyagi, *Names We Call Home: Autobiography on Racial Identity* (1996) and *Beyond a Dream Deferred: Multicultural Education and the Politics of Excellence* (1993). She is an associate professor of sociology at Simmons College where she teaches courses in African American studies, women's studies, and sociology.

Bulimia, anorexia, binging, and extensive dieting are among the many health issues women have been confronting in the last 20 years. Until recently, however, there has been almost no research about eating problems among African-American, Latina, Asian-American, or Native American women; working-class women; or lesbians.[1] In fact, according to the normative epidemiological portrait, eating problems are largely a white, middle- and upper-class heterosexual phenomenon. Further, while feminist research has documented how eating problems are fueled by sexism, there has been almost no attention to how other systems of oppression may also be implicated in the development of eating problems.

In this article, I reevaluate the portrayal of eating problems as issues of appearance based in the "culture of thinness." I propose that eating problems begin as ways women cope with various traumas including sexual abuse, racism, classism, sexism, heterosexism, and poverty. Showing the interface between these traumas and the onset of eating problems explains why women may use eating to numb pain and cope with violations to their bodies. This theoretical shift also permits an understanding of the economic, political, social, educational, and cultural resources that women need to change their relationship to food and their bodies.

Existing Research on Eating Problems

There are three theoretical models used to explain the epidemiology, etiology, and treatment of eating problems. The biomedical model offers important scientific research about possible physiological causes of eating problems and the physiological dangers of purging and starvation (Copeland 1985; Spack 1985). However, this model adopts medical treatment strategies that may disempower and traumatize women (Garner 1985; Orbach 1985). In addition, this model ignores many social, historical, and cultural factors that influence women's eating patterns. The psychological model identifies eating problems as "multidimensional disorders" that are influenced by biological, psychological, and cultural factors (Garfinkel and Garner 1982). While useful in its exploration of effective therapeutic treatments, this model, like the biomedical one, tends to neglect women of color, lesbians, and working-class women.

The third model, offered by feminists, asserts that eating problems are gendered. This model explains why the vast majority of people with eating problems are women, how gender socialization and sexism may relate to eating problems, and how masculine models of psychological development have shaped theoretical interpretations. Feminists offer the culture of thinness model as a key reason why eating problems predominate among women. According to this model, thinness is a culturally, socially, and economically enforced requirement for female beauty. This imperative makes women vulnerable to cycles of dieting, weight loss, and subsequent weight gain, which may lead to anorexia and bulimia (Chernin 1981; Orbach 1978, 1985; Smead 1984).

Feminists have rescued eating problems from the realm of individual psychopathology by showing how the difficulties are rooted in systematic and pervasive attempts to control women's body sizes and appetites. However, researchers have yet to give significant attention to how race, class, and sexuality influence women's understanding of their bodies and appetites. The handful of epidemiological studies that include African-American women and Latinas casts doubt on the accuracy of the normative epidemiological portrait. The studies suggest that this portrait reflects which particular populations of women have been studied rather than actual prevalence (Andersen and Hay 1985; Gray, Ford, and Kelly 1987; Hsu 1987; Nevo 1985; Silber 1986).

More important, this research shows that bias in research has consequences for women of color. Tomas Silber (1986) asserts that many well-trained professionals have either misdiagnosed or delayed their diagnoses of eating problems among African-American and Latina women due to stereotypical thinking that these problems are restricted to white women. As a consequence, when African-American women or Latinas are diagnosed, their eating problems tend to be more severe due to extended processes of starvation prior to intervention. In her autobiographical account of her eating problems, Retha Powers (1989), an African-American woman, describes being told not to worry about her eating problems since "fat is more acceptable in the Black community" (p. 78). Stereotypical perceptions held by her peers and teachers of the "maternal Black woman" and the "persistent mammy-brickhouse Black woman image" (p. 134) made it difficult for Powers to find people who took her problems with food seriously.

Recent work by African-American women reveals that eating problems often relate to women's struggles against a "simultaneity of oppression" (Clarke 1982; Naylor 1985; White 1991). Byllye Avery (1990), the founder of the National Black Women's Health Project, links the origins of eating problems among African-American women to the daily stress of being undervalued and overburdened at home and at work. In Evelyn C. White's (1990) anthology, *The Black Woman's Health Book: Speaking for Ourselves,* Georgiana Arnold (1990) links her eating problems partly to racism and racial isolation during childhood.

Recent feminist research also identifies factors that are related to eating problems among lesbians (Brown 1987; Dworkin 1989; Iazzetto 1989; Schoenfielder and Wieser 1983). In her clinical work, Brown (1987) found that lesbians who have internalized a high degree of homophobia are more likely to accept negative attitudes about fat than are lesbians who have examined their internalized homophobia. Autobiographical accounts by lesbians have also indicated that secrecy about eating problems among lesbians partly reflects their fear of being associated with a stigmatized illness ("What's Important" 1988).

Attention to African-American women, Latinas, and lesbians paves the way for further research that explores the possible interface between facing multiple oppressions and the development of eating problems. In this way, this study is part of a larger feminist and sociological research agenda that seeks to understand how race, class, gender, nationality, and sexuality inform women's experiences and influence theory production.

Methodology

I conducted 18 life history interviews and administered lengthy questionnaires to explore eating problems among African-American, Latina, and white women. I employed a snowball sample, a method in which potential respondents often first learn about the study from people who have already participated. This method was well suited for the study since it enabled women to get information about me and the interview process from people they already knew. Typically, I had much contact with the respondents prior to the interview. This was particularly important given the secrecy associated with this topic (Russell 1986; Silberstein, Striegel-Moore, and Rodin 1987), the necessity of women of color and lesbians to be discriminating about how their lives are studied, and the fact that I was conducting across-race research.

To create analytical notes and conceptual categories from the data, I adopted Glaser and Strauss's (1967) technique of theoretical sampling, which directs the researcher to collect, analyze, and test hypotheses during the sampling process (rather than imposing theoretical categories onto the data). After completing each interview transcription, I gave a copy to each woman who wanted one. After reading their interviews, some of the women clarified or made additions to the interview text.

Demographics of the Women in the Study

The 18 women I interviewed included 5 African-American women, 5 Latinas, and 8 white women. Of these women, 12 are lesbian and 6 are heterosexual. Five women are Jewish, 8 are Catholic, and 5 are Protestant. Three women grew up outside of the United States. The women represented a range of class backgrounds (both in terms of origin and current class status) and ranged in age from 19 to 46 years old (with a median age of 33.5 years).

The majority of the women reported having had a combination of eating problems (at least two of the following: bulimia, compulsive eating, anorexia, and/or extensive dieting). In addition, the particular types of eating problems often changed during a woman's life span. (For example, a woman might have been bulimic during adolescence and anorexic as an adult.) Among the women, 28 percent had been bulimic, 17 percent had been bulimic and anorexic, and 5 percent had been anorexic. All of the women who had been anorexic or bulimic also had a history of compulsive eating and extensive dieting. Of the women, 50 percent were compulsive eaters and dieters (39 percent) or compulsive eaters (11 percent) but had not been bulimic or anorexic.

Two-thirds of the women have had eating problems for more than half of their lives, a finding that contradicts the stereotype of eating problems as transitory. The weight fluctuation among the women varied from 16 to 160 pounds, with an average fluctuation of 74 pounds. This drastic weight change illustrates the degree to which the women adjusted to major changes in body size at least once during their lives as they lost, gained, and lost weight again. The average age of onset was 11 years old, meaning that most of the women developed eating problems prior to puberty. Almost all of the women (88 percent) consider themselves as still having a problem with eating, although the majority believe they are well on the way to recovery.

The Interface of Trauma and Eating Problems

One of the most striking findings in this study was the range of traumas the women associated with the origins of their eating problems, including racism, sexual abuse, poverty, sexism, emotional or physical abuse, heterosexism, class injuries, and acculturation.[2] The particular constellation of eating problems among the women did not vary with race, class, sexuality, or nationality. Women from various race and class backgrounds attributed the origins of their eating problems to sexual abuse, sexism, and emotional and/or physical abuse. Among some of the African-American and Latina women, eating problems were also associated with poverty, racism, and class injuries. Heterosexism was a key factor in the onset of bulimia, compulsive eating, and extensive dieting among some of the lesbians. These oppressions are not the same nor are the injuries caused by them. And certainly, there are a variety of potentially harmful ways that women respond to oppression (such as using drugs, becoming a workaholic, or committing suicide). However, for all these women, eating was a way of coping with trauma.

Sexual Abuse

Sexual abuse was the most common trauma that the women related to the origins of their eating problems. Until recently, there has been virtually no research exploring the possible relationship between these two phenomena. Since the mid-1980s, however, researchers have begun identifying connections between the two, a task that is part of a larger feminist critique of traditional psychoanalytic symptomatology (DeSalvo 1989; Herman 1981; Masson 1984). Results of a number of incidence studies indicate that between one-third and two-thirds of women who have eating problems have been abused (Oppenheimer et al. 1985; Root and Fallon 1988). In addition, a growing number of therapists and researchers have offered interpretations of the meaning and impact of eating problems for survivors of sexual abuse (Bass and Davis 1988; Goldfarb 1987; Iazzetto 1989; Swink and Leveille 1986). Kearney-Cooke (1988) identifies dieting and binging as common ways in which women cope with frequent psychological consequences of sexual abuse (such as body image disturbances, distrust of people and one's own experiences, and confusion about one's feelings). Root and Fallon (1989) specify ways that victimized women cope with assaults by binging and purging: bulimia serves many functions, including anesthetizing the negative feelings associated with victimization. Iazzetto's innovative study (1989), based on in-depth interviews and art therapy sessions, examines how a woman's relationship to her body changes as a consequence of sexual abuse. Iazzetto discovered that the process of leaving the body (through progressive phases of numbing, dissociating, and denying) that often occurs during sexual abuse parallels the process of leaving the body made possible through binging.

Among the women I interviewed, 61 percent were survivors of sexual abuse (11 of the 18 women), most of whom made connections between sexual abuse and the beginning of their eating problems. Binging was the most common method of coping identified by the survivors. Binging helped women "numb out" or anesthetize their feelings. Eating sedated, alleviated anxiety, and combated loneliness. Food was something that they could trust and was accessible whenever they needed it. Antonia (a pseudonym) is an Italian-American woman who was first sexually abused by a male relative when she was four years old. Retrospectively, she knows that binging was a way she coped with the abuse. When the abuse began, and for many years subsequently, Antonia often woke up during the middle of the night with anxiety attacks or nightmares and would go straight to the kitchen cupboards to get food. Binging helped her block painful feelings because it put her back to sleep.

Like other women in the study who began binging when they were very young, Antonia was not always fully conscious as she binged. She described eating during the night as "sleep walking. It was mostly desperate—like I had to have it." Describing why she ate after waking up with nightmares, Antonia said, "What else do you do? If you don't have any coping mechanisms, you eat." She said that binging made her "disappear," which made her feel protected. Like Antonia, most of the women were sexually abused before puberty, four of them before they were five years old. Given their youth, food was the most accessible and socially acceptable drug available to them. Because all of the women endured the psychological consequences alone, it is logical that they coped with tactics they could do alone as well.

One reason Antonia binged (rather than dieted) to cope with sexual abuse is that she saw little reason to try to be the small size girls were supposed to be. Growing up as one of the only Italian Americans in what she described as a "very WASP town," Antonia felt that everything from her weight and size to having dark hair on her upper lip were physical characteristics she was supposed to hide. From a young age she knew she "never embodied the essence of the good girl. I don't like her. I have never acted like her. I can't be her. I sort of gave up." For Antonia, her body was the physical entity that signified her outsider status. When the sexual abuse occurred, Antonia felt she had lost her body. In her mind, the body she lived in after the abuse was not really hers. By the time Antonia was 11, her mother put her on diet pills. Antonia began to eat behind closed doors as she continued to cope with the psychological consequences of sexual abuse and feeling like a cultural outsider.

Extensive dieting and bulimia were also ways in which women responded to sexual abuse. Some women thought that the men had abused them because of their weight. They believed that if they were smaller, they might not have been abused. For example when Elsa, an Argentine woman, was sexually abused at the age of 11, she thought her chubby size was the reason the man was abusing her. Elsa said, "I had this notion that these old perverts liked these plump girls. You heard adults say this too. Sex and flesh being associated." Looking back on her childhood, Elsa believes she made fat the enemy partly due to the shame and guilt she felt about the incest. Her belief that fat was the source of her problems was also supported by her socialization. Raised by strict German governesses in an upper-class family, Elsa was taught that a woman's weight was a primary criterion for judging her worth. Her mother "was socially conscious of walking into places with a fat daughter and maybe people staring at her." Her father often referred to Elsa's body as "shot to hell." When asked to describe how she felt about her body when growing up, Elsa described being completely alienated from her body. She explained,

> Remember in school when they talk about the difference between body and soul? I always felt like my soul was skinny. My soul was free. My soul sort of flew. I was tied down by this big bag of rocks that was my body. I had to drag it around. It did pretty much what it wanted and I had a lot of trouble controlling it. It kept me from doing all the things that I dreamed of.

As is true for many women who have been abused, the split that Elsa described between her body and soul was an attempt to protect herself from the pain she believed her body caused her. In her mind, her fat body was what had "bashed in her dreams." Dieting became her solution, but, as is true for many women in the study, this strategy soon led to cycles of binging and weight fluctuation.

Ruthie, a Puerto Rican woman who was sexually abused from 12 until 16 years of age, described bulimia as a way she responded to sexual abuse. As a child, Ruthie liked her body. Like many Puerto Rican women of her generation, Ruthie's mother did not want skinny children, interpreting that as a sign that they were sick or being fed improperly. Despite her mother's attempts to make her gain weight, Ruthie remained thin through puberty. When a male relative began sexually abusing her, Ruthie's sense of her body changed dramatically. Although she weighed only 100 pounds, she began to feel fat and thought her size was causing the abuse. She had seen a movie on television about Romans who made themselves throw up and so she began doing it, in hopes that she could look like the "little kid" she was before the abuse began. Her symbolic attempt to protect herself by purging stands in stark contrast to the psychoanalytic explanation of eating problems as an "abnormal" repudiation of sexuality. In fact, her actions and those of many other survivors indicate a girl's logical attempt to protect herself (including her sexuality) by being a size and shape that does not seem as vulnerable to sexual assault.

These women's experiences suggest many reasons why women develop eating problems as a consequence of sexual abuse. Most of the survivors "forgot" the sexual abuse after its onset and were unable to retrieve the abuse memories until many years later. With these gaps in memory, frequently they did not know why they felt ashamed, fearful, or depressed. When sexual abuse memories resurfaced in dreams, they often woke feeling upset but could not remember what they had dreamed. These free-floating, unexplained feelings left the women feeling out of control and confused. Binging or focusing on maintaining a new diet were ways women distracted or appeased themselves, in turn, helping them regain a sense of control. As they grew older, they became more conscious of the consequences of these actions. Becoming angry at themselves for binging or promising themselves they would not purge again was a way to direct feelings of shame and self-hate that often accompanied the trauma.

Integral to this occurrence was a transference process in which the women displaced onto their bodies painful feelings and memories that actually derived from or were directed toward the persons who caused the abuse. Dieting became a method of trying to change the parts of their bodies they hated, a strategy that at least initially brought success as they lost weight. Purging was a way women tried to reject the body size they thought was responsible for the abuse. Throwing up in order to lose the weight they thought was making them vulnerable to the abuse was a way to try to find the body they had lost when the abuse began.

Poverty

Like sexual abuse, poverty is another injury that may make women vulnerable to eating problems. One woman I interviewed attributed her eating problems directly to the stress caused by poverty. Yolanda is a Black Cape Verdean mother who began eating compulsively when she was 27 years old. After leaving an abusive husband in her early 20s, Yolanda was forced to go on welfare. As a single mother with small children and few financial resources, she tried to support herself and her children on $539 a month. Yolanda began binging in the evenings after putting her children to bed. Eating was something she could do alone. It would calm her, help her deal with loneliness, and make her feel safe. Food was an accessible commodity that was cheap. She ate three boxes of macaroni and cheese when nothing else was available. As a single mother with little money, Yolanda felt as if her body was the only thing she had left. As she described it,

> I am here, [in my body] 'cause there is no where else for me to go,
> Where am I going to go? This is all I got . . . that probably
> contributes to putting on so much weight cause staying in your
> body, in your home, in yourself, you don't go out. You aren't
> around other people. . . . You hide and as long as you hide you
> don't have to face . . . nobody can see you eat. You are safe.

When she was eating, Yolanda felt a momentary reprieve from her worries. Binging not only became a logical solution because it was cheap and easy but also because she had grown up amid positive messages about eating. In her family, eating was a celebrated and joyful act. However, in adulthood, eating became a double-edged sword. While comforting her, binging also led to weight gain. During the three years Yolanda was on welfare, she gained seventy pounds.

Yolanda's story captures how poverty can be a precipitating factor in eating problems and highlights the value of understanding how class inequalities may shape women's eating problems. As a single mother, her financial constraints mirrored those of most female heads of households. The dual hazards of a race- and sex-stratified labor market further limited her options (Higginbotham 1986). In an article about Black women's health, Byllye Avery (1990) quotes a Black woman's explanation about why she eats compulsively. The woman told Avery,

> I work for General Electric making batteries, and, I know it's killing me. My old man is an alcoholic. My kid's got babies. Things are not well with me. And one thing I know I can do when I come home is cook me a pot of food and sit down in front of the TV and eat it. And you can't take that away from me until you're ready to give me something in its place. (p. 7)

Like Yolanda, this woman identifies eating compulsively as a quick, accessible, and immediately satisfying way of coping with the daily stress caused by conditions she could not control. Connections between poverty and eating problems also show the limits of portraying eating problems as maladies of upper-class adolescent women.

The fact that many women use food to anesthetize themselves, rather than other drugs (even when they gained access to alcohol, marijuana, and other illegal drugs), is partly a function of gender socialization and the competing demands that women face. One of the physiological consequences of binge eating is a numbed state similar to that experienced by drinking. Troubles and tensions are covered over as a consequence of the body's defensive response to massive food intake. When food is eaten in that way, it effectively works like a drug with immediate and predictable effects. Yolanda said she binged late at night rather than getting drunk because she could still get up in the morning, get her children ready for school, and be clearheaded for the college classes she attended. By binging, she avoided the hangover or sickness that results from alcohol or illegal drugs. In this way, food was her drug of choice since it was possible for her to eat while she continued to care for her children, drive, cook, and study. Binging is also less expensive than drinking, a factor that is especially significant for poor women. Another woman I interviewed said that when her compulsive eating was at its height, she ate breakfast after rising in the morning, stopped for a snack on her way to work, ate lunch at three different cafeterias, and snacked at her desk throughout the afternoon. Yet even when her eating had become constant, she was still able to remain employed. While her patterns of eating no doubt slowed her productivity, being drunk may have slowed her to a dead stop.

Heterosexism

The life history interviews also uncovered new connections between heterosexism and eating problems. One of the most important recent feminist contributions has been identifying compulsory heterosexuality as an institution which truncates opportunities for heterosexual and lesbian women (Rich

1986). All of the women interviewed for this study, both lesbian and hetero-sexual, were taught that heterosexuality was compulsory, although the versions of this enforcement were shaped by race and class. Expectations about heterosexuality were partly taught through messages that girls learned about eating and their bodies. In some homes, boys were given more food than girls, especially as teenagers, based on the rationale that girls need to be thin to attract boys. As the girls approached puberty, many were told to stop being athletic, begin wearing dresses, and watch their weight. For the women who weighed more than was considered acceptable, threats about their need to diet were laced with admonitions that being fat would ensure becoming an "old maid."

While compulsory heterosexuality influenced all of the women's emerging sense of their bodies and eating patterns, the women who linked hetero-sexism directly to the beginning of their eating problems were those who knew they were lesbians when very young and actively resisted heterosexual norms. One working-class Jewish woman, Martha, began compulsively eating when she was 11 years old, the same year she started getting clues of her lesbian identity. In junior high school, as many of her female peers began dating boys, Martha began fantasizing about girls, which made her feel utterly alone. Confused and ashamed about her fantasies, Martha came home every day from school and binged. Binging was a way she drugged herself so that being alone was tolerable. Describing binging, she said, "It was the only thing I knew. I was looking for a comfort." Like many women, Martha binged because it softened painful feelings. Binging sedated her, lessened her anxiety, and induced sleep.

Martha's story also reveals ways that trauma can influence women's experience of their bodies. Like many other women, Martha had no sense of herself as connected to her body. When I asked Martha whether she saw herself as fat when she was growing up she said, "I didn't see myself as fat. I didn't see myself. I wasn't there. I get so sad about that because I missed so much." In the literature on eating problems, *body image* is the term that is typically used to describe a woman's experience of her body. This term connotes the act of imagining one's physical appearance. Typically, women with eating problems are assumed to have difficulties with their body image. However, the term *body image* does not adequately capture the complexity and range of bodily responses to trauma experienced by the women. Exposure to trauma did much more than distort the women's visual image of themselves. These traumas often jeopardized their capacity to consider themselves as having bodies at all.

Given the limited connotations of the term *body image,* I use the term *body consciousness* as a more useful way to understand the range of bodily responses to trauma.[3] By body consciousness I mean the ability to reside comfortably in one's body (to see oneself as embodied) and to consider one's body as connected to oneself. The disruptions to their body consciousness that the women described included leaving their bodies, making a split between their body and mind, experiencing being "in" their bodies as painful, feeling unable to control what went in and out of their bodies, hiding in one part of their bodies, or simply not seeing themselves as having bodies. Binging, dieting, or purging were common ways women responded to disruptions to their body consciousness.

Racism and Class Injuries

For some of the Latinas and African-American women, racism coupled with the stress resulting from class mobility related to the onset of their eating problems. Joselyn, an African-American woman, remembered her white grandmother telling her she would never be as pretty as her cousins because they were lighter skinned. Her grandmother often humiliated Joselyn in front of others, as she made fun of Joselyn's body while she was naked and told her she was fat. As a young child, Joselyn began to think that although she could not change her skin color, she could at least try to be thin. When Joselyn was young, her grandmother was the only family member who objected to Joselyn's weight. However, her father also began encouraging his wife and daughter to be thin as the family's class standing began to change. When the family was working class, serving big meals, having chubby children, and keeping plenty of food in the house was a sign the family was doing well. But, as the family became mobile, Joselyn's father began insisting that Joselyn be thin. She remembered, "When my father's business began to bloom and my father was interacting more with white businessmen and seeing how they did business, suddenly thin became important. If you were a truly well-to-do family, then your family was slim and elegant."

As Joselyn's grandmother used Joselyn's body as territory for enforcing her own racism and prejudice about size, Joselyn's father used her body as the territory through which he channeled the demands he faced in the white-dominated business world. However, as Joselyn was pressured to diet, her father still served her large portions and bought treats for her and the neighborhood children. These contradictory messages made her feel confused about her body. As was true for many women in this study, Joselyn was told she was fat beginning when she was very young even though she was not overweight. And, like most of the women, Joselyn was put on diet pills and diets before even reaching puberty, beginning the cycles of dieting, compulsive eating, and bulimia.

The confusion about body size expectations that Joselyn associated with changes in class paralleled one Puerto Rican woman's association between her eating problems and the stress of assimilation as her family's class standing moved from poverty to working class. When Vera was very young, she was so thin that her mother took her to a doctor, who prescribed appetite stimulants. However, by the time Vera was eight years old, her mother began trying to shame Vera into dieting. Looking back on it, Vera attributed her mother's change of heart to competition among extended family members that centered on "being white, being successful, being middle class, . . . and it was always, 'Ay Bendito. She is so fat. What happened?'"

The fact that some of the African-American and Latina women associated the ambivalent messages about food and eating to their family's class mobility and/or the demands of assimilation while none of the eight white women expressed this (including those whose class was stable and changing) suggests that the added dimension of racism was connected to the imperative to be thin. In fact, the class expectations that their parents experienced exacerbated standards about weight that they inflicted on their daughters.

Eating Problems as Survival Strategies

Feminist Theoretical Shifts

My research permits a reevaluation of many assumptions about eating problems. First, this work challenges the theoretical reliance on the culture-of-thinness model. Although all of the women I interviewed were manipulated and hurt by this imperative at some point in their lives, it is not the primary source of their problems. Even in the instances in which a culture of thinness was a precipitating factor in anorexia, bulimia, or binging, this influence occurred in concert with other oppressions.

Attributing the etiology of eating problems primarily to a woman's striving to attain a certain beauty ideal is also problematic because it labels a common way that women cope with pain as essentially appearance-based disorders. One blatant example of sexism is the notion that women's foremost worry is about their appearance. By focusing on the emphasis on slenderness, the eating problems literature falls into the same trap of assuming that the problems reflect women's "obsession" with appearance. Some women were raised in families and communities in which thinness was not considered a criterion for beauty. Yet, they still developed eating problems. Other women were taught that women should be thin, but their eating problems were not primarily in reaction to this imperative. Their eating strategies began as logical solutions to problems rather than problems themselves as they tried to cope with a variety of traumas.

Establishing links between eating problems and a range of oppressions invites a rethinking of both the groups of women who have been excluded from research and those whose lives have been the basis of theory formation. The construction of bulimia and anorexia as appearance-based disorders is rooted in a notion of femininity in which white middle- and upper-class women are portrayed as frivolous, obsessed with their bodies, and overly accepting of narrow gender roles. This portrayal fuels women's tremendous shame and guilt about eating problems—as signs of self-centered vanity. This construction of white middle- and upper-class women is intimately linked to the portrayal of working-class white women and women of color as their opposite: as somehow exempt from accepting the dominant standards of beauty or as one step away from being hungry and therefore not susceptible to eating problems. Identifying that women may binge to cope with poverty contrasts the notion that eating problems are class bound. Attending to the intricacies of race, class, sexuality, and gender pushes us to rethink the demeaning construction of middle-class femininity and establishes bulimia and anorexia as serious responses to injustices.

Understanding the link between eating problems and trauma also suggests much about treatment and prevention. Ultimately, their prevention depends not simply on individual healing but also on changing the social conditions that underlie their etiology. As Bernice Johnson Reagon sings in Sweet Honey in the Rock's song "Oughta Be a Woman," "A way outa no way is too much to ask/too much of a task for any one woman" (Reagon 1980).[4] Making it possible for women to have healthy relationships with their bodies and eating is a comprehensive task. Beginning steps in this direction include ensuring that (1) girls can grow up without being sexually abused, (2) parents have adequate resources to raise their children, (3) children of color grow up free of racism, and (4) young lesbians have the chance to see their reflection in their teachers and community leaders. Ultimately, the prevention of eating problems depends on women's access to economic, cultural, racial, political, social, and sexual justice.

NOTES

Author's Note: The research for this study was partially supported by an American Association of University Women Fellowship in Women's Studies. An earlier version of this article was presented at the New England Women's Studies Association Meeting in 1990 in Kingston, Rhode Island. I am grateful to Margaret Andersen, Liz Bennett, Lynn Davidman, Mary Gilfus, Evelynn Hammonds, and two anonymous reviewers for their comprehensive and perceptive comments on earlier versions of this article. Reprint requests: Becky Wangsgaard Thompson, Dept. of Sociology, Simmons College, 300 The Fenway, Boston, MA 02115.

1. I use the term *eating problems* as an umbrella term for one or more of the following: anorexia, bulimia, extensive dieting, or binging. I avoid using the term *eating disorder* because it categorizes the problems as individual pathologies, which deflects attention away from the social inequalities underlying them (Brown 1985). However, by using the term *problem* I do not wish to imply blame. In fact, throughout, I argue that the eating strategies that women develop begin as logical solutions to problems, not problems themselves.

2. By trauma I mean a violating experience that has long-term emotional, physical, and/or spiritual consequences that may have immediate or delayed effects. One reason the term *trauma* is useful conceptually is its association with the diagnostic label Post Traumatic Stress Disorder (PTSD) (American Psychological Association 1987). PTSD is one of the few clinical diagnostic categories that recognizes social problems (such as war or the Holocaust) as responsible for the symptoms identified (Trimble 1985). This concept adapts well to the feminist assertion that a woman's symptoms cannot be understood as solely individual, considered outside of her social context, or prevented without significant changes in social conditions.

3. One reason the term *consciousness* is applicable is its intellectual history as an entity that is shaped by social context and social structures (Delphy 1984; Marx

1964). This link aptly applies to how the women described their bodies because their perceptions of themselves as embodied (or not embodied) directly relate to their material conditions (living situations, financial resources, and access to social and political power).
4. Copyright © 1980. Used by permission of Songtalk Publishing.

REFERENCES

American Psychological Association. 1987. *Diagnostic and statistical manual of mental disorders.* 3rd ed. rev. Washington, DC: American Psychological Association.

Andersen, Arnold, and Andy Hay. 1985. Racial and socioeconomic influences in anorexia nervosa and bulimia. *International Journal of Eating Disorders* 4:479–87.

Arnold, Georgiana. 1990. Coming home: One Black woman's journey to health and fitness. In *The Black women's health book: Speaking for ourselves,* edited by Evelyn C. White. Seattle, WA: Seal Press.

Avery, Byllye Y. 1990. Breathing life into ourselves: The evolution of the National Black Women's Health Project. In *The Black women's health book: Speaking for ourselves,* edited by Evelyn C. White. Seattle, WA: Seal Press.

Bass, Ellen, and Laura Davis. 1988. *The courage to heal: A guide for women survivors of child sexual abuse.* New York: Harper & Row.

Brown, Laura S. 1985. Women, weight and power: Feminist theoretical and therapeutic issues. *Women and Therapy* 4:61–71.

_____. 1987. Lesbians, weight and eating: New analyses and perspectives. In *Lesbian psychologies,* edited by the Boston Lesbian Psychologies Collective. Champaign: University of Illinois Press.

Chernin, Kim. 1981. *The obsession: Reflections on the tyranny of slenderness.* New York: Harper & Row.

Clarke, Cheryl. 1982. *Narratives.* New Brunswick, NJ: Sister Books.

Copeland, Paul M. 1985. Neuroendocrine aspects of eating disorders. In *Theory and treatment of anorexia nervosa and bulimia: Biomedical sociocultural and psychological perspectives,* edited by Steven Wiley Emmett. New York: Brunner/Mazel.

Delphy, Christine. 1984. *Close to home: A materialist analysis of women's oppression.* Amherst: University of Massachusetts Press.

DeSalvo, Louise. 1989. *Virginia Woolf: The impact of childhood sexual abuse on her life and work.* Boston, MA: Beacon.

Dworkin, Sari H. 1989. Not in man's image: Lesbians and the cultural oppression of body image. In *Loving boldly: Issues facing lesbians,* edited by Ester D. Rothblum and Ellen Cole. New York: Harrington Park Press.

Garfinkel, Paul E., and David M. Garner. 1982. *Anorexia nervosa: A multidimensional perspective.* New York: Brunner/Mazel.

Garner, David. 1985. Iatrogenesis in anorexia nervosa and bulimia nervosa. *International Journal of Eating Disorders* 4:701–26.

Glaser, Barney G., and Anselm L. Strauss. 1967. *The discovery of grounded theory: Strategies for qualitative research.* New York: Aldine DeGruyter.

Goldfarb, Lori. 1987. Sexual abuse antecedent to anorexia nervosa, bulimia and compulsive overeating: Three case reports. *International Journal of Eating Disorders* 6:675–80.

Gray, James, Kathryn Ford, and Lily M. Kelly. 1987. The prevalence of bulimia in a Black college population. *International Journal of Eating Disorders* 6:733–40.

Herman, Judith. 1981. *Father-daughter incest.* Cambridge, MA: Harvard University Press.

Higginbotham, Elizabeth. 1986. We were never on a pedestal: Women of color continue to struggle with poverty, racism and sexism. In *For crying out loud,* edited by Rochelle Lefkowitz and Ann Withorn. Boston, MA: Pilgrim Press.

Hsu, George. 1987. Are eating disorders becoming more common in Blacks? *International Journal of Eating Disorders* 6:113–24.

Iazzetto, Demetria. 1989. When the body is not an easy place to be: Women's sexual abuse and eating problems. Ph.D. diss., Union for Experimenting Colleges and Universities, Cincinnati, Ohio.

Kearney-Cooke, Ann. 1988. Group treatment of sexual abuse among women with eating disorders. *Women and Therapy* 7:5–21.

Marx, Karl. 1964. *The economic and philosophic manuscripts of 1844.* New York: International.

Masson, Jeffrey. 1984. *The assault on the truth: Freud's suppression of the seduction theory.* New York: Farrar, Strauss & Giroux.

Naylor, Gloria. 1985. *Linden Hills.* New York: Ticknor & Fields.

Nevo, Shoshana. 1985. Bulimic symptoms: Prevalence and ethnic differences among college women. *International Journal of Eating Disorders* 4:151–68.

Oppenheimer, R., K. Howells, R. L. Palmer, and D. A. Chaloner. 1985. Adverse sexual experience in childhood and clinical eating disorders: A preliminary description. *Journal of Psychiatric Research* 19:357–61.

Orbach, Susie. 1978. *Fat is a feminist issue.* New York: Paddington.

_____. 1985. Accepting the symptom: A feminist psychoanalytic treatment of anorexia nervosa. In *Handbook of psychotherapy for anorexia nervosa and bulimia,* edited by David M. Garner and Paul E. Garfinkel. New York: Guilford.

Powers, Retha. 1989. Fat is a Black women's issue. *Essence,* Oct., 75, 78, 134, 136.

Reagon, Bernice Johnson. 1980. Oughta be a woman. On Sweet Honey in the Rock's album, *Good News.* Music by Bernice Johnson Reagon; lyrics by June Jordan. Washington, DC: Songtalk.

Rich, Adrienne. 1986. Compulsory heterosexuality and lesbian existence. In *Blood, bread and poetry.* New York: Norton.

Root, Maria P. P., and Patricia Fallon. 1988. The incidence of victimization experiences in a bulimic sample. *Journal of Interpersonal Violence* 3:161–73.

_____. 1989. Treating the victimized bulimic: The functions of binge-purge behavior. *Journal of Interpersonal Violence* 4:90–100.

Russell, Diana E. 1986. *The secret trauma: Incest in the lives of girls and women.* New York: Basic Books.

Schoenfielder, Lisa, and Barbara Wieser, eds. 1983. *Shadow on a tightrope: Writings by women about fat liberation.* Iowa City, IA: Aunt Lute Book Co.

Silber, Tomas. 1986. Anorexia nervosa in Blacks and Hispanics. *International Journal of Eating Disorders* 5:121–28.

Silberstein, Lisa, Ruth Striegel-Moore, and Judith Rodin. 1987. Feeling fat: A woman's shame. In *The role of shame in symptom formation,* edited by Helen Block Lewis. Hillsdale, NJ: Lawrence Erlbaum.

Smead, Valerie. 1984. Eating behaviors which may lead to and perpetuate anorexia nervosa, bulimarexia, and bulimia. *Women and Therapy* 3:37–49.

Spack, Norman. 1985. Medical complications of anorexia nervosa and bulimia. In *Theory and treatment of anorexia nervosa and bulimia: Biomedical sociocultural and psychological perspectives,* edited by Steven Wiley Emmett. New York: Brunner/Mazel.

Swink, Kathy, and Antoinette E. Leveille. 1986. From victim to survivor: A new look at the issues and recovery process for adult incest survivors. *Women and Therapy* 5:119–43.

Trimble, Michael. 1985. Post-traumatic stress disorder: History of a concept. In *Trauma and its wake: The study and treatment of post-traumatic stress disorder,* edited by C. R. Figley. New York: Brunner/Mazel.

What's important is what you look like. 1988. *Gay Community News,* July, 24–30.

White, Evelyn C., ed. 1990. *The Black women's health book: Speaking for ourselves.* Seattle, WA: Seal Press.

_____. 1991. Unhealthy appetites. *Essence,* Sept., 28, 30.

20

JUST WALK ON BY
A Black Man Ponders His Power
to Alter Public Space

BRENT STAPLES

Brent Staples is assistant metropolitan editor of the *New York Times*.

M y first victim was a woman—white, well dressed, probably in her early twenties. I came upon her late one evening on a deserted street in Hyde Park, a relatively affluent neighborhood in an otherwise mean, impoverished section of Chicago. As I swung onto the avenue behind her, there seemed to be a discreet, uninflammatory distance between us. Not so. She cast back a worried glance. To her, the youngish black man— a broad six feet two inches with a beard and billowing hair, both hands shoved into the pockets of a bulky military jacket—seemed menacingly close. After a few more quick glimpses, she picked up her pace and was soon running in earnest. Within seconds she disappeared into a cross street.

That was more than a decade ago. I was 22 years old, a graduate student newly arrived at the University of Chicago. It was in the echo of that terrified woman's footfalls that I first began to know the unwieldy inheritance I'd come into—the ability to alter public space in ugly ways. It was clear that she thought herself the quarry of a mugger, a rapist, or worse. Suffering a bout of insomnia, however, I was stalking sleep, not defenseless wayfarers. As a softy who is scarcely able to take a knife to a raw chicken—let alone hold it to a person's throat—I was surprised, embarrassed, and dismayed all at once. Her flight made me feel like an accomplice in tyranny. It also made it clear that I was indistinguishable from the muggers who occasionally seeped into the area from the surrounding ghetto. That first encounter, and those that followed, signified that a vast, unnerving gulf lay between nighttime pedestrians—particularly women—and me. And I soon gathered that being perceived as dangerous is a hazard in itself. I only needed to turn a corner into a dicey situation, or crowd some frightened, armed person in a foyer somewhere, or make an errant move after being pulled over by a policeman. Where fear and weapons meet—and they often do in urban America—there is always the possibility of death.

Brent Staples, "Just Walk On By: A Black Man Ponders His Power to Alter Public Space" from *Ms.* (September 1986). Reprinted with the permission of the author.

In that first year, my first away from my hometown, I was to become thoroughly familiar with the language of fear. At dark, shadowy intersections in Chicago, I could cross in front of a car stopped at a traffic light and elicit the *thunk, thunk, thunk, thunk* of the driver—black, white, male, female—hammering down the door locks. On less-traveled streets after dark, I grew accustomed to but never comfortable with people who crossed to the other side of the street rather than pass me. Then there were the standard unpleasantries with police, doormen, bouncers, cab drivers, and others whose business it is to screen out troublesome individuals *before* there is any nastiness.

I moved to New York nearly two years ago and I have remained an avid night walker. In central Manhattan, the near-constant crowd cover minimizes tense one-on-one street encounters. Elsewhere—visiting friends in SoHo, where sidewalks are narrow and tightly spaced buildings shut out the sky—things can get very taut indeed.

Black men have a firm place in New York mugging literature. Norman Podhoretz in his famed (or infamous) 1963 essay, "My Negro Problem—And Ours," recalls growing up in terror of black males; they "were tougher than we were, more ruthless," he writes—and as an adult on the Upper West Side of Manhattan, he continues, he cannot constrain his nervousness when he meets black men on certain streets. Similarly, a decade later, the essayist and novelist Edward Hoagland extols a New York where once "Negro bitterness bore down mainly on other Negroes." Where some see mere panhandlers, Hoagland sees "a mugger who is clearly screwing up his nerve to do more than just *ask* for money." But Hoagland has "the New Yorker's quick-hunch posture for broken-field maneuvering," and the bad guy swerves away.

I often witness that "hunch posture," from women after dark on the warrenlike streets of Brooklyn where I live. They seem to set their faces on neutral and, with their purse straps strung across their chests bandolier style, they forge ahead as though bracing themselves against being tackled. I understand, of course, that the danger they perceive is not a hallucination. Women are particularly vulnerable to street violence, and young black males are drastically overrepresented among the perpetrators of that violence. Yet these truths are no solace against the kind of alienation that comes of being ever the suspect, against being set apart, a fearsome entity with whom pedestrians avoid making eye contact.

It is not altogether clear to me how I reached the ripe old age of 22 without being conscious of the lethality nighttime pedestrians attributed to me. Perhaps it was because in Chester, Pennsylvania, the small, angry industrial town where I came of age in the 1960s, I was scarcely noticeable against a backdrop of gang warfare, street knifings, and murders. I grew up one of the good boys, had perhaps a half-dozen fist fights. In retrospect, my shyness of combat has clear sources.

Many things go into the making of a young thug. One of those things is the consummation of the male romance with the power to intimidate. An infant discovers that random flailings send the baby bottle flying out of the crib and crashing to the floor. Delighted, the joyful babe repeats those motions again and again, seeking to duplicate the feat. Just so, I recall the points at which some of my boyhood friends were finally seduced by the perception of themselves as tough guys. When a mark cowered and surrendered his money without resistance, myth and reality merged—and paid off. It is, after all, only manly to embrace the power to frighten and intimidate. We, as men, are not supposed to give an inch of our lane on the highway; we are to seize the fighter's edge in work and in play and even in love; we are to be valiant in the face of hostile forces.

Unfortunately, poor and powerless young men seem to take all this nonsense literally. As a boy, I saw countless tough guys locked away; I have since buried several, too. They were babies, really—a teenage cousin, a brother of 22, a childhood friend in his mid-twenties—all gone down in episodes of bravado played out in the streets. I came to doubt the virtues of intimidation early on. I chose, perhaps even unconsciously, to remain a shadow—timid, but a survivor.

The fearsomeness mistakenly attributed to me in public places often has a perilous flavor. The most frightening of these confusions occurred in the late 1970s and early 1980s when I worked as a journalist in Chicago. One day, rushing into the office of a magazine I was writing for with a deadline story in hand, I was mistaken for a burglar. The office manager called security and, with an ad hoc posse, pursued me through the labyrinthine halls, nearly to my editor's door. I had no way of proving who I was. I could only move briskly toward the company of someone who knew me.

Another time I was on assignment for a local paper and killing time before an interview. I entered a jewelry store on the city's affluent Near North Side. The proprietor excused herself and returned with an enormous red Doberman pinscher straining at the end of a leash. She stood, the dog extended toward me, silent to my questions, her eyes bulging nearly out of her head. I took a cursory look around, nodded, and bade her good night. Relatively speaking, however, I never fared as badly as another black male journalist. He went to nearby Waukegan, Illinois, a couple of summers ago to work on a story about a murderer who was born there. Mistaking the reporter for the killer, police hauled him from his car at gunpoint and but for his press credentials would have tried to book him. Such episodes are not uncommon. Black men trade tales like this all the time.

In "My Negro Problem—And Ours," Podhoretz writes that the hatred he feels for blacks makes itself known to him through a variety of avenues—one being his discomfort with that "special brand of paranoid touchiness" to which he says blacks are prone. No doubt he is speaking here of black men. In time, I learned to smother the rage I felt at so often being taken for a criminal. Not to do so would surely have led to madness—via that special "paranoid touchiness" that so annoyed Podhoretz at the time he wrote the essay.

I began to take precautions to make myself less threatening. I move about with care, particularly late in the evening. I give a wide berth to nervous people on the subway platforms during the wee hours, particularly when I have exchanged business clothes for jeans. If I happen to be entering a building behind some people who appear skittish, I may walk by, letting them clear the lobby before I return, so as not to seem to be following them. I have been calm and extremely congenial on those rare occasions when I've been pulled over by the police.

And on late-evening constitutionals along streets less traveled by, I employ what has proved to be an excellent tension-reducing measure: I whistle melodies from Beethoven and Vivaldi and the more popular classical composers. Even steely New Yorkers hunching toward nighttime destinations seem to relax, and occasionally they even join in the tune. Virtually everybody seems to sense that a mugger wouldn't be warbling bright, sunny selections from Vivaldi's *Four Seasons*. It is my equivalent of the cowbell that hikers wear when they know they are in bear country.

21

TAKING IT

LEONARD KRIEGEL

Leonard Kriegel, author of the novel *Quitting Time* and of the collection of essays *Falling,* is a professor of English and director of the Center for Worker Education at the City University of New York.

In 1944, at the age of eleven, I had polio. I spent the next two years of my life in an orthopedic hospital, appropriately called a reconstruction home. By 1946, when I returned to my native Bronx, polio had reconstructed me to the point that I walked very haltingly on steel braces and crutches.

But polio also taught me that, if I were to survive, I would have to become a man—and become a man quickly. "Be a man!" my immigrant father urged, by which he meant "become an American." For, in 1946, this country had very specific expectations about how a man faced adversity. Endurance, courage, determination, stoicism—these might right the balance with fate.

"I couldn't take it, and I took it," says the wheelchair-doomed poolroom entrepreneur William Einhorn in Saul Bellow's *The Adventures of Augie*

Leonard Kriegel, "Taking It" from *The New York Times Magazine* (1995). Copyright © 1995 by The New York Times Company. Reprinted with permission.

March. "And I *can't* take it, yet I do take it." In 1953, when I first read these words, I knew that Einhorn spoke for me—as he spoke for scores of other men who had confronted the legacy of a maiming disease by risking whatever they possessed of substance in a country that believed that such risks were a man's wagers against his fate.

How one faced adversity was, like most of American life, in part a question of gender. Simply put, a woman endured, but a man fought back. You were better off struggling against the effects of polio as a man than as a woman, for polio was a disease that one confronted by being tough, aggressive, decisive, by assuming that all limitations could be overcome, beaten, conquered. In short, by being "a man." Even the vocabulary of rehabilitation was masculine. One "beat" polio by outmuscling the disease. At the age of eighteen, I felt that I was "a better man" than my friends because I had "overcome a handicap." And I had, in the process, showed that I could "take it." In the world of American men, to take it was a sign that you were among the elect—an assumption my "normal" friends shared. "You're lucky," my closest friend said to me during an intensely painful crisis in his own life. "You had polio." He meant it. We both believed it.

Obviously, I wasn't lucky. By nineteen, I was already beginning to understand—slowly, painfully, but inexorably—that disease is never "conquered" or "overcome." Still, I looked upon resistance to polio as the essence of my manhood. As an American, I was self-reliant. I could create my own possibilities from life. And so I walked mile after mile on braces and crutches. I did hundreds of push-ups every day to build my arms, chest, and shoulders. I lifted weights to the point that I would collapse, exhausted but strengthened, on the floor. And through it all, my desire to create a "normal" life for myself was transformed into a desire to become the man my disease had decreed I should be.

I took my heroes where I found them—a strange, disparate company of men: Hemingway, whom I would write of years later as "my nurse"; Peter Reiser, whom I dreamed of replacing in Ebbets Field's pastures and whose penchant for crashing into outfield walls fused in my mind with my own war against the virus; Franklin Delano Roosevelt, who had scornfully faced polio with aristocratic disdain and patrician distance (a historian acquaintance recently disabused me of that myth, a myth perpetrated, let me add, by almost all of Roosevelt's biographers); Henry Fonda and Gary Cooper, in whose resolute Anglo-Saxon faces Hollywood blended the simplicity, strength and courage a man needed if he was going to survive as a man; any number of boxers in whom heart, discipline and training combined to stave off defeats the boy's limitations made inevitable. These were the "manly" images I conjured up as I walked those miles of Bronx streets, as I did those relentless push-ups, as I moved up and down one subway staircase after another by turning each concrete step into a personal insult. And they were still the images when, fifteen years later, married, the father of two sons of my own, a Fulbright professor in the Netherlands, I would grab hold of vertical poles in a train in The Hague and swing my brace-bound body across the dead space between platform and carriage, filled with self-congratulatory vanity as amazement spread over the features of the Dutch conductor.

It is easy to dismiss such images as adolescent. Undoubtedly they were. But they helped remind me, time and time again, of how men handled their diseases and their pain. Of course, I realized even then that it was not the idea of manhood alone that had helped me fashion a life out of polio. I might write of Hemingway as "my nurse," but it was an immigrant Jewish mother—already transformed into a cliché by scores of male Jewish writers—who serviced my crippled body's needs and who fed me love, patience and care even as I fed her the rhetoric of my rage.

But it was the need to prove myself an American man—tough, resilient, independent, able to take it—that pulled me through the war with the virus. I have, of course, been reminded again and again of the price extracted for such ideas about manhood. And I am willing to admit that my sons may be better off in a country in which "manhood" will mean little more than, say, the name for an after-shave lotion. It is forty years since my war with the virus began. At fifty-one, even an American man knows that mortality is the only legacy and defeat the only guarantee. At fifty-one, my legs still encased in braces and crutches still beneath my shoulders, my elbows are increasingly arthritic from all those streets walked and weights lifted and stairs climbed. At fifty-one, my shoulders burn with pain from all those push-ups done so relentlessly. And at fifty-one, pain merely bores—and hurts.

Still, I remain an American man. If I know where I'm going, I know, too, where I have been. Best of all, I know the price I have paid. A man endures his diseases until he recognizes in them his vanity. He can't take it, but he takes it. Once, I relished my ability to take it. Now I find myself wishing that taking it were easier. In such quiet surrenders do we American men call it quits with our diseases.

22

DO YOU REMEMBER ME?

BARBARA MACDONALD

Barbara MacDonald was an Anglo-European lesbian feminist theorist and lecturer who died at age 86 in June 2000. *Look Me in the Eye: Old Women, Aging, and Ageism* (Spinsters Ink, 1983) has recently appeared in an expanded edition (2001).

I am less than five feet high and except that I may have shrunk a quarter of an inch or so in the past few years, I have viewed the world from this height for sixty-five years. I have taken up some space in the world; I weigh about a hundred and forty pounds and my body is what my mother used to call dumpy. My mother didn't like her body and so of course didn't like mine. My mother was not always rational and her judgment was further impaired because she was a recluse, but the "dumpy" was her word, and just as I have had to keep the body, somehow I have had to keep the word— thirty-eight-inch bust, no neck, no waistline, fat hips—that's dumpy.

My hair is grey, white at the temples, with only a little of the red cast of earlier years showing through. My face is wrinkled and deeply lined. Straight lines have formed on the upper lip as though I had spent many years with my mouth pursed. This has always puzzled me and I wonder what years those were and why I can't remember them. My face has deep lines that extend from each side of the nose down the face past the corners of my mouth. My forehead is wide and the lines across my forehead and between my eyes are there to testify that I was often puzzled and bewildered for long periods of time about what was taking place in my life. My cheekbones are high and become more noticeably so as my face is drawn further and further down. My chin is small for such a large head and below the chin the skin hangs in a loose vertical fold from my chin all the way down to my neck where it meets a horizontal scar. The surgeon who made the scar said that the joints of my neck were worn out from looking up so many years. For all kinds of reasons, I seldom look up to anyone or anything anymore.

My eyes are blue and my gaze is usually steady and direct. But I look away when I am struggling with some nameless shame, trying to disclaim parts of myself. My voice is low and my speech sometimes clipped and rapid if I am uncomfortable; otherwise I have a pleasant voice. I like the sound of it from in here where I am. When I was younger, some people, lovers mostly, enjoyed my singing, but I no longer have the same control of my voice and sing only occasionally now when I am alone.

My hands are large and the backs of my hands begin to show the brown spots of aging. Sometimes lately, holding my arms up reading in bed or lying with my arms clasped around my lover's neck, I see my own arms with the skin hanging loosely from my own forearm and cannot believe that the arm I see is really my own. It seems disconnected from me; it is someone else's, it is the arm of an old woman. It is the arm of such old women as I myself have seen, sitting on benches in the sun with their hands folded in their laps; old women I have turned away from. I wonder now, how and when these arms I see came to be my own—arms I cannot turn away from. . . .

The truth is I like growing old. Oh, it isn't that I don't feel at moments the sharp irrevocable knowledge that I have finally grown old. That is evident every time I stand in front of the bathroom mirror and brush my teeth. I may begin as I often do, wondering if those teeth that are so much a part of myself, teeth I've clenched in anger all my life, felt with my own tongue with a feeling of possession, as a cat licks her paw lovingly just because it is hers—wondering, will these teeth always be mine? Will they stay with me loyally and die with me, or will they desert me before the Time comes? But I grow dreamy brushing my teeth and find myself, unaware, planning as I always have when I brush my teeth—that single-handed crossing I plan to make. From East to West, a last stop in the Canaries and then the trade winds. What will be the best time of year? What boat? How much sail? I go over again the list of supplies, uninterrupted until some morning twinge in my left shoulder reminds me with uncompromising regret that I will never make that single-handed crossing—probably. That I have waited too long. That there is no turning back.

But I always say probably. Probably I'll never make that single-handed crossing. Probably, I've waited too long. Probably, I can't turn back now. But I leave room now, at sixty-five, for the unexpected. That was not always true of me. I used to feel I was in a kind of linear race with life and time. There were no probablies; it was a now or never time of my life. There were landmarks placed by other generations and I had to arrive on time or fail in the whole race. If I didn't pass—if the sixth grade went on to the seventh without me, I would be one year behind for the rest of my life. If I graduated from high school in 1928, I had to graduate from college in 1932. When I didn't graduate from college until 1951, it took me twenty years to realize the preceding twenty years weren't lost. But now I begin to see that I may get to have the whole thing and that no experience longed for is really going to be missed.

"I like growing old." I say it to myself with surprise. I had not thought that it could be like this. There are days of excitement when I feel almost a kind of high with the changes I feel taking place in my body, even though I know the inevitable course my body is taking will lead to debilitation and death. I say to myself frequently in wonder, "This is my body doing this thing." I cannot stop it, I don't even know what it is doing, I wouldn't know how to direct it; my own body is going through a process that only my body knows about. I never grew old before; never died before. I don't really know how it's done, I wouldn't know where to begin, and God knows, I certainly wouldn't know when to begin—for no time would be right. And then I realize, lesbian or straight, I belong to all the women who carried my cells for generations and my body remembers how for each generation this matter of ending is done.

Cynthia tells me now about being a young girl, watching and enjoying what her body was doing in preparation for her life. Seeing her breasts develop, watching the cleft disappear behind a cushion of dark pubic hair, discovering her own body making a bright red stain, feeling herself and seeing herself in the process of becoming.

When I was young, I watched this process with dread, seeing my breasts grow larger and larger and my hips widen. I was never able to say, "This is my body doing this wonderful unknown thing." I felt fear with every visible change, I felt more exposed, more vulnerable to attack. My swelling breasts, my widening hips, my growing pubic hair and finally the visible bleeding wound, all were acts of violence against my person, and could only bring me further acts of violence. I never knew in all the years of living in my woman's body that other women had found any pleasure in that early body experience, until Cynthia told me. But now, after a lifetime of living, my body has taken over again. I have this second chance to feel my body living out its own plan, to watch it daily change in the direction of its destiny. . . .

I wanted a different body when I was young. I have lived in this body for sixty-five years. "It is a good body, it is mine."

I wanted another mother and another beginning when I was young. I wanted a mother who liked herself, who liked her body and so would like mine. "My mother did not like herself and she did not like me; that is part of the definition of who she was and of who I am. She was my mother."

When I was fifty-two, my lover left me after fourteen years of living our lives together. I wanted her to return. I waited for many years and she did not come back. "I am the woman whose lover did not return."

I was lonely for years of my life and I wandered in search of a lover. "I am a person who loves again. I am a woman come home."

So often we think we know how an experience is going to end so we don't risk the pain of seeing it through to the end. We think we know the outcome so we think there is no need to experience it, as though to anticipate an ending were the same as living the ending out. We drop the old and take up the new—drop an idea and take up a new one—drop the middle-aged and old and start concentrating on the young, always thinking somehow it's going to turn out better with a new start. I have never had a child, but sometimes I see a young woman beginning to feel the urge to have a child at about the same time she feels some disappointment at how her own life is turning out. And soon the young mother feels further disappointment when her own mother withdraws her loving investment in her daughter to pour it into her grandchild. I see how all are devalued, the grandmother devalued by society, devalued by her own self, the daughter devalued by her mother, and the granddaughter, valued not for who she is but for who she may become, racing for the landmarks, as I once did.

We never really know the beginning or the middle, until we have lived out an ending and lived on beyond it.

Of course, this time, for me, I am not going to live beyond this ending. The strangeness of that idea comes to me at the most unexpected moments and always with surprise and shock; sometimes I am immobilized by it. Standing before the mirror in the morning, I feel that my scalp is tight. I see that the skin hangs beneath my jaw, beneath my arm; my breasts are pulled low against my body; loose skin hangs from my hips, and below my stomach a new horizontal crease is forming over which the skin will hang like the hem of a skirt turned under. A hem not to be "let down," as once my skirts were, because I was "shooting up," but a widening hem to "take up" on an old garment that has been stretched. Then I see that my body is being drawn into the earth—muscle, tendon, tissue and skin is being drawn down by the earth's pull back to the loam. She is pulling me back to herself; she is taking back what is hers.

Cynthia loves bulbs. She digs around in the earth every fall, looking for the rich loamy mold of decayed leaves and vegetation, and sometimes as she takes a sack of bone meal and works it into the damp earth, I think, "Why not mine? Why not?"

I think a lot about being drawn into the earth. I have the knowledge that one day I will fall and the earth will take back what is hers. I have no choice, yet I choose it. Maybe I won't buy that boat and that list of supplies; maybe I will. Maybe I will be able to write about my life; maybe I won't. But uncertainty will not always be there, for this is like no other experience I have ever had—I can count on it. I've never had anything before that I could really count on. My life has been filled with uncertainties, some were not of my making and many were: promises I made myself I did not keep, promises I made others I did not keep, hopes I could not fulfill, shame carried like a weight heavier by the years, at my failure, at my lack of clear purpose. But this time I can rely on myself, for life will keep her promise to me. I can trust her. She isn't going to confuse me with a multitude of other choices and beckon me down other roads with vague promises. She will give me finally only one choice, one road, one sense of possibility. And in exchange for the multitude of choices she no longer offers, she gives me, at last, certainty. Nor do I have to worry this time that I will fail myself, fail to pull it off. This time, for sure I am going to make that single-handed crossing.

23

I'M NOT FAT, I'M LATINA

CHRISTY HAUBEGGER

Christy Haubegger, a Mexican-American native of Houston, attended the University of Texas at Austin and received a B.A. in philosophy. She attended Stanford
Law School and was president of her class. Frustrated with the lack of positive
media portrayal of Latinas in the United States, she put her law degree under her
bed to pursue the entrepreneurial venture of creating a magazine for women like
herself. Essence magazine and Alegre Enterprises, of which Haubegger is the chief
executive officer, formed a new joint venture, Latina Publications, to publish *Latina*
magazine, the first bilingual lifestyle magazine for Latinas in the United States.

I recently read a newspaper article that reported that nearly 40 percent of
Hispanic and African-American women are overweight. At least I'm in
good company. Because according to even the most generous height and
weight charts at the doctor's office, I'm a good 25 pounds overweight. And
I'm still looking for the panty-hose chart that has me on it (according to
Hanes, I don't exist). But I'm happy to report that in the Latino community,
my community, I fit right in.

Latinas in this country live in two worlds. People who don't know us
may think we're fat. At home, we're called *bien cuidadas* (well cared for).

I love to go dancing at Cesar's Latin Palace here in the Mission District
of San Francisco. At this hot all-night salsa club, it's the curvier bodies like
mine that turn heads. I'm the one on the dance floor all night while some of
my thinner friends spend more time waiting along the walls. Come to think
of it, I wouldn't trade my body for any of theirs.

But I didn't always feel this way. I remember being in high school and
noticing that none of the magazines showed models in bathing suits with
bodies like mine. Handsome movie heroes were never hoping to find a
chubby damsel in distress. The fact that I had plenty of attention from Latino
boys wasn't enough. Real self-esteem cannot come from male attention alone.

My turning point came a few years later. When I was in college, I made
a trip to Mexico, and I brought back much more than sterling-silver bargains
and colorful blankets.

I remember hiking through the awesome ruins of the Maya and the
Aztecs, civilizations that created pyramids as large as the ones in Egypt. I

loved walking through temple doorways whose clearance was only two inches above my head, and I realized that I must be a direct descendant of those ancient priestesses for whom those doorways had originally been built.

For the first time in my life, I was in a place where people like me were the beautiful ones. And I began to accept, and even like, the body that I have.

I know that medical experts say that Latinas are twice as likely as the rest of the population to be overweight. And yes, I know about the health problems that often accompany severe weight problems. But most of us are not in the danger zone; we're just bien cuidadas. Even the researchers who found that nearly 40 percent of us are overweight noted that there is a greater "cultural acceptance" of being overweight within Hispanic communities. But the article also commented on the cultural-acceptance factor as if it were something unfortunate, because it keeps Hispanic women from becoming healthier. I'm not so convinced that we're the ones with the problem.

If the medical experts were to try and get to the root of this so-called problem, they would probably find that it's part genetics, part enchiladas. Whether we're Cuban-American, Mexican-American, Puerto Rican or Dominican, food is a central part of Hispanic culture. While our food varies from fried plaintains to tamales, what doesn't change is its role in our lives. You feed people you care for, and so if you're well cared for, *bien cuidada,* you have been fed well.

I remember when I used to be envious of a Latina friend of mine who had always been on the skinny side. When I confided this to her a while ago, she laughed. It turns out that when she was growing up, she had always wanted to look more like me. She had trouble getting dates with Latinos in high school, the same boys that I dated. When she was little, the other kids in the neighborhood had even given her a cruel nickname: la seca, "the dry one." I'm glad I never had any of those problems.

Our community has always been accepting of us well-cared-for women. So why don't we feel beautiful? You only have to flip through a magazine or watch a movie to realize that beautiful for most of this country still means tall, blond and underfed. But now we know it's the magazines that are wrong. I, for one, am going to do what I can to make sure that *mis hijas,* my daughters, won't feel the way I did.

24

THE TYRANNY OF THE ESTHETIC
Surgery's Most Intimate Violation

MARTHA COVENTRY

Martha Coventry, when asked by a photographer what culture she came from that would clitoridectomize its daughters, laughed and answered, "WASP culture." A middle-aged midwestern mother of two daughters, Coventry writes and speaks about intersexuality in order to change a world that treats different bodies as wrong bodies.

Big clitorises aren't allowed in America. By big, I mean over three-eighths of an inch for newborns, about the size of a pencil eraser. Tiny penises, under one inch, aren't allowed either.[1] A big clitoris is considered too capable of becoming alarmingly erect, and a tiny penis is not quite capable enough. Such genitals are confounding to the strictly maintained and comforting social order in America today, which has everyone believing that bodies come in only two ways: perfectly female and perfectly male. But genitals are surprisingly ambiguous. At least one out of every 2,000 babies is born with genitals that don't elicit the automatic "It's a girl!" or "It's a boy!"[2] Many more have genitals that are perceived as "masculinized" or "feminized," although the child's sex is not in doubt.

The American Academy of Pediatrics recommends surgically altering these children between the ages of six weeks and 15 months to fashion their bodies into something closer to perfection.[3] Everyone can then breathe easier, except for the child, who may well spend the rest of her or his life trying to let the breath flow easy and full through the fear and shame created by such devastating surgery.

On a November night in 1958, I was playing in the bathtub in the cheery, country home of my childhood. I was six years old. My mother came in and sat on the edge of the tub, her kind face looking worried. I glanced up at her, wondering, "Time to get out so soon?" She told me that I had to go to the hospital the next day for an operation. I knew this was about something between my legs. My chest felt tight and there was a rushing sound in my ears. I begged not to go. Please. But my mother told me only that I must. Not a word was said about what was going to happen or why. The next day, it took the surgeon 30 minutes to make a U-shaped incision around my half-inch clitoris,

Martha Coventry, "The Tyranny of the Esthetic: Surgery's Most Intimate Violation" from *On the Issues* (Summer 1998). Reprinted with the permission of the author.

remove it, and put it in a specimen dish to send to the lab. He then closed the wound and stitched the skin up over the stump.

Take no comfort in the fact that this took place 40 years ago. Today, most parents and doctors in this country are still unable to see that a child has a right to her or his own sexual body, even if that body is deemed "abnormal" by their standards. If a parent is uncomfortable, a doctor can be found who will be willing to make irreversible changes in the child's body, in order to ease that discomfort. My gynecologist told me about a case in which he had been involved the year before: A woman brought her five-year-old daughter to his office in Minneapolis; the mother felt that the child's clitoris was too big. He examined the girl and assured the mother that her daughter would grow into her clitoris, which was no longer than the end of his little finger. The mother left. A few weeks later, he was called into an operating room to help another doctor who had run into trouble during a surgical procedure. On the table, he found the same little girl he had seen earlier. She was hemorrhaging from a clitorectomy attempted by the second doctor, from instructions he had read in a medical text. My physician stopped the bleeding, and managed to keep the girl's clitoris mostly intact.

It is not new in our culture to remove or alter the clitoris. Not so long ago, such surgery was commonly practiced to prevent masturbation and "unnatural sexual appetites." Although such justifications still lurk in the minds of parents and doctors ("Won't she become a lesbian?" is a concern of many mothers whose daughters have big clitorises), clitorectomies gained new status toward the end of the 1950s, as a "legitimate" way to make a child with atypical genitals feel and appear more normal. Surgical techniques learned during World War II led to advances in the field of cosmetic genital surgery; at about the same time, a new medical discipline—endocrinology, the study of the hormonal system—was established at Johns Hopkins University Medical School. A child's body could now be successfully altered by surgery and hormones to look just about any way you wanted it to look. And the controversial research into sex and gender roles by Johns Hopkins' John Money, Ph.D., led doctors to believe that by changing that body, you could make the child into a "normal" male or female, both physically and psychologically. Children could be made "right" if they were born "wrong." And American medicine, and our society at large, sees "imperfect" genitals as wrong.

That view is challenged by farsighted pediatric urologist Justine Schober, M.D., of Erie, Penn.: "Why should we say that, because this is a variation, that it is a wrong variation? If all their faculties work, their sexual sensitivities work, why should we presume that their body is wrong?"[4] But by seeing a child's body as wrong and by labeling such a child "intersexed," we turn a simple variation on a theme into a problem that can and should be fixed. And fixed it usually is, by surgery that sacrifices healthy erotic tissue for cosmetic reasons some five times a day in the U.S. The rules of the game are still the same as they were 40 years ago: Erase any sign of difference, tidy things up, and don't say another word.

After I had my clitorectomy, my innocent life became filled with fear and guilt. The secrecy surrounding my surgery began to undermine my entire sense of identity. I knew I had something between my legs cut off, and I could imagine only that it was a penis. Girls were Barbie-doll smooth, so there wasn't anything on a girl to cut off. Was I really a boy? Or perhaps the horrible thing I had somehow known about forever: hermaphrodite? The study of my father, a physician, was full of medical books, but I flipped through them quickly, drawn to the pictures of children with their eyes blacked out, knowing there was something we shared, yet terrified to find out what kind of freak I really was. Then, one night when I was 11 or 12, I found my parents, as they sat around the dining room table, looking at studio pictures of my sisters and me. My mother held up my photo and I heard her say the word "boy." My gut heaved. I was a boy. It was true. I blurted out, "What was that operation I had?" My father turned to me and said, "Don't be so self-examining." I never had the heart to tell this man who loved me so dearly that, by keeping the truth from me that night, by trying to protect me from my own wondering mind and wandering hands, he had sentenced me to a life of almost crippling fear in relation to my sexuality, even to a profound doubt of my right to be alive.

It would be 25 years before I could begin to start asking questions again. When I finally pressed my dying father as gently as I could for a reason why he and my mother wanted my clitoris removed, he said, "We didn't want you to be mistaken for a hermaphrodite." My father was a surgeon. No doctor had patronizingly spun to him tales of "improperly formed gonads," or lied to him about my medical condition, or told him I would become a lesbian if I had a big clitoris, or pretended that no other children like me existed. Just having a child with an abnormal body in Rochester, Minn., was bad enough for my parents. But doctors do lie—to parents and to children, in a gross insult to their intelligence and their right to the truth. Lying to children is a rule strictly adhered to, and enforced, by all but the most enlightened doctors. First, the surgery steals your body from you, then lies confirm that there is so little respect for you as a human being that you don't even deserve the truth.

X Marks the . . . .

Angela Moreno was a happy child growing up in the late seventies in Peoria, Ill. She was fairly sexually precocious with herself, and became very familiar with her clitoris: "I loved it, but had no name for it. I remember being amazed that there was a part of my body that was so intensely pleasurable. It felt wonderful under my hand. There was no fantasy, just pleasure—just me and my body." Life in the pleasure garden came to an abrupt end for Angela when, at age 12, her mother noticed her protruding clitoris while Angela was toweling off after a bath. After being examined by the family doctor, she was sent to an endocrinologist. The endocrinologist revealed to her parents that, instead of the two X chromosomes that characterize the female genotype, Angela had an X and a Y. She was "genetically male." She had the external genitalia of a female because the receptors for the "male" hormone testosterone did not function; that is, her body was unable to respond to the androgenizing or masculinizing hormones it produced. Her parents were assured that if surgeons removed Angela's internal testes, and shortened her clitoris, she would be a "very normal little girl," albeit one born without ovaries or a uterus. This was lie number one.

Just because your body may look "normal" is no guarantee that you will feel that way. The truth is that the very thing surgery claims to save us from — a sense of differentness and abnormality — it quite unequivocally creates.

Doctors then told Angela's parents that if she didn't have surgery she might kill herself when she found out that she was different from other girls. It had happened to another patient, the physicians said, and it could happen to Angela. Although such speculation is not a lie, it is also not the whole truth. In my talks with scores of people with atypical genitals, it is those who have been surgically altered as children and left alone with their trauma who most often become suicidal. The isolation from others who have experienced what we are going through, the loneliness, is what kills us. Angela's parents were justifiably frightened and agreed to the surgery.

The final lie was to Angela herself, with her distraught parents' complicity. She was told, at her physician's suggestion, that her nonexistent ovaries could become cancerous and that she would have to go into the hospital and have them removed.

In 1985, at a leading children's hospital in Chicago, doctors removed the testes from Angela's abdomen. The clitoris that had brought her so much joy was not merely shortened, it was all but destroyed. She woke up and discovered the extent of her deceit: "I put my hand down there and felt something like the crusty top of some horrible casserole, like dried caked blood where my clitoris was. I wondered why no one told me and I just figured it was the kind of thing decent people don't talk about."

Angela became depressed and severely bulimic. "I blamed my body. My body had betrayed me. Made me someone worthy of that kind of treatment. I just studied and puked." She was a straight-A student in high school, but otherwise, her adolescence was a nightmare. She avoided becoming close to other girls her age, afraid she would be asked questions about the menstrual period she knew she would never have. The uncomplicated sexuality she had reveled in before the clitorectomy was gone, and she was desolated by the loss of erotic sensation. In an attempt to find out the truth, she returned to her original endocrinologist, who told her that her gonads had not formed properly, and her clitoris had grown because of an abnormal level of hormones. She did not tell Angela about her XY status or her testes. Angela fell deeper into darkness, sensing that she had not been given the whole story. Finally, at 20, weakened by chronic and near-lethal bingeing and purging, and suicidal, she checked herself into a psychiatric unit.

After her release, she began seeing a therapist who finally hit on the connection between her bulimia and the control she lost over her body at the time of surgery. Angela knew she had to find out the mystery of her body in order to get well. By now she was 23 and could legally obtain her medical records, yet it took a year for her to find the courage to write for them. When she received them and read the truth about herself, she could begin at last to save her own life. "Although the doctors had claimed that knowing the truth would make me self-destructive, it was *not* knowing what had been done to me—and why—that made me want to die."

In my case, I have XX chromosomes, and my outsized clitoris was the only part of my body that was not like that of most other girls.

Do these facts make you want to differentiate me from Angela? To say, "Wait a minute. You were simply a girl born with a big clitoris, but Angela had a real pathological condition." But the doctors removed Angela's clitoris for exactly the same reason they removed mine—they thought it offensively large. Her chromosomes and her abdominal testes had no bearing on the decision.

If you rush to see Angela as fundamentally different from me, if you see her as a real intersexual and me as just a normal woman, you do two very damaging things: You may see it as justified to perform cosmetic surgery on her and not on me because she really is "abnormal," and you separate us from each other and deny our right to find solace and strength in the sameness of our experience.

The doctor who was kind enough to help me begin to explore my early surgery did just that to me. I found the Intersex Society of North America on my own several months after my initial visit with him, and told him later how healing it had been to find others who knew intimately what my life had been like.[5] He had known about ISNA all along, he said, but didn't pass the information on to me because I was not intersexed. I was a real woman. He had tried to save me from a pathologizing label, but ended up enforcing my isolation instead.

New and Improved?

When a baby is born today with genitals that are ambiguous, a team of surgeons, pediatric endocrinologists, and social workers scramble to relieve what is called a "psychosocial emergency." Tests are done and orifices explored to determine as nearly as possible the baby's "true sex." Then, in almost all cases, doctors perform surgery to make the child look more like a girl, because, they say, the surgery required is easier to perform than trying to make the child look like a boy.

The form this feminizing surgery most often takes is the dissection and removal of healthy clitoral tissue—a clitorectomy, also known as "clitoral recession," "clitoral reduction," and "clitoroplasty." Sensitive, erectile tissue is stripped away from the shaft of the clitoris, and the glans is tucked away so expertly that all you see is the cute little love button that is the idealized clitoris.

But the pleasure is almost gone, or gone completely, for the owner of that dainty new clit. If orgasms are possible, and they aren't for many women subjected to clitoral surgery, the intensity is greatly diminished. One woman whose clitoris was "recessed" writes: "If orgasms before the recession were a deep purple, now they are a pale, watery pink."[6]

Doctors maintain that modern surgery retains more clitoral sensation than the older forms of surgery, but they base their assurance on nerve impulses measured by machines — supposedly accurate and unbiased information — and not the real experience of thousands and thousands of women in this country. This is because no long-term post-surgical studies have been done. I, who had the old-style surgery, have clitoral sensation and orgasmic function, while those subjected to more modern surgeries often have neither. How much do doctors truly care about a child's sexual future if they decimate the one organ in the body designed solely for pleasure?

In 1965, Annie Green, then three years old, took a car trip with her father from the small town in Idaho where she lived to Spokane, Wash. She sat in the back seat with her stuffed animal, unaware that she was on her way to the hospital. The next day doctors removed her inch-long clitoris. She was never given any explanation of her surgery. As she got older, her attempts to find pleasure in masturbation failed, and she began to suspect she was very different from other girls. Then, during a visit to her sister's house as a teenager, she found the book *Our Bodies, Ourselves:* "I studied the female anatomy and read about sex from that book. That was when I learned I didn't have a clitoris. I remember looking at the diagram, feeling myself, and reading what a clitoris was over and over. My God, I couldn't figure out why I didn't have one. I couldn't fathom anyone removing it if it was that important. I was stunned, and I held it all in. I was only 14. I became depressed. I was disgusted with my body, and I thought there was no hope that I would ever be loved by anyone. I became a little teenage alcoholic. I drank heavily every weekend. I really blew it because I had been a really good athlete and an honor student."

Clitoral surgery on children is brutal and illogical, and no matter what name you give it, it is a mutilation. When I use the word mutilation, I can hear doors slamming shut in the minds of doctors all over this country. John Gearhart, a pediatric urologist at Johns Hopkins, has said, "To compare genital mutilation of young girls in Africa to reconstructive surgery of a young baby is a giant, giant leap of misrepresentation."[7] But neither Dr. Gearhart, nor anyone else, has ever bothered to ask those of us subjected to clitoral surgery as children if being taken to the hospital without explanation, having your healthy genitals cut and scarred, then left alone with the results feels like mutilation or "reconstructive surgery." Gearhart's mistake is to judge surgery only by the surgeon's intent and not by the effect on the child. I spoke with a woman recently who is young enough to be my daughter. With great effort, she told me of her clitoral surgery as a child. She implored me, "Why do they have to cut so deep, Martha? Why do they do that?"

Of the notable feminist voices raised long and loud in outrage over traditional genital surgeries practiced in parts of Africa, which are now denounced as "female genital mutilation" (FGM), not a single woman has said a word about the equally mutilating practice of surgically destroying the healthy genitals of children in their own country. Like Gearhart, they shrink when we describe our surgeries as mutilation. But do they believe that African mothers, any more than American surgeons, cut their children out of malicious intent? Could their silence be because they don't know what is happening in American hospitals? It's possible, but the issue has received media coverage in the past year, and many of them have had the facts explained to them in person or in writing.

I could speculate that these women don't want to take on a foe as formidable and familiar as the medical profession, and that it is simpler to point fingers at more barbaric countries. They may not want to dilute their cause with the sticky subjects of sex and gender that surround the issue of ambiguous genitalia. Or perhaps they don't want to be aligned with children they can only see as freaks of nature. Even the liberal-thinking Joycelyn Elders, the former Surgeon General, refers to children who blur gender lines in a less-than-humane way. When Elders, a professor of pediatric endocrinology who continues to promote "reconstructive surgery" for girls with big clitorises, was asked about the wisdom of genital surgery on such children, she responded with, "Well, you just can't have an *it!*"[8]

Each woman has her own reasons for turning away from this issue. But I challenge them to pay attention to the fact that in hospitals just down the street in any big American city, five children a day are losing healthy, erotic parts of their bodies to satisfy a social demand for "normalcy." There is no federal ban to save them. The surgery is left out of the law against FGM because it is deemed "necessary to the health of the child on whom it is performed."[9] But as social psychologist Suzanne Kessler at the State University of New York at Purchase points out, "Genital ambiguity is corrected not because it is threatening to the infant's life, but because it is threatening to the infant's culture."[10]

Doctors and parents believe society will reject a child with atypical genitals, and the child is made to pay with her or his body for the shortcoming of our culture. What is happening in American hospitals to healthy children is just as mutilating to the bodies—no matter how exquisite the surgical craftsmanship—and violating to the souls of these children as FGM. And frequently, the surgical craftsmanship falls far short of exquisite.

The strict sexual agenda for bodies in America extends to little boys as well. To grow up to be a real man, a boy will have to be able to do two things—pee standing up and penetrate a vagina with his penis. If a little boy has to sit like a girl to urinate because his urethra exits somewhere along the shaft of his penis rather than the tip (a condition that can occur in as many as 8 out of 1,000),[11] he may be subjected to many disheartening surgeries over the course of his childhood to correct this "defect," and be left with a lifetime of chronic infections and emotional trauma. And if the baby is born with a "too-small" penis that doctors decide will never be big enough to "successfully" penetrate a woman, physicians will probably make him into a "girl" through surgery and hormone treatments, because, in the words of one surgeon, "It's easier to poke a hole than to build a pole."

In the 40 years since surgical intervention to "correct" genitals that are viewed as abnormal was first prescribed, treatment protocols have been rarely questioned. After all, it is much more comfortable for doctors to assume all is well than to start digging around to find out if it's really true. Until recently, all discussions of what is done to people's sexual bodies have been hidden safely away in the pages of medical texts, where real lives are only "interesting cases," and pictures of genitals are disembodied curiosities or teaching tools. Many doctors would like to keep things that way. For example, Dr. Kenneth Glassberg, a pediatric urologist associated with the American Academy of Pediatrics (AAP), insists that people who speak up and tell their stories are doing a disservice by "scaring patients away."[12]

In a blatant disregard for patient feedback not seen in any other medical field, the AAP still advocates early surgery and insists that the "management" of children with atypical genitals has improved over the past several decades. Their refusal to consider the reality of the lives of people who have been treated by this protocol can be likened to an astronomer gazing at Mars through his telescope while ignoring the real live Martian tugging at his sleeve. The messy truth of what happens to children treated with surgery and hormones is simply ignored by the AAP, as they stubbornly cling to a treatment paradigm that has never been anything but experimental.

Cosmetic genital surgery on children is out of control. As the practice has careened along unexamined for decades, illustrious careers and reputations have been made, consciences have been swallowed, and terrific damage has been done. For a doctor even to hesitate before operating takes tremendous effort and self-reflection. The need for babies to have genitals that look typical has been perceived as so unquestionable that surgeons travel all over the world to perform surgery on children free of charge as a "humanitarian gesture."

Dr. Justine Schober challenges her fellow surgeons to realize that "when you do [this kind of] surgery on someone, you are responsible for them for the rest of their lives."[13] In less than two hours in a sterile operating room, a child's personal and sexual destiny can be changed forever. The stakes are excruciatingly high for the sake of appearances. Angela's story, Annie's story, and my own tell only the smallest fraction of the terrible fallout from these surgeries. No one is naive enough to say that life in a body seen as abnormal is a ticket to bliss. But it is not the bodies of these children that are wrong, it is the way people see them. And if these children grow up and want to change their bodies one day, that will be their right. Nobody, but nobody, no matter how loving, no matter how well intentioned, should have the power to steal precious parts of a body from a child before she or he even gets started in life.

NOTES

1. Suzanne J. Kessler, "Meanings of Genital Variability," a paper presented as part of a plenary symposium titled "Genitals, Identity, and Gender." The Society for the Scientific Study of Sexuality, November 1995, San Francisco. Further reference: Barbara C. McGillivray, "The Newborn with Ambiguous Genitalia," *Seminars in Perinatology* 16, no. 6 (1992): 365–68.
2. Melanie Blackless, Anthony Charuvastra, Amanda Derryck, Anne Fausto-Sterling, Karl Lauzanne, Ellen Lee, "How sexually dimorphic are we? Review and synthesis." *American Journal of Human Biology* Vol. 12, Issue 2, Date: March/April 2000, pp. 151–166.
3. News release from the American Academy of Pediatrics (American Academy of Pediatrics, 141 Northwest Point Blvd., Elk Grove, IL 60009-0927) distributed to the press on October 26, 1996.
4. Justine Schober, personal communication, March 1998.
5. Intersex Society of North America, PO Box 31791, San Francisco, CA, 415/575-3885 (email:info@isna.org, web:www.isna.org). ISNA is a peer-support and advocacy group operated by and for individuals born with anatomy or physiology that differs from cultural ideals of female and male.
6. Cheryl Chase, "Winged Labia: Deformity or Gift?" *Hermaphrodites with Attitude*, a publication of the Intersex Society of North America, 1, no. 1 (Winter 1994): 3–4.
7. Monika Bauerlein, "The Unkindest Cut," *Utne Reader* (September/October 1996): 16.
8. Joycelyn Elders, personal communication, September 1997.
9. Federal Prohibition of Female Genital Mutilation Act of 1995.
10. Suzanne J. Kessler, "The Medical Construction of Gender: Case Management of Intersexual Infants," *Signs: Journal of Women in Culture and Society* 16, no. 1 (1990): 3–26.
11. Justine Schober, personal communication, March 1998.
12. Geoffrey Cowley, "Gender Limbo," *Newsweek* (May 19, 1997): 64–66.
13. Justine Shober, personal communication, March 1998.

PART IV
Communication

Individuals, groups, institutions, systems, governments, world organizations, and the mass media all engage in communication, sometimes face-to-face and often in other ways — via phone, TV, in print, via the Internet, etc. At the interpersonal level, telling the truth about one's experience is one task of communicating with others. The other task, frequently more challenging than the first, is listening carefully, empathizing, and trying to understand other people without being defensive or interrupting. Most people have a sense of how difficult this can be. A growing literature, especially related to counseling and psychotherapy, focuses on basic communication skills, such as listening, and on multicultural communication skills which include acknowledging how the various intersections of gender, race, class, ethnicity, disability, sexual orientation, and age affect communication. The task of becoming multiculturally competent takes time and effort, and it is necessary for all groups since most people are intimately familiar with only their own cultures.[1]

Communication patterns reflect power relationships. Those who have more power control what is communicated including what gets media attention; they especially control the extent to which people with less power are listened to and seen for who they are without prejudice. In an examination of African American and Latina women in film, for example, Elizabeth Hadley Freydberg concludes that despite active protest from these two communities, the film industry continues to portray Latinas and African American women in stereotyped, insulting roles.

Theories of the limited images of women in the media examine, among other things, the absence of women in positions of power in the communications industries, as well as the capitalist system that sells products and avoids offending potential consumers with more realistic images.[2] If we add race, sexual orientation, class, disability, and age to what is missing in the centers of power, this absence of many underrepresented groups serves to eliminate accurate images of many groups of people in the media.[3]

The dream that the Internet might create a more level communication playing field, where demographic traits mattered less, has not become a reality. Access to the Internet is still tied to social class, race and ethnicity, and education, and women's roles in cyber-related activities and industries are not equal to those of men. High-level computer science jobs are male-dominated, and gender differences in interaction in chat rooms seems to parallel gender differences in other realms of communication. Women are responding to this by establishing technology programs and Internet resources for girls and women generally, for people with disabilities, for low-income people, and for people of color, in order to increase access and to develop web sites and e-mail lists and bulletins that are designed to be empowering.[4] Although men's use of cyberspace to enhance their access to pornography, sex tours, and sex with children has incensed some feminists who had hoped for better things from the Internet,[5] feminists are finding ways to use this resource creatively.[6]

Literature from men's studies addresses the challenge of men's connections with each other, identifying various aspects of male-male communication that facilitate or impede close friendships. Sociologist Clyde Franklin,[7] for example, identified ways in which upward mobility interrupts Black men's friendships. Michael Messner, in a study of athletes, concluded that male athletes' "covert intimacy"—an intimacy based on doing things together rather than by intimate talk about personal issues—inhibits their ability to develop egalitarian relationships with either men or women.[8] Even when differences like race and class are not present and power between the people involved is relatively equal, difficulty sharing feelings, heavy competition for success, and fear of admitting dependency or vulnerability combine with homophobia to keep men apart in many circumstances in U.S. society.[9]

Finally, communication is difficult because the array of prejudices we learn in childhood frequently follows us into adulthood, often unconsciously. As children, we learn attitudes in situations in which we have little or no control, and we frequently live in families in which communication is far from ideal.[10] Until schools and communities routinely work to help people appreciate diversity, acknowledge differences of power and privilege, listen to each other, and learn peaceful methods of dispute resolution, we are on our own as individuals to improve communication across differences.

As you read the selections in this part, you might want to think about your own interpersonal relationships as they compare to or contrast with the relationship challenges described by Pat Parker, Deborah Tannen and Phil Petrie. Have you observed what Douglas and Michaels call the "New Momism?" Have you been involved in any Internet organizing as described by Shireen Lee? Where do you stand on the ways in which women and men are presented in Hip Hop? Finally, have you noticed any feminist commentators on TV or in major newspapers, the absence of which is observed by Laura Zimmerman?

NOTES

1. See for example Joseph G. Ponterotto et al., eds. *Handbook of Multicultural Counseling* (Thousand Oaks: Sage, 1995); Larry A. Samovar and Richard E. Porter, eds., *Intercultural Communication: A Reader* (Belmont, CA: Wadsworth, 1991). For a report of how different ethnic groups in the United States see each other, including the stereotypes their members hold about each other, see *Taking America's Pulse: Summary Report of the National Conference Survey on Inter-Group Relations* (New York: The National Conference of Christians and Jews, 1994).

2. For a summary of these theoretical perspectives, see Margaret L. Andersen, *Thinking about Women: Sociological Perspectives on Sex and Gender,* 3rd ed. (New York: Macmillan, 1993), pp. 54–62.

3. For an examination of these issues, see Gail Dines and Jean M. Humez, eds., *Gender, Race, and Class in Media: A Text-Reader* (Thousand Oaks, CA: Sage, 2003).

4. Joyce Slaton, "Mind the Gap: Three Women Working to Close the Digital Divide in Their Own Communities" *Ms.* (April–May 2001), pp. 42–44.

5. Donna Hughes, "The Internet and the Global Prostitution Industry," in Susan Hawthorne and Renate Klein, eds., *Cyberfeminism: Connectivity, Critique, and Creativity* (North Melbourne, Vic, Australia: Spinifex, 1999).

6. Susan Hawthorne and Renate Klein, eds., *Cyberfeminism: Connectivity, Critique, and Creativity* (North Melbourne, Vic, Australia: Spinifex, 1999).

7. Clyde Franklin, "'Hey, Home—Yo, Bro': Friendship among Black Men" in Peter Nardi, ed., *Men's Friendships* (Thousand Oaks: Sage, 1992), pp. 201–214.

8. Michael A. Messner, "Like Family: Power, Intimacy, and Sexuality in Male Athletes' Friendships" in Peter Nardi, ed., *Men's Friendships* (Thousand Oaks: Sage, 1992), pp. 215–237.

9. Michael S. Kimmel and Michael A. Messner, eds., *Men's Lives*, 3rd ed. (Boston: Allyn & Bacon, 1995), p. 323; Gregory K. Lehne, "Homophobia among Men: Supporting and Defining the Male Role," in Kimmel and Messner, *Men's Lives*, pp. 325–336.

10. In my years as a teacher and psychotherapist, I have met only a small proportion of people who would like to continue using the communication patterns of the adults in the households in which they grew up; more frequently, they experienced successful communication with siblings—enjoying the relative equality of power that allowed for more open communication.

25

FOR THE WHITE PERSON WHO WANTS TO KNOW HOW TO BE MY FRIEND

PAT PARKER

Pat Parker, Black lesbian poet, feminist medical administrator, mother of two daughters, lover of women, softball devotee, and general progressive troublemaker, died of breast cancer on June 17, 1989, at the age of 45. Her 1978 work, *Movement in Black,* has recently been republished by Firebrand Books.

> The first thing you do is to forget that i'm black.
> Second, you must never forget that i'm black.
>
> You should be able to dig Aretha,
> but don't play her every time i come over.
> And if you decide to play Beethoven — don't tell me
> his life story. They make us take music appreciation too.
>
> Eat soul food if you like it, but don't expect me
> to locate your restaurants
> or cook it for you.
>
> And if some Black person insults you,
> mugs you, rapes your sister, rapes you,
> rips your house or is just being an ass —
> please, do not apologize to me
> for wanting to do them bodily harm.
> It makes me wonder if you're foolish.
>
> And even if you really believe Blacks are better lovers than
> Whites — don't tell me. I start thinking of charging stud fees.
>
> In other words — if you really want to be my friend — *don't*
> make a labor of it. I'm lazy. Remember.

26

YOU JUST DON'T UNDERSTAND
Women and Men in Conversation

DEBORAH TANNEN

Deborah Tannen, a professor of linguistics at Georgetown University, has published sixteen books, as well as essays, poems, and plays. She has appeared on such television and radio shows as *Oprah, Good Morning America, 20/20,* and *Larry King Live.* Born and bred in Brooklyn, New York, she is proud that her parents were born in Russia and Poland.

*I*ntimacy is key in a world of connection where individuals negotiate complex networks of friendship, minimize differences, try to reach consensus, and avoid the appearance of superiority, which would highlight differences. In a world of status, *independence* is key, because a primary means of establishing status is to tell others what to do, and taking orders is a marker of low status. Though all humans need both intimacy and independence, women tend to focus on the first and men on the second. It is as if their lifeblood ran in different directions.

These differences can give women and men differing views of the same situation, as they did in the case of a couple I will call Linda and Josh. When Josh's old high-school chum called him at work and announced he'd be in town on business the following month, Josh invited him to stay for the weekend. That evening he informed Linda that they were going to have a houseguest, and that he and his chum would go out together the first night to shoot the breeze like old times. Linda was upset. She was going to be away on business the week before, and the Friday night when Josh would be out with his chum would be her first night home. But what upset her the most was that Josh had made these plans on his own and informed her of them, rather than discussing them with her before extending the invitation.

Linda would never make plans, for a weekend or an evening, without first checking with Josh. She can't understand why he doesn't show her the same courtesy and consideration that she shows him. But when she protests, Josh says, "I can't say to my friend, 'I have to ask my wife for permission'!"

To Josh, checking with his wife means seeking permission, which implies that he is not independent, not free to act on his own. It would make him feel like a child or an underling. To Linda, checking with her husband has nothing to do with permission. She assumes that spouses discuss their plans with each other because their lives are intertwined, so the actions of one have consequences for the other. Not only does Linda not mind telling someone, "I have to check with Josh"; quite the contrary—she likes it. It makes her feel good to know and show that she is involved with someone, that her life is bound up with someone else's.

Linda and Josh both felt more upset by this incident, and others like it, than seemed warranted, because it cut to the core of their primary concerns. Linda was hurt because she sensed a failure of closeness in their relationship: He didn't care about her as much as she cared about him. And he was hurt because he felt she was trying to control him and limit his freedom.

A similar conflict exists between Louise and Howie, another couple, about spending money. Louise would never buy anything costing more than a hundred dollars without discussing it with Howie, but he goes out and buys whatever he wants and feels they can afford, like a table saw or a new power mower. Louise is disturbed, not because she disapproves of the purchases, but because she feels he is acting as if she were not in the picture.

Many women feel it is natural to consult with their partners at every turn, while many men automatically make more decisions without consulting their partners. This may reflect a broad difference in conceptions of decision making. Women expect decisions to be discussed first and made by consensus. They appreciate the discussion itself as evidence of involvement and communication. But many men feel oppressed by lengthy discussions about what they see as minor decisions, and they feel hemmed in if they can't just act without talking first. When women try to initiate a freewheeling discussion by asking, "What do you think?" men often think they are being asked to decide. . . .

Asymmetries: Women and Men Talking at Cross-Purposes

Eve had a lump removed from her breast. Shortly after the operation, talking to her sister, she said that she found it upsetting to have been cut into, and that looking at the stitches was distressing because they left a seam that had changed the contour of her breast. Her sister said, "I know. When I had my operation I felt the same way." Eve made the same observation to her friend Karen, who said, "I know. It's like your body has been violated." But when she told her husband, Mark, how she felt, he said, "You can have plastic surgery to cover up the scar and restore the shape of your breast."

Eve had been comforted by her sister and her friend, but she was not comforted by Mark's comment. Quite the contrary, it upset her more. Not only didn't she hear what she wanted, that he understood her feelings, but, far worse, she felt he was asking her to undergo more surgery just when she was telling him how much this operation had upset her. "I'm not having any more surgery!" she protested. "I'm sorry you don't like the way it looks." Mark was hurt and puzzled. "I don't care," he protested. "It doesn't bother me at all." She asked, "Then why are you telling me to have plastic surgery?" He answered, "Because you were saying *you* were upset about the way it looked."

Eve felt like a heel: Mark had been wonderfully supportive and concerned throughout her surgery. How could she snap at him because of what he said—"just words"—when what he had done was unassailable? And yet she had perceived in his words metamessages that cut to the core of their relationship. It was self-evident to him that his comment was a reaction to her complaint, but she heard it as an independent complaint of his. He thought he was reassuring her that she needn't feel bad about her scar because there was something she could *do* about it. She heard his suggestion that she do something about the scar as evidence that *he* was bothered by it. Furthermore, whereas she wanted reassurance that it was normal to feel bad in her situation, his telling her that the problem could easily be fixed implied she had no right to feel bad about it.

Eve wanted the gift of understanding, but Mark gave her the gift of advice. He was taking the role of problem solver, whereas she simply wanted confirmation for her feelings.

A similar misunderstanding arose between a husband and wife following a car accident in which she had been seriously injured. Because she hated being in the hospital, the wife asked to come home early. But once home, she suffered pain from having to move around more. Her husband said, "Why didn't you stay in the hospital where you would have been more comfortable?" This hurt her because it seemed to imply that he did not want her home. She didn't think of his suggestion that she should have stayed in the hospital as a response to her complaints about the pain she was suffering; she thought of it as an independent expression of his preference not to have her at home.

"They're My Troubles—Not Yours"

If women are often frustrated because men do not respond to their troubles by offering matching troubles, men are often frustrated because women do. Some men not only take no comfort in such a response; they take offense. For example, a woman told me that when her companion talks about a personal concern—for example, his feelings about growing older—she responds, "I know how you feel; I feel the same way." To her surprise and chagrin, he gets annoyed; he feels she is trying to take something away from him by denying the uniqueness of his experience.

A similar miscommunication was responsible for the following interchange, which began as a conversation and ended as an argument:

He: I'm really tired. I didn't sleep well last night.
She: I didn't sleep well either. I never do.
He: Why are you trying to belittle me?
She: I'm not! I'm just trying to show that I understand!

This woman was not only hurt by her husband's reaction; she was mystified by it. How could he think she was belittling him? By "belittle me," he meant "belittle my experience." He was filtering her attempts to establish connection through his concern with preserving independence and avoiding being put down.

"I'll Fix It for You"

Women and men are both often frustrated by the other's way of responding to their expression of troubles. And they are further hurt by the other's frustration. If women resent men's tendency to offer solutions to problems, men complain about women's refusal to take action to solve the problems they complain about. Since many men see themselves as problem solvers, a complaint or a trouble is a challenge to their ability to think of a solution, just as a woman presenting a broken bicycle or stalling car poses a challenge to their ingenuity in fixing it. But whereas many women appreciate help in fixing mechanical equipment, few are inclined to appreciate help in "fixing" emotional troubles. . . .

Trying to solve a problem or fix a trouble focuses on the message level of talk. But for most women who habitually report problems at work or in friendships, the message is not the main point of complaining. It's the metamessage that counts: Telling about a problem is a bid for an expression of understanding ("I know how you feel") or a similar complaint ("I felt the same way when something similar happened to me"). In other words, troubles talk is intended to reinforce rapport by sending the metamessage "We're the same; you're not alone." Women are frustrated when they not only don't get this reinforcement but, quite the opposite, feel distanced by the advice, which seems to send the metamessage "We're not the same. You have the problems; I have the solutions."

Furthermore, mutual understanding is symmetrical, and this symmetry contributes to a sense of community. But giving advice is asymmetrical. It frames the advice giver as more knowledgeable, more reasonable, more in control—in a word, one-up. And this contributes to the distancing effect. . . .

Matching Troubles

The very different way that women respond to the telling of troubles is dramatized in a short story, "New Haven," by Alice Mattison. Eleanor tells Patsy that she has fallen in love with a married man. Patsy responds by first displaying understanding and then offering a matching revelation about a similar experience:

> "Well," says Patsy. "I know how you feel."
> "You do?"
> "In a way, I do. Well, I should tell you. I've been sleeping with a married man for two years."

Patsy then tells Eleanor about her affair and how she feels about it. After they discuss Patsy's affair, however, Patsy says:

> "But you were telling me about this man and I cut you off. I'm sorry. See? I'm getting self-centered."
> "It's OK." But she is pleased again.

The conversation then returns to Eleanor's incipient affair. Thus Patsy responds first by confirming Eleanor's feelings and matching her experience, reinforcing their similarity, and then by encouraging Eleanor to tell more. Within the frame of Patsy's similar predicament, the potential asymmetry inherent in revealing personal problems is avoided, and the friendship is brought into balance.

What made Eleanor's conversation with Patsy so pleasing to Eleanor was that they shared a sense of how to talk about troubles, and this reinforced their friendship. Though Eleanor raised the matter of her affair, she did not elaborate on it until Patsy pressed her to do so. In another story by the same author, "The Knitting," a woman named Beth is staying with her sister in order to visit her sister's daughter Stephanie in a psychiatric hospital. While there, Beth receives a disturbing telephone call from her boyfriend, Alec. Having been thus reminded of her troubles, she wants to talk about them, but she refrains, because her sister doesn't ask. She feels required, instead, to focus on her sister's problem, the reason for her visit:

> She'd like to talk about her muted half-quarrels with Alec of the last weeks, but her sister does not ask about the phone call. Then Beth thinks they should talk about Stephanie.

The women in these stories are balancing a delicate system by which troubles talk is used to confirm their feelings and create a sense of community.

When women confront men's ways of talking to them, they judge them by the standards of women's conversational styles. Women show concern by following up someone else's statement of trouble by questioning her about it. When men change the subject, women think they are showing a lack of sympathy—a failure of intimacy. But the failure to ask probing questions could just as well be a way of respecting the other's need for independence. When Eleanor tells Patsy that she is in love with Peter, Patsy asks, "Are you sleeping with him?" This exploration of Eleanor's topic could well strike many men—and some women—as intrusive, though Eleanor takes it as a show of interest that nourishes their friendship.

Women tend to show understanding of another woman's feelings. When men try to reassure women by telling them that their situation is not so bleak, the women hear their feelings being belittled or discounted. Again, they encounter a failure of intimacy just when they were bidding to reinforce it. Trying to trigger a symmetrical communication, they end up in an asymmetrical one.

27

REAL MEN DON'T CRY . . . AND OTHER "UNCOOL" MYTHS

PHIL W. PETRIE

Phil W. Petrie is a freelance writer in New Jersey.

Things were not going well. Do they ever for young couples struggling to understand each other, raise a family, pay the mortgage and at least keep the Joncses in sight? I had wanted to comfort my pregnant wife, soothe her with words that would temper the harshness of our reality. The baby was due in two months and my employer had just informed me that I didn't have hospitalization coverage for childbirth. I was frustrated and wanted to scream, lay my head in my wife's lap and cry. I needed to be soothed as well as she. She wanted to talk about our predicament, needed to talk it out. So did I, but I couldn't. I felt that I had failed her. Guilt stood at my side. But how could she know any of that, since all I did was to turn on the stereo system— my electronic security blanket—and listen to Miles Davis. I was cool. Her words shot through the space of "All Blues." "You're a cold SOB," she hissed.

She's being emotional again, I thought, *Just like a woman.* I, on the other hand, was controlling the situation because I was cool— which in reality was only a few degrees away from being cold. Wasn't that what she really wanted from me as head of the

Phil W. Petrie, "Real Men Don't Cry . . . and Other 'Uncool' Myths" from *Essence* (November 1982). Reprinted with the permission of the author.

household—control? Wasn't Freud correct when he proclaimed that our anatomy was our destiny (that is, our genitals determine our behavior)? In spite of her protestations that we had to talk, there was nothing in my upbringing that negated for me the power of coolness. I knew by the example of my elders that men controlled themselves and women did not.

In Mt. Olive, the Baptist church of my youth, it was expected that the "sisters" would "carry on" at church services. And they did. Moved by something that the preacher had said or by the mystery of a song, they would leap from their seats, run, scream, hurtle down the aisles. Transformed. Private feeling was suddenly public spectacle. Ushers came. White-gloved hands brushed away the tears. The men of the church, the elders, sat glued to their seats. I watched, instructed by this example of male control. I watched in silence but wished that I could know the electric transformation that moved those souls to dance.

"The larger culture creates expectations for males," says Dr. Walter Tardy, a psychiatrist in New York City. "In spite of the Women's Liberation Movement, men still live in a very macho culture and role play. Women tend to display their feelings more."

One of the roles men play is that of the rational being devoid of strong emotions. Profound feelings, it is thought, will interfere with the male task, whether that means making it at the nine-to-five or making it at war. Objective decisions must be made without distracting emotions, which women are thought to be prone to—even by some other women. For many persons, "being a man" is synonymous with being emotionless—cool.

One need not be told this. Like air, it seems to be a pervasive part of the male atmosphere. If one missed it at church (as I did not), one might pick it up at the barbershop or the playground—places where the elements of the culture are passed on without the benefit of critical examination.

Didn't Wimpy Sheppard tell me at Tom Simon's Barbershop that only babies, women and sissies cried? A man, he said, ain't supposed to cry. That's why my father, at the death of his mother, slipped out to the backyard away from his family to sit among the chickens and wail. How could I explain to my wife—to myself— that I couldn't rest my head in her lap and weep? I had to protect my masculinity. Asking me to cry, to drop my cool, was asking me to redefine my life.

Says Margo Williams, a widow residing in San Diego, California, with her two children, "If you can't let down to your mate, friend or what have you, then you have to ask yourself what the relationship is all about—is it worth being involved with? For me, it's not about my man being strong and hard. I want him to be a human being—warm, sensitive and willing to share his life with me."

What if he balks? Williams is asked. "If the relationship is a serious one, I would urge him to let us try to work through the problems," she says. "I would want to establish a relationship wherein we could express to each other our needs and wants—even express our dislikes. We have to establish an honest relationship."

Dr. Tardy cautions that "there are degrees of honesty. Do you tell the truth all of the time, or is a white lie something appropriate? One can only be just so honest. The truth may set you free, but some truths should be withheld because they can hurt more than they help. But even if you don't tell it all, you must tell *something*. Communication is the key."

Therein lies the danger of being cool and playing roles. In doing this, one reveals a persona rather than a person, plays a part rather than being part of the relationship. Communication, by its root definition, means "sharing, making something common between people." It is this fear of sharing—giving up something—that drives some men into being noncommunicative except in the area of sex.

Robert Staples, a sociologist, states in his book *Black Masculinity* (Black Scholar Press) that when Black men "have been unable to achieve status in the workplace, they have exercised the privilege of their manliness and attempted to achieve it [power] in the bedroom. Feeling a constant need to affirm their masculinity, tenderness and compassion are eschewed as signs of weakness, which leaves them vulnerable to the ever-feared possibility of female domination."

It could be argued that in today's climate of women's liberation, all men are on the defensive because of the developing assertiveness of women. No doubt some men—if not many—use sex as a controlling force. "But," says Wilbur Suesberry, a pediatrician practicing in Compton, California, "I don't believe that sex is racially restrictive. Black sexuality is a myth started and supported by whites and perpetuated by Blacks. Men find it difficult to express their inner feelings but they must find a way to do it. If you have things pent up inside of you and they do not come out in a healthy way, then they exit in an unhealthy way. Sex as an outlet for your emotions is not good. To communicate you can't sulk or take to the bed, you must talk." Talk? Yes, talk is a more precise method of communicating than sex, intuition or an "understanding."

"The birth is due in two months," she persisted. "What are we going to do?" Annoyed, not at her but at the apparent futility of the situation, I turned up the record player and went deeper into myself. Didn't she *understand* me well enough to know that I would do something? Hadn't I always? Couldn't she look at me and see that I was worried too? Didn't she *trust* me well enough to know that I would do something? All of those questions might have been eliminated with my telling her simply and directly what my feelings really were. How could she really know them unless she were a mind reader, just as I didn't know what she felt? Screaming and crying isn't quite the same thing as communicating effectively. I pulled her to me, caressed her.

Hugging and kissing are not substitutes for words, for language. Talking to each other allows us to bring order to the disruption and confusion engendered by silence. *Talk to me,* Little Willie John used to sing, *talk to me in your own sweet gentle way.*

This simple verbal act is made all the more difficult for men (and women, for that matter) if we don't know (or won't admit) what our feelings really are. We can't talk about things if we can't conceptualize them. Communication is more than mouthing words or rapping. I see it as defining an aspect of one's life by framing that aspect into words and then sharing it with someone. It is not only a problem for lovers; it also bedevils fathers and sons, mothers and daughters. It is problematic because it drives you within. The first act of communication is with your self—"the private self," Dr. Tardy calls it. This journey within involves both introspection and openness.

Yet what I face within myself—if indeed I face it—may never be completely shared with anyone. An insistence that I communicate *all* of my feelings is asking too much. We men are now being urged not only to redefine our roles and relationships with our mates and society but also to become vulnerable by revealing our private selves to another public, although it may be a public of only one. The degree to which I can do this—express *some* of my feelings—is determined by the self-awareness I have of myself and the trust I have for my spouse.

I closet my feelings out of self-protection and fear of the unknown. Women in their newfound drive for liberation have the example of men to direct them. It seems that all women are asking for are some of the prerogatives once claimed by men only. But what is to be the model for me? White men? I think not. Granted they are the movers and shakers within this society, but the madness of the world that they have created does not make them legitimate role models. Yet for many Black women the term *man* is synonymous with *white man.* I resent being asked to pattern myself after a man whose reality—full of avarice and destruction—is so antithetical to mine. I hold on to my cool.

For Black men, being cool is not just an attitude; it becomes a political stance, a metaphor for power. To give that up is, in effect, to render oneself powerless—to lose control. For Black men, who control so little, to lose this cool is to lose a weapon in their arsenal for survival. Do Black women know that?

"Maybe you could call somebody [white?] who can help," she suggested, determined to get a word out of me. And if I can't find someone white to help us with my problems, I thought, then I can fold up and cry to you. Ugh. Is this what you ask of me: to imitate white men or act like women (that is, take control or cry)? What brave new world are you asking me to enter into by dropping my cool, discarding my role as leader, drowning my strength with tears? It is a scenario that no other group of men in history has ever played. Yet you ask me, the most politically weak person within the society, to lead the way to this new world. How can you ask me that, baby? And if I go, will you cast me aside as being weak? You scream about a man who is strong enough to cry, strong enough to admit weaknesses, and at the same time you want a "take-charge" person, a man who won't let anyone run over him. Caught between such confusion, I turn to the ball game, to the television, to the silence within myself. Love is withheld. Restrained. Tentative.

"I think that our generation is too tentative," says Lee Atkins, a publishing-company sales representative living in Chicago. "Those of us born in the 1940's and before were given too many caveats. Black men or boys were told not to do this and not to do that. Avoid the police. Stay out of trouble. All of this was done to protect us in an extremely racist and hostile society. In effect, we were being told: behave or you will be destroyed." That made us cautious and we are now paying the price for all that caution. As men we find that we are too careful, too private, not open and not willing to explore. We find it difficult to open up even to those we care about the most.

"Those kids born in the 1950's and 1960's," Atkins continues, "were born into a world where the expectations for the Black male were more positive. A whole set of new possibilities was suddenly available. Sexually, things were more permissive, and in the do-your-own-thing attitude of the 1960's and 1970's Black men were actually encouraged to be more unconventional, to open up."

This has led to young Black men who are more candid about their feelings, more carefree in their attitudes. "I would be surprised," says Dr. Tardy, "if these young adults weren't more open in their dealings with each other. The drawback may be that they don't want to establish the permanent relations that were expected in the past. I can imagine that many young women will say that the young men today aren't 'serious' or are too much into themselves. That's the legacy of hanging loose."

Whether we are young or old, one thing is certain: we men cannot expect to go through a lifetime in silence, repressing our feelings, denying our emotions, without being run down by frustrations, failed opportunities and unfulfilled promises. And why would we do this? Is it because of the protrusion dangling between our legs? Is it because we hold on to a fixed role in a changing world? Or is it because of our fear of losing an imagined power? Perhaps the answer is all of the above. If so, we must rush to get rid of these contrived ghosts. In the real world our women are calling to us. How long will they keep it up before they give up? Or as writer Amiri Baraka asks, "How long till the logic of our lives runs us down?"

She stood before me pleading, belly swollen with my seed. She wasn't asking for much, just that I talk to her. She was richly human and was demanding that I be nothing less, saying that I couldn't be a man until I showed that I was human—warm, tender, compassionate, feeling, and able to express that feeling. It was difficult, but with a guide so dedicated to my good health I began the journey from within to without that day. We found the money for the hospital. But more important, I found that I could talk to her about me, could share my life in trust with her. I write this as a souvenir of remembrance—a gift for her.

28

THE NEW MOMISM

SUSAN J. DOUGLAS • MEREDITH W. MICHAELS

Susan J. Douglas is the Catherine Neafie Kellogg Professor of Communication Studies at the University of Michigan. She is author of *Listening In: Radio and the American Imagination,* which won the Hacker Prize in 2000 for the best popular book about technology and culture; *Where the Girls Are: Growing Up Female with the Mass Media;* and *Inventing American Broadcasting, 1899–1922.* Her writing has appeared in *The Nation, Ms., In These Times, TV Guide,* and *The Progressive.* She lives in Ann Arbor, Michigan, with her husband and daughter.

Meredith W. Michaels teaches philosophy at Smith College and writes about ethics and ideologies of reproduction and parenthood. She and her husband, Lee Bowie, have five children and live in Amherst, Massachusetts.

It's 5:22 P.M. You're in the grocery checkout line. Your three-year-old is writhing on the floor, screaming, because you have refused to buy her a Teletubby pinwheel. Your six-year-old is whining, repeatedly, in a voice that could saw through cement, "But mommy, puleeze, puleeze" because you have not bought him the latest "Lunchables," which features, as the four food groups, Cheetos, a Snickers, Cheez Whiz, and Twizzlers. Your teenager, who has not spoken a single word in the past four days except, "You've ruined my life," followed by "Everyone else has one," is out in the car, sulking, with the new rap-metal band Piss on the Parentals blasting through the headphones of a Discman.

To distract yourself, and to avoid the glares of other shoppers who have already deemed you the worst mother in America, you leaf through *People* magazine. Inside, Uma Thurman gushes "Motherhood Is Sexy."[1] Moving on to *Good Housekeeping,* Vanna White says of her child, "When I hear his cry at six-thirty in the morning, I have a smile on my face, and I'm not an early riser."[2] Another unexpected source of earth-mother wisdom, the newly maternal Pamela Lee, also confides to *People,* "I just love getting up with him in the middle of the night to feed him or soothe him."[3] Brought back to reality by stereophonic whining, you indeed feel as sexy as Rush Limbaugh in a thong.

You drag your sorry ass home. Now, if you were a "good" mom, you'd joyfully empty the shopping bags and transform the process of putting the groceries away into a fun game your kids love to play (upbeat Raffi songs would provide a lilting soundtrack). Then, while you steamed the broccoli and poached the chicken breasts in Vouvray and Evian water, you and the kids would also be doing jigsaw puzzles in the shape of the United Arab Emirates so they learned some geography. Your cheerful teenager would say, "Gee, Mom, you gave me the best advice on that last homework assignment." When your husband arrives, he is so overcome with admiration for how well you do it all that he looks lovingly into your eyes, kisses you, and presents you with a diamond anniversary bracelet. He then announces that he has gone on flex time for the next two years so that he can split childcare duties with you fifty-fifty. The children, chattering away happily, help set the table, and then eat their broccoli. After dinner, you all go out and stencil the driveway with autumn leaves.

But maybe this sounds slightly more familiar. "I won't unpack the groceries! You can't make me," bellows your child as he runs to his room, knocking down a lamp on the way. "Eewee—gross out!" he yells and you discover that the cat has barfed on his bed. You have fifteen minutes to make dinner because there's a school play in half an hour. While the children fight over whether to watch *Hot Couples* or people eating larvae on *Fear Factor,* you zap some Prego spaghetti sauce in the microwave and boil some pasta. *You* set the table. "Mommy, Mommy, Sam losted my hamster," your daughter wails. Your ex-husband calls to say he won't be taking the kids this weekend after all because his new wife, Buffy, twenty-three, has to go on a modeling shoot in Virgin Gorda for the *Sports Illustrated* swimsuit issue, and "she really needs me with her." You go to the TV room to discover the kids watching transvestites punching each other out on *Jerry Springer.* The pasta boils over and scalds the hamster, now lying prostrate on the floor with its legs twitching in the air. "Get your butts in here this instant or I'll murder you immediately," you shriek, by way of inviting your children to dinner. "I hate this pasta—I only like the kind shaped like wagon wheels!" "Mommy, you killded my hamster!"

If you're like us—mothers with an attitude problem—you may be getting increasingly irritable about this chasm between the ridiculous, honey-hued ideals of perfect motherhood in the mass media and the reality of mothers' everyday lives. And you may also be worn down by media images that suggest that however much you do for and love your kids, it is never enough. The love we feel for our kids, the joyful times we have with them, are repackaged into unattainable images of infinite patience and constant adoration so that we fear, as Kristin van Ogtrop put it movingly in *The Bitch in the House*, "I will love my children, but my love for them will always be imperfect."[4]

From the moment we get up until the moment we collapse in bed at night, the media are out there, calling to us, yelling, "Hey you! Yeah, you! Are you *really* raising your kids right?" Whether it's the cover of *Redbook* or *Parents* demanding "Are You a Sensitive Mother?" "Is Your Child Eating Enough?" "Is Your Baby Normal?" (and exhorting us to enter its pages and have great sex at 25, 35, or 85), the nightly news warning us about missing children, a movie trailer hyping a film about a cross-dressing dad who's way more fun than his stinky, careerist wife (*Mrs. Doubtfire*), or Dr. Laura telling some poor mother who works four hours a week that she's neglectful, the siren song blending seduction and accusation is there all the time. Mothers are subjected to an onslaught of beatific imagery, romantic fantasies, self-righteous sermons, psychological warnings, terrifying movies about losing their children, even more terrifying news stories about abducted and abused children, and totally unrealistic advice about how to be the most perfect and revered mom in the neighborhood, maybe even in the whole country. (Even *Working Mother*—which should have known better—had a "Working Mother of the Year Contest." When Jill Kirschenbaum became the editor in 2001, one of the first things she did was dump this feature, noting that motherhood should not be a "competitive sport.") We are urged to be fun-loving, spontaneous, and relaxed, yet, at the same time, scared out of our minds that our kids could be killed at any moment. No wonder 81 percent of women in a recent poll said it's harder to be a mother now than it was twenty or thirty years ago, and 56 percent felt mothers were doing a worse job today than mothers back then.[5] Even mothers who deliberately avoid TV and magazines, or who pride themselves on seeing through them, have trouble escaping the standards of perfection, and the sense of threat, that the media ceaselessly atomize into the air we breathe.

We are both mothers, and we adore our kids—for example, neither one of us has ever locked them up in dog crates in the basement (although we have, of course, been tempted). The smell of a new baby's head, tucking a child in at night, receiving homemade, hand-scrawled birthday cards, heart-to-hearts with a teenager after a date, seeing *them* become parents—these are joys parents treasure. But like increasing numbers of women, we are fed up with the myth—shamelessly hawked by the media—that motherhood is eternally fulfilling and rewarding, that it is *always* the best and most important thing you do, that there is only a narrowly prescribed way to do it right, and that if you don't love each and every second of it there's something really wrong with you. At the same time, the two of us still have been complete suckers, buying those black-and-white mobiles that allegedly turn your baby into Einstein Jr., feeling guilty for sending in store-bought cookies to the class bake sale instead of homemade like the "good" moms, staying up until 2:30 A.M. making our kids' Halloween costumes, driving to the Multiplex 18 at midnight to pick up teenagers so they won't miss the latest outing with their friends. We know that building a scale model of Versailles out of mashed potatoes may not be quite as crucial to good mothering as *Martha Stewart Living* suggests. Yet here we are, cowed by that most tyrannical of our cultural icons, Perfect Mom. So, like millions of women, we buy into these absurd ideals at the same time that we resent them and think they are utterly ridiculous and oppressive. After all, our parents—the group Tom Brokaw has labeled "the greatest generation"—had parents who whooped them on the behind, screamed stuff at them like "I'll tear you limb from limb," told them babies came from cabbage patches, never drove them four hours to a soccer match, and yet they seemed to have nonetheless saved the western world.

This book is about the rise in the media of what we are calling the "new momism": the insistence that no woman is truly complete or fulfilled unless she has kids, that women remain the best primary caretakers of children, and that to be a remotely decent mother, a woman has to devote her entire physical, psychological, emotional, and intellectual being, 24/7, to her children. The new momism is a highly romanticized and yet demanding view of motherhood in which the standards for success are impossible to meet. The term "momism" was initially coined by the journalist Philip Wylie in his highly influential 1942 bestseller *Generation of Vipers,* and it was a very derogatory term. Drawing from Freud (who else?), Wylie attacked the mothers of America as being so smothering, overprotective, and invested in their kids, especially their sons, that they turned them into dysfunctional, sniveling weaklings, maternal slaves chained to the apron strings, unable to fight for their country or even stand on their own two feet.[6] We seek to reclaim this term, rip it from its misogynistic origins, and apply it to an ideology that has snowballed since the 1980s and seeks to return women to the Stone Age.

The "new momism" is a set of ideals, norms, and practices, most frequently and powerfully represented in the media, that seem on the surface to celebrate motherhood, but which in reality promulgate standards of perfection that are beyond your reach. The new momism is the direct descendant and latest version of what Betty Friedan famously labeled the "feminine mystique" back in the 1960s. The new momism *seems* to be much more hip and progressive than the feminine mystique, because now, of course, mothers can and do work outside the home, have their own ambitions and money, raise kids on their own, or freely choose to stay at home with their kids rather than being forced to. And unlike the feminine mystique, the notion that women should be subservient to men is not an accepted tenet of the new momism. Central to the new momism, in fact, is the feminist insistence that women have choices, that they are active agents in control of their own destiny, that they have autonomy. But here's where the distortion of feminism occurs. The only truly enlightened choice to make as a woman, the one that proves, first, that you are a "real" woman, and second, that you are a decent, worthy one, is to become a "mom" and to bring to child rearing a combination of selflessness and professionalism that would involve the cross cloning of Mother Teresa with Donna Shalala. Thus the new momism is deeply contradictory: It both draws from and repudiates feminism.

The fulcrum of the new momism is the rise of a really pernicious ideal in the late twentieth century that the sociologist Sharon Hays has perfectly labeled "intensive mothering."[7] It is no longer okay, as it was even during the heyday of June Cleaver, to let (or make) your kids walk to school, tell them to stop bugging you and go outside and play, or, God forbid, serve them something like Tang, once the preferred beverage of the astronauts, for breakfast. Of course many of our mothers baked us cookies, served as Brownie troop leaders, and chaperoned class trips to Elf Land. But today, the standards of good motherhood are really over the top. And they've gone through the roof at the same time that there has been a real decline in leisure time for most Americans.[8] The yuppie work ethic of the 1980s, which insisted that even when you were off the job you should be working—on your abs, your connections, your portfolio, whatever—absolutely conquered motherhood. As the actress Patricia Heaton jokes in *Motherhood & Hollywood*, now mothers are supposed to "sneak echinacea" into the "freshly squeezed, organically grown orange juice" we've made for our kids and teach them to "download research for their kindergarten report on 'My Family Tree—The Early Roman Years.'"[9]

Intensive mothering insists that mothers acquire professional-level skills such as those of a therapist, pediatrician ("Dr. Mom"), consumer products safety inspector, and teacher, and that they lavish every ounce of physical vitality they have, the monetary equivalent of the gross domestic product of Australia, and, most of all, every single bit of their emotional, mental, and psychic energy on their kids. We must learn to put on the masquerade of the doting, self-sacrificing mother and wear it at all times. With intensive mothering, everyone watches us, we watch ourselves and other mothers, and we watch ourselves watching ourselves. How many of you know someone who swatted her child on the behind in a supermarket because he was, say, opening a pack of razor blades in the toiletries aisle, only to be accosted by someone she never met who threatened to put her up on child-abuse charges? In 1997, one mother was arrested for child neglect because she left a ten-year-old and a four-year-old home for an hour and a half while she went to the supermarket.[10] Motherhood has become a psychological police state.

Intensive mothering is the ultimate female Olympics: We are all in powerful competition with each other, in constant danger of being trumped by the mom down the street, or in the magazine we're reading. The competition isn't just over who's a good mother—it's over who's the best. We compete with each other; we compete with ourselves. The best mothers always put their kids' needs before their own, period. The best mothers are the main caregivers. For the best mothers, their kids are the center of the universe. The best mothers always smile. They always understand. They are never tired. They never lose their temper. They never say, "Go to the neighbor's house and play while Mommy has a beer." Their love for their children is boundless, unflagging, flawless, total. Mothers today cannot just respond to their kids' needs, they must predict them—and with the telepathic accuracy of Houdini. They must memorize verbatim the books of all the child-care experts and know which approaches are developmentally appropriate at different ages. They are supposed to treat their two-year-olds with "respect." If mothers screw up and fail to do this on any given day, they should apologize to their kids, because any misstep leads to permanent psychological and/or physical damage. Anyone who questions whether this is *the* best and *the* necessary way to raise kids is an insensitive, ignorant brute. This is just common sense, right?[11]

The new momism has become unavoidable, unless you raise your kids in a yurt on the tundra, for one basic reason: Motherhood became one of the biggest media obsessions of the last three decades, exploding especially in the mid-1980s and continuing unabated to the present. Women have been deluged by an ever-thickening mudslide of maternal media advice, programming, and marketing that powerfully shapes how we mothers feel about our relationships with our own kids and, indeed, how we feel about ourselves. These media representations have changed over time, cutting mothers some real slack in the 1970s, and then increasingly closing the vise in the late 1980s and after, despite important rebellions by Roseanne and others. People don't usually notice that motherhood has been such a major media fixation, revolted or hooked as they've been over the years by other media excesses like the O. J. Simpson trials, the Lewinsky-Clinton imbroglio, the Elian Gonzalez carnival, *Survivor,* or the 2002 Washington-area sniper killings in which "profilers" who knew as much as SpongeBob SquarePants nonetheless got on TV to tell us what the killer was thinking.

But make no mistake about it—mothers and motherhood came under unprecedented media surveillance in the 1980s and beyond. And since the media traffic in extremes, in anomalies—the rich, the deviant, the exemplary, the criminal, the gorgeous—they emphasize fear and dread on the one hand and promote impossible ideals on the other. In the process, *Good Housekeeping, People,* E!, Lifetime, *Entertainment Tonight,* and *NBC Nightly News* built an interlocking, cumulative image of the dedicated, doting "mom" versus the delinquent, bad "mother." There have been, since the early 1980s, several overlapping media frameworks that have fueled the new momism. First, the media warned mothers about the external threats to their kids from abductors and the like. Then the "family values" crowd made it clear that supporting the family was not part of the government's responsibility. By the late 1980s, stories about welfare and crack mothers emphasized the internal threats to children from mothers themselves. And finally, the media brouhaha over the "Mommy Track" reaffirmed that businesses could not or would not budge much to accommodate the care of children. Together, and over time, these frameworks produced a prevailing common sense that only you, the individual mother, are responsible for your child's welfare: The buck stops with you, period, and you'd better be a superstar.

Of course there has been a revolution in fatherhood over the past thirty years, and millions of men today tend to the details of child rearing in ways their own fathers rarely did. Feminism prompted women to insist that men change diapers and pack school lunches, but it also gave men permission to become more involved with their kids in ways they have found to be deeply satisfying. And between images of cuddly, New Age dads with babies asleep on their chests (think old Folger's ads), movies about hunky men and a baby (or clueless ones who shrink the kids), and sensational news stories about "deadbeat dads" and men who beat up their sons' hockey coaches, fathers too have been subject to a media "dad patrol." But it pales in comparison to the new momism. After all, a dad who knows the name of his kids' pediatrician and reads them stories at night is still regarded as a saint; a mother who doesn't is a sinner.

Once you identify it, you see the new momism everywhere. The recent spate of magazines for "parents" (i.e., mothers) bombard the anxiety-induced mothers of America with reassurances that they can (after a $100,000 raise and a personality transplant) produce bright, motivated, focused, fun-loving, sensitive, cooperative, confident, contented kids just like the clean, obedient ones on the cover. The frenzied hypernatalism of the women's magazines alone (and that includes *People*, *Us*, and *InStyle*), with their endless parade of perfect, "sexy" celebrity moms who've had babies, adopted babies, been to sperm banks, frozen their eggs for future use, hatched the frozen eggs, had more babies, or adopted a small Tibetan village, all to satisfy their "baby lust," is enough to make you want to get your tubes tied. (These profiles always insist that celebs all love being "moms" much, much more than they do their work, let alone being rich and famous, and that they'd spend every second with their kids if they didn't have that pesky blockbuster movie to finish.) Women without children, wherever they look, are besieged by ridiculously romantic images that insist that having children is the most joyous, fulfilling experience in the galaxy, and if they don't have a small drooling creature who likes to stick forks in electrical outlets, they are leading bankrupt, empty lives. Images of ideal moms and their miracle babies are everywhere, like leeches in the Amazon, impossible to dislodge and sucking us dry.

There is also the ceaseless outpouring of books on toilet training, separating one sibling's fist from another sibling's eye socket, expressing breast milk while reading a legal brief, helping preschoolers to "own" their feelings, getting Joshua to do his homework, and raising teenage boys so they become Sensitive New Age Guys instead of rooftop snipers or Chippendale dancers. Over eight hundred books on motherhood were published between 1970 and 2000; only twenty-seven of these came out between 1970 and 1980, so the real avalanche happened in the past twenty years.[12] We've learned about the perils of "the hurried child" and "hyperparenting," in which we schedule our kids with so many enriching activities that they make the secretary of state look like a couch spud. But the unhurried child probably plays too much Nintendo and is out in the garage building pipe bombs, so you can't underschedule them either.

Then there's the Martha Stewartization of America, in which we are meant to sculpt the carrots we put in our kids' lunches into the shape of peonies and build funhouses for them in the backyard; this has raised the bar to even more ridiculous levels than during the June Cleaver era. Most women know that there was a massive public relations campaign during World War II to get women into the workforce, and then one right after the war to get them to go back to the kitchen. But we haven't fully focused on the fact that another, more subtle, sometimes unintentional, more long-term propaganda campaign began in the 1980s to redomesticate the women of America through motherhood.[13] Why aren't all the mothers of America leaning out their windows yelling "I'm mad as hell and I'm not going to take it anymore"?

So the real question is how did the new momism—especially in the wake of the women's movement—become part of our national common sense? Why have mothers—who have entered the workforce in droves at exactly the same time that intensive mothering conquered notions of parenting—bought into it? Are there millions of us who conform to the ideals of the new momism on the outside, while also harboring powerful desires for rebellion that simply can't be satisfied by a ten-minute aromatherapy soak in the bathtub?

There are several reasons why the new momism—talk about the wrong idea for the wrong time—triumphed when it did. Baby boom women who, in the 1970s, sought to enter schools and jobs previously reserved for men knew they couldn't be just as good as the guys—they had to be better, in part to dispel the myths that women were too stupid, irrational, hysterical, weak, flighty, or unpredictable during "that time of the month" to manage a business, report the news, wear a stethoscope, or sell real estate. Being an overachiever simply went with the terrain of breaking down barriers, so it wouldn't be surprising to find these women bringing that same determination to motherhood. And some of us did get smacked around as kids, or had parents who crushed our confidence, and we did want to do a better job than that. One brick in the wall of the new momism.

Many women, who had started working in the 1970s and postponed having children, decided in the 1980s to have kids. Thus, this was a totally excellent time for the federal government to insist that it was way too expensive to support any programs for families and children (like maternity leave or subsidized, high-quality day care or even decent public schools) because then the U.S. couldn't afford that $320 billion appropriation to the Pentagon, which included money for those $1600 coffee makers and $600 toilet seats the military needed so badly in 1984.[14] (Imagine where we'd be today if the government had launched the equivalent of the G.I. bill for mothers in the 1980s!) Parents of baby boomers had seen money flow into America's schools because of the Sputnik scare that the Russkies were way ahead of the U.S. in science and technology; thus the sudden need to reacquaint American kids with a slide rule. Parents in the 1980s saw public schools hemorrhaging money. So the very institutions our mothers had been able to count on now needed massive CPR, while the prospect of any new ones was, we were told, out of the question. Guess who had to take up the slack? Another brick in the wall of the new momism.

The right wing of the Republican party — which controlled the White House from 1980 to 1992, crucial years in the evolution of motherhood — hated the women's movement and believed all women, with the possible exception of Phyllis Schlafly, should remain in the kitchen on their knees polishing their husband's shoes and golf clubs while teaching their kids that Darwin was a very bad man. (Unless the mothers were poor and black — those moms had to get back to work ASAP, because by staying home they were wrecking the country. . . .) We saw, in the 1980s and beyond, the rise of what the historian Ruth Feldstein has called "mother-blaming," attacks on mothers for failing to raise physically and psychologically fit future citizens.[15] See, no one, not even Ronald Reagan, said explicitly to us, "The future and the destiny of the nation are in your hands, oh mothers of America. And you are screwing up." But that's what he meant. Because not only are mothers supposed to reproduce the nation biologically, we're also supposed to regenerate it culturally and morally. Even after the women's movement, mothers were still expected to be the primary socializers of children.[16] Not only were our individual kids' well-being our responsibility, but also the entire fate of the nation supposedly rested on our padded and milk-splotched shoulders. So women's own desires to be good parents, their realization that they now had to make up for collapsing institutions, and all that guilt-tripping about "family values" added many more bricks to the wall.

But we are especially interested in the role that the mass media played, often inadvertently, and often, mind you, in the name of *helping* mothers — in making the new momism a taken-for-granted, natural standard of how women should imagine their lives, conceive of fulfillment, arrange their priorities, and raise their kids. After all, the media have been and are the major dispenser of the ideals and norms surrounding motherhood: Millions of us have gone to the media for nuts-and-bolts child-rearing advice. Many of us, in fact, preferred media advice to the advice our mothers gave us. We didn't want to be like our mothers and many of us didn't want to raise our kids the way they raised us (although it turns out they did a pretty good job in the end).

Thus, beginning in the mid-1970s, working mothers became the most important thing you can become in the United States: a market. And they became a market just as niche marketing was exploding—the rise of cable channels, magazines like *Working Mother, Family Life, Child,* and *Twins,* all supported by advertisements geared specifically to the new, modern mother. Increased emphasis on child safety, from car seats to bicycle helmets, increased concerns about Johnny not being able to read, the recognition that mothers bought cars, watched the news, and maybe didn't want to tune into one TV show after the next about male detectives with a cockatoo or some other dumbass mascot saving hapless women—all contributed to new shows, ad campaigns, magazines, and TV news stories geared to mothers, especially affluent, upscale ones. Because of this sheer increase in output and target marketing, mothers were bombarded as never before by media constructions of the good mother. The good mother bought all this stuff to stimulate, protect, educate, and indulge her kids. She had to assemble it, install it, use it with her child, and protect her child from some of its features. As all this media fare sought to advise mothers, flatter them, warn them and, above all, sell to them, they collaborated in constructing, magnifying, and reinforcing the new momism.

Here's the rub about the new momism. It began to conquer our psyches just as mothers entered the workforce in record numbers, so those of us who work (and those of us who don't) are pulled between two rather powerful and contradictory cultural riptides: Be more doting and self-sacrificing at home than Bambi's mother, yet more achievement-oriented at work than Madeleine Albright.[17] The other set of values that took hold beginning in the 1980s was "free-market ideology": the notion that competition in "the marketplace" (which supposedly had the foresight and wisdom of Buddha) provided the best solutions to all social, political, and economic problems. So on the job we were—and are—supposed to be highly efficient, calculating, tough, judgmental and skeptical, competitive, and willing to do what it takes to promote ourselves, our organization, and beat out the other guys. Many work environments in the 1980s and '90s emphasized increased productivity and piled on more work, kids or no kids, because that's what "the market" demanded. Television shows offered us role models of the kind of tough broads who succeeded in this environment, from the unsmiling, take-no-prisoners DA Joyce Davenport on *Hill Street Blues* to Judge Judy and the no-nonsense police lieutenant Anita Van Buren on *Law & Order.* So the competitive go-getter at work had to walk through the door at the end of the day and, poof, turn into Carol Brady: selfless doormat at home. No wonder some of us feel like Sybil when we get home: We have to move between these riptides on a daily basis. And, in fact, many of us want to be both women: successful at work, successful as mothers.

Now, here's the real beauty of this contorting contradiction. Both working mothers *and* stay-at-home mothers get to be failures. The ethos of intensive mothering has lower status in our culture ("stay-at-home mothers are boring"), but occupies a higher moral ground ("working mothers are ne-glectful").[18] So, welcome to the latest media catfight: the supposed war be-tween working mothers and stay-at-home mothers. Why analyze all the ways in which our country has failed to support families while inflating the work ethic to the size of the *Hindenburg* when you can, instead, project this paradox onto what the media have come to call, incessantly, "the mommy wars." The "mommy wars" puts mothers into two, mutually exclusive cate-gories—working mother versus stay-at-home mother, and never the twain shall meet. It goes without saying that they allegedly hate each other's guts. In real life, millions of mothers move between these two categories, have been one and then the other at various different times, creating a mosaic of work and child-rearing practices that bears no resemblance to the supposed ironclad roles suggested by the "mommy wars."[19] Not only does this media catfight pit mother against mother, but it suggests that all women be reduced to their one role—mother—or get cut out of the picture entirely.

At the same time that the new momism conquered the media outlets of America, we also saw mothers who talked back. *Maude*, Ann Romano on *One Day at a Time*, Erma Bombeck, Peg Bundy, *Roseanne*, Brett Butler, Marge Simpson, and the mothers in *Malcolm in the Middle* and *Everybody Loves Ray-mond* have all given the new momism a big Bronx cheer. They have repre-sented rebellious mothering: the notion that you can still love your kids and be a good mother without teaching them Origami, explaining factor analy-sis to them during bath time, playing softball with them at six A.M., or mak-ing sure they have a funny, loving note in their lunch box each and every day. Since 1970, because of money and politics, the new momism has con-quered much of the media, and thus our own self-esteem. But it has not done so uncontested. The same media that sell and profit from the new momism have also given us permission—even encouraged us—to resist it. However, it is important to note that much of this rebellion has occurred in TV sitcoms which, with a few exceptions, offer primarily short-term catharsis, a brief respite from the norms in dramatic programming, the news, and advice columns that bully us so effectively.

• • •

Because the media always serve up heroes and villains, there had to be the terrible mothers, the anti-Madonnas, the hideous counterexamples good mothers were meant to revile. We regret to report that nearly all of these women were African American and were disproportionately featured as failed mothers in news stories about "crack babies," single, teen mothers, and welfare mothers. One of the worst things about the new momism is that it is like a club, where women without kids, or women deemed "bad" moth-ers, like poor women and welfare mothers, don't belong. It is—with a few exceptions, like Clair Huxtable on *The Cosby Show*—a segregated club.

At the very same time that we witnessed the explosion of white celebrity moms, and the outpouring of advice to and surveillance of middle-class mothers, the welfare mother, trapped in a "cycle of dependency," became ubiquitous in our media landscape, and she came to represent everything wrong with America. She appeared not in the glossy pages of the women's magazines but rather as the subject of news stories about the "crisis" in the American family and the newly declared "war" on welfare mothers. Whatever ailed America—drugs, crime, loss of productivity—was supposedly her fault. She was portrayed as thumbing her nose at intensive mothering. Even worse, she was depicted as bringing her kids into the realm of market values, as putting a price on their heads, by allegedly calculating how much each additional child was worth and then getting pregnant to cash in on them. For middle-class white women in the media, by contrast, their kids were priceless.[20] These media depictions reinforced the divisions between "us" (minivan moms) and "them" (welfare mothers, working-class mothers, teenage mothers), and did so especially along the lines of race.

For example, one of the most common sentences used to characterize the welfare mother was, "Tanya, who has _____ children by _____ different men" (you fill in the blanks). Like zoo animals, their lives were reduced to the numbers of successful impregnations by multiple partners. So it's interesting to note that someone like Christie Brinkley, who has exactly the same reproductive MO, was never described this way. Just imagine reading a comparable sentence in *Redbook*. "Christie B., who has three children by three different men." But she does, you know.

At the same time that middle- and upper-middle-class mothers were urged to pipe Mozart into their wombs when they're pregnant so their kids would come out perfectly tuned, the government told poor mothers to get the hell out of the house and get to work—no more children's aid for them. Mothers like us—with health care, laptops, and Cuisinarts—are supposed to replicate the immaculate bedrooms we see in Pottery Barn Kids catalogs, with their designer sheets and quilts, one toy and one stuffed animal atop a gleaming white dresser, and a white rug on the floor that has never been exposed to the shavings from hamster cages, Magic Markers accidentally dropped with their caps off, or Welch's grape juice. At the same time, we've been encouraged to turn our backs on other mothers who pick their kids' clothes out of other people's trash and sometimes can't buy a can of beans to feed them. How has it come to seem perfectly reasonable—even justified—that one class of mother is supposed to sew her baby's diapers out of Egyptian cotton from that portion of the Nile blessed by the god Osiris while another class of mother can't afford a single baby aspirin?

NOTES

1. *People,* September 21, 1998.
2. *Good Housekeeping,* January 1995.
3. *People,* July 8, 1996.
4. Kristin van Ogtrop, "Attila the Honey I'm Home," *The Bitch in the House* (New York: William Morrow, 2002), p. 169.

5. "Motherhood Today — A Tougher Job, Less Ably Done," The Pew Research Center for the People & the Press, March 1997.

6. Philip Wylie, *Generation of Vipers* (New York: Holt, Rinehart and Winston, 1942). See also Ruth Feldstein's excellent discussion of momism in *Motherhood in Black and White: Race and Sex in American Liberalism, 1930–1965* (Ithaca: Cornell University Press, 2000), especially chapter 2.

7. Hays's book is must reading for all mothers, and we are indebted to her analysis of intensive mothering, from which this discussion draws. Sharon Hays, *The Cultural Contradictions of Motherhood* (New Haven: Yale University Press, 1996), p. 4.

8. For an account of the decline in leisure time see Juliet B. Schorr, *The Overworked American* (New York: Basic Books, 1992).

9. Patricia Heaton, *Motherhood & Hollywood* (New York: Villard Books, 2002), pp. 48–49.

10. See Katha Pollitt's terrific piece "Killer Moms, Working Nannies" in *The Nation*, November 24, 1997, p. 9.

11. Hays, pp. 4–9.

12. Based on an On-line Computer Library Center, Inc., search under the word *motherhood*, from 1970–2000.

13. Susan Faludi, in her instant classic *Backlash*, made this point, too, but the book focused on the various and multiple forms of backlash, and we will be focusing only on the use of motherhood here.

14. Robert Lekachman, *Visions and Nightmares: America after Reagan* (New York: Collier Books, 1988), pp. 118–121.

15. For a superb analysis of the role of mother-blaming in American politics, see Ruth Feldstein, *Motherhood in Black and White*, especially pp. 7–9.

16. V. Spike Peterson, "Gendered Nationalism: Reproducing 'Us' versus 'Them,'" in Lois Ann Lorentzen and Jennifer Turpin, eds., *The Women and War Reader* (New York: New York University Press, 1998).

17. This contradiction is central to Hays's argument.

18. Hays, p. 9.

19. Ibid.

20. Hays, p. 8.

29

CLAIMING JEZEBEL:
Black Female Subjectivity and Sexual Expression in Hip-Hop

AYANA BYRD

Ayana Byrd is a writer and editor living in Brooklyn, New York. She is an entertainment journalist whose work has appeared in *Vibe, Rolling Stone, Honey, TV Guide,* and *Paper* magazines. She is the coauthor of *Hair Story: Untangling the Roots of Black Hair in America.*

A ll it used to take was one "bitch" reference in a song, one gratuitous ass shake in a video and I was on a roll, criticizing the sexism of black men, denouncing the misogynistic societal structures set up by white men who supported it from their music industry corner offices, lamenting the misrepresented ways that black female bodies were on display. It didn't take much to get me back on my soapbox. But that, apparently, was a long time ago. Because today, allowed a receptive audience and the opportunity to wax passionately and even philosophically about the state of women in hip-hop — the art form that I once believed most defined me — I draw a big blank, barely able to muster up a half-hearted "You won't believe what I just heard . . ."

What happened since my rankled ire over Snoop Doggy Dogg's 1993 *Doggystyle* album cover of a black female behind wiggling, naked, out of a doghouse? Things haven't gotten any better. The "feminist rapper" Queen Latifah now uses the once taboo B word in her lyrics. Alongside Chaka Khan, who sings the hook for "It's All Good," the onetime "conscious" group De La Soul had a video complete with a Jacuzzi overflowing with near-naked women. Since the debut of rap videos, outfits in videos are skimpier, the sexual references lewder, and the complicity by women in their own exploitation more widespread. Yet all I generally feel is an apathy.

I can now listen to a song with the hook "Hoes/I've got hoes/in different area codes" and instead of cringing at thoughts of debasement, chuckle at the artist Ludacris's witty delivery. Maybe it's that I've defined my own sexuality and know for sure what I only suspected in the past—that these men aren't talking about me. The problem is, *they* don't know they're not talking about me. Further, a lot of women, particularly girls and young adults, aren't sure that they don't want to be talked about in this way. These songs, and the videos that illustrate them, offer the most broadly distributed examples of seemingly independent black women that many young and sexually pubescent girls see. And unfortunately few girls transitioning into womanhood understand that the representation of female bodies in rap videos is not an empowering power-of-the-pussy but a fleeting one.

Because I grew up in the 1970s and '80s, I find it easy to list all the people who looked like me that were on television. There was Penny on *Good Times,* Tootie from *The Facts of Life,* and the occasional appearance of Charlene on *Diff'rent Strokes.* In the mid-eighties, there were as well the wholesome Huxtable daughters of *The Cosby Show.* Those of us who came of age then had a near void of images upon which to draw for representations of black women our age, negative or positive. It was a decade devoted both to saving and to condemning the "Endangered Black Male." But teen pregnancy was skyrocketing, and often the predominant young black female faces on television were in public service spots against babies having babies. Yet there were few policies or social organizations that were addressing their need to be saved or uplifted.

As the eighties progressed, things didn't get much better. In film as well as television, portrayals of black women were at either extreme of the sexual spectrum. In Spike Lee's *She's Gotta Have It,* which has been raked over the coals by feminists since its release, the lead, Nola Darling, was, among other atrocities, raped by one of her lovers (the supposed nice one) and got back together with him for a short time. On *The Cosby Show,* the television program that perhaps came closest to engaging and entertaining an entire generation of black kids, the female characters were completely desexed. On one episode we learn that Denise, the "wild child" of the family, was a virgin until her wedding night. Though their cousin Pam and her friend Charmaine both flirt with the idea of "giving it up" to their boyfriends, they seem less interested in actually having sex than in keeping their mates happy.

As popular culture weighed in on young black female sexuality, there were also deeply embedded societal stereotypes with which to contend. The lingering effects of the Moynihan Report, the controversial paper by Daniel Patrick Moynihan, who would later become a U.S. Senator, were still being felt. It asserted that black social immobility was caused by a crisis in the black family, and that Black Superwomen had emasculated black men, causing a fissure in the normal family setting.[1] President Reagan had effectively constructed the idea of the Welfare Mother: a black woman who refused to get a job and be a normal contributor to society but instead sat at home all day (most likely in the projects), maybe hitting the crack pipe, having babies by a host of men, living off welfare checks that came out of the pockets of decent, hardworking (white) Americans. Outside of academic conferences, few observers pointed out that the majority of women in the country on welfare were white, and that most women stayed on public assistance for two years or less.

By the early nineties there were other messages in which black women were made into villains. While the media highlighted the Tawana Brawley case, in which the fifteen-year-old black girl alleged a racist attack by white police officers but was found by a grand jury to be lying,[2] they virtually ignored the 1990 case of five white student athletes who were charged with sodomy and sexual abuse for repeatedly sexually assaulting a Jamaican woman in a fraternity house at St. John's University. In the latter case, there was more than enough evidence to convict, but according to one juror, the acquittal was based on the jury's desire to save the boys' lives from "ruin." Together the cases colluded in delegitimizing claims of rape by black women. There was also Mike Tyson's 1991 conviction for raping Desiree Washington. As vehemently as the white press sought to turn Tyson into a beast, many blacks cried foul to the champ's imprisonment. "What was she doing in his room anyway?" "That bitch set him up!" "How was she laughing and smiling at the show if just the night before he had raped her?" There was often more talk about how he had been framed than about the fact that Tyson had a history of physical abuse toward women. Around the same time, Clarence Thomas's self-declared "high-tech lynching" was played out on television screens across the nation, although it was women—Anita Hill and black women in particular—who were left feeling like the ones hanging from the tree of political, if not necessarily public, opinion.

So what does any of this have to do with hip-hop? It is telling that the women—whether they're the rappers topping the charts or the dancers in the videos—formed their own identities at a time when black female sexuality in the cultural marketplace was not at all positive. The way black women experience and interpret the world has indeed been determined by our having to wage constant battles in order to determine our subjectivity—to say that we are not whores à la Desiree Washington, tricksters and liars à la Tawana Brawley, or disgruntled spinsters à la Anita Hill. In *Black Looks* the cultural theorist bell hooks writes, "The extent in which Black women feel devalued, objectified, dehumanized in this society determines the scope and texture of their looking relations. Those Black women whose identities were constructed in resistance, by practices that oppose the dominant order, were most inclined to develop an oppositional gaze."[3] Yet those women whose identities were instead constructed in compliance with the status quo were most inclined to absorb these images and make these representations and stereotypes of heterosexual black female sexuality their own.

Today, through the music video, there are so many black female bodies on view on any given day of watching television that it is impossible to list them. In many ways that is probably the point. Through the constant barrage of hypersexualized images, the young, black female has ceased to be an anomaly in the marketplace and is now back in the slave era position of anonymous chattel. Hooks sums it up in *Black Looks* when she writes, "Just as nineteenth-century representations of Black female bodies were constructed to emphasize that these bodies were expendable, contemporary images (even those created in black cultural production) give a similar message."[4] The hip-hop video has taken rap music to a level never imagined during its roots in the house parties of the 1970s Bronx. Early rap videos were overwhelmingly low-budget affairs. But in the late 1980s, *Video Music Box*—now the longest-running hip-hop video show in New York City—debuted from Miami and collided with the national explosion of that same city's 2 Live Crew, forever changing hip-hop video.

Before Luther Campbell and his 2 Live Crew, there were countless images of scantily clad women in music videos. Bands like Van Halen and Mötley Crüe had perfected the art of the gratuitous bikini shot long before rappers. The difference was that these women were white. And they were not being depicted in a genre proclaiming itself to be politically charged and revolutionary. As the rap historian Tricia Rose explains in her seminal work *Black Noise*, "Rap music is a black cultural expression that prioritizes black voices from the margins of urban America."[5] During the Reagan and Bush administrations, as prisons went up as rapidly as homelessness and drug use, and police brutality spread across the country, hip-hop became the medium for the disenfranchised citizens of the inner city to state their rage, vent their concerns, educate themselves about political issues, and fight back against government propaganda. Public Enemy, whose lyrics advised the disenfranchised to "fight the power," or spoke to controversial urban realities ("I don't wanna be called yo nigga"), were by far the most visible political rappers, but they were hardly the only ones.

By the time of the "Me So Horny"s and "Baby Got Back"s of the rap world, there were legions of hip-hop tunes that were not deep or meaningful in their lyrical content. But the accompanying videos, with images of women with DD cups washing soapy car windows with their breasts, were groundbreaking. "The visualization of music has far-reaching effects on musical culture and popular culture generally, not the least of which is the increase in visual interpretations of sexist power relationships,"[6] Rose wrote. In short, it became as easy as the click of the cable remote to see images of black women as so sexually licentious, so insatiably horny that Van Halen's "Hot for Teacher" looked almost tame.

In the early days of the booty video, the depiction of women in the music was overwhelmingly cut-and-dried. With a few notable exceptions, they were portrayed as gold-digging vixens. Hip-hop music extended the idea with videos that showed women dressed in G-strings, bikinis, and stripper outfits, oftentimes in situations that had nothing to do with the beach or a strip club. It was a time when many feminists and other interested onlookers noted that, as misconstrued and narrow as the representation of black women in rap music was, it would most likely be balanced once more women became viable, popular rappers. The idea was that, given the space to define themselves, female rappers would construct an image of black womanhood which encompassed a more realistic scope of sexuality, not to mention give voice to the day-to-day struggles of women living in the urban arenas that were typically the focus of hip-hop music.

The meteoric rise of Lil' Kim's career was the likely starting point for the muddying of the waters that has taken place for me and many others who once felt that there were only two sides in the sexual war of hip-hop. She is arguably the female rapper closest to achieving iconic status. And although she has attracted many fans based on interest in her music, Kim's real infamy stems from the public way she has lived her life. Nothing has been deemed too private for the diminutive rapper from Brooklyn. She's admitted that she never had her dad's acceptance and that as a teen she used sex and her body to survive. After the Notorious B.I.G., the man who had been her mentor as well as her married lover, died, she told *People* magazine how she kissed his urn each morning. On her sophomore album, *Notorious KIM,* she revealed how she aborted a pregnancy from her rap Svengali. We have watched Kim publicly wrestle with weight, undergo two breast enlargements, a nose job, blond hair, and blue contact lenses.

In 1995 Kim and her then-friend Foxy Brown opened the door for the public's acceptance of sexual female rappers. Before them, those relatively few women who were sexually brazen in hip-hop—groups like Hoes with Attitudes and Bytches Wit Problems are good examples—were often dismissed by cultural critics and feminists as willing participants in their own dehumanization. Instead, there was a perceived transgressiveness in Kim's and Foxy's acts of asserting desire and sexual wants in a culture where female sexuality is not typically linked with the pursuit of pleasure.

Yet while these two performers challenged notions of what it meant to be a woman in hip-hop, it could be argued that they were simultaneously supporting an image of black female sexuality that the white patriarchy had been trying to sell us since slavery. During the whole of the nineteenth century, for example, depictions of black female bodies were often sexualized in ways that white women's never were.[7] The black female was a licentious counterpart to the white woman's virtue, in fact making that virtue possible. The supposed sexuality of black women was the thing that white women could set themselves against. One of the most emblematic (and bizarre) representations of black female sexuality was the Hottentot Venus, whose "grossly overdeveloped labia," "enlarged clitoris," and large buttocks were seen as evidence of the "primitive sexuality of African women."[8] Like the African Hottentot, the black female body not only had a divergent sexual physiology made up of more pronounced sexual organs but a divergent sexual psychology that dictated uncontrollable "primitive" sexual desire. Although the Hottentot Venus was a medical myth, it was presented to the public as pure fact. Such fictions, whether they pertain to the hypersexual Hottentot or her diametrical opposite, the sexless archmother mammy, are all too powerful images. Contemporary black women are forced to negotiate the traces left by these contaminated constructions of black female sexuality.

Many black women who have always felt a need to strive for re-spectability in a culture that hypersexualizes them almost from birth see in Lil' Kim the freedom of "acting out" their sexuality. She not only refuses to shy away from the male gaze by desexing herself but openly preens for the male gaze while returning it. As bell hooks would say, she looks back. Some like to assert that rappers like Kim are intimidating men, shaking the very foundations of male sexuality by demanding that female sexual urgency and female pleasure be taken into account. Yet alongside demanding that they be sexually pleased, many female rappers convey a parallel overriding message in their lyrics: that the men who sexually satisfy them should also provide money, cash, and clothes.

By comparing the majority of female rappers in the entertainment mar-ketplace with the undisputed queen of commercialized female sexual agency, Madonna, it becomes clearer how precariously drawn the line is be-tween self-determination and coconspiring in one's own exploitation. "Madonna provides a perfect example of the postmodern, feminist heroine, selling the virtues of political indeterminacy in her insistent play with sex-ual expression," wrote Roseann M. Mandzuik in her essay "Feminist Politics and Postmodern Seductions." "Yet in her discourse as a postmodern icon, [there is] something [very] familiar in her transformation of politics into pleasure: Madonna sounds the same old cultural message that a woman's place is to be sensual, stylish and self-involved."[9] Underscoring this point and bringing it back to female rappers is Lil' Kim's video "How Many Licks," in which she turns herself into a doll with replaceable parts, a move so infused with self-objectification that it seems almost laughable in its ob-viousness. The question must be asked: What kind of transgressiveness is Kim enacting when she performs a femininity that mimics misogynistic pa-triarchal desires? In another song, she denounces her previous fear of fella-tio: "Now I throw lips to the shit/Handle it like a real bitch." Can sexual em-powerment be articulated by making oneself a powerful agent in the familiar pornographic images of sexual acts?

It would be easy to state that had these women, had all of us, been privy to more realistic images of black women in popular culture as we were growing up, things would be different today. But it's not that simple. There is a market impetus behind these images. "The artistry takes a backseat to the image," said Faith Newman, vice president of A&R at Jive Records, in the hip-hop publication *Blaze*. "Men control [these] women's careers, and it seems like if [the women] aren't looking like sluts or some hardcore dykes — excuse the expression — they aren't going to get the necessary push."[10] The commodification of blackness in the entertainment industry rewards black women much more readily for reactionary or regressive thinking about gen-der and sexuality. Both Foxy Brown and Lil' Kim, who were molded by older, already popular male rappers, have stated repeatedly that in the be-ginning of their careers they were pretty much told what their image would be and how they needed to play it up to sell records, whether this was how they chose to be depicted or not. "At sixteen I was just so happy to have a nice car and a nice home that I didn't complain about [my image]," Foxy said in *Essence* magazine. "I had all the influences around me, and I wasn't always strong enough to come back like, 'No. I don't want to do that.'"[11]

Back in 1999, when my soapbox preaching had harshly turned on female rappers as the real problem, I wrote a review of Foxy Brown's second album, *Chyna Doll*. I declared that if we were supposed to believe Foxy was any kind of doll at all, it was of the blow-up variety, willing and ready at all times to be the receptacle for a man's sexual pleasures. While it was hardly a nuanced, subtle statement, it seemed, at the time, fitting to explain what appeared to be going on. Rappers like Trina, Hurricane G, and Charli Baltimore (another mistress of the Notorious B.I.G.), alongside Foxy and Kim, were reveling in the narrow confines of this Pussy Free-For-All. Because while, yes, these assertions of female sexual agency were a direct challenge to the notion that black male sexuality within hip-hop exists as a conquering force over women, it was, to put it in blunt vernacular, getting tired. While these female rappers were perhaps providing a voice for those who had been silent sexual objects in male hip-hop, the rules had not been overturned in how they were being read by the rest of the society. So though it may at first be shocking or new to assert that you, a woman, want sex *and* oral sex *and* a man who can last for a long time, after a few similarly themed songs, the shock has worn off and what is left is confirmation of something that many men of all races and quite a few non-black women had always suspected: black women are whores.

The near-total lack of media images depicting the real lives of working class, inner city black girls in the 1980s left a void, and that space was filled with male-centered constructs of the licentious black female. What will be the effect on a young black girl today as she is bombarded with images of black female asses, breasts, and dirty talk? A group of teen black girls at the mall dressed as if they had just finished taping a video could arguably be not much different from white girls in the eighties donning see-through lace getups and scaring their parents with recitations of "Like a Virgin." But it could also be said that more is at stake: the very grim realities of sexually transmitted diseases, AIDS, teen pregnancy, and sexual assault and abuse. Just as important, mainstream American culture interprets black cultural articulations of misogyny, sexism, and unbridled female sexuality differently from their white counterparts. In the 1990s, during the fiercest criticisms of teen pop star Britney Spears for sporting bare midriffs and see-through pants, she professed to be a virgin. When Foxy Brown came onto the scene, at age fifteen, she was featured on a song called "Ain't No Nigga," rhyming, "Ain't no nigga like the one I got/sleeps around but he gives me a lot," and very few people expressed disgust, or even shock, at her age. And with white suburban youth being one of the biggest consumer bases for rap music, it is safe to say that while some of the kids buying the CDs may have never met a black woman, they've all seen at least one (probably quite a few) wrap her legs around a pole and dance to a hip-hop tune during an afternoon spent watching BET, MTV, or the Box.

Of course, black women aren't the only ones being sexualized in the new millennium. Magazines like *Maxim* and *Rolling Stone* enjoy massive sales due in large part to the soft porn shots of white celebrities that grace their covers. Within all levels and substrata of society, women are dabbling with a hypersexual, yet decidedly pro-woman persona, epitomized by the characters on the popular HBO show *Sex and the City*. (Incidentally, the show's stylist, Patricia Fields, has admitted that Lil' Kim is a major influence for the wardrobe of Carrie, the Upper East Side, fashion-fabulous protagonist.)

And, of course, not all women rappers are playing out triple X-rated fantasies, just as not every video contains a bevy of near-naked ladies. Lauryn Hill has earned fans, respect, critical acclaim and awards with her mix of earthy sensuality and political and social awareness. Her themes run the gamut from love, motherhood, and simple reminiscing to the current state of gender relations. In "Lost Ones," Hill rhymes, "Don't be a hardrock when you really are a gem / Baby girl, respect is just the minimum," as she encourages women to seek their true selves and demand respect at the very least. The rapper Eve does not hesitate to admit that for a short time before her rap career she was a stripper. Yet it is told not as a way to entice but simply as a fact, and Eve seems to be very much in control of her current image, which is part pop star sass, part round-the-way-girl tough, and part sexy plaything.

So now, as I find myself humming along to a catchy "ho" anthem, I'm curious about what happened to my once-rankled ire. A few months ago, when I began thinking about this essay, I would probably have argued that my apathy was proof that while sexism and self-objectification still existed, there was a balance that allowed me to breathe easier. That maybe it was because women rappers have come into the industry, and while it's not the utopia of sexual equality I had hoped for, at the very least we are there, pushing the envelope, being recognized. Or that there's a likely chance the next song on the radio could be, if not redeeming, at least inoffensive to women. That for every thug love ode like the one by Bonnie Shyne, there's a "my beautiful queen" song by a "conscious" rapper like Common.

But now I can say that it's nothing like that. More likely I have calmed down because the powers that be—the programming executives, the music industry bigwigs, the video casting agents—have achieved a major goal. Through a saturation of the market with tramplike black women, I, too, have fallen victim to the normalizing effects of visual and lyrical hoochie overkill.

In order to see if that was the case, I took time off from being a pop culture consumer—I turned off the cable television and never listened to the radio unless I needed a weather update. I wanted to test whether I'd climb back up on the soapbox, newly charged with disgust and anger once I'd stopped being so used to all the ass. During my hiatus, Puffy became P. Diddy and made a public statement of apology to any Asian women he may have unintentionally offended with one line from his song "Diddy," yet offered nothing to the black women he's been insulting throughout his career.

Vibe magazine printed an article on the current state of hip-hop for its 2001 year-end issue, and a full-page photo accompanying the piece was of a black woman's behind, even though the story never made any reference to it.

Two nights ago I found myself at a party for the rapper Jay Z's clothing line, Rocawear, where my time-out officially came to an end. The models, mostly men, were positioned inside cases meant to look like store window displays. And each black woman who was featured was wearing too-small shorts that let a portion of butt cheek peek out as she danced around a pole in front of excessively dressed men (coats, baggy pants, boots, hats) who offered her dollars. I looked around at the crowd and saw that few looked irritated or even seemed to question the ludicrousness of the setup. At the very least I hoped that some would find it passé. Just as I began searching for my car keys, more than aware that it was time for me to leave, the deejay put on the song that started all of this: "I've got hoes/I've got hoes/in different area codes." I didn't sing along, nor did I applaud Ludacris's linguistic wit. Instead I walked through the dancing bodies and headed out the door, wishing for a space in hip-hop where sex could be sexy and not insulting and women could be Smart and Interesting as well as Sexy. On that cold February night, it seemed like a goal that would be a long time coming.

NOTES

1. Officially titled "The Negro Family: The Case for National Action" and written in 1965.
2. In 1987 Tawana Brawley was found in upstate New York covered with racial slurs and charcoal. She alleged that a gang of six white police officers had "abducted and held her for four days in the woods, raping her repeatedly, writing KKK and NIGGER on her belly, smearing her with dog feces and leaving her in a plastic garbage bag outside an apartment complex where her family had once lived," but a grand jury found her story to lack credibility. See http://www.time.com/time/magazine/1998/dom/980727/file.stories_sacred_lies18.html.
3. bell hooks, *Black Looks: Race and Representation* (Boston: South End Press, 1992), 127.
4. Ibid., 64.
5. Tricia Rose, *Black Noise: Rap Music and Black Culture in Contemporary America* (Middletown, Conn.: Wesleyan University Press, 1994), 2.
6. Ibid., 9.
7. The stereotypical depiction of the black female body as licentious during the nineteenth century was one of two primary stereotypes.
8. Jan Nederveen Pieterse, *White on Black: Images of Africa and Blacks in Western Popular Culture* (New Haven: Yale University Press, 1992), 181.
9. Roseann M. Mandzuik, "Feminist Politics and Postmodern Seductions: Madonna and the Struggle," in *The Madonna Connection: Representational Politics, Subcultural Identities, and Cultural Theory,* ed. Cathy Schwichtenberg (Boulder, Colo.: Westview Press, 1993), 183–84.
10. Quoted in Charisse Nikole, "Invisible Women," *Blaze,* April 1999, 68.
11. Michelle Buford and Christopher John Farley, "Foxy's Dilemma," *Essence,* August 1999, 72.

30

THE NEW GIRLS NETWORK:
Women, Technology, and Feminism

SHIREEN LEE

Shireen Lee is an advocate for the empowerment of girls and young women and
helped to start SportsBridge, a nonprofit organization for girls, in 1995. In 2001 she
also served on an advisory board for the Asian Pacific American Women's Leadership Institute. Internationally, she was one of the founding members of the Youth
Caucus of the UN Commission on the Status of Women. She served on the International NGO Coordinating Committee for the UN General Assembly Special Session
on Beijing + 5, an appointed body of twenty-five international women activists. She
holds a bachelor of applied science honors degree in engineering science from the
University of Toronto and a master's degree in public administration from San
Francisco State University.

Virtual Organizing, Global Activism

After I left engineering, I joined a group of women who use technology for
feminist empowerment. I bought a one-way train ticket from Toronto to San
Francisco to help start a non-profit organization for girls. Five years later,
while I am fully immersed in local, national, and international advocacy for
girls and young women, technology remains an integral part of my work,
but like other women, I have redefined my involvement with it. Now, as one
of the cofounders of the Youth Caucus of the United Nations Commission on
the Status of Women, I use Internet technologies to fight for women's rights.
In a sense, I have come full circle. I left a job in technology because there was
no gender awareness or sensitivity there, and I now use the Internet to organize young women activists from around the world.

   The Internet has revolutionized the way we organize. While e-mail,
websites, Listservs, search engines, and newsgroups have improved communications for all groups, they have been particularly effective in serving a
women's political agenda. All over the world, women's groups tend to be

small, helping communities on a local, grassroots level. Historically they have worked in isolation, having little communication with one another. In the past three years, as access to the Internet worldwide has grown exponentially, this circumstance has changed drastically. Even in poor rural communities women may now have access to a computer with an online connection, albeit not with the frequency that we take for granted in the United States. Nonetheless, even sporadic access has globally facilitated information-sharing and coalition-building among women's groups in unprecedented numbers. Through Listservs that help build online communities, young women activists from Nigeria and Bosnia share learning about peer education models in HIV-AIDS prevention, and youth activists from Kenya and India exchange information about the state of girls' and young women's education in their countries.

The Internet offers possibilities for inclusion, diversity, and transparency that feminists have always aspired to but have sometimes had difficulty achieving. New technologies have sped up our communications, allowed us to share information on a grand scale, and given an immediacy to what we do. My favorite image of these new practices remains the computer room set up for the thousands of women's activists who converged on the UN in June 2000 for the Special Session of the General Assembly, also known as Beijing + 5. At each of the twenty or so computer terminals sat a women's rights activist from a different country e-mailing the latest information about the negotiations in New York back to her colleagues at home while hearing feedback on lobbying strategy from the dozens of activists from her country who could not be at the United Nations. If information is power, then that little room was power central.

The Internet has also changed how we interact with government, making it easier for us to influence legislation, demand accountability, and promote democratic participation. Women who have been reluctant to take a visible role in the women's movement now have the option of being "armchair activists" who can have an impact without leaving their homes or sacrificing anonymity. Rebecca Tadikonda epitomizes this new breed of women's activist. "I got an e-mail from a friend of mine about [the appointment of Attorney General John] Ashcroft and clicked on to the website," she says. "It only took five minutes—I wouldn't have done it if it was longer. I ended up forwarding the e-mail to a bunch of my women friends. Then I got another activist e-mail from another woman friend that I had forwarded the e-mail to. It creates networks and is an easy and personal way to get people involved in political activism—*especially* if the e-mail comes from someone you know."[1]

The Internet has definitely brought more women into the political process. According to Jennifer Pozner, founder and executive director of Women In Media News (WIMN), a media watchdog group, since President George W. Bush's inauguration, women have been embracing technology as a means of activism like never before. When President Bush reinstated the "global gag rule," which prevents government agencies from giving funds to private family planning programs outside the United States even if the money is not going to be used for abortion, Patt Morrison wrote a column in the *Los Angeles Times* denouncing it. Morrison sent the president a card that read, "President George W. Bush, in honor of President's Day, a donation has been made to Planned Parenthood in your name." People began forwarding the column via e-mail, asking that donations to Planned Parenthood be made in Bush's name. The e-mail spread like wildfire, and Planned Parenthood received $500,000.[2]

Toward an Empowered Future

When we think of technology, we often think more of the *use* of technology — using computers, e-mail, cell phones — and less of the *creation* of technology — designing computer software and hardware. The distinction is important because women now relate to technology much differently than men do. Women tend to be users more than creators of technology, whereas men are as much creators as they are users. Women have clearly used technology to their advantage in their activist work and business lives, but they are often shut out from creating the technology. Being good at using technology and adapting it for our political activism and financial independence is a huge step forward. But women must also play an integral part in creating the technology. To ensure that women are not left behind, we must develop ways to educate and graduate more women engineers and computer scientists and facilitate their participation in the workforce. Bridging this gap will ensure that future generations of feminists will not only express their activism from the outside, through existing technology, but also from within, through new technologies that are created with a gender lens and communities of color in mind.

How exactly will creating technology benefit women? Let's imagine. Thanks to new communications technologies, working from home at least part of the time is a growing phenomenon. This arrangement benefits women, particularly those with families, more than any other demographic group. Could this flexible approach to work have come about even earlier if women were responsible for designing the computers, networks, and faxes that make it all possible? Does it surprise anyone that when more women entered the medical profession, we started seeing more research on the impact of diseases on women and using women subjects rather than the male standard?

According to the Institute for Women and Technology, most product designers create products with themselves in mind.[3] As a result, most new products reflect the desires of the single, eighteen- to thirty-five-year-old men who design them. What if women were at the forefront of creating technology? We can imagine a spectrum of changes from the trivial — keyboards to fit women's smaller hands — to products with broad societal consequences. Will women engineers choose to perpetuate the multibillion-dollar military industry that keeps us locked in war games all over the globe? Or will they apply their intelligence and expertise to solving more pressing global problems?

As a movement, young feminists must continue to fight for meaningful representation and participation in the technology workforce and, equally important, continue to create their own workforces. But there is much work to be done. Gender equity in computer access, knowledge, and use cannot be measured solely by how many women send e-mail, surf the Net, or perform basic functions on the computer. The new benchmark should emphasize computer fluency—being able to interpret the information that technology makes available, mastering analytical skills and computer concepts, employing technology proactively, and imagining innovative uses for technology across a wide range of problems and subjects.[4]

NOTES

1. Women all over the United States protested the appointment of John Ashcroft as attorney general because of his dismal record on women's issues. Rebecca Tadikonda, interview with the author, 19 April 2001.
2. Robin Clewley, "Women Power Web of Protests," *Wired Online,* 16 April 2001, http://www.wired.com/news/politics/0,1283,43063,00.html.
3. Institute for Women and Technology, http://www.iwt.org/home.html.
4. AAUW Educational Foundation, *Tech-Savvy: Educating Girls in the New Computer Age* (Washington, D.C., 2000), http://www.aauw.org/research/girls_education/techsavvy.cfm.

31

WHERE ARE THE WOMEN?
The Strange Case of the Missing Feminists.
When Was the Last Time You Saw One on TV?

LAURA ZIMMERMAN

Laura Zimmerman is cofounder and codirector of the Center for New Words (formerly New Worlds Bookstore in Cambridge, MA), a nonprofit organization promoting women's voices and ideas.

"The neutral voice in America is the white male," The *Nation* columnist Katha Pollitt recently told me when I asked her about political opinion-making in the US since 9/11. "Everyone else is providing color commentary. A woman's opinion about Iraq or the budget is seen as a woman's opinion. The same for a black person. And white men just don't have the idea that they are affected by the fact that they are white men."

For decades, this spurious claim to "neutrality" has justified a white male monopoly of the air waves and the printed page. In today's media-driven culture, these "experts" deliver the opinions that shape our lives and the country's political system. Frequently, it's the op-ed pages, elite opinion journals, and Sunday morning news programs that explicate, promote, and even guide national decisions. When women are excluded from these venues, we're excised from the public policy-making loop. At the same time, our exclusion confirms our apparent lack of authority to speak about critical political issues. Consciously or not, audiences become habituated to male voices and bylines and dependent on white male gravitas to explain what's happening in the world. As we witnessed at the time of 9/11 and later during the wars in Afghanistan and Iraq, national emergencies push women even further to the sidelines. "To feel voiceless in a democracy in so difficult a time," prize-winning journalist Geneva Overholser said on National Public Radio in November 2001, "is very close to feeling disenfranchised."

Many women have felt a renewed sense of second-class citizenry in the past two years. By muting women's voices, the media has belittled our authority and leadership and removed us from the public conversation. We have also been robbed of the platform to assert political opinions that specifically affect women. "News agencies do not gather the facts about issues of concern to women," Rita Henley Jensen, editor in chief of Women's eNews, an Internet news service for e-mail subscribers and major media outlets, told me. "They do not hear women's voices, literally. And by not having access to the media, women's organizations and advocates cannot build their communities of interest." Jensen has all-too-often witnessed male editors' unlikely concepts of "women's issues." In the late 1990s, at a public talk given by a top decision maker at *The Los Angeles Times,* Jensen asked how the paper was reaching out to women readers. He replied, "We have a brand-new lifestyle and home decorating section."

In the months following 9/11, women wrote only 8 percent of the op-ed articles in *The Washington Post, The New York Times,* and *USA Today.* During the wars in Afghanistan and Iraq, biased editorial choices persisted. "It hasn't been this bad for women scholars and journalists wanting to influence the national public agenda since the pre-women's movement days when women were completely invisible," Caryl Rivers, author and journalism professor at Boston University, wrote in an April 2003 commentary published by Women's eNews. More recently, Rivers confirmed that these conditions are still at an all-time low. "We're being systematically overlooked," she said. "I'm not talking about fringe people. People who have enjoyed access to the media are feeling very much frozen out. In the best of times women face a high barrier. Now they may be less inclined to keep hurling themselves against the barricades."

Indeed, as Rivers mentions in her article, even Pulitzer Prize winner and syndicated columnist Ellen Goodman "complained . . . about getting bumped too often" at *The Washington Post.* Jill Nelson, best-selling author and the first black woman on *The Washington Post Magazine's* staff, says she lost $10,000 in freelance work after 9/11. "It was an immediate post 9/11 paradigm shift," Nelson said. "If you weren't on the government-sponsored white male reaction page, you were not going to be heard." Previously contacted for commentary by CNN or other outlets every six weeks or so, Nelson went an entire year with only an occasional call—and those were to cover insignificant events such as OJ's most recent arrest.

At best, many editors are afflicted with a "one-woman-only" mentality. Currently, for example, the op-ed page of *The New York Times* carries Maureen Dowd. Before her, it had Anna Quindlen and before that, Flora Lewis. Before Lewis, it had no women columnists at all. "This is true in many newspapers and magazines," said Pollitt. "There's one star woman columnist. Editors don't have the 50/50 picture at all. They have the picture: men plus one woman, or maybe two." After an editor for a weekly or monthly magazine commissions one long piece by a woman, he or she has done the affirmative action for that issue. This unacknowledged quota system caps the number of accomplished women writers in major venues and all but eliminates the up and coming. Additionally, male editors tend to look for someone to father and mentor. Typically, it's another man who closely resembles them.

And then there's television. In December 2001, the White House Project, a national group advocating women's political leadership, announced that the frequency of women guests on Sunday morning talk shows dropped in the month following 9/11 from only 10.7 percent of guests to an even worse 9.4 percent. Among repeat appearances—the true measure of authoritative presence—women were a mere seven percent. The study showed that we were also afforded less airtime, placed in later segments, and underrepresented in every professional category. Nightly newscasts were equally imbalanced: A 2002 Fairness and Accuracy in Reporting (FAIR) study showed that in 2001, US sources interviewed on the three major networks were 92 percent white and 85 percent male. Women constituted only 15 percent of all sources, and in the categories of professional and political sources (think of all the qualified feminists you know who could have filled those seats!) a mere nine percent.

Television producers, like print editors, dislike risk-taking. As a rule, they seek sources who have been used previously, either on the air or in print—a perfect method to keep the circle of opinion-makers small and closed, making it an old-boy's network. Perhaps this stems as much from lack of imagination as from deliberate exclusion. No doubt the motives are varied and complex. But the result is clear: Television and print media suppress the views of women commentators on critical subjects like the effect of war and peace on women's lives, sexual violence and trafficking of women, how globalization affects women's lives, or what low wage earning women endure. Women commentators discussing subjects like these would cast a critical eye on the news and shake up the standard male-chosen topics.

Media leaders perpetuate sameness, exclude outsiders, and enforce unspoken quotas. Add to these norms a corporate structure that all but eliminates women from the top of the decision-making pyramid, and we're looking at a structure that nearly guarantees exclusion of feminist commentators. Especially in today's hyper-masculine, conservative culture, when progressive voices in general have been marginalized, feminists are barred from view. "I'm worried that elite journals like *The Atlantic* are looking for women to say provocative things," said Rivers. "That means you smash other women, dump on feminism, or say that the real victims are men. And you can't find a feminist with a show of her own on cable television and very few on talk radio."

What you can find, of course, are right-wing commentators like Laura Ingraham and Ann Coulter filling women's allotted air time and print space. Chances are, they will be mocking Hillary Clinton, attacking feminist "misfits," or asserting outrageous opinions, such as Coulter's that McCarthyism wasn't so bad after all. Recent articles in *The New York Times Magazine* and *The Nation* have analyzed the conservative machine that grooms and sponsors journalists (especially on college campuses), endows media think tanks, and operates a highly organized, long-term campaign to control and manipulate the media. "Our side has nothing like it," Pollitt said. "It doesn't spend the money. And when it does, it's much mushier. There's a deficiency of sharkiness." Jensen also spoke about the vast sums conservatives have poured into the media, adding that women's organizations have moved in the opposite direction by diverting their resources into direct service. The result, Jensen believes, is the stifling of women's chances to affect the political workings of the country.

By themselves, these cultural and political forces present huge hurdles to progressive women. Add to these the personal ones. Many women distrust what is required of political commentators. We are not inclined to be thunderous and simplistic. In our eagerness to be fair-minded, we obsessively research subjects and worry too much about how we are received. Of course, we can also be bombastic, smart-alecky, and combative. But that's not our typical tone. "Commentary, punditry, op-ed writing, and also the web lend themselves to being brash and quick," media activist, journalist, and broadcaster Laura Flanders told me. "Historically, women have not been given to practice this. It's more acceptable for a man than a woman to be outrageous—but this seems to be changing on the right, not on the left."

Even people who write letters to the editor tend to be overwhelmingly male—and women also make fewer contacts with media ombudspersons. "It's not because women aren't reading the papers," said Overholser. "If you compare the percentage of women who read the paper with the percent of letter-writers, the numbers are very skewed." Other journalists, mentioning that women also submit fewer unsolicited manuscripts to magazine slush piles, speculated that we too quickly shy away from being told no, or dislike pestering people in charge—or that our lives have become so overwhelmingly busy we don't have time even to write a note. Perhaps we're not well-enough endowed with a trait that Katha Pollitt calls undiscourageability. Men are definitely not better writers, Pollitt says, and their perseverance does not necessarily win friends. But undaunted by dozens of rejections, they do increase their odds of getting published.

Then there's the problem that even those few women who have successfully entered the arena of mainstream commentary often conceal their feminist leanings. "If a female journalist does begin to advocate for women or to promote a related story, she loses credibility in the newsroom," said Jensen. "It's the same experience that African Americans and Latinas have. No one asks white men to give up their interest in sports or the military. But if a woman were to advocate running a story every day on the front page of a major newspaper about defunding rape crisis centers, she might likely be asked, 'Do you have a hang-up about this?' Her credibility would definitely be challenged." As a result, with a few well-known exceptions, feminist spokespersons mostly publish or broadcast in independent media, such as alternative websites, community radio, *The Village Voice*, *The Progressive*, and others.

There was a time when US feminists viewed the media as too abstract and elitist to claim top priority. Pained and outraged by institutions that thwarted women's lives—racism, domestic violence, the law, medicine, theology, politics, academia—we directed our attention to these. At the same time, we helped build an environmental movement, a gay rights movement, and a human rights movement. We were not slackers. We simply had enough to do.

But the days of letting the media off the hook are over. Increasingly, a vast industry run by a handful of corporate executives saturates our public and personal lives with narrow, biased ideas and opinions. And in times of crisis, like 9/11 and the war in Iraq, it goes berserk with the sound of its own voice and the sight of its own face.

For decades, a number of prescient feminists have been warning us that a state of emergency for women and people of color exists in the media industry. "A serious effort to match the right's media assault with comparable vigor is crucial," wrote Laura Flanders years before most of us were thinking about this problem, "if only to respond to those newspaper editors and TV anchors who claim they don't hear from feminists as they do from their opponents."

How to win access to both the mainstream and alternative media, how to use it to advance equality, how to exert influence—these are the big questions. But backing away from their magnitude would be a mistake. So would assuming simple answers. Nothing should stop us from talking among ourselves, making a public clamor, or joining with media activists already in gear. "What's holding us back is access," Flanders writes in the concluding pages of her book. "But so what else is new? . . . The right to communicate is like any right. And like any right, it will not be given. It must be won."

PART V
Sexuality

The social construction of gender greatly affects how sexuality emerges in humans. Without the constraints put upon sexuality by gender, expressions of human sexuality would probably look very different than they currently do. In spite of these constraints, however, human sexuality encompasses a wide range of behaviors and identities. The expectation in mainstream U.S. society that feminine, heterosexual women and masculine, heterosexual men will have sex only with each other and by mutual agreement is challenged by many people who do not conform to the dominant norms. It is also challenged by the rates of abusive sexual exploitation perpetrated by the more powerful on the less powerful, most frequently by men against women, children, and less powerful men.

The combinations and permutations of biological sex, gender, and sexual orientation are many. A person could be, for example, genetically and biologically female, actively heterosexual, and "masculine" in appearance, identity, or behavior (whatever masculine means in her social and cultural context). The American Psychiatric Association (APA) took on this issue when it reversed its designation of gay men and lesbians as mentally ill. Deciding that homosexuality was not, in itself, pathological, they did define as mentally ill those children who preferred to behave like people of the other gender. Reinforcing the assumption that sex and gender should match, "gender identity disorder" became the pathological label for feminine boys and masculine girls. Thus, Tommi Avicolli and Linnea Due (Part II) would probably have been labeled sick—Avicolli for his preference for jump rope and his manner of walking and Due for her too-masculine presentation and her wish to marry a woman. There is no suggestion by the APA that the boys who teased and ostracized Avicolli or the teachers who ignored them or the scout leader who rejected Due because of her "masculinity" might, in fact, be the sick ones. In part in response to this labeling, some gay men take on very masculine identities in adulthood, effectively distancing themselves from the "sissy" boys now considered pathological by the APA.[1] It is interesting to note that when high school football player Corey Johnson courageously came out as gay to his team, he was accepted and defended in an unusual example of community support; his masculinity seems to have bought him some privilege that Avicolli could not enjoy.[2]

When we acknowledge that one's genetic makeup is the only aspect of sexuality that is immutable, and that sexual behavior, sexual orientation, and gender do not necessarily line up in a predictable pattern, the options for the expression of gender and sexuality are many. Psychologist Carla Golden, in a study of undergraduates at an elite women's college in the Northeast, found that students' sexual identities did not necessarily match their sexual behavior.

For example, some women who identified themselves as heterosexual were exclusively involved sexually with women; some who had never had a same-sex sexual experience nevertheless identified themselves as bisexual because they perceived in themselves the potential for same-sex attraction and sexual activity. Golden also interviewed women who identified themselves as "political lesbians" whose sexual behavior was exclusively heterosexual. Golden concludes that the congruence between sexual feelings, behavior, and identity is often lacking, and she urges people to acknowledge the complex expressions of sexuality and sexual identity that result.[3]

Apart from examining the complex ways in which people define and express their sexuality, passionate debates and interesting topics abound in the field of sexuality. The origins of sexual orientations have been the subject of much research, as scholars explore the extent to which genetic predispositions or cultural influences might cause people to become heterosexual, gay, lesbian, or bisexual, or to change sexual orientation.[4] Heated debate ensues about whether pornography that is violent and degrading should continue to be legal in the United States.[5] Others argue for or against butch-femme roles in lesbian and gay communities.[6] Still others debate the pros and cons of sadomasochistic sexual practices.[7]

The debate about sex education in schools has created conflict in school districts in many parts of the United States (Should it exist? If so, with what content and starting at what age?).[8] Federal funding for sex education is currently limited to abstinence-only sex education. This program is designed to advocate for the psychological and physical benefits of abstinence and to present sex within heterosexual marriage as the only acceptable sexual expression. The American Civil Liberties Union has argued that this is a breach of freedom of speech; puts young people at risk for sexually transmitted diseases since half are not abstinent during high school; and discriminates against gay and lesbian youth. Schools that provide comprehensive sex education cannot qualify for federal funds. A survey of adults in 2004 suggests that only 15% think that abstinence only is the way to go. About half (46%) argue for abstinence-plus, teaching teens that abstinence is best but that if they are going to have sex, to know what is happening and do so responsibly. Another 36% recommend comprehensive sex education. The United States has the highest teen pregnancy rate in the developed world.[9]

The emergence of Viagra has provoked interest in women's sexuality, as researchers explore whether it or a similar drug could increase women's sexual responses as well.[10] It has also provoked debate among pharmaceutical companies and feminist health advocates as the definition of "sexual dysfunction" is addressed. It is unclear to what extent women's sexual dysfunction even exists; whether, if it exists, it is similar to erectile dysfunction; and whether doctors and pharmaceutical companies are truly concerned about women's sexual well-being or simply concerned with profits. Feminist critics are worried that emphasis on sexual physiology and performance could obscure the complex psychosocial aspects of sexuality, and they question the alleged "equal opportunity" in the attempt to develop a female arousal drug.[11] A recent attempt by Procter and Gamble to market Intrinsa, a testosterone patch for women billed as a female Viagra, was unanimously rejected by a U.S. Food and Drug Administration advisory panel in December 2004. The drug had been tested for only 6 months on a limited group of women—those who had experienced surgical menopause and had low sexual drive. The lessons learned from the failure to do long-term studies on hormone replacement therapy before marketing it to millions of women seem to have had an effect: experts called for longer-term research with a diverse group of women before allowing the drug to be marketed.[12] The emergence of Viagra has also raised questions about insurance coverage of this male-specific, voluntary drug, especially in light of the fact that most health plans do not cover the costs of contraception.[13]

Recently the reproductive technology that makes it possible for postmenopausal women to give birth has raised questions about the double standard related to women bearing children after their typical childbearing years. A sixty-three-year-old woman who gave birth in California was criticized for doing so, while men who become fathers at sixty-three are more likely to be cheered on.[14]

The sexual use and abuse of women, children, and disempowered men (especially in prison, see Kupers, Part IX) is a major issue in the study of sexuality. Human beings' potential for healthy, nonexploitive, enjoyable sexual expression with others is heavily influenced by the level of decision-making power we have over our own bodily expressions and the kind of caring (or lack thereof) that surrounds us as children.[15] The high rates of childhood sexual abuse (estimated at one in four girls, one in seven boys), followed by the rates of rape over a lifetime (estimated at one in three women and one in six men.[16] *Sex Roles: A Journal of Research* (March, 2002) suggest that sexual pleasure will be severely curtailed for a large proportion of the U.S. population. Boys seem to have an especially difficult time dealing with sexual abuse, in part because of homophobia. Many worry that they will be called gay if the perpetrator were male (and the perpetrator usually is male) or that they will be called unmanly if they didn't automatically enjoy forced sex with a woman, since many men and boys are socialized to accept and like heterosexual activity whatever the circumstance. If, in fact, children are gendered female by male perpetrators, a boy is apt to feel like a "girl" and have a difficult time admitting it.[17]

The widespread abuse of women in prostitution, trafficking, pornography, and interpersonal relationships leaves millions of women worldwide in a state of long-term sexual victimization. For that population, the choices related to sexual orientation and identity, freedom of sexual expression, and gender bending become largely irrelevant against a backdrop of the need to survive.[18] We have recently seen increased attention to "comfort women" who were forced into prostitution by the Japanese army during World War II, as these now-elderly women find their voices and tell the truth about what they experienced.[19] The use of prostitutes, including child prostitutes by the U.S. military abroad, has led to an effort to end soldiers' use of child prostitutes.[20] Publicity about international sex trafficking is bringing this issue to more readers in the United States, as illustrated by a recent report of female sex slaves from China in Chicago.[21]

HIV and AIDS have curtailed the sexual activity and, literally, the lives of a large segment of the world's population, leaving millions of people infected or dead. Young men ages 20–24 in the United States are currently at highest risk for sexually transmitted infections (STIs), tied, in part, to their commitment to the risk-taking aspects of masculinity.[22] An estimated one in four people in the United States will contract a sexually transmitted infection, some of which are without symptoms and can cause infertility and cancer.[23] AIDS and STIs have forced many people to communicate about sex in ways they didn't need to before, and they have stimulated changed sexual practices for a large proportion of the U.S. population, although some people are still in denial about the importance of condom use, even when they have access to condoms.[24] Even the Catholic Church is considering easing up on its policy against condom use, as the reality of the transmission of AIDS takes on a life of its own. A new perspective on condoms defines them as disease control rather then birth control, especially in developing countries with high rates of AIDS. It remains to be seen to what extent permission or recommendation for condom use will become church policy, especially in places where AIDS is not devastating the population.[25] Silvana Paternostro, a journalist who grew up in Colombia, reports that AIDS in Latin America is often spread by heterosexually identified men who have unprotected sex with other men and infect their unsuspecting female partners; their lack of identification as gay and their consequent denial of the risks of same-sex unprotected sexual activity leave them at high risk both for the illness itself and to become agents of its transmission.[26]

All the above sexual issues are embedded in cultural, racial, and class contexts. Sociologist Patricia Hill Collins, for example, examined pornography, prostitution, and rape in the context of race, class, and gender oppression. She provides data about, and analysis of, the long-term sexual exploitation of African American women.[27]

In oppressed communities, there is sometimes pressure to not break rank with one's cultural group. Thus, sometimes women of color or women in small white ethnic communities are pressured not to address sexism within those communities. For similar reasons, gays, lesbians, bisexuals, and transgendered people sometimes feel pressured not to address homophobia or transphobia. The larger, mostly white, movements that are fighting for gay/lesbian/bi/transgender rights and women's rights have a history of racism that renders those movements uncomfortable, unsafe, or unacceptable for many people of color. Gays and lesbians of color, then, frequently deal with two communities that fail to acknowledge their whole selves: a gay /lesbian/bisexual/transgender community that fails to address racism and a racial/ethnic community that fails to address heterosexism.[28]

In an interesting and moving account of what it's like to be the only Black person in a group of white lesbians, writer Paula Ross reports,

> There is rarely a time when I can attend to my self as lesbian apart from my self as black, a diasporic offspring, one of the millions of Africa's daughters dispersed by imperialism, greed, and an overweening appetite for colonization. I stand around this campfire with fifteen other lesbians. We are all erotically and sexually connected to other women. My lover's butch and my femme identities are not questioned for an instant. But even here, I cannot forget about race. They can forget — perhaps at their own peril, but they do have the option.[29]

Homophobia thrives in many contexts. In a recent well-publicized trial in Egypt that was denounced by various human rights groups, twenty-three men were jailed for one to five years for homosexual activity.[30] In fact, in response to the homophobic atmosphere that exists in most places, many gays and lesbians wish they were straight. The ex-gay movement in the United States has attempted to assist with conversions to heterosexuality, with mixed success. Recently, some active spokespersons for the ex-gay movement have resumed their lives as gays, creating an ex-ex-gay movement.[31]

This part of this book addresses sexuality from a range of perspectives, including questioning whether sexuality needs to be linked to gender (John Stoltenberg); looking at male athletes' approaches to sexuality (Don Sabo); issues of reproductive rights and sexuality for women with disabilities (Marsha Saxton); the difficulties faced by bisexual people from various racial and ethnic groups (Paula Rust); and a creative look at the potential for erotic energy in various aspects of women's lives (Audre Lorde). The authors in this part would like to see a world that is free of sexual exploitation and in which people are free to be sexual or erotic in any nonexploitative ways they choose. Some also make clear how difficult it would be to achieve this ideal.

As you explore these readings, you might want to think about your own sexuality. How closely is it tied to your gender? How does your ethnic/cultural context affect your understanding of, and your experience with, your sexuality? Do the men you know have anything in common with Sabo and his teammates in the locker room? Have you thought much about people with disabilities and sexuality or reproduction? Finally, what does erotic mean to you and what sense do you make of Lorde's understanding of the erotic?

NOTES

1. For an interesting discussion of the process by which the American Psychiatric Association removed homosexuality from the pathology list and simultaneously added "gender identity disorder of childhood," see Eve Kosofsky Sedgwick, "How to Bring Your Kids Up Gay," in *Tendencies* (Durham, NC: Duke University Press, 1993), pp. 154–164.

2. Rick Reilly, "The Biggest Play of His Life," *Sports Illustrated* 92, 19, p. 114.

3. Carla Golden, "Diversity and Variability in Women's Sexual Identities," in the Boston Lesbian Psychologies Collective, eds., *Boston Lesbian Psychologies Collective, Lesbian Psychologies: Exploration and Challenges* (Chicago: University of Illinois Press, 1987), pp. 19–34.

4. For discussions of causes of sexual orientation and the development of sexual identity see Alan P. Bell and Martin S. Weinberg, *Homosexualities: A Study of Human Diversity* (South Melbourne, Victoria: Macmillan, 1978); Jan Clausen, *Beyond Gay or Straight: Understanding Sexual Orientation* (New York: Chelsea House, 1997); Ronald C. Fox, "Bisexuality in Perspective: A Review of Theory and Research" in Beth A. Firestein, ed., *Bisexuality: The Psychology and Politics of an Invisible Minority* (Thousand Oaks, CA: Sage, 1996), pp. 3–50; Martin S. Weinberg, *Dual Attraction: Understanding Bisexuality* (New York: Oxford University Press, 1994).

5. For a discussion of class and pornography, see Laura Kipnis, "(Male) Desire and (Female) Disgust: Reading Hustler," in Lawrence Grossberg, Cary Nelson, and Paula Treichler, *Cultural Studies* (New York: Routledge, 1992), pp. 373–391. For a presentation of the anti-pornography position in the feminist pornography debate, see Dorchen Leidholdt and Janice G. Raymond, eds., *The Sexual Liberals and the Attack on Feminism* (New York: Pergamon Press, 1990); Laura Lederer and Richard Delgado, eds., *The Price We Pay: The Case against Racist Speech, Hate Propaganda, and Pornography* (New York: Hill and Wang, 1995). For a discussion of the feminist position in support of pornography, see Lisa Duggan and Nan D. Hunter, eds., *Sex Wars: Sexual Dissent and Political Culture* (New York: Routledge, 1995). For a recent attempt to bridge these two positions, see Gail Dines, Robert Jensen, and Ann Russo, *Pornography: The Production and Consumption of Inequality* (New York: Routledge, 1998). For an example from Queer studies of the role of racism in gay pornographic videos, see Richard Fung, "Looking for My Penis: The Eroticized Asian in Gay Video Porn," in Bad Object-Choices, ed., *How Do I Look? Queer Film and Video* (Seattle, WA: Bay Press, 1991).

6. For a discussion of butch-femme roles in the lesbian community, see Joan Nestle, "Butch-Femme Relationships: Sexual Courage in the 1950s," in *A Restricted Country* (Ithaca, NY: Firebrand, 1987), pp. 100–109.

7. For a discussion of sadomasochism, see Robin Ruth Linden et al., eds., *Against Sadomasochism: A Radical Feminist Analysis* (San Francisco: Frog in the Well, 1982); Pat Califia, *Sapphistry: The Book of Lesbian Sexuality* (Tallahassee, FL: Naiad Press, 1980).

8. See Pepper Schwartz and Virginia Rutter, *The Gender of Sexuality* (Thousand Oaks, CA: Pine Forge, 1998), pp. 20–21.

9. www.aclu.org/ReproductiveRights/ReproductiveRights.cfm?ID=10781&c=227; womensissues.about.com/od/healthsexuality/i/isabstinenceonl.htm.

10. Jennifer Babson, "At BU, a Fresh Look at Viagra—for Women" *Boston Sunday Globe* 254, no. 12 (July 12, 1998), pp. A1, A20.

11. Meika Loe, "Female Sexual Dysfuction: For Women or For Sale?" *The Network News* (January–February 2000), pp. 1, 6 (published by the National Women's Health Network).

12. Kathleen Phalen Tomaselli, "Intrinsa stalled by concerns about safety," *American Medical News*, January 17, 2005, http://www.ama-assn.org/amednews/2005/01/17/hlsc0117.htm.

13. www.ppnyc.org/facts/facts/contraceptive.html

14. Pepper Schwartz and Virginia Rutter, *The Gender of Sexuality* (Thousand Oaks, CA: Pine Forge Press, 1998), p. xiv.

15. Aline P. Zoldbrod, *Sex Smart: How Your Childhood Shaped Your Sexual Life and What to Do About It* (Oakland, CA: New Harbinger Publications, 1998).

16. Bradley H. White and Sharon E. Robinson Kurpius (2002) "Effects of Victim Sex and Sexual Orientation on Perceptions of Rape." *Sex Roles: A Journal of Research* (March).

17. I would like to acknowledge sociologist Gail Dines of Wheelock College for the idea that children are gendered female.

18. Kathleen Barry, *The Prostitution of Sexuality: The Global Exploitation of Women* (New York: NYU Press, 1995).

19. Cynthia Enloe, *Manueuvers: The International Politics of Militarizing Women's Lives* (Berkeley: University of California Press, 2000); Maria Rosa Henson, *Comfort Woman: A Filipina's Story of Prostitution and Slavery under the Japanese Military* (Lanham, MD: Rowman & Littlefield, 1999).

20. Cynthia Enloe, *Manueuvers: The International Politics of Militarizing Women's Lives* (Berkeley: University of California Press, 2000).

21. Charity Crouse, "Slaves of Chicago: International Sex Trafficking Is Becoming Big Business," *In These Times* 25, no. 3 (January 8, 2001), pp. 7–8.

22. John Stoltenberg, "Of Microbes and Men," *Ms.* 10, no. 5 (August–September 2000), pp. 60–62.

23. Angela Bonavoglia, "Making Love in the Dark," *Ms.* 10, no. 5 (August–September 2000), pp. 54–59.

24. Jill Lewis, "'So How Did Your Condom Use Go Last Night, Daddy?' Sex Talk and Daily Life" in Lynne Segal, ed., *New Sexual Agendas* (New York: New York University Press, 1997), pp. 238–252; Carla Willig, "Trust as Risky Practice," in Lynne Segal, ed., *New Sexual Agendas* (New York: New York University Press, 1997), pp. 125–153.

25. Raphael Lewis, "Cleric Calls Condom Use 'Lesser Evil' in HIV Fight," *The Boston Globe* 258, no. 78 (September 16, 2000), p. A1ff.

26. Silvana Paternostro, *In the Land of God and Man: A Latin Woman's Journey* (New York: Penguin Putnam, Inc., 1998).

27. Patricia Hill Collins, *Black Feminist Thought,* 2nd ed. (New York: Routledge, 2000).

28. Connie S. Chan, "Issues of Identity Development among Asian-American Lesbians and Gay Men," *Journal of Counseling and Development* 68, no. 1 (September–October 1989), pp. 16–20; Surina Kahn, "The All-American Queer Pakistani Girl," in Gwen Kirk and Margo Okazawa-Rey, eds., *Women's Lives: Multicultural Perspectives,* 2nd ed. (Mountain View, CA: Mayfield Publishing, 2001).

29. Paula Ross, "What's Race Got to Do with It?" in Karla Jay, ed., *Dyke Life* (New York: Basic Books, 1995), p. 142.

30. Sarah El Deeb, "23 Jailed after Trial for Gay Sex," *The Boston Globe* (November 15, 2001), p. A8.

31. Tatsha Robertson, "Gays Return to the Fold: Many Cite Flaws of 'Conversion'" *The Boston Globe* (September 9, 2000), pp. B1, B4.

32

HOW MEN HAVE (A) SEX

JOHN STOLTENBERG

John Stoltenberg is the author of *Refusing to Be a Man: Essays on Sex and Justice* (Meridian, 1990), *The End of Manhood: A Book for Men of Conscience* (Plume, 1994), and *What Makes Pornography "Sexy"?* (Milkweed Editions, 1994). He was born in Minneapolis in 1944 to working-class parents—his mother is German, and his father is Norwegian. He grew up queer, and lived with the writer Andrea Dworkin from 1974 until her death in 2005.

An address to college students

In the human species, how many sexes are there?
Answer A: *There are two sexes.*
Answer B: *There are three sexes.*
Answer C: *There are four sexes.*
Answer D: *There are seven sexes.*
Answer E: *There are as many sexes as there are people.*

I'd like to take you, in an imaginary way, to look at a different world, somewhere else in the universe, a place inhabited by a life form that very much resembles us. But these creatures grow up with a peculiar knowledge. They know that they have been born in an infinite variety. They know, for instance, that in their genetic material they are born with hundreds of different chromosome formations at the point in each cell that we would say determines their "sex." These creatures don't just come in XX or XY; they also come in XXY and XYY and XXX plus a long list of "mosaic" variations in which some cells in a creature's body have one combination and other cells have another. Some of these creatures are born with chromosomes that aren't even quite X or Y because a little bit of one chromosome goes and gets joined to another. There are hundreds of different combinations, and though all are not fertile, quite a number of them are. The creatures in this world enjoy their individuality; they delight in the fact that they are not divisible into distinct categories. So when another newborn arrives with an exoterically rare chromosomal formation, there is a little celebration: "Aha," they say, "another sign that we are each unique."

These creatures also live with the knowledge that they are born with a vast range of genital formations. Between their legs are tissue structures that vary along a continuum, from clitorises with a vulva through all possible combinations and gradations to penises with a scrotal sac. These creatures live with an understanding that their genitals all developed prenatally from exactly the same little nub of embryonic tissue called a genital tubercle, which grew and developed under the influence of varying amounts of the hormone androgen. These creatures honor and respect everyone's natural-born genitalia—including what we would describe as a microphallus or a clitoris several inches long. What these creatures find amazing and precious is that because everyone's genitals stem from the same embryonic tissue, the nerves inside all their genitals got wired very much alike, so these nerves of touch just go crazy upon contact in a way that resonates completely between them. "My gosh," they think, "you must feel something in your genital tubercle that intensely resembles what I'm feeling in my genital tubercle." Well, they don't exactly *think* that in so many words; they're actually quite heavy into their feelings at that point; but they do feel very connected— throughout all their wondrous variety.

I could go on. I could tell you about the variety of hormones that course through their bodies in countless different patterns and proportions, both before birth and throughout their lives—the hormones that we call "sex hormones" but that they call "individuality inducers." I could tell you how these creatures think about reproduction: For part of their lives, some of them are quite capable of gestation, delivery, and lactation; and for part of their lives, some of them are quite capable of insemination; and for part or all of their lives, some of them are not capable of any of those things—so these creatures conclude that it would be silly to lock anyone into a lifelong category based on a capability variable that may or may not be utilized and that in any case changes over each lifetime in a fairly uncertain and idiosyncratic way. These creatures are not oblivious to reproduction; but nor do they spend their lives constructing a self-definition around their variable reproductive capacities. They don't have to, because what is truly unique about these creatures is that they are capable of having a sense of personal identity without struggling to fit into a group identity based on how they were born. These creatures are quite happy, actually. They don't worry about sorting *other* creatures into categories, so they don't have to worry about whether they are measuring up to some category they themselves are supposed to belong to.

These creatures, of course, have sex. Rolling and rollicking and robust sex, and sweaty and slippery and sticky sex, and trembling and quaking and tumultuous sex, and tender and tingling and transcendent sex. They have sex fingers to fingers. They have sex belly to belly. They have sex genital tubercle to genital tubercle. They *have* sex. They do not have *a* sex. In their

erotic lives, they are not required to act out their status in a category system—because there is *no* category system. There are no sexes to belong to, so
sex between creatures is free to be between genuine individuals—not representatives of a category. They have sex. They do not have a sex. Imagine life
like that.

Perhaps you have guessed the point of this science fiction: Anatomically,
each creature in the imaginary world I have been describing could be an
identical twin of every human being on earth. These creatures, in fact, *are
us*—in every way except socially and politically. The way they are born is the
way we are born. And we are not born belonging to one or the other of two
sexes. We are born into a physiological continuum on which there is no discrete and definite point that you can call "male" and no discrete and definite
point that you can call "female." If you look at all the variables in nature that
are said to determine human "sex," you can't possibly find one that will unequivocally split the species into two. Each of the so-called criteria of sexedness is itself a continuum—including chromosomal variables, genital and
gonadal variations, reproductive capacities, endocrinological proportions,
and any other criterion you could think of. Any or all of these different variables may line up in any number of ways, and all of the variables may vary
independently of one another.[1]

What does all this mean? It means, first of all, a logical dilemma: Either
human "male" and human "female" actually exist in nature as fixed and discrete entities and you can credibly base an entire social and political system
on those absolute natural categories, or else the variety of human sexedness
is infinite. As Andrea Dworkin wrote in 1974:

> The discovery is, of course, that "man" and "woman" are fictions,
> caricatures, cultural constructs. As models they are reductive,
> totalitarian, inappropriate to human becoming. As roles they are
> static, demeaning to the female, dead-ended for male and female
> both.[2]

The conclusion is inescapable:

> We are, clearly, a multisexed species which has its sexuality spread
> along a vast continuum where the elements called male and female
> are not discrete.[3]

"We are . . . a multisexed species." I first read those words a little over ten
years ago—and that liberating recognition saved my life.

All the time I was growing up, I knew that there was something really
problematical in my relationship to manhood. Inside, deep inside, I never
believed I was fully male—I never believed I was growing up enough of a
man. I believed that someplace out there, in other men, there was something
that was genuine authentic all-American manhood—the real stuff—but I
didn't have it: not enough of it to convince *me* anyway, even if I managed to

be fairly convincing to those around me. I felt like an impostor, like a fake. I agonized a lot about not feeling male enough, and I had no idea then how much I was not alone.

Then I read those words—those words that suggested to me for the first time that the notion of manhood is a cultural delusion, a baseless belief, a false front, a house of cards. It's not true. The category I was trying so desperately to belong to, to be a member of in good standing—it doesn't exist. Poof. Now you see it, now you don't. Now you're terrified you're not really part of it; now you're free, you don't have to worry anymore. However removed you feel inside from "authentic manhood," it doesn't matter. What matters is the center inside yourself—and how you live, and how you treat people, and what you can contribute as you pass through life on this earth, and how honestly you love, and how carefully you make choices. Those are the things that really matter. Not whether you're a real man. There's no such thing.

The idea of the male sex is like the idea of an Aryan race. The Nazis believed in the idea of an Aryan race—they believed that the Aryan race really exists, physically, in nature—and they put a great deal of effort into making it real. The Nazis believed that from the blond hair and blue eyes occurring naturally in the human species, they could construe the existence of a separate *race*—a distinct category of human beings that was unambiguously rooted in the natural order of things. But traits do not a race make; traits only make traits. For the idea to be real that these physical traits comprised a race, the race had to be socially constructed. The Nazis inferiorized and exterminated those they defined as "non-Aryan." With that, the notion of an Aryan race began to seem to come true. That's how there could be a political entity known as an Aryan race, and that's how there could be for some people a personal, subjective sense that they belonged to it. This happened through hate and force, through violence and victimization, through treating millions of people as things, then exterminating them. The belief system shared by people who believed they were all Aryan could not exist apart from that force and violence. The force and violence created a racial class system, *and* it created those people's membership in the race considered "superior." The force and violence served their class interests in large part because it created and maintained the class itself. But the idea of an Aryan race could never become metaphysically true, despite all the violence unleashed to create it, because there simply *is* no Aryan race. There is only the idea of it—and the consequences of trying to make it seem real. The male sex is very like that.

Penises and ejaculate and prostate glands occur in nature, but the notion that these anatomical traits comprise a sex—a discrete class, separate and distinct, metaphysically divisible from some other sex, *the* "other sex"—is simply that: a notion, an idea. The penises exist; the male sex does not. The male sex is socially constructed. It is a political entity that flourishes only through acts of force and sexual terrorism. Apart from the global inferiorization and subordination of those who are defined as "nonmale," the idea of personal membership in the male sex class would have no recognizable meaning. It would make no sense. No one could be a member of it and no one would think they *should* be a member of it. There would be no male sex to belong to. That doesn't mean there wouldn't still be penises and ejaculate and prostate glands and such. It simply means that the center of our selfhood would not be required to reside inside an utterly fictitious category — a category that only seems real to the extent that those outside it are put down.

We live in a world divided absolutely into two sexes, even though nothing about human nature warrants that division. We are sorted into one category or another at birth based solely on a visual inspection of our groins, and the only question that's asked is whether there's enough elongated tissue around your urethra so you can pee standing up. The presence or absence of a long-enough penis is the primary criterion for separating who's to grow up male from who's to grow up female. And among all the ironies in that utterly whimsical and arbitrary selection process is the fact that *anyone* can pee both sitting down and standing up.

Male sexual identity is the conviction or belief, held by most people born with penises, that they are male and not female, that they belong to the male sex. In a society predicated on the notion that there are two "opposite" and "complementary" sexes, this idea not only makes sense, it *becomes* sense; the very idea of a male sexual identity produces sensation, produces the meaning of sensation, becomes the meaning of how one's body feels. The sense and the sensing of a male sexual identity is at once mental and physical, at once public and personal. Most people born with a penis between their legs grow up aspiring to feel and act unambiguously male, longing to belong to the sex that is male and daring not to belong to the sex that is not, and feeling this urgency for a visceral and constant verification of their male sexual identity — for a fleshy connection to manhood — as the driving force of their life. The drive does not originate in the anatomy. The sensations derive from the idea. The idea gives the feelings social meaning; the idea determines which sensations shall be sought.

People born with penises must strive to make the idea of male sexual identity personally real by doing certain deeds, actions that are valued and chosen because they produce the desired feeling of belonging to a sex that is male and not female. Male sexual identity is experienced only in sensation and action, in feeling and doing, in eroticism and ethics. The feeling of belonging to a male sex encompasses both sensations that are explicitly "sexual" and those that are not ordinarily regarded as such. And there is a tacit social value system according to which certain acts are chosen because they make an individual's sexedness feel real and certain other acts are eschewed because they numb it. That value system is the ethics of male sexual identity — and it may well be the social origin of all injustice.

Each person experiences the idea of sexual identity as more or less real, more or less certain, more or less true, depending on two very personal phenomena: one's feelings and one's acts. For many people, for instance, the act of fucking makes their sexual identity feel more real than it does at other times, and they can predict from experience that this feeling of greater certainty will last for at least a while after each time they fuck. Fucking is not the only such act, and not only so-called sex acts can result in feelings of certainty about sexual identity; but the act of fucking happens to be a very good example of the correlation between *doing* a specific act in a specific way and *sensing* the specificity of the sexual identity to which one aspires. A person can decide to do certain acts and not others just because some acts will have the payoff of a feeling of greater certainty about sexual identity and others will give the feedback of a feeling of less. The transient reality of one's sexual identity, a person can know, is always a function of what one does and how one's acts make one feel. The feeling and the act must conjoin for the idea of the sexual identity to come true. We all keep longing for surety of our sexedness that we can feel; we all keep striving through our actions to make the idea real.

In human nature, eroticism is not differentiated between "male" and "female" in any clear-cut way. There is too much of a continuum, too great a resemblance. From all that we know, the penis and the clitoris are identically "wired" to receive and retransmit sensations from throughout the body, and the congestion of blood within the lower torso during sexual excitation makes all bodies sensate in a remarkably similar manner. Simply put, we all share all the nerve and blood-vessel layouts that are associated with sexual arousal. Who can say, for instance, that the penis would not experience sensations the way that a clitoris does if this were not a world in which the penis is supposed to be hell-bent on penetration? By the time most men make it through puberty, they believe that erotic sensation is supposed to *begin* in their penis; that if engorgement has not begun there, then nothing else in their body will heat up either. There is a massive interior dissociation from sensations that do not explicitly remind a man that his penis is still there. And not only there as sensate, but *functional and operational*.

So much of most men's sexuality is tied up with gender-actualizing — with feeling like a real man — that they can scarcely recall an erotic sensation that had no gender-specific cultural meaning. As most men age, they learn to cancel out and deny erotic sensations that are not specifically linked to what they think a real man is supposed to feel. An erotic sensation unintentionally experienced in a receptive, communing mode — instead of in an aggressive and controlling and violative mode, for instance — can shut down sensory systems in an instant. An erotic sensation unintentionally linked to the "wrong" sex of another person can similarly mean sudden numbness. Acculturated male sexuality has a built-in fail-safe: Either its political context reifies manhood or the experience cannot be felt as sensual. Either the act creates his sexedness or it does not compute as a sex act. So he tenses up, pumps up, steels himself against the dread that he be found not male enough. And his dread is not stupid; for he sees what happens to people when they are treated as nonmales.

My point is that sexuality does not *have* a gender; it *creates* a gender. It creates for those who adapt to it in narrow and specified ways the confirmation for the individual of belonging to the idea of one sex or the other. So-called male sexuality is a learned connection between specific physical sensations and the idea of a male sexual identity. To achieve this male sexual identity requires that an individual *identify with* the class of males—that is, accept as one's own the values and interests of the class. A fully realized male sexual identity also requires *nonidentification with* that which is perceived to be nonmale, or female. A male must not identify with females; he must not associate with females in feeling, interest, or action. His identity as a member of the sex class men absolutely depends on the extent to which he repudiates the values and interests of the sex class "women."

I think somewhere inside us all, we have always known something about the relativity of gender. Somewhere inside us all, we know that our bodies harbor deep resemblances, that we are wired inside to respond in a profound harmony to the resonance of eroticism inside the body of someone near us. Physiologically, we are far more alike than different. The tissue structures that have become labial and clitoral or scrotal and penile have not forgotten their common ancestry. Their sensations are of the same source. The nerve networks and interlock of capillaries throughout our pelvises electrify and engorge as if plugged in together and pumping as one. That's what we feel when we feel one another's feelings. That's what can happen during sex that is mutual, equal, reciprocal, profoundly communing.

So why is it that some of us with penises think it's sexy to pressure someone into having sex against their will? Some of us actually get harder the harder the person resists. Some of us with penises actually believe that some of us without penises want to be raped. And why is it that some of us with penises think it's sexy to treat other people as objects, as things to be bought and sold, impersonal bodies to be possessed and consumed for our sexual pleasure? Why is it that some of us with penises are aroused by sex tinged with rape, and sex commoditized by pornography? Why do so many of us with penises want such antisexual sex?

There's a reason, of course. We have to make a lie seem real. It's a very big lie. We each have to do our part. Otherwise the lie will look like the lie that it is. Imagine the enormity of what we each must do to keep the lie alive in each of us. Imagine the awesome challenge we face to make the lie a social fact. It's a lifetime mission for each of us born with a penis: to have sex in such a way that the male sex will seem real—and so that we'll feel like a real part of it.

We all grow up knowing exactly what kind of sex that is. It's the kind of sex you can have when you pressure or bully someone else into it. So it's a kind of sex that makes your will more important than theirs. That kind of sex helps the lie a lot. That kind of sex makes you feel like someone important and it turns the other person into someone unimportant. That kind of sex makes you feel real, not like a fake. It's a kind of sex men have in order to feel like a real man.

There's also the kind of sex you can have when you force someone and hurt someone and cause someone suffering and humiliation. Violence and hostility in sex help the lie a lot too. Real men are aggressive in sex. Real men get cruel in sex. Real men use their penises like weapons in sex. Real men leave bruises. Real men think it's a turn-on to threaten harm. A brutish push can make an erection feel really hard. That kind of sex helps the lie a lot. That kind of sex makes you feel like someone who is powerful and it turns the other person into someone powerless. That kind of sex makes you feel dangerous and in control—like you're fighting a war with an enemy and if you're mean enough you'll win but if you let up you'll lose your manhood. It's a kind of sex men have *in order to have* a manhood.

There's also the kind of sex you can have when you pay your money into a profit system that grows rich displaying and exploiting the bodies and body parts of people without penises for the sexual entertainment of people with. Pay your money and watch. Pay your money and imagine. Pay your money and get real turned on. Pay your money and jerk off. That kind of sex helps the lie a lot. It helps support an industry committed to making people with penises believe that people without are sluts who just want to be ravished and reviled—an industry dedicated to maintaining a sex-class system in which men believe themselves sex machines and men believe women are mindless fuck tubes. That kind of sex helps the lie a lot. It's like buying Krugerrands as a vote of confidence for white supremacy in South Africa.

And there's one more thing: That kind of sex makes the lie indelible—burns it onto your retinas right adjacent to your brain—makes you remember it and makes your body respond to it and so it makes you believe that the lie is in fact true: You really are a real man. That slavish and submissive creature there spreading her legs is really not. You and that creature have nothing in common. That creature is an alien inanimate thing, but your penis is completely real and alive. Now you can come. Thank God almighty—you have a sex at last.

Now, I believe there are many who are sick at heart over what I have been describing. There are many who were born with penises who want to stop collaborating in the sex-class system that needs us to need these kinds of sex. I believe some of you want to stop living out the big lie, and you want to know how. Some of you long to touch truthfully. Some of you want sexual relationships in your life that are about intimacy and joy, ecstasy and equality—not antagonism and alienation. So what I have to say next I have to say to you.

When you use sex to have a sex, the sex you have is likely to make you feel crummy about yourself. But when you have sex in which you are not struggling with your partner in order to act out "real manhood," the sex you have is more likely to bring you close.

This means several specific things:

1. *Consent is absolutely essential.* If both you and your partner have not freely given your informed consent to the sex you are about to have,

you can be quite certain that the sex you go ahead and have will make you strangers to each other. How do you know if there's consent? You ask. You ask again if you're sensing any doubt. Consent to do one thing isn't consent to do another. So you keep communicating, in clear words. And you don't take anything for granted.

2. *Mutuality is absolutely essential.* Sex is not something you do *to* someone. Sex is not a one-way transitive verb, with a subject, you, and an object, the body you're with. Sex that is mutual is not about doing and being done to; it's about being-with and feeling-with. You have to really be there to experience what is happening between and within the two of you—between every part of you and within both your whole bodies. It's a matter of paying attention—as if you are paying attention to someone who matters.

3. *Respect is absolutely essential.* In the sex that you have, treat your partner like a real person who, like you, has real feelings—feelings that matter as much as your own. You may or may not love—but you must always respect. You must respect the integrity of your partner's body. It is not yours for the taking. It belongs to someone real. And you do not get ownership of your partner's body just because you are having sex—or just because you have had sex.

For those who are closer to the beginning of your sex lives than to the middle or the end, many things are still changing for you about how you have sex, with whom, why or why not, what you like or dislike, what kind of sex you want to have more of. In the next few years, you are going to discover and decide a lot. I say "discover" because no one can tell you what you're going to find out about yourself in relation to sex—and I say "decide" because virtually without knowing it you are going to be laying down habits and patterns that will probably stay with you for the rest of your life. You're at a point in your sexual history that you will never be at again. You don't know what you don't know yet. And yet you are making choices whose consequences for your particular sexuality will be sealed years from now.

I speak to you as someone who is closer to the middle of my sexual history. As I look back, I see that I made many choices that I didn't know I was making. And as I look at men who are near my age, I see that what has happened to many of them is that their sex lives are stuck in deep ruts that began as tiny fissures when they were young. So I want to conclude by identifying what I believe are three of the most important decisions about your sexuality that you can make when you are at the beginning of your sexual history. However difficult these choices may seem to you now, I promise you they will only get more difficult as you grow older. I realize that what I'm about to give is some quite unsolicited nuts-and-bolts advice. But perhaps it will spare you, later on in your lives, some of the obsessions and emptiness that have claimed the sexual histories of many men just a generation before you. Perhaps it will not help, I don't know; but I hope very much that it will.

First, you can start choosing now not to let your sexuality be manipulated by the pornography industry. I've heard many unhappy men talk about how they are so hooked on pornography and obsessed with it that they are virtually incapable of a human erotic contact. And I have heard even more men talk about how, when they do have sex with someone, the pornography gets in the way, like a mental obstacle, like a barrier preventing a full experience of what's really happening between them and their partner. The sexuality that the pornography industry needs you to have is not about communicating and caring; it's about "pornographizing" people—objectifying and conquering them, not being with them as a person. You do not have to buy into it.

Second, you can start choosing now not to let drugs and alcohol numb you through your sex life. Too many men, as they age, become incapable of having sex with a clear head. But you need your head clear—to make clear choices, to send clear messages, to read clearly what's coming in on a clear channel between you and your partner. Sex is no time for your awareness to sign off. And another thing: Beware of relying on drugs or alcohol to give you "permission" to have sex, or to trick your body into feeling something that it's not, or so you won't have to take responsibility for what you're feeling or for the sex that you're about to have. If you can't take sober responsibility for your part in a sexual encounter, you probably shouldn't be having it—and you certainly shouldn't be zonked out of your mind *in order* to have it.

Third, you can start choosing now not to fixate on fucking—especially if you'd really rather have sex in other, noncoital ways. Sometimes men have coital sex—penetration and thrusting then ejaculating inside someone—not because they particularly feel like it but because they feel they *should* feel like it: It's expected that if you're the man, you fuck. And if you don't fuck, you're not a man. The corollary of this cultural imperative is that if two people don't have intercourse, they have not had real sex. That's baloney, of course, but the message comes down hard, especially inside men's heads: Fucking is *the* sex act, the act in which you act out what sex is supposed to be—and what sex you're supposed to be.

Like others born with a penis, I was born into a sex-class system that requires my collaboration every day, even in how I have sex. Nobody told me, when I was younger, that I could have noncoital sex and that it would be fine. Actually, much better than fine. Nobody told me about an incredible range of other erotic possibilities for mutual lovemaking—including rubbing body to body, then coming body to body; including multiple, nonejaculatory orgasms; including the feeling you get when even the tiniest place where you and your partner touch becomes like a window through which great tidal storms of passion ebb and flow, back and forth. Nobody told me about the sex you can have when you stop working at having a sex. My body told me, finally. And I began to trust what my body was telling me more than the lie I was supposed to make real.

I invite you too to resist the lie. I invite you too to become an erotic traitor to male supremacy.

NOTES

1. My source for the foregoing information about so-called sex determinants in the human species is a series of interviews I conducted with the sexologist Dr. John Money in Baltimore, Maryland, in 1979 for an article I wrote called "The Multisex Theorem," which was published in a shortened version as "Future Genders" in *Omni* magazine, May 1980, pp. 67–73ff.
2. Dworkin, Andrea, *Woman Hating* (New York: Dutton, 1974), p. 174.
3. Dworkin, *Woman Hating*, p. 183.

33

THE MYTH OF THE SEXUAL ATHLETE

DON SABO

Don Sabo, Ph.D., is professor of sociology at D'Youville College in Buffalo, New York. His latest books include (with Michael Messner) *Sex, Violence & Power in Sport* (Crossing Press) and (with Dave Gordon) *Men's Health & Illness: Gender, Power, & the Body* (Sage Publishers). He coauthored the 1997 President's Council on Physical Fitness and Sport report *Physical Activity and Sport in the Lives of Girls*. He directed the nationwide Women's Sports Foundation study *Sport and Teen Pregnancy* (1998).

The phrase "sexual athlete" commonly refers to male heterosexual virtuosity in the bedroom. Images of potency, agility, technical expertise, and an ability to attract and satisfy women come to mind. In contrast, the few former athletes who have seriously written on the subject, like Dave Meggyesy and Jim Bouton, and films such as *Raging Bull* and *North Dallas Forty*, depict the male athlete as sexually uptight, fixated on early adolescent sexual antics and exploitative of women. The former image of athletic virility, however, remains fixed within the popular imagination. Partly for this reason, little has been said about the *real* connections between sports and male sexuality.

Locker-Room Sex Talk

Organized sports were as much a part of my growing up as Cheerios, television, and homework. My sexuality unfolded within the all-male social world of sports where sex was always a major focus. I remember, for example, when as prepubertal boys I and my friends pretended to be shopping for baseball cards so we could sneak peeks at *Playboy* and *Swank* magazines at the newsstand. After practices, we would talk endlessly about "boobs" and what it must feel like to kiss and neck. Later, in junior high, we teased one another in the locker room about "jerking off" or being virgins, and there were endless interrogations about "how far" everybody was getting with their girlfriends.

Eventually, boyish anticipation spilled into *real* sexual relationships with girls, which, to my delight and confusion, turned out to be a lot more complex than I ever imagined. While sex (kissing, necking, and petting) got more exciting, it also got more difficult to figure out and talk about. Inside, all the boys, like myself, needed to love and be loved. We were awkwardly reaching out for intimacy. Yet we were telling one another to "catch feels," be cool, connect with girls but don't allow yourself to depend on them. When I was a high-school junior, the gang in the weight room once accused me of being wrapped around my girlfriend's finger. Nothing could be further from the truth, I assured them, and to prove it I broke up with her. I felt miserable about this at the time, and I still feel bad about it.

Within the college jock subculture, men's public protests against intimacy sometimes became exaggerated and ugly. I remember two teammates, drunk and rowdy, ripping girls' blouses off at a party and crawling on their bellies across the dance floor to look up skirts. Then there were the late Sunday morning breakfasts in the dorm. We jocks would usually all sit at one table listening to one braggart or another describe his sexual exploits of the night before. Though a lot of us were turned off by such boasting, ego-boosting tactics, we never openly criticized it. Stories of raunchy, or even abusive sex, real or fabricated, were also assumed to "win points." A junior fullback claimed to have defecated on a girl's chest after she passed out during intercourse. There were also some laughing reports of "gang-bangs."

When sexual relationships were "serious," that is, tempered by love and commitment, the unspoken rule was silence. Rarely did we young men share our feeling about women, our uncertainty about sexual performance, or our disdain for the crudeness and insensitivity of some of our teammates. I now see the tragic irony in this: we could talk about casual sex and about using, trivializing, or debasing women, but frank discussions about sexuality that unfolded within a loving relationship were taboo. Within the locker-room subculture, sex and love were seldom allowed to mix. There was a terrible split between our inner needs and outer appearances, between our desire for love from women and our feigned indifference toward them.

Sex as a Sport

Organized sports provide a social setting in which gender (i.e., masculinity and femininity) learning melds with sexual learning. Our sense of "femaleness" or "maleness" influences the ways we see ourselves as sexual beings. Indeed, as we develop, sexual identity emerges as an extension of an already formed gender identity, and sexual behavior tends to conform to cultural norms. To be manly in sports, traditionally, means to be competitive, successful, dominating, aggressive, stoical, goal-directed, and physically strong. Many athletes accept this definition of masculinity and apply it in their relationships with women. Dating becomes a sport in itself, and "scoring," or having sex with little or no emotional involvement, is a mark of masculine achievement. Sexual relationships are games in which women are seen as opponents, and his scoring means her defeat. Too often, women are pawns in men's quests for status within the male pecking order. For many of us jocks, sexual relationships are about man as a hunter and woman as prey.

Why is this? What transforms us from boys who depend on women to men who misunderstand, alienate ourselves from, and sometimes mistreat women? One part of the problem is the expectation that we are supposed to act as though we want to be alone, like the cowboy who always rides off into the sunset alone. In sports, there is only one "most valuable player" on the team.

Too often this prevents male athletes from understanding women and their life experiences. Though women's voices may reach men's ears from the sidelines and grandstands, they remain distant and garbled by the clamor of male competition. In sports, communication gaps between the sexes are due in part to women's historical exclusion, from refusal to allow girls to play along with boys, and coaching practices which quarantine boys from the "feminizing" taint of female influence. One result of this isolation is that sexual myths flourish. Boys end up learning about girls and female sexuality from other males, and the information that gets transmitted within the male network is often inaccurate and downright sexist. As boys, we lacked a vocabulary of intimacy, which would have enabled us to better share sexual experiences with others. The locker-room language that filled our adolescent heads did not exactly foster insights into the true nature of women's sexuality—or our own, for that matter.

Performance and Patriarchy

Traditional gender learning and locker-room sexual myths can also shape men's lovemaking behavior. Taught to be "achievement machines," many athletes organize their energies and perceptions around a performance ethic that influences sexual relations. Men apply their goal-directedness and preoccupation with performance to their lovemaking. In the movie *Joe,* a sexually liberated woman tells her hard-hat lover that "making love isn't like running a fifty-yard dash."

Making intercourse the chief goal of sex limits men's ability to enjoy other aspects of sexual experience. It also creates problems for both men and their partners. Since coitus requires an erection, men pressure themselves to get and maintain erections. If erections do not occur, or men ejaculate too quickly, their self-esteem as lovers and men can be impaired. In fact, sex therapists tell us that men's preoccupation and anxieties about erectile potency and performance can cause the very sexual dysfunctions they fear.

It is important to emphasize that not only jocks swallow this limiting model of male sexuality. Sports are not the only social setting that promotes androcentrism and eroticism without emotional intimacy. Consider how male sexuality is developed in fraternities, motorcycle gangs, the armed forces, urban gangs, pornography, corporate advertising, MTV, magazines like *Playboy* or *Penthouse,* and the movies—to name but a few examples. These are not random and unrelated sources of traditional masculine values. They all originate in patriarchy.

Sexual relations between men and women in Western societies have been conducted under the panoply of patriarchal power. The sexual values that derive from patriarchy emphasize male dominance and the purely physical dimensions of the sex act while reducing women to delectable but expendable objects. An alternative conception of human sexuality, however, is also gaining ascendancy within the culture. Flowing out of women's experiences and based on egalitarian values, it seeks to integrate eroticism with love and commitment. It is deeply critical of the social forces that reduce women (and men) to sex objects, depersonalize relationships, and turn human sexuality into an advertising gimmick or commodity to be purchased. This is the sexual ethos proffered by the women's movement.

Today's young athletes don't seem as hooked as their predecessors on the hypermasculine image traditional sports have provided. Perhaps this is because alternative forms of masculinity and sexuality have begun to enter the locker-room subculture. More girls are playing sports than ever before, and coeducational athletic experiences are more common. As more women enter the traditionally male settings of sports, business, factories, and government, men are finding it more difficult to perceive women in only one dimension. Perhaps we are becoming better able to see them as fellow human beings and, in the process, we are beginning to search for alternative modes of being men.

What Do Men Really Want (or Need)?

Most of us do not really know what it is we want from our sexual lives. Men seem torn between yearning for excitement and longing for love and intimacy. On one side, we feel titillated by the glitter of corporate advertising. Eroticism jolts our minds and bodies. We're sporadically attracted by the simple hedonism of the so-called sexual revolution and the sometimes slick, sometimes sleazy veil of pornography, soft and hard. Many of us fantasize about pursuing eroticism without commitment; some actually live the fantasy. Yet more men are recently becoming aware of genuine needs for intimate relationships. We are beginning to recognize that being independent, always on the make and emotionally controlled, is not meeting our needs. Furthermore, traditional masculine behavior is certainly not meeting women's expectations or satisfying their emotional needs. More and more men are starting to wonder if sexuality can be a vehicle for expressing and experiencing love.

In our culture many men are suffering from sexual schizophrenia. Their minds lead them toward eroticism while their hearts pull them toward emotional intimacy. What they think they want rarely coincides with what they need. Perhaps the uneasiness and the ambivalence that permeate male sexuality are due to this root fact: the traditional certainties that men have used to define their manhood and sexuality no longer fit the realities of their lives. Until equality between the sexes becomes more of a social reality, no new model of a more humane sexuality will take hold.

As for me, I am still exploring and redefining my sexuality. Although I don't have all the answers yet, I do have direction. I am listening more closely to women's voices, turning my head away from the sexist legacy of the locker room, and pursuing a profeminist vision of sexuality. I feel good to have stopped pretending that I enjoy being alone. I never did like feeling alone.

34

REPRODUCTIVE RIGHTS
A Disability Rights Issue

MARSHA SAXTON

Marsha Saxton, Ph.D. teaches Disability Studies at the University of California, Berkeley, School of Public Health, and works as a researcher at the World Institute on Disability in Oakland, California. She has special interests in women's issues, genetic technologies and personal assistance services. She has published many articles about disability rights, women's health, and genetic screening issues.

I n recent years, the women's movement has broadened its definition of "reproductive rights" to include not only abortion, but all aspects of sexuality, procreation, and parenthood. The priorities of the National Abortion Reproductive Rights Action League also reveal this broader agenda: protecting adolescent reproductive health, preventing unintended pregnancy and sexually transmitted disease, eliminating restrictive or coercive reproductive health policies, and promoting healthy pregnancy and early childhood health.

Some women may take for granted birth control, reproductive health care, and sex education, forgetting that people with different life experiences based on class, race, or physical or mental ability may not have access to these fundamental aspects of reproductive freedom. But for people with disabilities, *all* the reproductive rights are still at stake.

For centuries, the oppression of people with disabilities has denied us "choice": choice about who should be regarded as "a sexual being," who should have babies, which babies should be born, which babies should be allowed to live after they're born, who should raise these babies into adulthood. These choices were made, for the most part, by others. People with disabilities are beginning to demand a say in these decisions now that the Americans with Disabilities Act (ADA) has forced the public to perceive our issues as civil rights issues. In the decades to come, we hope to see a transformation in the public's perception of disability and of people with disabilities. The issue of reproductive rights can serve as a catalyst for this transformation.

The stereotype of asexuality is slowly lifting. There are now a few disabled characters in the popular literature and media who are portrayed as sexual beings participating in intimate activities. (Some of these movie personalities,

Marsha Saxton, "Reproductive Rights: A Disability Rights Issue," from *Sojourner: The Women's Forum* (1995). Reprinted with the permission of the author.

such as actress Marlee Maitlin, themselves are deaf or have physical disabilities. However, most disabled characters on TV or in the movies are still
played by non-disabled actors.)

New and complex issues are emerging in regard to disability and procreation. Many relate to new developments in reproductive technologies.
Others reflect changing social values. What follows is a discussion of how
these new issues affect people with disabilities.

Reproductive Health Care

Because of patronizing attitudes about disabled people, many medical practitioners and health care facilities do not consider offering reproductive
health care services to their patients who have disabilities. Many people with
disabilities or with chronic illness, because of the "preexisting condition" exclusion in most health insurance, have been denied access to *any* health care,
not only reproductive health care. There are few medical or nursing schools
that offer any training on the reproductive health of people with disabilities.
Only in the last five years has there been any research on the effects of various birth control methods for people with different kinds of disabilities or
chronic illness, and these studies are limited, often focusing only on spinal
cord injury. Even people with the more common disabling conditions like diabetes, arthritis, or multiple sclerosis have little or no information about
whether they should or shouldn't use particular methods of birth control.

In Chicago, a group of disabled women have created a "disability accessible" gynecological clinic through the Chicago Rehabilitation Institute and
the Prentice Women's Hospital, staffed with practitioners who have been
trained to serve disabled women. The Health Resource Center for Women
with Disabilities is unique. One day a week, it offers accessible core gyn
services for women with disabilities and now serves more than 200 women.
The staff includes nurse practitioners and midwives; and a nurse who has a
disability has been hired. The clinic program plans to expand its resources to
include a project director to monitor clinic services and to oversee a library
with health-related videos and publications. It will also add an 800 telephone number staffed by a woman with a disability to respond to questions
about accessible health care services. The center has initiated research directed at documenting the medical experiences of women with disabilities
and improving services for traditionally underserved populations, including
developmentally disabled, learning disabled, and mentally retarded women.

Sex Education

Disabled children and adults need information about dating, sex, menstrua-
tion, pregnancy, birth control, AIDS, and other sexually transmitted diseases.
Attitudes have changed, and increasingly, parents and educators are recog-

nizing that disabled children need sex education. But this is not the norm. Disabled children are still often overprotected by adults who don't know how to teach them about "the facts of life." Questions such as the following tend to provoke confusion: how can blind children be given information about gender anatomy? How should retarded children be told about AIDS? How can deaf children, children who use wheelchairs, or any child who may have felt the stigma of disability be encouraged to interact positively with non-disabled and disabled peers and to learn positive sexual self-esteem? Many disabled adults never received important information about sex. They are vulnerable to confusing or dangerous misinformation and serious difficulties with their own sexuality, difficulties that result not from actual physical limitations but simply from exclusion from information and experience.

Marriage Disincentives

In the United States, people with disabilities who receive certain kinds of Social Security or Medicaid benefits are discouraged from getting married by threat of reduced or eliminated benefits. These "marriage disincentives" (like "employment disincentives," which discourage disabled people from employment by threat of reduced medical coverage) reveal the serious disability discrimination fundamentally built into our disability policies. If an SSI (Supplemental Security Income) recipient marries, his or her spouse's earnings are considered income, thus reducing the recipient's benefits, jeopardizing essential medical and personal care attendant services, and often placing enormous financial burden on the couple to finance prohibitively expensive services or equipment. The current law has the effect of forcing people with disabilities to accept "living together" as temporary sweethearts rather than an adult, community-sanctioned marriage. A recent attempt by disability rights advocates to urge Donna Shalala of the federal Department of Health and Human Services to legislate a more equitable system failed. While the outward rationale for the law is to save taxpayer money on people who could be supported by a spouse (based on the assumption that two can live as cheaply as one), social scientists and disability rights activists suspect that drafters of these marriage disincentive laws were also intending to thwart marriage and potential procreation for disabled people.

"Reproducing Ourselves"

The very idea of disabled persons as parents scares some people and exposes discriminatory attitudes that might otherwise remain hidden. Acceptance of disabled people as parents simply requires the larger community's acceptance of us as human beings. By denying our rights to be mothers and fathers, it is not only our competence to care for our young, but our very existence, our desire to "reproduce ourselves," that is forbidden.

In late 1991, TV news anchor Bree Walker, who has a genetic disability and who was pregnant, became the brunt of a call-in radio talk show when the host Jane Norris asked listeners, "Should disabled people have children?" Callers aired their opinions about whether Walker should have her baby or, as Norris posed the question, "Is it 'fair' to bring a child with a disability into the world?" The incident became the focal point of the disabled women's community's challenge to the idea that people with disabilities should not be born.

Qualifications for Parenthood

The Earls are a married Michigan couple, both severely disabled with cerebral palsy. They had a baby, Natalie, and sought assistance from the Michigan Home Help Program in providing physical care for the infant. Their desire to raise their own child and to demonstrate their competence as loving parents was thwarted by state regulations that bar the personal care assistant (PCA) of a disabled client from touching the client's child during paid work hours. One result of this regulation seems to be that disabled people who rely on the PCA program for help in daily living cannot have children.

Of course, people with disabilities must take seriously the responsibilities of adult sexuality and the potential for pregnancy and parenthood. We must also educate ourselves, the disability community, and our families and friends about what it means to be a parent and be disabled. And we must be prepared to take on the discriminatory policies of a variety of institutions: medical, social services, legal, and media. But we must also do battle within ourselves. We must overcome the voices we've internalized that say, "You can't possibly do this, you can't be good parents, and you don't deserve the benefits or the assistance required to raise your own children."

In Berkeley, California, an agency called Through the Looking Glass offers the first program specifically designed to assist parents with disabilities in skills development, community resources, and peer support. Looking Glass also publishes a newsletter, which can be ordered at: 2198 Sixth St., Suite 100, Berkeley, CA 94710.

Custody Struggles

Tiffany Callo is a young woman who wanted to raise her newborn son. Because of her cerebral palsy, the California Department of Social Services challenged her ability to care for the child. Armed with lawyers and court orders, the department refused to allow her to demonstrate her parenting skills in an appropriate environment that would enable her to show the creative approaches she had developed to handle the baby. *Newsweek* reporter Jay Mathews picked up her story, and Callo became a spokesperson for the cause of mothers with disabilities who fight for the right to raise their own children. Social service and child protection agency professionals need training and awareness to allow them to perceive the *abilities* of disabled parents, not only the stereotyped limitations.

Adoption

A large number of children adopted or waiting for adoption are disabled. Many disabled adults were adopted or placed in foster homes. It is still largely the case that adoption agencies do not consider disabled people as prospective parents for either disabled or non-disabled children. We need to challenge this stereotype that people with disabilities cannot be good adoptive parents. A few adoption agencies are changing policies, allowing disabled people to adopt, and in some cases even encouraging disabled adults to adopt children with disabilities. For example, Adoption Resource Associates in Watertown, Massachusetts, has taken a special interest in prospective disabled parents and makes specific mention in their brochure that they do not discriminate on the basis of disability in their placement services.

Sterilization Abuse

Consider this story of a woman with a psychiatric disability: "When I was twenty, I got pregnant by my boyfriend at the state mental school. Of course, there was no birth control for patients. We weren't allowed to have sex, but it went on all the time, even between patients and attendants. A doctor forced my mother to sign a paper giving me an abortion, even though I wanted to give up the baby for adoption. When I woke up, I found out I had had a hysterectomy. Maybe I couldn't take care of the baby then, but nobody even asked me what I wanted to do, or what I hoped for when I got older."

When a guardian or medical professional decides that people labeled retarded, mentally ill, or with other disabilities should not be parents, sterilization without consent may occur. Often, guardians or other decision makers who intervene on behalf of these disabled people have little exposure to the Independent Living Movement, or other community disability resources. As disabled people, we need to be empowered to make our own decisions regarding sexuality and procreation.

Abortion

Women with disabilities have reported significant difficulties with regard to abortion. These include being pressured to undergo an abortion because it is assumed that a disabled woman could not be a good parent, or, conversely, being denied access to abortion because a guardian decides the woman was incapable of making her own reproductive choices. Sometimes, after birth, a disabled woman's child is taken away from her. Women with disabilities experience the same kinds of abortion access difficulties as non-disabled women, but these difficulties are often magnified by disability discrimination.

Prenatal Screening

Scientific advances in the field of genetics have created technologies that can detect an increasing number of genetic conditions in the womb. While the general public seems to regard this medical technology as a wonderful advance and a way to reduce the incidence of disability and improve the quality of life, people with disabilities often have a very different view. As revealed in the Bree Walker case mentioned above, the unchallenged assumption often accompanying the use of these screening tests is that the lives of people with genetically related disabilities (such as muscular dystrophy, Down syndrome, cystic fibrosis, sickle cell anemia, and spina bifida) are simply not worth living and are a burden that families and society would rather not endure. The options to abort a fetus who might die early in life, or to abort in order to preclude the birth of a child with severe disabilities, are framed as "reproductive options." But in this era of health care cost containment, the notion of controlling costs by eliminating births of disabled babies may become a requirement, rather than an option. Then it ceases to be reproductive freedom and becomes quality control of babies—eugenics. The availability of these tests reinforces these notions, and the tests are actually marketed to women and to health care providers on this basis. Women are increasingly pressured to abort a fetus identified as disabled. Real choice must include the right to bear children with disabilities.

We in the disabled community must voice our ideas about selective abortion and attest to the true value of our lives. Only when a valid picture of the quality of our lives is available can prospective parents make choices about the use of tests for genetic disabilities in fetuses.

The Reproductive Rights Movement

The women's movement has begun to reach out to women with disabilities as a group. Women's organizations have begun to understand and challenge their own discriminatory attitudes and behaviors. More and more events in the women's movement are beginning to be wheelchair accessible and interpreted for the hearing impaired. But we have a long way to go to make the women's community fully welcoming of disabled people. This is a good time to get involved and share our thinking and energies. To be fully integrated into society, we must get involved and take leadership in all movements, and the movement for reproductive health care and real choice is an especially important one for people with disabilities to take on.

As disabled people, we have unique perspectives to share. Our views can enlighten everyone about the fundamental issues of sexuality and reproduction. We have gained much knowledge and experience with medical intervention, asking for and effectively managing help, dealing with bureaucracy, and fighting for access and power. Other controversial issues to which we can contribute our thinking include surrogate motherhood, population concerns, birthing technologies, artificial insemination, and *in vitro* fertilization.

The movement for reproductive rights needs to include people with disabilities as much as disabled people need to be included in the movement.

35

THE IMPACT OF MULTIPLE MARGINALIZATION

PAULA C. RUST

Paula C. Rust, Ph.D., is assistant professor of sociology at Hamilton College in Clinton, New York, where she teaches LesBiGayTrans studies. She is author of *Bisexuality and the Challenge to Lesbian Politics: Sex, Loyalty, and Revolution.*

One's sexuality is affected not only by the sexual norms of one's culture of origin but also by the position of one's culture of origin vis-à-vis the dominant culture of the United States. For individuals who belong to marginalized racial-ethnic, religious, or socioeconomic groups, the effects are numerous. Marginalized groups sometimes adopt the attitudes of the mainstream; other times, they reject these attitudes as foreign or inapplicable. McKeon (1992) notes that both processes shape the sexual attitudes of the white working class. On the one hand, the working class absorbs the homophobic attitudes promoted by the middle- and upper-class controlled media. At the same time, working-class individuals are rarely exposed to "liberal concepts of tolerance" taught in institutions of higher education which help moderate overclass heterosexism. On the other hand, working-class sexual norms are less centered around the middle-class notion of "pro-priety"—a value that working-class individuals cannot as readily afford. The result is a set of sexual norms that differs in complex ways from those facing middle- and upper-class bisexuals.

In marginalized racial and ethnic groups, racism interacts with cultural monosexism and heterosexism in many ways. In general, the fact of racism strengthens ethnic communities' desires to preserve ethnic values and tradi-tions, because ethnicity is embodied and demonstrated via the preservation of these values and traditions. Tremble, Schneider, and Appathurai (1989) wrote, "After all, one can abandon traditional values in Portugal and still be Portuguese. If they are abandoned in the New World, the result is assimila-tion" (p. 225). Thus, ethnic minorities might cling even more tenaciously to traditional cultures than Euro-Americans do, because any cultural change reflects not a change in ethnic culture but a loss of ethnic culture. To the ex-tent that ethnic values and traditions restrict sexual expression to heterosex-uality, ethnic minority bisexuals will be under particular pressure to deny same-sex feelings in demonstration of ethnic loyalty and pride. Attempts to challenge these values and traditions by coming out as bisexual will be in-terpreted as a challenge to ethnic culture and identity in general.

Because homosexuality represents assimilation, it is stigmatized as a "white disease" or, at least, a "white phenomenon." Individuals who claim a bisexual, lesbian, or gay identity are accused of buying into white culture and thereby becoming traitors to their own racial or ethnic group. Previous researchers have found the attitude that lesbian or gay identity is a white thing among African Americans and Hispanics and the attitude that homo-sexuality is a "Western" behavior among Asian Americans (Chan, 1989; Espin, 1987; H., 1989; Icard, 1986; Matteson, 1994; Morales, 1989). In the cur-rent study, the association of gayness with whiteness was reported most often by African American respondents. One African American woman wrote that "when I came out, it was made clear to me that my being queer was in some sense a betrayal of my 'blackness.' Black women just didn't do 'these' kinds of things. I spent a lot of years thinking that I could not be me and be 'really' black too." Morales (1990) found that Hispanic men choose to identify as bisexual even if they are exclusively homosexual, because they see gay identity as representing "a white gay political movement rather than a sexual orientation or lifestyle" (p. 215). A Mexican woman in the current study wrote that she has "felt like . . . a traitor to my race when I acknowl-edge my love of women. I have felt like I've bought into the White 'disease' of lesbianism." A Puerto Rican woman reported that in Puerto Rico homo-sexuality is considered an import from the continental States. Chan (1989) found that Asian Americans tend to deny the existence of gays within the Asian American community, Wooden et al. (1983) reported this attitude among Japanese Americans, and Carrier et al. (1992) found denial of the ex-istence of homosexuality among Vietnamese Americans who considered homosexuality the result of seduction by Anglo-Americans. Tremble et al. (1989) suggested that viewing homosexuality as a white phenomenon might permit ethnic minority families to accept their LesBiGay members, while transferring guilt from themselves to the dominant society.

Ironically, whereas racism can strengthen commitment to ethnic values and traditions, it can also pressure ethnic minorities to conform to mainstream values in an effort to gain acceptance from culturally dominant groups. Because members of ethnic minorities are often perceived by Euro-Americans as representatives of their entire ethnic group, the nonconformist behavior of one individual reflects negatively on the whole ethnic group. For example, African American respondents reported that homosexuality is considered shameful for the African American community because it reflects badly on the whole African American community in the eyes of Euro-Americans. A similar phenomenon exists among lesbians and gays, some of whom chastise their more flamboyant members with "How can you expect heterosexual society to accept us when you act like *that!?*" As one Black bisexual woman put it, "Homosexuality is frowned upon in the black community more than in the white community. It's as if I'm shaming the community that is trying so hard to be accepted by the white community."

The fact of ethnic oppression also interacts with particular elements of ethnic minority culture in ways that affect bisexuals. Specifically, the emphasis on the family found in many ethnic minority cultures is magnified by ethnic oppression in two ways. First, oppression reinforces the prescription to marry and have children among minorities which, for historical reasons, fear racial genocide (Greene, 1994; Icard, 1986). Second, the fact of racism makes the support of one's family even more important for ethnic minority individuals. As Morales (1989) put it, the "nuclear and extended family plays a key role and constitutes a symbol of their ethnic roots and the focal point of their ethnic identity" (p. 225). Ethnic minority individuals learn techniques for coping with racism and maintaining a positive ethnic identity from their families and ethnic communities; to lose the support of this family and community would mean losing an important source of strength in the face of the ethnic hostility of mainstream society (Almaguer, 1993; Chan, 1992; Icard, 1986). Thus, ethnic minority bisexuals have more to lose if they are rejected by their families than do Euro-American bisexuals. At the same time, they have less to gain because of the racism of the predominantly Euro-American LesBiGay community. Whereas Euro-American bisexuals who lose the support of their families can count on receiving support from the LesBiGay community instead (albeit limited by the monosexism of that community), ethnic minority bisexuals cannot be assured of this alternative source of support.

Because of fear of rejection within their own racial, ethnic, or class communities, many bisexuals — like lesbians and gay men — remain in the closet among people who share their racial, ethnic, and class backgrounds. For example, an African American–Chicana "decided to stay in the closet instead of risk isolation and alienation from my communities." Sometimes, individuals who remain closeted in their own racial-ethnic or class communities participate in the mainstream lesbian, gay, and bisexual community, which is primarily a Euro-American middle-class lesbian and gay community. Such individuals have to juggle two lives in two different communities, each of which is a valuable source of support for one aspect of their identity, but neither of which accepts them completely. Among people of their own racial, ethnic, or class background, they are not accepted and often not known as bisexuals, and among Euro-American lesbians and gays, they encounter both monosexism and class and racial prejudice or, at the least, a lack of support and understanding for the particular issues that arise for them because of their race, ethnicity, or class. Simultaneously, like other members of their racial, ethnic, or class community, they have to be familiar enough with mainstream Euro-American heterosexual culture to navigate daily life as a racial or ethnic minority; so they are, in effect, tricultural (Lukes & Land, 1990; Matteson, 1994; Morales, 1989). This situation leads not only to a complex social life but might also promote a fractured sense of self, in which one separates one's sexual identity from one's racial identity from one's American identity and experiences these identities as being in conflict with each other, just as are the communities that support each identity. Some individuals attempt to resolve this dilemma by prioritizing allegiances to these communities (Espin, 1987; Johnson, 1982; Morales, 1989), a response that Morales (1989, 1992) sees as a developmental stage preceding full integration of one's ethnic and sexual identities. More detailed descriptions of the antagonism between ethnic and gay communities and its effect on sexual minority individuals can be found in Gutiérrez and Dworkin (1992), Icard (1986), and Morales (1989, 1992).

Other bisexuals respond to the conflict between their racial/ethnic, class, and sexual communities by leaving their communities of origin in favor of mainstream LesBiGay communities. For most ethnic minority bisexuals, however, this does not solve the problem. For example, an Orthodox Jew who grieves her lost connection to the Jewish community wrote, "I still do not feel that my Jewish life and my queer life are fully integrated and am somewhat at a loss." This is true despite the large numbers of Jewish bisexuals, gays, and lesbians she has met, because "most Jewish people in the queer community are highly assimilated and are no help to me." The identities available for ethnic minorities in the LesBiGay community sometimes consist of racialized sexual stereotypes. Icard (1986), for example, describes the "Super Stud" and "Miss Thing" identities available for African American men in the gay male community. Such stereotypical identities limit and distort the potential for integrated identity development among ethnic minority bisexuals.

Finally, some people from cultures that stigmatize homosexuality choose neither to closet themselves nor to leave their cultures and communities of origin but to remain within their communities as "out" bisexuals, lesbians, or gays to challenge homophobic and biphobic attitudes. In fact, some react positively to their own stigmatization with increased pride. A Korean American immigrant woman explained that the "Asian shun of homosexuality/bisexuality . . . makes me even more defensive yet proud of my orientation." The African American–Chicana mentioned earlier eventually decided to come out within the Latin and African American communities and now uses her "'outness' within [her] communities as a testimony to . . . diversity and to the strength [she has] developed from being raised Latina and African American."

A positive integration of one's racial, ethnic, or class identity with one's sexual identity is greatly facilitated by support from others who share an individual's particular constellation of identities. For some, finding kindred spirits is made difficult by demographic and cultural realities. But as more and more people come out, there are inevitably more "out" members of racial and ethnic minorities and among these, more bisexuals. Many respondents described the leap forward in the development of their sexual identities that became possible when they finally discovered a community of bisexuals, lesbians, or gays with a similar racial or ethnic background. A Jewish Chicana reported that she is "finding more people of my ethnic backgrounds going through the same thing. This is affirming." Similarly, a Chicano is "just now starting to integrate my sexuality and my culture by getting to know other gays/bis of color." An African American woman reported that "it wasn't until I lived in Washington, D.C., for a number of years and met large numbers of Black lesbians that I was able to resolve this conflict for myself." Many Jewish respondents commented on the fact that there are many Jewish bisexuals, lesbians, and gays, and noted that receiving support from these peers was important in the development and maintenance of their positive sexual identities. One man, when asked to describe the effect of his racial or ethnic cultural heritage on his sexuality, said simply, "I'm a Jewish Agnostic Male-oriented Bisexual. There are lots of us." Some Jewish respondents also commented that being racially white facilitated their acceptance in the mainstream LesBiGay community and permitted them to receive support from this community that was not as available to individuals of other racial and ethnic backgrounds. Of course, it is this same assimilationist attitude that caused the Orthodox Jewish woman quoted earlier to find a lack of support among Jewish LesBiGays.

For individuals who belong to racial or ethnic minorities, the discovery that one is bisexual is a discovery that one is a double or triple minority. It is even more the case for bisexuals than for lesbians and gays, because bisexuals are a political and social minority within the lesbian and gay community. Many racial and ethnic minority individuals experience their coming out as a process of further marginalization from the mainstream, that is, as an exacerbation of an already undesirable position. An African American woman described being bi as "just one other negative thing I have to deal with. My race is one and my gender another." This can inhibit coming out for individuals who are reluctant to take on yet another stigmatized identity. For example, Morales (1990) reported that some Hispanic men limit their coming out, because they do not want to risk experiencing double discrimination in their careers and personal lives. A Black woman in the current study said that she is "unwilling to come too far 'out' as I already have so many strikes against me."

Many respondents found, however, that their experiences as racial or ethnic minorities facilitated their recognition and acceptance of their sexuality. This was most common among Jewish respondents, many of whom explained that their history as an oppressed people sensitized them to other issues of oppression. One man wrote, "The Jewish sense of being an outsider or underdog has spurred my rebelliousness; the emphasis on learning and questioning has helped to open my mind." A woman wrote, "My Jewish ethnicity taught me about oppression and the need to fight it. It gave me the tools to be able to assert that the homophobes (like the anti-Semites) are wrong." Some non-Jewish respondents also found that their experiences as ethnic minorities facilitated their coming out as bisexual. For example, a woman of Mexican, Dutch, and Norwegian descent wrote that her cultural background "has made me less afraid to be different." She was already ethnically different, so she was better prepared to recognize and accept her sexual difference. Similarly, an Irish Tsalagi Indian man found being outside the mainstream to be a liberating position; he wrote, "I have always felt alienated from the cultural norm, so I'm only affected in the sense that this alienation has allowed me the freedom to visualize myself on my own terms."

Many bisexuals of mixed race or ethnicity feel a comfortable resonance between their mixed heritage and their bisexuality. In a society where both racial-ethnic and sexual categories are highly elaborated, individuals of mixed heritage or who are bisexual find themselves straddling categories that are socially constructed as distinct from one another. The paradox presented by this position was described by a bisexual woman of Native American, Jewish, and Celtic heritage who wrote, "Because I am of mixed ethnicity, I rotate between feeling 'left out' of every group and feeling 'secretly' qualified for several racial/cultural identities. I notice the same feeling regarding my sexual identity." Other respondents of mixed racial and ethnic backgrounds also saw connections between their ethnic heritage and their bisexuality. For example, an Asian European woman wrote,

> Being multiracial, multicultural has always made me aware of
> nonbipolar thinking. I have always been outside people's
> categories, and so it wasn't such a big leap to come out as bi, after
> spending years explaining my [racial and cultural] identity rather
> than attaching a single label [to it].

A Puerto Rican who grew up alternately in Puerto Rico and a northeastern state explained,

> The duality of my cultural upbringing goes hand in hand with the
> duality of my sexuality. Having the best of both worlds (ethnically

speaking—I look white but am Spanish) in my everyday life might
have influenced me to seek the best of both worlds in my sexual
life—relationships with both a man and a woman.

A Black Lithuanian Irish Scottish woman with light skin, freckles, red curly
hair, and a "Black political identity," who is only recognized as Black by
other Blacks, wrote, "As with my race, my sex is not to be defined by others
or absoluted by myself. It is a spectrum."

However, individuals whose mixed heritages have produced unresolved cultural difficulties sometimes transfer these difficulties to their bisexuality. A "Latino-Anglo" who was raised to be a "regular, middle-class,
all-American," and who later became acculturated to Latin culture, wrote,

> Since I am ethnically confused and pass as different from what I
> am, as I do in sexual orientation also, I spend a lot of time
> underground. . . . I think it has definitely been a major factor in the
> breakup of two very promising long-term relations.

Similarly, a transgendered bisexual respondent of mixed European, Native
American, and North African heritage believes that the pressures she feels as
a transgenderist and a bisexual are closely related to the fact that her parents
"felt it necessary to hide a large part of their ethnic and racial heritage," although she did not elaborate on the nature of these pressures.

In contrast to bisexuals from marginalized racial-ethnic, religious, or class
backgrounds, middle- or upper-class Protestant Euro-Americans experience
relatively few difficulties integrating their sexual identities with their cultural
backgrounds and other identities. Euro-American bisexuals might have difficulty developing a positive bisexual identity in a monosexist culture, but unlike Bisexuals of Color, they have no particular problems integrating their
sexual identity with their racial identity, because these identities are already
integrated in the LesBiGay community. Being Euro-American gives them
the luxury of not dealing with racial identity. Not surprisingly, when asked
how their racial-ethnic background had affected their sexuality, most Euro-
Americans did not mention their race at all. Instead, Euro-Americans tended
to attribute their sexual upbringing to the peculiarities of their parents, their
religion, their class, or their geographic location within the United States. One
woman explained,

> I do not associate my racial-ethnic cultural background and my
> sexuality. Undoubtedly I would think and feel differently if I were
> of a different background but I'm not able to identify the effect of
> my background on my sexuality.

REFERENCES

Almaguer, T. (1993). Chicano men: A cartography of homosexual identity and behavior. In H. Abelove, M. A. Barale, & D. M. Halperin (Eds.), *The lesbian and gay
studies reader*. New York: Routledge.

Carrier, J., Nguyen, B., & Su, S. (1992). Vietnamese American sexual behaviors and HIV infection. *Journal of Sex Research, 29*(4), 547–560.

Chan, C. S. (1989). Issues of identity development among Asian American lesbians and gay men. *Journal of Counseling and Development, 68*(1), 16–21.

Chan, C. S. (1992). Cultural considerations in counseling Asian American lesbians and gay men. In S. H. Dworkin & F. Guitérrez (Eds.), *Counseling gay men and lesbians* (pp. 115–124). Alexandria, VA: American Association for Counseling and Development.

Espin, O. (1987). Issues of identity in the psychology of Latina lesbians. In Boston Lesbian Psychologies Collective (Eds.), *Lesbian psychologies: Explorations and challenges* (pp. 35–51). Urbana: University of Illinois Press.

Greene, B. (1994). Ethnic-minority lesbians and gay men: Mental health and treatment issues. *Journal of Consulting and Clinical Psychology, 62*(2), 243–251.

Guitérrez, F. J., & Dworkin, S. H. (1992). Gay, lesbian, and African American: Managing the integration of identities. In Dworkin & Gutiérrez (Eds.), *Counseling gay men and lesbians* (pp. 141–155).

H., P. (1989). Asian American lesbians: An emerging voice in the Asian American community. In Asian Women United of California (Eds.), *Making waves: An anthology of writings by and about Asian American women* (pp. 282–290). Boston: Beacon.

Icard, L. (1986). Black gay men and conflicting social identities: Sexual orientation versus racial identity. *Journal of Social Work and Human Sexuality, 4*(1/2), 83–92.

Johnson, J. (1982). *The influence of assimilation on the psychosocial adjustment of Black homosexual men.* Unpublished dissertation, California School of Professional Psychology, Berkeley.

Lukes, C. A., & Land, H. (1990, March). Biculturality and homosexuality. *Social Work,* 155–161.

Matteson, D. R. (1994). *Bisexual behavior and AIDS risk among some Asian American men.* Unpublished manuscript.

McKeon, E. (1992). To be bisexual and underclass. In E. R. Weise (Ed.), *Closer to home: Bisexuality & feminism* (pp. 27–34). Seattle, WA: Seal.

Morales, E. S. (1989). Ethnic minority families and minority gays and lesbians. *Marriage and Family Review, 14*(3/4), 217–239.

Morales, E. S. (1990). HIV infection and Hispanic gay and bisexual men. *Hispanic Journal of Behavioral Sciences, 12*(2), 212–222.

Morales, E. S. (1992). Counseling Latino gays and Latina lesbians. In Dworkin, S. H. and Gutiérrez, F. (Eds.), *Counseling gay men and lesbians: Journey to the end of the rainbow* (pp. 125–139).

Tremble, B., Schneider, M., & Appathurai, C. (1989). Growing up gay or lesbian in a multicultural context. *Journal of Homosexuality, 17*(1–4), 253–267.

Wooden, W. S., Kawasaki, H., & Mayeda, R. (1983). Lifestyles and identity maintenance among gay Japanese American males. *Alternative Lifestyles, 5*(4), 236–243.

36

USES OF THE EROTIC: THE EROTIC AS POWER

AUDRE LORDE

Audre Lorde, who passed away in 1992, grew up in the West Indian community of Harlem in the 1930s, the daughter of immigrants from Grenada. She attended Hunter College (later becoming professor of English there), ventured to the American expatriate community in Mexico, and participated in the Greenwich Village scene of the early 1950s. She is a major figure in the lesbian and feminist movements. Among her works are *Sister Outsider, Zami: A New Spelling of My Name, Uses of the Erotic, Chosen Poems Old and New, The Black Unicorn,* and *From a Land Where Other People Live.*

T here are many kinds of power, used and unused, acknowledged or otherwise. The erotic is a resource within each of us that lies in a deeply female and spiritual plane, firmly rooted in the power of our unexpressed or unrecognized feeling. In order to perpetuate itself, every oppression must corrupt or distort those various sources of power within the culture of the oppressed that can provide energy for change. For women, this has meant a suppression of the erotic as a considered source of power and information within our lives.

We have been taught to suspect this resource, vilified, abused, and devalued within western society. On the one hand, the superficially erotic has been encouraged as a sign of female inferiority; on the other hand, women have been made to suffer and to feel both contemptible and suspect by virtue of its existence.

It is a short step from there to the false belief that only by the suppression of the erotic within our lives and consciousness can women be truly strong. But that strength is illusory, for it is fashioned within the context of male models of power.

As women, we have come to distrust that power which rises from our deepest and nonrational knowledge. We have been warned against it all our lives by the male world, which values this depth of feeling enough to keep women around in order to exercise it in the service of men, but which fears this same depth too much to examine the possibilities of it within themselves. So women are maintained at a distant/inferior position to be psychically milked, much the same way ants maintain colonies of aphids to provide a life-giving substance for their masters.

But the erotic offers a well of replenishing and provocative force to the woman who does not fear its revelation, nor succumb to the belief that sensation is enough.

The erotic has often been misnamed by men and used against women. It has been made into the confused, the trivial, the psychotic, the plasticized sensation. For this reason, we have often turned away from the exploration and consideration of the erotic as a source of power and information, confusing it with its opposite, the pornographic. But pornography is a direct denial of the power of the erotic, for it represents the suppression of true feeling. Pornography emphasizes sensation without feeling.

The erotic is a measure between the beginnings of our sense of self and the chaos of our strongest feelings. It is an internal sense of satisfaction to which, once we have experienced it, we know we can aspire. For having experienced the fullness of this depth of feeling and recognizing its power, in honor and self-respect we can require no less of ourselves.

It is never easy to demand the most from ourselves, from our lives, from our work. To encourage excellence is to go beyond the encouraged mediocrity of our society is to encourage excellence. But giving in to the fear of feeling and working to capacity is a luxury only the unintentional can afford, and the unintentional are those who do not wish to guide their own destinies.

This internal requirement toward excellence which we learn from the erotic must not be misconstrued as demanding the impossible from ourselves nor from others. Such a demand incapacitates everyone in the process. For the erotic is not a question only of what we do; it is a question of how acutely and fully we can feel in the doing. Once we know the extent to which we are capable of feeling that sense of satisfaction and completion, we can then observe which of our various life endeavors bring us closest to that fullness.

The aim of each thing which we do is to make our lives and the lives of our children richer and more possible. Within the celebration of the erotic in all our endeavors, my work becomes a conscious decision—a longed-for bed which I enter gratefully and from which I rise up empowered.

Of course, women so empowered are dangerous. So we are taught to separate the erotic demand from most vital areas of our lives other than sex. And the lack of concern for the erotic root and satisfactions of our work is felt in our disaffection from so much of what we do. For instance, how often do we truly love our work even at its most difficult?

The principal horror of any system which defines the good in terms of profit rather than in terms of human need, or which defines human need to the exclusion of the psychic and emotional components of that need — the principal horror of such a system is that it robs our work of its erotic value, its erotic power and life appeal and fulfillment. Such a system reduces work to a travesty of necessities, a duty by which we earn bread or oblivion for ourselves and those we love. But this is tantamount to blinding a painter and then telling her to improve her work, and to enjoy the act of painting. It is not only next to impossible, it is also profoundly cruel.

As women, we need to examine the ways in which our world can be truly different. I am speaking here of the necessity for reassessing the quality of all the aspects of our lives and of our work, and of how we move toward and through them.

The very word *erotic* comes from the Greek word *eros,* the personification of love in all its aspects — born of Chaos, and personifying creative power and harmony. When I speak of the erotic, then, I speak of it as an assertion of the lifeforce of women; of that creative energy empowered, the knowledge and use of which we are now reclaiming in our language, our history, our dancing, our loving, our work, our lives.

There are frequent attempts to equate pornography and eroticism, two diametrically opposed uses of the sexual. Because of these attempts, it has become fashionable to separate the spiritual (psychic and emotional) from the political, to see them as contradictory or antithetical. "What do you mean, a poetic revolutionary, a meditating gunrunner?" In the same way, we have attempted to separate the spiritual and the erotic, thereby reducing the spiritual to a world of flattened affect, a world of the ascetic who aspires to feel nothing. But nothing is farther from the truth. For the ascetic position is one of the highest fear, the gravest immobility. The severe abstinence of the ascetic becomes the ruling obsession. And it is one not of self-discipline but of self-abnegation.

The dichotomy between the spiritual and the political is also false, resulting from an incomplete attention to our erotic knowledge. For the bridge which connects them is formed by the erotic — the sensual — those physical, emotional, and psychic expressions of what is deepest and strongest and richest within each of us, being shared: the passions of love, in its deepest meanings.

Beyond the superficial, the considered phrase, "It feels right to me," acknowledges the strength of the erotic into a true knowledge, for what that means is the first and most powerful guiding light toward any understanding. And understanding is a handmaiden which can only wait upon, or clarify, that knowledge, deeply born. The erotic is the nurturer or nursemaid of all our deepest knowledge.

The erotic functions for me in several ways, and the first is in providing the power which comes from sharing deeply any pursuit with another person. The sharing of joy, whether physical, emotional, psychic, or intellectual, forms a bridge between the sharers which can be the basis for understanding much of what is not shared between them, and lessens the threat of their difference.

Another important way in which the erotic connection functions is the open and fearless underlining of my capacity for joy. In the way my body stretches to music and opens into response, hearkening to its deepest rhythms, so every level upon which I sense also opens to the erotically satisfying experience, whether it is dancing, building a bookcase, writing a poem, examining an idea.

That self-connection shared is a measure of the joy which I know myself to be capable of feeling, a reminder of my capacity for feeling. And that deep and irreplaceable knowledge of my capacity for joy comes to demand from all of my life that it be lived within the knowledge that such satisfaction is possible, and does not have to be called *marriage,* nor *god,* nor *an afterlife.*

This is one reason why the erotic is so feared, and so often relegated to the bedroom alone, when it is recognized at all. For once we begin to feel deeply all the aspects of our lives, we begin to demand from ourselves and from our life-pursuits that they feel in accordance with that joy which we know ourselves to be capable of. Our erotic knowledge empowers us, becomes a lens through which we scrutinize all aspects of our existence, forcing us to evaluate those aspects honestly in terms of their relative meaning within our lives. And this is a grave responsibility, projected from within each of us, not to settle for the convenient, the shoddy, the conventionally expected, nor the merely safe.

During World War II, we bought sealed plastic packets of white, uncolored margarine, with a tiny, intense pellet of yellow coloring perched like a topaz just inside the clear skin of the bag. We would leave the margarine out for a while to soften, and then we would pinch the little pellet to break it inside the bag, releasing the rich yellowness into the soft pale mass of margarine. Then taking it carefully between our fingers, we would knead it gently back and forth, over and over, until the color had spread throughout the whole pound bag of margarine, thoroughly coloring it.

I find the erotic such a kernel within myself. When released from its intense and constrained pellet, it flows through and colors my life with a kind of energy that heightens and sensitizes and strengthens all my experience.

We have been raised to fear the *yes* within ourselves, our deepest cravings. But, once recognized, those which do not enhance our future lose their power and can be altered. The fear of our desires keeps them suspect and indiscriminately powerful, for to suppress any truth is to give it strength beyond endurance. The fear that we cannot grow beyond whatever distortions we may find within ourselves keeps us docile and loyal and obedient, externally defined, and leads us to accept many facets of our oppression as women.

When we live outside ourselves, and by that I mean on external directives only rather than from our internal knowledge and needs, when we live away from those erotic guides from within ourselves, then our lives are limited by external and alien forms, and we conform to the needs of a structure that is not based on human need, let alone an individual's. But when we begin to live from within outward, in touch with the power of the erotic within ourselves, and allowing that power to inform and illuminate our actions upon the world around us, then we begin to be responsible to ourselves in the deepest sense. For as we begin to recognize our deepest feelings, we begin to give up, of necessity, being satisfied with suffering and self-negation, and with the numbness which so often seems like their only alternative in our society. Our acts against oppression become integral with self, motivated and empowered from within.

In touch with the erotic, I become less willing to accept powerlessness, or those other supplied states of being which are not native to me, such as resignation, despair, self-effacement, depression, self-denial.

And yes, there is a hierarchy. There is a difference between painting a back fence and writing a poem, but only one of quantity. And there is, for me, no difference between writing a good poem and moving into sunlight against the body of a woman I love.

This brings me to the last consideration of the erotic. To share the power of each other's feelings is different from using another's feelings as we would use a kleenex. When we look the other way from our experience, erotic or otherwise, we use rather than share the feelings of those others who participate in the experience with us. And use without consent of the used is abuse.

In order to be utilized, our erotic feelings must be recognized. The need for sharing deep feeling is a human need. But within the european-american tradition, this need is satisfied by certain proscribed erotic comings-together. These occasions are almost always characterized by a simultaneous looking away, a pretense of calling them something else, whether a religion, a fit, mob violence, or even playing doctor. And this misnaming of the need and the deed give rise to that distortion which results in pornography and obscenity — the abuse of feeling.

When we look away from the importance of the erotic in the development and sustenance of our power, or when we look away from ourselves as we satisfy our erotic needs in concert with others, we use each other as objects of satisfaction rather than share our joy in the satisfying, rather than make connection with our similarities and our differences. To refuse to be conscious of what we are feeling at any time, however comfortable that might seem, is to deny a large part of the experience, and to allow ourselves to be reduced to the pornographic, the abused, and the absurd.

The erotic cannot be felt secondhand. As a Black lesbian feminist, I have a particular feeling, knowledge, and understanding for those sisters with whom I have danced hard, played, or even fought. This deep participation has often been the forerunner for joint concerted actions not possible before.

But this erotic charge is not easily shared by women who continue to operate under an exclusively european-american male tradition. I know it was not available to me when I was trying to adapt my consciousness to this mode of living and sensation.

Only now, I find more and more women-identified women brave enough to risk sharing the erotic's electrical charge without having to look away, and without distorting the enormously powerful and creative nature of that exchange. Recognizing the power of the erotic within our lives can give us the energy to pursue genuine change within our world, rather than merely settling for a shift of characters in the same weary drama.

For not only do we touch our most profoundly creative source, but we do that which is female and self-affirming in the face of a racist, patriarchal, and anti-erotic society.

PART VI

Families

The structures of families reflect gender expectations within particular cultures, and cultures themselves are shaped by surrounding or embedded social forces such as sexism, poverty, and homophobia. For example, the wish to have male offspring who are expected to support parents in old age affects whether or not girls even get born in some cultures. In China and in parts of India, sex-selective abortion has changed the gender ratio in favor of boys. An estimated 50 to 80 million more girls and women might be alive today in India and China if discrimination against girls and women had not occurred. One-child policies in China have especially encouraged sex-selective abortions. Sex selection occurs in India even though sex tests on fetuses and sex-selective abortions are illegal there.[1]

Attention to changing gender expectations within families is on many people's minds, especially in the United States. People in the U.S. women's and men's movements have been talking about this issue for decades, but today people from all walks of life are addressing it. Even the National Conference of Catholic Bishops has urged married couples to move beyond gender stereotypes and develop more equality in marriages through shared decision making, shared household duties when both spouses are employed, fathers who are actively engaged in their children's lives, and the expression of feeling by both spouses.[2] Explicit attention to fathers has increased as more single fathers enjoy and embrace their roles,[3] as divorced fathers fight for custody,[4] and as young fathers join mentoring programs to help them learn parenting skills.[5]

In 1998, 59.5 percent of married women were in the labor force. The task of balancing paid work and family work now affects women across the economic spectrum; it is no longer a challenge only for poor and working-class women, who have always been in the paid workforce. In 1998, for example, 66.5 percent of women college graduates with a child under one year of age were in the labor force. At the end of the twentieth century, the husband worked outside the home and the wife did unpaid work at home in only 19 percent of families.[6] However, women who work outside the home are most likely to be responsible for arranging child care, and they continue to do most of the housework, working what sociologist Arlie Hochschild called the "second shift."[7]

Family life requires complex negotiations and compromises that are often hidden from view. For example, in a family studied by Arlie Hochschild and Anne Machung, the wife gave up her ideal of a marriage in which household tasks and child care would be shared; she redefined what her husband was willing to do as acceptable in order to keep the marriage together. He was unwilling to take on much responsibility at home and would have preferred that she work part time so she could handle the work at home with less conflict. Committed to her career, she did not want to work part time. The image of the happy professional mother, her child in one hand and a briefcase in the other, is seldom what it appears to be, even for professional women with enough money to hire people to serve as nannies or housekeepers at home.[8] The reality of the effects of having children on women's wages has finally hit home, leading researcher Ann Crittendon (Part VIII) to refer to mothers as "society's involuntary philanthropists."[9] The ideology of what sociologist Sharon Hays calls "intensive mothering" reinforces the gender divide since this ideology advises women to spend a lot of time, energy, and money on their children. This frequently results in conflicts with employers since the ideology of the workplace is at odds with the ideology of intensive mothering.[10] (See Douglas and Michaels, Part IV)

Sociologist Scott Coltrane, after taking a careful look at changing gender roles in families, concludes that gradually men have begun to share more equally in family life, especially in the area of child care, and he predicts that this trend toward equality in family life will continue, though perhaps gradually and with resistance on both sides.[11] An intergenerational study of Mexican men's roles in the early 1990s by anthropologist Matthew Gutmann found that younger Mexican men were participating more in housework and childrearing as a result of women working outside the home and were not needing to have a lot of children in order to prove their masculinity.[12] The data in this field are being debated, however, related to changes in men's contributions to housework. Sociologists Julie Press and Eleanor Townsley found that a careful look at two large surveys that have informed the literature on housework participation (not childcare) revealed overreporting of time spent on housework by both husbands and wives. They conclude, also, that ". . . the overreport we document is large enough to cast doubt on the conclusion that husbands have increased their supply of domestic labor to the household in the past 25 years."[13]

The stress and turmoil that poverty imposes on families is well documented.[14] Sociologist Anne R. Roschelle, in an analysis of families of color in the 1987–88 National Survey of Families and Households, argues that one powerful effect of poverty on communities of color has been to weaken support networks, calling into question the assumption that cuts in welfare support will simply force people to lean on their support networks. Those networks, previously documented in the social science literature (see also Collins, this part), appear to have weakened to some extent.[15] The risk of becoming homeless is a pernicious presence for poor families. Many families that are able to escape homelessness function at the margins of the social order, living in crowded conditions and working, at times, in the informal economy—outside the realm of W-2 forms, benefits, and any protection from exploitation by employers.[16] The negative effects of humiliating, illness-inducing work are often brought home in the form of exhaustion, drunkenness, and violence.[17]

In response to the conditions of poor families, especially single mothers with children, professor of education Valerie Polakow asks, ". . . where are our commitments to the existential futures of children as we approach the twenty-first century?" Clearly, the structure of the economy is wreaking havoc in many families, though, as Pokalow argues, homelessness and poverty are often pathologized causing victims of poverty to be labeled and blamed for their conditions. Rather, she argues, society should focus on the economic structure as the source of blame and potential solutions.[18] Political scientist Shirley M. Geiger, examining the public perceptions and public policies concerning African American single mothers argues that their poverty is a result of both conscious action and inaction that is damaging to all poor families, 40 percent of which are headed by white men.[19] Frank F. Furstenberg comes to a similar conclusion regarding poor single fathers, arguing that unless the social order provides adequate incomes for young fathers, most will continue to stay disengaged from their children.[20] Later in this book, the situations of poor families are addressed in more depth (Sharon Hays, Part VIII).

The movement to establish the right of gay men and lesbians to marry or at least establish civil unions provides an example of changing attitudes and changing family arrangements in various countries, as discussed in the Introduction to this book and in a reading in this part by E. J. Graff. Although many gay and lesbian couples might choose not to marry, their support of the right to do so is strong.[21] Many same-sex couples in Massachusetts find themselves in a quandry over same-sex marriage. On the one hand, they celebrate the new state-level rights and benefits now available and applaud the decision from a civil rights perspective. On the other, the structure of marriage with its many benefits rankles fair-minded people who believe that all family structures—single parents, unmarried couples of any kind, other household compositions—deserve the supports that marriage often brings, such as access to a partner's health insurance coverage, hospital visitation rights, tax benefits, inheritance, etc.[22] Although some legal protections for same-sex couples are available, such as joint adoptions so that both partners can become legal parents of the children involved,[23] many other benefits are lacking. For example, in the aftermath of September 11, many surviving partners have gone unrecognized by both their partners' families and by agencies providing financial relief to surviving spouses or next of kin.[24] The struggle for the right of same-sex couples to marry continues in all states except Massachusetts. As this book was going to press, the U.S. Supreme Court had just refused to hear a conservative challenge to the Massachusetts law. The Supreme Court decision was expected, since the Court typically leaves marriage policies to the states. It will be interesting to follow how the Court deals with the Defense of Marriage Act (DOMA), passed by 38 states, which defines marriage as between one man and one woman. Objections to DOMA are already in the courts.

The readings in this part address a range of family issues including gender arrangements in working-class families from various ethnic groups (Lillian B. Rubin); various family and child-care arrangements in African American communities (Patricia Hill Collins); men's experiences as involved fathers (Kathleen Gerson); the challenges of raising an African American son in a lesbian family (Audre Lorde); the challenge of breaking away from a father whose definition of "manhood" is unacceptable (Raul E. Ybarra); and a defense of same-sex marriage (E. J. Graff). The authors in this chapter give voice to many of the challenging aspects of family life today. Embedded in their stories and research are implications for changes in personal relationships and policy, including sharing household and child-rearing tasks; support for fathers' caring involvement in family life; the elimination of poverty; the development of jobs that pay enough to keep families going; and the legitimation of same-sex marriage.

As you read these essays, you might want to think about the family contexts in which you were raised. To what extent do the various authors speak to your experience or contradict it? Where do you stand on same-sex marriage?

NOTES

1. Celia W. Dugger, "Modern Asia's Anomoly: The Girls Who Don't Get Born," *The New York Times* (May 6, 2001), p. 4 (WK); Agence France-Presse, "India Cracks Down on Sex Tests for Fetuses," *The New York Times* (May 6, 2001), p. 14 (NE).

2. National Conference of Catholic Bishops, *Follow the Way of Love* (Washington, DC: United States Catholic Conference, 1994), pp. 20–21.

3. Doris Sue Wong, "Single Fathers Embrace Role, Fight Stereotype," *The Boston Globe* (July 5, 1999), p. A1.

4. Kate Zernike, "Divorced Dads Emerge as a Political Force," *The Boston Globe* 253, no. 139 (Tuesday, May 19, 1998), p. A1.

5. Erica Thesing, "Mentoring Programs Focusing on Fatherhood," *The Boston Globe* (Saturday, June 17, 2000), p. B4.

6. All data in this paragraph are from Barbara Reskin and Irene Padavic, *Women and Men at Work*, 2nd ed. (Thousand Oaks, CA: Pine Forge Press, 2002), pp. 149–150.

7. Ibid., pp. 149–53. See also Arlie Russell Hochschild with Anne Machung, *The Second Shift: Working Parents and the Revolution at Home* (New York: Avon Books, 1990).

8. Hochschild and Machung, *The Second Shift.*

9. Ann Crittendon, *The Price of Motherhood: Why the Most Important Job in the World Is Still the Least Valued* (New York: Henry Holt and Co., 2001), p. 9.

10. Sharon Hays, *The Cultural Contradictions of Motherhood* (New Haven: Yale University Press, 1996).

11. Scott Coltrane, "The Future of Fatherhood: Social, Demographic, and Economic Influences on Men's Family Involvements," in William Marsiglio, ed., *Fatherhood: Contemporary Theory, Research, and Social Policy* (Thousand Oaks, CA: Sage, 1995), pp. 255–74.

12. Matthew C. Gutmann, "The Meaning of Macho," in Louise Lamphere, Heléna Ragoné, and Patricia Zavella, eds., *Situated Lives: Gender and Culture in Everyday Life* (New York: Routledge, 1997), pp. 223–34.

13. Julie E. Press and Eleanor Townsley, "Wives' and Husbands' Housework Reporting: Gender, Class, and Social Desirability," *Gender & Society* 12, no. 2 (April 1998), p. 214.

14. Elliot Liebow, *Tell Them Who I Am: The Lives of Homeless Women* (New York: Penguin, 1993); Valerie Polakow, *Lives on the Edge: Single Mothers and Their Children in the Other America* (Chicago: University of Chicago Press, 1994); Doug A. Timmer, Stanley D. Eitzen, and Kathryn D. Talley, *Paths to Homelessness: Extreme Poverty and the Urban Housing Crisis* (Boulder, CO: Westview Press, 1994).

15. Anne R. Roschelle, *No More Kin: Exploring Race, Class, and Gender in Family Networks* (Thousand Oaks, CA: Sage, 1997), pp. 199–202.

16. See for example, "Patchworking: Households in the Economy," in Nazli Kibria, *Family Tightrope: The Changing Lives of Vietnamese Americans* (Princeton: Princeton University Press, 1993), pp. 73–107.

17. See for example, Sue Doro, "The Father Poem," in Janet Zandy, ed., *Calling Home: Working-Class Women's Writings: An Anthology* (New Brunswick: Rutgers University Press, 1990), pp. 132–38.

18. Polakow, *Lives on the Edge,* p. 3.

19. Shirley M. Geiger, "African-American Single Mothers: Public Perceptions and Public Policies," in Kim Marie Vaz, ed., *Black Women in America* (Thousand Oaks, CA: Sage, 1995), pp. 244–57.

20. Frank F. Furstenburg, Jr., "Fathering in the Inner City: Paternal Participation and Public Policy," in William Marsiglio, ed., *Fatherhood: Contemporary Theory, Research, and Social Policy* (Thousand Oaks, CA: Sage, 1995), pp. 119–47.

21. Gretchen A. Stiers, *From This Day Forward: Commitment, Marriage, and Family in Lesbian and Gay Relationships* (New York: St. Martin's Griffin, 1999).

22. Martha Ackelsberg and Judith Plaskow, "Why We're Not Getting Married" (June 1, 2004), CommonDreams.org.

23. Associated Press, "N.J. Gay Parents Exchange Vows," *The Boston Globe* (Monday, June 22, 1998), p. A4.

24. Kathleen Burge, "Sept. 11 Leaves Same-Sex Partners Adrift," *The Boston Globe* (March 18, 2002), p. B1

37

THE TRANSFORMATION OF FAMILY LIFE

LILLIAN B. RUBIN

Lillian B. Rubin, as a girl growing up in an immigrant working-class family, experienced firsthand the injuries this society inflicts on those who are born outside the golden circle of gender and class privilege. Since receiving her doctorate in 1971, she has published nine books, all dealing with some aspect of gender and class.

"I know my wife works all day, just like I do," says Gary Braunswig, a twenty-nine-year-old white drill press operator, "but it's not the same. She doesn't *have* to do it. I mean, she *has* to because we need the money, but it's different. It's not really her job to have to be working; it's mine." He stops, irritated with himself because he can't find exactly the words he wants, and asks, "Know what I mean? I'm not saying it right; I mean, it's the man who's supposed to support his family, so I've got to be responsible for that, not her. And that makes one damn big difference."

"I mean, women complain all the time about how hard they work with the house and the kids and all. I'm not saying it's not hard, but that's her responsibility, just like the finances are mine."

"But she's now sharing that burden with you, isn't she?" I remark.

"Yeah, and I do my share around the house, only she doesn't see it that way. Maybe if you add it all up, I don't do as much as she does, but then she doesn't bring in as much money as I do. And she doesn't always have to be looking for overtime to make an extra buck. I got no complaints about that, so how come she's always complaining about me? I mean, she helps me out financially, and I help her out with the kids and stuff. What's wrong with that? It seems pretty equal to me."

Cast that way, his formulation seems reasonable: They're each responsible for one part of family life; they each help out with the other. But the abstract formula doesn't square with the lived reality. For him, helping her adds relatively little to the burden of household tasks he *must* do each day. A recent study by University of Wisconsin researchers, for example, found that in families where both wife and husband work full-time, the women average over twenty-six hours a week in household labor, while the men do about ten.[1] That's because there's nothing in the family system to force him to accountability or responsibility on a daily basis. He may "help her out with the kids and stuff" one day and be too busy or preoccupied the next.

But for Gary's wife, Irene, helping him means an extra eight hours every working day. Consequently, she wants something more consistent from him than a helping hand with a particular task when he has the time, desire, or feels guilty enough. "Sure, he helps me out," she says, her words tinged with resentment. "He'll give the kids a bath or help with the dishes. But only when I ask him. He doesn't have to *ask* me to go to work every day, does he? Why should I have to ask him?"

"Why should I have to ask him?" — words that suggest a radically different consciousness from the working-class women I met twenty years ago. Then, they counted their blessings. "He's a steady worker; he doesn't drink; he doesn't hit me," they told me by way of explaining why they had "no right to complain."[2] True, these words were reminders to themselves that life could be worse, that they shouldn't take these things for granted — reminders that didn't wholly work to obscure their discontent with other aspects of the marriage. But they were nevertheless meaningful statements of value that put a brake on the kinds of demands they felt they could make of their men, whether about the unequal division of household tasks or about the emotional content of their lives together.

Now, the same women who reminded themselves to be thankful two decades ago speak openly about their dissatisfaction with the role divisions in the family. Some husbands, especially the younger ones, greet their wives' demands sympathetically. "I try to do as much as I can for Sue, and when I can't, I feel bad about it," says twenty-nine-year-old Don Dominguez, a Latino father of three children, who is a construction worker.

Others are more ambivalent. "I don't know, as long as she's got a job, too, I guess it's right that I should help out in the house. But that doesn't mean I've got to like it," says twenty-eight-year-old Joe Kempinski, a white warehouse worker with two children.

Some men are hostile, insisting that their wives' complaints are unreasonable, unjust, and oppressive. "I'm damn tired of women griping all the time; it's nothing but nags and complaints," Ralph Danesen, a thirty-six-year-old white factory worker and the father of three children, says indignantly. "It's enough! You'd think they're the only ones who've got it hard. What about me? I'm not living in a bed of roses either."

"Christ, what does a guy have to do to keep a wife quiet these days? What does she want? It's not like I don't do anything to help her out, but it's never enough."

In the past there was a clear understanding about the obligations and entitlements each partner took on when they married. He was obliged to work outside the home; she would take care of life inside. He was entitled to her ministrations, she to his financial support. But this neat division of labor with its clear-cut separation of rights and obligations no longer works. Now, women feel obliged to hold up their share of the family economy — a partnership men welcome. In return, women believe they're entitled to their husbands' full participation in domestic labor. And here is the rub. For while men enjoy the fruits of their wives' paid work outside the home, they have been slow to accept the reciprocal responsibilities—that is, to become real partners in the work inside the home.

The women, exhausted from doing two days' work in one, angry at the need to assume obligations without corresponding entitlements, push their men in ways unknown before. The men, battered by economic uncertainty and by the escalating demands of their wives, feel embattled and victimized on two fronts—one outside the home, the other inside. Consequently, when their wives seem not to see the family work they do, when they don't acknowledge and credit it, when they fail to appreciate them, the men feel violated and betrayed. "You come home and you want to be appreciated a little. But it doesn't work that way, leastwise not here anymore," complains Gary Braunswig, his angry words at odds with the sadness in his eyes. "There's no peace, I guess that's the real problem; there's no peace anywhere anymore."

The women often understand what motivates their husbands' sense of victimization and even speak sympathetically about it at times. But to understand and sympathize is not to condone, especially when they feel equally assaulted on both the home and the economic fronts. "I know I complain a lot, but I really don't ask for that much. I just want him to help out a little more," explains Ralph Danesen's wife, Helen, a thirty-five-year-old office worker. "It isn't like I'm asking him to cook the meals or anything like that. I know he can't do that, and I don't expect him to. But every time I try to talk to him, you know, to ask him if I couldn't get a little more help around here, there's a fight."

One of the ways the men excuse their behavior toward family work is by insisting that their responsibility as breadwinner burdens them in ways that are alien to their wives. "The plant's laying off people left and right; it could be me tomorrow. Then what'll we do? Isn't it enough I got to worry about that? I'm the one who's got all the worries; she doesn't. How come that doesn't count?" demands Bob Duckworth, a twenty-nine-year-old factory worker.

But, in fact, the women don't take second place to their men in worrying about what will happen to the family if the husband loses his job. True, the burden of finding another one that will pay the bills isn't theirs—not a trivial difference. But the other side of this truth is that women are stuck with the reality that the financial welfare of the family is out of their control, that they're helpless to do anything to prevent its economic collapse or to rectify it should it happen. "He thinks I've got it easy because it's not my job to support the family," says Bob's wife, Ruthanne. "But sometimes I think it's worse for me. I worry all the time that he's going to get laid off, just like he does. But I can't do anything about it. And if I try to talk to him about it, you know, like maybe make a plan in case it happens, he won't even listen. How does he think *that* makes me feel? It's my life, too, and I can't even talk to him about it."

Not surprisingly, there are generational differences in what fuels the conflict around the division of labor in these families. For the older couples—those who grew up in a different time, whose marriages started with another set of ground rules—the struggle is not simply around how much men do or about whether they take responsibility for the daily tasks of living without being pushed, prodded, and reminded. That's the overt manifestation of the discord, the trigger that starts the fight. But the noise of the explosion when it comes serves to conceal the more fundamental issue underlying the dissension: legitimacy. What does she have a *right* to expect? "What do I know about doing stuff around the house?" asks Frank Moreno, a forty-eight-year-old foreman in a warehouse. "I wasn't brought up like that. My pop, he never did one damn thing, and my mother never complained. It was her job; she did it and kept quiet. Besides, I work my ass off every day. Isn't that enough?"

For the younger couples, those under forty, the problem is somewhat different. The men may complain about the expectation that they'll participate more fully in the care and feeding of the family, but talk to them about it quietly and they'll usually admit that it's not really unfair, given that their wives also work outside the home. In these homes, the issue between husband and wife isn't only who does what. That's there, and it's a source of more or less conflict, depending upon what the men actually do and how forceful their wives are in their demands. But in most of these families there's at least a verbal consensus that men *ought* to participate in the tasks of daily life. Which raises the next and perhaps more difficult issue in contest between them: Who feels responsible for getting the tasks done? Who regards them as a duty, and for whom are they an option? On this, tradition rules.

Even in families where husbands now share many of the tasks, their wives still bear full responsibility for the organization of family life. A man may help cook the meal these days, but a woman is most likely to be the one who has planned it. He may take the children to child care, but she virtually always has had to arrange it. It's she also who is accountable for the emotional life of the family, for monitoring the emotional temperature of its members and making the necessary corrections. It's this need to be responsible for it all that often feels as burdensome as the tasks themselves. "It's not just doing all the stuff that needs doing," explains Maria Jankowicz, a white twenty-eight-year-old assembler in an electronics factory. "It's worrying all the time about everything and always having to arrange everything, you know what I mean. It's like I run the whole show. If I don't stay on top of it all, things fall apart because nobody else is going to do it. The kids can't and Nick, well, forget it," she concludes angrily.

If, regardless of age, life stage, or verbal consensus, women usually still carry the greatest share of the household burdens, why is it important to notice that younger men grant legitimacy to their wives' demands and older men generally do not? Because men who believe their wives have a right to expect their participation tend to suffer guilt and discomfort when they don't live up to those expectations. And no one lives comfortably with guilt. "I know I don't always help enough, and I feel bad about it, you know, guilty sometimes," explains Bob Beardsley, a thirty-year-old white machine operator, his eyes registering the discomfort he feels as he speaks.

"Does it change anything when you feel guilty" I ask.

A small smile flits across his face, and he says, "Sometimes. I try to do a little more, but then I get busy with something and forget that she needs me to help out. My wife says I don't pay attention, that's why I forget. But I don't know. Seems like I've just got my mind on other things."

It's possible, of course, that the men who speak of guilt and rights are only trying to impress me by mouthing the politically correct words. But even if true, they display a sensitivity to the issue that's missing from the men who don't speak those words. For words are more than just words. They embody ideas; they are the symbols that give meaning to our thoughts; they shape our consciousness. New ideas come to us on the wings of words. It's words that bring those ideas to life, that allow us to see possibilities unrecognized before we gave them words. Indeed, without words, there is no conscious thought, no possibility for the kind of self-reflection that lights the path of change.[3]

True, there's often a long way between word and deed. But the man who feels guilty when he disappoints his wife's expectations has a different consciousness than the one who doesn't—a difference that usually makes for at least some small change in his behavior. Although the emergence of this changing male consciousness is visible in all the racial groups in this study, there also are differences among them that are worthy of comment.

Virtually all the men do some work inside the family—tending the children, washing dishes, running the vacuum, going to the market. And they generally also remain responsible for those tasks that have always been traditionally male—mowing the lawn, shoveling the snow, fixing the car, cleaning the garage, doing repairs around the house. Among the white families in this study, 16 percent of the men share the family work relatively equally, almost always those who live in families where they and their wives work different shifts or where the men are unemployed. "What choice do I have?" asks Don Bartlett, a thirty-year-old white handyman who works days while his wife is on the swing shift. "I'm the only one here, so I do what's got to be done."

Asian and Latino men of all ages, however, tend to operate more often on the old male model, even when they work different shifts or are unemployed, a finding that puzzled me at first. Why, I wondered, did I find only two Asian men and one Latino who are real partners in the work of the family? Aren't these men subject to the same social and personal pressures others experience?

The answer is both yes and no. The pressures are there, but, depending upon where they live, there's more or less support for resisting them. The

Latino and Asian men who live in ethnic neighborhoods—settings where they are embedded in an intergenerational community and where the language and culture of the home country is kept alive by a steady stream of new immigrants—find strong support for clinging to the old ways. Therefore, change comes much more slowly in those families. The men who live outside the ethnic quarter are freer from the mandates and constraints of these often tight-knit communities, and therefore are more responsive to the winds of change in the larger society.

These distinctions notwithstanding, it's clear that Asian and Latino men generally participate least in the work of the household and are the least likely to believe they have much responsibility there beyond bringing home a paycheck. "Taking care of the house and kids is my wife's job, that's all," says Joe Gomez flatly.

"A Chinese man mopping a floor? I've never seen it yet," says Amy Lee angrily. Her husband, Dennis, trying to make a joke of the conflict with his wife, says with a smile, "In Chinese families men don't do floors and windows. I help with the dishes sometimes if she needs me to or," he laughs, "if she screams loud enough. The rest, well, it's pretty much her job."

The commonly held stereotype about black men abandoning women and children, however, doesn't square with the families in this study. In fact, black men are the most likely to be real participants in the daily life of the family and are more intimately involved in raising their children than any of the others. True, the men's family work load doesn't always match their wives', and the women are articulate in their complaints about this. Nevertheless, compared to their white, Asian, or Latino counterparts, the black families look like models of egalitarianism.

Nearly three-quarters of the men in the African-American families in this study do a substantial amount of the cooking, cleaning, and child care, sometimes even more than their wives do. All explain it by saying one version or another of: "I just figure it's my job, too"—which simply says what is, without explaining how it came to be that way.

To understand that, we have to look at family histories that tell the story of generations of African-American women who could find work and men who could not, and to the family culture that grew from this difficult and painful reality. "My mother worked six days a week cleaning other people's houses, and my father was an ordinary laborer, when he could find work, which wasn't very often," explains thirty-two-year-old Troy Payne, a black waiter and father of two children. "So he was home a lot more than she was, and he'd do what he had to do around the house. The kids all had to do their share, too. It seemed only fair, I guess."

Difficult as the conflict around the division of labor is, it's only one of the many issues that have become flash points in family life since mother went to work. Most important, perhaps, is the question: Who will care for the children? For the lack of decent, affordable facilities for the care of the children creates unbearable problems and tensions for these working-class families.

It's hardly news that child care is an enormous headache and expense for all two-job families. In many professional middle-class families, where the child-care bill can be $1,500–2,000 a month, it competes with the mortgage payment as the biggest single monthly expenditure. Problematic as this may be, however, these families are the lucky ones when compared to working-class families, many of whom don't earn much more than the cost of child care for these upper-middle-class families. Even the families in this study at the highest end of the earnings scale, those who earn $42,000 a year, can't dream of such costly arrangements.

For most working-class families, therefore, child care often is patched together in ways that leave parents anxious and children in jeopardy. "Care for the little ones, that's a real big problem," says Beverly Waldov, a thirty-year-old white mother of three children—the youngest two; products of a second marriage, under three years old. "My oldest girl is nine, so she's not such a problem. I hate the idea of her being a latchkey kid, but what can I do? We don't even have the money to put the little ones in one of those good day-care places, so I don't have any choice with her. She's just *got* to be able to take care of herself after school," she says, her words a contest between anxiety and hope.

"We have a kind of complicated arrangement for the little kids. Two days a week, my mom takes care of them. We pay her, but at least I don't have to worry when they're with her; I know it's fine. But she works the rest of the time, so the other days we take them to this woman's house. It's the best we can afford, but it's not great because she keeps too many kids, and I know they don't get good attention. Especially the little one; she's just a baby, you know." She pauses and looks away, anguished. "She's so clingy when I bring her home; she can't let go of me, like nobody's paid her any mind all day. But it's not like I have a choice. We barely make it now; if I stop working, we'd be in real trouble."

Even such makeshift solutions don't work for many families. Some speak of being unable to afford day care at all. "We couldn't pay our bills if we had to pay for somebody to take care of the kids."

Some say they're unwilling to leave the children in the care of strangers. "I just don't believe someone else should be raising our kids, that's all."

Some have tried a variety of child-care arrangements, only to have them fail in a moment of need. "We tried a whole bunch of things, and maybe they work for a little while," says Faye Ensey, a black twenty-eight-year-old office worker. "But what happens when your kid gets sick? Or when the baby sitter's kids get sick? I lost two jobs in a row because my kids kept getting sick and I couldn't go to work. Or else I couldn't take my little one to the baby sitter because her kids were sick. They finally fired me for absenteeism. I didn't really blame them, but it felt terrible anyway. It's such a hassle, I sometimes think I'd be glad to just stay home. But we can't afford for me not to work, so we had to figure out something else."

For such families, that "something else" is the decision to take jobs on different shifts—a decision made by one-fifth of the families in this study.

With one working days and the other on swing or graveyard, one parent is home with the children at all times. "We were getting along okay before Daryl junior was born, because Shona, my daughter, was getting on. You know, she didn't need somebody with her all the time, so we could both work days," explains Daryl Adams, a black thirty-year-old postal clerk with a ten-year-old daughter and a nine-month-old son. "I used to work the early shift—seven to three—so I'd get home a little bit after she got here. It worked out okay. But then this here big surprise came along." He stops, smiles down fondly at his young son and runs his hand over his nearly bald head.

"Now between the two of us working, we don't make enough money to pay for child care and have anything left over, so this is the only way we can manage. Besides, both of us, Alesha and me, we think it's better for one of us to be here, not just for the baby, for my daughter, too. She's growing up and, you know, I think maybe they need even more watching than when they were younger. She's coming to the time when she could get into all kinds of trouble if we're not here to put the brakes on."

But the cost such arrangements exact on a marriage can be very high. When I asked these husbands and wives when they have time to talk, more often than not I got a look of annoyance at a question that, on its face, seemed stupid to them. "Talk? How can we talk when we hardly see each other?" "Talk? What's that?" "Talk? Ha, that's a joke."

Mostly, conversation is limited to the logistics that take place at shift-changing time when children and chores are handed off from one to the other. With children dancing around underfoot, the incoming parent gets a quick summary of the day's or night's events, a list of reminders about things to be done, perhaps about what's cooking in the pot on the stove. "Sometimes when I'm coming home and it's been a hard day, I think: Wouldn't it be wonderful if I could just sit down with Leon for half an hour and we could have a quiet beer together?" thirty-one-year-old Emma Guerrero, a Latina baker, says wistfully.

But it's not to be. If the arriving spouse gets home early enough, there may be an hour when both are there together. But with the pressures of the work-day fresh for one and awaiting the other, and with children clamoring for parental attention, this isn't a promising moment for any serious conversation. "I usually get home about forty-five minutes or so before my wife has to leave for work," says Ralph Jo, a thirty-six-year-old Asian repairman, whose children, ages three and five, are the product of a second marriage. "So we try to take a few minutes just to make contact. But it's hard with the kids and all. Most days the whole time gets spent with taking care of business—you know, who did what, what the kids need, what's for supper, what bill collector was hassling her while I was gone—all the damn garbage of living. It makes me nuts."

Most of the time even this brief hour isn't available. Then the ritual changing of the guard takes only a few minutes—a quick peck on the cheek in greeting, a few words, and it's over. "It's like we pass each other. He comes in; I go out; that's it."

Some of the luckier couples work different shifts on the same days, so they're home together on weekends. But even in these families there's so little time for normal family life that there's hardly any room for anyone or anything outside. "There's so much to do when I get home that there's no time for anything but the chores and the kids," says Daryl's wife, Alesha Adams. "I never get to see anybody or do anything else anymore and, even so, I'm always feeling upset and guilty because there's not enough time for them. Daryl leaves a few minutes after I get home, and the rest of the night is like a blur—Shona's homework, getting the kids fed and down for the night, cleaning up, getting everything ready for tomorrow. I don't know; there's always something I'm running around doing. I sometimes feel like— What do you call them?—one of those whirling dervishes, rushing around all the time and never getting everything done.

"Then on the weekends, you sort of want to make things nice for the kids—and for us, too. It's the only time we're here together, like a real family, so we always eat with the kids. And we try to take them someplace nice one of the days, like to the park or something. But sometimes we're too tired, or there's too many other catch-up things you have to do. I don't even get to see my sister anymore. She's been working weekends for the last year or so, and I'm too busy week nights, so there's no time.

"I don't mean to complain; we're lucky in a lot of ways. We've got two great kids, and we're a pretty good team, Daryl and me. But I worry sometimes. When you live on this kind of schedule, communication's not so good."

For those whose days off don't match, the problems of sustaining both the couple relationship and family life are magnified enormously. "The last two years have been hell for us," says thirty-five-year-old Tina Mulvaney, a white mother of two teenagers. "My son got into bad company and had some trouble, so Mike and I decided one of us had to be home. But we can't make it without my check, so I can't quit.

"Mike drives a cab and I work in a hospital, so we figured one of us could transfer to nights. We talked it over and decided it would be best if I was here during the day and he was here at night. He controls the kids, especially my son, better than I do. When he lays down the law, they listen." She interrupts her narrative to reflect on the difficulty of raising children. "You know, when they were little, I used to think about how much easier it would be when they got older. But now I see it's not true; that's when you really have to begin to worry about them. This is when they need someone to be here all the time to make sure they stay out of trouble."

She stops again, this time fighting tears, then takes up where she left off. "So now Mike works days and I work graveyard. I hate it, but it's the only answer; at least this way somebody's here all the time. I get home about 8:30 in the morning. The kids and Mike are gone. It's the best time of the day because it's the only time I have a little quiet here. I clean up the house a little, do the shopping and the laundry and whatever, then I go to sleep for a couple of hours until the kids come home from school.

"Mike gets home at five; we eat; then he takes over for the night, and I go back to sleep for another couple of hours. I try to get up by 9 so we can all have a little time together, but I'm so tired that I don't make it a lot of times. And by 10, he's sleeping because he has to be up by 6 in the morning. So if I don't get up, we hardly see each other at all. Mike's here on weekends, but I'm not. Right now I have Tuesday and Wednesday off. I keep hoping for a Monday–Friday shift, but it's what everybody wants, and I don't have the seniority yet. It's hard, very hard; there's no time to live or anything," she concludes with a listless sigh.

NOTES

1. James Sweet, Larry Bumpass, and Vaugn Call, *National Survey of Families and Households* (Madison, Wisc.: Center for Demography and Ecology, University of Wisconsin, 1988). This study featured a probability sample of 5,518 households and included couples with and without children. See also Joseph Pleck, *Working Wives/Working Husbands* (Beverly Hills: Sage Publications, 1985), who summarizes time-budget studies; and Iona Mara-Drita, "The Effects of Power, Ideology, and Experience on Men's Participation in Housework," unpublished paper (1993), whose analysis of Sweet, Bumpass, and Call's data shows that when housework and employment hours are added together, a woman's work week totals 69 hours, compared to 52 hours for a man.
2. Lillian Rubin, *Worlds of Pain* (New York: Basic Books, 1992), p. 93.
3. See Daniel Stern, *The Interpersonal World of the Infant* (New York: Basic Books, 1985), who argues that a child's capacity for self-reflection coincides with the development of language.

38

BLOODMOTHERS, OTHERMOTHERS, AND WOMEN-CENTERED NETWORKS

PATRICIA HILL COLLINS

Patricia Hill Collins is the Charles Taft Professor of Sociology in the Department of African-American Studies at the University of Cincinnati. She is also the author of *Fighting Words: Black Women and the Search for Justice.* Her first edition of *Black Feminist Thought* won the Association for Women in Psychology's Distinguished Publication Award, the Society for the Study of Social Problems' C. Wright Mills Award, and the Association of Black Women Historians' Letitia Woods Brown Memorial Book Prize.

In many African-American communities, fluid and changing boundaries often distinguish biological mothers from other women who care for children. Biological mothers, or bloodmothers, are expected to care for their children. But African and African-American communities have also recognized that vesting one person with full responsibility for mothering a child may not be wise or possible. As a result, othermothers—women who assist bloodmothers by sharing mothering responsibilities—traditionally have been central to the institution of Black motherhood (Troester 1984).

The centrality of women in African-American extended families reflects both a continuation of African-derived cultural sensibilities and functional adaptations to intersecting oppressions of race, gender, class, and nation (Tanner 1974; Stack 1974; Martin and Martin 1978; Sudarkasa 1981b; Reagon 1987). Women's centrality is characterized less by the *absence* of husbands and fathers than by the significance of women. Though men may be physically present or have well-defined and culturally significant roles in the extended family, the kin unit tends to be woman-centered. Bebe Moore Campbell's (1989) parents separated when she was small. Even though she spent the school year in the North Philadelphia household maintained by her grandmother and mother, Campbell's father assumed an important role in her life. "My father took care of me," Campbell remembers. "Our separation didn't stunt me or condemn me to a lesser humanity. His absence never made me a fatherless child. I'm not fatherless now" (p. 271). In woman-centered kin units such as Campbell's—whether a mother-child household unit, a married couple household, or a larger unit extending over several households—the centrality of mothers is not predicated on male powerlessness (Tanner 1974, 133).

Organized, resilient, women-centered networks of bloodmothers and othermothers are key in understanding this centrality. Grandmothers, sisters, aunts, or cousins act as othermothers by taking on child-care responsibilities for one another's children. Historically, when needed, temporary child-care arrangements often turned into long-term care or informal adoption (Stack 1974; Gutman 1976). These practices continue in the face of changing social pressures. Andrea Hunter's (1997) research on Black grandmothers explores how Black parents rely on grandmothers for parenting support. This traditional source of support became even more needed in the 1980s and 1990s, when increasing numbers of Black mothers saw their teenage children fall victim to drugs and the crime associated with it. Many witnessed their sons killed or incarcerated, while their daughters became addicts. In many cases, these young men and women left behind children, who often ended up in foster care. Other children did not, primarily because their grandmothers took responsibility for raising them, often under less than optimal conditions.

In many African-American communities these women-centered networks of community-based child care have extended beyond the boundaries of biologically related individuals to include "fictive kin" (Stack 1974). Civil rights activist Ella Baker describes how informal adoption by othermothers functioned in the rural Southern community of her childhood:

> My aunt who had thirteen children of her own raised three more. She had become a midwife, and a child was born who was covered with sores. Nobody was particularly wanting the child, so she took the child and raised him . . . and another mother decided she didn't want to be bothered with two children. So my aunt took one and raised him . . . they were part of the family. (Cantarow 1980, 59)

Stanlie James recounts how othermother traditions work with notions of fictive kin within her own extended family. James notes that the death of her grandmother in 1988 reunited her family, described as a host of biological and fictive kin. James's rendition of how one female family member helped James's nine-year-old daughter deal with the loss of her great-grandmother illustrates the interactions among women-centered extended kin networks, fictive kin, and othermother traditions. The woman who helped James's daughter was not a blood relative but had been "othermothered" by James's grandmother and was a full member of the extended family. James's grandmother believed that because all children must be fed, clothed, and educated, if their biological parents could not discharge these obligations, then some other member of the community should accept that responsibility. As James points out, "This fictive kin who stepped in to counsel my daughter was upholding a family tradition that had been modeled by my grandmother some fifty years before" (James 1993, 44).

Even when relationships are not between kin or fictive kin, African-American community norms traditionally were such that neighbors cared for one another's children. Sara Brooks, a Southern domestic worker, describes the importance that the community-based child care a neighbor offered her daughter had for her: "She kept Vivian and she didn't charge me nothin either. You see, people used to look after each other, but now its not that way. I reckon its because we all was poor, and I guess they put theirself in the place of the person that they was helpin'" (Simonsen 1986, 181). Brooks's experiences demonstrate how the African-American cultural value placed on cooperative child care traditionally found institutional support in the adverse conditions under which so many Black women mothered.

Othermothers can be key not only in supporting children but also in helping bloodmothers who, for whatever reason, lack the preparation or desire for motherhood. In confronting racial oppression, maintaining community-based child care and respecting othermothers who assume child-care responsibilities can serve a critical function in African-American communities. Children orphaned by sale or death of their parents under slavery, children conceived through rape, children of young mothers, children born into extreme poverty or to alcoholic or drug-addicted mothers, or children who for other reasons cannot remain with their bloodmothers have all been supported by othermothers, who, like Ella Baker's aunt, take in additional children even when they have enough of their own.

Young women are often carefully groomed at an early age to become othermothers. As a 10-year-old, Ella Baker learned to be an othermother by caring for the children of a widowed neighbor: "Mama would say, 'You must take the clothes to Mr. Powell's house, and give so-and-so a bath.' The children were running wild. . . . The kids . . . would take off across the field. We'd chase them down, and bring them back, and put 'em in the tub, and wash 'em off, and change clothes, and carry the dirty ones home, and wash them. Those kind of things were routine" (Cantarow 1980, 59).

Many Black men also value community-based child care but historically have exercised these values to a lesser extent. During slavery, for example, Black children under age 10 experienced little division of labor. They were dressed alike and performed similar tasks. If the activities of work and play are any indication of the degree of gender role differentiation that existed among slave children, "then young girls probably grew up minimizing the difference between the sexes while learning far more about the differences between the races" (D. White 1985, 94). Because they are often left in charge of younger siblings, many young Black men learn how to care for children. Geoffrey Canada (1995) recounts how he had to learn how to fight in his urban neighborhood. The climate of violence that he and his two brothers encountered mandated developing caretaking skills, especially since his single mother had to work and could not offer them the protection that they needed. Thus, differences among Black men and women in behaviors concerning children may have more to do with male labor force patterns and similar factors. As Ella Baker observes, "My father took care of people too, but . . . my father had to work" (Cantarow 1980, 60).

Historically, within Black diasporic societies, community-based child care and the relationships among bloodmothers and othermothers in women-centered networks have taken diverse institutional forms. In some polygynous West African societies, the children of the same father but different mothers referred to one another as brothers and sisters. While a strong bond existed between the biological mother and her child — one so strong that, among the Ashanti for example, "to show disrespect toward one's mother is tantamount to sacrilege" (Fortes 1950, 263) — children could be disciplined by any of their "mothers." Cross-culturally, the high status given to othermothers and the cooperative nature of child-care arrangements among bloodmothers and othermothers in Caribbean and other Black diasporic societies gives credence to the importance that people of African descent place on mothering (Sudarkasa 1981a).

Although the political economy of slavery brought profound changes to Africans enslaved in the United States, beliefs in the importance of motherhood and the value of cooperative approaches to child care continued. During slavery, while older women served as nurses and midwives, their most common occupation was caring for the children of parents who worked (D. White 1985). Informal adoption of orphaned children reinforced the importance of social motherhood in African-American communities (Gutman 1976). The relationship between bloodmothers and othermothers also survived the transition from a slave economy to post-emancipation Southern rural agriculture. Children in Southern rural communities were not solely the responsibility of their biological mothers. Aunts, grandmothers, and others who had time to supervise children served as othermothers (Dougherty 1978). The significant status that women enjoyed in family networks and in African-American communities continued to be linked to their bloodmother and othermother activities.

In the 1980s, the entire community structure of bloodmothers and othermothers came under assault. Racial desegregation as well as the emergence of class-stratified Black neighborhoods greatly altered the fabric of Black civil society. African-Americans of diverse social classes found themselves in new residential, school, and work settings that tested this enduring theme of bloodmothers, othermothers, and woman-centered networks. In many inner-city, working-class neighborhoods, the very fabric of African-American community life eroded when crack cocaine flooded the streets. African-American children and youth often formed the casualties of this expanding market for drugs, from the increasing number of Black children in foster care (Nightingale 1993), to children threatened by violence (Canada

1995), to those killed. Residents of Central Harlem interviewed by anthropologist Leith Mullings repeatedly expressed concern about losing the community's children, leading Mullings to observe, "The depth of worry about children growing up in these conditions is difficult to convey" (Mullings 1997, 93). Given this situation, it is remarkable that even in the most troubled communities, remnants of the othermother tradition endure. Bebe Moore Campbell's 1950s North Philadelphia neighborhood underwent startling changes in the 1980s. Increases in child abuse and parental neglect left many children without care. But some residents, such as Miss Nee, continued the othermother tradition. After raising her younger brothers and sisters and five children of her own, Miss Nee cared for three additional children whose families fell apart. Moreover, on any given night Miss Nee's house may have been filled by up to a dozen children because she had a reputation for never turning away a needy child ("Children of the Underclass" 1989).

Black middle-class women and their families found challenges from another direction. In some fundamental ways, moving into the middle class means adopting the values and lifestyles of White middle-class families. While the traditional family ideal is not the norm, the relative isolation of such families from others is noteworthy. U.S. middle-class family life is based on privatization—buying a big house so that one need not cooperate with one's neighbors, or even see them. American middle-class families participate in the privatization of everything, from schools and health care, to for-fee health clubs and private automobiles. Working-class African-Americans who experience social mobility thus may encounter a distinctly different value system. Not only are woman-centered networks of bloodmothers and othermothers much more difficult to sustain structurally—class-stratified residential and employment patterns mean that middle-class Black women often see working-class and poor Black women only as their employees or clients—such ideas are often anathema to the ethos of achievement. From the security firms that find ways to monitor nannies, to the gated-communities of suburbia, purchasing services appears to be the hallmark of American middle-class existence. In this context, stopping to help others to whom one is not related and doing it for free can be seen as rejecting the basic values of the capitalist market economy.

In this context, these relationships among bloodmothers and othermothers and the persistence of woman-centered networks may have greater theoretical importance than currently recognized. The traditional family ideal assigns mothers full responsibility for children and evaluates their performance based on their ability to procure the benefits of a nuclear family household. Within this capitalist marketplace model, those women who "catch" legal husbands, who live in single-family homes, who can afford private school and music lessons for their children, are deemed better mothers than those who do not. In this context, those African-American women who continue community-based child care challenge one fundamental assumption underlying the capitalist system itself: that children are "private property" and can be disposed of as such. Under the property model that accompanies the traditional family ideal, parents may not literally assert that their children are pieces of property, but their parenting may reflect assumptions analogous to those they make in connection with property. For example, the exclusive parental "right" to discipline children as parents see fit, even if discipline borders on abuse, parallels the widespread assumption that property owners may dispose of their property without consulting members of the larger community.

By seeing the larger *community* as responsible for children and by giving othermothers and other nonparents "rights" in child rearing, those African-Americans who endorse these values challenge prevailing capitalist property relations. In Harlem, for example, Black women are increasingly the breadwinners in their families, and rates of households maintained by single mothers remain high. These families are clearly under stress, yet to see the household formation itself as an indication of decline in Black family organization misreads a more complex situation. Leith Mullings suggests that many of these households participate in fluid, familylike networks that have different purposes. Women activate some networks for socialization, reproduction, and consumption, and others for emotional support, economic cooperation, and sexuality. The networks may overlap, but they are not coterminous (Mullings 1997, 74).

The resiliency of women-centered family networks and their willingness to take responsibility for Black children illustrates how African-influenced understandings of family have been continually reworked to help African-Americans as a collectivity cope with and resist oppression. Moreover, these understandings of woman-centered kin networks become critical in understanding broader African-American understandings of community. At the same time, the erosion of such networks in the face of the changing institutional fabric of Black civil society points to the need either to refashion these networks or develop some other way of supporting Black children. For far too many African-American children, assuming that a grandmother or "fictive kin" will care for them is no longer a reality.

REFERENCES

Campbell, Bebe Moore. 1989. *Sweet Summer: Growing Up with and without My Dad.* New York: Putnam.

Canada, Geoffrey. 1995. *First Stick Knife Gun: A Personal History of Violence in America.* Boston: Beacon.

Cantarow, Ellen. 1980. *Moving the Mountain: Women Working for Social Change.* Old Westbury, NY: Feminist Press.

"Children of the Underclass." 1989. *Newsweek.* September 11, 16–27.

Dougherty, Molly C. 1978. *Becoming a Woman in Rural Black Culture.* New York: Holt, Rinehart and Winston.

Fortes, Meyer. 1950. "Kinship and Marriage among the Ashanti." In *African Systems of Kinship and Marriage,* ed. A. R. Radcliffe-Brown and Daryll Forde, 252–84. New York: Oxford University Press.

Gutman, Herbert, 1976. *The Black Family in Slavery and Freedom,* 1750–1925. New York: Random House.

Hunter, Andrea. 1997. "Counting on Grandmothers: Black Mothers' and Fathers' Reliance on Grandmothers for Parenting Support." *Journal of Family Issues* 18 (3): 251–69.

James, Stanlie. 1993. "Mothering: A Possible Black Feminist Link to Social Transformation?" In *Theorizing Black Feminisms: The Visionary Pragmatism of Black Women,* ed. Stanlie James and Abena Busia, 44–54. New York: Routledge.

Martin, Elmer, and Joanne Mitchell Martin. 1978. *The Black Extended Family.* Chicago: University of Chicago Press.

Mullings, Leith. 1997. *On Our Own Terms: Race, Class, and Gender in the Lives of African American Women.* New York: Routledge.

Nightingale, Carl Husemoller. 1993. *On the Edge: A History of Poor Black Children and Their American Dreams.* New York: Basic Books.

Reagon, Bernice Johnson. 1987. "African Diaspora Women: The Making of Cultural Workers." In *Women in Africa and the African Diaspora,* ed. Rosalyn Terborg-Penn, Sharon Harley, and Andrea Benton Rushing, 167–80. Washington, D.C.: Howard University Press.

Simonsen, Thordis, ed. 1986. *You May Plow Here: The Narrative of Sara Brooks.* New York: Touchstone.

Stack, Carol D. 1974. *All Our Kin: Strategies for Survival in a Black Community.* New York: Harper and Row.

Sudarkasa, Niara. 1981a. "Female Employment and Family Organization in West Africa." In *The Black Woman Cross-Culturally,* ed. Filomina Chioma Steady, 49–64. Cambridge, MA: Schenkman.

———. 1981b. "Interpreting the African Heritage in Afro-American Family Organization." In *Black Families,* ed. Harriette Pipes McAdoo, 37–53. Beverly Hills, CA: Sage.

Tanner, Nancy. 1974. "Matrifocality in Indonesia and Africa and among Black Americans." In *Woman, Culture, and Society,* ed. Michelle Z. Rosaldo and Louise Lamphere, 129–56. Stanford, CA: Stanford University Press.

Troester, Rosalie Riegle. 1984. "Turbulence and Tenderness: Mothers, Daughters, and 'Othermothers' in Paule Marshall's *Brown Girl, Brownstones.*" *Sage: A Scholarly Journal on Black Women* 1 (2): 13–16.

White, Deborah Gray. 1985. *Ar'n't I a Woman? Female Slaves in the Plantation South.* New York: W. W. Norton.

39

DILEMMAS OF INVOLVED FATHERHOOD

KATHLEEN GERSON

Kathleen Gerson is professor of sociology at New York University and the author of several books, including *No Man's Land: Men's Changing Commitments to Family and Work* (Basic Books, 1993), *Hard Choices: How Women Decide about Work, Career, and Motherhood* (University of California Press, 1985), and *The Time Divide: Work Family, and Gender Inequality* (with Jerry A. Jacobs), (Harvard University Press, 2004). She lives with her spouse, John Mollenkopf, and their daughter, Emily, in New York City.

> *Work's a necessity, but the things that really matter are spending time with my family. If I didn't have a family, I don't know what I would have turned to. That's why I say you're rich in a lot of ways other than money. I look at my daughter and think, "My family is everything."*
>
> — *CARL, A THIRTY-FOUR-YEAR-OLD UTILITIES WORKER*

Social disapproval and economic inequality put full-time domesticity out of reach for almost all men. Yet most also found that economic necessity and employer intransigence made anything less than full-time work an equally distant possibility. Few employers offered the option of part-time work, especially in male-dominated fields. Arthur, a married sanitation worker planning for fatherhood, complained:

> If it was feasible, I would love to spend more time with my child. That would be more important to me than working. I'd love to be able to work twenty-five hours a week or four days a week and have three days off to spend with the family, but most jobs aren't going to accommodate you that way.

Yet, even if part-time work were available, involved fathers still needed the earnings that only full-time and overtime work could offer. Lou, the sewage worker who worked the night shift in order to spend days with his young daughter, could not accept lower wages or fewer benefits:

If I knew that financially everything would be set, I'd stay home. I'd like to stay more with my daughter. It's a lot of fun to be with a very nice three-year-old girl. But if I work less, I would equate it to less money and then I wouldn't be taking care of my family. If it meant less work and the same or more money, I'd say, "Sure!" I'd be dumb if I didn't.

Dean, the driver for a city department of parks, agreed that his economic obligations could not take a backseat to his nurturing ones:

It always comes down to the same thing: I would like to have more time to spend with my children, but if I didn't have money, what's the sense of having time off? If I could work part-time and make enough money, that would be fine and dandy.

Since involved fathers tried to nurture as well as support their children, they made an especially hard choice between money and time. Like many mothers, they had to add caretaking onto full-time workplace responsibilities, but employers are generally reluctant to recognize male (or female) parental responsibility as a legitimate right or need.[1] Worse yet, paternal leaves are rarely considered a legitimate option for men even if they formally exist. Involved fathers wished to take time off for parenting, but like most men they were reluctant to do so for fear of imperiling their careers.[2] And even though most employers allow health-related leaves with impunity, they have not been so flexible when it comes to the job of parenting. Workers receive the message that illness is unavoidable, but parenting is voluntary — an indication of a lack of job commitment. Our current corporate culture thus makes parenting hazardous to anyone's career, and choosing a "daddy track" can be just as dangerous as the much-publicized "mommy track." Juan, a financial analyst, knew he could not pull back from his job for more than a few days or a week without jeopardizing his job security. To parental leave,

I'd say yes, but realistically no. It would be a problem because it's very difficult for me to tell my boss that I have to leave at such a time. I have deadlines to meet. If I leave the office for two or three months, my job is in jeopardy.

Because employers did not offer flexible options for structuring work on a daily basis or over the course of a career, some involved fathers looked to self-employment or home-based work for more flexibility and control. Craig, the ex-dancer currently working in an office, hoped he would be able to integrate work and parenting by working at home:

I would like to find myself in the situation where I'm not locked into a nine-to-five schedule. Ultimately, I hope I'm doing consulting on my own at home, which means time close to the family. So that in the middle of my own workday, at the house, I'm available. I can just put my work aside and play Daddy.

Most could not even entertain this option. They had to fit parenting in around the edges of their work lives.[3]

Domestic arrangements also impede full equality. Child rearing remains an undervalued, isolating, and largely invisible accomplishment for *all* parents. This has fueled women's flight from domesticity and also dampened men's motivation to choose it. Russell, the legal-aid attorney and father of two, recognized that child rearing was less valued than employment:

> I think I would feel somewhat meaningless to not be engaged in
> any form of productive work—although certainly raising children
> is productive work. But I couldn't be responsible for that on a full-
> time basis. While I love my guys, I don't think I could be around
> them all the time.

Child rearing can be invisible as well as undervalued. Unlike the size of a paycheck or the title one holds at work, there are few socially recognized rewards for the time a parent devotes to raising a child or the results it produces. This made only the most dedicated, like Hank, willing to consider full-time parenting:

> Nobody will know the time and the effort I put in the family. They
> will look down on it. I would devote time, hours, and nobody will
> be happy with it except me because I'll know what I was trying for.

The forces pulling women out of the home are stronger than the forces pulling men into it. Since the social value of public pursuits outstrips the power and prestige of private ones, men are likely to resist full-time domesticity even as women move toward full-time employment. This process is similar to the one pulling women into male-dominated occupations while leaving men less inclined to enter female-dominated ones. In addition, just as women in male-dominated occupations face prejudice and discrimination, fathers who become equal or primary parents are stigmatized—treated as "tokens" in a female-dominated world.[4] Roger shied away from the pervasive questioning about his life as a custodial parent:

> I think I've become somewhat more introverted than I used to be—
> because I get tired of explaining my situation at home. . . . The
> thing that blows all the kids' minds—they're all living with
> Mommy and my kids are living with Daddy.

In the face of such disincentives, most involved fathers rejected staying home for the same reasons many women do and more. Female breadwinning and male homemaking did not seem acceptable even when they made economic sense. Robin, a stockbroker, rejected domesticity precisely because his poor work prospects left him in no state to bear the additional stigma of becoming a househusband. Although he was making a lot less money than his wife was, he felt too "demoralized" to consider staying home. "I'm not secure enough, I guess, to stay home and be a househusband."

Of course, involved fathers actively resisted the discrimination they encountered. They asserted their nurturing competence and insisted on being taken as seriously as female parents are. The prevailing skepticism about men's parental abilities, however, made this an uphill battle. Ernie complained:

> I believe I have as much right in raising the child as she does, but I found a lot of reverse discrimination—people assuming that the mother takes care of the child. It's a lot of stereotyping, a lot that's taken for granted. Like pediatricians: they speak to my wife; they won't speak to me. I say, "Hey, I take care of her, too." They look at me like I'm invisible. The same thing with the nursery school. I went out on all the interviews. They looked at me like, "What're *you* doing here?"

Economic, social, and ideological arrangements thus made involved fatherhood difficult. The lack of workplace and domestic supports diluted and suppressed the potential for involvement even among the most motivated men. In the absence of these hurdles, fathers who wished to be involved might have participated far more than they actually did. They might, in fact, have made choices that now remain open to a rapidly diminishing number of women. Ernie wished he had options that only full-time mothers enjoy:

> I'm not the type that has career aspirations and is very goal-oriented. If I didn't have to work, I wouldn't. But I would volunteer. I would work in a nursery school. I would do a lot more volunteer work with my daughter's school. I would love to go on trips like the mothers who don't work, be more active in the P.T.A. I would love that. But I can't.

As the supports for homemaking mothers erode, supports for equal and primary fathers have not emerged to offset the growing imbalance between children's needs and families' resources. Fathers have had to depend on paid help, relatives, and already overburdened wives even when they did not wish to do so.

These obstacles not only left mothers giving up more. They also made involved fathers appear heroic about *whatever* they did. Comparisons with other men could be used to ward off complaints and resist further change. Ernie maintained:

> Sometimes she didn't think I did enough. I couldn't stand that because I thought I was doing too much. I really felt I was doing more than I should, whatever that means. I told her to go talk to some of her friends and see what their husbands are doing.

Nurturing fathers faced deeply rooted barriers to full equality in parenting. Social arrangements at work and in the home dampened even willing men's ability to share equally. The truncated range of choices open to most of these men limited the options of their wives, ex-wives, and partners as well. We can only guess how many mothers' helpers would become equal parents if these obstacles did not exist or, better yet, were replaced by positive supports for involved fatherhood.

Benefiting from the Loss of Privilege: Incentives for Change

If full equality remained beyond the reach of most involved fathers, they nevertheless moved a notable distance toward it. They were not simply forced to make concessions; nor were they just being altruistic. They also perceived offsetting, if unheralded, benefits. After all, parenting can be its own reward—offering intrinsic pleasures and a powerful sense of accomplishment. Rick explained:

> I have an extremely close relationship with my kids, and that makes me feel good. The fact that they're both doing very well in school—I know that at least a little bit of that comes from having been with them when they were young. So there's all those interactions in seeing them on their way to being healthy and vibrant kids.

These feelings took on added significance when other avenues for building self-esteem were blocked. Todd, the aspiring actor who became a construction worker, hoped his talents could be channeled toward his daughter instead of his job:

> If there's any Creator at all up there, She or It or They're going to ask for some sort of accounting at the end. They're going to be pleased if they gave you a certain amount of gifts and you were able to do something with them. I'd still like to be a part of something more meaningful than putting in a new fire hydrant—I guess through my influence on this little one's life.

If children offered a source of pride for those whose workplace aspirations had not been met, this was not just a concern for passing on genes or the family name. Contributions of time and emotions counted more. Carl, who chose utility repair work so that he could care for his daughter after school, saw his "investment" reflected in her talents and achievements:

> I've had a lot of compliments on her, and I take them as a compliment also. It's something that became part of you—teaching them different things, helping them grow up. They'll do something, and it's like seeing a reflection of you.

As work opportunities stall in an age of stagnant economic growth, parenting offers men another avenue for developing self-esteem. But economically successful fathers also reaped benefits from involvement because it balanced lives that would otherwise have been more narrowly focused on paid work. For Charles, the attorney with a young son, caretaking provided a legitimate reason for limiting the demands of work: "I'm working a little less hard, taking on fewer responsibilities. . . . But I think it's great. I don't need all the other shit."

Children also provided the hope of permanence in an age of divorce. Even happily married fathers came to see their children as the bedrock of stability in a shaky world, the one bond that could not be severed or assailed. Having been reared by a single mother, Juan viewed his children rather than his wife as the best chance for enduring emotional ties: "What if one day my wife and I get sick of each other after so many years? So I would like to have children."

Involved fatherhood also provided emotional supports by creating a bond between husbands and wives. Married men were less likely to feel rejected by their wives and excluded from the new relationships that form with the birth of a child. Timothy, the worker at a city dump, could not understand why less-involved fathers complained of being rejected when a new baby arrived:

> They have these books about how fathers are supposed to go
> through blues because the wife is giving her attention to the child.
> Is this some kind of maniac that wrote this? I take care of him just
> as much as she does.

Sharing the load of caring for a newborn also seemed to decrease the chances that a mother would feel overwhelmed and alone during a critical, and trying, turning point in a marriage.[5] Carlos hoped that sharing the caretaking would help him avoid the hostility that he felt unequal arrangements would generate:

> I think it's a great burden to have one parent do all the caretaking.
> It would burn out that person, and they're not going to be able to
> respond to you. Then I would start feeling resentment towards her
> and possibly the child. So the only way I could see avoiding that is
> by sharing the responsibility.

Since involved fathers believed that a satisfying relationship depended on both partners being able to meet their needs, thwarting a partner's dreams by refusing to participate seemed to be a Pyrrhic victory. The costs of not sharing appeared greater than the costs of sharing. Carl was pleased to escape his parents' pattern:

> My parents are the old school. He never really touched a dish. I
> like what I'm doing better. The older way, I feel the woman will
> think, "I never really had an opportunity to do things." She will
> become resentful later on. Where my wife can't say nothing
> because she's had her freedom, she's worked, she's not stayed in

the kitchen barefoot and pregnant, and I did what I had to do. I feel in the long run it pays off. The other way, maybe she would have left.

Involved fatherhood thus offered two ways of coping with the risks of marriage in an era of divorce. It provided another source of emotional sustenance in the event that the marital bond did not survive. And it offered a way to build less rancorous relationships by reducing wives' resentment. Indeed, there is growing evidence that egalitarian relationships do provide benefits to husbands and wives. In one report, wives whose husbands participate in domestic duties showed lower rates of depression than those with husbands who don't, while another found that the more housework a husband does, the lower are the chances that his wife has considered divorce.[6]

Emotional gratification and marital peace were not the only payoffs. In agreeing to share the domestic load, men can also share the economic load. Their wives' income lessens the pressure to work long hours and take on second jobs. Wesley was pleased to exchange extra hours at work for domestic sharing:

> If Cindy wants to be home, she can stay home. But that would probably mean I would have to either get myself another job or work overtime on the job I have. I would do it. She knows that. But she doesn't want me to. We spend more time with each other this way.

Involved fathers also believed their children would benefit in both the short and long runs—perceptions that research on both married and divorced fathers supports.[7] Larry observed:

> Having spent a lot of time with both of us, she's not really dependent on either one of us. Mommy's like daddy; daddy's like mommy. At times I am her mother. It's good to switch roles. She don't run to mommy or run to daddy. She runs to both of us.

They hoped their example would help their daughters and sons develop a flexible approach to building their own lives. Ernie decided his involvement created a better domestic environment for his daughter:

> The sharing—it's a good role model for her. She sees me cook. I'm trying to teach her baking, and I think it's nice my daughter is learning baking from her father. So I'm hoping she sees that it's split and not that just the wife does this and the man does that.

He also hoped his participation would give his daughter a sense of self-reliance, agreeing with a growing group of psychologists who argue that girls no less than boys need their fathers. Both sexes identify in varying degrees with both parents, and girls look to fathers as well as mothers to provide models for living:[8]

Raising my child, that is my priority—seeing that she's raised well
in the sense of preparing her to face the world, trying to get her
exposed as much as possible, so she may find out what she likes to
pursue. I hope she has a career. I hope she finds something she
really likes and works for it.

These men concluded that their domestic arrangements would also benefit their sons, echoing recent research showing that sons of involved fathers
are likely to show a more developed capacity for empathy.[9] Wesley thus concluded that his two sons "feel close to the two of us. Maybe when they get
married, they'll share in the house."

Just as these fathers created families that differed from the households in
which they were reared, so their children will take the lessons of their childhood into unknown futures. Involved fathers' belief in the advantages of domestic sharing cannot guarantee a similar response in their children, but it
can and did strengthen their own resolve to create a more egalitarian household. As more fathers become involved, their growing numbers should
prompt wider social acceptance of egalitarian households, bolstering the option to make such choices.

Ultimately, however, men's movement toward domestic equality will
depend on their ability to overcome the obstacles to change and their desire
to resist the social pressures to conform. Equal fathers were willing and able
to defy social expectations, to overcome social constraints, and to reject the
pathways of the past. There is good reason to believe that their outlooks and
choices reflect a simmering mood among many American men, who long for
more work flexibility and fewer work demands. There is even reason to believe many would be willing to relinquish some earnings in exchange for
spending more time with their families. A *Time* survey found that 56 percent
of a random sample of men said they would forfeit up to one-fourth of their
salaries "to have more family and personal time," and 45 percent "said they
would probably refuse a promotion that involved sacrificing hours with
their families."[10] Carl reflects this mood:

It's amazing how many people don't understand the way I feel. I
would prefer to be home than work overtime, where they would
kill to get it. They say, "What are you, rich?" No, but you only
need a certain amount of money to live. God forbid you walk
down the street and get struck by a car, or whatever, and it's over. I
don't want to say, "Why didn't I spend more time with my
family?" It's not going to happen to me. You can control it.

By focusing on the advantages and discounting the drawbacks of their
choices, men are able to overcome some of the social and ideological barriers to equal parenting. In adding up the sacrifices and the gains, Larry spoke
for the group: "I've given some things up, sure, but the changes in my
lifestyle are eighty or ninety percent in the positive."

Though few in number, equal fathers demonstrate that men can discover or acquire nurturing skills and find pleasure in using them. Those men who did find support for being an equal father made contingent choices just like those who did not. In both instances, different circumstances could easily have produced different outcomes. It is not surprising that Rick found his rare and unexpected path to be a matter of chance:

> I have very conservative attitudes in many respects. The fact that we got married and had children was very conservative. The fact that within those parameters, we shared, co-shared, work and family — that was not conservative. We've never discussed it, but I feel that the outcome is built much more on chance. I may not have always felt that way, but my own experiences confirmed it.

Chance, however, is just another way of saying that his choice was based on unusual and unexpected opportunities. Given how rare are the supports for involved fathering and how pervasive the obstacles, its rise is even more significant than its limited nature. For the potential of the many men who wish to be more involved to be realized, however, the unusual circumstances that now prompt only a small fraction of men to become equal parents must become real for a much larger group.

NOTES

1. See Lawson, Carol. 1991. "Baby Beckons: Why Is Daddy at Work?" *New York Times* (May 16); C1, C8. The Family Leave Act that finally became law in 1993 is an important first step, but much more will be needed for men to feel able to choose equal parenting.

2. Joseph H. Pleck. 1983. "Husbands' Paid Work and Family Roles: Current Research Trends," *Research in the Interweave of Social Roles: Jobs and Families* 3: 251–333.

3. Barbara J. Risman and Maxine P. Atkinson. 1990. "Gender in Intimate Relationships: Toward a Dialectical Structural Theory." Paper presented at the National Council on Family Relations Theory, Construction, and Research Methodology Workshop (November), Seattle, Washington. According to Risman and Atkinson: "No matter how involved 'new feminist' fathers become in child-care, they . . . are expected to work harder and are constrained from leaving less than optimal jobs because of their economic responsibilities. When they do care for their children after work, they are praised highly by friends, family members, and wives as wonderful, modern, 'involved' fathers" (pp. 15–16).

4. Hal Strauss. 1989. "Freaks of Nature." *American Health* (January–February): 70–71; Rosabeth M. Kanter. 1977. *Men and Women of the Corporation.* New York: Basic Books; Bryan E. Robinson. 1986. "Men Caring for the Young: A Profile." In *Men's Changing Roles in the Family,* pp. 151–61. Edited by Robert A. Lewis and Marvin B. Sussman. New York: Haworth Press. Men who become primary parents face barriers similar to those faced by the first female managers, who had to cope with being "tokens." Strauss discusses the stigmatization and social isolation of househusbands. Kanter analyzes how the first female managers were tokens in the corporation. Robinson, 1986, reports that male caregivers who work in nursery schools and day-care programs also faced discrimination and stigma from employers, co-workers, and even parents.

5. See Alice A. Rossi. 1960. "Transition to Parenthood." *Journal of Marriage and the Family* 30: 26–39.

6. Joan Huber and Glenna Spitze. 1983. *Sex Stratification: Children, Housework, and Jobs.* New York: Academic Press; Catherine E. Ross, John Mirowsky, and Joan Huber. 1983. "Dividing Work, Sharing Work, and In-Between: Marriage Patterns and Depression." *American Sociological Review* 48 (6) (December): 809–23; See also Michael E. Lamb, Joseph H. Pleck, and James A. Levine. 1987. "Effects of Increased Paternal Involvement on Fathers and Mothers." In *Reassessing Fatherhood: New Observations on Fathers and the Modern Family,* pp. 103–25. Edited by Charlie Lewis and Margaret O'Brien. Newberry Park, CA: Sage Publications; Arlie R. Hochschild with Anne Machung. 1989. *The Second Shift: Working Parents and the Revolution at Home.* New York: Viking.

7. See Frank F. Furstenberg, Jr., S. Phillip Morgan, and Paul D. Allison. 1987. "Paternal Participation and Children's Well-Being After Marital Dissolution." *American Sociological Review* 52(5):695–701; Shirley M. H. Hanson. 1986. "Father/Child Relationships: Beyond *Kramer vs. Kramer.*" In *Men's Changing Roles in the Family,* pp. 135–50. Edited by Robert A. Lewis and Marvin B. Sussman. New York: Haworth Press; Michael E. Lamb, ed. 1976. *The Role of the Father in Child Development.* New York: Wiley; J. W. Santrock and R. A. Warshak. 1979. "Father Custody and Social Development in Boys and Girls." *Journal of Social Issues* 32: 112–25; J. W. Santrock, R. A. Warshak, and G. L. Elliot. 1982. "Social Development and Parent-Child Interaction in Father-Custody and Stepmother Families." In *Nontraditional Families: Parenting and Child Development,* pp. 289–314. Edited by Michael E. Lamb. Hillside, NJ: Lawrence Erlbaum.

8. Victoria Secunda. 1992. *Women and Their Fathers: The Sexual and Romantic Impact of the First Man in Your Life.* New York: Delacorte Press.

9. Daniel Goleman. 1990. "Surprising Findings about the Development of Empathy in Children." *New York Times* (July 10): C1.

10. Reported in Judith Stacey. 1991. "Backwards toward the Post-Modern Family." In *America at Century's End,* pp. 17–34. Edited by Alan Wolfe. Berkeley and Los Angeles: University of California Press. See also Phyllis Moen and Donna I. Dempster-McClain. 1987. "Employed Parents: Role Strain, Work Time, and Preferences for Working Less." *Journal of Marriage and the Family* 49 (3): 579–90; Eli Chinoy. 1955. *Automobile Workers and the American Dream.* New York: Random House. If Chinoy found that automobile workers in the 1950s dreamed about retiring, inheriting wealth, or opening their own businesses as an alternative to dead-end factory jobs, then the decline of well-paying, secure manufacturing jobs over the last decade has given this dream of independence through self-employment new life.

40

MAN CHILD
A Black Lesbian Feminist's Response

AUDRE LORDE

Audre Lorde, who passed away in 1992, grew up in the West Indian community of Harlem in the 1930s, the daughter of immigrants from Grenada. She attended Hunter College (later becoming professor of English there), ventured to the American expatriate community in Mexico, and participated in the Greenwich Village scene of the early 1950s. She is a major figure in the lesbian and feminist movements. Among her works are *Sister Outsider, Zami: A New Spelling of My Name, Uses of Erotic, Chosen Poems Old and New, The Black Unicorn,* and *From a Land Where Other People Live.*

This article is not a theoretical discussion of Lesbian Mothers and their Sons, nor a how-to article. It is an attempt to scrutinize and share some pieces of that common history belonging to my son and to me. I have two children: a fifteen-and-a-half-year-old daughter Beth, and a fourteen-year-old son Jonathan. This is the way it was/is with me and Jonathan, and I leave the theory to another time and person. This is one woman's telling.

I have no golden message about the raising of sons for other lesbian mothers, no secret to transpose your questions into certain light. I have my own ways of rewording those same questions, hoping we will all come to speak those questions and pieces of our lives we need to share. We are women making contact within ourselves and with each other across the restrictions of a printed page, bent upon the use of our own/one another's knowledges.

The truest direction comes from inside. I give the most strength to my children by being willing to look within myself, and by being honest with them about what I find there, without expecting a response beyond their years. In this way they begin to learn to look beyond their own fears.

All our children are outriders for a queendom not yet assured.

My adolescent son's growing sexuality is a conscious dynamic between Jonathan and me. It would be presumptuous of me to discuss Jonathan's sexuality here, except to state my belief that whomever he chooses to explore this area with, his choices will be nonoppressive, joyful, and deeply felt from within, places of growth.

One of the difficulties in writing this piece has been temporal; this is the summer when Jonathan is becoming a man, physically. And our sons must become men—such men as we hope our daughters, born and unborn, will be pleased to live among. Our sons will not grow into women. Their way is more difficult than that of our daughters, for they must move away from us, without us. Hopefully, our sons have what they have learned from us, and a howness to forge it into their own image.

Our daughters have us, for measure or rebellion or outline or dream; but the sons of lesbians have to make their own definitions of self as men. This is both power and vulnerability. The sons of lesbians have the advantage of our blueprints for survival, but they must take what we know and transpose it into their own maleness. May the goddess be kind to my son, Jonathan.

Recently I have met young Black men about whom I am pleased to say that their future and their visions, as well as their concerns within the present, intersect more closely with Jonathan's than do my own. I have shared vision with these men as well as temporal strategies for our survivals and I appreciate the spaces in which we could sit down together. Some of these men I met at the First Annual Conference of Third World Lesbians and Gays held in Washington, D.C., in October, 1979. I have met others in different places and do not know how they identify themselves sexually. Some of these men are raising families alone. Some have adopted sons. They are Black men who dream and who act and who own their feelings, questioning. It is heartening to know our sons do not step out alone.

When Jonathan makes me angriest, I always say he is bringing out the testosterone in me. What I mean is that he is representing some piece of myself as a woman that I am reluctant to acknowledge or explore. For instance, what does "acting like a man" mean? For me, what I reject? For Jonathan, what he is trying to redefine?

Raising Black children—female and male—in the mouth of a racist, sexist, suicidal dragon is perilous and chancy. If they cannot love and resist at the same time, they will probably not survive. And in order to survive they must let go. This is what mothers teach—love, survival—that is, self-definition and letting go. For each of these, the ability to feel strongly and to recognize those feelings is central: how to feel love, how to neither discount fear nor be overwhelmed by it, how to enjoy feeling deeply.

I wish to raise a Black man who will not be destroyed by, nor settle for, those corruptions called *power* by the white fathers who mean his destruction as surely as they mean mine. I wish to raise a Black man who will recognize that the legitimate objects of his hostility are not women, but the particulars of a structure that programs him to fear and despise women as well as his own Black self.

For me, this task begins with teaching my son that I do not exist to do his feeling for him.

Men who are afraid to feel must keep women around to do their feeling for them while dismissing us for the same supposedly "inferior" capacity to feel deeply. But in this way also, men deny themselves their own essential humanity, becoming trapped in dependency and fear.

As a Black woman committed to a liveable future, and as a mother loving and raising a boy who will become a man, I must examine all my possibilities of being within such a destructive system.

Jonathan was three and one half when Frances, my lover, and I met; he was seven when we all began to live together permanently. From the start, Frances' and my insistence that there be no secrets in our household about the fact that we were lesbians has been the source of problems and strengths for both children. In the beginning, this insistence grew out of the knowledge, on both parts, that whatever was hidden out of fear could always be used either against the children or ourselves—one imperfect but useful argument for honesty. The knowledge of fear can help make us free.

> for the embattled
> there is no place
> that cannot be
> home
> nor is.[1]

For survival, Black children in America must be raised to be warriors. For survival, they must also be raised to recognize the enemy's many faces. Black children of lesbian couples have an advantage because they learn, very early, that oppression comes in many different forms, none of which have anything to do with their own worth.

To help give me perspective, I remember that for years, in the name-calling at school, boys shouted at Jonathan not—"your mother's a lesbian"—but rather—"your mother's a nigger."

When Jonathan was eight years old and in the third grade, we moved, and he went to a new school where his life was hellish as a new boy on the block. He did not like to play rough games. He did not like to fight. He did not like to stone dogs. And all this marked him early on as an easy target.

When he came in crying one afternoon, I heard from Beth how the corner bullies were making Jonathan wipe their shoes on the way home whenever Beth wasn't there to fight them off. And when I heard that the ringleader was a little boy in Jonathan's class his own size, an interesting and very disturbing thing happened to me.

My fury at my own long-ago impotence, and my present pain at his suffering, made me start to forget all that I knew about violence and fear, and blaming the victim, I started to hiss at the weeping child. "The next time you come in here crying . . . ," and I suddenly caught myself in horror.

This is the way we allow the destruction of our sons to begin—in the name of protection and to ease our own pain. *My* son get beaten up? I was about to demand that he buy that first lesson in the corruption of power, that might makes right. I could hear myself beginning to perpetuate the age-old distortions about what strength and bravery really are.

And no, Jonathan didn't have to fight if he didn't want to, but somehow he did have to feel better about not fighting. An old horror rolled over me of being the fat kid who ran away, terrified of getting her glasses broken.

About that time a very wise woman said to me, "Have you ever told Jonathan that once you used to be afraid, too?"

The idea seemed far-out to me at the time, but the next time he came in crying and sweaty from having run away again, I could see that he felt shamed at having failed me, or some image he and I had created in his head of mother/woman. This image of woman being able to handle it all was bolstered by the fact that he lived in a household with three strong women, his lesbian parents and his forthright older sister. At home, for Jonathan, power was clearly female.

And because our society teaches us to think in an either/or mode—kill or be killed, dominate or be dominated—this meant that he must either surpass or be lacking. I could see the implications of this line of thought. Consider the two western classic myth/models of mother/son relationships: Jocasta/Oedipus, the son who fucks his mother, and Clytemnestra/Orestes, the son who kills his mother.

It all felt connected to me.

I sat down on the hallway steps and took Jonathan on my lap and wiped his tears. "Did I ever tell you about how I used to be afraid when I was your age?"

I will never forget the look on that little boy's face as I told him the tale of my glasses and my after-school fights. It was a look of relief and total disbelief, all rolled into one.

It is as hard for our children to believe that we are not omnipotent as it is for us to know it, as parents. But that knowledge is necessary as the first step in the reassessment of power as something other than might, age, privilege, or the lack of fear. It is an important step for a boy, whose societal destruction begins when he is forced to believe that he can only be strong if he doesn't feel, or if he wins.

I thought about all this one year later when Beth and Jonathan, ten and nine, were asked by an interviewer how they thought they had been affected by being children of a feminist.

Jonathan said that he didn't think there was too much in feminism for boys, although it certainly was good to be able to cry if he felt like it and not to have to play football if he didn't want to. I think of this sometimes now when I see him practicing for his Brown Belt in Tae Kwon Do.

The strongest lesson I can teach my son is the same lesson I teach my daughter: how to be who he wishes to be for himself. And the best way I can do this is to be who I am and hope that he will learn from this not how to be me, which is not possible, but how to be himself. And this means how to move to that voice from within himself, rather than to those raucous, persuasive, or threatening voices from outside, pressuring him to be what the world wants him to be.

And that is hard enough.

Jonathan is learning to find within himself some of the different faces of courage and strength, whatever he chooses to call them. Two years ago, when Jonathan was twelve and in the seventh grade, one of his friends at school who had been to the house persisted in calling Frances "the maid." When Jonathan corrected him, the boy then referred to her as "the cleaning woman." Finally Jonathan said, simply, "Frances is not the cleaning woman, she's my mother's lover." Interestingly enough, it is the teachers at this school who still have not recovered from his openness.

Frances and I were considering attending a Lesbian/Feminist conference this summer, when we were notified that no boys over ten were allowed. This presented logistic as well as philosophical problems for us, and we sent the following letter:

> Sisters:
>
> Ten years as an interracial lesbian couple has taught us both the dangers of an oversimplified approach to the nature and solutions of any oppression, as well as the danger inherent in an incomplete vision.
>
> Our thirteen-year-old son represents as much hope for our future world as does our fifteen-year-old daughter, and we are not willing to abandon him to the killing streets of New York City while we journey west to help form a Lesbian-Feminist vision of the future world in which we can all survive and flourish. I hope we can continue this dialogue in the near future, as I feel it is important to our vision and our survival.

The question of separatism is by no means simple. I am thankful that one of my children is male, since that helps to keep me honest. Every line I write shrieks there are no easy solutions.

I grew up in largely female environments, and I know how crucial that has been to my own development. I feel the want and need often for the society of women, exclusively. I recognize that our own spaces are essential for developing and recharging.

As a Black woman, I find it necessary to withdraw into all-Black groups at times for exactly the same reasons—differences in stages of development and differences in levels of interaction. Frequently, when speaking with men and white women, I am reminded of how difficult and time-consuming it is to have to reinvent the pencil every time you want to send a message.

But this does not mean that my responsibility for my son's education stops at age ten, any more than it does for my daughter's. However, for each of them, that responsibility does grow less and less as they become more woman and man.

Both Beth and Jonathan need to know what they can share and what they cannot, how they are joined and how they are not. And Frances and I, as grown women and lesbians coming more and more into our power, need to relearn the experience that difference does not have to be threatening.

When I envision the future, I think of the world I crave for my daughters and my sons. It is thinking for survival of the species—thinking for life.

Most likely there will always be women who move with women, women who live with men, men who choose men. I work for a time when women with women, women with men, men with men, all share the work of a world that does not barter bread or self for obedience, nor beauty, nor love. And in that world we will raise our children free to choose how best to fulfill themselves. For we are jointly responsible for the care and raising of the young, since *that* they be raised is a function, ultimately, of the species.

Within that tripartite pattern of relating/existence, the raising of the young will be the joint responsibility of all adults who choose to be associated with children. Obviously, the children raised within each of these three relationships will be different, lending a special savor to that eternal inquiry into how best can we live our lives.

Jonathan was three and a half when Frances and I met. He is now fourteen years old. I feel the living perspective that having lesbian parents has brought to Jonathan is a valuable addition to his human sensitivity.

Jonathan has had the advantage of growing up within a nonsexist relationship, one in which this society's pseudo-natural assumptions of ruler/ruled are being challenged. And this is not only because Frances and I are lesbians, for unfortunately there are some lesbians who are still locked into patriarchal patterns of unequal power relationships.

These assumptions of power relationships are being questioned because Frances and I, often painfully and with varying degrees of success, attempt to evaluate and measure over and over again our feelings concerning power, our own and others'. And we explore with care those areas concerning how it is used and expressed between us and between us and the children, openly and otherwise. A good part of our biweekly family meetings are devoted to this exploration.

As parents, Frances and I have given Jonathan our love, our openness, and our dreams to help form his visions. Most importantly, as the son of lesbians, he has had an invaluable model—not only of a relationship—but of relating.

Jonathan is fourteen now. In talking over this paper with him and asking his permission to share some pieces of his life, I asked Jonathan what he felt were the strongest negative and the strongest positive aspects for him in having grown up with lesbian parents.

He said the strongest benefit he felt he had gained was that he knew a lot more about people than most other kids his age that he knew, and that he did not have a lot of the hang-ups that some other boys did about men and women.

And the most negative aspect he felt, Jonathan said, was the ridicule he got from some kids with straight parents.

"You mean, from your peers?" I said.

"Oh no," he answered promptly. "My peers know better. I mean other kids."

NOTE

1. From "School Note" in *The Black Unicorn* (W. W. Norton and Company, New York, 1978), p. 55.

41

I AM A MAN

RAUL E. YBARRA

Raul E. Ybarra, Ph.D. says about himself: Somehow I managed to receive my bachelors in Plant Science and masters in English Composition from California State University Fresno. I then graduated with my doctorate from the University of Illinois at Chicago, specializing in language, literacy and rhetoric. I am currently an associate professor at the College of Public and Community Service at the University of Massachusetts Boston. This excerpt is from a much larger piece entitled *I Am A Man* in which I chronicle my struggles to get my formal education. I often come to school early on my teaching days at the University of Massachusetts Boston. I go to the Wits End Cafe, buy a cup of black coffee and sit alone trying to prepare mentally for the day's events. This is also the time when I most often think about home, about how I managed to end up 3,000 miles from home. I think about what I've done, what I have accomplished.

Even though it was difficult, I continued working as a janitor at night and went to school during the day. On weekends I worked out in the fields doing anything from planting the crops to irrigating, to harvesting, and anything in between. I was not able to keep any of the money, however. My father took most of it. "For room and board," he'd say. Then he'd give me about forty dollars back. Then he'd tell me to give half of the forty to my brothers. My younger brothers did not have to work; all they needed to do was go to school. In addition, I had to go looking for my younger brothers when they were off at football or basketball games, dances, or whatever.

Whenever my father saw that I was the only one in my room, he asked me where my brothers were. "I don't know," was my usual answer. "Ve a buscarlos. And don't come back until you find them," was his usual command.

I'd get in his little, light blue Chevy Luv and go into town. Most of the time I didn't have any idea where to look for them, so I'd drive around until I got tired or ran low on gas. Then I'd stop at the local 7-11 store for a Diet Pepsi and play video games.

As soon as I stepped inside the store, the sales clerk, who was usually a high school student, would jokingly say "No, they're not here," and laugh.

I'd laugh along with him even though I didn't like it. But I knew that there was nothing I could do. Most of the students knew who I was and what I was doing. So I'd put a burrito in the microwave and eat it while I played games.

"Eating frozen burritos again?" the boy behind the counter joked. "Why don't you tell your mother to make you some? Be a man about it."

I'd just ignore him and continue playing Pac Man or Star Blaster. All the time I was there, I knew I was the butt of many jokes about looking for my brothers and eating food made by a machine. Sometimes I did know where my brothers were, but I still didn't look for them, even though I knew I was going to get in trouble for not finding them.

"¡Estúpido!" my father called me as soon as he saw me get out of the pickup alone. I knew what would follow before he even said it. "Did you look for them? Why couldn't you find them? You go to school, and you can't do anything right!"

All the time he yelled at me, I didn't say anything back. I just stared at him, at his feet. They were swollen with a couple of toenails missing, and their color was more yellow than the rest of his skin.

"Tu no sabes hacer nada," he continued yelling. "You're useless. Go to bed."

Then I'd slowly walk to my bedroom, angry—angry at my brothers for getting me into trouble, angry at my father for making me do his work, angry at myself for being too scared to say anything back. I'd just lie in my bed listening to my breathing as I slowly calmed down. Later I'd hear my brothers come home giggling and laughing, and I'd pretend to be asleep. The noise, however, usually woke my father up. "Raul, why can't you keep them quiet?" he'd yell. That was enough most of the time to calm my brothers down, so I didn't have to say anything. But one night I answered back, "Because they're not my sons."

The entire house suddenly became quiet. My brothers' breathing became very loud as they pretended to be asleep. The floor creaked louder and louder as my father walked toward our bedroom. When the door opened, it seemed to whine. The color of my father's skin made it difficult for me to see him clearly, but I made out his outline standing in the doorway. He was in his white underwear with a belt in his hand.

"¿Que dijites?" he asked.

"Nada," I answered, also shaking my head.

"Levantate."

I slowly pulled the blanket off of me and stood.

"¡Mentiroso!" he said as he swung his belt across my face. "I don't want lies." Then he left the room.

Tears poured down my face, stinging the mark on my cheek, as I stood clenching my teeth and gripping the bedpost. "Hombres no lloran," I remembered my father saying. I wanted to prove I was a man. I didn't want to cry, so I closed my eyes, but that only made the tears come faster. I got back in bed without turning, pulled the blanket over me and stared at the bunk above, forcing myself not to think of anything.

Back then I wondered why my younger brothers didn't have to work, why I started working at ten years of age and they didn't. I had no idea. Now I do. Albert and I were the older ones. We had to support our younger brothers. But Albert wasn't there; I was. I was quiet, didn't complain, kept my grades up. My brothers did none of these. I wanted to leave, to do what Albert and my sisters did, but I didn't. And I knew the reason. My father was a big man to me still. I was scared.

A month later, I graduated from high school and, according to my father, it was time to go and work like a man. I started the summer like the summers before: weeds in June, sweet potatoes in July, and grapes in August. In late August, I wanted to start college, but my father took me with him to knock almonds. He began by banging the trees with a rubber mallet, and I followed with a twenty-foot bamboo pole in my hands, knocking the almonds that clung to the tree. We worked fifteen hours a day that week. We started at eight to give the sun time to dissipate the moisture and worked until eleven at night, using spotlights after dark. At the end of the day, we went home tired, sweaty, and covered with dust. I just wanted to clean myself up and go to bed.

On Saturday, after we had gotten off work, I sat down in a chair, thankful that the next day was Sunday. I didn't have to get up. I started taking off my shoes when my father whistled. I thought about pretending I didn't hear, but I realized that would just get him angry. I got up slowly and dragged myself over to him.

"Tráigame una cerveza," he said.

I was tired, tired of working long hours, tired of following his orders. I wanted to say, "No. Go get it yourself," but I went to the kitchen, grabbed a beer, and started taking it to him.

I was almost to him when he yelled, "¡Andale pronto!"

All I could think about was how my father treated me. I realized I wasn't a man to him. He never wanted me to be a man, only a slave like my mother. I was there to bring him his beer, bring him his shoes, work for him. Now I saw why my brother and sisters had left. They too didn't like the way they were treated, and they too were scared of him. But they left anyway. I realized now why Anna let herself get pregnant, why Margaret went to live with a man, why Albert just left without saying anything to anybody, why he never bothered to tell anybody where he went. Fear. I knew why I was still there, still being his slave. . . . I didn't say anything; I didn't go anywhere; I followed orders. Gripping the beer can tightly, I gave it to him. He didn't even look at me. Instead, he reached down and patted Tico.

I was angry, angry at the dog. He was better treated, petted when he did something right. I never got that attention.

I don't remember everything that happened next. I do remember white foam splashing from the can that hit the floor. I remember Jose coming between us pushing me away as I went for my father.

"Pinche Perro. Hijo de perra," my father kept yelling at me over and over.

Jose and Richard held me back, while I yelled, "Fuck you! Fuck you!" at the same time struggling to break loose. "I ain't your fucking slave no more." Then I saw my mother crying, holding onto my father's arm, trying to calm him down.

My brothers were holding me back, telling me, "Calm down, man. Calm down. Man, what's you trying to do?"

"Let go," I yelled, trying to free myself from their grip. But they just held tighter, too afraid to let go for fear I'd attack my father. My mother walked over, stopped in front of me, and slapped my face.

I looked at her. I saw the dog jumping wildly, barking. I looked at my father. He was the same height as I was, his skin a dull brown, his hair now more grey than black. He didn't look proud or menacing with his belly sticking out and his shoulders slouched. I realized then that this was my father, the man I had patterned myself after, the man I had wanted to be.

After they saw I was calm enough, my brothers let me go. I turned to leave, and one of them gave me a helping push. I quickly shoved the arm away and glared at them.

I heard my mother say "ya no Raul." I walked out the door and down the street, kicking and hitting anything in my way. I ended up at a house of a friend, Don Mier, one of the few instructors who had helped me through high school.

By the time I got there, my right hand was swollen to where I couldn't close it, but I was calm enough to start worrying about where I was going to stay. Don wasn't at home, so I sat on his patio table to think about what I was going to do next. When I woke, it was already daylight, and Don still wasn't home, so I broke into his house, washed up, ate, and was gone before he came. The next night I did the same thing, slept on the patio table, but he saw me in the morning. He never asked any questions. He just told me I could stay there as long as I wanted, but I would have to pay rent when I could afford it.

"I only need a couple of days," I remember telling him, "to figure out what I'm going to do."

42

WHAT IS MARRIAGE FOR?

E. J. GRAFF

E. J. Graff is contributing editor to *The American Prospect* and *Out* magazines, and a visiting scholar at the Brandeis Women's Studies Research Center. Her work has appeared in such publications as *The Boston Globe, The New York Times Magazine, Ms., The Nation, The Village Voice, The Women's Review of Books,* and more than a dozen anthologies. This address is based on her book entitled *What Is Marriage For: The Strange Social History of Our Most Intimate Institution* (Beacon Press, 1999).

Back in the 1970s, when I first fell in love, I knew I would never get married. As did most of my friends during the 1980s, I expected we would live together without the intrusion of law. And besides, who ever imagined two women marrying?

But today my marriage—or rather, the possibility of its legal recognition—is being debated around the world. Three countries—the Netherlands, Belgium, and Canada—now offer same-sex couples full civil marriage rights. The Massachusetts Supreme Judicial Court has said that full marriage rights must be made available to our state's same-sex couples beginning May 17, 2004. Other countries—including all six Scandinavian countries, Germany, and South Africa—offer lesbian and gay couples just about everything about marriage except the word. Many more countries, provinces, and states give us roughly half of full marriage's legal obligations, recognitions, rights, and responsibilities: Australia, New Zealand, Hungary, Israel, Portugal, France, eleven out of seventeen provinces in Spain, and two provinces in Argentina. And more countries and states are on their way in the next two or three years. Taiwan has said it will pass a same-sex marriage law. South Africa, Sweden, Spain, and New Jersey are all strong contenders for full marriage rights. Switzerland, England, and Scotland will soon add "all-but-marriage" systems that offer just about everything but the word. California is expanding its domestic partnership registry to be essentially the equal of Vermont's civil unions, and I expect more Argentinian and Brazilian states and provinces to follow suit.

My job here is to give some historical background to all this discussion. How is it that for the first time in western history, the world is debating whether to recognize a life commitment between two women or two men? And, second, why do same-sex couples—or different-sex couples, for that matter—need or want marriage?

To answer the first question, I want to examine the idea that marriage is some solid, immovable pillar of society; that what we see in 1950s sitcom re-runs is exactly what marriage has always been. False. Here is the first key point of my talk, and of my book: Marriage has always been a social battle-ground, its rules constantly shifting to fit each culture and class, each era and economy. Let me give you some examples. Did you know that Abraham and Sarah, that founding couple in the Torah or Bible, were half-siblings, sharing a father? That only the upper-class third of Romans had the right to marry legally—everyone else lived together outside the law? That a Jewish man whose wife did not give birth within the first ten years of marriage was, in some parts of the world, required by Jewish law to marry again, with or without divorcing his first wife? That Christianity for its first five hundred to a thousand years ignored marriage, considering it tainted and secular, and did not declare it a sacrament until 1215?

There is a lot more "Ripley's Believe It Or Not" to marriage's history, but for the rest, you will have to read my book.

The point is this: Marriage has not been one revered, immutable, monog-amous thing for 6000 years. Rather, marriage has always been hot political territory, constantly redefined to fit every time societies change. Neverthe-less, a big historical shift did have to take place for us to stop thinking mar-riage meant boy plus girl equals baby and to start talking about girl plus girl equals love.

That change really exploded in the mid-nineteenth century. The phrase "traditional marriage," which is thrown around so easily on editorial pages, really should be used only to mean marriage for money. Traditionally, the engagement feast was the moment that the two families finished negotia-tions and finally signed, witnessed, and notarized the marriage contract (and maybe the two started living together). The marriage ceremony was when property actually changed hands, a ceremony that was often overseen by a notary, rather than a priest. If your family had property, they found an-other family with whom you exchanged it. And if you worked—if your an-cestors, like mine, came from the class of butchers, bakers, and candlestick makers—marriage was your complete plan of labor. The farmer required a farmwife; the fisherman required a fishwife to get his goods to market. The German guilds would not let a man move up from journeyman to master until he had a wife, the business partner who would feed the apprentices, keep the books, and oversee the cleaning of the shop. As one historian wrote, "for many centuries marriage for love was the dubious privilege of those without property"—that bottom quintile who were near starvation, who did not even have two dresses and a cookpot to bring to the marriage as dowry.

Of course the pair cared for each other, unless they irritated each other to death—do you not care for, or hate, your coworkers? But everyone ex-pected you to talk about the important money matters first, and assumed that afterwards, you could work out such details as affection, sex, and maybe even love.

But a funny thing happened to marriage on the way to the twentieth century. Marriage stopped being the way you exchanged those limited resources, land or labor. Today we are expected to make a living by making individual decisions about which talents or inclinations to trust. And—here is a key point—once you can make your own living, you can also make your own bed. Capitalism pushed marriage through the looking glass: Now we expect people to talk about love first, and money last—maybe very last, when they are getting a divorce.

That change led to some ferocious nineteenth and twentieth century battles over marriage's rules, battles that all lead directly to same-sex marriage. For instance, after a very nasty battle, and despite almost seventy-five years of ferocious opposition by the Catholic Church and the mainline Protestant hierarchy, and some ugly federal laws, contraception is now legal—which tells us that our society believes marriage is justified by making intimacy, not just by making babies. And if marriage isn't for making babies, then why can't same-sex couples marry?

After an even nastier battle, divorce is legal for other causes than the traditional Protestant causes of adultery and attempted murder—because society now believes that the heart is what makes and unmakes a marriage. We no longer see marriage as a labor contract but as a love commitment. When you love, you are married . . . when you can no longer love, you are no longer married—a very new idea in history. And if our society believes that a couple marries for love, why can't same-sex couples marry?

After equally nasty battles, our societies consider men and women to be formally equal—a woman can vote and own property, a man can raise children. Sometimes that equality is very theoretical in individual marriages, but it is absolutely true in law. Except for the entrance requirement, we no longer have gender requirements within marriage. And if the sexes are equal—if marriage doesn't automatically turn one partner into lord and master and the other partner into Laura Petrie—why can't same-sex couples marry?

All of these changes were revolutionary in their time. And here is the point: lesbians and gay men are following, not leading, the massive changes that were made between 1850 and 1950 in our public marriage philosophy. Sex for intimacy; marriage for love; gender equality; me and my gal.

Let me make that point a little more strongly. It is no more radical for a girl to fall in love with mathematics or basketball than to fall in love with another girl. If she can commit herself to any career she wants, why can she not commit herself to any spouse she wants? The battle against same-sex marriage is a battle against basic feminism—and even more, a battle against the choices opened to us by our highly mobile capitalism. But today's economy, like today's marriages, cannot live by feudal rules. In our world, we believe that the talents and hopes and inclinations that we find inside ourselves count—whether in work or in love.

Which brings us to another question: Why should same-sex couples want to marry, and why should society care? Not every same-sex couple wants to marry. Some want to remain outside the institution, just as some different-sex couples decide never to visit a justice of the peace. The question is whether people should be free to make their own choices about whether or not to register their bonds publicly, and not have that choice ruled out by the government.

But same-sex couples want and need marriage, when we do, for the same reasons that different-sex couples do. When we talk about this, it is important to remember that marriage is an incredibly overstuffed suitcase of a word, meaning four overlapping but separate things. Today we are not talking about the inner bond, the commitment, freely entered into by two people, which I have. We are not talking about the wedding, the ceremony, which celebrates the bond between two people and their communities, and which I have already had. We are not . . . debating changes to religious marriage, which each religion defines vastly differently. Just imagine locking a Catholic, an Orthodox Jew, and a Southern Baptist in a room and refusing to let them out until they agree on the rules of divorce. Ha! That is a bloody fantasy, which would reprise the history of Western Europe, which gave us the concept of a strict separation between church beliefs and civil law.

Today we are talking about the governmental, legal recognition of the bond made between two people. And for that—for civil marriage—the most important purpose is justice. Civil marriage, legal marriage, is the way society adjudicates an incredible array of disputes over who counts to whom. If I am hit by a car when traveling in Utah, would a Salt Lake City hospital let the woman I consider my spouse oversee my care, or would it force me to go through that alone? If I had been killed on September 11, would the woman I consider my spouse, and who relies on and makes it possible for me to earn my income, be eligible for governmental aid or my social security benefits? When I die, who gets to decide whether to donate my organs? If I win the Massachusetts lottery, who can I will it to? As a later panel will tell you, civil unions or domestic partnership will not cut it; in American law, only the M-word covers it all.

Obviously, some of these are incredibly petty, and some very large. That is the point. The rules of marriage have accumulated over centuries to cover an astonishing array of contingencies. As a result, civil marriage is an unbelievably comprehensive shorthand, a shared legal mailbox that lets the state, employers, courts, pension programs, life insurers, health insurers, car rental companies, frequent flyer programs, jails, hospitals, food stamp programs, banks, cemeteries—and more—decide which relationships to take seriously.

Our medieval ancestors did not need civil marriage. Most of them lived in small villages where everyone knew who was married—with or without a ceremony—and who was not. We need civil marriage. We live in a highly complex world, in which each of us regularly bumps into dozens of institutional strangers. For today's couples to fulfill the vows that make wedding guests weep—to care for each other in sickness and in health, for richer or for poorer, and even after the moment of crisis that is death—their bond must be marked and recognizable for the institutions around them.

And the watermark of marriage really does matter. I know far too many heartbreaking stories that have happened to couples who did not have that state stamp. Let me tell you just two. In October 2000, Bobby Daniel and William Flanigan were visiting Bobby's family back east when Bobby, who had AIDS, got ill and was sent to the Maryland Shock Trauma Center in Baltimore. There, as Bobby spent six hours sliding into a coma before he died, the hospital refused to allow William into his beloved's room—until Bobby's sister showed up and insisted that William could go in. The two men were both 34 years old, were registered as domestic partners in California, and carried with them the power of attorney that said William should oversee Bobby's healthcare. By the time William got into Bobby's room, it was too late. He never regained consciousness; they never got to say goodbye. Bobby's mother put it this way: "My son Bobby not only suffered in his final hours, but he suffered alone."

In Pennsylvania a few years ago, Sherry Barone and Cynthia Friedman had been together 13 years when Friedman got cancer. They signed as many legal documents as they could to ensure Barone would be in charge: wills; powers of attorney; health proxies; written instructions giving rights to the survivor to carry out any wishes. But after Friedman died, the cemetery refused to follow Barone's instructions to inscribe the epitaph Friedman had requested. The widowed Barone had to go to court for a year of legal wrangling before she could honor her dead spouse's wishes. Imagine doing that while you are grieving.

As we have just seen in the Terri Schiavo right-to-die case in Florida, when there is a crisis, a spouse can be overridden by the government. But only a spouse has standing in the debate. Had Terri Schiavo's spouse instead been female, she would have had no legal voice, no standing in court.

Unfortunately, the history of humanity is the history of disagreement. Lesbian and gay couples and our families are neither better nor worse than others: We too squabble over inheritances, epitaphs, hospital decisions, breakups. The purpose of the civil institution of marriage, in Western law, is to apply a just consensus to private disputes. Given that all human beings occasionally need such Solomonic intervention, same-sex couples belong.

And to close again with our main point: Marriage has been a kind of Jerusalem, an archaeological site on which the present is constantly building over the past, so that history's many layers twist and tilt into today's walls and floors. Many people believe theirs is the one true claim to this holy ground. But marriage has always been a battleground, owned and defined first by one group and then another. While marriage may retain its ancient name, very little else in this city has remained the same—not its boundaries, boulevards, or daily habits—except the fact that it is inhabited by human beings like me.

PART VII
Education

There is substantial agreement in the United States that equal opportunity is something worth providing to our citizens and that the education system is the central institution that should prepare people for equal opportunity.[1] Even in the face of tension and competition between various racial and ethnic groups, the value of an adequate education for all is shared by nearly everyone. For example, in a 1994 survey conducted by the National Conference of Christians and Jews (now called the National Conference for Community and Justice), about 90 percent of the 3,000 Asian, Black, Latino, and white respondents said they would be willing to work with members of other racial or ethnic groups, even those with whom they felt the least in common, in order to "help schools teach kids what they really need to learn to succeed."[2]

Many changes in the U.S. education system during the past several decades have been implemented with the goal of eliminating the education gap between white students and students of color, between poor children and wealthier ones, and between boys and girls and men and women. Sociologist Roslyn Mickelson and political scientist Stephen Smith have taken a close look at the effects of some of these changes. Programs designed to increase the education level of poor children have helped to equalize levels of education. For example, compensatory education (such as Head Start), and various other initiatives, have helped to create a situation where Black and white women and men, on average, achieve similar levels of education (about 13 years), in spite of the fact that a majority of children in the United States still attend schools segregated by race, ethnicity, and class. A look at income, however, reveals continuing disparity, with whites earning more than Blacks and men earning more than women. And a close look at class issues within groups reveals large differences. For example, in the eighties, a child of a Black farmer completed less than 9 years of schooling, while children of Black professionals averaged 14 years of schooling.[3]

Mickelson and Smith consider three issues related to inequality: equality, equality of educational opportunity, and equality of educational outcomes. They conclude that the United States has no interest in equality and has failed to establish equality of educational outcomes. Thus, as a country we support equal educational opportunity but have not designed an economy that would guarantee a living wage for everyone who achieves a certain level of education.

On an individual level, research demonstrates that race, class, and gender continue to affect students' experiences in spite of efforts to the contrary. Jonathan Kozol, for example, describes how race and poverty intersect in brutally impoverished schools in several U.S. cities, severely limiting learning.[4] Jorge Noriega looks at the history of American Indian education in the

United States and concludes that it has been, and continues to be (with minor exceptions), a cultural disaster, designed primarily for indoctrination to the white majority culture and limiting career options to vocational ones.[5]

Reports on gender and education reveal troublesome results for students of both genders. A report entitled "How Schools Shortchange Girls," commissioned by the American Association of University Women Educational Foundation, documents how gender, race, and class all affect educational achievement. Some of the data suggest that class is the most important of these three variables.[6] Bernice Sandler, director of the Project on the Status and Education of Women at the Association of American Colleges and Universities, discovered that men in college were given both overt and subtle support, whereas women were undermined in both overt and subtle ways. Studying interaction in classrooms, Sandler found frequent cases of disparaging remarks about women, such as sexist jokes made by male professors, and she found subtle differences in the treatment of male and female students, such as men being called on more frequently than women, by faculty of both genders.[7]

Educators David and Myra Sadker, concluding overall that girls experience discrimination in schools, nevertheless observed that although boys receive more attention than girls at both the elementary and secondary levels, that attention does not necessarily lead to success. They reported that boys are more likely to receive lower grades, to suffer from learning disabilities, to be assigned to special education classes, to be suspended, and to drop out than are girls.[8] Similar findings have been reported by other researchers working on the situations of boys.[9] Some of these writers and educators are exploring ways to allow boys to express their traditionally high energy without pathologizing it. Some recommend all-boy environments to support and nurture boys, a suggestion that troubles others who have fought for coeducation at all levels. Recent federal guidelines on single-sex education allow the development of single-sex schools as long as comparable course work and facilities are available for both sexes.[10]

What these data on boys obscure, however, is the reality that boys generally achieve higher grades on standardized tests and are more economically successful into adulthood, in spite of the difficult time that some of them have in school. Clearly, some boys need more help than others. Although women outnumber men as college students, this gender discrepancy is most pronounced at lower-status institutions; men tend to major in more lucrative fields like engineering, computer science, business, and physics; and the five occupations most likely to be held by women include secretary, receptionist, bookkeeper, nurse, and hairdresser/cosmetologist.[11] In short, all children need more effective educations in contexts that promote equality related to gender, class, race, ability, and culture (see Sadker & Sadker and Kimmel, this part).

The choice of which fields women and men pursue is obviously a crucial aspect of education as it relates to occupational outcomes. Thus, some scholars have attempted to analyze the effects of race and gender on educational outcomes while others have looked at the experience of women and people of color in various careers.[12] Programs designed to encourage the study of math and science by boys and girls of color and white girls have also emerged with the goal of addressing the underrepresentation of white women and women and men of color in mathematical and scientific careers.[13] Programs designed to support white female graduate students and graduate students of color in math and science have also emerged in recent years.[14]

A recent issue of *The Journal of Men's Studies* focuses on African American men in academia. Among the range of issues addressed, one article focuses on the importance of preparing African American boys for academic track careers via a project aimed at younger men entitled Gentlemen on the Move (PGOTM).[15] Another article looks at African American men studying engineering. The authors found that an essential aspect of persistence in the engineering program was a commitment to prove critics wrong by working extra hard.[16] In short, in spite of illusions to the contrary, there is much work to do in overcoming the effects of racism when people of color enter fields of study and work that have been predominantly white.

Other educators have documented ways that subtle and overt stereotypes are reinforced in the curriculum, and many have worked toward eliminating them. For example, substantial attention has been given to gendered images in children's books, and now attention is focusing on the intersections of gender with other factors.[17] Other scholars are examining the success or failure of the testing system for various groups. For example, in a recent finding that helps explain why bright Black students do not perform as well as expected on tests, Claude Steele, a social psychologist at Stanford University, identified what he calls "stereotype vulnerability"—the tendency for group members to perform badly when they think their performance is a reflection of their group. Concerned that even highly qualified Black students tended to earn increasingly lower grades as they progressed through college, Steele set out to identify the cause. He found that when Black Stanford University undergraduates were given a difficult verbal test, those who were told that it was a "genuine test of your verbal abilities and limitations" received lower scores than the white students also being tested. But when another group of Black students taking the same test was told that it was designed to study "psychological factors involved in solving verbal problems," they performed as well as the white students. Steele repeated this experiment in various places and formats, documenting that stereotype vulnerability also affected women when they were told that a given math test showed "gender differences." It even affected white men who were told that Asians tended to outperform whites on a difficult math test.[18]

The context of test taking is just one aspect of the hidden curriculum—the myriad messages, subtle and obvious, that affect students' attitudes and performance, apart from course content. Classroom interaction has been the subject of much research, as educators attempt to establish more gender-equal classrooms.[19] Other scholars observe the social environment on campuses. In an ethnographic study of Black and white women on two college campuses, anthropologists Dorothy Holland and Margaret Eisenhart found that peer culture eroded career plans for many women in both groups as romance became more important than their studies.[20]

Pressure to conform in K–12 classrooms puts pressure on many kinds of young people, from girls who are "too masculine," to Black girls who are "too loud," to boys who are "too feminine." Students who fail to conform to white heterosexist hegemonic expectations, for whatever reasons, are defined as "other" and pay a high price. Anthropologist Signithia Fordham argues that educators need to accept a range of behavior in students and not expect conformity to narrow standards; after intensive research in an urban school in Washington DC, she was especially concerned about Black children who were expected to conform to white expectations ("acting white"), rather than be supported to develop their own ways of expressing themselves within the context of a challenging academic program.[21]

Pressure for gender conformity can be especially difficult. In a study of schooling in England, educator Máirtín Mac an Ghaill recounts an incident in a schoolyard that shook the gender rules: a male student, happy over passing his exams, brought flowers to Mac an Ghaill. Mac an Ghaill was scolded for the incident.[22] In two recently reported cases in the United States, boys who were acting "too effeminate" were the subject of ridicule in schools. In one case, the boy was expelled from his private school for cross-dressing.[23] In another case, the Center for Constitutional Rights helped a grandmother intervene in a situation in which her grandson had been referred to as a girl and called "girlish" by his teacher and his peers. The intervention succeeded in convincing the teacher to apologize and in convincing the school to institute seminars on sexual harassment and gender-based name calling for fifth and sixth graders.[24] According to the Supreme Court, schools receiving federal funds are responsible for student-on-student harassment if they know about it and do not intervene and if it is severe enough to interfere with the victim's education.[25] As a result, schools are becoming more proactive in preventing harassment, including harassment of gay and lesbian young people.[26] In yet another case, a Massachusetts child who is physically male and diagnosed as transgendered challenged a school's decision to disallow female dress. Many months later, the city finally agreed to allow her to come to school in female attire.[27] Transgendered teachers are an issue as well, as schools and parents grapple with whether or not to support the hiring or continued employment of transgendered teachers, and as states debate whether transgender rights deserve protection.[28]

Frequently, prejudice against gay teenagers is so strong that these teenagers drop out of school. The Hetrick-Martin Institute in New York City was founded to serve lesbian and gay youth, offering an alternative high school for those who cannot tolerate mainstream schooling. Hetrick-Martin also provides a wide array of other programs including a shelter to house some of the estimated 8,000 homeless gay and lesbian youth in New York City who have been kicked out of their homes because they are gay.[29] In Massachusetts, state law has mandated support for gay and lesbian students in high schools in order to create a climate that will be more welcoming, especially given the high suicide rate of gay teens. K–12 schools, it seems, have become a primary battleground for gay, lesbian, and transgender rights.[30]

College campuses serve as a battleground for gender equality as well. The September 2000 issue of *Men's Health* ranked colleges based on how male-friendly they were; issues such as the presence of a large women's studies department were cause for a low ranking.[31] A woman who wanted to play football at Duke University was awarded $2 million in damages when she was cut from the team by a coach who had suggested that she participate in beauty pageants instead of football.[32]

Affirmative action, which requires employers and educational institutions to "actively seek inclusion of qualified minorities among their pool of applicants,"[33] is another issue affecting higher education. Laws, voter petitions, and executive orders in various parts of the United States have undercut or eliminated affirmative action programs, arguing that they are no longer necessary. An effect in some areas of the country is "resegregation."[34] Ironically, once the state of Texas eliminated affirmative action, the state legislature passed a law mandating that all students in the top 10 percent of their high school class be granted automatic admission to institutions of higher education in Texas. Because of the high level of school segregation in Texas, the effect of the legislation has been to increase the level of diversity in undergraduate colleges in Texas. In states with more integrated schools, this sort of alternative to affirmative action would not succeed in diversifying the student body. Some colleges are changing admissions procedures to include examining a range of factors such as SAT score, class rank, race/ethnicity, and life experience such as overcoming adversity. The goal of such policies is to have a diverse student body for educational purposes (supporting a university's mission), rather than to right past discrimination.[35]

The Texas alternative did not affect graduate schools. With the elimination of affirmative action, applications to the University of Texas School of Law immediately dropped among Blacks, Mexican Americans, Asian Americans, and whites, with the largest decline occurring among Blacks—66 percent. Admissions of Black and Latino students to law school in both Texas and California—the two states that had eliminated affirmative action at the time of the study—dropped considerably at that time. This provoked attorney Robert J. Grey, chair of the House of Delegates of the American Bar Association, to express concern over the decline in minority lawyers that will result if fewer people of color continue to apply to law school.[36] In the midst of fluctuations in applications by students of color, the legality of taking race into account as a factor in admission was in the courts, related to two lawsuits against the University of Michigan. The U.S. Supreme Court ultimately decided that the use of race as *a factor* in admissions was acceptable in the University of Michigan Law School but that the University of Michigan undergraduate system of awarding points for race was not constitutional.[37] Other colleges are now revising their affirmative action procedures to put their admissions policies in line with the Court's decisions.

While the truth-seeking traditions outlined in the introduction to this book have led to a voluminous literature designed to eliminate the invisibility of many groups in the curriculum at the university level, many members of those groups now risk being shut out of higher education. The likelihood of changing the low proportion of people of color and white women at the upper ranks of higher education is not high if people of color and white women are not allowed into institutions of higher education, especially at the graduate level.[38] And, once there, these institutions are frequently not the most welcoming of environments for white women and people of color.[39]

The readings in this part of the book address issues in both K–12 and higher education including interaction (and lack thereof) of boys and girls in elementary schools (Sadker and Sadker), the debate about the situation of boys in schools (Michael S. Kimmel), and conflicts and discrimination on college campuses (Ruth Sidel and bell hooks). The messages in this chapter echo many that have been heard throughout this book so far: people need validation of their varied experiences; knowledge is incomplete without a broad range of voices and perspectives; and discrimination greatly interferes with people's abilities to move freely in the world and achieve their goals. Some of these themes will be heard again in Part VIII in the context of paid work and unemployment.

As you consider these articles, think about how your own school experience reflects, or doesn't, that described by the authors. For example, if you have been in gender-mixed classrooms, do women and men/girls and boys speak in proportion to their numbers in the class? Are teachers less likely to call on girls? Have boys seemed more at risk for not doing well or dropping out? Who had higher SAT scores? In college, have you observed any of the dynamics reported by hooks or Sidel?

NOTES

1. Mickelson and Smith, "Education and the Struggle against Race, Class, and Gender Inequality," in Berch Berberoglu, ed., *Critical Perspectives in Sociology: A Reader* (Dubuque, IA: Kendall-Hunt, 1991).
2. "Taking America's Pulse: A Summary Report of the National Conference Survey on Inter-Group Relations" (New York: paper from the National Conference of Christians and Jews, 1994), p. 11.
3. Mickelson and Smith, "Education and the Struggle."
4. Jonathan Kozol, *Savage Inequalities* (New York: Crown, 1991).
5. Jorge Noriega, "American Indian Education in the United States: Indoctrination for Subordination to Colonialism," in M. Annette Jaimes, ed., *The State of Native America* (Boston: South End Press, 1992), pp. 371–402.

6. American Association of University Women Educational Foundation, *How Schools Shortchange Girls* (New York: Marlowe & Company, 1995).

7. Bernice Resnick Sandler, "The Classroom Climate: Still a Chilly One for Women," in Carol Lasser, ed., *Educating Men and Women Together: Coeducation in a Changing World* (Urbana: University of Illinois Press in conjunction with Oberlin College, 1987). Reprinted in Karin Bergstrom Costello, *Gendered Voices: Readings from the American Experience* (New York: Harcourt Brace, 1996), pp. 359–68. Sandler does not discuss the intersections of gender with other factors.

8. Myra Sadker and David Sadker, *Failing at Fairness: How Our Schools Cheat Girls* (New York: Simon & Schuster, 1994).

9. Carey Goldberg, "After Girls Get Attention, Focus Shifts to Boys' Woes," *The New York Times* (April 22, 1998), p. A1; Christina Hoff Sommers, *The War against Boys: How Misguided Feminism Is Harming Our Young Men* (New York: Simon & Schuster, 2000).

10. Greg Toppo, "US to Boost Single-Sex Schools: Education Dept. Offers Rules to Encourage Growth," *The Boston Globe* (May 9, 2002), p. A4.

11. David Sadker, "Gender Games," *The Washington Post* (July 31, 2000), p. A19.

12. Lisa M. Frehill, "Subtle Sexism in Engineering," in Nijole V. Benokraitis, ed., *Subtle Sexism: Current Practices and Prospects for Change* (Thousand Oaks, CA: Sage, 1997), pp. 117–35.

13. David Johnson, ed., *Minorities and Girls in School: Effects on Achievement and Performance* (Thousand Oaks, CA: Sage, 1997).

14. For a description of one such program, contact the New England Board of Higher Education, 45 Temple Place, Boston, MA 02111.

15. Daryl Bailey, "Preparing African-American Males for Postsecondary Options." *The Journal of Men's Studies* 12, no. 1 (Fall 2003), pp. 15–24.

16. James L. Moore III, Octavia Madison-Colmore, and Dionne M. Smith, "The Prove-Them-Wrong Syndrome: Voices from Unheard African-American Males in Engineering Disciplines," *The Journal of Men's Studies* 12, no. 1 (Fall 2003), pp. 61–73.

17. For a recent look at gendered images in children's books and references to prior work in this area, see Roger Clark, Rachel Lennon, and Leanna Morris, "Of Caldecotts and Kings: Gendered Images in Recent American Children's Books by Black and Non-Black Illustrators," *Gender & Society* 7, no. 2 (June 1993), pp. 227–45.

18. See Claude Steele and Joshua Aronson, "Stereotype Threat and the Intellectual Test Performance of African Americans," *Journal of Personality and Social Psychology* 69, no. 5 (Fall 1995), pp. 797ff. For a discussion of bias, especially gender bias, in standardized college entrance tests (PSAT and SAT), see Myra Sadker and David Sadker, "Test Drive," in Sadker and Sadker, eds., *Failing at Fairness.*

19. Magda Lewis, "Interrupting Patriarchy: Politics, Resistance, and Transformation in the Feminist Classroom," *Harvard Educational Review* 60, no. 4 (November 1990), pp. 467–88; Sara N. Davis, Mary Crawford, and Jadwiga Sebrechts, eds., *Coming into Her Own: Educational Success in Girls and Women* (San Francisco: Jossey-Bass, 1999); Berenice Malka Fisher, *No Angel in the Classroom* (Lanham, MD: Rowman & Littlefield, 2001); Sharon Bernstein, "Feminist Intentions: Race, Gender and Power in a High School Classroom," *NWSA Journal* 7, no. 2 (1995), pp. 18–34.

20. Dorothy C. Holland and Margaret A. Eisenhart, *Educated in Romance: Women, Achievement, and College Culture* (Chicago: University of Chicago Press, 1990).

21. Signithia Fordham, *Blacked Out: Dilemmas of Race, Identity and Success at Capital High* (Chicago: Chicago University Press, 1996).

22. For an extended discussion of this see Máirtín Mac an Ghaill, *The Making of Men: Masculinities, Sexualities and Schooling* (Buckingham, UK: Open University Press, 1994).

23. "Feminine Boy Shakes Up Small School" *New York Times* (October 29, 1998).

24. Margaret Carey, "In re Minor Child," *Center for Constitutional Rights Docket* (New York: Center for Constitutional Rights, 1998), p. 76.

25. Mary Leonard, "Schools Can Be Liable if Pupils Harass," *The Boston Globe* (May 25, 1999), p. A1.

26. Anna Gorman, "Educators Taking Steps to Protect Homosexual Pupils," *The Boston Globe* 258, no. 77 (September 15, 2000), p. A29.

27. Rick Klein, "Brockton Boy Still at Home: Talks Continue on Class Return," *The Boston Globe* (October 18, 2000), p. B2; "Student Allowed to Wear Female Clothing," *The Boston Globe* (May 17, 2001), p. B2.

28. Stephanie Simon, "Transgender Protection Debated in Minn.," *The Boston Globe* (April 10, 1999), p. A9.

29. For more information contact the Hetrick-Martin Institute, 2 Astor Place, New York, NY 10003.

30. Eric Rofes, "Gay Issues, Schools, and the Right-Wing Backlash," *Resist* 8, no. 5 (June 1999), pp. 1–3.

31. Lawrence Roy Stains, "The Best and Worst Colleges for Men," *Men's Health* 15, no. 3, p. 120.

32. "Title IX Victory," *Outlook* 95, no. 1 (2001), p. 9.

33. A. E. Sadler, ed., *Affirmative Action* (San Diego, CA: Greenhaven Press, 1996), p. 6.

34. Doreen Iudica Vigue, "Schools Segregating Anew, Harvard Researchers Report," *The Boston Globe* (June 12, 1999), p. A3.

35. Arthur L. Coleman, "'Affirmative Action' through a Different Looking Glass," *Diversity Digest* 5, no. 3 (Spring 2001), pp. 1ff.

36. Evelyn Apgar, "Impact of California, Texas Decisions," *The New Jersey Lawyer* (Sept. 7, 1998), p. 1.

37. CNN, "Narrow use of affirmative action preserved in college admissions" (Thursday, December 25, 2003). www.cnn.com/2003/LAW/06/23/scotus.affirmative. action/.

38. For a look at the numbers of women at various levels of academia, including students and faculty, see Margaret L. Andersen, *Thinking about Women: Sociological Perspectives on Sex and Gender,* 3rd ed. (New York: Macmillan, 1993), p. 64. Andersen draws on data from Charles J. Andersen, Deborah J. Carter, and Andrew Malizio, *1989–90 Fact Book on Higher Education* (New York: Macmillan, 1989).

39. Judith E. Owen Blakemore, Jo Young Switzer, Judith A. DiLorio, and David L. Fairchild, "Exploring the Campus Climate for Women Faculty," in Nijole V. Benokraitis, ed., *Subtle Sexism: Current Practices and Prospects for Change* (Thousand Oaks, CA: Sage, 1997), pp. 54–71; Teresa Córdova, "Power and Knowledge: Colonialism in the Academy," in Carla Trujillo, ed., *Living Chicana Theory* (Berkeley, CA: Third Woman Press, 1998), pp. 17–45.

43

MISSING IN INTERACTION

MYRA SADKER   •   DAVID SADKER

David Sadker is a professor at American University (Washington, DC) and, along with his late wife *Myra Pollack Sadker* (1943–1995) gained a national reputation for work in confronting gender bias and sexual harassment. He has directed more than a dozen federal education grants and has authored five books and more than seventy-five articles. His research and writing document sex bias from the classroom to the boardroom. Dr. Myra Pollack Sadker pioneered much of the research documenting gender bias in America's schools.

As the snapshots continue, the underlying gender messages become clear. The classroom consists of two worlds: one of boys in action, the other of girls' inaction. Male students control classroom conversation. They ask and answer more questions. They receive more praise for the intellectual quality of their ideas. They get criticized. They get help when they are confused. They are the heart and center of interaction. Watch how boys dominate the discussion in this upper elementary class about presidents.

The fifth-grade class is almost out of control. "Just a minute," the teacher admonishes. "There are too many of us here to all shout out at once. I want you to raise your hands, and then I'll call on you. If you shout out, I'll pick somebody else."

Order is restored. Then Stephen, enthusiastic to make his point, calls out.

Stephen: I think Lincoln was the best president. He held the country together during the war.
Teacher: A lot of historians would agree with you.
Mike: (seeing that nothing happened to Stephen, calls out): I don't. Lincoln was okay, but my Dad liked Reagan. He always said Reagan was a great president.
David: (calling out): Reagan? Are you kidding?
Teacher: Who do you think our best president was, Dave?
David: FDR. He saved us from the depression.
Max: (calling out): I don't think it's right to pick one best president. There were a lot of good ones.

Teacher: That's interesting.
Kimberly: (calling out): I don't think the presidents today are as good as the ones we used to have.
Teacher: Okay, Kimberly. But you forgot the rule. You're supposed to raise your hand.

The classroom is the only place in society where so many different, young, and restless individuals are crowded into close quarters for an extended period of time day after day. Teachers sense the undertow of raw energy and restlessness that threatens to engulf the classroom. To preserve order, most teachers use established classroom conventions such as raising your hand if you want to talk.

Intellectually, teachers know they should apply this rule consistently, but when the discussion becomes fast-paced and furious, the rule is often swept aside. When this happens and shouting out begins, it is an open invitation for male dominance. Our research shows that boys call out significantly more often than girls. Sometimes what they say has little or nothing to do with the teacher's questions. Whether male comments are insightful or irrelevant, teachers respond to them. However, when girls call out, there is a fascinating occurrence. Suddenly the teacher remembers the rule about raising your hand before you talk. And then the girl, who is usually not as assertive as the male students, is deftly and swiftly put back in her place.

Not being allowed to call out like her male classmates during the brief conversation about presidents will not psychologically scar Kimberly; however, the system of silencing operates covertly and repeatedly. It occurs several times a day during each school week for twelve years, and even longer if Kimberly goes to college, and, most insidious of all, it happens subliminally. This micro-inequity eventually has a powerful cumulative impact.

On the surface, girls appear to be doing well. They get better grades and receive fewer punishments than boys. Quieter and more conforming, they are the elementary school's ideal students. "If it ain't broke, don't fix it" is the school's operating principle as girls' good behavior frees the teacher to work with the more difficult-to-manage boys. The result is that girls receive less time, less help, and fewer challenges. Reinforced for passivity, their independence and self-esteem suffer. As victims of benign neglect, girls are penalized for doing what they should and lose ground as they go through school. In contrast, boys get reinforced for breaking the rules; they are rewarded for grabbing more than their fair share of the teacher's time and attention.

Even when teachers remember to apply the rules consistently, boys are still the ones who get noticed. When girls raise their hands, it is often at a right angle, arm bent at the elbow, a cautious, tentative, almost insecure gesture. At other times they raise their arms straight and high, but they signal silently. In contrast, when boys raise their hands, they fling them wildly in the air, up and down, up and down, again and again. Sometimes these hand signals are accompanied by strange noises, "Ooh! Ooh! Me! Me! Ooooh!"

Occasionally they even stand beside or on top of their seats and wave one or both arms to get attention. "Ooh! Me! Mrs. Smith, call on me." In the social studies class about presidents, we saw boys as a group grabbing attention while girls as a group were left out of the action.

When we videotape classrooms and play back the tapes, most teachers are stunned to see themselves teaching subtle gender lessons along with math and spelling. The teacher in the social studies class about presidents was completely unaware that she gave male students more attention. Only after several viewings of the videotape did she notice how she let boys call out answers but reprimanded girls for similar behavior. Low-achieving boys also get plenty of attention, but more often it's negative. No surprise there. In general, girls receive less attention, but there's another surprise: Unlike the smart boy who flourishes in the classroom, the smart girl is the student who is least likely to be recognized.

When we analyzed the computer printouts for information about gender and race, an intriguing trend emerged. The students most likely to receive teacher attention were white males; the second most likely were . . . males [of color]; the third, white females; and the least likely, . . . females [of color]. In elementary school, receiving attention from the teacher is enormously important for a student's achievement and self-esteem. Later in life, in the working world, the salary received is important, and the salary levels parallel the classroom: white males at the top and . . . females [of color] at the bottom. In her classroom interaction studies, Jacqueline Jordan Irvine found that black girls were active, assertive, and salient in the primary grades, but as they moved up through elementary school, they became the most invisible members of classrooms.

In our research in more than one hundred classrooms, . . . boys were more likely to be praised, corrected, helped, and criticized—all reactions that foster student achievement. Girls received the more superficial "Okay" reaction, one that packs far less educational punch. In her research, Jacqueline Jordan Irvine found that black females were least likely to receive clear academic feedback.

At first teachers are surprised to see videotapes where girls are "Okay'd" and boys gain clear feedback. Then it begins to make sense, "I don't like to tell a girl anything is wrong because I don't want to upset her," many say. This vision of females as fragile is held most often by male teachers." What if she cries? I wouldn't know how to handle it."

The "Okay" response is well meaning, but it kills with kindness. If girls don't know when they are wrong, if they don't learn strategies to get it right, then they never will correct their mistakes. And if they rarely receive negative feedback in school, they will be shocked when they are confronted by it in the workplace.

• • •

Ashley Reiter, National Winner of the 1991 Westinghouse Talent Competition for her sophisticated project on math modeling, remembers winning her first math contest. It happened at the same time that she first wore her contact lenses. Triumphant, Ashley showed up at school the next day without glasses and with a new medal. "Everybody talked about how pretty I looked," Ashley remembers. "Nobody said a word about the math competition."

The one area where girls are recognized more than boys is appearance. Teachers compliment their outfits and hairstyles. We hear it over and over again — not during large academic discussions but in more private moments, in small groups, when a student comes up to the teacher's desk, at recess, in hallways, at lunchtime, when children enter and exit the classroom: "Is that a new dress?" "You look so pretty today." "I love your new haircut. It's so cute." While these comments are most prevalent in the early grades, they continue through professional education: "That's a great outfit." "You look terrific today."

When teachers talk with boys about appearance, the exchanges are brief — quick recognition and then on to something else. Or teachers use appearance incidents to move on to a physical skill or academic topic. In one exchange, a little boy showed the teacher his shiny new belt buckle. Her response: "Cowboys wore buckles like that. They were rough and tough and they rode horses. Did you know that?"

●   ●   ●

Boy Bastions—Girl Ghettos

Raphaela Best spent four years as an observer in an elementary school in one of Maryland's most affluent counties. She helped the children with schoolwork, ate lunch with them, and played games with them in class and at recess. As an anthropologist, she also took copious notes. After more than one thousand hours of living with the children, she concluded that elementary school consists of separate and unequal worlds. She watched segregation in action firsthand. Adult women remember it well.

A college student recalled, "When I was in elementary school, boys were able to play basketball and kick ball. They had the side of the playground with the basketball hoops." Another college woman remembers more formal segregation: "I went to a very small grammar school. At recess and gym the boys played football and the girls jumped rope. All except one girl and one boy — they did the opposite. One day they were pulled aside. I'm not exactly sure what they were told, but the next day the schoolyard was divided in two. The boys got the middle and the girls got the edge, and neither sex was allowed on the other's part."

A third grader described it this way: "Usually we separate ourselves, but my teacher begins recess by handing a jump rope to the girls and a ball to the boys." Like the wave of a magic wand, this gesture creates strict gender lines. "The boys always pick the biggest areas for their games," she says. "We have what's left over, what they don't want."

Every morning at recess in schoolyards across the country, boys fan out over the prime territory to play kick ball, football, or basketball. Sometimes girls join them, but more often it's an all-male ball game. In the typical schoolyard, the boys' area is ten times bigger than the girls'. Boys never ask if it is their right to take over the territory, and it is rarely questioned. Girls huddle along the sidelines, on the fringe, as if in a separate female annex. Recess becomes a spectator sport.

Teachers seldom intervene to divide space and equipment more evenly, and seldom attempt to connect the segregated worlds—not even when they are asked directly by the girls.

"The boys won't let us play," a third grader said, tugging at the arm of the teacher on recess duty. "They have an all-boys club and they won't let any girls play."

"Don't you worry, honey," the teacher said, patting the little girl's hair. "When you get bigger, those boys will pay you all the attention you want. Don't you bother about them now."

As we observed that exchange, we couldn't help but wonder how the teacher would have reacted if the recess group had announced "No Catholics" or if white children had blatantly refused to play with Asians.

Barrie Thorne, a participant observer in elementary schools in California and Michigan whose students are mainly from working-class families, captured the tiny incidents that transform integrated classes into gender-divided worlds: Second-grade girls and boys eat lunch together around a long rectangular table. A popular boy walks by and looks the scene over. "Oooh, too many girls," he says, and takes a place at another table. All the boys immediately pick up their trays and abandon the table with girls, which has now become taboo.

Although sex segregation becomes more pervasive as children get older, contact points remain. School life has its own gender rhythm as girls and boys separate, come together, and separate again. But the points of contact, the together games that girls and boys play, often serve to heighten and solidify the walls of their separate worlds.

"You can't get me!" "Slobber Monster!" With these challenges thrown out, the game begins. It may be called "Girls Chase the Boys" or "Boys Chase the Girls," or "Chase and Kiss." It usually starts out one on one, but then the individual boy and girl enlist same-sex peers. "C'mon, let's get that boy." "Help, a girl's gonna get me!"

Pollution rituals are an important part of these chases. Children treat one another as if they were germ carriers. "You've got cooties" is the cry. (Substitute other terms for different cultures or different parts of the country.) Elaborate systems are developed around the concept of cooties. Transfer occurs when one child touches another. Prepared for such attack, some protect themselves by writing C. V. (cooties vaccination) on their arms.

Sometimes boys give cooties to girls, but far more frequently girls are the polluting gender. Boys fling taunts such as "girl stain" or "girl touch" or "cootie girl." The least-liked girls, the ones who are considered fat or ugly or poor, become "cootie queens," the real untouchables of the class, the most contaminating females of all.

Chasing, polluting, and invasions, where one gender attacks the play area of the other, all function as gender intensifiers, heightening perceived differences between female and male to an extreme degree. The world of children and the world of adults is composed of *different* races, but each gender is socially constructed as so different, so alien that we use the phrase "the *opposite* sex."

It is boys who work hardest at raising the walls of sex segregation and intensifying the difference between genders. They distance themselves, sending the message that girls are not good enough to play with them. Watch which boys sit next to the girls in informally sex-segregated classrooms and lunchrooms; they are the ones most likely to be rejected by male classmates. Sometimes they are even called "girls." A student at The American University remembers his school lunchroom in Brooklyn:

> At lunch our class all sat together at one long table. All the girls sat
> on one side, and the boys sat on the other. This was our system.
> Unfortunately, there were two more boys in my class than seats on
> the boys' side. There was no greater social embarrassment for a
> boy in the very hierarchical system we had set up in our class than
> to have to sit on the girls' side at lunch. It happened to me once,
> before I moved up the class social ladder. Boys climbed the rungs
> of that ladder by beating on each other during recess. To this day,
> twenty years later, I remember that lunch. It was horrible.

Other men speak, also with horror, of school situations when they became "one of the girls." The father of a nine-year-old daughter remembered girls in elementary school as "worse than just different. We considered them a subspecies." Many teachers who were victims of sexist schooling themselves understand this system and collaborate with it; they warn noisy boys of a humiliating punishment: "If you don't behave, I'm going to make you sit with the girls."

Most little girls—five, six, seven, or eight—are much too young to truly understand and challenge their assignment as the lower-caste gender. But without challenge over the course of years, this hidden curriculum in second-class citizenship sinks in. Schools and children need help—intervention by adults who can equalize the playing field.

We have found that sex segregation in the lunchroom and schoolyard spills over into the classroom. In our three-year, multi-state study of one hundred classrooms, our raters drew "gender geography" maps of each class they visited. They found that more than half of the classes were segregated by gender. There is more communication across race than across gender in elementary schools.

We have seen how sex segregation occurs when children form self-selected groups. Sometimes the division is even clearer, and so is the impact on instruction.

The students are seated formally in rows. There are even spaces between the rows, except down the middle of the room where the students have created an aisle large enough for two people standing side by side to walk down. On one side of the aisle, the students are all female; on the other side, all male. Black, white, Hispanic, and Asian students sit all around the room, but no student has broken the gender barrier.

The teacher in the room is conducting a math game, with the right team (boys) against the left team (girls). The problems have been put on the board, and members of each team race to the front of the room to see who can write the answer first. Competition is intense, but eventually the girls fall behind. The teacher keeps score on the board, with two columns headed "Good Girls" and "Brilliant Boys."

The gender segregation was so formal in this class that we asked if the teacher had set it up. "Of course not." She looked offended. "I wouldn't think of doing such a thing. The students do it themselves." It never occurred to the well-meaning teacher to raise the issue or change the seats.

In our research we have found that gender segregation is a major contributor to female invisibility. In sex-segregated classes, teachers are pulled to the more talkative, more disruptive male sections of the classroom or pool. There they stay, teaching boys more actively and directly while the girls fade into the background.

44

"WHAT ABOUT THE BOYS?"
What the Current Debates Tell Us—
and Don't Tell Us—About Boys in School

MICHAEL S. KIMMEL

Michael S. Kimmel is professor of Sociology at SUNY at Stony Brook. His books include *The Gendered Society* (2004), *The Gendered Society Reader* (2004), *Changing Men* (1987), *Men Confront Pornography* (1990), *Men in the United States* (1992), *Manhood in America* (1996), and *The Politics of Manhood* (1996). He is the editor of *Men and Masculinities,* a scholarly journal, and National Spokesperson for the National Organization for Men Against Sexism (NOMAS).

I've placed the question contained in my title—"what about the boys?"—in quotation marks. In that way, I can pose two different questions to frame the discussion of boys in school. First, the question within the quotation marks is the empirical one: What *about* the boys? What's going on with them? The second question, expressed by the question *and* the quotation marks, is cultural and political: Why is the question "what about the boys?" such a pressing question on the cultural agenda? Why is the question popping up increasingly in the cultural conversation about gender? Why has it become one of the litany of questions that compose the backlash against feminism?

I believe that the answers to both questions are linked. But first let's look at each separately.

What about the Boys?

Are boys in trouble in school? At first glance, the statistics would suggest that they are. Boys drop out of school, are diagnosed as emotionally disturbed, and commit suicide four times more often than girls; they get into fights twice as often; they murder ten times more frequently and are 15 times more likely to be the victims of a violent crime. Boys are six times more likely to be diagnosed with Attention Deficit Disorder (see, for example, Knickerbocker).

Michael S. Kimmel, "'What About the Boys?' What the Current Debates Tell Us (and Don't Tell Us) About Boys in School" from *Michigan Feminist Studies* 14 (1999): 1–28. Copyright © 1999 by Michael S. Kimmel. Reprinted with permission.

If they can manage to sit still and not get themselves killed, the argument seems to go, boys get lower grades on standardized tests of reading and writing, and have lower class rank and fewer honors than girls (Kleinfeld).

Finally, if they succeed in dodging the Scylla of elementary and high school, they're likely to dash themselves against the Charybdis of collegiate male bashing. We read that women now constitute the majority of students on college campuses, passing men in 1982, so that in eight years women will earn 58 percent of bachelor's degrees in U.S. colleges. One reporter tells us that if present trends continue, "the graduation line in 2068 will be all females." (That's like saying that if the enrollment of black students at Ol' Miss was 1 in 1964, 24 in 1968 and 400 in 1988, that by 1994 there should have been no more white students there.) Doomsayers lament that women now outnumber men in the social and behavioral sciences by about three to one, and that they've invaded such traditionally male bastions as engineering, where they now make up about 20 percent of all students, and biology and business, where the genders are virtually on par (see Lewin; Koerner).

So, the data might seem to suggest that there are fewer and fewer boys, getting poorer grades, with increasing numbers of behavioral problems. Three phenomena—numbers, achievement and behavior—compose the current empirical discussion about where the boys are and what they are doing.

"What about the Boys?"

These three themes—numbers, grades, behavior—frame the political debate about boys as well. (Now I'm going to include the quotation marks.) Given these gender differences, it's not surprising that we're having a national debate. After all, boys seem not only to be doing badly, but they are also doing worse than girls. What may be surprising, though, is the way the debate is being framed.

To hear some tell it, there's a virtual war against boys in America. Bestsellers' subtitles counsel us to "protect" boys, to "rescue" them. Inside these books, we read how boys are failing at school, where their behavior is increasingly seen as a problem. We read that boys are depressed, suicidal, emotionally shut down. Therapists advise anguished parents about boys' fragility, their hidden despondence and depression, and issue stern warnings about the dire consequences if we don't watch our collective cultural step.

But if there is a "war against boys" who has declared it? What are the sides of the conflict? Who is to blame for boys' failures? What appears to be a concern about the plight of boys actually masks a deeper agenda—a critique of feminism. And I believe that in the current climate, boys need defending against precisely those who claim to defend them; they need rescuing from precisely those who would rescue them.

The arguments of these jeremiads go something like this: First, we hear, feminism has already succeeded in developing programs for girls, enabling and encouraging girls to go into the sciences, to continue education, to imagine careers outside the home. But, in so doing, feminists have over-emphasized the problems of girls, and distorted the facts. Particularly objectionable are the findings of the American Association of Unversity Women (AAUW) reports on the "chilly classroom climate." According to these critics, the salutary effects of paying attention to girls have been offset by the increasing problematization of boys. It was feminists, we hear, who pitted girls against boys, and in their efforts to help girls, they've "pathologized" boyhood.

Elementary schools, we hear, are "anti-boy," emphasizing reading and restricting the movements of young boys. They "feminize" boys, forcing active, healthy and naturally rambunctious boys to conform to a regime of obedience, "pathologizing what is simply normal for boys," as psychologist Michael Gurian put it (qtd. in Zachary 1). In *The Wonder of Boys,* Gurian argues that with testosterone surging through their little limbs, we demand that they sit still, raise their hands, and take naps. We're giving them the message, he says, that "boyhood is defective" (qtd. in Zachary 1). . . .

Today, women teachers are still to blame for boys' feminization. "It's teachers' job to create a classroom environment that accommodates both male and female energy, not just mainly female energy," explains the energetic therapist Michael Gurian (qtd. in Knickerbocker 2). Since women also may run those boy scout troops and may actually run circles around the boys on the soccer field, men may be feeling a tad defensive these days. Not to worry — we can always retreat into our den to watch "The Man Show" and read *Men's Health* magazine.

In this way, the problem of boys is a problem caused entirely by women who both feminize the boys and pathologize them in their rush to help girls succeed. I'll return to these issues later, but for now, let me turn to what I see are the chief problems with the current "what about the boys?" debate.

What's Wrong with the "What about the Boys?" Debate

First, it creates a false opposition between girls and boys, pretending that the educational reforms undertaken to enable girls to perform better actually hindered boys' educational development. But these reforms — new initiatives, classroom configurations, teacher training, increased attentiveness to students' processes and individual learning styles — actually enable larger numbers of boys to get a better education.

And since, as Susan McGee Bailey and Patricia Campbell point out in their comment on "The Gender Wars in Education" in the January, 2000 issue of the *WCW Research Report,* "gender stereotypes, particularly those related to education, hurt both girls and boys," the challenging of those stereotypes, decreased tolerance for school violence and bullying, and increased attention to violence at home actually enables *both* girls *and* boys to feel safer at school (13).

Second, the critics all seem to be driven to distraction by numbers—the increasing percentages of women in high education and the growing gender gap in test scores. But here's a number they don't seem to factor in: zero—as in zero dollars of *any* new public funding for school programs for the past twenty years, the utter dearth of school bond issues that have passed, money from which might have developed remedial programs, intervention strategies, and teacher training. Money that might have prevented cutting school sports programs and after-school extra-curricular activities. Money that might have enabled teachers and administrators to do more than "store" problem students in separate classes.

Nor do the critics mention managed care health insurance, which virtually demands that school psychologists diagnose problem behavior as a treatable medical condition so that drugs may be substituted for costly, "unnecessary" therapy. These numbers—numbers of dollars—don't seem to enter the discussion about boys, and yet they provide the foundation for everything else. But even the numbers they *do* discuss—numbers and test scores—don't add up. For one thing, more *people* are going to college than ever before. In 1960, 54 percent of boys and 38 percent of girls went directly to college; today the numbers are 64 percent of boys and 70 percent of girls (Mortenson).

And while some college presidents fret that to increase male enrollments they'll be forced to lower standards (which is, incidentally, exactly the opposite of what they worried about 25 years ago when they all went coeducational) no one seems to find gender disparities going the other way all that upsetting. Of the top colleges and universities in the nation, only Stanford sports a 50–50 gender balance. Harvard and Amherst enroll 56 percent men, Princeton and Chicago 54 percent men, Duke and Berkeley 52 percent and Yale 51 percent. And that doesn't even begin to approach the gender disparities at Cal Tech (65 percent male, 35 percent female) or MIT (62 percent male, 38 percent female) (Gose "Liberal Arts Colleges Ask"). Nor does anyone seem driven to distraction about the gender disparities in nursing, social work, or education. Did somebody say "what about the girls?" Should we lower standards to make sure they're gender balanced?

In fact, much of the great gender difference we hear touted in actually what sociologist Cynthia Fuchs Epstein calls a "deceptive distinction," a difference that appears to be about gender but is actually about something else—in this case, class or race (see Epstein *Deceptive Distinctions*). Girls' vocational opportunities are far more restricted than boys' are. Their opportunities are from the service sector, with limited openings in manufacturing or construction. A college-educated woman earns about the same as a high-school educated man, $35,000 to $31,000 (Gose "Colleges Look for Ways").

The shortage of male college students is also actually a shortage of *non-white* males. The gender gap between college-age white males and white females is rather small, 51 percent women to 49 percent men. But only 37 percent of black college students are male, and 63 percent female, and 45 percent of Hispanic students are male, compared with 55 percent female (Lewin). (If this is a problem largely of class and race, why do the books that warn of this growing crisis have cute little white boys on their covers?)

These differences among boys—by race, or class, for example—do not typically fall within the radar of the cultural critics who would rescue boys. These differences are incidental because, in their eyes, all boys are the same: aggressive, competitive, rambunctious little devils. And this is perhaps the central problem and contradiction in the work of those who would save boys. They argue that it's testosterone that makes boys into boys, and a society that paid attention to boys would have to acknowledge testosterone. We're making it impossible for boys to be boys. . . .

Feminist emphases on gender discrimination, sexual harassment, or date rape only humiliate boys and distract us from intervening constructively. These misdiagnoses lead to some rather chilling remedies. Gurian suggests reviving corporal punishment, both at home and at school—but only when administered privately with cool indifference and never in the heat of adult anger. He calls it "spanking responsibly" (*A Fine Young Man* 175), though school boards and child welfare agencies might call it child abuse. . . .

What's Missing from the Debate about Boys

I believe that it is *masculinity* that is missing in the discussions of both fathers and sons. Though we hear an awful lot about *males*, we hear very little about *masculinity*, about the cultural meanings of the biological fact of maleness. Raising the issue of masculinity, I believe, will enable us to resolve many of these debates.

When I say that masculinity is invisible in the discussion, what could I possibly mean? How is masculinity invisible? Well, let me ask you this: when I say the word "gender," what gender do you think of? In our courses and our discourses, we act as if women alone "had" gender. This is political; this is central. . . .

Let me give you two . . . illustrations of this. . . . In a recent article about the brutal homophobic murder of Mathew Shepard, the reporter for the *New York Times* writes that "[y]oung men account for 80 percent to 90 percent of people arrested for 'gay bashing' crimes, says Valerie Jenness, a sociology professor who teaches a course on hate crimes" at U. C. Irvine. Then the reporter quotes Professor Jenness directly: "'This youth variable tells us they are working out identity issues, making the transition away from home into adulthood" (Brooke A16). Did you hear it disappear? The *Times* reporter says "young men" account for . . . ," the sociologist, the expert, is quoted as saying, "this youth variable." That is what invisibility looks like.[1]

. . . Here's one more illustration of the invisibility of masculinity in the discussion of young boys, and how that invisibility almost always plays out as a critique of feminism. Asked to comment on the school shootings at Columbine and other high schools, House Majority Leader Tom DeLay said that guns "have little or nothing to do with juvenile violence" but rather, that the causes were daycare, the teaching of evolution, and "working mothers who take birth control pills" (qtd. in *The Nation* 5).

Some of the recent boy books do get it; they get that masculinity—not feminism, not testosterone, not fatherlessness, and not the teaching of evolution—is the key to understanding boyhood and its current crisis. For example, in *Raising Cain,* Dan Kindlon and Michael Thompson write that male peers present a young boy with a "culture of cruelty" in which they force him to deny emotional neediness, "routinely disguise his feelings," and end up feeling emotionally isolated (89). And in *Real Boys,* therapist William Pollack calls it the "boy code" and the "mask of masculinity"—a kind of swaggering posture that boys embrace to hide their fears, suppress dependency and vulnerability, and present a stoic, impervious front.

What exactly is that "boy code?" Twenty-five years ago, psychologist Robert Brannon described the four basic rules of manhood.

1. "No Sissy Stuff"—one can never do anything that even remotely hints of femininity; masculinity is the relentless repudiation of the feminine.
2. "Be a Big Wheel"—Wealth, power, status are markers of masculinity. We measure masculinity by the size of one's pay-check. In the words of that felicitous Reagan-era phrase, "He who has the most toys when he dies, wins."
3. "Be a Sturdy Oak"—what makes a man a man is that he is reliable in a crisis, and what makes a man reliable in a crisis is that he resembles an inanimate object. Rocks, pillars, trees are curious masculine icons.
4. "Give em Hell!"—exude an aura of daring and aggression. Live life on the edge. Take risks (Brannon and David).

Of course, these four rules are elaborated by different groups of men and boys in different circumstances. There are as sizable differences among different groups of men as there are differences between women and men. Greater in fact. Just because we make masculinity visible doesn't mean that we make other categories of experience—race, class, ethnicity, sexuality, age—invisible. What it means to be a 71-year-old, black, gay man in Cleveland is probably radically different from what it means to a 19-year-old, white, heterosexual farm boy in Iowa.

. . . [W]e can't forget that all masculinities are not created equal. All American men must also contend with a singular vision of masculinity, a particular definition that is held up as the model against which we all measure ourselves. We thus come to know what it means to be a man in our culture by setting our definitions in opposition to a set of "others"—racial minorities, sexual minorities, and, above all, women. As the sociologist Erving Goffman once wrote:

In an important sense there is only one complete unblushing male
in America: a young, married, white, urban, northern,
heterosexual, Protestant, father, of college education, fully
employed, of good complexion, weight, and height, and a recent
record in sports. . . . Any male who fails to qualify in any one of
these ways is likely to view himself—during moments at least—as
unworthy, incomplete, and inferior. (128)

I think it's crucial to listen carefully to those last few words. When men
feel that they do not measure up, Goffman argues, they are likely to feel "unworthy, incomplete and inferior." It is, I believe, from this place of unwor-
thiness, incompleteness and inferiority that boys begin their efforts to prove
themselves as men. And the ways they do it—based on misinformation and
disinformation—is what is causing the problems for girls and boys in school.

How Does the Perspective on Masculinity Transform the Debate?

Introducing masculinities into the discussion alleviates several of the problems with the "what about the boys?" debate. It enables us to explore the
ways in which class and race complicate the picture of boys' achievement
and behaviors, for one thing. For another, it reveals that boys and girls are
on the same side in this struggle, not pitted against each other.

For example, when Kindlon and Thompson describe the things that *boys*
need, they are really describing what *children* need. Adolescent boys, Kindlon and Thompson inform us, want to be loved, get sex, and not be hurt
(195–6). And girls don't? Parents are counseled to: allow boys to have their
emotions (241); accept a high level of activity (245); speak their language and
treat them with respect (247); teach that empathy is courage (249); use discipline to guide and build (253); model manhood as emotionally attached
(255); and teach the many ways a boy can be a man (256). Aside from the obvious tautologies, what they advocate is exactly what feminist women have
been advocating for girls for some time.

Secondly, a focus on masculinity explains what is happening to those
boys in school. Consider again the parallel for girls. Carol Gilligan's astonishing and often moving work on adolescent girls describes how these assertive, confident and proud young girls "lose their voices" when they hit
adolescence (see, for example, Brown and Gilligan). At the same moment,
William Pollack notes, boys become *more* confident, even beyond their abilities. You might even say that boys *find* their voices, but it is the inauthentic
voice of bravado, of constant posturing, of foolish risk-taking and gratuitous
violence. The "boy code" teaches them that they are supposed to be in
power, and thus begin to act like it. . . .

What's the cause of all this posturing and posing? It's not testosterone, but privilege. In adolescence, both boys and girls get their first real dose of gender inequality: girls suppress ambition, boys inflate it.

Recent research on the gender gap in school achievement bears this out. Girls are more likely to undervalue their abilities, especially in the more traditionally "masculine" educational arenas such as math and science. Only the most able and most secure girls take such courses. Thus, their numbers tend to be few, and their grades high. Boys, however, possessed of this false voice of bravado (and many facing strong family pressure) are likely to *over-value* their abilities, to remain in programs though they are less qualified and capable of succeeding. This difference, and not some putative discrimination against boys, is the reason that girls' mean test scores in math and science are now, on average, approaching that of boys. Too many boys who over-value their abilities remain in difficult math and science courses longer than they should; they pull the boys' mean scores down. By contrast, few girls, whose abilties and self-esteem are sufficient to enable them to "trespass" into a male domain, skew female data upwards.

A parallel process is at work in the humanities and social sciences. Girls' mean test scores in English and foreign languages, for example, also outpace boys. But this is not the result of "reverse discrimination"; rather, it is because the boys bump up against the norms of masculinity. Boys regard English as a "feminine" subject. Pioneering research in Australia by Wayne Martino found that boys are uninterested in English because of what it might say about their (inauthentic) masculine pose (see, for example, Martino "Gendered Learning Practices," "'Cool Boys'"; see also Yates "Gender Equity," "The 'What About the Boys' Debate"; Lesko). "Reading is lame, sitting down and looking at words is pathetic," commented one boy. "Most guys who like English are faggots" (Martino "Gendered Learning Practices" 132). The traditional liberal arts curriculum is seen as feminizing: as Catharine Stimpson recently put it sarcastically, "real men don't speak French" (qtd. in Lewin A26).

Boys tend to hate English and foreign languages for the same reasons that girls love it. In English, they observe, there are no hard and fast rules, but rather one expresses one's opinion about the topic and everyone's opinion is equally valued. "The answer can be a variety of things, you're never really wrong," observed one boy. "It's not like math and science where there is one set answer to everything." Another boy noted:

> I find English hard. It's because there are no set rules for reading texts . . . English isn't like math where you have rules on how to do things and where there are right and wrong answers. In English you have to write down how you feel and that's what I don't like. (Martino "Gendered Learning Practices" 133)

Compare this to the comments of girls in the same study:

I feel motivated to study English because . . . you have freedom in English—unlike subjects such as math and science—and your view isn't necessarily wrong. There is no definite right or wrong answer and you have the freedom to say what you feel is right without it being rejected as a wrong answer. (Martino "Gendered Learning Practices" 134)

It is not the school experience that "feminizes" boys, but rather the ideology of traditional masculinity that keeps boys from wanting to succeed. "The work you do here is girls' work," one boy commented to a researcher. "It's not real work" (Mac an Ghaill 59; for additional research on this, see Lesko). . . .

The Real Boy Crisis Is a Crisis of Masculinity

Making masculinity visible enables us to understand what I regard as the *real* boy crisis in America. The real boy crisis usually goes by another name. We call it "teen violence," "youth violence," "gang violence," "suburban violence," "violence in the schools." Just who do we think are doing it—girls?

Imagine if all the killers in the schools in Littleton, Pearl, Paducah, Springfield, and Jonesboro were all black girls from poor families who lived instead in New Haven, Newark, or Providence. We'd be having a national debate about inner-city, poor, black girls. The entire focus would be on race, class, and gender. The media would invent a new term for their behavior, as with "wilding" a decade ago. We'd hear about the culture of poverty, about how living in the city breeds crime and violence, about some putative natural tendency among blacks towards violence. Someone would even blame feminism for causing girls to become violent in a vain imitation of boys. Yet the obvious fact that these school killers were all middle-class, white boys seems to have escaped everyone's notice.

Let's face facts: Men and boys are responsible for 95 percent of all violent crimes in this country. Every day 12 boys and young men commit suicide—seven times the number of girls. Every day 18 boys and young men die from homicide—ten times the number of girls (see Kimmel *The Gendered Society*). From an early age, boys learn that violence is not only an acceptable form of conflict resolution, but one that is admired. Four times more teenage boys than teenage girls think fighting is appropriate when someone cuts into the front of a line. Half of all teenage boys get into a physical fight each year.

And it's been that way for many years. No other culture developed such a violent "boy culture," as historian E. Anthony Rotundo calls it in his book, *American Manhood*. Where else did young boys, as late as the 1940s, actually carry little chips of wood on their shoulders daring others to knock it off so that they might have a fight? It may be astonishing to readers that "carrying a chip on your shoulder" is literally true—a test of manhood for adolescent boys.

In what other culture did some of the reigning experts of the day actually *prescribe* fighting for young boys' healthy masculine development? The celebrated psychologist, G. Stanley Hall, who invented the term "adolescence," believed that a non-fighting boy was a "nonentity," and that it was "better even an occasional nose dented by a fist . . . than stagnation, general cynicism and censoriousness, bodily and psychic cowardice" (154).

And his disciples vigorously took up the cause. Here, for example is J. Adams Puffer in 1912, from his successful parental advice book, *The Boy and His Gang:*

> There are times when every boy must defend his own rights if he
> is not to become a coward, and lose the road to independence and
> true manhood. . . . The strong willed boy needs no inspiration to
> combat, but often a good deal of guidance and restraint. If he
> fights more than, let us say, a half-dozen times a week—except of
> course, during his first week at a new school—he is probably over-
> quarrelsome and needs to curb. (91)

Boys are to fight an average of once a day, except during the first week at a new school, during which, presumably they would have to fight more often!

From the turn of the century to the present day, violence has been part of the meaning of manhood, part of the way men have traditionally tested, demonstrated and proved their manhood. Without another cultural mechanism by which young boys can come to think of themselves as men, they've eagerly embraced violence as a way to become men.

I remember one little childhood game called "Flinch" that we played in the school yard. One boy would come up to another and pretend to throw a punch at his face. If the second boy flinched—as any *reasonable* person would have done—the first boy shouted "you flinched" and proceeded to punch him hard on the arm. It was his right; after all, the other boy had failed the test of masculinity. Being a man meant never flinching.

In the recent study of youthful violent offenders, psychologist James Garbarino locates the origins of men's violence in the ways boys swallow anger and hurt. Among the youthful offenders he studied, "[d]eadly petulance usually hides some deep emotional wounds, a way of compensating through an exaggerated sense of grandeur for an inner sense of violation, victimization, and injustice" (128). In other words, as that famous Reagan-era bumper-sticker put it, "I don't just get mad, I get even." Or, as one prisoner said, "I'd rather be wanted for murder than not wanted at all" (132).

James Gilligan is even more specific. In his book *Violence,* one of the most insightful studies of violence I've ever read, he argues that violence has its origins in "the fear of shame and ridicule, and the overbearing need to prevent others from laughing at oneself by making them weep instead" (77).

Recall those words by Goffman again—"unworthy, incomplete, inferior." Now listen to these voices: First, here is Evan Todd, a 255-pound defensive lineman on the Columbine football team, an exemplar of the jock culture that Dylan Klebold and Eric Harris—the gunmen at Columbine High School—found to be such an interminable torment: "Columbine is a clean, good place, except for those rejects," Todd says. "Sure we teased them. But what do you expect with kids who come to school with weird hairdos and horns on their hats? It's not just jocks; the whole school's disgusted with them. They're a bunch of homos, grabbing each others' private parts. If you want to get rid of someone, usually you tease 'em. So the whole school would call them homos" (qtd. in Gibbs and Roche 50–51). Harris says people constantly made fun of "my face, my hair, my shirts" (44). Klebold adds, "I'm going to kill you all. You've been giving us s__ for years" (44).

Our Challenge

If we really want to rescue boys, protect boys, promote boyhood, then our task must be to find ways to reveal and challenge this ideology of masculinity, to disrupt the facile "boys will be boys" model, and to erode boys' sense of entitlement. Because the reality is that it is this ideology of masculinity that is the problem for *both* girls *and* boys. And seen this way, our strongest ally, it seems to me, is the women's movement.

To be sure, feminism opened the doors of opportunity to women and girls. And it's changed the rules of conduct: in the workplace, where sexual harassment is no longer business as usual; on dates, where attempted date rape is no longer "dating etiquette"; and in schools, where both subtle and overt forms of discrimination against girls—from being shuffled off to Home Economics when they want to take physics, excluded from military schools and gym classes, to anatomy lectures using pornographic slides—have been successfully challenged. And let's not forget the legal cases that have confronted bullying, and sexual harassment by teachers and peers.

More than that, feminism has offered a blueprint for a new boyhood and masculinity based on a passion for justice, a love of equality, and expression of a fuller emotional palette. So naturally, feminists will be blamed for male bashing—feminists imagine that men (and boys) can do better (see, for example, Miedzian; Silverstein and Rashbaum).

And to think feminists are accused of male bashing! Actually, I think the anti-feminist right wing are the real male bashers. Underneath the anti-feminism may be perhaps the most insulting image of masculinity around. Males, you see, are savage, predatory, sexually omnivorous, violent creatures, who will rape, murder and pillage unless women perform their civilizing mission and act to constrain us. "Every society must be wary of the unattached male, for he is universally the cause of numerous social ills," writes David Popenoe (12). When they say that boys will be boys, they mean boys will be uncaged, uncivilized animals. Young males, conservative critic

Charles Murray wrote recently, are "essentially barbarians for whom marriage . . . is an indispensible civilizing force" (23). And what of evolutionary psychologist Robert Wright, who recently "explained" that women and men are hard-wired by evolutionary imperatives to be so different as to come from different planets. "Human males," he wrote, "are by nature oppressive, possessive, flesh-obsessed pigs" (22). Had any radical feminist said these words, anti-feminist critics would howl with derision about how feminists hated men!

And here's that doyenne of talk radio, Dr. Laura Schlesinger: "Men would not do half of what they do if women didn't let them," she told an interviewer for *Modern Maturity* magazine recently. "That a man is going to do bad things is a fact. That you keep a man who does bad things in your life is your fault" (qtd. in Goodman 68).

Now it seems to me that the only rational response to these insulting images of an unchangeable, hard-wired, violent manhood is, of course, to assume they're true. Typically when we say that boys will be boys, we assume that propensity for violence is innate, the inevitable fruition of that prenatal testosterone cocktail. So what? That only begs the question. We still must decide whether to organize society so as to maximize boys' "natural" predisposition toward violence, or to minimize it. Biology alone cannot answer that question, and claiming that boys will be boys, helplessly shrugging our national shoulders, abandons our political responsibility.

Besides, one wants to ask, which biology are we talking about? Therapist Michael Gurian demands that we accept boy's "hard wiring." This "hard wiring," he informs us, is competitive and aggressive. "Aggression and physical risk taking are hard wired into a boy," he writes. Gurian claims that he likes the kind of feminism that "is not anti-male, accepts that boys are who they are, and chooses to love them rather than change their hard wiring" (*A Fine Young Man* 53–4).

That's too impoverished a view of feminism—and of boys—for my taste. I think it asks far too little of us, to simply accept boys and this highly selective definition of their hard-wiring. Feminism asks more of us—that we *not* accept those behaviors that are hurtful to boys, girls, and their environment—because we can do better than what this *part* of our hard wiring might dictate. We are also, after all, hard-wired towards compassion, nurturing and love, aren't we?

Surely we wouldn't insult men the way the right-wing insults men, by arguing that only women are hard-wired for love, care-giving, and nurturing, would we? (I am sure that those legions of men's rights types, demanding custody wouldn't dare do so!) I'm reminded of a line from Kate Millett's path-breaking book, *Sexual Politics,* more than thirty years ago:

> Perhaps nothing is so depressing an index of the inhumanity of the
> male supremacist mentality as the fact that the more genial human

traits are assigned to the underclass: affection, response to sympathy, kindness, cheerfulness. (324–6)

The question, to my mind, is not whether or not we're hard wired, but rather which hard wiring elements we choose to honor and which we choose to challenge.

I remember one pithy definition that feminism was the radical idea that women are people. Feminists also seem to believe the outrageous proposition that, if given enough love, compassion and support, boys—as well as men—can also be people. That's a vision of boyhood I believe is worth fighting for.

NOTES

This paper began as the keynote address at the 6th annual K–12 Gender Equity in Schools Conference, Wellesley College Center for Research on Women, Wellesley College, January, 2000. A revised version was also presented at The Graduate School of Education, Harvard University, May, 2000. Although modified and revised, I have tried to retain the language and feeling of the original oral presentation. I am grateful to Susan McGee Bailey and Carol Gilligan for inviting me, and to Amy Aronson, Peggy McIntosh, Martin Mills, and Nan Stein, for their comments and support, and to the editors at *Michigan Feminist Studies,* and especially Laura Citrin, for their patience and editorial precision.

1. In fairness to Professor Jenness, whose work on gay bashing crimes I admire, it is possible that her quotation was only part of what she said, and that it was the newspaper, not the expert, who again rendered masculinity invisible.

REFERENCES

American Association of University Women. *How Schools Shortchange Girls: The AAUW Report, A Study of Major Findings on Girls and Education.* Washington, DC: American Association of University Women Educational Foundation, 1992.

Bailey, Susan McGee, and Patricia B. Campbell, "The Gender Wars in Education." *WCW Research Report.* Wellesley, MA: Wellesley Center for Research on Women, 1999/2000.

Brannon, Robert, and Deborah David. "Introduction" to *The Forty-Nine Per Cent Majority.* Reading, MA: Addison, Wesley, 1976.

Brooke, James. "Men Held in Beating Lived on the Fringes." *The New York Times,* 16 October 1998: A16.

Brown, Lyn Mikeal, and Carol Gilligan. *Meeting at the Cross-roads.* New York: Ballantine, 1992.

Epstein, Cynthia Fuchs. *Deceptive Distinctions.* New Haven: Yale UP, 1988.

Garbarino, James. *Lost Boys: Why Our Sons Turn Violent and How We Can Save Them.* New York: The Free P, 1999.

Gibbs, Nancy, and Timothy Roche. "The Columbine Tapes." *Time* 154 (25), 20 December 1999: 40–51.

Gilligan, Carol. *In a Different Voice.* Cambridge: Harvard UP, 1982.

Gilligan, James. *Violence.* New York: Vintage, 1997.

Goffman, Erving. *Stigma: Notes on the Management of Spoiled Identity.* Englewood Cliffs, NJ: Prentice-Hall, 1963.

Goodman, Susan. "Dr. No." *Modern Maturity,* September-October, 1999.

Gose, Ben. "Liberal Arts Colleges Ask: Where Have the Men Gone?" *Chronicle of Higher Education,* 6 June 1997: A35–6.

_____. "Colleges Look for Ways to Reverse a Decline in Enrollment of Men." *Chronicle of Higher Education,* 26 November 1999: A73.

Gurian, Michael. *A Fine Young Man: What parents, mentors, and educators can do to shape adolescent boys into exceptional men.* New York: Jeremy P. Tarcher/Putnam, 1998.

_____. *The Wonder of Boys: What parents, mentors, and educators can do to shape boys into exceptional men.* New York: Jeremy P. Tarcher/Putnam, 1996.

Hall, G. Stanley. "The Awkward Age." *Appleton's Magazine,* August 1900.

Kimmel, Michael. *The Gendered Society.* New York: Oxford UP, 2000.

Kindlon, Dan, and Michael Thompson. *Raising Cain: Protecting the Emotional Life of Boys.* New York: Ballantine, 1999.

Kleinfeld, Judith. "Student Performance: Males Versus Females." *The Public Interest,* Winter 1999.

Knickerbocker, Brad. "Young and Male in America: It's Hard Being a Boy." *Christian Science Monitor,* 29 April 1999.

Koerner, Brendan. "Where the Boys Aren't." *U.S. News and World Report,* 8 February 1999.

Lesko, Nancy, ed. *Masculinities and Schools.* Newbury Park, CA: Sage Publications, 2000.

Lewin, Tamar. "American Colleges Begin to Ask, Where Have All the Men Gone?" *The New York Times,* 6 December 1998.

Mac an Ghaill, Mairtin. *The Making of Men: Masculinities, Sexualities and Schooling.* London: Open UP, 1994.

_____. "'What About the Boys?': Schooling, Class and Crisis Masculinity." *Sociological Review,* 44 (3), 1996.

Martino, Wayne. "Gendered Learning Practices: Exploring the Costs of Hegemonic Masculinity for Girls and Boys in Schools." *Gender Equity: A Framework for Australian Schools,* Canberra: np, 1997.

_____. "'Cool Boys,' 'Party Animals', 'Squids,' and 'Poofters': Interrogating the Dynamics and Politics of Adolescent Masculinities in School." *British Journal of Sociology of Education,* 20 (2), 1999.

Miedzian, Myriam. *Boys will be Boys: Breaking the Link between Masculinity and Violence.* New York: Doubleday, 1991.

Millett, Kate. *Sexual Politics.* New York: Random House, 1969.

Mills, Martin. "Disrupting the 'What about the Boys?' Discourse: Stories from Australia" paper presented at the Men's Studies Conference, SUNY at Stony Brook, 6 August 1998.

Mortenson, Thomas. "Where Are the Boys? The Growing Gender Gap in Higher Education." *The College Board Review,* 188, August 1999.

Murray, Charles. "The Emerging British Underclass." London: IEA Health and Welfare Unit, 1990.

The Nation. "News of the Week in Review." 15 November 1999.

Pollack, William. *Real Boys: Rescuing Our Sons from the Myths of Boyhood.* New York: Henry Holt, 1998.

Popenoe, David. *Life Without Father.* New York: The Free Press, 1996.

Priest, R., A. Vitters, and H. Prince. "Coeducation at West Point." *Armed Forces and Society,* 4 (4), 1978.

Puffer, J. Adams. *The Boy and His Gang.* Boston: Houghton, Mifflin, 1912.

Rotundo, E. Anthony. *American Manhood: Transformations of Masculinity from the Revolution to the Present Era.* New York: BasicBooks, 1993.

Silverstein, Olga, and Beth Rashbaum. *The Courage to Raise Good Men.* New York: Penguin, 1995.

Wright, Robert. "The Dissent of Woman: What Feminists Can Learn from Darwinism." *Matters of Life and Death: Demos Quarterly,* 10, 1996.

Yates, Lyn. "Gender Equity and the Boys Debate: What Sort of Challenge Is It?" *British Journal of Sociology of Education,* 18 (3), 1997.

_____. "The 'What About the Boys?' Debate as a Public Policy Issue." Ed. Nancy Lesko. *Masculinities and Schools.* Newbury Park, CA: Sage Publications, 2000.

Zachary, G. Pascal. "Boys Used to Be Boys, But Do Some Now See Boyhood as a Malady." *The Wall Street Journal,* 2 May 1997.

45

CONFLICT WITHIN THE IVORY TOWER

RUTH SIDEL

Ruth Sidel is professor of sociology at Hunter College. She has long been concerned about the well-being of women, children, and families in the United States and in other countries. Her most recent book is *Keeping Women and Children Last: America's War on the Poor* (Penguin).

> *Either/or dichotomous thinking categorizes people, things, and ideas in terms of their difference from one another. . . . This emphasis on quantification and categorization occurs in conjunction with the belief that either/or categories must be ranked. The search for certainty of this sort requires that one side of a dichotomy be privileged while its other is denigrated. Privilege becomes defined in relationship to its other.*[1]

PATRICIA HILL COLLINS,
BLACK FEMINIST THOUGHT:
KNOWLEDGE, CONSCIOUSNESS, AND THE
POLITICS OF EMPOWERMENT

Admission to college or university is, as has been noted, a first but crucial step in an individual's preparation for meaningful participation in the social, economic, and political life of postindustrial America. But admission is merely the first hurdle a student must clear in higher education. Financing college education, achieving academically, and maneuvering around the multitude of social, psychological, and political obstacles that impede the path to a bachelor's degree are often much higher hurdles than admission. Among the barriers that many students have had to face in recent years are virtually continuous clashes stemming from prejudice, ethnocentrism, and fear—fear of the unknown, of the stranger among us. At root these clashes are about entitlement and power, and about students' concerns with the precariousness of their position in the social structure.

Although colleges and universities have since the end of the Second World War been to a considerable extent transformed from elite bastions of privilege to increasingly open, heterogeneous communities, a wave of overt intolerance has recently swept over the academic community. There is little doubt that students today are more tolerant than their grandparents and their parents, yet clashes—some involving vocal or written assaults, some involving violence—continue to plague academic institutions and to shock observers. One of the reasons these so-called hate incidents are so shocking is the increasing unacceptability of overtly racist, sexist, anti-Semitic, and homophobic language and behavior in much of the wider society; another is the contrast between the violence of these incidents and the open expression of hatred and bigotry on the one hand, and the expectation of at least minimal civility in academic settings on the other.

Two relatively recent incidents that deal with the incendiary combination of race and gender point up the depth and pervasiveness of intergroup hostility on campuses all over the country. In the small rural town of Olivet, Michigan, at Olivet College, a school founded in 1844 by the abolitionist minister the Reverend John Shipherd as a "bastion of racial tolerance,"[2] a "racial brawl" involving approximately forty white students and twenty black students broke out one night in early April 1992. According to one report:

> Racial epithets were shouted at the black students as the two sides rumbled on the gray linoleum. Two students, one black, one white, were injured and briefly hospitalized.
>
> Afterward, blacks and whites who had crammed together for midterms and shared lunch money and dormitory rooms could not look each other in the face and were no longer on speaking terms.[3]

This incident was the culmination of increasing hostility among black and white students at Olivet. In the months prior to the incident, white male students had become more openly resentful of black men dating white women. Then, on April 1, a white female student claimed she had been attacked by four black students and left unconscious in a field near the campus. She was not hospitalized, and, despite a police investigation, no arrests were made. College officials were said to be skeptical about her accusations. Nonetheless, word spread, and later that night two trash cans were set on fire outside the dormitory rooms of black student leaders.

The specific incident that precipitated the brawl occurred the next night and again involved a white female student and black male students. Three male students, two black and one white, knocked on a female student's door to ask about a paper she was typing for one of the black students. The men later described the conversation as "civil." The woman, a sorority member, called her brother fraternity for help, saying she was being harassed by some male students. Within a few minutes, about fifteen members of the white fraternity Phi Alpha Pi arrived and confronted the two black men. More whites joined in, and black female students called more black males to even the numbers. Who threw the first punch is unclear; black students claim it was a white fraternity member. "What is clear," according to one report of the incident, "is that instead of seeing a roommate or a fellow sophomore, the students saw race."[4] Davonne Pierce, a dormitory resident assistant who is black, stated that his white friends shouted racial epithets at him as he was trying to break up the fight. He said to them, "How can you call me that when we were friends, when I let you borrow my notes?" But, he later recalled, "At that point, it was white against black. It was disgusting."[5]

After the incident, most of the fifty-five black students, who said they feared for their safety, left the college and went home. They made up 9 percent of the student body. Davonne Pierce stayed on campus but stated, "Obviously they don't want us here."[6] Dave Cook, a white junior who was one of the fraternity members involved in the fight, later said, "There were a lot of bonds that were broken that didn't need to be broken." He talked about his friendship with a black female student: "We would high-five each other and study for tests. But I don't know what she thinks about me. I don't know whether she's hating me or what. I didn't say one word to her, and she didn't say one word to me. Now she's gone."[7]

Racist behavior on college campuses is, of course, not limited to students. An incident involving a campus in New York State reveals the deep-seated stereotyping and bigotry of some college administrators, police officers, and citizens in communities all over the country. In the early morning of September 4, 1992, a seventy-seven-year-old woman was attacked in the small town of Oneonta, New York. She told the state police that she thought her attacker was a black man who used a "stiletto-style" knife and that his hands and arms were cut when she fended him off.[8] In response to a request from the police, the State University of New York at Oneonta gave the police a list of all of the black and Hispanic males registered at the college. Armed with the list, state and city police, along with campus security, tracked down the students "in their dormitories, at their jobs and in the shower." Each student was asked his whereabouts at the time the attack occurred, and each had to show his hands and his arms.

Michael Christian, the second of five children from a family headed by a single mother, grew up in the Bronx. His mother encouraged him to go to Oneonta to get him away from the problems of the city. Shortly after the attack, two state-police officers and representatives of campus security went to his dormitory room and woke him at 10:00 A.M. After asking him where he was at the time of the attack and demanding to see his hands, they said they wanted to question him downtown, and then they left. His roommate, Hopeton Gordon, a Jamaican student who had gone to high school in the Bronx with Mr. Christian, was questioned in front of other students from their dormitory. When the police asked to see his hands and he demanded their reasons, they responded, "Why? Do you have something to hide?" He said that he had felt humiliated in front of his suite mates and in front of female students.

This is not the first time black students, faculty, and administrators have been humiliated and have seen their civil rights trampled in Oneonta. Edward I. (Bo) Whaley, who went to the small town in upstate New York in 1968 as a student, remained, and is currently an instructor and counselor in the school's Educational Opportunity Program for disadvantaged students, recalls being followed by salespeople in Oneonta shops because they feared he would shoplift. He remembers the two minority ball players—one of whom he was trying to recruit—who were picked up as suspects in a rape case and had to pay for DNA testing even though someone else was convicted for the crime.

An admissions coordinator, Sheryl Champen, who is also black, was herself stopped by the state police the night of the attack. They demanded to see her identification before she could board a bus to New York City. It is unclear why the police questioned her and three other black women traveling with children, who also had to show identification before boarding the bus, since the attacked woman had reported that the person who assaulted her was a man. Their only common characteristic was race. When she heard about the treatment of the students of color, Ms. Champen said, "I was devastated, ashamed of being an admissions coordinator. Am I setting them up?" She feels that the behavior of the police was not an example of overeagerness to solve a crime. After recounting thirteen years of incidents that had begun when she was a first-year student at SUNY/Oneonta, she stated, "I know what it was. It was a chance to humiliate niggers."[9]

The release of the names of the 125 black and Hispanic students not only violated their privacy (and their right to be presumed innocent until proven guilty) but also violated the Family Educational Rights and Privacy Act of 1974 (also known as the Buckley Amendment). Following the incident, the vice-president who authorized the release of the names was suspended for one month without pay and demoted. The president of SUNY/Oneonta called using the list in the investigation "an affront to individual dignity and human rights."[10]

Though each of these events is unique and a product of the particular social environment, demographics, personalities, and stresses at the particular institution, during the late 1980s and early 1990s campuses were rife with similar episodes. A Brown student describes one incident at her university:

It was April 25, 1989, the end of spring term. . . . Students . . . were preparing for Spring Weekend, an annual fling before final exams.

That day, found scrawled in large letters across an elevator door in Andrews dormitory were the words, NIGGERS GO HOME. Over the next 24 hours, similar racial epithets were found on the doors of several women of color living in that hall; on the bathroom doors WOMEN was crossed out and replaced with NIGGERS, MEN was crossed out, replaced with WHITE. And in that same women's bathroom, a computer-printed flyer was found a day later which read: "Once upon a time Brown was a place where a white man could go to class without having to look at little black faces or little yellow faces or little brown faces except when he went to take his meals. Things have been going downhill since the kitchen help moved into the classroom. Keep white supremcy [sic] alive! Join the Brown Chapter of the KKK."[11]

Seven years earlier, the *Dartmouth Review* had set the standard for racist denigration by publishing an article ridiculing black students. The article was entitled "Dis Sho' Ain't No Jive, Bro," and read in part: "Dese boys be saying that we be comin hee to Dartmut an' not takin' the classics. . . . We be culturally 'lightened, too. We be takin hard courses in many subjects, like Afro-Am studies . . . and who bee mouthin' bout us not bein' good read?"[12]

During the late 1980s, the University of Michigan experienced several racist incidents. One of the most infamous took place in 1988, when a poster mocking the slogan of the United Negro College Fund was hung in a classroom. It read "Support the K.K.K. College Fund. A mind is a terrible thing to waste—especially on a nigger."[13]

Violent behavior has also been part of the cultural climate over the past decade. In February 1991, two black students from the University of Maine were allegedly assaulted by nine white men. The two students, both twenty-one, were driving in downtown Orono when approximately a dozen white men attacked their car and shouted, "Nigger, get out of here." When they got out of the car to see what was going on, the two men were kicked and beaten. Three students from the university were among those who attacked the students.[14]

Incidents have not been limited to one kind of school, but have occurred at private as well as public, urban and rural, large and small, at Ivy League as well as less prestigious, little-known institutions. . . .

According to the Anti-Defamation League, anti-Semitic incidents on college campuses have risen sharply in recent years, from fifty-four in 1988 to over double that number, 114, in 1992.[15] In February 1990, at American University in Washington, D.C., anti-Semitic graffiti were spray-painted on the main gate and on a residence hall. On the gate were painted a Star of David, an equal sign, and a swastika. On the dormitory was sprayed an expletive followed by "Israel Zionist."[16] In 1991, at California State University at Northridge, a ceremonial hut used to celebrate the Jewish holiday of Sukkoth was vandalized with anti-Semitic writing. In addition to swastikas,

"Hi' [sic] Hitler" and "Fuckin [sic] Jews" defaced the informative signs and flyers that decorated the hut.[17] Two months earlier, Dr. Leonard Jeffries, Jr., then chair of the African-American Studies department at the City College of New York, delivered a speech at a black cultural festival in which he spoke of "a conspiracy, planned and plotted and programmed out of Hollywood" by "people called Greenberg and Weisberg and Trigliani." He went on to say that "Russian Jewry had a particular control over the movies and their financial partners, the Mafia, put together a financial system of destruction of black people."[18]

Gay bashing has also been widely visible on college campuses. A Syracuse University fraternity, Alpha Chi Rho, was suspended by its national organization in 1991 for selling T-shirts with antihomosexual slogans, including one advocating violence against gays. On the front the shirts said "Homophobic and Proud of It!" and on the back, "Club Faggots Not Seals!" The picture illustrating the words was of a muscled crow, the fraternity's symbol, holding a club and standing over a faceless figure lying on the ground. Next to them is a seal hoisting a mug of beer.[19]

During the same year, *Peninsula,* a conservative campus magazine at Harvard, published an issue entirely devoted to the subject of homosexuality. The magazine called homosexuality a "bad alternative" to heterosexuality and stated in its introduction that "homosexuality is bad for society."[20] Within one hour of the magazine's distribution, the door of a gay student's room was defaced with antihomosexual words.

But, of course, discrimination does not need to be physical or perpetrated by students to wound, and to exclude some from mainstream college life. The football coach at the University of Colorado has called homosexuality "an abomination" and has supported a statewide group working to limit gay rights.[21] In 1992, the governor of Alabama signed legislation prohibiting gay student groups from receiving public money or using buildings at state universities.[22]

Sexual harassment and assault have been reported on campuses across the country. . . . Perhaps the most disturbing account of sexual harassment has been described by Carol Burke, currently an associate dean at Johns Hopkins University, about events at the U.S. Naval Academy, where she taught for seven years.[23] Marching chants—or "cadence calls," as they are called in the navy—provide a window into the macho male culture fostered at the academy, a culture that simultaneously celebrates the power of men and violence toward women. As Burke states:

> Cadence calls not only instill mutual solidarity but resurrect the
> Casey Jones of American ballad tradition as a brave pilot who
> survives the crash of his plane only to subdue women with greater
> ferocity:
>
> > Climbed all out with his dick in his hand.
> > Said, "Looky here, ladies, I'm a hell of a man."

> Went to his room and lined up a hundred . . .
> Swore up and down he'd fuck everyone.
> Fucked ninety-eight till his balls turned blue.
> Then he backed off, jacked off, and fucked the other two.

Members of the academy's Male Glee Club while away the hours on bus trips back from concerts by singing a particularly sadistic version of the song "The Candy Man":

> THE S&M MAN
>
> Who can take a chain saw,
> Cut the bitch in two,
> Fuck the bottom half
> and give the upper half to you. . . .
>
> The S&M Man, the S&M Man
> The S&M Man cause he mixes it with love
> and makes the hurt feel good!
>
> Who can take a bicycle,
> Then take off the seat,
> Set his girlfriend on it
> Ride her down a bumpy street. . . .
>
> Who can take an ice pick
> Ram it through her ear
> Ride her like a Harley,
> As you fuck her from the rear. . . .

Lest we think that such lyrics are sung only at the U.S. Naval Academy, the following incident took place at the Phi Kappa Psi fraternity at UCLA in 1992:

> A group of fraternity brothers waited outside the door. They serenaded the rape victim inside, cheering a brother on as if it were a football game. To the tune of "The Candy Man," they sang, "Who can take his organ / Dip it in vaseline / Ram it up inside you till it tickles your spleen / The S and M man, the S and M man / The S and M man can / cause he mixes it with love and / makes the hurtin feel good."
>
> UCLA's administration looked the other way this spring as Phi Kappa Psi fraternity brothers distributed a songbook with lyrics glorifying necrophilia, rape and violent torture of women. Although a 1991 suspension for violation of alcohol and other policies forced the fraternity to implement pledge education programs and forums on sexism and homophobia, the recent songbook controversy reveals the inadequacies of such programs.[24]

In March 1992, *Together,* a feminist magazine at UCLA, "exposed" the songbook that was left anonymously in their office.[25] When asked about the songs, an assistant vice-chancellor of the university first responded, "What's the problem? They are just erotic lyrics." Later, when questioned by the media, he stated, "I was horrified, revolted, shocked and embarrassed. This book is sexist, homophobic and promoted violence." The president of Phi Kappa Psi claimed that the "lyrics are a joke [and] so exaggerated that it is . . . ridiculous to say these songs promote violence against women."

Nevertheless, it is clear that fraternities have been in the forefront of bias-related incidents. Among the most serious incidents occurred at a University of Rhode Island fraternity. An eighteen-year-old female first-year student claimed she was raped during a fraternity party while at least five other men watched. During the investigation a former student committed suicide just hours before he was to be questioned by the police. In this case, as in many others, not only had the fraternity members been drinking heavily but often the victims as well. . . .[26]

Over the past several years, an increasing number of rapes have been reported at campuses across the country. . . . Most studies indicate that alcohol is involved, on the part of the victim as well as the perpetrator. A national study of women at thirty-two institutions of higher education in the U.S. found that 15 percent of college women said they had experienced attempted intercourse by the threat of force and 12 percent said they had experienced attempted intercourse by the use of alcohol or drugs.[27] Recent data plus in-depth studies of individual cases have made it clear that acquaintance rape is far more common than stranger rape in the United States. According to David Beatty, the public-policy director of the National Victim Center, a Washington-based advocacy group, "There is no question that acquaintance rape is more common than stranger rape. No one has the exact numbers, but the consensus is that probably in 80 to 85 percent of all rape cases, the victim knows the defendant."[28]

Many questions have been raised about acquaintance rape since the surge of reported cases has been noted across the country. Notorious cases such as the one involving William Kennedy Smith, in which rape was not proved, and the one involving Mike Tyson, in which the verdict was guilty, have also raised many questions: What is rape? Must physical force be used? When does "no" mean "no" and when is it part of a mating ritual? What about plying a woman with drugs or alcohol and then, when she is too inebriated or out of control to protest effectively, having sex with her? Is that rape?

An incident that came to be known as the "St. John's case" is a vivid and heart-wrenching example of the difficulties of establishing the parameters of acquaintance rape and of prosecuting the alleged perpetrators:

> As she recalled it, the evening of March 1, 1990, a Thursday, began
> ordinarily enough: the St. John's University student took target

practice with another member of the school's rifle club and bantered with him and the coach about everything from the coach's shabby clothing to the other student's love life.

But when the evening ended about seven hours later, as the 22-year-old woman later testified, she had been "forced" to drink nearly three cups of mixture of orange soda and vodka and had been disrobed, ogled, fondled, berated and sodomized by at least seven St. John's students, including her acquaintance from the rifle club. The debauchery began in a house near the Jamaica, Queens, campus; then she was transported, semiconscious and disheveled, to a second house where a party was underway and the assault continued.

Later, she said, she heard the men debating what to do with her. One asked, "What if she talks?" Another replied: "So what? Remember Tawana Brawley? Nobody believed her. Nobody will believe this one."[29]

And, of course, he was partially right. After months of publicity and an extensive trial, after two students pleaded guilty to lesser charges while essentially corroborating the young woman's story, three of the defendants were found not guilty and the final defendant interrupted his trial to plead guilty to sharply reduced charges but, in so doing, admitted that he had done everything he had been accused of.

As newspaper accounts stressed, the case "rocked" the ten-thousand-student university, the country's largest Roman Catholic institution of higher education, and the surrounding community. Adding to the explosive nature of the accusations — that someone the female student knew took her back to a house where several of the accused lived and plied her with alcohol, and then, when she was on the couch with her eyes closed, appearing helpless, he and other male students fondled the woman and made her perform oral sex on them — all six defendants were white and the young woman was black. None of the six defendants were convicted of the original felony charges against them.

Perhaps the most disturbing analysis of rape on college campuses is anthropologist Peggy Reeves Sanday's shocking study of fraternity gang rape. Also known as "gang banging," the phenomenon of "pulling train" refers to a "group of men lining up like train cars to take turns having sex with the same woman."[30] Bernice Sandler, one of the authors of a report issued in 1985 by the American Association of American Colleges, has reported finding more than seventy-five documented cases of gang rape in recent years. These incidents, which occurred at all kinds of institutions — "public, private, religiously affiliated, Ivy League, large and small" — share a common pattern:

> A vulnerable young woman, one who is seeking acceptance or who is high on drugs or alcohol, is taken to a room. She may or may not agree to have sex with one man. She then passes out, or is

too weak or scared to protest, and a train of men have sex with her. Sometimes the young woman's drinks are spiked without her knowledge, and when she is approached by several men in a locked room, she reacts with confusion and panic. Whether too weak to protest, frightened, or unconscious, as has been the case in quite a number of instances, anywhere from two to eleven or more men have sex with her.[31]

The specific case that is the centerpiece of Sanday's study involves a young woman, Laurel, who was known to have serious drinking and drug problems. The evening in question, she was drunk on beer and had taken "four hits of LSD" before going to a fraternity-house party. According to her account, she fell asleep after the party in a room on the first floor. When she awoke, she was undressed. One of the fraternity members dressed her and carried her upstairs, where she claimed she was raped by five or six "guys." She said, in Sanday's words, that she was "barely conscious and lacked the strength to push them off her."[32] This account was corroborated by another woman, a friend of the fraternity members, who felt that, because Laurel was incapable of consenting to sex, she had been raped. The fraternity brothers never publicly admitted to any wrongdoing; they claimed throughout the investigation that Laurel had "lured" them into a "gang bang," which they preferred to call an "express."

In this study, Sanday claims that "coercive sexual behavior" is prevalent on college campuses and that rape is "the means by which men programmed for violence and control use sexual aggression to display masculinity and to induct younger men into masculine roles."[33] Sanday continues her analysis:

> [The] male participants brag about their masculinity and . . . [the] female participants are degraded to the status of what the boys call "red meat" or "fish." The whole scenario joins men in a no-holds-barred orgy of togetherness. The woman whose body facilitates all of this is sloughed off at the end like a used condom. She may be called a "nympho" or the men may believe that they seduced her — a practice known as "working a yes out" — through promises of becoming a little sister, by getting her drunk, by promising her love, or by some other means. Those men who object to this kind of behavior run the risk of being labeled "wimps" or, even worse in their eyes, "gays" or "faggots."[34]

As we have seen, a variety of groups have been perceived and treated as "the Other" — in Patricia Hill Collins' words, "viewed as an object to be manipulated and controlled"[35] — on college campuses over the past few years. Though many of the bias incidents have involved racial enmity and misunderstanding, anti-Semitism, homophobia, and blatant sexism have also been catalysts for hostile acts. Many academic institutions, concerned about oveitly demeaning, sometimes violent behavior as well as the far more subtle denigration of women and other minority groups, have attempted to address these problems through a variety of measures: speech codes; orientation programs for entering students that stress respect for diversity and the importance of civility; curriculum changes that focus on multiculturalism; hiring policies whose goals are to increase the number of women and members of minority groups on the faculty and staff of the institution; and the recruitment of more students of color. These measures, often employed to counter the ignorance, ethnocentrism, and anger within the college community, have themselves become the subject of controversy and debate. Both academic and popular discourse have focused far more on political correctness, on affirmative action, and on changes in the curriculum than on the hate incidents and violence that continue to occur. Speech codes at the universities of Wisconsin and Michigan became front-page news; discussions of what and who was p.c. seemed ubiquitous; and the pros and cons of a multicultural curriculum have been debated in university governing bodies and editorial meetings across the country.

NOTES

1. Patricia Hill Collins, *Black Feminist Thought: Knowledge, Consciousness, and the Politics of Empowerment* (Boston: Unwin Hyman, 1990), pp. 68, 225.
2. Isabel Wilkerson, "Racial Tension Erupts Tearing a College Apart," *New York Times*, April 13, 1992.
3. Ibid.
4. Ibid.
5. Ibid.
6. Ibid.
7. Ibid.
8. Diana Jean Schemo, "Anger over List Divides Blacks and College Town," *New York Times*, September 27, 1992.
9. Ibid.
10. "College Official Who Released List of Black Students Is Demoted," *New York Times*, September 18, 1992.
11. N'Tanya Lee, "Racism on College Campuses," *Focus* (monthly magazine of the Joint Center for Political Studies), Special Social Policy Issue, August/September 1989.
12. Ibid.
13. Michele Collison, "For Many Freshmen, Orientation Now Includes Efforts to Promote Racial Understanding," *Chronicle of Higher Education*, September 7, 1988.
14. Denise Goodman, "Racial Attack Jolts U. of Maine," *Boston Globe*, February 23, 1991.
15. "ADL 1992 Audit of Anti-Semitic Incidents: Overall Numbers Decrease but Campus Attacks Are Up," *On the Frontline* (monthly newsletter published by the Anti-Defamation League), March 1993.
16. "Anti-Semitic Slurs Are Painted: Campus Reacts," *New York Times*, February 11, 1990.

17. Sharon Kaplan, "Hillel Hut Vandalized with Anti-Semitic Graffiti," *Daily Sundial* (California State University, Northridge), September 26, 1991.

18. James Barron, "Professor Steps off a Plane into a Furor over His Words," *New York Times,* August 15, 1991.

19. "Anti-Gay Shirts Oust Syracuse Fraternity," *USA Today,* June 28, 1991.

20. "Magazine Issue on Homosexuality Leads to Rallies," *New York Times,* December 22, 1991.

21. Dirk Johnson, "Coach's Anti-Gay Stand Ignites Rage," *New York Times,* March 15, 1992.

22. "Alabama Denies Aid to Gay Student Groups," *New York Times,* May 16, 1992.

23. Carol Burke, "Dames at Sea," *New Republic,* August 17, 24, 1992, pp. 16–20.

24. Katrina Foley, "Terror on Campus: Fraternities Training Grounds for Rape and Misogyny," *New Directions for Women,* September/October 1992, pp. 15, 29.

25. Ibid.

26. William Celis, 3d, "After Rape Charge, 2 Lives Hurt and 1 Destroyed," *New York Times,* November 12, 1990.

27. Peggy Reeves Sanday, *Fraternity Gang Rape: Sex, Brotherhood, and Privilege on Campus* (New York: New York University Press, 1990), pp. 23–24.

28. Tamar Lewin, "Tougher Laws Mean More Cases Are Called Rape," *New York Times,* May 27, 1991.

29. E. R. Shipp, "St. John's Case Offers 2 Versions of Events," *New York Times,* July 6, 1991.

30. Sanday, *Fraternity Gang Rape,* p. 1.

31. Ibid., pp. 1–2.

32. Ibid., p. 6.

33. Ibid., pp. 8–9.

34. Ibid., p. 11.

35. Collins, *Black Feminist Thought,* p. 69.

46

BLACK AND FEMALE
Reflections on Graduate School

bELL hOOKS

bell hooks (nee Gloria Watkins) is Distinguished Professor of English at City College in New York. Although hooks is mainly known as a feminist thinker, her writings cover a broad range of topics on gender, race, teaching and the significance of media for contemporary culture. She is the author of many books, the most recent of which is *We Real Cool: Black Men and Masculinity* (2004).

Searching for material to read in a class about women and race, I found an essay in *Heresies: Racism is the Issue* that fascinated me. I realized that it was one of the first written discussions of the struggles black English majors (and particularly black women) face when we study at predominantly white universities. The essay, "On Becoming A Feminist Writer," is by Carole Gregory. She begins by explaining that she has been raised in racially segregated neighborhoods but that no one had ever really explained "white racism or white male sexism." Psychically, she was not prepared to confront head-on these aspects of social reality, yet they were made visible as soon as she registered for classes:

> Chewing on a brown pipe, a white professor said, "English departments do not hire Negroes or women!" Like a guillotine, his voice sought to take my head off. Racism in my hometown was an economic code of etiquette which stifled Negroes and women.
>
> "If you are supposed to explain these courses, that's all I want," I answered. Yet I wanted to kill this man. Only my conditioning as a female kept me from striking his volcanic red face. My murderous impulses were raging.

Her essay chronicles her struggles to pursue a discipline which interests her without allowing racism or sexism to defeat and destroy her intellectual curiosity, her desire to teach. The words of this white male American Literature professor echo in her mind years later when she finds employment difficult,

bell hooks (1989), "Black and Female: Reflections on Graduate School" from *Talking Back: Thinking Feminist, Thinking Black*. Reprinted with the permission of South End Press and Between the Lines.

when she confronts the reality that black university teachers of English are rare. Although she is writing in 1982, she concludes her essay with the comment:

> Many years ago, an American Literature professor had cursed the destiny of "Negroes and women." There was truth in his ugly words. Have you ever had a Black woman for an English teacher in the North? Few of us are able to earn a living. For the past few years, I have worked as an adjunct in English. Teaching brings me great satisfaction; starving does not. . . . I still remember the red color of the face which said, "English departments do not hire Negroes or women." Can women change this indictment? These are the fragments I add to my journal.

Reading Carole Gregory's essay, I recalled that in all my years of studying in English department classes, I had never been taught by a black woman. In my years of teaching, I have encountered students both in English classes and other disciplines who have never been taught by black women. Raised in segregated schools until my sophomore year of high school, I had wonderful black women teachers as role models. It never occurred to me that I would not find them in university classrooms. Yet I studied at four universities—Stanford, University of Wisconsin, University of Southern California, and the University of California, Santa Cruz—and I did not once have the opportunity to study with a black woman English professor. They were never members of the faculty. I considered myself lucky to study with one black male professor at Stanford who was visiting and another at the University of Southern California even though both were reluctant to support and encourage black female students. Despite their sexism and internalized racism, I appreciated them as teachers and felt they affirmed that black scholars could teach literature, could work in English departments. They offered a degree of support and affirmation, however relative, that countered the intense racism and sexism of many white professors.

Changing hiring practices have meant that there are increasingly more black professors in predominantly white universities, but their presence only mediates in a minor way the racism and sexism of white professors. During my graduate school years, I dreaded talking face-to-face with white professors, especially white males. I had not developed this dread as an undergraduate because there it was simply assumed that black students, and particularly black female students, were not bright enough to make it in graduate school. While these racist and sexist opinions were rarely directly stated, the message was conveyed through various humiliations that were aimed at shaming students, at breaking our spirit. We were terrorized. As an undergraduate, I carefully avoided those professors who made it clear that the presence of any black students in their classes was not desired. Unlike Carole Gregory's first encounter, they did not make direct racist statements. Instead, they communicated their message in subtle ways—forgetting to call your name when reading the roll, avoiding looking at you, pretending they do not hear you when you speak, and at times ignoring you altogether.

The first time this happened to me I was puzzled and frightened. It was clear to me and all the other white students that the professor, a white male, was directing aggressive mistreatment solely at me. These other students shared with me that it was not likely that I would pass the class no matter how good my work, that the professor would find something wrong with it. They never suggested that this treatment was informed by racism and sexism; it was just that the professor had for whatever "unapparent" reason decided to dislike me. Of course, there were rare occasions when taking a course meant so much to me that I tried to confront racism, to talk with the professor; and there were required courses. Whenever I tried to talk with professors about racism, they always denied any culpability. Often I was told, "I don't even notice that you are black."

In graduate school, it was especially hard to choose courses that would not be taught by professors who were quite racist. Even though one could resist by naming the problem and confronting the person, it was rarely possible to find anyone who could take such accusations seriously. Individual white professors were supported by white-supremacist institutions, by racist colleagues, by hierarchies that placed the word of the professor above that of the student. When I would tell the more supportive professors about racist comments that were said behind closed doors, during office hours, there would always be an expression of disbelief, surprise, and suspicion about the accuracy of what I was reporting. Mostly they listened because they felt it was their liberal duty to do so. Their disbelief, their refusal to take responsibility for white racism made it impossible for them to show authentic concern or help. One professor of 18th century literature by white writers invited me to his office to tell me that he would personally see to it that I would never receive a graduate degree. I, like many other students in the class, had written a paper in a style that he disapproved of, yet only I was given this response. It was often in the very areas of British and American literature where racism abounds in the texts studied that I would encounter racist individuals.

Gradually, I began to shift my interest in early American literature to more modern and contemporary works. This shift was influenced greatly by an encounter with a white male professor of American literature whose racism and sexism was unchecked. In his classes, I, as well as other students, was subjected to racist and sexist jokes. Any of us that he considered should not be in graduate school were the objects of particular scorn and ridicule. When we gave oral presentations, we were told our work was stupid, pathetic, and were not allowed to finish. If we resisted in any way, the situation worsened. When I went to speak with him about his attitude, I was told that I was not really graduate school material, that I should drop out. My anger surfaced and I began to shout, to cry. I remember yelling wildly, "Do you love me? And if you don't love me then how can you have any insight about my concerns and abilities? And who are you to make such suggestions on the basis of one class?" He of course was not making a suggestion. His was a course one had to pass to graduate. He was telling me that I could avoid the systematic abuse by simply dropping out. I would not drop out. I continued to work even though it was clear that I would not succeed, even as the persecution became more intense. And even though I constantly resisted.

In time, my spirits were more and more depressed. I began to dream of entering the professor's office with a loaded gun. There I would demand that he listen, that he experience the fear, the humiliation. In my dreams I could hear his pleading voice begging me not to shoot, to remain calm. As soon as I put the gun down he would become his old self again. Ultimately in the dream the only answer was to shoot, to shoot to kill. When this dream became so consistently a part of my waking fantasies, I knew that it was time for me to take a break from graduate school. Even so I felt as though his terrorism had succeeded, that he had indeed broken my spirit. It was this feeling that led me to return to graduate school, to his classes, because I felt I had given him too much power over me and I needed to regain that sense of self and personal integrity that I allowed him to diminish. Through much of my graduate school career, I was told that "I did not have the proper demeanor of a graduate student." In one graduate program, the black woman before me, who was also subjected to racist and sexist aggression, would tell me that they would say she was not as smart as me but she knew her place. I did not know my place. Young white radicals began to use the phrase "student as nigger" precisely to call attention to the way in which hierarchies within universities encouraged domination of the powerless by the powerful. At many universities the proper demeanor of a graduate student is exemplary when that student is obedient, when he or she does not challenge or resist authority.

During graduate school, white students would tell me that it was important not to question, challenge, or resist. Their tolerance level seemed much higher than my own or that of other black students. Critically reflecting on the differences between us, it was apparent that many of the white students were from privileged class backgrounds. Tolerating the humiliations and degradations we were subjected to in graduate school did not radically call into question their integrity, their sense of self-worth. Those of us who were coming from underprivileged class backgrounds, who were black, often were able to attend college only because we had consistently defied those who had attempted to make us believe we were smart but not "smart enough"; guidance counselors who refused to tell us about certain colleges because they already knew we would not be accepted; parents who were not necessarily supportive of graduate work, etc. White students were not living daily in a world outside campus life where they also had to resist degradation, humiliation. To them, tolerating forms of exploitation and domination in graduate school did not evoke images of a lifetime spent tolerating abuse. They would endure certain forms of domination and abuse, accepting it as an initiation process that would conclude when they became the person in power. In some ways they regarded graduate school and its many humiliations as a game, and they submitted to playing the role of subordinate. I and many other students, especially non-white students from non-privileged backgrounds, were unable to accept and play this "game." Often we were ambivalent about the rewards promised. Many of us were not seeking to be in a position of power over others. Though we wished to teach, we did not want to exert coercive authoritarian rule over others. Clearly those students who played the game best were usually white males and they did not face discrimination, exploitation, and abuse in many other areas of their lives.

Many black graduate students I knew were concerned about whether we were striving to participate in structures of domination and were uncertain about whether we could assume positions of authority. We could not envision assuming oppressive roles. For some of us, failure, failing, being failed began to look like a positive alternative, a way out, a solution. This was especially true for those students who felt they were suffering mentally, who felt that they would never be able to recover a sense of wholeness or well-being. In recent years, campus awareness of the absence of support for international students who have many conflicts and dilemmas in an environment that does not acknowledge their cultural codes has led to the development of support networks. Yet there has been little recognition that there are black students and other non-white students who suffer similar problems, who come from backgrounds where we learned different cultural codes. For example, we may learn that it is important not to accept coercive authoritarian rule from someone who is not a family elder—hence we may have difficulties accepting strangers assuming such a role.

Not long ago, I was at a small party with faculty from a major liberal California university, which until recently had no black professors in the English department who were permanent staff, though they were sometimes visiting scholars. One non-white faculty member and myself began to talk about the problems facing black graduate students studying in English departments. We joked about the racism within English departments, commenting that other disciplines were slightly more willing to accept study of the lives and works of non-white people, yet such work is rarely affirmed in English departments, where the study of literature usually consists of many works by white men and a few by white women. We talked about how some departments were struggling to change. Speaking about his department, he commented that they have only a few black graduate students, sometimes none, that at one time two black students, one male and one female, had been accepted and both had serious mental health problems. At departmental meetings, white faculty suggested that this indicated that black students just did not have the wherewithal to succeed in this graduate program. For a time, no black students were admitted. His story revealed that part of the burden these students may have felt, which many of us have felt, is that our performance will have future implications for all black students and this knowledge heightens one's performance anxiety from the very beginning.

Unfortunately, racist biases often lead departments to see the behavior of one black student as an indication of the way all black students will perform academically. Certainly, if individual white students have difficulty adjusting or succeeding within a graduate program, it is not seen as an indication that all other white students will fail.

The combined forces of racism and sexism often make the black female graduate experience differ in kind from that of the black male experience. While he may be subjected to racial biases, his maleness may serve to mediate the extent to which he will be attacked, dominated, etc. Often it is assumed that black males are better able to succeed at graduate school in English than black females. While many white scholars may be aware of a black male intellectual tradition, they rarely know about black female intellectuals. African-American intellectual traditions, like those of white people, have been male-dominated. People who know the names of W.E.B. Du Bois or Martin Delaney may have never heard of Mary Church Terrell or Anna Cooper. The small numbers of black women in permanent positions in academic institutions do not constitute a significant presence, one strong enough to challenge racist and sexist biases. Often the only black woman white professors have encountered is a domestic worker in their home. Yet there are no sociological studies that I know of which examine whether a group who has been seen as not having intellectual capability will automatically be accorded respect and recognition if they enter positions that suggest they are representative scholars. Often black women are such an "invisible presence" on campuses that many students may not be aware that any black women teach at the universities they attend.

Given the reality of racism and sexism, being awarded advanced degrees does not mean that black women will achieve equity with black men or other groups in the profession. Full-time, non-white women comprise less than 3 percent of the total faculty on most campuses. Racism and sexism, particularly on the graduate level, shape and influence both the academic performance and employment of black female academics. During my years of graduate work in English, I was often faced with the hostility of white students who felt that because I was black and female I would have no trouble finding a job. This was usually the response from professors as well if I expressed fear of not finding employment. Ironically, no one ever acknowledged that we were never taught by any of these black women who were taking all the jobs. No one wanted to see that perhaps racism and sexism militate against the hiring of black women even though we are seen as a group that will be given priority, preferential status. Such assumptions, which are usually rooted in the logic of affirmative action hiring, do not include recognition of the ways most universities do not strive to attain diversity of faculty and that often diversity means hiring one non-white person, one black person. When I and other black women graduate students surveyed English departments in the United States, we did not see masses of black women and rightly felt concerned about our futures.

Moving around often, I attended several graduate schools but finally finished my work at the University of California, Santa Cruz, where I found support despite the prevalence of racism and sexism. Since I had much past experience, I was able to talk with white faculty members before entering the program about whether they would be receptive and supportive of my desire to focus on African-American writers. I was given positive reassurance that proved accurate. More and more, there are university settings where black female graduate students and black graduate students can study in supportive atmospheres. Racism and sexism are always present, yet they do not necessarily shape all areas of graduate experience. When I talk with black female graduate students working in English departments, I hear that many of the problems have not changed, that they experience the same intense isolation and loneliness that characterized my experience. This is why I think it is important that black women in higher education write and talk about our experiences, about survival strategies. When I was having a very difficult time, I read *Working It Out.* Despite the fact that the academics who described the way in which sexism had shaped their academic experience in graduate school were white women, I was encouraged by their resistance, by their perseverance, by their success. Reading their stories helped me to feel less alone. I wrote this essay because of the many conversations I have had with black female graduate students who despair, who are frustrated, who are fearful that the experiences they are having are unique. I want them to know that they are not alone, that the problems that arise, the obstacles created by racism and sexism are real—that they do exist—they do hurt but they are not insurmountable. Perhaps these words will give solace, will intensify their courage, and renew their spirit.

PART VIII

Paid Work and Unemployment

Equality of educational opportunity, as discussed previously in the introduction to the readings on education, cannot produce equality in society. Once people enter or attempt to enter the workforce, they face three major obstacles. First, the economic structure blocks many people from finding any type of work at all. Second, the economic structure fails to provide enough jobs that pay a decent wage. Third, discrimination in the workplace limits the progress of many, either by keeping people out or by blocking their upward mobility. Our economic system privileges a small proportion of the population with large amounts of wealth and leaves a huge proportion with varying degrees of economic difficulty, including brutal poverty. This discrepancy is getting larger. In the United States in the 1990s, the richest 1 percent of households had more wealth than the bottom 95 percent. The net worth of the median U.S. household in 1997 was $49,900, down from $54,600 about 10 years earlier (adjusted for inflation). The net worth of the poorest fifth of households was negative $5,600 in 1997, while in 1983 it was negative $3,000. In 1995, nearly a fifth of U.S. households (18.5 percent) had zero net worth (e.g., had more debt than assets); this was up from 15.5 percent in 1983.[1] The racial wealth gap is even wider: whites enjoy a median net worth 10 times that of Blacks ($106,400 compared to $10,700), while Latinos' net worth is even lower—$3,000; 26 percent of Native Americans and 13 percent of Asian Americans are poor compared to 8 percent of whites.[2]

Many women on welfare struggle to provide basic needs for themselves and their children and face cutoffs when they reach the maximum time allowed on Temporary Assistance for Needy Families (TANF), the 1996 replacement for Aid to Families with Dependent Children (AFDC).

Progressive economists debate ways to redistribute U.S. wealth more fairly by creating a more socialistic economic structure, closing tax loopholes that benefit the rich, or redistributing some of the defense budget to social services and education. But politicians continue to support benefits for the rich and to cut social services. This situation has been exacerbated following September 11, 2001, as a larger proportion of federal and state budgets is now spent on defense and security and as tax revenues dropped following the downturn in the stock market.

Many people face the effects of discrimination in the workplace on the basis of gender, race, ability, sexual orientation, or other factors. This discrimination includes sexual and other harassment, blocked access to jobs or promotions, or wage gaps that privilege the earnings of certain groups over others. For example, occupations dominated by women or people of color generally have lower pay scales.[3] Discrimination and prejudice are sometimes confusingly subtle but often there nonetheless.[4] Disability or being gay or lesbian can serve as the kiss of death in some work situations.[5] Some recent examples include women earning 76.5 percent of men's wages for the same full-time work in 1999;[6] the exclusion of women from roles as ministers in the Southern Baptist Convention in June 2000;[7] the persistently different experiences of Black and white women in the business world;[8] the persistent harassment of gays and lesbians in the military, leading to more discharges than before the "don't ask, don't tell" policy;[9] and the dismal record of hiring women in most fire departments (not to mention the harassment the few women firefighters typically receive).[10] Around the world, the use of computers has left women segregated at the bottom of the technology hierarchy, as they have become the "data and keyboard drones" of the information world.[11] As an illustration of the pace at which women's wages are catching up with men's, sociologists Irene Padavik and Barbara Reskin report "Since 1964 when Congress outlawed pay discrimination based on sex, women have been catching up with men's earnings at a little less than a half cent per year. If this rate of progress continues, the sexes will not earn equal pay until 2055."[12]

The dearth of high-paying jobs combined with systematic discrimination against many groups leaves large numbers of people in the United States either without work or without adequate income. Even middle-class people are struggling to hold their own, no longer able to assume that they will do as well as their parents. Although home ownership is up because of very low interest rates, many people cannot afford to buy houses like the ones they grew up in, and others cannot buy houses at all.[13]

Even in high-paying contexts, sex discrimination continues. For example, Morgan Stanley recently decided to settle a sex discrimination case, paying $54 million to a group of past and present female employees in one of its securities divisions. Although denying guilt, it chose not to go to trial. It also agreed to provide diversity training focused on enhancing women's success in the firm. Other large securities firms (Merrill Lynch and Smith Barney) have reportedly paid more than $200 million to settle discrimination suits to women who worked for them.[14] Professional occupations can be especially stressful for upwardly-mobile people of color. In a study of middle class African American women, Veronica Chambers,[15] addressed the conflicts of upward mobility among black heterosexual women. The women she interviewed experienced isolation, feeling not at home in either white or black communities although some expressed satisfaction at overcoming obstacles.

Sexual harassment in the workplace is a very common experience for women and affects some men as well. In a study of women physicians, 32 percent reported unwanted sexual attention, and 48 percent reported the use of sexist teaching materials during their training.[16] In a 1991 survey by the U.S. Navy, 44 percent of enlisted women and 33 percent of female officers reported sexual harassment within the year prior to responding to the survey. By comparison, 8 percent of enlisted men and 2 percent of male officers reported sexual harassment in the same time period.[17] Work contexts obviously vary in relation to this issue, ranging from a pervasive sexualized atmosphere aimed at many women (as in the Mitsubishi case that settled for $34 million[18]), to isolated cases of harassment. The Supreme Court decided for the first time in

1998 that a male-male case of sexual harassment did qualify as sexual harassment under federal law, and other cases followed,[19] even though some people question the appropriateness of that definition of sexual harassment.[20]

Where a person is situated in the workplace affects their perception and experience of how fair the workplace is. In the Navy survey just mentioned, men perceived the equal opportunity climate in the Navy to be more positive than did women; white male officers had the most positive perceptions with African American women holding the least positive perceptions; and women who had been sexually harassed had more negative perceptions of the climate than did those who had not been sexually harassed. In another study that compared Black and white women in professional and managerial positions, sociologists Lynn Weber and Elizabeth Higginbotham found that the vast majority of white women perceived no race discrimination in their various workplaces, whereas a large majority of Black women did.[21]

By contrast, some equality gains have been made as Israeli women in 2000 won the right to serve in any army position including combat units;[22] as Japanese women won, in 2000, a sex discrimination case related to promotion and pay that was filed in 1987;[23] as boys have braved teasing and ridicule to become ballet dancers;[24] and as Pride at Work, a national organization of gay, lesbian, bisexual and transgendered labor activists, became an official constituency group of the AFL-CIO in August 1997.[25]

The conflict between work and family is a persistent and unresolved issue facing parents who work outside the home. Women's increased participation in the workforce has exacerbated this.[26] Some corporations are developing "family friendly" policies including such options as flex time, job sharing, child care, and paid family leave. But according to a recent study of one of the top 100 companies for working mothers identified by *Working Woman* magazine, policies that look good on paper are frequently not available to all workers; often this is a result of mothers being pressured not to use the policies.[27] Sociologist Arlie Hochschild, in her recent book *The Time Bind*, looks at the relationship between work and family and concludes that corporate culture, with its pressure to put in long hours at the office, is to blame for the bind most families are in. She argues for new social values that would encourage spending less time at work and more time with children, family, and community. In support of her position, she cites corporate experiments that have increased efficiency while saving time.[28]

The fate of Social Security is especially important to women. If President Bush succeeds in getting support to set up private investment accounts as alternatives to Social Security, women will end up proportionally worse off than men, according to the Institute for Women's Policy Research (IWPR). Among many reasons why the current system is better, IWPR points out that: "Women rely on Social Security for a larger part of their income in retirement than do men, because women are less likely to have income from pensions than men (30 percent vs. 47 percent) and their pension benefits are less than half of men's on average. Social Security provides more generous benefits to lower earnings for the amount of taxes paid, as compared with higher earnings. Because women have lower earnings on average than men, they benefit from this re-distribution toward lower earners. Since women's life expectancy is nearly five years longer than men (80 vs. 75), women rely disproportionately on survivors' benefits, and on the full cost of living adjustment in Social Security, which protects them from inflation as they age. Social Security provides benefits to living and surviving spouses. Despite their increasing employment and improved lifetime earnings, 34 percent of women still rely on the spouse benefits (based on their husbands' or ex-husbands' earnings records) for their retirement security." According to IWPR, the changes proposed by the Bush administration do not provide these same protections and are likely to greatly increase poverty levels among older women.[29]

The situation of women workers around the world varies depending on the social support offered by governments. Within Europe, for example, the number of women in paid work is highest in Scandinavia, apparently because of the availability of publicly funded child care. Women in Sweden and Finland had more children than in other European countries for the same reason.[30] On the other hand, some analysts observe that the presence of supportive family leave policies can reinforce gender segregation in the workplace.[31]

Globalization has had a huge impact on workers worldwide. U.S. corporations have moved many factories to parts of the world where wages are lower (see Enloe, this part). The plight of women who cannot earn a decent living in their home countries and who come to the United States as domestic workers is gaining attention, revealing situations in which the workers live isolated, lonely lives while someone else cares for their children far away in their home countries.[32] These immigrants share many of the experiences of invisibility and disempowerment experienced by Black domestic workers in the United States as described by sociologist Judith Rollins.[33]

An estimated 50,000 undocumented workers are trafficked to the United States each year to work as prostitutes, agricultural workers, sweatshop laborers, or domestic workers. Many are enslaved by their employers, have few rights, and often fear for their lives. Only in the late 1990s was there a serious move to prosecute perpetrators of involuntary servitude, especially sexual slavery.[34] Many women work in sweatshop conditions in both the United States and abroad, particularly in the garment industry.[35]

This part of this book looks at welfare reform (Sharon Hays), the effects of motherhood on earnings (Ann Crittendon), workplace discrimination against Asian American men (Ben Fong-Torres), affirmative action (Barbara Reskin), the effect of globalization on women's work and lives worldwide (Ehrenreich and Hochschild), the situation of enslaved domestic workers (Joy M. Zarembka), and the global sneaker industry (Cynthia Enloe). Implied or stated in these pieces are suggestions for empowerment at personal, organizational, and policy levels.

As you consider these readings, think about the economic issues that you and your family and friends have faced. Do you know anyone struggling with poverty? Have you observed income drop among parents who are primary caretakers for their children? How does Reskin's presentation of affirmative action compare to the ideas you had about affirmative action before you read her essay? Have you ever seen an Asian anchorman on TV? Do you think about domestic workers and the risks some of them run living in the U.S.? Do you ever think about who made your sneakers and what they got paid to do that? Finally, does the state of the economy seem to be affecting your ability to pay for your education?

NOTES

1. Holly Sklar, Chuck Collins, and Betsy Leondar-Wright, *Shifting Fortunes: The Perils of the Growing American Wealth Gap* (Boston, MA: United for a Fair Economy, 1999). www.faireconomy.org.

2. Meizhu Lui, *Doubly Divided: The Racial Wealth Gap* (Boston, MA: United for a Fair Economy, 2004). www.faireconomy.org.

3. Irene Padavik and Barbara Reskin, *Women and Men at Work*, 2nd Edition (Thousand Oaks, CA: Pine Forge Press, 2002), pp. 108–112.

4. Yanick St. Jean and Joe R. Feagin, "Racial Masques: Black Women and Subtle Gendered Racism," in Nijole V. Benokraitis, ed., *Subtle Sexism: Current Practices and Prospects for Change* (Thousand Oaks, CA: Sage, 1997), pp. 179–200.

5. For a discussion of discrimination against gay men in the workforce, see Martin P. Levine, "The Status of Gay Men in the Workplace," in Michael S. Kimmel and Michael A. Messner, eds., *Men's Lives*, 3rd ed. (Boston: Allyn & Bacon, 1995), pp. 212–24. Michelle Fine and Adrienne Asch report that it is estimated that between 65% and 76% of women with disabilities are unemployed: "Disabled Women: Sexism without the Pedestal," in Mary Jo Deegan and Nancy A. Brooks, eds., *Women and Disability: The Double Handicap* (New Brunswick, NJ: Transaction, 1985), pp. 6–22.

6. Associated Press, "Women Said to Earn 76.5% of Men's Wage," *The Boston Globe* (May 27, 2000), p. A10.

7. Brad Liston and Michael Paulson, "Southern Baptists Deliver a 'No' on Women as Pastors," *The Boston Globe* 257, no. 167 (June 15, 2000), p. A1.

8. Ella J. E. Bell and Stella M. Nkomo, *Our Separate Ways: Black and White Women and the Struggle for Professional Identity* (Boston: Harvard Business School Press, 2001).

9. Debbie Emery, "The Mother of All Witch Hunts," *Out* (June 1996), p. 176.

10. Joseph P. Kahn, "Under Fire," *The Boston Globe Magazine* (December 7, 1997), pp. 19ff; David Armstrong, "Brotherhood Under Fire: Big-City Departments Facing Reform of Closed Culture and Old-Boy Traditions," *The Boston Globe* (January 9, 2000), pp. A1ff.

11. Christa Wichterich, *The Globalized Woman: Reports from a Future of Inequality* (New York: Zed Books, 2000), p. 47.

12. Padavik and Reskin, *Women and Men at Work*, p. 146.

13. Katherine S. Newman, *Declining Fortunes: The Withering of the American Dream* (New York: Basic Books, 1993).

14. Patrick McGeehan, "Morgan Stanley Settles Bias Suit with $54 Million" *New York Times* (July 13, 2004), on-line version.

15. Veronica Chambers, *Having It All? Black Women and Success.* (New York: Doubleday, 2003).

16. M. Catherine Vukovich, "The Prevalence of Sexual Harassment among Female Family Practice Residents in the United States," *Violence and Victims* 11, no. 2 (1996), pp. 175–80.

17. Carol E. Newell, Paul Rosenfeld, and Amy L. Culbertson, "Sexual Harassment Experiences and Equal Opportunity Perceptions of Navy Women," *Sex Roles: A Journal of Research* 32 no. 3–4 (February 1995), pp. 159–68.

18. Harriet Brown, "After the Suit, How Do Women Fit in at Mitsubishi?" *Ms.* IX, no. 2 (September/October 1998), pp. 32–36.

19. Thomas M. Sipkins and Joseph G. Schmitt, "Same-Sex Harassers Get Equal Time; After 'Oncale,' Employers Should Consider Implementing Sexual Harassment Policies That Deal with Same-Sex Perpetrators," *The National Law Journal* 20, no. 41 (June 8, 1998), p. B7, col. 1; Stephanie Ebbert, "Man Wins Same-Sex Lawsuit Judgment," *The Boston Globe* (June 19, 1998), p. D40.

20. Elizabeth Pryor Johnson and Michael A. Puchades, "Same-Gender Sexual Harassment: But Is It Discrimination Based on Sex?" *Florida Bar Journal* (December, 1995), pp. 79–160.

21. Lynn Weber and Elizabeth Higginbotham, "Black and White Professional-Managerial Women's Perceptions of Racism and Sexism in the Workplace," in Elizabeth Higginbotham and Mary Romero, eds., *Women and Work: Exploring Race, Ethnicity, and Class* (Thousand Oaks, CA: Sage, 1997), pp. 153–75.

22. Associated Press, "Israeli Law Lifts Barriers for Women Soldiers," *The Boston Globe* (January 5, 2000), p. 14.

23. Yuri Kageyama, "Women Win Bias Case in Japan," *The Boston Globe* (December 23, 2000), p. A16.

24. Stephen Kiehl, "Difficult Journey of Dance: Braving Taunts, More Boys Turn to Art of Ballet," *The Boston Globe* (August 2, 1998), p. B1.

25. Carol Schachet, "Gay and Lesbian Labor Gains a Voice: Pride at Work Is Officially Recognized by the AFL-CIO," *Resist* 7, no. 5 (June 1998), pp. 1–3.

26. For a history of women's participation in the paid labor force see Elizabeth Higginbotham, "Introduction" in Elizabeth Higginbotham and Mary Romero, eds., *Women and Work: Exploring Race, Ethnicity, and Class* (Thousand Oaks, CA: Sage, 1997), pp. xv–xxxii.

27. Jane Kiser, "Behind the Scenes at a 'Family Friendly' Workplace," *Dollars and Sense*, no. 215 (January/February 1998), pp. 19–21.

28. Arlie Russell Hochschild, *The Time Bind: When Work Becomes Home and Home Becomes Work* (New York: Metropolitan Books, 1997).

29. Institute for Women's Policy Research, "Women and Social Security," 2005. http://womenandsocialsecurity.org/Women%5FSocial%5Security.

30. Christa Wichterich, *The Globalized Woman: Reports from a Future of Inequality* (New York: Zed Books, 2000), p. 99.

31. Deborah Figart and Ellen Mutari, "It's About Time: Will Europe Solve the Work/Family Dilemma?" *Dollars and Sense* (January/February 1998), pp. 27–31.

32. Pierette Hondagneu-Sotelo, *Doméstica: Immigrant Workers Cleaning and Caring in the Shadows of Affluence* (Berkeley, CA: University of California Press, 2001); Rhacel Salazar Parreñas, *Servants of Globalization: Women, Migration, and Domestic Work* (Stanford, CA: Stanford University Press, 2001); Grace Chang, *Disposable Domestics: Immigrant Women Workers in the Global Economy* (Boston: South End Press, 2000).

33. Judith Rollins, *Between Women: Domestics and Their Employers* (Philadelphia: Temple University Press, 1985).

34. Michelle Herrera Mulligan, "Fields of Shame," *Latina* (May 2000), pp. 110ff.

35. Miriam Ching Yoon Louie, *Sweatshop Warriors: Immigrant Women Workers Take on the Global Factory* (Boston: South End Press, 2001).

47
_____

THE "SUCCESS" OF WELFARE REFORM

SHARON HAYS

Sharon Hays is Professor in the Department of Sociology and Women's Studies at the University of Virginia and the author of *The Cultural Contradictions of Motherhood*.

Most welfare mothers have not been activists for the rights of the poor. Some have joined or established poverty advocacy groups to publicly protest the Personal Responsibility Act. Others have individually lodged their complaints against changes in the system, with the quiet determination of Nadia or the louder frustration of Sandra. But the majority of welfare mothers, like the majority of Americans, have expressed their support for the "end to welfare as we know it."[1]

Poor mothers' support for welfare reform is the single most striking indication that welfare mothers are not the social "outsiders" portrayed in the Personal Responsibility Act. Most welfare mothers share the core values of most Americans. They share a concern with contemporary problems in work and family life and a commitment to finding solutions—including the overhaul of the welfare system. The trouble is, welfare reform was founded on the assumption that welfare mothers do not share American values and are, in fact, personally responsible for *undermining* our nation's moral principles. The policies and procedures instituted by welfare reform have thus been aimed at "fixing" these women.

This paradoxical state of affairs raises questions of just who has the right to fix whom, and what, exactly, is broken and in need of repair. Still, . . . the problems in work and family life that informed welfare reform are real problems that have impacted us all. Similarly, the broader moral principles implied in the cultural logic of reform—principles of independence, productivity, citizenship, strong families, community spirit, and obligations to others—are worthy and widely shared. Yet from the start, welfare reform was also plagued by cultural distortions, exclusionary stereotypes, and a narrowly drawn and internally inconsistent vision of what counts as the proper commitment to work, family, and nation. And the policies instituted by welfare reform have left the nation's poorest mothers in a position in which no matter how committed they are to the work ethic and family values, under current conditions, the majority will remain unable to achieve either the model of the happily married homemaker or the model of the successful supermom, just as the majority will remain unable to lift their families out of poverty.

The inadequacies of welfare reform clearly follow from structured inequalities in American society. But the inadequacies of welfare reform also follow from a serious problem in the cultural logic of personal responsibility itself.

The notion of personal responsibility denies the embeddedness of all individuals in the wider society and their reliance on it. It is an image of unfettered individualism—of every man, woman, and child as an island unto themselves. This logic most obviously neglects the "dependency" of children and the fact that no parent is "unfettered." It also neglects the importance, the reality, and the necessity of wider social ties and connections. It makes invisible, in other words, our interdependence.

It is this failure to take account of the full measure of our interdependence that allows for the construction of "us-versus-them" scenarios that not only demonize welfare recipients but also call into question the values and behaviors of all of us who find ourselves unable to mimic the mythological model of perfected self-reliance: seamlessly juggling our multiple commitments without ever needing to depend on our friends, our families, our neighbors, or the nation to support us. This individualistic logic similarly undergirds our privatization of the work of caring for others, leaving it hidden, undervalued, and inadequately supported. And this logic upholds the privatization of the labor market, leaving it insufficiently regulated by the public and allowing competitive, profit-seeking employers to ignore the existence of children, circumvent the minimum standards for sustenance, and exploit the most vulnerable among us.

All this explains why, in the long run, the Personal Responsibility Act will not be a law we can proudly hail as a national "success." Women, children, . . . people of color, and the poor will be hardest hit. But the consequences of reform will leave nearly all of us losers, in economic, political, and moral terms. To make sense of this and to examine how the road to hell can, in fact, be paved with good intentions (or at least a mix of good intentions, harsh realities, and incomplete moral reasoning), let me begin again, with the principles and problems that initially prompted this massive change in law.

Shared Values, Symbolic Boundaries, and the Politics of Exclusion

In responding to welfare reform, the welfare mothers I met often offered a perfect mirror of the complex mix of higher values, genuine concerns, exclusionary judgments, and cultural distortions that informed the Personal Responsibility Act. One mother, Denise, captured nearly all these elements in her response, offering the full range of the more prominent patterns I encountered and mimicking the words of [many other] welfare mothers. . . . A black woman with two daughters, at the time I met her Denise was recently employed at Mailboxes-R-Us for $6.50 an hour and was making ends meet with the help of welfare reform's (time-limited) income supplement, transportation vouchers, and childcare subsidy. This is what she had to say when I asked her for her overall assessment of reform:

> When I was younger, years ago, anybody could get on welfare. And I think that's what's good about welfare reform. People have to show some sort of *initiative*. Before, the welfare office didn't pressure you to find a job, but now they do. And I think that's a good system. They've really helped me out a lot.
>
> Plus, I think people are sick of having to pay their tax money. They say, "Look, I am out here working, and I don't make that much money, and I have kids of my own. I'm tired of having to take care of your babies." People are getting upset and it's rightly so. I think it's rightly so.
>
> And lots of people abuse the system. You see it every day. A lot of people that you run into and lot of people that live in your neighborhood—I mean a lot of people do hair and get paid in cash. And I hear about these people who had children just to get a welfare check, just because they didn't want to go out and work. I've seen women that's on welfare, they're looking good and their children look poorly. I see that happening.
>
> Some of them are lazy and don't want to work. I think that some just want to stay home with their kids. But then they should have thought about that before they had the children.

At this point in her argument, Denise had hit upon nearly all the concerns of hardworking Americans who conscientiously pay their taxes, raise their children, and struggle to make it all work. She had also hit upon nearly all the well-worn stereotypes of poor mothers—implicitly labeling them as welfare cheats, lazy couch potatoes, promiscuous breeders, and lousy parents. But Denise wasn't finished.

> I think some people on welfare are being greedy—taking away from people that are homeless, people that really need the help. I mean there are truly people out there living at the Salvation Army. I hear tell that there are people who can't get in those shelters because they're so full. And I think that's the sad part about it. Those women that don't really need welfare shouldn't be taking money away from the homeless.
>
> But there are gonna be problems. Like, there are women that want to go out there and get a job, but who's gonna watch their kids? And there are people who will still need that little extra help

to pay the bills. So that's a glitch in the system. And some of these women are already pregnant, and they're already poor, and they really do need the help. I think that we have to weigh things and maybe investigate a bit more. There are a lot of people that are disabled and need welfare; there are women who have been abused. Some of those people that are in a lot of trouble, you know, their kids are gonna be the ones you see on TV, shooting up the schools and everything.[2]

I know a lot of people say that this welfare reform is a good thing—and it is really gonna help a lot of people. But in the end things are probably gonna get worse. There's gonna be more crime 'cause people can't get on welfare and they're not gonna have any money and they're gonna go out and rob people, and kill people. And it happens, it happens. So that's a problem with the system.

If Denise had been responding to a national survey, "Do you approve of welfare reform?" her answer would simply be coded as a "yes." Yet you can't help noticing that she has a number of mixed feelings on this question.

This same sort of ambivalence is evident in Americans' response to welfare reform. Although most are positive about reform, the majority of Americans also say that they are "very" concerned about poverty. Most additionally believe that the national standards for poverty are set too low, stating that a family of four with an income of less than $20,000 is, in fact, "poor," even if the federal government does not label them as such. More significantly, a majority of Americans are in favor of further aid to the poor—including the expansion of job opportunities, tax credits, medical coverage, subsidies for childcare and housing, and the provision of better schools. Still, Americans worry about the government's ability to appropriately and effectively provide that aid, and many don't want to have to pay higher taxes to subsidize the poor.[3]

Denise is also much like most Americans in that the central moral categories she uses to frame her response are work and family values, independence and commitment to others, self-sufficiency and concern for the common good. Women should take the "initiative," they should work, they should not rely on the help of others, they should support their own children, they should think twice before they give birth to children they cannot afford to raise. At the same time, people should not be "greedy," they should care for those who are more vulnerable than themselves, and they should consider the impact of their actions on the nation as a whole. All this makes perfect sense, and all this resonates perfectly with our nation's values. The trouble is that managing these commitments is hard enough if you have a spouse, a house in the suburbs, two cars in the garage, good health insurance, reliable childcare, a willingness to make compromises, a great deal of determination, empathy, and energy, and a household income of $60,000. The more items on this list that you lack, the tougher it becomes to live up to this demanding system of values. Denise, like most Americans, implicitly understands these "glitches." Yet her reasoning becomes a bit cloudy at this point—in large measure, I would argue, because of the loophole provided by the final significant element in her response to welfare reform.

It is hard to miss that Denise's support for the Personal Responsibility Act is predicated on the construction of a moral distinction between herself and all those "other" bad welfare mothers who fail to live up to social standards. Denise is making use of what Michèle Lamont has called "symbolic boundaries" to develop an implicit hierarchy of social worth. Like most people who use this strategy, she is not simply engaging in a mean-spirited attack on others or a self-interested attempt to highlight her own virtues. These symbolic boundaries also allow her to positively affirm shared values and specify the proper way to live one's life.[4]

Yet, given that many observers consider Denise herself a member of the deviant group she describes, the fact that she and other welfare mothers persist in this technique is curious. It testifies not just to the power and ubiquity of boundary making as a social strategy, it also speaks to the power and ubiquity of the demonization of poor single mothers. When welfare mothers distinguish themselves from those other "bad" women, they are calling on widely disseminated negative images of welfare mothers. These images seem to match all those strangers, those loud neighbors, those people who appear to spend their lives hanging out on street corners. The lives of the women they actually know, on the other hand, seem much more complex, their actions more understandable, their futures more redeemable.

The demonization of welfare mothers and the dichotomy between "us" and "them" can thus provide a dividing line that allows Denise and other Americans to say, if some welfare mothers can't make it, it's not because the problems they encounter in trying to manage work and family and still keep their heads above water are that bad or that widespread; it's because they didn't try hard enough or weren't good enough. Symbolic boundaries thus become *exclusionary* boundaries—simultaneously offering a means to affirm shared values and a means to think of "outsiders" in terms of individual blame. The obvious problem, in Denise's case, is that her own logic might ultimately leave her as one of the "accused." In broader terms, this exclusionary process means that all those Americans who are suffering from childcare woes, second shifts, inadequate health insurance, precarious jobs, unmanageable debt, and unstable communities are left to feel that their problems are *personal* problems for which no public solutions can be found.

Reading the Good News

In the months and years following welfare reform, newspaper headlines offered a seemingly unequivocal vision of success: "10,000 Welfare Recipients Hired by Federal Agencies." "Number on Welfare Dips Below 10 Million." "White House Releases Glowing Data on Welfare." "Businesses Find Success in Welfare-to-Work Program." "The Welfare Alarm That Didn't Go Off."

"Most Get Work after Welfare."[5] The message was clearly upbeat, congratulatory. It seemed that one could almost hear the clucking sounds emanating from Capitol Hill.

Yet the newspapers also followed a second story, one more cautious and disturbing: "Most Dropped from Welfare Don't Get Jobs." "New York City Admits Turning away Poor." "Penalties Pushing Many Off Welfare." "Mothers Pressed into Battle for Child Support." "As Welfare Rolls Shrink, Load on Relatives Grows." "Welfare Policies Alter the Face of Food Lines."[6] The bigger picture, the one that could put a damper on all the celebrations, was carried in the stories behind these headlines. But overall, this reality seemed drowned out by the first story, the good news.

Given the inadequacies of the Personal Responsibility Act—the relentless bureaucracy, the sanctions, the unpaid work placements, the grossly insufficient childcare subsidies, the policies that operate at cross-purposes, and the genuine hardship suffered by current and former welfare recipients—why has welfare reform been deemed such a success? Part of the reason, as I've argued, is that the cultural message of reform has always been more important than its practical efficacy. A simpler answer is that the success of welfare reform has been measured by the decline of the welfare rolls. The trimming of the rolls from 12.2 million recipients at the start of reform to 5.3 million in 2001 is read as a sign that all those former welfare recipients are going to work, getting married, or otherwise taking care of themselves in the same (mysterious) way the poor have always taken care of themselves. But what, exactly, is behind the decline of the welfare rolls?

Financial success is clearly not the central reason that so many have left welfare. Although the booming economy of the 1990s had a crucial impact on welfare mothers' ability to get off the rolls and find some kind of work, even in that prosperous decade, the majority of former welfare recipients were not faring well. Between 1996 and 2000, the number of families living in desperate (welfare-level) poverty declined by only 15 percent, yet the number of welfare recipients declined by over half.[7] Although all the answers are not yet in, from the work of policy institutes, scholars, journalists and my own research, I can piece together the following portrait. In the context of a highly favorable economy, the welfare rolls were cut in half for four central reasons:

1. More welfare clients were getting jobs more quickly than they did under the old system.
2. More poor families were being discouraged from using welfare than was true under AFDC.
3. More were leaving welfare faster and returning more slowly than they did in the past.
4. More welfare mothers were being sanctioned or otherwise punished off the welfare rolls.

The best news in all this is the number of welfare mothers who have gotten jobs. Nationwide, as I've noted, researchers estimate that approximately

60 percent of all the adults who left welfare since reform were working, at least part of the time, in 2002. This reality not only offered good news to the proponents of reform; it also offered, for a time at least, a real sense of hope to many welfare mothers. On the other hand, only half of the former welfare recipients who found work were actually making sufficient money to raise their families out of poverty. Only one-third were able to remain employed continuously for a full year. A good number would thus end up, at one time or another, among the 40 percent of former welfare recipients who had neither work nor welfare. Some of those would go back to the welfare office again and start the process anew: policy analysts suggest that over one-third of those who left since reform had already returned to welfare at least once by 2002. In any case, even among those who were employed during that prosperous decade, according to federal statistics their earnings averaged only $598 a month for the support of themselves and their children. Other researchers have estimated average hourly wages at $7.00 an hour and average annual earnings at between $8,000 and $10,800.[8]

With the economy no longer booming, there is reason to worry that many will be unable to sustain even these levels of work and income over time. No matter how you look at it, such facts indicate very difficult living conditions for families. And most of the low-wage jobs acquired by former welfare recipients . . . are without health insurance, many are without sick and vacation leave, a good proportion are at odd or fluctuating hours, and many are only part time.[9] When the problems implied by these facts are coupled with the hardship of trying to find and keep affordable childcare and housing, worries about family health, how to pay the utility bills, and the everyday distress that comes with managing life in the debit column, then one can understand why Barbara Ehrenreich, in *Nickel and Dimed,* referred to the lives of low-wage workers as not just a situation of chronic distress and insecurity but as a "state of emergency."[10]

The second group contributing to the decline of the welfare rolls is even less upbeat. This is the relatively invisible group of discouraged welfare clients—those poor mothers who have left or avoided welfare rather than face the increased stigma and the demanding "rigmarole" of rules and regulations that came with reform. This includes, first, all those mothers and children who never show up on any paperwork but have nonetheless been deeply affected by the law. These are the mothers who went to Sunbelt City's "diversionary workshop" and just headed back home without ever filling out an application. These are all the potential applicants in New York City and elsewhere who, by state rules, were not allowed to apply until they had completed their job search, many of whom simply never went back to the welfare office. These are also all those very poor families who have heard the stories on the streets and on the news and are now more reluctant to go to the welfare office than they were in the past. Finally, this group includes all the welfare clients who have filled out the forms, begun their job search, started the workshops, or taken a workfare placement, but then just stopped showing up—depressed, ill, angry, without children, without hope, unable or unwilling to meet the new standards. Some proportion of these women will eventually find jobs, and if they made it through the application process and if researchers are able to track them, they will be counted in the first category of "successes," working somewhere, for some period of time, for that $598 a month, no benefits.[11] For those who go long stretches without work or welfare, it is difficult to determine precisely how they and their children will survive (although I will speculate on their fate in a moment).

Once it becomes clear that welfare reform has resulted in both encouragement and discouragement, the third reason behind the decline of the rolls can be surmised. The Personal Responsibility Act has effectively transformed the process of "cycling." As I've noted, long before reform, most welfare clients cycled on and off the welfare rolls, moving between jobs and welfare. Now that welfare reform has instituted the "carrots" of supportive services and the "sticks" of time limits, sanctions, and work rules, the process of cycling has been altered—speeded up at the exiting end and slowed down at the return end. That is, poor mothers are now getting jobs or getting off welfare faster than they would have in the past, and they are also entering or returning to the welfare office more slowly and reluctantly. Given that welfare rolls are counted from moment to moment, on paper this speed up/slow down appears as an absolute decline in the welfare rolls.[12] It says nothing, however, about the health and well-being of poor mothers and their kids.

Finally, about one-quarter of welfare recipients are now sanctioned or denied benefits for failure to comply with welfare rules. A 50-state Associated Press survey in 1999 found wide variations by state, with 5 to 60 percent of welfare recipients sanctioned (or procedurally penalized) at any given time in any given state—with rates twice as high as they were prior to reform. In one careful study of three major U.S. cities, 17 percent of clients had their benefits stopped or reduced as a result of sanctions or procedural penalties. In Wisconsin, the most carefully analyzed welfare program in the nation, 31 percent of the caseload was sanctioned in 1999, 21 percent in 2000. (Of those Wisconsin clients who had the wherewithal to appeal their cases, 70 percent of appeals were resolved in favor of clients, suggesting that many of these penalties were unfounded or improperly administered). Federal statistics find just 5 percent of clients under sanction but also note that 23 percent of cases are "procedural closures" (many of which could be penalties for noncompliance).[13]

These sanctioning practices, along with discouragement, faster cycling, and below-poverty wages explain why the number of welfare-eligible families who actually receive welfare benefits has fallen at a much faster pace than the rate of dire poverty. It is clear, in other words, that a substantial portion of desperately poor mothers and children are being punished, worn down, or frightened off the welfare rolls.

Putting it all together, in the context of a booming economy *more than two-thirds of the mothers and children who left welfare have either disappeared or are working for wages that do not meet federal standards for poverty.* At best, only 30 percent of the decline of the welfare rolls represents a "successful" escape from poverty—and many of those successes are only temporary, and many would have occurred with or without reform. The state of Wisconsin, marked as the most outstanding welfare program in the nation, matches these proportions precisely.[14]

In the meantime, there are still millions of poor women and children on welfare and hundreds of thousands coming in anew—or coming back again, unable to find or keep work or to establish some other means of survival under the terms of welfare reform. All of them are desperately poor.

That all this information on the declining welfare rolls still leaves many questions unanswered is one indication that it will take many, many years before we can comprehend the full impact of reform. And almost all of what we now know pertains only to the period of economic boom and only to welfare mothers who had not yet faced the time limits on welfare receipt. Given that time limits do not result in a massive exodus from the rolls but rather a (relatively) slow trickle, it will take a very long time before all the consequences of "the end of entitlement" are surmised.[15]

One final related note is in order.[16] For those who were worried about the consequences of reform from the start, one source of protection against hardship appeared to be the federal rule allowing states to "exempt" up to 20 percent of their caseloads from the time limits. These exemptions, however, have proven severely inadequate. . . . Some states have made the rules so complex and demanding that few clients can qualify. Other states have used all the exemptions available and still cannot fully protect all those recipients with serious physical disabilities and mental health problems, let alone all those who are at risk for domestic violence or who cannot find or afford childcare.[17] The number of families protected over the long haul will vary greatly depending on the rigidity or generosity of state and federal policies. But given what we know about those who have left already, it is clear that the exemptions available in 2002 are not enough to spare all the women and children faced with extreme poverty.

Looking on the brighter side, welfare reform, and the money that came with it—the income supplements, childcare subsidies, bus vouchers, work clothing, and for the lucky ones, the new eyeglasses, the help in buying used cars or making a down payment on an apartment—has been truly helpful, improving the lives of many poor mothers and children, at least for a time. Further, in some cases reform has meant that mothers are getting *better* jobs than they would have in the past, thanks to the education and mentoring offered by some state welfare programs. As I've suggested, as many as 10 to 15 percent of welfare mothers are in a better position now than they would have been had this law not been passed. Perhaps equally important, though harder to quantify, is the positive sense of hope and social inclusion that many recipients experienced (in the short term at least) as a result of the supportive side of welfare reform.

The number of families that have been genuinely helped by reform is neither insignificant nor superfluous. At a practical as well as moral level, the services and income supports offered by the Personal Responsibility Act have clearly been positive. Yet in the long run and in the aggregate, poor mothers and children are worse off now than they were prior to reform. Among those who are working and still poor, among those without work or welfare, and among those who are still facing constant and intense pressure to find work and figure out some way to care for their children, we can only guess what impact this law will have on their ability to retain hope over the long term. Even the U.S. Census Bureau (not anyone's idea of a bleeding heart organization) has found itself answering the question, "Is work better than welfare?" in the negative, at least for those without substantial prior education and work experience.[18] With a slower economy and increasing numbers of poor families due to hit their time limits in coming years, there are reasons to expect that conditions will become increasingly difficult.

Empathy for the downtrodden is one reason to worry about these results. As the following sections will emphasize, enlightened self-interest, a concern with financial costs, and a commitment to our collective future are also very good reasons to be troubled by the consequences of welfare reform.

Winners and Losers

The extent to which the facts about the declining welfare rolls are read as a success ultimately depends on one's primary goals. If the goal of reform was solely to trim the rolls, then it has surely succeeded. If the goal was to place more single mothers in jobs regardless of wages, that goal has been met. If we sought to ensure that more welfare mothers would face a double shift of paid work and childcare, placing them on an "equal" footing with their middle-class counterparts, then some celebrations are in order. If the aim was to ensure that poor men are prosecuted for failure to pay child support, then welfare reform has been relatively effective. If the goal was to make low-income single mothers more likely to seek out the help of men, no matter what the costs, there is some (inconclusive) evidence that this strategy may be working.[19] If the goal was to decrease poverty overall, there is no indication that anything but the cycle of the economy has had an impact. Beyond this, the answers are more complicated.

Thinking about losers, one can start with the families who have left welfare. One-half are sometimes without enough money to buy food. One-third have to cut the size of meals. Almost half find themselves unable to pay their rent or utility bills. Many more families are turning to locally funded services, food banks, churches, and other charities for aid. Many of those charities are already overburdened. In some locales, homeless shelters and housing assistance programs are closing their doors to new customers, food banks are running out of food, and other charities are being forced to tighten their eligibility requirements.[20]

Among the former welfare families who are now living with little or no measurable income, will those charities be enough? At ground level, Nancy, the supervisor in Arbordale's welfare office, told me more than once that she was deeply concerned about these families, particularly the children. Melissa, the supervisor in Sunbelt City, on the other hand, repeatedly responded to my questions regarding the fate of former welfare recipients with the simple statement, "They have other resources." Melissa was referring not only to all those (overloaded) charities, but also to all the boyfriends and family members who could help in paying the bills, and to all those unreported or underreported side jobs (doing hair, cleaning houses, caring for other people's children, selling sex or drugs).[21] Between these two welfare supervisors, both of whom have spent many years working with poor mothers, who is right? And what about Denise, who both agreed with Melissa that many welfare mothers didn't *really* need the help, and who predicted that welfare reform would result in frightening hardship, including a rise in crime?

Consider the "other resources" available to the women I have introduced in this book. In the case of Sheila, the Sunbelt mother who was caring for her seven-year-old daughter and her terminally ill mother, the three of them might be able to survive somehow on her mom's disability check (about $550 per month) with the help of food stamps and local charities. If worse came to worst, she might be able to find some work on the graveyard shift so that she wouldn't have to leave her mom and daughter alone during the day (but she would be faced with leaving them alone at night in that very dangerous housing project). Diane, the Sunbelt mother with a three-year-old son and a long history of severe depression and domestic violence, could go back to operating that illegal flophouse and taking under-the-table housecleaning work (though it is not clear what impact this would have on her son, not to mention Diane). Nadia, the Arbordale mother with four children and no work experience, might rejoin her old friends in petty thievery and prostitution, or she could put further pressure on her employed aunt or the two unemployed fathers of her children, or she might consider turning her children over to relatives or to the foster care system (a worst case scenario recognized by many of the mothers I talked to). Monique, the second-generation Arbordale recipient who'd had her first child at 17, could probably manage on her current job, though one might be a little concerned that her abusive ex-husband would return, force her to move, and throw the fragile balance of her life into chaos. Of course, there are also women like Sonya, the compulsive house rearranger (and incest survivor), who have no family, no work experience, no marketable skills, and no idea about how to make use of local charitable institutions. Someone would surely notice such women eventually, if only because their children missed school or appeared too ill-kept or malnourished.

Most welfare mothers *do* have other resources. Yet many of those resources are only temporary, and many are, at best, inadequate. Most will likely add greater instability and uncertainty to the lives of these families. And nearly all these resources have their own price tags — practical, emotional, moral, and social.

As these negative effects begin to overburden ever-larger numbers of women, we can expect to see more crime, drug abuse, prostitution, domestic violence, mental health disorders, and homelessness. More children will end up in foster care, residing with relatives other than their parents, or living on the streets. These children will also be at greater risk for malnutrition, illness, and delinquency. At the same time, more sick and disabled relatives who once relied on the care of welfare mothers will find their way into state-supported facilities or be left to fend for themselves. Caseworkers in Arbordale told me that they were already noticing the rise in foster care cases and in child-only welfare cases (where mothers had relinquished their children to relatives — making those children eligible for welfare benefits until age 18).* In Sunbelt City, welfare clients told me they were already witnessing rising rates of hunger, drug abuse, prostitution, and crime among sanctioned or discouraged former welfare mothers they knew.

All this hardship will affect poor men as well as women. Not only are these men faced with a more rigid and unforgiving child support system, but they are also very likely to face pressure from the mothers of their children and from the recognition that their children may go hungry or become homeless.[22] The desperation of some of these men could result in a greater incidence of violence, crime, and drug abuse among a low-wage, chronically underemployed male population that is already suffering from severe hardship.

The long-term consequences of welfare reform will also place a tremendous burden on other working-poor and working-class families. The upper classes can rest (fairly) assured that most desperately poor mothers won't come knocking on their doors, asking for cash, a meal, a place to stay, or the loan of a car. But many poor mothers will (reluctantly) knock on the doors of the working-poor and working-class people who are their friends and relatives. It is these people who will share their homes, their food, and their incomes and provide practical help with childcare and transportation. These good deeds won't appear on any income tax forms, welfare case reports, or analyses of charitable spending. But this burden on low-income working people will be one of the very real, and largely invisible, costs of welfare reform. And it will surely exacerbate existing income inequalities.

In the end, it is simultaneously true that most welfare mothers have other resources, many will face frightening hardship, and some proportion will turn to desperate measures. If nothing changes and welfare reform isn't itself reformed, by the close of the first decade of the twenty-first century, we will see the beginnings of measurable impacts on prison populations, mental health facilities, domestic violence shelters, children's protective services, and the foster care system.

---

*According to the rules of reform, there are no time limits on welfare benefits to children who live with relatives (or other adults) who are not themselves receiving welfare. This policy thereby offers welfare mothers an *incentive* to give up their children to other family members, since it means continued financial assistance for those children. Among "streetwise" welfare recipients, this is already a well-known rule. And the number of child-only welfare cases has, in fact, been on the rise since reform (U.S. House of Representatives 2000, see also Bernstein 2002).

NOTES

1. See Abramovitz (1999) for welfare mothers' activism; see Public Agenda (2001), Wertheimer et al. (2001), Draut (2001), and Seccombe et al. (1999) for welfare mothers' opinions regarding welfare.

2. Denise is referring to then-prominent news stories on the Columbine school shooting and the other school shootings that followed.

3. See National Public Radio et al. (2001).

4. On symbolic boundaries, see Lamont (1992, 2000). For a connected, yet distinct, treatment of "moral boundaries," see Tronto (1993). For an analysis of the construction of welfare mothers as the "other" in the division between "us" and "them," see Gans (1995), Handler and Hasenfeld (1997).

5. In order, these newspaper articles are Pear (1999A), Pear (1998), Pear (1999B), Havemann and Vobejda (1998), Goldberg (1999).

6. In order, these newspaper articles are Hernandez (1998), Swarns (1999), Associated Press (1999), DeParle (1999A), Rivera (1997), Revkin (1999).

7. Dalaker (2001), Lamison-White (1997), Pear (2002).

8. See U.S. Department of Health and Human Services (1999A), Holzer and Stoll (2001), Acs and Loprest (2001), Moffit (2002).

9. See Parrot (1998), Loprest (1999), Moffit (2002), National Campaign for Jobs and Income Support (2001A, 2001B). Arguably, the majority of jobs that pay sufficient wages to allow a woman to raise children on her own require at least an associate degree. Women with an associate degree average $12.46 an hour, almost double the $6.69 earned by women who haven't completed high school, and $3.34 more than women with a high school diploma (Sherman et al. 1998). According to a report by the Economic Policy Institute, a "living wage" for a family of one adult and two children is $14 per hour (Ehrenreich 2001:213).

10. Ehrenreich (2001: 214).

11. Over 30 states nationwide either use diversionary programs or require prospective clients to complete specified work requirements *before* they may apply for benefits (Moffit 2002). See also Loprest (1999), Swarns (1999), and National Campaign for Jobs and Income Support (2001A, 2001B).

12. As noted, prior to reform, the process of cycling meant that the majority of welfare clients never stayed on welfare for longer than two years, though many would eventually return (e.g., Bane and Ellwood 1994; Harris 1993, 1996). There is no irrefutable statistical evidence to confirm or disconfirm my point regarding the speed up/slow down process caused by reform, though virtually all the larger trends suggest this reality, as did my experience in the welfare office.

13. See Associated Press (1999), Cherlin et al. (2000), Wisconsin Joint Legislative Audit Committee (2001), U.S. Department of Health and Human Services (1999A), Goldberg (2001), National Campaign for Jobs and Income Support (2001A). Putting this all together—and mimicking my analysis of the speed up/slow down—one report notes that the decline in welfare caseloads is not just a matter of the "best" or "easiest" clients (most educated and most employable) making their way off the rolls. Rather, welfare reform has effected a decline at both ends—with the most employable and the least employable leaving at the same rate. One could surmise that most of those in the former group leave with jobs, most in the latter group as a result of discouragement and sanctions (Cherlin et al. 2000).

14. See Wisconsin Joint Legislative Audit Committee (2001).

15. As of April 2001, just 120,000 welfare clients nationwide had lost their TANF benefits as a result of time limits (National Campaign for Jobs and Income Support 2001A).

16. Actually, one further note is in order. Although official government reports state that there is no change in the racial composition of the welfare rolls once population changes are taken into account, some commentators have argued that whites are leaving the rolls faster than other groups. The changing racial composition of the welfare rolls from 1996 to 1999 was as follows: whites at 30.3 percent, down from 35 percent; blacks at 38 percent up from 37 percent; and Hispanics with the largest increase: 24.5 percent, up from 21 percent. See U.S. Department of Health and Human Services (1999A, 1999B); DeParle (1998).

17. See Schott (2001:4) on state rules for hardship exemptions. See also Moffit (2002), National Campaign for Jobs and Income Support (2001A).

18. See Bauman (2000); Edin and Lein (1997) were the first to clearly demonstrate this point. Of course, the proponents of welfare reform disagree with this assessment. For a reasonable, careful, and well-informed positive assessment of reform, see Moffit (2002).

19. See Sorenson and Zibman (2000); Cherlin and Fomby (2002).

20. See Loprest (1999), Boushev and Gunderson (2001), Sherman et al. (1998), National Campaign for Jobs and Income Support (2001A, 2001B). A study of major U.S. cities found that from 2000 to 2001, requests for food had increased by 23 percent and requests for emergency housing were up by 13 percent (U.S. Conference of Mayors 2001).

21. See Edin and Lein (1997).

22. See especially Waller (1999), Garfinkel et al. (2001), and McLanahan et al. (2001) on the ongoing ties between welfare children and their fathers.

REFERENCES

Abramovitz, Mimi. 1999. "Toward a Framework for Understanding Activism Among Poor and Working-Class Women in Twentieth-Century America," pp. 214–248 in *Whose Welfare?* edited by Gwendolyn Mink. Ithaca, NY: Cornell University Press.

Acs, Gregory and Pamela Loprest. 2001. *Initial Synthesis Report of the Findings from ASPE's "Leavers" Grants.* Washington, DC: Urban Institute.

Associated Press. 1999. "Penalties Pushing Many Off Welfare." *Poughkeepsie Journal,* March 29: A2.

Bane, Mary Jo and David T. Ellwood. 1994. *Welfare Realities: From Rhetoric to Reform.* Cambridge, MA: Harvard University Press.

Bauman, Kurt J. 2000. *The Effect of Work and Welfare on Living Conditions in Single Parent Households.* U.S. Bureau of the Census, Population Division, Working Paper Series No. 46 (August). Washington, DC: U.S. Government Printing Office.

Bernstein, Nina. 2002. "Side Effect of Welfare Law: The No Parent Family." *New York Times,* July 29: A1.

Boushev, Heather and Bethney Gunderson. 2001. *When Work Just Isn't Enough: Measuring Hardships Faced by Families after Moving from Welfare to Work.* Washington, DC: Economic Policy Institute.

Cherlin, Andrew J., Linda Burton, Judith Francis, Jane Henrici, Laura Lein, James Quane, and Karen Bogen. 2000. *Sanctions and Case Closings for Noncompliance: Who is Affected and Why.* Welfare, Children, and Families: A Three-City Study, Policy Brief 01–1. Baltimore, MD: Johns Hopkins University.

Cherlin, Andrew J. and Paula Fomby. 2002. *A Closer Look at Changes in Children's Living Arrangements.* Welfare, Children, and Families: A Three-City Study, Working Paper 02–01. Baltimore, MD: Johns Hopkins University.

Dalaker, Joseph. 2001. *Poverty in the United States.* U.S. Census Bureau, Current Population Reports, Series P60-214. Washington, DC: U.S. Government Printing Office.

DeParle, Jason. 1998. "Shrinking Welfare Rolls Leave Record High Share of Minorities." *New York Times,* July 27: A1.

DeParle, Jason. 1999. "As Welfare Rolls Shrink, Load on Relatives Grows." *New York Times,* February 21: A1.

Draut, Tammy. 2001. *New Opportunities? Public Opinion on Poverty, Income Inequality and Public Policy: 1996–2001.* New York: Demos.

Edin, Kathryn and Laura Lein. 1997. *Making Ends Meet: How Single Mothers Survive Welfare and Low-Wage Work.* New York: Russell Sage Foundation.

Ehrenreich, Barbara. 2001. *Nickel and Dimed: On (Not) Getting By in America.* New York: Metropolitan Books.

Gans, Herbert J. 1995. *The War Against the Poor: The Underclass and Antipoverty Policy.* New York: Basic Books.

Garfinkel, Irwin, Sara S. McLanahan, Marta Tienda, and Jeanne Brooks-Gunn. 2001. "Fragile Families and Welfare Reform: An Introduction." *Children and Youth Services Review* 23 (4/5): 277–301.

Goldberg, Carey. 1999. "Most Get Work After Welfare, Studies Suggest." *New York Times,* April 17: A1.

Goldberg, Heidi. 2001. *A Compliance-Oriented Approach to Sanctions in State and County TANF Programs.* Washington, DC: Center on Budget and Policy Priorities.

Handler, Joel F. and Yeheskel Hasenfeld. 1997. *We the Poor People: Work, Poverty, and Welfare.* New Haven, CT: Yale University Press.

Harris, Kathleen Mullan. 1993. "Work and Welfare Among Single Mothers in Poverty," *American Journal of Sociology* 99 (September): 317–52.

Harris, Kathleen Mullan. 1996. "Life after Welfare: Women, Work, and Repeat Dependency," *American Sociological Review* 61 (June): 407–426.

Havemann, Judith and Barbara Vobejda. 1998. "The Welfare Alarm that Didn't Go Off." *Washington Post,* October 1: A1.

Hernandez, Raymond. 1998. "Most Dropped from Welfare Don't Get Jobs." *New York Times,* March 23: A1.

Holzer, Harry J. and Michael A. Stoll. 2001. *Meeting the Demand: Hiring Patterns of Welfare Recipients in Four Metropolitan Areas.* Washington, DC: Brookings Institution.

Lamison-White, Leatha. 1997. *Poverty in the United States: 1996.* U.S. Bureau of the Census, Current Population Reports, Series P60-198. Washington, DC: U.S. Government Printing Office.

Lamont, Michèle. 1992. *Money, Morals, and Manners.* Chicago: University of Chicago Press.

Lamont, Michèle. 2000. *The Dignity of Working Men: Morality and the Boundaries of Race, Class, and Immigration.* New York: Russell Sage Foundation.

Loprest, Pamela. 1999. *Families Who Left Welfare: Who Are They and How Are They Doing?* Washington, DC: Urban Institute.

McLanahan, Sara, Irwin Garfinkel, and Ronald B. Mincy. 2001. *Fragile Families, Welfare Reform, and Marriage.* Welfare Reform and Beyond: Policy Brief No. 10. Washington, DC: Brookings Institution.

Moffitt, Robert A. 2002. *From Welfare to Work: What the Evidence Shows.* Welfare Reform and Beyond: Policy Brief #13. Washington, DC: Brookings Institution.

National Campaign for Jobs and Income Support. 2001A. *A Recession Like No Other: New Analysis Finds Safety Net in Tatters as Economic Slump Deepens.* Washington, DC: National Campaign for Jobs and Income Support.

National Campaign for Jobs and Income Support. 2001B. *Leaving Welfare, Left Behind: Employment Status, Income, and Well-Being of Former TANF Recipients.* Washington, DC: National Campaign for Jobs and Income Support.

National Public Radio, Kaiser Family Foundation, and Kennedy School of Government. 2001. *Poverty in America.* Washington, DC: National Public Radio.

Parrot, Sharon. 1998. *Welfare Recipients Who Find Jobs: What Do We Know About Their Employment and Earnings?* Washington, DC: Center on Budget and Policy Priorities.

Pear, Robert. 1998. "Number on Welfare Dips Below 10 Million." *New York Times*, January 21: A12.

Pear, Robert. 1999A. "White House Releases Glowing Data on Welfare." *New York Times*, August 1: A12.

Pear, Robert. 1999B. "10,000 Welfare Recipients Hired by Federal Agencies." *New York Times*, March 1: A12.

Pear, Robert. 2002. "Governors Want Congress to Ease Welfare's Work Rule." *New York Times*, February 24.

Public Agenda. 2001. "Welfare: Public Opinion." http://www.publicagenda.org/issues.

Revkin, Andrew C. 1999. "Welfare Policies Alter the Face of Food Lines." *New York Times*, February 26: A1.

Rivera, Carla. 1997. "Mothers Pressed into Battle for Child Support." *Los Angeles Times*, March 24: A1.

Schott, Liz. 2001. *Ways that States Can Serve Families that Reach Welfare Time Limits.* Washington, DC: Center on Budget and Policy Priorities.

Seccombe, Karen, Kimberly Battle Walters, and Delores James. 1999. "'Welfare Mothers' Welcome Reform, Urge Compassion." *Family Relations* 48: 197–206.

Sherman, Arloc, Cheryl Amey, Barbara Duffield, Nancy Ebb, and Deborah Weinstein. 1998. *Welfare to What? Early Findings on Family Hardship and Well-Being.* National Coalition for the Homeless. Washington, DC: Children's Defense Fund.

Sorensen, Elaine and Chava Zibman. 2000. *Child Support Offers Some Protection Against Poverty.* Assessing the New Federalism, Series B, No. B-10. Washington, DC: Urban Institute.

Swarns, Rachel L. 1999. "New York City Admits Turning Away Poor." *New York Times*, January 22: B3.

Tronto, Joan C. 1993 [1994]. *Moral Boundaries: A Political Argument for an Ethic of Care.* New York: Routledge.

U.S. Bureau of the Census. 2001A. *Families by Presence of Own Children Under 18: 1950 to Present.* (FM-1.) Washington, DC: U.S. Government Printing Office.

U.S. Bureau of the Census. 2001B. *Net Worth of Nation's Households Unchanged.* http://www.census.gov/hhes/www/wealth.html.

U.S. Conference of Mayors. 2001. *A Status Report on Hunger and Homelessness in America's Cities:* A 27-City Survey. Washington, DC: Conference of Mayors.

U.S. Department of Health and Human Services. 1999A. *Characteristics and Financial Circumstances of TANF Recipients.* Washington, DC: U.S. Government Printing Office.

U.S. Department of Health and Human Services. 1999B. *Temporary Assistance for Needy Families Program: Second Annual Report to Congress.* Washington, DC: U.S. Government Printing Office.

U.S. House of Representatives, Committee on Ways and Means. 2000. *Green Book: Overview of Entitlement Programs.* Washington, DC: U.S. Government Printing Office.

Waller, Maureen R. 1999. "Meanings and Motives in New Family Stories: The Separation of Reproduction and Marriage Among Low-Income Black and White Parents," pp. 182–218 in *The Cultural Territories of Race: Black and White Boundaries*, edited by Michèle Lamont. Chicago: University of Chicago Press.

Wertheimer, Richard, Melissa Long, and Sharon Vandivere. 2001. *Welfare Recipients' Attitudes Toward Welfare, Nonmarital Childbearing, and Work: Implications for Reform?* Series B, No. B-37. Washington, DC: Urban Institute.

Wisconsin Joint Legislative Audit Committee. 2001. *An Evaluation: Wisconsin Works (W-2) Program, Department of Workforce Development.* Madison, WI: Legislative Audit Bureau.

48

─────────

SIXTY CENTS TO A MAN'S DOLLAR

ANN CRITTENDEN

Ann Crittenden is the author of *Killing the Sacred Cows: Bold Ideas for a New Economy.*
A former reporter for *The New York Times* and a Pulitzer Prize nominee, she has also
been a reporter for *Fortune,* a financial writer for *Newsweek,* a visiting lecturer at
M.I.T. and Yale, and an economics commentator for CBS News. Her articles have
appeared in *The Nation, Foreign Affairs, McCall's,* and *Working Woman,* among others.
She lives with her husband and son in Washington, DC.

In the Bible, in Leviticus, God instructs Moses to tell the Israelites that
women, for purposes of tithing, are worth thirty shekels while men are
worth fifty—a ratio of 60 percent.[1] For fifty years, from about 1930 to
1980, the value of employed women eerily reflected that biblical ratio: The
earnings of full-time working women were only 60 percent of men's earnings. In the 1980s, that ratio began to change. By 1993, women working full-
time were earning an average of seventy-seven cents for every dollar men
earned. (In 1997, the gap widened again, as the median weekly earnings of
full-time working women fell to 75 percent of men's earnings.)

But lo and behold, when we look closer, we find the same old sixty cents
to a man's dollar. The usual way to measure the gender wage gap is by comparing the hourly earnings of men and women who work full-time year-round.
But this compares only the women who work like men with men—a method
that neatly excludes most women. . . . [O]nly about half of the mothers of children under eighteen have full-time, year-round paying jobs.[2]

To find the real difference between men's and women's earnings, one
would have to compare the earnings of *all* male and female workers, both
full- and part-time. And guess what one discovers? The average earnings of
all female workers in 1999 were 59 percent of men's earnings.[3] Women who
work for pay are still stuck at the age-old biblical value put on their labor.

My research turned up other intriguing reflections of the 60 percent ratio:
A survey of 1982 graduates of the Stanford Business School found that ten
years after graduation, the median income of the full- and part-time employed
female M.B.A.s amounted to $81,300, against the men's median income of
$139,100. Again, the women's share is 58 percent. Another study, of 1974

───────

graduates of the University of Michigan Law School, revealed that in the late 1980s the women's average earnings were 61 percent of the men's—despite the fact that 96 percent of the women were working, and that the men and women were virtually identical in terms of training. The authors of this study concluded that the women's family responsibilities were "certainly the most important single cause of sex differences in earnings."[4]

Conservatives frequently tout women's economic gains in order to charge that women's advocates who haven't folded their tents and gone home must be making up things to complain about. In a polemic titled *Who Stole Feminism?* Christina Hoff Sommers lambasts feminist activists for wearing a button stating that women earn fifty-nine cents to a man's dollar, which, she claims, is "highly misleading and now egregiously out of date."[5] Sommers is right if we skim over what she calls such "prosaic matters" as the fact that people who have primary responsibility for a child have different work patterns from people without caring responsibilities. But if we are interested in the real differences in the earnings of employed men and women, those buttons still tell the real story.

The Cost of Being a Mother

A small group of mostly female academic economists has added another twist to the story. Their research reveals that working mothers not only earn less than men, but also less per hour than childless women, even after such differences as education and experience are factored out. The pay gap between mothers and nonmothers under age thirty-five is now larger than the wage gap between young men and women.

The first comprehensive estimates of the cost of motherhood in terms of lost income were made in England by Heather Joshi of the City University in London and Hugh Davies of Birkbeck College of the University of London. The two economists estimated that a typical middle-class British mother of two forfeits almost *half* of her potential lifetime earnings.[6]

In the United States, similar work has been done by Jane Waldfogel at Columbia University. Waldfogel set out to assess the opportunity cost of motherhood by asking exactly how much of the dramatic wage gains made by women in the 1980s went to women without family responsibilities. How many of the female winners in the 1980s were people like Donna Shalala, Janet Reno, Elizabeth Dole, and Carole Bellamy, the director of UNICEF: childless women whose work patterns were indistinguishable from those of traditional males.

Back in the late 1970s, Waldfogel found, the difference between men's and women's pay was about the same for all women. Nonmothers earned only slightly higher wages. But over the next decade things changed.[7] By 1991, thirty-year-old American women without children were making 90 percent of men's wages, while comparable women with children were making only 70 percent. Even when Waldfogel factored out all the women's differences, the disparity in their incomes remained—something she dubbed the "family wage gap."[8]

———————

Why do working mothers earn so much less than childless women? Academic researchers have worried over this question like a dog over a bone but haven't turned up a single, definitive answer.[9]

Waldfogel argues that the failure of employers to provide paid maternity leaves is one factor that leads to the family wage gap in the United States. This country is one of only six nations in the world that does not require a paid leave. (The others are Australia, New Zealand, Lesotho, Swaziland, and Papua New Guinea.)[10] With no right to a paid leave, many American mothers who want to stay at home with a new baby simply quit their jobs, and this interruption in employment costs them dearly in terms of lost income. Research in Europe reveals that when paid maternity leaves were mandated, the percentage of women remaining employed rose, and women's wages were higher, unless the leaves lasted more than a few months.[11]

In the United States as well, women who are able to take formal paid maternity leave do not suffer the same setback in their wages as comparably placed women who do not have a right to such leaves. This is a significant benefit to mothers in the five states, including California, New York, and New Jersey, that mandate temporary disability insurance coverage for pregnancy and childbirth.[12]

Paid leaves are so valuable because they don't seem to incur the same penalties that employers impose on even the briefest of unpaid career interruptions. A good example is the experience of the 1974 female graduates of the University of Michigan Law School. During their first fifteen years after law school, these women spent an average of only 3.3 months out of the workplace, compared with virtually no time out for their male classmates. More than one-quarter of the women had worked part-time, for an average of 10.1 months over the fifteen years, compared with virtually no part-time work among the men. While working full-time, the women put in only 10 percent fewer hours than full-time men, again not a dramatic difference.

But the penalties for these slight distinctions between the men's and women's work patterns were strikingly harsh. Fifteen years after graduation, the women's average earnings were not 10 percent lower, or even 20 percent lower, than the men's, but almost 40 percent lower. Fewer than one-fifth of the women in law firms who had worked part-time for more than six months had made partner in their firms, while more than four-fifths of the mothers with little or no part-time work had made partner.[13]

Another survey of almost 200 female M.B.A.s found that those who had taken an average of only 8.8 months out of the job market were less likely to reach upper-middle management and earned 17 percent less than comparable women who had never had a gap in their employment.[14]

Working-class women are also heavily penalized for job interruptions, although these are the very women who allegedly "choose" less demanding occupations that enable them to move in and out of the job market without undue wage penalties. The authors of one study concluded that the negative repercussions of taking a little time out of the labor force were still discernible after twenty years.[15] In blue-collar work, seniority decides who is eligible for better jobs, and who is "bumped" in the event of layoffs. Under current policies, many women lose their seniority forever if they interrupt their employment, as most mothers do. Training programs, required for advancement, often take place after work, excluding the many mothers who can't find child care.[16]

Mandatory overtime is another handicap placed on blue-collar mothers. Some 45 percent of American workers reported in a recent survey that they had to work overtime with little or no notice.[17] In 1994 factory workers put in the highest levels of overtime ever reported by the Bureau of Labor Statistics in its thirty-eight years of tracking the data. Where does that leave a woman who has to be home in time for dinner with the kids? Out of a promotion and maybe out of a job. Increasingly in today's driven workplace, whether she is blue- or white-collar, a woman who goes home when she is supposed to go home is going to endanger her economic well-being.

The fact that many mothers work part-time also explains some of the difference between mother's and comparable women's hourly pay. (About 65 percent of part-time workers are women, most of whom are mothers.)[18] Employers are not required to offer part-time employees equal pay and benefits for equal work. As a result, nonstandard workers earn on average about 40 percent less an hour than full-time workers, and about half of that wage gap persists even for similar workers in similar jobs.

Many bosses privately believe that mothers who work part-time have a "recreational" attitude toward work, as one Maryland businessman assured me. Presumably, this belief makes it easier to justify their exploitation. But the working conditions they face don't sound very much like recreation. A recent survey by Catalyst, a research organization focused on women in business, found that more than half of the people who had switched to part-time jobs and lower pay reported that their workload stayed the same. Ten percent reported an increase in workload after their income had been reduced. Most of these people were mothers.[19]

Another factor in the family wage gap is the disproportionate number of mothers who operate their own small businesses, a route often taken by women who need flexibility during the child-rearing years. Female-owned small businesses have increased twofold over small businesses owned by men in recent years.[20] In 1999, women owned 38 percent of all U.S. businesses, compared with only 5 percent in 1972, a remarkable increase that is frequently cited as evidence of women's economic success. One new mother noted that conversations at play groups "center as much on software and modems as they do on teething and ear infections."[21]

Less frequently mentioned is the fact that many of these women-owned businesses are little more than Mom-minus-Pop operations: one woman trying to earn some money on the side, or keep her career alive, during the years when her children have priority. Forty-five percent of women-owned businesses are home-based. And the more than one-third of businesses owned by women in 1996 generated only 16 percent of the sales of all U.S. businesses in that year.[22]

In 1997, although women were starting new businesses at twice the rate of men, they received only 2 percent of institutional venture capital, a principal source of financing for businesses with serious prospects for growth. Almost one-quarter of female business owners financed their operations the same way that they did their shopping: with their credit cards.[23]

Some researchers have suggested that mothers earn less than childless women because they are less productive. This may be true for some mothers who work at home and are subject to frequent interruptions, or for those who are exhausted from having to do most of the domestic chores, or distracted by creaky child-care arrangements. But the claim that mothers have lower productivity than other workers is controversial and unproven. It is easier to demonstrate that working mothers face the same old problem that has bedeviled women in the workplace for decades.

It's Discrimination, Stupid

It is revealing that those occupations requiring nurturing skills, such as child care, social work, and nursing, are the most systematically underpaid, relative to their educational and skill demands.[24] These are also, of course, the occupations with the highest percentage of females. But men who are primary caregivers also pay a heavy price: a "daddy tax," if you will. This suggests that at least part of the huge tax on mothers' earnings is due to work rules and practices and habits of mind that discriminate against anyone, of either sex, who cannot perform like an "unencumbered" worker. In other words, discrimination against all good parents, male or female.

Surveys have found that wives may adore husbands who share the parenting experience, but employers distinctly do not. A majority of managers believe that part-time schedules and even brief parental leaves are inappropriate for men.[25] When Houston Oiler David Williams missed one Sunday game to be with his wife after the birth of their first child, he was docked $111,111.

A survey of 348 male managers at twenty Fortune 500 companies found that fathers from dual-career families put in an average of *two* fewer hours per week—or about 4 percent less—than men whose wives were at home. That was the only difference between the two groups of men. But the fathers with working wives, who presumably had a few more domestic responsibilities, earned almost 20 percent less. There it is again: a 20 percent family wage gap.[26]

"Face time still matters as much or more than productivity in many companies," Charles Rodgers, a management consultant in Boston, said.

Rodgers told me about a man in a high-tech company who regularly came to work two hours early so that he could occasionally leave early for Little League games with his son. He was given a poor performance rating.[27]

Such discrimination is hard to quantify, but it is potentially a powerful political issue. When the Clinton administration announced that it was banning employment discrimination against *parents* working in the federal government, there were so many calls to a White House staffer assigned to the case that her machine stopped taking messages.

Only eight states currently have laws prohibiting discrimination against parents in the workplace. Examples include taking a primary parent off a career track out of an assumption that the individual couldn't do the work; hiring someone without children over a more qualified person with children; forcing a primary parent to work overtime, or else; and refusing to hire a single parent, though the employer hires single, childless people. In the course of my reporting, I encountered numerous mothers who felt that their employer's refusal to arrange a shorter workweek, particularly after the birth of a second baby, amounted to career-destroying discrimination.

NOTES

1. Amity Shales, "What Does Woman Want?" *Women's Quarterly* (summer 1996): 10.
2. According to June O'Neill, an economist and former head of the Congressional Budget Office, "Full-time year-round workers are not likely to be representative of all workers. Women are less likely to be in this category than men." See June O'Neill and Solomon Polachek, "Why the Gender Gap in Wages Narrowed in the 1980s," *Journal of Labor Economics* 2, no. 1, pt. 1 (1993): 208–9.
3. U.S. Bureau of the Census, Current Population Reports, *Money Income in the U.S.: 1995*, Washington, D.C., March 2000, P60-209, pp. 46–49.
4. Robert G. Wood, Mary E. Corcoran, and Paul N. Courant, "Pay Differentials Among the Highly-Paid: The Male-Female Earnings Gap in Lawyers' Salaries," *Journal of Labor Economics* 11, no. 3 (1993): 417–41.
5. Christina Hoff Sommers, *Who Stole Feminism?* (New York: Simon & Schuster, 1994), p. 240.
6. The estimate of a 47 percent loss of lifetime earnings was presented by Hugh Davies at a session of the Allied Social Science Association in New York City on January 4, 1999. It is based on the British Household Poll Survey of 1994. Using earlier data, Davies and Joshi calculated that the mommy tax on a typical British secretary was the equivalent of $324,000 — not counting lost pension benefits. See Heather Joshi, "Sex and Motherhood as Handicaps in the Labour Market," in *Women's Issues in Social Policy,* ed. Mavis Maclean and Dulcie Grove (London: Routledge, 1991), p. 180. See also Heather Joshi, "The Cost of Caring," in *Women and Poverty in Britain: The 1990's,* ed. Carol Glendenning and Jane Millar (New York: Harvester Wheatsheaf, 1992), p. 121. Also see Heather Joshi and Pierella Paci, *Unequal Pay for Men and Women* (Cambridge, Mass.: M.I.T. Press, 1998).
7. Jane Waldfogel, "Women Working for Less: Family Status and Women's Pay in the US and UK," Malcolm Wiener Center for Social Policy Working Paper D-94-1, Harvard University, 1994.
8. Jane Waldfogel, "Understanding the 'Family Gap' in Pay for Women with Children," *Journal of Economic Perspectives* 12, no. 1 (winter 1998): 137–56. See also

Waldfogel, "The Family Gap for Young Women in the United States and Britain," *Journal of Labor Economics* 11 (1998): 505–19. Looking at two different cohorts of young women, one averaging age thirty in 1981 and the other about thirty in 1990, Waldfogel found that the nonmothers' wages rose from 72 percent to 90 percent of men's between 1981 and 1990. But the wages of mothers rose less, from 60 percent to only 70 percent of men the same age during the same period. The more children a woman had, the lower her earnings, even with all other factors being equal.

   Waldfogel also uncovered a wage gap of 20 percentage points for young women in the United Kingdom. Nonmothers at age thirty-three earn 84 percent of men's pay, while mothers earn only 64 percent. See Jane Waldfogel, "The Family Gap for Young Women in the US and UK: Can Maternity Leave Make a Difference?" Malcolm Wiener Center for Social Policy, Harvard University, October 1994, pp. 1, 20.

9. See Paula England and Michelle Budig, "The Effects of Motherhood on Wages in Recent Cohorts: Findings from the National Longitudinal Survey of Youth," unpublished paper, 1999.

10. Elizabeth Olson, "U.N. Surveys Paid Leave for Mothers," *New York Times*, February 16, 1998.

11. Christopher J. Ruhm, "The Economic Consequences of Parental Leave Mandates: Lessons from Europe," *Quarterly Journal of Economics* CXIII, no. 1 (1998): 285–317. Ruhm found that longer leaves (of nine months or more) were associated with a slight reduction in women's relative wages, but Waldfogel discovered that mothers in Britain who exercised their right to a ten-month paid maternity leave and returned to their original employer had wages no different from those of childless women.

   See also "Working Mothers Then and Now: A Cross-Cohort Analysis of the Effects of Maternity Leave on Women's Pay," in *Gender and Family Issues in the Workplace,* ed. Francine Blau and Ronald Ehrenberg (New York: Russell Sage Foundation, 1997).

12. Heidi Hartmann, Institute for Women's Policy Research, personal communication, January 8, 1995. Hartmann's research has shown that fully 11 percent of women who have no paid leave have to go on public assistance during their time with a new baby.

13. Wood, Corcoran, and Courant, "Pay Differentials," pp. 417–28.

14. This 1993 study was coauthored by Joy Schneer of Rider University's College of Business Administration and Frieda Reitman, professor emeritus at Pace University's Lubin School of Business.

15. Joyce Jacobsen and Arthur Levin, "The Effects of Intermittent Labor Force Attachment on Female Earnings," *Monthly Labor Review* 118, no. 9 (September 1995): 18.

16. For a good discussion of the obstacles to mothers' employment in relatively well-paying blue-collar work, see Joan Williams, *Unbending Gender: Why Family and Work Conflict and What to Do About It* (New York: Oxford University Press, 2000), pp. 76–81.

17. This survey of 1,000 workers was conducted by researchers at the University of Connecticut and Rutgers University, and was reported in the *Wall Street Journal,* May 18, 1999.

18. A survey of more than 2,000 people in four large corporations found that 75 percent of the professionals working part-time were women who were doing so because of child-care obligations. Only 11 percent of the male managers surveyed expected to work part-time at some point in their careers, compared with 36 percent of

women managers. *A New Approach to Flexibility: Managing the Work/Time Equation* (New York: Catalyst, 1997), pp. 25–26.

19. There is other evidence that many so-called part-timers are increasingly working what used to be considered full-time—thirty-five to forty hours a week—for lower hourly pay than regular full-timers. See Reed Abelson, "Part-time Work for Some Adds Up to Full-Time Job," *New York Times,* November 2, 1998.

20. In the five years from 1988 through 1992, the number of women-owned sole proprietorships, partnerships, and similar businesses soared 43 percent, compared with overall growth of 26 percent in such businesses. *Wall Street Journal,* January 29, 1996.

21. Tracy Thompson, "A War Inside Your Head," *Washington Post Magazine,* February 15, 1998, p. 29.

22. Information on women-owned businesses provided by the National Foundation for Women Business Owners in Washington, D.C., September 2000.

23. Noelle Knox, "Women Entrepreneurs Attract New Financing," *New York Times,* July 26, 1998.

24. For the relatively low value placed on the caring professions, see Paula England, George Farkas, Barbara Kilbourne, Kurt Beron, and Dorothea Weir, "Returns to Skill, Compensating Differentials, and Gender Bias: Effects of Occupational Characteristics on Wages of White Women and Men," *American Journal of Sociology* 100, no. 3 (November 1994): 689–719.

25. On corporate attitudes toward part-time work for men, see the study cited in note 17. Another study found that 63 percent of large employers thought it was inappropriate for a man to take *any* parental leave, and another 17 percent thought it unreasonable unless the leave was limited to two weeks or less. Martin H. Malin, "Fathers and Parental Leave," *Texas Law Review* 72 (1994): 1047, 1089; cited in Williams, *Unbending Gender,* p. 100

26. This study, by Linda Stroh of Loyola University, was reported by Tamar Lewin, "Fathers Whose Wives Stay Home Earn More and Get Ahead, Studies Find," *New York Times,* October 12, 1994.

27. Charles Rodgers, personal communication, October 1993.

49

WHY ARE THERE NO MALE ASIAN ANCHORMEN ON TV?

BEN FONG-TORRES

Ben Fong-Torres is a journalist in the San Francisco Bay area. His most recent book is *The Rice Room: Growing Up Chinese-American.*

Connie Chung, the best-known Asian TV newswoman in the country, is a co-anchor of *1986,* a prime-time show on NBC. Ken Kashiwahara, the best-known Asian TV newsman, has been chief of ABC's San Francisco bureau for seven years; his reports pop up here and there on ABC's newscasts and other news-related programs.

Wendy Tokuda, the best-known Asian TV newswoman in the Bay Area, is a co-anchor of KPIX's evening news. David Louie, the most established Asian TV newsman, is a field reporter, covering the Peninsula for KGO.

And that's the way it is: among Asian American broadcasters, the glamour positions—the anchor chairs, whose occupants earn more than $500,000 a year in the major markets—go to the women; the men are left outside, in the field, getting by on reporters' wages that top out at about $80,000.

The four Bay Area television stations that present regular newscasts (Channels 2, 4, 5 and 7) employ more than 40 anchors. Only two are Asian Americans: Tokuda and Emerald Yeh, a KRON co-anchor on weekends. There is no Asian male in an anchor position, and there has never been one. (Other Asian women who have anchored locally are Linda Yu [KGO] and Kaity Tong [KPIX], now prime-time anchors in Chicago and New York.)

None of the two dozen broadcasters this reporter spoke to could name a male Asian news anchor working anywhere in the United States.

Don Fitzpatrick, a TV talent headhunter whose job it has been for four years to help television stations find anchors and reporters, maintains a video library in his San Francisco office of 9000 people on the air in the top 150 markets.

There are, in fact, several reasons proposed by broadcasters, station executives, talent agents and others.

- Asian men have been connected for generations with negative stereotypes. Asian women have also been saddled with false images, but,

---

Ben Fong-Torres, "Why Are There No Male Asian Anchormen on TV?" from *San Francisco Chronicle* (July 13, 1986). Reprinted with permission.

according to Tokuda, "In this profession, they work for women and against men."

- Asian women are perceived as attractive partners for the typical news anchor: a white male. "TV stations," says Henry Der, director of Chinese for Affirmative Action, "have discovered that having an Asian female with a white male is an attractive combination." And, adds Sam Chu Lin, a former reporter for both KRON and KPIX, "they like the winning formula. If an Asian woman works in one market, then another market duplicates it. So why test for an Asian male?"
- Asian women allow television stations to fulfill two equal-opportunity slots with one hiring. As Mario Machado, a Los Angeles-based reporter and producer puts it, "They get two minorities in one play of the cards. *They* hit the jackpot."
- Asian males are typically encouraged by parents toward careers in the sciences and away from communications.
- Because there are few Asian men on the air, younger Asian males have no racial peers as role models. With few men getting into the profession, news directors have a minuscule talent pool from which to hire.

And, according to Sumi Haru, a producer at KTLA in Los Angeles, the situation is worsening as stations are being purchased and taken over by large corporations. At KTTV, the ABC affiliate, "The affirmative action department was the first to go." At her own station, the public affairs department is being trimmed. "We're concerned with what little Asian representation we have on the air," said Haru, an officer of the Association of Asian-Pacific American Artists.

Honors Thesis

Helen Chang, a communications major at UC Berkeley now working in Washington, DC, made the missing Asian anchorman the subject of her honors thesis. Chang spoke with Asian anchorwomen in Los Angeles, Chicago and New York as well as locally. "To capsulize the thesis," she says, "it is an executive decision based on a perception of an Asian image. On an executive decision level, the image of the Asian woman is acceptable."

"It's such a white bread medium; it's the survival of the blandest," says a male Asian reporter who asked to remain anonymous. A native San Franciscan, this reporter once had ambitions to be an anchor, but after several static years at his station, "I've decided to face reality. I have a white man's credentials but it doesn't mean a thing. I'm not white. How can it not be racism?"

"Racism is a strong word that scares people," says Tokuda.

"But whatever's going on here is some ugly animal. It's not like segregation in the south. What it is is very subtle . . . bias."

To Mario Machado, it's not that subtle. Machado, who is half Chinese and half Portuguese, is a former daytime news anchor in Los Angeles who's had the most national television exposure after Kashiwahara. Being half Chinese, he says, has given him no advantage in getting work. "It's had no bearing at all. There's a move on against Asians, period, whether part-Asian or full-Asian."

TV executives, he charges, "don't really want minority males to be totally successful. They don't want minority men perceived as strong, bright, and articulate. We can be cute second bananas, like Robert Ito on *Quincy.* But having an Asian woman—that's always been the feeling from World War II, I guess. You bring back an Asian bride, and she's cute and delicate. But a strong minority man with authority and conviction—I don't think people are ready for that."

War Image

Bruno Cohen, news director at KPIX, agrees that "for a lot of people, the World War II image of Japanese, unfortunately, is the operative image about what Asian males are all about."

That image, says Serena Chen, producer and host of Asians Now! on KTVU, was one of danger. "They may be small, but they're strong. So watch out, white women!"

The Vietnam war and recent movies like *Rambo,* Machado says, add to the historic negativity. "You never went to war against Asian women," he says. "You always went to war against Asian men."

Today, says Tokuda, Asian men are saddled with a twin set of stereotypes. "They're either wimpy—they have real thick glasses and they're small and they have an accent and they're carrying a lot of cameras—or they're a murderous gangster." "Or," says Les Kumagai, a former KPIX intern now working for a Reno TV station, "they're businessmen who are going to steal your jobs."

"The Asian woman is viewed as property, and the Asian male has been denied sexuality," says Chen. "Eldridge Cleaver created a theory of the black male being superglorified in the physical and superdecreased in the mental. It's very difficult for people to see a successful black male unless he's an athlete or a performer. If he's in a corporate situation, everyone says, 'Wow, he's the product of affirmative action.' That theory holds that in this society, people who have potential to have power have to be male, and have both mental and physical [strength] to be the superior male. In this society, they took away the black male's mental and gave him his physical. The Asian male has been denied the physical and given the mental."

Veteran KRON reporter Vic Lee listens to a tally of stereotypes and images associated with Asian men. "All those reasons limit where an Asian American can work. I've always said to my wife, if I'm fired here, there're only a couple of cities I can go to and get a job based on how well I do my work, not how I look or what color my skin is. There are cities with Asian American populations, and you can count them on one hand: Seattle, Los Angeles, New York, Boston, and possibly Washington.

"The rest of the country? You might as well forget Detroit. They *killed* a [Chinese] guy just 'cause he looked Japanese." Lee is referring to Vincent Chin, who was beaten to death by two white auto workers who mistook him for a Japanese and blamed him for their unemployment.

"Exotic" Females

In contrast to the threatening Asian male, says Les Kumagai, "Females are 'exotic.' They're not threatening to non-Asian females and they're attractive to non-Asian males. You're looking to draw the 18-to-45-year-old female demographic for advertising. You just won't get that draw from an Asian male."

To Tokuda, the Asian woman's persisting stereotype is more insidious than exotic. "It's the Singapore girl: not only deferential but submissive. It's right next to the geisha girl."

At KGO, says one newsroom employee, "somebody in management was talking about [recently hired reporter] Janet Yee and blurted out, 'Oh, she's so cute.' They don't care about her journalistic credentials. . . . That type of thinking still persists."

Aggressive

Janet Yee says she can take the comment as a compliment, but agrees that it is "a little dehumanizing." Yee, who is half Chinese and half Irish-Swedish, says she doesn't get the feeling, at KGO, that she was hired for her looks. Stereotypes "are the things I've fought all my life," she says, adding that she isn't at all submissive and deferential. "I'm assertive and outgoing, and I think that's what got me the job."

Emerald Yeh, who worked in Portland and at CNN (Cable News Network) in Atlanta before joining KRON, says she's asked constantly about the part being an Asian woman played in her landing a job. "The truth is that it's a factor, but at the same time, there is absolutely no way I can keep my job virtually by being Asian."

Despite the tough competition for jobs in television, Yeh, like Tokuda and several peers in Los Angeles, is vocal about the need to open doors to Asian men. "People think Asians have done so well," she says, "but how can you say that if one entire gender group is hardly visible?"

George Lum, a director at KTVU who got into television work some 30 years ago at Channel 5, has a theory of his own. "The Asian male is not as aggressive as the Asian female. In this business you have to be more of an extrovert. Men are a little more passive."

Headhunter Don Fitzpatrick agrees. "Watching my tapes, women in general are much more aggressive than men. . . . My theory on that is that— say a boy and girl both want to get into television, and they have identical SATs and grade point averages. Speakers tell them, you'll go to Chico or Medford and start out making $17,000 to $18,000 a year. A guy will say, 'This is bull. If I stay in school and get into accounting or law . . . ' And they have a career change. A woman will go to Chico or Medford and will get into LA or New York."

"In Helen Chang's paper," recalls Tokuda, "she mentions the way Asian parents have channeled boys with a narrow kind of guidance."

"With Japanese kids," says Tokuda, "right after the war, there was a lot of pressure on kids to get into society, on being quiet and working our way back in." In Seattle, she says, "I grew up with a whole group of Asian American men who from the time they were in junior high knew that they were going to be doctors—or at least that they were gonna be successful. There was research that showed that they were very good in math and sciences and not good in verbal skills. With girls there's much less pressure to go into the hard sciences."

Most of the men who do make it in broadcasting describe serendipitous routes into the field, and all of them express contentment with being reporters. "Maybe I'm covering my butt by denying that I want to anchor," says Kumagai, "but I do get a bigger charge being out in the field."

Still, most Asian male reporters do think about the fame and fortune of an anchor slot. Those thoughts quickly meet up against reality.

David Louie realizes he has little chance of becoming the 6 o'clock anchor. "I don't have the matinee idol look that would be the most ideal image on TV. Being on the portly side and not having a full head of hair, I would be the antithesis of what an anchorman is supposed to look like."

Kind of like KPIX's Dave McElhatton? Louie laughs. "But he's white," he says, quickly adding that McElhatton also has 25 years of experience broadcasting in the Bay Area.

At least Louie is on the air. In Sacramento, Lonnie Wong was a reporter at KTXL (Channel 40), and Jan Minagawa reported and did part-time anchoring at KXTV (Channel 10). Both have been promoted into newsroom editing and production jobs. And neither is thrilled to be off the air.

Wong, who says he was made an assignment editor because, among reporters, he had "the most contacts in the community," says his new job is "good management experience. But I did have a reservation. I was the only minority on the air at the station; and I know that's valuable for a station."

Minagawa's station, KXTV, does have an Asian on the air: a Vietnamese woman reporter named Mai Pham. "That made the decision easier," says Minagawa, who had been a reporter and fill-in anchor for seven years. A new news director, he says, "had a different idea of what should be on the air" and asked him to become a producer. "I didn't like it, but there was nothing I could do."

Mitch Farris rejects any notion of a conspiracy by news directors against Asian American men. In fact, he says they are "desperate" for Asian male applicants. "Just about any news director would strive to get an Asian on the air and wouldn't mind a man."

To which Machado shouts, "We're here! We're here! We're looking for work."

50

THE EFFECTS OF AFFIRMATIVE ACTION ON OTHER STAKEHOLDERS

BARBARA RESKIN

Barbara Reskin is a professor of sociology at Harvard University, having formerly taught at several Big Ten universities. She was drawn to sociology because it provides a framework for studying the factors that contribute to and reduce race and sex inequality. Her goal is to bring sociological knowledge on inequality to policymakers, and she has occasionally served as an expert witness in discrimination cases. Her research and teaching focus primarily on sex, race, and ethnic inequality at work. She brings personal experience to her research: before becoming a sociologist, she held a variety of jobs in the "real world."

Affirmative action policies and practices reduce job discrimination against minorities and white women, although their effects have not been large. Some critics charge that affirmative action's positive effects have been offset by its negative effects on white men, on productivity, and on the merit system. The research examined in this chapter shows that affirmative action rarely entails reverse discrimination, and neither hampers business productivity nor unduly increases the costs of doing business. Both theoretical and empirical research suggest that it enhances productivity by encouraging employment practices that better utilize workers' skills.

Barbara F. Reskin (1998), "The Effects of Affirmative Action on Other Stakeholders" from *The Realities of Affirmative Action in Employment*. Reprinted with the permission of the American Sociological Association.

Reverse Discrimination

For many people, the most troubling aspect of affirmative action is that it may discriminate against majority-group members (Lynch 1997). According to 1994 surveys, 70 to 80 percent of whites believed that affirmative action sometimes discriminates against whites (Steeh and Krysan 1996, p. 139). Men are more likely to believe that a woman will get a job or promotion over an equally or more qualified man than they are to believe that a man will get a promotion over an equally or more qualified women (Davis and Smith 1996). In short, many whites, especially white men, feel that they are vulnerable to reverse discrimination (Bobo and Kluegel 1993). When asked whether African Americans or whites were at greater risk of discrimination at work, respondents named whites over African Americans by a margin of two to one (Steeh and Krysan 1996, p. 140). In addition, 39 percent of respondents to a 1997 *New York Times*/CBS News poll said that whites losing out because of affirmative action was a bigger problem than African Americans losing out because of discrimination (Verhovek 1997, p. 32).

Several kinds of evidence indicate that whites' fears of reverse discrimination are exaggerated. Reverse discrimination is rare both in absolute terms and relative to conventional discrimination.[1] The most direct evidence for this conclusion comes from employment-audit studies: On every measured outcome, African-American men were much more likely than white men to experience discrimination, and Latinos were more likely than non-Hispanic men to experience discrimination (Heckman and Siegelman 1993, p. 218). Statistics on the numbers and outcomes of complaints of employment discrimination also suggest that reverse discrimination is rare.

According to national surveys, relatively few whites have experienced reverse discrimination. Only 5 to 12 percent of whites believe that their race has cost them a job or promotion, compared to 36 percent of African Americans (Steeh and Krysan 1996, pp. 139–40). Of 4,025 Los Angeles workers, 45 percent of African Americans and 16 percent of Latinos said that they had been refused a job because of their race, and 16 percent of African Americans and 8 percent of Latinos reported that they had been discriminated against in terms of pay or a promotion (Bobo and Suh 1996, table 1). In contrast, of the 863 whites surveyed, less than 3 percent had ever experienced discrimination in pay or promotion, and only one mentioned reverse discrimination. Nonetheless, two-thirds to four-fifths of whites (but just one-quarter of African Americans) surveyed in the 1990s thought it likely that less qualified African Americans won jobs or promotions over more qualified whites (Taylor 1994a; Davis and Smith 1994; Steeh and Krysan 1996, p. 139).[2]

Alfred Blumrosen's (1996, pp. 5–6) exhaustive review of discrimination complaints filed with the Equal Employment Opportunity Commission offers additional evidence that reverse discrimination is rare. Of the 451,442 discrimination complaints filed with the EEOC between 1987 and 1994, only 4 percent charged reverse discrimination (see also Norton 1996, pp. 44–5).[3]

Of the 2,189 discrimination cases that Federal appellate courts decided between 1965 and 1985, less than 5 percent charged employers with reverse discrimination (Burstein 1991, p. 518).

Statistics on the more than 3,000 cases that reached district and appeals courts between 1990 and 1994 show an even lower incidence of reverse-discrimination charges: Less than 2 percent charged reverse discrimination (U.S. Department of Labor, Employment Standards Administration n.d., p. 3). The small number of reverse discrimination complaints by white men does not appear to stem from their reluctance to file complaints: They filed more than 80 percent of the age discrimination complaints that the EEOC received in 1994. Instead, as former EEOC chair Eleanor Holmes Norton (1996, p. 45) suggested, white men presumably complain most about the kind of discrimination that they experience most and least about discrimination they rarely encounter.

Allegations of reverse discrimination are less likely than conventional discrimination cases to be supported by evidence. Of the approximately 7,000 reverse-discrimination complaints filed with the EEOC in 1994, the EEOC found only 28 credible (Crosby and Herzberger 1996, p. 55). Indeed, U.S. district and appellate courts dismissed almost all the reverse-discrimination cases they heard between 1990 and 1994 as lacking merit.

Although rare, reverse discrimination does occur. District and appellate courts found seven employers guilty of reverse discrimination in the early 1990s (all involved voluntary affirmative action programs), and a few Federal contractors have engaged in reverse discrimination, according to the Office of Federal Contract Compliance Program's (OFCCP) director for Region II (Stephanopoulos and Edley 1995, section 6.3).[4]

The actions and reports of Federal contractors are inconsistent with the belief that goals are *de facto* quotas that lead inevitably to reverse discrimination. In the first place, the fact that contractors rarely meet their goals means that they do not view them as quotas (Leonard 1990, p. 56). Second, only 2 percent of 641 Federal contractors the OFCCP surveyed in 1994 complained that the agency required quotas or reverse discrimination (Stephanopoulos and Edley 1995, section 6.3).

How can we reconcile the enormous gulf between whites' perceptions that they are likely to lose jobs or promotions because of affirmative action and the small risk of this happening? The white men who brought reverse discrimination suits presumably concluded that their employers' choices of women or minorities could not have been based on merit, because men are accustomed to being selected for customarily male jobs (*New York Times*, March 31, 1995).[5] Most majority-group members who have not had a first-hand experience of competing unsuccessfully with a minority man or woman or a white woman cite media reports as the source of their impression that affirmative action prompts employers to favor minorities and women (Hochschild 1995, pp. 144, 308).[6] It seems likely that politicians' and the media's emphasis on "quotas" has distorted the public's understanding of what is required and permitted in the name of affirmative action (Entman 1997). It is also likely that the public does not distinguish affirmative action in employment from affirmative action in education which may include preferences or in the awarding of contracts which have included set-asides.

Affirmative Action and American Commerce

Does affirmative action curb productivity, as some critics have charged? On the one hand, affirmative action could impede productivity if it forces employers to hire or promote marginally qualified and unqualified workers, or if the paperwork associated with affirmative action programs is burdensome. On the other hand, employers who assign workers to jobs based on their qualifications rather than their sex or race should make more efficient use of workers' abilities and hence should be more productive than those who use discriminatory employment practices (Becker 1971; Leonard 1984c; Donohue 1986). Affirmative action could also increase profitability by introducing varied points of view or helping firms broaden their markets (Cox and Blake 1991; Watson, Kumar, and Michaelsen 1993).

Effects on Productivity

There is no evidence that affirmative action reduces productivity or that workers hired under affirmative action are less qualified than other workers. In the first place, affirmative action plans that compromise valid educational and job requirements are illegal. Hiring unqualified workers or choosing a less qualified person over a more qualified one because of their race or sex is illegal and is not condoned in the name of affirmative action (U.S. Department of Labor, Employment Standards Administration n.d., p. 2). Second, to the extent that affirmative action gives women and minority men access to jobs that more fully exploit their productive capacity, their productivity and that of their employers should increase.

Although many Americans believe that affirmative action means that less qualified persons are hired and promoted (Verhovek 1997, p. 32), the evidence does not bear this out. According to a study of more than 3,000 workers hired in entry-level jobs in a cross-section of firms in Atlanta, Boston, Detroit, and Los Angeles, the performance evaluations of women and minorities hired under affirmative action did not differ from those of white men or female or minority workers for whom affirmative action played no role in hiring (Holzer and Neumark 1998). In addition, Columbus, Ohio, female and minority police officers hired under an affirmative action consent decree performed as well as white men (Kern 1996). Of nearly 300 corporate executives surveyed in 1979, 72 percent believed that minority hiring did not impair productivity (*Wall Street Journal* 1979); 41 percent of CEOs surveyed in 1995 said affirmative action improved corporate productivity (Crosby and Herzberger 1996, p. 86).[7]

Of the handful of studies that address the effect of affirmative action on productivity, none suggests a negative affect of the employment of women or minorities on productivity. First, the increasing representation of female and minority male workers between 1966 and 1977 and between 1984 and 1988 did not affect firms' productivity (Leonard 1984c; Conrad 1995). Second, in the context of policing, the proportions of minority or female officers are unrelated to measures of departments' effectiveness (Lovrich, Steel, and Hood 1986, p. 70; Steel and Lovrich 1987, p. 67). Third, according to a sophisticated analysis of 1990 data on establishments' and workers' characteristics, there is no relationship between firms' employment of women and their productivity in smaller plants, but in plants with more market power (and hence the capacity to discriminate), the more women plants employed, the better the firms' performance (Hellerstein, Neumark, and Troske 1998).

Studies assessing the effect of firms' racial makeup on their profits also show no effects of affirmative action on productivity. An analysis of 100 of Chicago's largest firms over a 13-year period found no statistically significant relationship between the firms' share of minority workers and their profit margins or return on equity (McMillen 1995). This absence of an association is inconsistent with companies using lower standards when hiring African American employees. Finally, according to a study that compared the market performance of the 100 firms with best and worst records of hiring and promoting women and minorities, the former averaged an 18-percent return on investments, whereas the latter's average returns were below 8 percent (Glass Ceiling Commission 1995, pp. 14, 61).[8]

Costs to Business

Estimates of the price tag of affirmative action range from a low of hundreds of millions of dollars to a high of $26 billion (Brimelow and Spencer 1993).[9] More realistic estimates put enforcement and compliance costs at about $1.9 billion (Leonard 1994, p. 34; Conrad 1995, pp. 37–8). According to Andrew Brimmer (1995, p. 12), former Governor of the Federal Reserve Board, the inefficient use of African Americans' productive capacity (as indicated by their education, training, and experience) costs the economy 70 times this much: about $138 billion annually, which is about 2.15 percent of the gross national product. Adding the cost of sex discrimination against white women would substantially increase the estimated cost of discrimination because white women outnumber African American men and women in the labor force by about three to one. The more affirmative action reduces race and sex discrimination, the lower its costs relative to the savings it engenders.

The affirmative action that the Federal executive order requires of Federal contractors adds to their paperwork. Companies with at least $50,000 in Federal contracts that employ at least 50 employees must provide written affirmative action plans that include goals and timetables, based on an annual analysis of their utilization of their labor pool. They must also provide specified information to the OFFCP and keep detailed records on the composition of their jobs and job applicants by race and sex. In response to an OFCCP survey soliciting their criticisms of the program, about one in eight Federal contractors complained about the paperwork burden (Stephanopoulos and Edley 1995, section 6.3). Keeping the records required by the OFCCP encourages the bureaucratization of human resource practices. As noted, informal employment practices, while cheaper in the short run, are also more subject to discriminatory bias and hence cost firms efficiency. Thus, implicit in the logic of the OFCCP's requirements is the recognition that formalizing personnel practices helps to reduce discrimination.

Business Support

U.S. business has supported affirmative action for at least 15 years. The Reagan administration's efforts to curtail the contract compliance program in the early 1980s drew strong opposition from the corporate sector (Bureau of National Affairs 1986). Among the groups that went on record as opposing cutbacks in Federal affirmative action programs was the National Association of Manufacturers, a major organization of U.S. employers (*The San Diego Union-Tribune* 1985, p. AA-2). All but six of 128 heads of major corporations indicated that they would retain their affirmative action plans if the Federal government ended affirmation action (Noble 1986, p. B4). A 1996 survey showed similar levels of corporate support for affirmative action: 94 percent of CEOs surveyed said that affirmative action had improved their hiring procedures, 53 percent said it had improved marketing, and—as noted above—41 percent said it had improved productivity (Crosby and Herzberger 1996, p. 86). The business community's favorable stance toward affirmative action is also seen in the jump in stock prices for firms recognized by the OFCCP for their effective affirmative action programs (Wright et al. 1995, p. 281).

Perhaps the most telling sign of business support for affirmative action is the diffusion of affirmative action practices from Federal contractors to noncontractors. As noncontractors have recognized the efficiency or market payoffs associated with more objective employment practices and a more diverse workforce, many have voluntarily implemented some affirmative action practices (Fisher 1985).

Affirmative Action and Other Stakeholders

The consequences of affirmative action reach beyond workers and employers by increasing the pools of skilled minority and female workers. When affirmative action prompts employers to hire minorities or women for positions that serve the public, it can bring services to communities that would otherwise be undeserved. For example, African-American and Hispanic physicians are more likely than whites and Anglos to practice in minority communities (Komaromy et al. 1996). Graduates of the Medical School at the University of California at San Diego who were admitted under a special admissions program were more likely to serve inner-city and rural communities and saw more poor patients than those admitted under the regular procedures (Penn, Russell, and Simon 1986).

Women's and minorities' employment in nontraditional jobs also raises the aspirations of other members of excluded groups by providing role models and by signaling that jobs are open to them. Some minorities and women do not pursue jobs or promotions because they expect to encounter discrimination (Mayhew 1968, p. 313). By reducing the perception that discriminatory barriers block access to certain lines of work, affirmative action curtails this self-selection (Reskin and Roos 1990, p. 305). In addition, the economic gains provided by better jobs permit beneficiaries to invest in the education of the next generation.

Affirmative Action, Meritocracy, and Fairness

Affirmative action troubles some Americans for the same reasons discrimination does: They see it as unfair and inconsistent with meritocracy (Nacoste 1990). The evidence summarized above indicates that employers very rarely use quotas and that affirmative action does not lead to the employment of unqualified workers. We know too that many employers implement affirmative action by expanding their recruiting efforts, by providing additional training, and by formalizing human resource practices to eliminate bias. By eliminating cronyism, drawing on wider talent pools, and providing for due process, these practices are fairer to all workers than conventional business practices (*Harvard Law Review* 1989, pp. 668–70; Dobbin et al. 1993, pp. 401–6). After all, managers who judge minority and female workers by their race or sex instead of their performance may judge white workers by arbitrary standards as well (Rand 1996, p. 72).

Available research does not address how often employers take into account race and gender in choosing among equally qualified applicants. Although the courts have forbidden race- and gender-conscious practices in layoffs, they have allowed employers to take into account race or gender in selecting among qualified applicants in order to remedy the consequences of having previously excluded certain groups from some jobs. Such programs trouble some Americans, as we can see from the research evidence presented in the next section.

Americans' Views of Affirmative Action

The passage of the 1996 California Civil Rights Initiative, which barred this state from engaging in affirmative action, has been interpreted as signaling mounting public opposition to affirmative action. In reality, whites' and

African Americans' views of affirmative action are both more nuanced and more positive than the California election result suggests. People's responses to opinion polls depend largely on how pollsters characterize affirmative action (Kravitz et al. 1997).[10] About 70 percent of Americans support affirmative action programs that pollsters describe as not involving "quotas" or "preferences" (Steeh and Krysan 1996, pp. 132, 134; Entman 1997, p. 37). Like a red flag, the term "quota" also triggers strong negative reactions. This happens because people view quotas as inconsistent with merit-based hiring and because quotas provoke fear of unfairly losing a job or promotion by members of groups that are not covered by affirmative action. As a result, most whites and African Americans oppose quotas (Bobo and Kluegel, 1993; Steeh and Krysan 1996, pp. 132–3, 148).

A casual reading of newspaper reports indicates considerable instability in Americans' attitudes toward affirmative action and a fair amount of opposition to affirmative action. For example, fewer than one in eight Americans surveyed in a 1995 Gallup poll approved of affirmative action programs that involve hiring quotas, and only 40 to 50 percent of Americans endorsed affirmative action programs designed to give African Americans or women preferential treatment (Moore 1995). However, polls that show low levels of support for affirmative action in the workplace typically ask about practices that are illegal and hence rare in actual affirmative action programs (Kravitz et al. 1997, p. xi). When pollsters ask about affirmative action in general or about the practices that actual affirmative action programs include, the majority of whites and African Americans are supportive.

In national polls conducted in the mid-1990s, about 70 percent of respondents endorsed affirmative action either as currently practiced or with reforms (Entman 1997, p. 37). For example, almost three-quarters of the respondents to a 1995 Gallup poll approved of employers using outreach efforts to recruit qualified minorities and women (Steeh and Krysan 1996, pp. 132, 134). Most whites and African Americans support such practices as targeted recruitment, open advertising, monitoring diversity, job training, and educational assistance designed to allow minorities to compete as individuals (e.g., training programs). More than three out of four white respondents and 85 percent of African-American respondents to a 1991 Harris survey agreed that "as long as there are no rigid quotas, it makes sense to give special training and advice to women and minorities so that they can perform better on the job" (Bobo and Kluegel 1993; Bruno 1995, p. 24).

We do not know how Americans feel about the kinds of race- or gender-conscious affirmative action that EEOC guidelines and Supreme Court rulings allow. When asked about "preferential hiring," most Americans disapprove. For example, only one-sixth to one-fifth of respondents surveyed during the 1990s favored the preferential hiring and promotion of African Americans because of past discrimination (about 10 to 17 percent of whites and about half to three-quarters of African Americans; Steeh and Krysan 1996, pp. 146–7). Just one survey phrased the question so that it approximately corresponded to what race- and gender-conscious affirmative action entails: giving a prefer-ence to a woman or minority over an equally qualified white man. Three-quarters of respondents did not view this practice as discriminatory (Roper Center for Public Opinion 1995).

Overall, the public is less concerned with affirmative action than media accounts would have us believe (Entman 1997). For example, respondents to a 1996 *Wall Street Journal*/NBC News poll ranked affirmative action second to last in importance out of 16 issues.[11] As Robert Entman (1997) argued, the media's framing of affirmative action as controversial exaggerates white op-position to and public discord over it.

In sum, the polls reveal that the majority of whites and African Ameri-cans have supported affirmative action since the early 1970s. Most Ameri-cans support the affirmative action procedures that employers actually use, such as taking extra efforts to find and recruit minorities and women. The broadest support is for practices that expand the applicant pool, but ignore race or gender in the selection process. Thus, Americans' first choice is en-hancing equal opportunity without using race- or gender-conscious mecha-nisms. What most Americans oppose is quotas, an employment remedy that courts impose only under exceptional circumstances. Thus, the kinds of af-firmative action practices most Americans support are in sync with what most affirmative action employers do.

Conclusion

Some critics charge that any positive effects of affirmative action come at too high a price. However, the evidence suggests that the predominant effects of affirmative action on American enterprise are neutral, and some are positive. Contrary to popular opinion, reverse discrimination is rare. Workers for whom affirmative action was a hiring consideration are no less productive than other workers. There is no evidence that affirmative action impairs productivity, and there is some evidence that, when properly implemented, affirmative action increases firms' efficiency by rationalizing their business practices. These neutral to positive effects of affirmative action contribute to the broad support it enjoys in corporate America. The affirmative action practices that appear to be most common—such as special training pro-grams or efforts to expand recruitment pools (Bureau of National Affairs 1986)—have the support of the majority of whites and people of color.

Although most affirmative action practices are neutral with respect to race and gender (e.g., eliminating subjectivity from evaluation systems), some employers take into account race and sex as "plus factors" in choosing among qualified candidates in order to reduce imbalances stemming from their past employment practices. Race- and gender-conscious practices are legal if they are part of court-ordered or voluntary affirmative action pro-grams designed to correct a serious imbalance resulting from past exclusionary practices and as long as they are properly structured so that they do not unnecessarily or permanently limit the opportunities of groups not protected under affirmative action. At least one in four Americans oppose such race- and gender-conscious practices. More generally, any departure from strict reliance on merit troubles some Americans. Others favor taking into account group membership in order to eradicate America's occupational caste system, enhance equal opportunity, and strengthen the U.S. democracy (Steinberg 1995).

The tension between affirmative action and merit is the inevitable result of the conflict between our national values and what actually occurs in the nation's workplaces. As long as discrimination is more pervasive than affirmative action, it is the real threat to meritocracy. But because no one will join the debate on behalf of discrimination, we end up with the illusion of a struggle between affirmative action and merit.

NOTES

1. Lynch's (1989, p. 53) search for white male Southern Californians who saw themselves as victims of reverse discrimination turned up only 32 men.
2. Younger whites, those from more privileged backgrounds, and those from areas with larger black populations—especially black populations who were relatively well off—were most likely to believe that blacks benefited from preferential treatment (Taylor 1994b).
3. Two percent were by white men charging sex, race, or national origin discrimination (three-quarters of these charged sex discrimination), and 1.8 percent were by white women charging race discrimination (Blumrosen 1996, p. 5).
4. In the early years of affirmative action, some federal contractors implemented quotas; since then the OFCCP has made considerable effort to ensure that contractors understand that quotas are illegal.
5. Occupational segregation by sex, race, and ethnicity no doubt contribute to this perception by reinforcing the notion that one's sex, color, or ethnicity is naturally related to the ability to perform a particular job.
6. The disproportionate number of court-ordered interventions to curtail race and sex discrimination in cities' police and fire departments (Martin 1991) and the large number of court challenges by white men (Bureau of National Affairs 1995, pp. 5–12) probably contributed to the public's impression that hiring quotas are common.
7. No data were provided on the proportion who believed that affirmative action hampered productivity.
8. Although firms' stock prices fall after the media report a discrimination suit, they rebound within a few days (Hersch 1991; Wright et al. 1995).
9. The $26 billion estimate includes the budgets of the OFCCP, the EEOC, other federal agencies' affirmative action–related activities, and private firms' compliance costs estimated at $20 million for each million of public funds budgeted for enforcement (Brimelow and Spencer 1993). Arguably, the EEOC's budget—indeed all enforcement costs—should be chalked up to the cost of discrimination, not the cost of affirmative action.
10. Several factors affect Americans' response to surveys about affirmative action in the workplace: whether their employer practices affirmative action (Taylor 1995), their own conception of what affirmative action means (one-third of white respondents

to a 1995 CBS/*New York Times* poll acknowledged that they were not sure what affirmative action is; Steeh and Krysan 1996, p. 129), whether the question also asks about affirmative action in education, whether the question asks about race- or sex-based affirmative action (although contractors are also obliged to provide affirmative action for Vietnam-era veterans and disabled persons, these groups are invisible in opinion polls), the respondents' own race and sex, the reasons respondents think racial inequality exists, and their level of racial prejudice (Bobo and Kluegel 1993). For full reviews, see Steeh and Krysan (1996) and Kravitz et al. (1997).

11. Only 1 percent of respondents named affirmative action as the most important problem our country faces (Entman 1997, p. 38).

REFERENCES

Becker, Gary S. 1971. *A Theory of Discrimination*. 2d ed. Chicago, IL: University of Chicago Press.

Blumrosen, Alfred W. 1996. *Declaration*. Statement submitted to the Supreme Court of California in Response to Proposition 209, September 26.

Bobo, Lawrence and James R. Kluegel. 1993. "Opposition to Race Targeting." *American Sociological Review* 58:443–64.

Bobo, Larry and Susan A. Suh. 1996. "Surveying Racial Discrimination: Analyses from a Multi-Ethnic Labor Market." Working Paper No. 75, Russell Sage Foundation, New York.

Brimelow, Peter and Leslie Spencer. 1993. "When Quotas Replace Merit, Everybody Suffers." *Forbes,* February 15, pp. 80–102.

Brimmer, Andrew F. 1995. "The Economic Cost of Discrimination against Black Americans." Pp. 11–29 in *Economic Perspectives on Affirmative Action,* edited by M. C. Simms. Washington, DC: Joint Center for Political and Economic Studies.

Bruno, Andorra. 1995. *Affirmative Action in Employment*. CRS Report for Congress. Washington, DC: Congressional Research Service.

Bureau of National Affairs. 1986. *Affirmative Action Today: A Legal and Political Analysis. A BNA Special Report*. Washington, DC: The Bureau of National Affairs.

————. 1995. *Affirmative Action after Adarand: A Legal, Regulatory, Legislative Outlook*. Washington, DC: The Bureau of National Affairs.

Burstein, Paul. 1991. "'Reverse Discrimination' Cases in the Federal Courts: Mobilization by a Countermovement." *Sociological Quarterly* 32:511–28.

Conrad, Cecilia. 1995. "The Economic Cost of Affirmative Action." Pp. 33–53 in *Economic Perspectives on Affirmative Action,* edited by M. C. Simms. Washington, DC: Joint Center for Political and Economic Studies.

Cox, Taylor H. and Stacy Blake. 1991. "Managing Cultural Diversity: Implications for Organizational Competitiveness." *Academy of Management Executive* 5:45–56.

Crosby, Faye J. and Sharon D. Herzberger. 1996. "For Affirmative Action." Pp. 3–109 in *Affirmative Action: Pros and Cons of Policy and Practice,* edited by R. J. Simon. Washington, DC: American University Press.

Davis, James A. and Tom W. Smith. 1994. *General Social Survey* [MRDF]. Chicago IL: National Opinion Research Center [producer, distributor].

————. 1996. *General Social Survey* [MRDF]. Chicago IL: National Opinion Research Center [producer, distributor].

Dobbin, Frank, John Sutton, John Meyer, and W. Richard Scott. 1993. "Equal Opportunity Law and the Construction of Internal Labor Markets." *American Journal of Sociology* 99:396–427.

Donohue, John J. 1986. "Is Title VII Efficient?" *University of Pennsylvania Law Review* 134:1411–31.

Entman, Robert M. 1997. "Manufacturing Discord: Media in the Affirmative Action Debate." *Press/Politics* 2:32–51.

Fisher, Ann B. 1985. "Businessmen Like to Hire by the Numbers." *Fortune Magazine,* September 16, pp. 26, 28–30.

Glass Ceiling Commission. See U.S. Department of Labor, Office of Federal Contract Compliance Programs, Glass Ceiling Commission.

Harvard Law Review. 1989. "Rethinking Weber: The Business Response to Affirmative Action." *Harvard Law Review* 102:658–71.

Heckman, James J. and Peter Siegelman. 1993. "The Urban Institute Audit Studies: Their Methods and Findings." Pp. 187–229 in *Clear and Convincing Evidence: Measurement of Discrimination in America,* edited by M. Fix and R. J. Struyk. Washington, DC: The Urban Institute.

Hellerstein, Judith K., David Neumark, and Kenneth R. Troske. 1998. "Market Forces and Sex Discrimination." Department of Sociology, University of Maryland, College Park. Unpublished manuscript.

Hersch, Joni. 1991. "Equal Employment Opportunity Law and Firm Profitability." *Journal of Human Resources* 26:139–53.

Hochschild, Jennifer. 1995. *Facing Up to the American Dream.* Princeton, NJ: Princeton University Press.

Holzer, Harry J. and David Neumark. Forthcoming 1998. "Are Affirmative Action Hires Less Qualified? Evidence from Employer-Employee Data on New Hires." *Journal of Labor Economics.*

Kern, Leesa. 1996. "Hiring and Seniority: Issues in Policing the Post-Judicial Intervention Period." Department of Sociology, Ohio State University, Columbus, OH: Unpublished manuscript.

Komaromy, Miriam, Kevin Grumbach, Michael Drake, Karen Vranizan, Nicole Lurie, Dennis Keane, and Andrew Bindman. 1996. "The Role of Black and Hispanic Physicians in Providing Health Care in Undeserved Populations." *New England Journal of Medicine* 334:1305–10.

Kravitz, David A., David A. Harrison, Marlene E. Turner, Edward L. Levine, Wanda Chaves, Michael T. Brannick, Donna L. Denning, Craig J. Russell, and Maureen A. Conrad. 1997. *Affirmative Action: A Review of Psychological and Behavioral Research.* Bowling Green, OH: Society for Industrial and Organizational Psychology.

Leonard, Jonathan S. 1984c. "Anti-Discrimination or Reverse Discrimination: The Impact of Changing Demographics, Title VII, and Affirmative Action on Productivity." *Journal of Human Resources* 19:145–74.

_____. 1990. "The Impact of Affirmative Action Regulation and Equal Employment Law on Black Employment." *Journal of Economic Perspectives* 4:47–63.

_____. 1994. "Use of Enforcement Techniques in Eliminating Glass Ceiling Barriers." Report to the Glass Ceiling Commission, April, U.S. Department of Labor, Washington, DC.

Lovrich, Nicholas P., Brent S. Steel, and David Hood. 1986. "Equity versus Productivity: Affirmative Action and Municipal Police Services." *Public Productivity Review* 39:61–72.

Lynch, Frederick R. 1989. *Invisible Victims: White Males and the Crisis of Affirmative Action.* New York: Greenwood.

_____. 1997. *The Diversity Machine: The Drive to Change the White Male Workplace.* New York: Free Press.

Martin, Susan E. 1991. "The Effectiveness of Affirmative Action: The Case of Women in Policing." *Justice Quarterly* 8:489–504.

Mayhew, Leon. 1968. *Law and Equal Opportunity: A Study of Massachusetts Commission against Discrimination.* Cambridge, MA: Harvard University Press.

McMillen, Liz. 1995. "[Affirmative Action] Policies Said to Help Companies Hire Qualified Workers at No Extra Cost." *Chronicle of Higher Education,* November 17, p. A7.

Moore, David W. 1995. "Americans Today Are Dubious about Affirmative Action." *The Gallup Poll Monthly,* March, pp. 36–8.

Nacoste, Rupert Barnes. 1990. "Sources of Stigma: Analyzing the Psychology of Affirmative Action." *Law & Policy* 12:175–95.

New York Times. 1995. "Reverse Discrimination Complaints Rare, Labor Study Reports." *New York Times,* March 31, p. A23.

Noble, Kenneth. 1986. "Employers Are Split on Affirmative Goals." *New York Times,* March 3, p. B4.

Norton, Elenor Holmes. 1996. "Affirmative Action in the Workplace." Pp. 39–48 in *The Affirmative Action Debate,* edited by G. Curry. Reading, MA: Addison-Wesley.

Penn, Nolan E., Percy J. Russell, and Harold J. Simon. 1986. "Affirmative Action at Work: A Survey of Graduates of the University of California at San Deigo Medical School." *American Journal of Public Health* 76:1144–46.

Rand, A. Barry. 1996. "Diversity in Corporate America." Pp. 65–76 in *The Affirmative Action Debate,* edited by G. Curry. Reading, MA: Addison-Wesley.

Reskin, Barbara F. and Patricia Roos. 1990. *Job Queues, Gender Queues.* Philadelphia, PA: Temple University Press.

Roper Center for Public Opinion. 1995. *Poll Database:* Question ID USGALLUP.95MRW1.R32[MRDF]. Storrs, Ct: Roper Center for Public Opinion [producer, distributor].

San Diego Union-Tribune. 1985. "Groups at Odds Over Affirmative Action Revisions." *San Diego Union-Tribune,* September 13, p. AA-2.

Steeh, Charlotte, and Maria Krysan. 1996. "The Polls—Trends: Affirmative Action and the Public, 1970–1995." *Public Opinion Quarterly* 60:128–58.

Steel, Brent S. and Nicholas P. Lovrich. 1987. "Equality and Efficiency Tradeoffs in Affirmative Action—Real or Imagined? The Case of Women in Policing." *Social Science Journal* 24:53–70.

Steinberg, Steven. 1995. *Turning Back: Retreat from Racial Justice in American Thought.* Boston, MA: Beacon.

Stephanopoulos, George and Christopher Edley, Jr. 1995. "Affirmative Action Review." *Report to the President,* Washington, DC.

Taylor, Marylee C. 1994a. "Beliefs about the Preferential Hiring of Black Applicants: Sure It Happens, But I've Never Seen It." Pennsylvania State University, University Park, PA. Unpublished manuscript.

———. 1994b. "Impact of Affirmative Action on Beneficiary Groups: Evidence from the 1990 General Social Survey." *Basic and Applied Social Psychology* 15:143–78.

———. 1995. "White Backlash to Workplace Affirmative Action: Peril or Myth?" *Social Forces* 73:1385–1414.

U.S. Department of Labor, Employment Standards Administration, Office of Federal Contract Compliance Programs [cited as OFCCP]. n.d. "The Rhetoric and the Reality about Federal Affirmative Action at the OFCCP." Washington, DC: U.S. Department of Labor.

U.S. Department of Labor, Office of Federal Contract Compliance Programs, Glass Ceiling Commission. 1995. *Good for Business: Making Full Use of the Nation's Human Capital/The Environmental Scar.* Washington, DC: U.S. Government Printing Office.

Verhovek, Sam Howe. 1997. "In Poll, Americans Reject Means but Not Ends of Racial Diversity." *New York Times,* December 14, pp. 1, 32.

Wall Street Journal. 1979. "Labor Letter: A Special News Report on People and Their Jobs in Offices, Fields, and Factories: Affirmative Action Is Accepted by Most Corporate Chiefs." *Wall Street Journal,* April 3, p. 1.

Watson, Warren E., Kamalesh Kumar, and Larry K. Michaelsen. 1993. "Cultural Diversity's Impact on Interaction Process and Performance: Comparing Homogeneous and Diverse Task Groups." *Academy of Management Journal* 36:590–602.

Wright, Peter, Stephen P. Ferris, Janine S. Hiller, and Mark Kroll. 1995. "Competitiveness through Management of Diversity: Effects on Stock Price Valuation." *Academy of Management Journal* 38:272–87.

51

GLOBAL WOMAN

BARBARA EHRENREICH • ARLIE RUSSELL HOCHSCHILD

Barbara Ehrenreich is the author of *Nickel and Dimed: On (Not) Getting by in America, Blood Rites: Origins and History of the Passions of War,* and numerous other works.

Arlie Russell Hochschild is the author of *The Second Shift, The Time Bind,* and the forthcoming *Commercialization of Intimate Life and Other Essays.* She teaches sociology at the University of California at Berkeley.

"Whose baby are you?" Josephine Perera, a nanny from Sri Lanka, asks Isadora, her pudgy two-year-old charge in Athens, Greece. Thoughtful for a moment, the child glances toward the closed door of the next room, in which her mother is working, as if to say, "That's my mother in there."

"No, you're *my* baby," Josephine teases, tickling Isadora lightly. Then, to settle the issue, Isadora answers, "Together!" She has two mommies—her mother and Josephine. And surely a child loved by many adults is richly blessed.

In some ways, Josephine's story—which unfolds in an extraordinary documentary film, *When Mother Comes Home for Christmas,* directed by Nilita Vachani—describes an unparalleled success. Josephine has ventured around the world, achieving a degree of independence her mother could not have imagined, and amply supporting her three children with no help from her ex-husband, their father. Each month she mails a remittance check from Athens to Hatton, Sri Lanka, to pay the children's living expenses and school fees. On her Christmas visit home, she bears gifts of pots, pans, and dishes. While she makes payments on a new bus that Suresh, her oldest son, now drives for a living, she is also saving for a modest dowry for her daughter, Norma. She dreams of buying a new house in which the whole family can live. In the meantime, her work as a nanny enables Isadora's parents to devote themselves to their careers and avocations.

But Josephine's story is also one of wrenching global inequality. While Isadora enjoys the attention of three adults, Josephine's three children in Sri

Lanka have been far less lucky. According to Vachani, Josephine's youngest child, Suminda, was two—Isadora's age—when his mother first left home to work in Saudi Arabia. Her middle child, Norma, was nine; her oldest son, Suresh, thirteen. From Saudi Arabia, Josephine found her way first to Kuwait, then to Greece. Except for one two-month trip home, she has lived apart from her children for ten years. She writes them weekly letters, seeking news of relatives, asking about school, and complaining that Norma doesn't write back.

Although Josephine left the children under her sister's supervision, the two youngest have shown signs of real distress. Norma has attempted suicide three times. Suminda, who was twelve when the film was made, boards in a grim, Dickensian orphanage that forbids talk during meals and showers. He visits his aunt on holidays. Although the oldest, Suresh, seems to be on good terms with his mother, Norma is tearful and sullen, and Suminda does poorly in school, picks quarrels, and otherwise seems withdrawn from the world. Still, at the end of the film, we see Josephine once again leave her three children in Sri Lanka to return to Isadora in Athens. For Josephine can either live with her children in desperate poverty or make money by living apart from them. Unlike her affluent First World employers, she cannot both live with her family and support it.

Thanks to the process we loosely call "globalization," women are on the move as never before in history. In images familiar to the West from television commercials for credit cards, cell phones, and airlines, female executives jet about the world, phoning home from luxury hotels and reuniting with eager children in airports. But we hear much less about a far more prodigious flow of female labor and energy: the increasing migration of millions of women from poor countries to rich ones, where they serve as nannies, maids, and sometimes sex workers. In the absence of help from male partners, many women have succeeded in tough "male world" careers only by turning over the care of their children, elderly parents, and homes to women from the Third World. This is the female underside of globalization, whereby millions of Josephines from poor countries in the south migrate to do the "women's work" of the north—work that affluent women are no longer able or willing to do. These migrant workers often leave their own children in the care of grandmothers, sisters, and sisters-in-law. Sometimes a young daughter is drawn out of school to care for her younger siblings.

This pattern of female migration reflects what could be called a worldwide gender revolution. In both rich and poor countries, fewer families can rely solely on a male breadwinner. In the United States, the earning power of most men has declined since 1970, and many women have gone out to "make up the difference." By one recent estimate, women were the sole, primary, or coequal earners in more than half of American families.[1] So the question arises: Who will take care of the children, the sick, the elderly? Who will make dinner and clean house?

While the European or American woman commutes to work an average twenty-eight minutes a day, many nannies from the Philippines, Sri Lanka, and India cross the globe to get to their jobs. Some female migrants from the Third World do find something like "liberation," or at least the chance to become independent breadwinners and to improve their children's material lives. Other, less fortunate migrant women end up in the control of criminal employers—their passports stolen, their mobility blocked, forced to work without pay in brothels or to provide sex along with cleaning and child-care services in affluent homes. But even in more typical cases, where benign employers pay wages on time, Third World migrant women achieve their success only by assuming the cast-off domestic roles of middle- and high-income women in the First World—roles that have been previously rejected, of course, by men. And their "commute" entails a cost we have yet to fully comprehend.

The migration of women from the Third World to do "women's work" in affluent countries has so far received little scholarly or media attention—for reasons that are easy enough to guess. First, many, though by no means all, of the new female migrant workers are women of color, and therefore subject to the racial "discounting" routinely experienced by, say, Algerians in France, Mexicans in the United States, and Asians in the United Kingdom. Add to racism the private "indoor" nature of so much of the new migrants' work. Unlike factory workers, who congregate in large numbers, or taxi drivers, who are visible on the street, nannies and maids are often hidden away, one or two at a time, behind closed doors in private homes. Because of the illegal nature of their work, most sex workers are even further concealed from public view.

At least in the case of nannies and maids, another factor contributes to the invisibility of migrant women and their work—one that, for their affluent employers, touches closer to home. The Western culture of individualism, which finds extreme expression in the United States, militates against acknowledging help or human interdependency of nearly any kind. Thus, in the time-pressed upper middle class, servants are no longer displayed as status symbols, decked out in white caps and aprons, but often remain in the background, or disappear when company comes. Furthermore, affluent careerwomen increasingly earn their status not through leisure, as they might have a century ago, but by apparently "doing it all"—producing a full-time career, thriving children, a contented spouse, and a well-managed home. In order to preserve this illusion, domestic workers and nannies make the house hotel-room perfect, feed and bathe the children, cook and clean up—and then magically fade from sight.

The lifestyles of the First World are made possible by a global transfer of the services associated with a wife's traditional role—child care, homemaking, and sex—from poor countries to rich ones. To generalize and perhaps oversimplify: in an earlier phase of imperialism, northern countries extracted natural resources and agricultural products—rubber, metals, and sugar, for example—from lands they conquered and colonized. Today, while still relying on Third World countries for agricultural and industrial labor, the wealthy countries also seek to extract something harder to measure and quantify, something that can look very much like love. Nannies like Josephine bring the distant families that employ them real maternal affection, no doubt enhanced by the heartbreaking absence of their own children in the poor countries they leave behind. Similarly, women who migrate from country to country to work as maids bring not only their muscle power but an attentiveness to detail and to the human relationships in the household that might otherwise have been invested in their own families. Sex workers offer the simulation of sexual and romantic love, or at least transient sexual companionship. It is as if the wealthy parts of the world are running short on precious emotional and sexual resources and have had to turn to poorer regions for fresh supplies.

There are plenty of historical precedents for this globalization of traditional female services. In the ancient Middle East, the women of populations defeated in war were routinely enslaved and hauled off to serve as household workers and concubines for the victors. Among the Africans brought to North America as slaves in the sixteenth through nineteenth centuries, about a third were women and children, and many of those women were pressed to be concubines, domestic servants, or both. Nineteenth-century Irishwomen—along with many rural Englishwomen—migrated to English towns and cities to work as domestics in the homes of the growing upper middle class. Services thought to be innately feminine—child care, housework, and sex—often win little recognition or pay. But they have always been sufficiently in demand to transport over long distances if necessary. What is new today is the sheer number of female migrants and the very long distances they travel. Immigration statistics show huge numbers of women in motion, typically from poor countries to rich. Although the gross statistics give little clue as to the jobs women eventually take, there are reasons to infer that much of their work is "caring work," performed either in private homes or in institutional settings such as hospitals, hospices, child-care centers, and nursing homes.

The statistics are, in many ways, frustrating. We have information on legal migrants but not on illegal migrants, who, experts tell us, travel in equal if not greater numbers. Furthermore, many Third World countries lack data for past years, which makes it hard to trace trends over time; or they use varying methods of gathering information, which makes it hard to compare one country with another. Nevertheless, the trend is clear enough for some scholars, including Stephen Castles, Mark Miller, and Janet Momsen, to speak of a "feminization of migration."[2] From 1950 to 1970, for example, men predominated in labor migration to northern Europe from Turkey, Greece, and North Africa. Since then, women have been replacing men. In 1946, women were fewer than 3 percent of the Algerians and Moroccans living in France; by 1990, they were more than 40 percent.[3] Overall, half of the world's 120 million legal and illegal migrants are now believed to be women.

Patterns of international migration vary from region to region, but women migrants from a surprising number of sending countries actually outnumber men, sometimes by a wide margin. For example, in the 1990s, women make up over half of Filipino migrants to all countries and 84 percent of Sri Lankan migrants to the Middle East.[4] Indeed, by 1993 statistics, Sri Lankan women such as Josephine vastly outnumbered Sri Lankan men as migrant workers who'd left for Saudi Arabia, Kuwait, Lebanon, Oman, Bahrain, Jordan, and Qatar, as well as to all countries of the Far East, Africa, and Asia.[5] About half of the migrants leaving Mexico, India, Korea, Malaysia, Cyprus, and Swaziland to work elsewhere are also women. Throughout the 1990s women outnumbered men among migrants to the United States, Canada, Sweden, the United Kingdom, Argentina, and Israel.[6]

Most women, like men, migrate from the south to the north and from poor countries to rich ones. Typically, migrants go to the nearest comparatively rich country, preferably one whose language they speak or whose religion and culture they share. There are also local migratory flows: from northern to southern Thailand, for instance, or from East Germany to West. But of the regional or cross-regional flows, four stand out. One goes from Southeast Asia to the oil-rich Middle and Far East—from Bangladesh, Indonesia, the Philippines, and Sri Lanka to Bahrain, Oman, Kuwait, Saudi Arabia, Hong Kong, Malaysia, and Singapore. Another stream of migration goes from the former Soviet bloc to western Europe—from Russia, Romania, Bulgaria, and Albania to Scandinavia, Germany, France, Spain, Portugal, and England. A third goes from south to north in the Americas, including the stream from Mexico to the United States, which scholars say is the longest-running labor migration in the world. A fourth stream moves from Africa to various parts of Europe. France receives many female migrants from Morocco, Tunisia, and Algeria. Italy receives female workers from Ethiopia, Eritrea, and Cape Verde.

Female migrants overwhelmingly take up work as maids or domestics. As women have become an ever greater proportion of migrant workers, receiving countries reflect a dramatic influx of foreign-born domestics. In the United States, African-American women, who accounted for 60 percent of domestics in the 1940s, have been largely replaced by Latinas, many of them recent migrants from Mexico and Central America. In England, Asian migrant women have displaced the Irish and Portuguese domestics of the past. In French cities, North African women have replaced rural French girls. In western Germany, Turks and women from the former East Germany have replaced rural native-born women. Foreign females from countries outside the European Union made up only 6 percent of all domestic workers in 1984. By 1987, the percentage had jumped to 52, with most coming from the Philippines, Sri Lanka, Thailand, Argentina, Colombia, Brazil, El Salvador, and Peru.[7]

The governments of some sending countries actively encourage women to migrate in search of domestic jobs, reasoning that migrant women are more likely than their male counterparts to send their hard-earned wages to their families rather than spending the money on themselves. In general, women send home anywhere from half to nearly all of what they earn. These remittances have a significant impact on the lives of children, parents, siblings, and wider networks of kin—as well as on cash-strapped Third World governments. Thus, before Josephine left for Athens, a program sponsored by the Sri Lankan government taught her how to use a microwave oven, a vacuum cleaner, and an electric mixer.

Over the last thirty years, as the rich countries have grown much richer, the poor countries have become—in both absolute and relative terms—poorer. Global inequalities in wages are particularly striking. In Hong Kong, for instance, the wages of a Filipina domestic are about fifteen times the amount she could make as a schoolteacher back in the Philippines. In addition, poor countries turning to the IMF or World Bank for loans are often forced to undertake measures of so-called structural adjustment, with disastrous results for the poor and especially for poor women and children. To qualify for loans, governments are usually required to devalue their currencies, which turns the hard currencies of rich countries into gold and the soft currencies of poor countries into straw. Structural adjustment programs also call for cuts in support for "noncompetitive industries," and for the reduction of public services such as health care and food subsidies for the poor. Citizens of poor countries, women as well as men, thus have a strong incentive to seek work in more fortunate parts of the world.

But it would be a mistake to attribute the globalization of women's work to a simple synergy of needs among women—one group, in the affluent countries, needing help and the other, in poor countries, needing jobs. For one thing, this formulation fails to account for the marked failure of First World governments to meet the needs created by its women's entry into the workforce. The downsized American—and to a lesser degree, western European—welfare state has become a "deadbeat dad." Unlike the rest of the industrialized world, the United States does not offer public child care for working mothers, nor does it ensure paid family and medical leave. Moreover, a series of state tax revolts in the 1980s reduced the number of hours public libraries were open and slashed school-enrichment and after-school programs. Europe did not experience anything comparable. Still, tens of millions of western European women are in the workforce who were not before—and there has been no proportionate expansion in public services.

Secondly, any view of the globalization of domestic work as simply an arrangement among women completely omits the role of men. Numerous studies, including some of our own, have shown that as American women took on paid employment, the men in their families did little to increase their contribution to the work of the home. For example, only one out of every five men among the working couples whom Hochschild interviewed for *The Second Shift* in the 1980s shared the work at home, and later studies suggest that while working mothers are doing somewhat less housework than their counterparts twenty years ago, most men are doing only a little more.[8] With divorce, men frequently abdicate their child-care responsibilities to their ex-wives. In most cultures of the First World outside the United States, power-ful traditions even more firmly discourage husbands from doing "women's work." So, strictly speaking, the presence of immigrant nannies does not en-able affluent women to enter the workforce; it enables affluent *men* to con-tinue avoiding the second shift.

The men in wealthier countries are also, of course, directly responsible for the demand for immigrant sex workers—as well as for the sexual abuse of many migrant women who work as domestics. Why, we wondered, is there a particular demand for "imported" sexual partners? Part of the an-swer may lie in the fact that new immigrants often take up the least desir-able work, and, thanks to the AIDS epidemic, prostitution has become a job that ever fewer women deliberately choose. But perhaps some of this de-mand, as we see in Denise Brennan's [work] on sex tourism, grows out of the erotic lure of the "exotic."[9] Immigrant women may seem desirable sexual partners for the same reason that First World employers believe them to be especially gifted as caregivers: they are thought to embody the traditional feminine qualities of nurturance, docility, and eagerness to please. Some men feel nostalgic for these qualities, which they associate with a bygone way of life. Even as many wage-earning Western women assimilate to the competitive culture of "male" work and ask respect for making it in a man's world, some men seek in the "exotic Orient" or "hot-blooded tropics" a woman from the imagined past.

Of course, not all sex workers migrate voluntarily. An alarming number of women and girls are trafficked by smugglers and sold into bondage. Be-cause trafficking is illegal and secret, the numbers are hard to know with any certainty. Kevin Bales estimates that in Thailand alone, a country of 60 mil-lion, half a million to a million women are prostitutes, and one out of every twenty of these is enslaved. As Bales's chapter in [*Global Woman*] shows, many of these women are daughters whom northern hill-tribe families have sold to brothels in the cities of the south. Believing the promises of jobs and money, some begin the voyage willingly, only to discover days later that the "arrangers" are traffickers who steal their passports, define them as debtors, and enslave them as prostitutes. Other women and girls are kidnapped, or sold by their impoverished families, and then trafficked to brothels. Even worse fates befall women from neighboring Laos and Burma, who flee crushing poverty and repression at home only to fall into the hands of Thai slave traders.[10]

If the factors that pull migrant women workers to affluent countries are not as simple as they at first appear, neither are the factors that push them. Certainly relative poverty plays a major role, but, interestingly, migrant women often do not come from the poorest classes of their societies.[11] In fact, they are typically more affluent and better educated than male migrants. Many female migrants from the Philippines and Mexico, for example, have high school or college diplomas and have held middle-class — albeit low-paid — jobs back home. One study of Mexican migrants suggests that the trend is toward increasingly better-educated female migrants. Thirty years ago, most Mexican-born maids in the United States had been poorly educated maids in Mexico. Now a majority have high school degrees and have held clerical, retail, or professional jobs before leaving for the United States.[12] Such women are likely to be enterprising and adventurous enough to resist the social pressures to stay home and accept their lot in life.

Noneconomic factors — or at least factors that are not immediately and directly economic — also influence a woman's decision to emigrate. By migrating, a woman may escape the expectation that she care for elderly family members, relinquish her paycheck to a husband or father, or defer to an abusive husband. Migration may also be a practical response to a failed marriage and the need to provide for children without male help. In the Philippines, . . . Rhacel Salazar Parreñas tells us, migration is sometimes called a "Philippine divorce."[13] And there are forces at work that may be making the men of poor countries less desirable as husbands. Male unemployment runs high in the countries that supply female domestics to the First World. Unable to make a living, these men often grow demoralized and cease contributing to their families in other ways. Many female migrants, including those in Michele Gamburd's [work], tell of unemployed husbands who drink or gamble their remittances away.[14] Notes one study of Sri Lankan women working as maids in the Persian Gulf: "It is not unusual . . . for the women to find upon their return that their Gulf wages by and large have been squandered on alcohol, gambling and other dubious undertakings while they were away."[15]

To an extent then, the globalization of child care and housework brings the ambitious and independent women of the world together: the career-oriented upper-middle-class woman of an affluent nation and the striving woman from a crumbling Third World or postcommunist economy. Only it does not bring them together in the way that second-wave feminists in affluent countries once liked to imagine — as sisters and allies struggling to achieve common goals. Instead, they come together as mistress and maid, employer and employee, across a great divide of privilege and opportunity.

This trend toward global redivision of women's traditional work throws new light on the entire process of globalization. Conventionally, it is the poorer countries that are thought to be dependent on the richer ones — a dependency symbolized by the huge debt they owe to global financial institutions. What we explore . . . , however, is a dependency that works in the other direction, and it is a dependency of a particularly intimate kind. Increasingly often, as affluent and middle-class families in the First World come to depend on migrants from poorer regions to provide child care, homemaking, and sexual services, a global relationship arises that in some ways mirrors the traditional relationship between the sexes. The First World takes on a role like that of the old-fashioned male in the family — pampered, entitled, unable to cook, clean, or find his socks. Poor countries take on a role like that of the traditional woman within the family—patient, nurturing, and self-denying. A division of labor feminists critiqued when it was "local" has now, metaphorically speaking, gone global.

To press this metaphor a bit further, the resulting relationship is by no means a "marriage," in the sense of being openly acknowledged. In fact, it is striking how invisible the globalization of women's work remains, how little it is noted or discussed in the First World. Trend spotters have had almost nothing to say about the fact that increasing numbers of affluent First World children and elderly persons are tended by immigrant care workers or live in homes cleaned by immigrant maids. Even the political groups we might expect to be concerned about this trend—antiglobalization and feminist activists—often seem to have noticed only the most extravagant abuses, such as trafficking and female enslavement. So if a metaphorically gendered relationship has developed between rich and poor countries, it is less like a marriage and more like a secret affair.

But it is a "secret affair" conducted in plain view of the children. Little Isadora and the other children of the First World raised by "two mommies" may be learning more than their ABC's from a loving surrogate parent. In their own living rooms, they are learning a vast and tragic global politics.[16] Children see. But they also learn how to disregard what they see. They learn how adults make the visible invisible. That is their "early childhood education."

NOTES

1. See Ellen Galinsky and Dana Friedman, *Women: The New Providers,* Whirlpool Foundation Study, Part 1 (New York: Families and Work Institute, 1995), p. 37.

2. Special thanks to Roberta Espinoza, who gathered and designed the flow maps shown in Appendix I. In addition to material directly cited, this introduction draws from the following works: Kathleen M. Adams and Sara Dickey, eds., *Home and Hegemony: Domestic Service and Identity Politics in South and Southeast Asia* (Ann Arbor: University of Michigan Press, 2000); Floya Anthias and Gabriella Lazaridis, eds., *Gender and Migration in Southern Europe: Women on the Move* (Oxford and New York: Berg, 2000); Stephen Castles and Mark J. Miller, *The Age of Migration: International Population Movements in the Modern World* (New York and London: The Guilford Press, 1998); Noeleen Heyzer, Geertje Lycklama à Nijehold, and Nedra Weerakoon, eds., *The Trade in Domestic Workers: Causes, Mechanisms, and Consequences of International Migration* (London: Zed Books, 1994); Eleanore Kofman, Annie Phizacklea, Parvati Raghuram, and Rosemary Sales, *Gender and International Migration in Europe: Employment, Welfare, and Politics* (New York and London: Routledge, 2000); Douglas S. Massey, Joaquin Arango, Graeme Hugo, Ali Kouaouci, Adela Pellegrino, and J. Edward Taylor, *Worlds in Motion: Understanding International Migration at the End of the Millennium* (Oxford: Clarendon Press, 1999); Janet Henshall Momsen, ed., *Gender, Migration, and Domestic Service* (London: Routledge, 1999); Katie Willis and Brenda Yeoh, eds., *Gender and Immigration* (London: Edward Elgar Publishers, 2000).

3. Illegal migrants are said to make up anywhere from 60 percent (as in Sri Lanka) to 87 percent (as in Indonesia) of all migrants. In Singapore in 1994, 95 percent of Filipino overseas contact workers lacked work permits from the Philippine

government. The official figures based on legal migration therefore severely underestimate the number of migrants. See Momsen, 1999, p. 7.

4. Momsen, 1999, p. 9.

5. Sri Lanka Bureau of Foreign Employment, 1994, as cited in G. Gunatilleke, *The Economic, Demographic, Sociocultural and Political Setting for Emigration from Sri Lanka International Migration,* vol. 23 (3/4), 1995, pp. 667–98.

6. Anthias and Lazaridis, 2000; Heyzer, Nijehold, and Weerakoon, 1994, pp. 4–27; Momsen, 1999, p. 21; "Wistat: Women's Indicators and Statistics Database," version 3, CD-ROM (United Nations, Department for Economic and Social Information and Policy Analysis, Statistical Division, 1994).

7. Geovanna Campani, "Labor Markets and Family Networks: Filipino Women in Italy," in Hedwig Rudolph and Mirjana Morokvasic, eds., *Bridging States and Markets: International Migration in the Early 1990s* (Berlin: Edition Sigma, 1993), p. 206.

8. For information on male work at home during the 1990s, see Arlie Russell Hochschild and Anne Machung, *The Second Shift: Working Parents and the Revolution at Home* (New York: Avon, 1997), p. 277.

9. Dennis Brennan, "Selling Sex for Visas: Sex Tourism as a Stepping-Stone to International Migration," *Global Woman: Nannies, Maids and Sex Workers in the New Economy,* eds. Barbara Ehrenreich and Arlie Hochschild (New York: Henry Holt, 2002), 154–168.

10. Kevin Bales, *Disposable People: New Slavery in the Global Economy* (Berkeley: University of California Press, 1999), p. 43. Kevin Bales, "Because She Looks Like a Child," in *Global Woman: Nannies, Maids and Sex Workers in the New Economy,* eds. Barbara Ehrenreich and Arlie Hochschild (New York: Henry Holt, 2002), 207–229.

11. Andrea Tyree and Katharine M. Donato, "A Demographic Overview of the International Migration of Women," in *International Migration: The Female Experience,* ed. Rita Simon and Caroline Bretell (Totowa, NJ: Rowman & Allanheld, 1986), p. 29. Indeed, many immigrant maids and nannies are more educated than the people they work for. See Pei-Chia Lan's paper in this volume.

12. Momsen, 1999, pp. 10, 73.

13. Rhacel Salazar Parreñas, "The Care Crisis in the Philippines: Children and Transnational Families in the New Global Economy," in *Global Woman: Nannies, Maids and Sex Workers in the New Economy,* eds. Barbara Ehrenreich and Arlie Hochschild (New York: Henry Holt, 2002), 39–54.

14. Michele Gamburd, "Breadwinners No More," in *Global Woman: Nannies, Maids and Sex Workers in the New Economy,* eds. Barbara Ehrenreich and Arlie Hochschild (New York: Henry Holt, 2002), 190–206.

15. Grete Brochmann, *Middle East Avenue: Female Migration from Sri Lanka to the Gulf* (Boulder, Colo.: Westview Press, 1993), pp. 179, 215.

16. On this point, thanks to Raka Ray, Sociology Department at the University of California, Berkeley.

52

AMERICA'S DIRTY WORK: MIGRANT MAIDS AND MODERN-DAY SLAVERY

JOY M. ZAREMBKA

Joy M. Zarembka, the daughter of a domestic worker from Kenya, is the director of Break the Chain Campaign. She is also the author of *The Pigment of Your Imagination: Mixed Race Families in Britain, Kenya, Zimbabwe and Jamaica* (www.ThePigment. com), which explores the various configurations of "race" in different countries.

Imagine you are locked away in a strange home. You do not speak your captor's language. On the rare occasions when you are escorted off the premises, you are forbidden to speak to anyone. You are often fed the leftover food of the children you are required to watch while completing your around-the-clock household duties. You have never been paid for your labors, and the woman of the house physically abuses you.

While this scenario seems to hark back to an earlier time in U.S. history, it describes Noreena Nesa's* recent working conditions in the Washington, D.C., area. Tucked behind the manicured lawns and closed doors of our wealthiest residents live some of the most vulnerable people in the United States: abused migrant domestic workers, who are sometimes the victims of slavery and human trafficking.

Marie Jose Perez, for example, left Bolivia in 1997, excited because she had always dreamed of flying on an airplane and hopeful that she would soon be able to support her family in Bolivia with her wages as a live-in maid. But once her plane landed in Washington, D.C., her employer, a human rights lawyer for the Organization of American States, confiscated her passport and forced her to work days more than twelve hours long, for less than one dollar per hour. She was not allowed to leave the house without her employer. When a friend of her employer's raped her, the human rights lawyer refused to take her to the hospital, claiming that medical care would be too expensive.

---

*Some names have been changed.

Ruth Gnizako, a fifty-two-year-old West African woman, says she was approached by a wealthy relative who worked for the World Bank. The relative promised her a house and a car if she would come serve as a housekeeper and nanny to his five children in suburban Maryland. When she arrived, she was required to sleep with a pair of one-year-old twins in her arms every night, essentially providing twenty-four-hour care with no days off. When the family went out, Ruth was forced to wait outside, in the hallway of the apartment building, until they returned. Both husband and wife repeatedly beat Ruth, and they igored her request to return to West Africa.

When neighbors heard Ruth screaming during the beatings, they called the Prince George's County Police Department. But the police were unable to understand her broken French, so they relied on her abusive employers for translation. Ruth attempted to reenact the beatings by gesturing physical blows to herself. Her employers, seeing an opportunity, told the police, "See, she's showing you how she beats herself. She's crazy." Ruth was taken to a local mental institution where she was forcibly sedated, her arms and legs tied to the bedposts. By the time the doctors contacted a French interpreter by phone, Ruth was feeling the effects of the psychoactive drugs, and, in her limited French, she could not manage to recount the traumatic events. Frustrated, the hospital staff called Ruth's employers and asked them to retrieve her.

When Ruth returned to the couple's home, they told her that if she upset them, they would call the police again and send her to the hospital permanently. They went on to claim that the security guard who patrolled the area was specifically sent to monitor her behavior and to make sure she did not harm their children. Intimidated by the barriers of language and culture, and still shaken from her terrifying experience at the mental institution, Ruth believed these threats. She suffered many more solitary months of beatings and servitude before the couple's neighbors finally managed to help her escape and contact the local authorities. In the end, Ruth found herself emotionally unable to participate in the U.S. Justice Department's criminal investigation of her former employers and returned home without collecting a dime.

Global Mothers

Noreena, Marie Jose, and Ruth are among a growing number of migrant women known to suffer under conditions that look very much like slavery after they legally enter the United States as domestic workers. The global economic changes that push women from developing nations to migrate for domestic work have also contributed to the recent rise of domestic worker abuse. Developed countries and international lending organizations such as the International Monetary Fund (IMF) and World Bank often prescribe preconditions for loans to developing countries that include cutting basic social services, devaluing local currencies, and imposing wage freezes. These structural adjustment programs create hardships that are borne most se-

verely by those at the bottom of the economic ladder, a significant proportion of whom are women. The world's poor are often faced with few better
options than to leave their home countries in search of work overseas, even
if they do so with no assurances and at grave personal risk. Once they arrive
in the United States, migrant women are sometimes forced into employment
situations to which they did not agree and from which they have no escape.

Modern-day slavery, trafficking, and migrant domestic worker abuse result from the illegal manipulation and deception of hopeful migrants, most of
whom believe they are going to the United States in order to better their situations. The new global economy permits transnational corporations and other
actors in developed countries to transport capital, labor, goods, and services
across state lines with relative ease. In the case of slavery and human trafficking, these goods, services, and labor become one: an unpaid or poorly paid person becomes a commodity that can be used again and again for accumulating
profit. Traffickers tell migrants that they will earn many times more money
abroad than they could at home. If they were employed by law-abiding people,
these workers could indeed increase their earnings. Dora Mortey, an articulate
Ghanaian schoolteacher, was one of those who believed the odds were on her
side. Little did she know she would be worked around the clock as a nanny and
housekeeper, and paid only around forty cents an hour.

Dora had signed an employment agreement with a World Bank official
in Ghana. Nonetheless, when she got to the Washington area, she was
handed a daily schedule that began at 5:45 A.M. and ended at 9:30 P.M., far exceeding the agreed-upon forty-hour workweek. After four months of working for only $100 a month, Dora asked that her contract be honored. The fam-
ily decided to terminate her services and put her on the next plane to Ghana.
She managed to escape from the moving car as her employer drove her to
the airport; but the employer scratched an 'X' across her visa and promptly
delivered her passport to the Immigration and Naturalization Service (INS),
requesting her immediate arrest and deportation. Uncertain what to do,
Dora took a cab from Washington to New Jersey to seek refuge with the one
person she knew in the United States. Back at the airport, an astute INS official suspected foul play. Eventually, Dora was granted a stay of deportation
while she pursued legal action against her former employers.

Each year, thousands of domestic workers like Dora enter the United
States on special visas issued by the U.S. State Department. Foreign nationals, diplomats, officials of international agencies, and, in some cases, U.S. citizens with permanent residency abroad, are permitted to "import" domestic
help on A-3, G-5, and B-1 visas. Nearly four thousand A-3 and G-5 visas are
issued annually—A-3 visas for household employees of diplomats and G-5
visas for employees of international agencies such as the World Bank, IMF,
and United Nations. The B-1 visa is a catch-all business category that, in
part, allows other foreign nationals and American citizens with permanent
residency abroad the option of bringing household employees with them
when they visit the United States. Every year, 200,000 B-1 visas are issued,

but the State Department does not keep records of B-1 domestic workers. As a result, their locations and working conditions remain particularly obscure. And the B-1 domestic workers may be at special risk for exploitation. All three visa types list the name of the worker's legal employer, but unlike the A-3 and G-5 visa holders, B-1 domestic workers have no option of legally transferring to another employer. They are left with few alternatives if they are enslaved or abused.

Even for A-3 and G-5 domestic workers, who are allowed to transfer to other diplomats or international officials, it is often difficult to find a suitable employer while suffering in an exploitative arrangement. Although the State Department, embassies, and international institutions involved (including the IMF, World Bank, and UN) keep records of the whereabouts of A-3 and G-5 domestic workers, this information is classified as confidential, for the privacy of the employer. Domestic violence and anti-incest advocates have challenged the privacy justification on the grounds that a lot of abuse occurs behind closed doors; other advocates have argued that in addition to being domiciles, these homes are also workplaces, subject to employment standards. Nonetheless, social service agencies remain uninformed of the whereabouts of domestic workers, which leaves them unable to prevent abuse or act on it before it is too late.

Patterns

Abuse and exploitation follow such uncannily predictable patterns that many in the social service world almost wonder if there is an "Abusers Manual" being circulated like samizdat. Typically, when the woman arrives in the United States, her employer illegally confiscates her passport and other travel documents. If the worker signed an official contract in a U.S. embassy abroad, that contract is often replaced with a new contract that stipulates longer hours and lower pay. Even the false contract is often subsequently ignored. Although U.S. labor law dictates that all workers be paid at least minimum wage, it is not uncommon to hear reports of women being paid fifty cents or a dollar an hour—in some cases, nothing at all. With yearly salaries at the World Bank and IMF averaging over $120,000 tax-free, the income disparity is striking, especially in situations where domestic workers are told that all or part of their meager wage is being withheld to offset their room and board.

Many women find themselves working nearly around the clock, seven days a week. The exploitative employer usually tells the worker that she may not leave the house unaccompanied, use the telephone, make friends, or even converse with others. The worker is often denied health insurance and social security, even if these benefits have been deducted from her pay. Some domestic workers are subjected to physical battery and sexual assault; others who have serious health conditions are denied medical treatment, which can result in long-term illness. Some domestic workers are given as gifts to the mistresses of diplomats, or traded and loaned out to American families who further exploit them. One Ghanaian woman reported that her employer's American wife referred to her not by name but rather as "the Creature." Yet another woman reported being called "the Slave." Others have been required to sleep on the floor, sometimes in the kitchen, laundry room, or unfurnished basement. An Ivy League professor, who paid her domestic worker $40 a month, slapped her for smoking outside. One domestic worker reported that she was made to kiss her employer's feet. A Malawian man recalls being forced to bathe in a bucket in the backyard rather than in the home of his American employer. A Filipina was forced to wear a dog collar and, at times, sleep outside with the family's dogs.

Typically, if an abused domestic worker complains, the employer threatens to send her home or turn her over to the police. The employer may also threaten to retaliate against her family if she speaks out; on several occasions, family members have been contacted and harassed after a domestic worker has escaped from an abusive situation. Legal issues in the United States also militate against leaving exploitative jobs: women who flee abusive employers are immediately considered "out of status," ineligible for other employment, and liable to be deported by the Immigration and Naturalization Service. As one neighbor who helped a Haitian domestic worker escape says, "When she ran away, she was out of a job, out of money, out of a home, out of status, and, quite frankly, out of her mind."

While some abusive employers use violence and the threat of violence to keep their domestic workers captive, others rely on psychological coercion. In one recent case, Hilda Rosa Dos Santos, a dark-skinned housekeeper from Brazil, was trapped for twenty years, with no pay and insufficient food, in the home of a Brazilian couple who convinced her that Americans disliked black people so intensely that she would likely be raped or killed if she went outside. Similarly, an Indonesian maid was informed by her Saudi Arabian bosses that Americans disliked Muslims so much that it was unsafe for her to leave the house. Abusive employers often point to violence on television to bolster claims about the dangers of American life. Unfamiliar with the English language or with American culture and laws, these women live as prisoners in the homes they clean.

Many women suffer in silence because they do not know their rights, nor do they have any idea where to go to seek help. Some may leave an abusive situation only to find themselves in even worse circumstances. Consider Tigris Bekele, who quickly found herself in jail on two felony counts of child abuse and grand larceny, all because she fled her job as a live-in maid after being exploited, sexually harassed, and threatened. Unfortunately, the day she decided to escape from her abusive employer, there was a bomb scare at the employer's children's school. The children were sent home at 10:00 A.M., a time when Tigris was not required to work as a nanny. But finding themselves alone, the children called the Virginia police. Tigris was arrested for leaving the children unattended.

The police record does not mention that Tigris was paid only $100 a week for around-the-clock chores because her Middle Eastern employer claimed that "that was enough money for a black person." Nowhere does it mention that the man of the house attempted to fondle and kiss her on various occasions. Nor does it mention that the woman of the house forced her to cut her hair and stop wearing makeup, threatening to kill Tigris if she had sex with her husband. Instead, the police record indicates that she is being held on $20,000 bail. It states that she allegedly stole a piece of jewelry, a claim that is often wielded against runaway domestic workers. Her employers had confiscated her passport and visa; when Tigris scoured the house to "steal" her belongings back, her employers accused her of stealing their personal effects.

Even though she came legally to the United States on a domestic worker visa program, if Tigris is convicted, she will be deported to her home country in East Africa, where she is fleeing political persecution. Tigris had been sending remittances to her father, and she has recently learned from relatives that she will be arrested if she returns because the government claims that the money is being used to launch political opposition. A felony conviction in the United States will automatically render it impossible for her to seek asylum here. While some domestic workers end up in court seeking judgments against their abusers, Tigris finds herself on the wrong side of the courtroom.

A Comparison

Some migrant workers who come to the United States to perform child care and light housework do so as participants in another, markedly different visa program. The congressionally sponsored au pair program—au pair means "an equal" in French—largely recruits young, middle-class women from Europe for "educational and cultural exchange" on J-1 visas. Ava Sudek, from the Czech Republic, experienced life in the United States both as a J-1 and as an A-3 visa holder. She thoroughly enjoyed her time as a J-1 au pair and thoroughly despised her time as an A-3 domestic worker. Ava's experience with the two visa programs highlights their striking dissimilarity.

When Ava arrived as an au pair, she was flown to a New York hotel for a week-long orientation session. There she was introduced to other nannies who would be living in the same region, so that they could form a network of friendships. Once she joined the employer's family, she attended another orientation program, where she received information on community resources and educational opportunities, as well as the contact numbers of other nannies in her local support network. Every month, she and her employers were required to check in with a counselor, who would help them resolve any disputes that arose or report any problems.

After completing a successful year with her au pair family, Ava decided to stay on an A-3 visa and work as a domestic worker for a French diplomat's family. There were no orientations, no information booklets, no contact numbers, no counselors, and no educational programs. In practice, for A-3 domestic workers, there is often no freedom. Ava felt like she was being held captive. She was not allowed to leave the house even during her off hours without a day's advance notice. Work hours and nonwork hours blurred together. When she asked for days off, her employers often refused to grant her request, telling her, "Perhaps another time." They did not pay her overtime. Within a month of obtaining her A-3 visa, Ava fled for the Czech Republic, where she dreamed of opening an au pair agency in her hometown. She did not bother to try to collect the overtime wages she was owed: her employer, as a high-level diplomat, was protected by diplomatic immunity.

Ava had the opportunity to hold both a J-1 and an A-3 visa, but few women of color from developing countries are so lucky. Most of them migrate on A-3, B-1, or G-5 visas, which do not come remotely close to offering the protections or the comforts J-1 visas provide European women. The different policies governing the temporary workers on these two visa programs are thick with racist and classist implications. Simply put, women of color in the domestic worker program deserve the same safety net and rigorous oversight granted to white women in the nanny program.

Solutions

Theoretically, the domestic worker visa program provides a window of opportunity for people from developing countries to enter the United States and earn a decent wage. What the program fails to do, however, is to ensure adequate protection for its visa holders. One simple improvement would be to establish independent monitoring and counseling like that which is provided to au pairs. Access to independent social workers, lawyers, and monitors would furnish live-in domestic workers with a system of safeguards to protect their legal rights and ensure employer compliance with contract conditions and labor laws.

By and large, migrant domestic workers belong to a hidden work force tucked away in private homes. Severe cases of domestic worker abuse differ from other cases of slavery and trafficking, such as those uncovered in brothels, farms, and sweatshops, because workers under the latter conditions have contact with one another. Each domestic worker, by contrast, is employed by an individual boss. Not only are the workers without peer support, but their cases involve no smuggling or trafficking rings for law enforcement to target for investigation. The result is that less attention is paid to these seemingly isolated incidents.

Far from their home countries, abused domestic workers are cut off from their families and their cultures, not to mention the protection that social networks and familiar institutions would provide. Many abusive employers incur the expense of hiring overseas precisely for this reason: they believe that they can increasily control non-English speaking help. Such workers are less likely to run away in the United States. Lack of familiarity with the American legal system also works to the disadvantage of abused domestic workers.

So where do these workers turn for help? A loose network of churches, lawyers, social service agencies, and good Samaritans have formed a modern-day underground railroad for women attempting to escape abusive employers. Because some domestic workers are only allowed out of the house on Sundays, churches are frequently a first stop on the path to freedom. One Catholic sister has files on several hundred G-5 and A-3 workers she has assisted over the years, beginning in the 1970s. Other good Samaritans have just happened to take initiatives when they've encountered domestic workers in need. Street vendors, taxicab drivers, neighbors, and complete strangers have been known to assist domestic workers in distress. Social service organizations and pro bono lawyers then help domestic workers with housing, medical care, mental health needs, and legal assistance.

Policy on matters affecting domestic workers has improved, but there are still troubling gaps in the protections these workers receive. Congress passed trafficking legislation in 2000 that allows federal law enforcement to convict not only traffickers who control their victims by force but also those who coerce workers by means of threats, psychological abuse, fraud, or deception. Domestic workers who bring criminal claims (such as sexual and physical abuse, or psychological coercion) against their former employers are granted work authorization, while domestic workers with civil claims (back pay, overtime, and the like) remain out of status and are considered illegal. Although the INS often turns a blind eye to out-of-status G-5, A-3, and B-1 domestic workers with civil claims, the threat of deportation and the lack of work authorization makes it unappealing for these workers to seek legal redress. It is time-consuming and difficult to find a pro bono lawyer, and migrants who come to the United States as temporary workers often have families to feed in their home countries; they are not really at liberty to sit around waiting for lengthy and uncertain court proceedings. Moreover, domestic workers with civil cases are so vulnerable and have so little bargaining power that they are sometimes re-enslaved as they wait out the long court process without job or housing options. It is certainly disheartening to think that a migrant domestic worker in a potentially violent situation is legally better off staying and getting beaten because she will later be able to receive a work permit, social services, and legal status. If she leaves before violence erupts, she receives nothing.

No shelters currently exist in the United States for trafficked women, and this remains one of the biggest obstacles facing nongovernmental organizations (NGOs) that attempt to assist domestic workers. NGOs sometimes have to ask women who are not in grave physical danger to stay in their exploitative situations while advocates scramble to find culturally appropriate housing. The Justice Department faces a small housing crisis every time a new criminal case involving trafficking is filed. On one occasion, police dropped a domestic worker on the private doorstep of an NGO worker in the middle of the night, for lack of housing alternatives.

Because few housing options are available to abused domestic workers, NGOs often turn to ethnic communities for assistance with housing, clothing, medical care, and mental health needs. Most of these communities are small and tight-knit. This presents a safety risk for some domestic workers, who find temporary housing in their ethnic communities only to be easily located by their abusers, who sometimes hail from the same background and know those communities well. Most domestic violence shelters will not accommodate domestic workers because they were not beaten by romantic partners; most homeless shelters refuse to assist due to language barriers and lack of beds. Domestic workers often end up relying on compassionate strangers — everyday people who open their homes and hearts to individuals in need.

Fortunately, advocates and domestic workers have been organizing to find solutions to these problems at both the policy and the grassroots levels. Groups such as CASA de Maryland's Mujeres Unidas de Maryland (United Women of Maryland) are forming workplace cooperatives to advocate for improved conditions for all workers. Former and current domestic workers take to the streets, parks, buses, and churches looking for potentially abused domestic workers and educating them about their rights, using Spanish-language legal literature. When a volunteer encounters an exploited employee, she directs her to bilingual legal assistance. The increase in outreach has resulted in an increase in the number of reported cases of domestic worker abuse. Mujeres Unidas has developed self-esteem classes, in which formerly abused or exploited domestic workers extend their support to others suffering under similar circumstances. The group has now formed a twenty-four-member, democratically controlled cleaning cooperative whose goal is to provide dignified day jobs and equitable working conditions. Most impressive, 10 percent of all the cleaning service's proceeds are funneled to social justice organizations.

While most members of Mujeres Unidas are Latina, other ethnically based organizations in the Washington, D.C., area are also engaged in efforts to curb domestic worker abuse; among them are a Filipina organization, Shared Communities, and the Ethiopian Community Development Council. More than twenty-five Washington-based organizations have joined forces to create the Campaign for Migrant Domestic Workers Rights (now Break the Chain Campaign), a coalition whose aim is to change public policy and to strengthen the safety net available to G-5, A-3, and B-1 domestic workers. These efforts involve lawyers, feminists, labor activists, human rights activists, community-based organizations, and social service agencies.

Related campaigns have sprung up elsewhere in the country. In New York, groups such as Andolan, Worker's Awaaz, and the Committee Against Anti-Asian Violence's Women Workers Project are working together; and in California, the Coalition Against Slavery and Trafficking, and the Korean Immigrant Workers Advocates, address similar issues. Workers rights' clinics in Washington, Los Angeles, and New York often provide relief to individuals escaping slavelike conditions. A nationwide Freedom Network (USA) to Empower Enslaved and Trafficked Persons recently formed in response to incidents of trafficking and slavery uncovered among laborers and sex workers.

Noreena, Marie Jose, Ruth, Dora, Hilda, Tigris, and Ava were all able to seek assistance from concerned neighbors, lawyers, and advocates. But it remains unclear how many other women currently toil in isolation, unpaid and abused. In the 1970s, the battered women's movement established a network of advocacy groups and shelters for women who were abused by their spouses; the movement even managed, through arduous grassroots efforts, to change public policy and public consciousness about domestic violence. Its work is not done. But the groups that have committed their time and resources to assisting trafficked and enslaved domestic workers have only now embarked on a similar movement: they are building a new underground railroad, one stretch of track at a time.

53

THE GLOBETROTTING SNEAKER

CYNTHIA ENLOE

Cynthia Enloe is Research Professor of International Development and Women's Studies at Clark University in Massachusetts. She teaches and writes about women, feminism, and international politics. Her recent books include *Bananas, Beaches and Bases: Making Feminist Sense of International Politics* (2000) and *Maneuvers: The International Politics of Militarizing Women's Lives* (2000). Her newest book is *The Curious Feminist: Searching for Women in A New Age of Empire* (2004).

Four years after the fall of the Berlin Wall marked the end of the Cold War, Reebok, one of the fastest-growing companies in United States history, decided that the time had come to make its mark in Russia. Thus it was with considerable fanfare that Reebok's executives opened their first store in downtown Moscow in July 1993. A week after the grand opening, store managers described sales as well above expectations.

Author's Note: This article draws from the work of South Korean scholars Hyun Sook Kim, Seung-kyung Kim, Katherine Moon, Seungsook Moon, and Jeong-Lim Nam.

Reebok's opening in Moscow was the perfect post-Cold War scenario: commercial rivalry replacing military posturing; consumerist tastes homogenizing heretofore hostile peoples; capital and managerial expertise flowing freely across newly porous state borders. Russians suddenly had the "freedom" to spend money on U.S. cultural icons like athletic footwear, items priced above and beyond daily subsistence: at the end of 1993, the average Russian earned the equivalent of $40 a month. Shoes on display were in the $100 range. Almost 60 percent of single parents, most of whom were women, were living in poverty. Yet in Moscow and Kiev, shoe promoters had begun targeting children, persuading them to pressure their mothers to spend money on stylish, Western sneakers. And as far as strategy goes, athletic shoe giants have, you might say, a good track record. In the U.S. many inner-city boys who see basketball as a "ticket out of the ghetto" have become convinced that certain brand-name shoes will give them an edge.

But no matter where sneakers are bought or sold, the potency of their advertising imagery has made it easy to ignore this mundane fact: Shaquille O'Neal's Reeboks are stitched by someone; Michael Jordan's Nikes are stitched by someone; so are your roommate's, so are your grandmother's. Those someones are women, mostly Asian women who are supposed to believe that their "opportunity" to make sneakers for U.S. companies is a sign of their country's progress—just as a Russian woman's chance to spend two months' salary on a pair of shoes for her child allegedly symbolizes the new Russia.

As the global economy expands, sneaker executives are looking to pay women workers less and less, even though the shoes that they produce are capturing an ever-growing share of the footwear market. By the end of 1993, sales in the U.S. alone had reached $11.6 billion. Nike, the largest supplier of athletic footwear in the world, posted a record $298 million profit for 1993—earnings that had nearly tripled in five years. And sneaker companies continue to refine their strategies for "global competitiveness"—hiring supposedly docile women to make their shoes, changing designs as quickly as we fickle customers change our tastes, and shifting factories from country to country as trade barriers rise and fall.

The logic of it all is really quite simple; yet trade agreements such as the North American Free Trade Agreement (NAFTA) and the General Agreement of Tariffs and Trade (GATT) are, of course, talked about in a jargon that alienates us, as if they were technical matters fit only for economists and diplomats. The bottom line is that all companies operating overseas depend on trade agreements made between their own governments and the regimes ruling the countries in which they want to make or sell their products. Korean, Indonesian, and other women workers around the world know this better than anyone. They are tackling trade politics because they have learned from hard experience that the trade deals their governments sign do little to improve the lives of workers. Guarantees of fair, healthy labor practices, of the rights to speak freely and to organize independently, will usually be left out of trade pacts—and women will suffer. The recent passage of both NAFTA

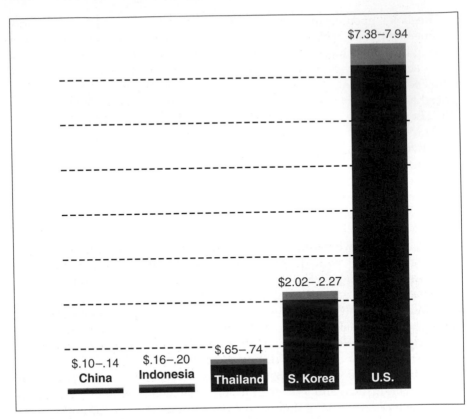

$7.38–7.94

$2.02–.2.27

$.10–.14
China

$.16–.20
Indonesia

$.65–.74
Thailand

S. Korea

U.S.

FIGURE 1   **Hourly Wages in Athletic Footwear Factories**

and GATT ensures that a growing number of private companies will now be competing across borders without restriction. The result? Big business will step up efforts to pit working women in industrialized countries against much lower-paid working women in "developing" countries, perpetuating the misleading notion that they are inevitable rivals in the global job market.

All the "New World Order" really means to corporate giants like athletic shoemakers is that they now have the green light to accelerate long-standing industry practices. In the early 1980s, the field marshals commanding Reebok and Nike, which are both U.S.-based, decided to manufacture most of their sneakers in South Korea and Taiwan, hiring local women. L.A. Gear, Adidas, Fila, and Asics quickly followed their lead. In short time, the coastal city of Pusan, South Korea, became the "sneaker capital of the world." Between 1982 and 1989 the U.S. lost 58,500 footwear jobs to cities like Pusan, which attracted sneaker executives because its location facilitated international transport. More to the point, South Korea's military government had an interest in suppressing labor organizing, and it had a comfortable military alliance with the U.S. Korean women also seemed accepting of Confucian

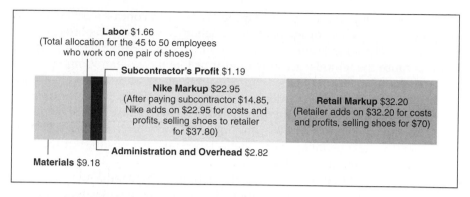

FIGURE 2   A $70 Pair of Nike Pegasus: Where the Money Goes

philosophy, which measured a women's morality by her willingness to work hard for her family's well-being and to acquiesce to her father's and husband's dictates. With their sense of patriotic duty, Korean women seemed the ideal labor force for export-oriented factories.

U.S. and European sneaker company executives were also attracted by the ready supply of eager Korean male entrepreneurs with whom they could make profitable arrangements. This fact was central to Nike's strategy in particular. When they moved their production sites to Asia to lower labor costs, the executives of the Oregon-based company decided to reduce their corporate responsibilities further. Instead of owning factories outright, a more efficient strategy would be to subcontract the manufacturing to wholly foreign-owned—in this case, South Korean—companies. Let them be responsible for workers' health and safety. Let them negotiate with newly emergent unions. Nike would retain control over those parts of sneaker production that gave its officials the greatest professional satisfaction and the ultimate word on the product: design and marketing. Although Nike was following in the footsteps of garment and textile manufacturers, it set the trend for the rest of the athletic footwear industry.

But at the same time, women workers were developing their own strategies. As the South Korean pro-democracy movement grew throughout the 1980s, increasing numbers of women rejected traditional notions of feminine duty. Women began organizing in response to the dangerous working conditions, daily humiliations, and low pay built into their work. Such resistance was profoundly threatening to the government, given the fact that South Korea's emergence as an industrialized "tiger" had depended on women accepting their "role" in growing industries like sneaker manufacture. If women reimagined their lives as daughters, as wives, as workers, as citizens, it wouldn't just rattle their employers; it would shake the very foundations of the whole political system.

At the first sign of trouble, factory managers called in government riot police to break up employees' meetings. Troops sexually assaulted women workers, stripping, fondling, and raping them "as a control mechanism for suppressing women's engagement in the labor movement," reported Jeong-Lim Nam of Hyosung Women's University in Taegu. It didn't work. It didn't work because the feminist activists in groups like the Korean Women Workers Association (KWWA) helped women understand and deal with the assaults. The KWWA held consciousness-raising sessions in which notions of feminine duty and respectability were tackled along with wages and benefits. They organized independently of the male-led labor unions to ensure that their issues would be taken seriously, in labor negotiations and in the pro-democracy movement as a whole.

The result was that women were at meetings with management, making sure that in addition to issues like long hours and low pay, sexual assault at the hands of managers and health care were on the table. Their activism paid off: in addition to winning the right to organize women's unions, their earnings grew. In 1980, South Korean women in manufacturing jobs earned 45 percent of the wages of their male counterparts; by 1990, they were earning more than 50 percent. Modest though it was, the pay increase was concrete progress, given that the gap between women's and men's manufacturing wages in Japan, Singapore, and Sri Lanka actually widened during the 1980s. Last, but certainly not least, women's organizing was credited with playing a major role in toppling the country's military regime and forcing open elections in 1987.

Without that special kind of workplace control that only an authoritarian government could offer, sneaker executives knew that it was time to move. In Nike's case, its famous advertising slogan—"Just Do It"—proved truer to its corporate philosophy than its women's "empowerment" ad campaign, designed to rally women's athletic (and consumer) spirit. In response to South Korean women workers' newfound activist self-confidence, the sneaker company and its subcontractors began shutting down a number of their South Korean factories in the late 1980s and early 1990s. After bargaining with government officials in nearby China and Indonesia, many Nike subcontractors set up shop in those countries, while some went to Thailand. China's government remains nominally Communist; Indonesia's ruling generals are staunchly anti-Communist. But both are governed by authoritarian regimes who share the belief that if women can be kept hard at work, low paid, and unorganized, they can serve as a magnet for foreign investors.

Where does all this leave South Korean women—or any woman who is threatened with a factory closure if she demands decent working conditions and a fair wage? They face the dilemma confronted by thousands of women from dozens of countries. The risk of job loss is especially acute in relatively mobile industries; it's easier for a sneaker, garment, or electronics manufacturer to pick up and move than it is for an automaker or a steel producer. In the case of South Korea, poor women had moved from rural villages into the cities searching for jobs to support not only themselves, but parents and siblings. The exodus of manufacturing jobs has forced more women into the growing "entertainment" industry. The kinds of bars and massage parlors offering sexual services that had mushroomed around U.S. military bases during the Cold War have been opening up across the country.

But the reality is that women throughout Asia are organizing, knowing full well the risks involved. Theirs is a long-term view; they are taking direct aim at companies' nomadic advantage, by building links among workers in countries targeted for "development" by multinational corporations. Through sustained grassroots efforts, women are developing the skills and confidence that will make it increasingly difficult to keep their labor cheap. Many are looking to the United Nations conference on women in Beijing, China, this September [1995], as a rare opportunity to expand their cross-border strategizing.

The Beijing conference will also provide an important opportunity to call world attention to the hypocrisy of the governments and corporations doing business in China. Numerous athletic shoe companies followed Nike in setting up manufacturing sites throughout the country. This included Reebok—a company claiming its share of responsibility for ridding the world of "injustice, poverty, and other ills that gnaw away at the social fabric," according to a statement of corporate principles.

Since 1988, Reebok has been giving out annual human rights awards to dissidents from around the world. But it wasn't until 1992 that the company adopted its own "human rights production standards"—after labor advocates made it known that the quality of life in factories run by its subcontractors was just as dismal as that at most other athletic shoe suppliers in Asia. Reebok's code of conduct, for example, includes a pledge to "seek" those subcontractors who respect workers' rights to organize. The only problem is that independent trade unions are banned in China. Reebok has chosen to ignore that fact, even though Chinese dissidents have been the recipients of the company's own human rights award. As for working conditions, Reebok now says it sends its own inspectors to production sites a couple of times a year. But they have easily "missed" what subcontractors are trying to hide—like 400 young women workers locked at night into an overcrowded dormitory near a Reebok-contracted factory in the town of Zhuhai, as reported last August in the *Asian Wall Street Journal Weekly.*

———

Nike's cofounder and CEO Philip Knight has said that he would like the world to think of Nike as "a company with a soul that recognizes the value of human beings." Nike, like Reebok, says it sends in inspectors from time to time to check up on work conditions at its factories; in Indonesia, those factories are run largely by South Korean subcontractors. But according to Donald Katz in a recent book on the company, Nike spokesman Dave Taylor told an in-house newsletter that the factories are "[the subcontractors'] business to run." For the most part, the company relies on regular reports from subcontractors regarding its "Memorandum of Understanding," which managers must sign, promising to impose "local government standards" for wages, working conditions, treatment of workers, and benefits.

In April, the minimum wage in the Indonesian capital of Jakarta will be $1.89 *a day*—among the highest in a country where the minimum wage varies by region. And managers are required to pay only 75 percent of the wage directly; the remainder can be withheld for "benefits." By now, Nike has a well-honed response to growing criticisms of its low-cost labor strategy. Such wages should not be seen as exploitative, says Nike, but rather as the first rung on the ladder of economic opportunity that Nike has extended to workers with few options. Otherwise, they'd be out "harvesting coconut meat in the tropical sun," wrote Nike spokesman Dusty Kidd, in a letter to the *Utne Reader.* The all-is-relative response craftily shifts attention away from reality: Nike didn't move to Indonesia to help Indonesians; it moved to ensure that its profit margin continues to grow. And that is pretty much guaranteed in a country where "local standards" for wages rarely take a worker over the poverty line. A 1991 survey by the International Labor Organization (ILO) found that 88 percent of women working at the Jakarta minimum wage at the time—slightly less than a dollar a day—were malnourished.

A woman named Riyanti might have been among the workers surveyed by the ILO. Interviewed by the *Boston Globe* in 1991, she told the reporter who had asked about her long hours and low pay: "I'm happy working here. . . . I can make money and I can make friends." But in fact, the reporter discovered that Riyanti had already joined her coworkers in two strikes, the first to force one of Nike's Korean subcontractors to accept a new women's union and the second to compel managers to pay at least the minimum wage. That Riyanti appeared less than forthcoming about her activities isn't surprising. Many Indonesian factories have military men posted in their front offices who find no fault with managers who tape women's mouths shut to keep them from talking among themselves. They and their superiors have a political reach that extends far beyond the barracks. Indonesia has all the makings for a political explosion, especially since the gap between rich and poor is widening into a chasm. It is in this setting that the government has tried to crack down on any independent labor organizing—a policy that Nike has helped to implement. Referring to a recent strike in a Nike-contracted factory, Tony Nava, Nike representative in Indonesia, told the *Chicago Tribune* in November 1994 that the "troublemakers" had been fired. When asked about Nike policy on the issue, spokesman Keith Peters struck a conciliatory note: "If the government were to allow and encourage independent labor organizing, we would be happy to support it."

Indonesian workers' efforts to create unions independent of governmental control were a surprise to shoe companies. Although their moves from South Korea have been immensely profitable [see chart], they do not have the sort of immunity from activism that they had expected. In May 1993, the murder of a female activist outside Surabaya set off a storm of local and international protest. Even the U.S. State Department was forced to take note in its 1993 worldwide human rights report, describing a system similar to that which generated South Korea's boom 20 years earlier: severely restricted union organizing, security forces used to break up strikes, low wages for men, lower wages for women—complete with government rhetoric celebrating women's contribution to national development.

Yet when President Clinton visited Indonesia last November, he made only a token effort to address the country's human rights problem. Instead, he touted the benefits of free trade, sounding indeed more enlightened, more in tune with the spirit of the post–Cold War era than do those defenders of protectionist trading policies who coat their rhetoric with "America first" chauvinism. But "free trade" as actually being practiced today is hardly *free* for any workers—in the U.S. or abroad—who have to accept the Indonesian, Chinese, or Korean workplace model as the price of keeping their jobs.

The not-so-new plot of the international trade story has been "divide and rule." If women workers and their government in one country can see that a sneaker company will pick up and leave if their labor demands prove more costly than those in a neighbor country, then women workers will tend to see their neighbors not as regional sisters, but as competitors who can steal their precarious livelihoods. Playing women off against each other is, of course, old hat. Yet it is as essential to international trade politics as is the fine print in GATT.

But women workers allied through the networks like the Hong Kong–based Committee for Asian Women are developing their own post–Cold War foreign policy, which means addressing women's needs: how to convince fathers and husbands that a woman going out to organizing meetings at night is not sexually promiscuous; how to develop workplace agendas that respond to family needs; how to work with male unionists who push women's demands to the bottom of their lists; how to build a global movement.

These women refuse to stand in awe of the corporate power of the Nike or Reebok or Adidas executive. Growing numbers of Asian women today have concluded that trade politics have to be understood by women on their own terms. They will be coming to Beijing this September [1995] ready to engage with women from other regions to link the politics of consumerism with the politics of manufacturing. If women in Russia and Eastern Europe can challenge Americanized consumerism, if Asian activists can solidify their alliances, and if U.S. women can join with them by taking on trade politics—the post–Cold War sneaker may be a less comfortable fit in the 1990s.

PART IX

Violence

Violence and abuse pervade U.S. society and put millions of people at risk for direct or indirect attack. When we combine the numbers of people who have been victims of violence with those whose loved ones have been victims and those who fear victimization, nearly everyone in this society is touched by violence. Add to that the attacks on the United States on September 11, 2001, the anthrax dispersion that followed, along with the U.S.-initiated wars in the Middle East, and we have a society infused with real or potential terror. However, as with the other issues addressed in this book, people's position in the matrix of domination and privilege affects their experiences.

A recent survey in Asian American communities suggests that domestic abuse is a major problem, with 69 percent of respondents reporting being hit by their parents while growing up and many people believing that divorce is not an option even in violent marriages. A code of silence seems to prevail about the violence.[1] A study of poor and working-class white women found that 92 percent had experiences with childhood and/or adult abuse and most told no one, again controlled by a code of silence. In the latter study, 68 percent of African American women reported domestic violence but were much more likely to have taken action in response to it by telling someone, finding alternate shelter, or getting the abuser out of the home.[2]

Although some people attempted to deny the reality of violence in the United States prior to September 11, 2001, it had become increasingly difficult to do so in the face of the many mass shootings in schools by white boys; whatever sense of safety that existed in suburban and rural areas has been shaken. And in all communities, many children are terrorized by adults, often by their parents or other family members, sometimes by pedophiles and kidnappers outside their families. Women are physically and sexually attacked and terrorized in many social contexts, especially in their own homes, primarily by men. Boys and men are frequently attacked and terrorized by each other, starting with school-yard fights, and continuing in violent sports, military training, street violence, gangs, war, and physically dangerous jobs. People and communities of color, Jewish communities, gay men, lesbians, bisexuals, and transgendered people are often victims of hate crimes.[3] Institutions and the people within them are increasingly becoming victims of terrorism, as evidenced by attacks on abortion clinics (including years of anthrax threats), on doctors who perform abortions, and on government institutions such as in the case of the 1995 Oklahoma City bombing and, of course, by the events of September 11.[4] Worldwide, women's low status correlates with high rates of rape, abuse, discrimination, death in childbirth, sexual slavery, sexually transmitted diseases, infanticide, and genital mutilation, all in a context of inadequate legal protection.[5] An estimated two out of five women in the United States will be physically or sexually assaulted in their lifetimes.[6]

Based on an analysis of the 1991 Federal Government's Uniform Crime Reports, attorney Sherri L. Schornstein reports that women are 10 times more likely than men to become victimized by intimates. Men, on the other hand, are much more likely to be victimized by someone outside their families, with only 5 percent of violent victimizations against men caused by family members. She reminds us of former Surgeon General C. Everett Koop's conclusion that domestic violence in the 1980s was the most serious health risk facing women, causing more injuries to women than car accidents, muggings, and rapes combined.[7] The crucial role of judges in granting restraining orders and helping to protect battered women is being examined, with the goal of making the judicial process more accountable to battered women.[8]

The daily crime reports in all urban areas and many suburban and rural ones suggest a country at war with itself. Many urban children are growing up in war zones, caught in the emotional and literal crossfire between warring teenagers and adults; many will, unfortunately, be pressed into gangs as their only option for a sense of meaning in life and into violence as their only means of self-defense.[9] Ironically, while gender socialization teaches women to fear violence and be vulnerable and teaches men to not fear it and be strong, men are at higher risk for every type of violence except sexual assault. Simultaneously, women are taught to fear attacks by strangers but, in fact, are much more likely to be attacked by people they know.[10] Children, too, taught to fear strangers, are most likely to be sexually assaulted by a relative or an acquaintance such as a teacher.[11] Recent outrage at the extent to which the Boston Archdiocese protected pedophile priests at children's expense may actually lead to some constructive changes as Massachusetts considers requiring clergy to become mandatory reporters of child abuse and as the Catholic Church is pressed to play a proactive role in sexual abuse prevention within its ranks.[12]

Although the rate of violent crime has gone down to some extent or stayed stable in recent years,[13] the rate of prison construction and imprisonment has gone up significantly, leading to what is now referred to as the prison-industrial complex in the United States. The United States now has the highest incarceration rate in the world.[14] Critics of this system focus especially on the physical, emotional, and sexual abuse that inmates, both men and women, experience and on the reality that prison is more apt to punish than "correct" in spite of the alleged philosophy of many departments of correction. Some critics also raise questions about why so many prisons are being built, suggesting that there are economic rather than correctional reasons behind the prison boom (e.g., creation of jobs).[15] (See Ward & Marable, Part XI.) The fact that community-based programs for male batterers are more effective than criminal justice interventions (lowering the incidence of violent incidents and controlling behaviors) suggests that an increase in these kinds of alternative programs would make more sense than construction of new prisons.[16] A recent study of women of color and law enforcement finds that the growth of law enforcement (including activity of the Immigration and Naturalization Service) has disproportionately affected women of color, leading to increased incarceration and detainment, abuse within these settings, and denial of reproductive and sexual autonomy. According to the study, between 1985 and 1996 the number of women of color imprisoned tripled and that of women detained by the INS doubled. The two fastest growing inmate populations are U.S.-born women of color and immigrants of color.[17]

A movement toward a new system of justice, called restorative justice, is gaining ground as people in various places in the judicial system along with community activists attempt to move toward community solutions to crime rather than punitive ones. With the goals of holding offenders accountable and also integrating them into the community rather than sending them to prison, meetings occur between offenders and their victims in an effort to educate offenders and provide an opportunity for them to "make things right" with the support of community members. The needs of people on both sides of the offense are addressed.[18]

The recent study of trauma has shed much light on violence and its effects on victims. Focusing on victims of war, torture, rape, incest, domestic violence, and other horrors, psychiatrist Judith Lewis Herman describes the dynamics of abuse and identifies symptoms experienced by survivors including posttraumatic stress, addictions, suicidal feelings, suicide attempts, and general life upheaval.[19] The rates of violence against women, for example, are even more upsetting when we consider the devastating pain, loss of time, and loss of quality of life that results from such violence. Most women who have been raped, for example, take at least a few months or, more frequently, several years to recover.[20] Thousands of veterans of the Vietnam and other wars have not been able to get their lives together since their war experiences. When I think about the profound waste of human potential and life due to violence, I often wonder how different the world would be without it. And it is not just the victims who suffer; their families and friends, as well as the families of the perpetrators of violence, are forced to turn their attention to violence rather than to more productive concerns. An estimated 325,000 children in the United States are sexually abused each year, and hundreds of thousands are involved as sex workers worldwide. These children are frequently left with permanent scars.[21] Concern about trafficking in children emerged after the 2004 tsunami as fear that some of the thousands of children whose parents were lost in the disaster would be sold into slavery under the guise of "adoption."[22]

Many institutions are blamed for violence against women. They include the system of gender inequality that creates an image of women as inferior objects worthy of disrespect; pornography, which sexualizes women's inferior status and presents women as fair game for sexual abuse; privacy, since it encourages a lot of violence to remain behind closed doors; women's unemployment and poverty, which keeps women from leaving abusive men;

and men's participation in sports.[23] The latter is a growing problem, according to writer Jeff Benedict, former director of research for the Center for the Study of Sport in Society at Northeastern University. In his study of both publicized and unpublicized cases of violence against women by college and professional athletes, he concludes that athletes commit more violence against women than their numbers would predict and expresses dismay at the fact that so many athlete role models are setting a poor example for boys and young men.[24]

The case of the gang rape of a retarded girl by a group of high school athletes in Glen Ridge, New Jersey, led the late writer Bernard Lefkowitz to conclude that the rape might only have been prevented if the community had taken a close look at what it was modeling for its children:

> Adults might have forstalled the unfolding tragedy in their town if they had questioned their own values, if they had challenged the assumptions of the culture that defined how people treated one another in Glen Ridge. . . . What happened to Leslie Faber is important because it reveals the extreme outcome of the behavior of young men who are made to feel omnipotent. If a culture is measured by how it treats its weakest members, the Glen Ridge case, first to last, revealed American culture at its basest.[25]

Another important theme to mention here is the high rate of civilian violence that men perpetrate against each other, particularly in prisons, in street warfare—gangs, etc.—and in other masculine institutions that involve initiations and hazing such as fraternities and sports. Violence against gay men and transgendered people by (presumably heterosexual) men, as in the recent murders of Matthew Shepard and Navajo gay/two-spirit teen Fred C. Martinez, is another aspect of men's violence against men, representing extreme and tragic examples of sociologist Michael Kimmel's hypothesis that masculinity is essentially about homophobia—about defining oneself as not a "sissy" and not a female.[26]

Finally, there is a growing literature on women's roles as perpetrators of violence, surrounded by much debate over many aspects of this issue. Researchers and activists are concerned with how to compute valid rates of female violence, how to understand the causes of violence, how to measure its effects in terms of harm and death, and the need to examine the purpose of the violence (e.g., women tend to use violence to stop or attempt to stop a violent event or relationship, whereas men tend to use violence as a means of control). Included in such discussions is the tendency for women to be more likely than men to admit to having used force against another person, therefore skewing the data.[27]

Prevention of violence is a central aspect of studies of violence at all levels (interpersonal, intergroup, and international). A "culture of peace" perspective on violence explores new ways of approaching violence prevention, and an examination of causes of male violence is a central aspect of this work.[28] Attention to men and boys as victims of violence, as mentioned in the introduction to this text, has received increasing attention, including within the culture of peace framework. Thus, in a Norwegian study that attempted to explain men's violence against women, Øystein Gullvåg Holter found that the predictors of male violence against women related not so much to their relationships with women or to masculine identity but to their relationships to men. They were more likely to be aggressive toward women if they had been bullied, especially in childhood or youth by boys or men or if they had experienced violence in the family of origin, particularly from their fathers. Holter also found that when men engage in care work (child care, etc.) they are more likely to have a positive attitude toward it and to be less violent. Men in Norway have the option of a month of paid paternity leave and most take it.[29]

The education and nurturance of boys and young men is a primary approach to violence prevention. The goals include helping boys to recognize their needs, to learn alternatives to violence, and to develop caring relationships with people of both sexes. The Oakland Men's Project in California has run antiviolence workshops for boys and men around the United States (see Robert Allen, this part). Other groups of men are getting together to tap the energy of the 25 percent of men who say they are willing to work toward stopping violence against women. Rather than simply treating batterers, they are working on prevention. For example, on Father's Day, 2004, the Founding Fathers Campaign (www.endabuse.org) took out a full-page ad in the Sunday *New York Times* for the second year in a row, signed by many celebrities. They also ran ads during the NBA playoffs, featuring young men. Their "Coaching Boys into Men" program (endabuse.org/cbim/) is aimed at educating men and boys about prevention of violence against women by changing attitudes and encouraging healthy, violence-free relationships. The Canadian White Ribbon Campaign to end violence against women has sponsored workshops in schools, corporations, and trade unions across Canada.[30]

Women in many parts of the world have been involved in efforts to end and/or prevent violence and to promote peace. Some have been involved in local efforts to stop violence and bring perpetrators to justice, such as in the case of the estimated 350 unsolved murders of women in Ciudad Juarez, Mexico, since 1993.[31] Others have attempted to end war in such places as Bosnia, Northern Ireland, and Israel/Palestine. In these particular peace efforts, women from different sides of the conflicts have come together to work toward peace (see Gila Svirsky, Part XI).[32]

This part of this book addresses everyday violence in a range of contexts including the war in Iraq. Self-defense for women (Melanie Kaye/Kantrowitz), trafficking in women (Jan Goodwin), racism and hate crimes (Helen Zia), and the rape of men in prison (Terry Kupers) provide a look at some of the ways that women and men are victims of violence on an ongoing basis. Then Robert Allen describes an approach to prevention of sexual harassment. Following these essays are several pieces related to the attacks on September 11 (Desiree Taylor), the war in Iraq (Cynthia Enloe), and masculinity in the current era of U.S.-initiated war (Stephen Ducat).

As you read these essays, think about your connections to them. Has violence touched your life? If so, how? Have you been affected by the war in Iraq? If so, how? To what extent does Cynthia Enloe's analysis of what happened at Abu Ghraib make sense to you? Have you ever analyzed the "climate" of an institution that you are involved in? To what extent do you find Stephen Ducat's arguments regarding fundamentalism, masculinity, and the blurring of the division between church and state convincing, or not? What kinds of additional data might you like to see before making up your mind on any of these issues?

NOTES

1. "Asian Family Violence Report Calls for Action," *New Moon: The Newsletter of the Asian Task Force against Domestic Violence* 11, no. 2 (2000), pp. 1, 3–5; "Asian Family Violence Report," www.atask.org.

2. Michelle Fine and Lois Weis, "Disappearing Acts: The State and Violence against Women in the Twentieth Century," *Signs* 25, no. 4 (Summer 2000), pp. 1139ff.

3. "Bias Incidents Reported During 1994," *Klanwatch Intelligence Report* 77 (March 1995), pp. 14ff.

4. For articles on clinic violence and the ongoing commitment to providing abortion to women who want one, see *Ms.* (May/June 1995), pp. 42–66; and (no author), "Welcome to My World," an interview with Merle Hoffman, founder and president of Choices Women's Medical Center in Queens, NY, *Women's Review of Books* XIX, no. 3 (December 2000), pp. 8–9; and Ruth Rosan, "Blind, Unpredictable Terror," *San Francisco Chronicle* (October 29, 2001). For a discussion of recent militia activity that threatens public officials, see "Extremists Pose Increasing Threat of Violence to Police, Other Public Officials," *Klanwatch Intelligence Report* 80 (October 1995), pp. 1ff.

5. Lyndsay Griffiths, "Hardships Plague Women Worldwide, UN Report Says," *The Boston Globe* (Thursday September 21, 2000), p. A14; Beth Gardiner, "Torture of Women Said to Be 'Global,'" *The Boston Globe* (Wednesday March 21, 2001), p. A12; Miami Herald, "Man Pleads Guilty to Sex-Slave Operation," 97th year, no. 124 (Saturday January 16, 1999), p. 5B.

6. Associated Press, "2 of 5 Women Encounter Sexual or Physical Abuse, Study Finds," *The Boston Globe* (Thursday May 6, 1999), p. A25.

7. Sherri L. Schornstein, *Domestic Violence and Health Care: What Every Professional Needs to Know* (Thousand Oaks, CA: Sage Publications, 1997), p. 2.

8. James Ptacek, *Battered Women in the Courtroom: The Power of Judicial Responses* (Boston: Northeastern University Press, 1999).

9. For a moving autobiography of gang life, see Luis Rodríguez, *Always Running* (New York: Simon & Schuster, 1993).

10. Jocelyn A. Hollander, "Vulnerability and Dangerousness: The Construction of Gender through Conversation about Violence," *Gender & Society* 15, no. 1 (February 2001), pp. 83–109; Jordana Hart, "Statistics Say Abuse Hits Close to Home: Most Young Victims Know Their Molester," *The Boston Globe* (Tuesday May 30, 2000), pp. B1, B8.

11. Raymond Hernandez, "Children's Sexual Exploitation Underestimated, Study Finds," *New York Times on the Web* (September 10, 2001), www.nytimes.com/ 2001/01/10/national/10CHIL.html?todaysheadlines=&pagewanted=print9/10 /01; Lee H. Bowker, "The Coaching Abuse of Teenage Girls," in Lee H. Bowker, ed., *Masculinities and Violence* (Thousand Oaks, CA: Sage, 1998).

12. Walter V. Robinson, "Scores of Priests Involved in Sex Abuse Cases: Settlements Kept Scope of Issue Out of Public Eye," *The Boston Globe* 261, no. 31 (January 31, 2002), pp. A1ff; Stephen Kurkjian and Farah Stockman, "DA Sees Lack of Priest Controls: Archdiocese Had No Rule on Abuse," *The Boston Globe* 261, no. 32 (February 1, 2002), pp. B1ff.

13. Eric Lichtblau, "Attacks between Partners Fall: Justice Dept. Data Seen as Encouraging," *The Boston Globe* (Thursday May 18, 2000), p. A3.

14. Silja J. A. Talvi, "The Craze of Incarceration," *The Progressive* (May 2001), pp. 40–4.

15. For a disturbing look at treatment of male inmates in a maximum security prison, see Mara Taub, "Super-Max Punishment in Prison," *Resist Newsletter* 9, no. 1, pp. 1–2. See also John Raymond Cook, *Asphalt Justice: A Critique of the Criminal Justice System in America* (Westport, CT: Praeger, 2001); Joseph T. Hallinan, *Going Up the River: Travels in a Prison Nation* (New York: Random House, 2001); Sue Pleming, "Abuse of Women Inmates Seen Rampant: Misconduct Found in All but One State, Amnesty USA says," *The Boston Globe* (Wednesday March 7, 2001), p. A7; and Don Sabo, Terry A. Kupers, and Willie London, eds., *Prison Masculinities* (Philadelphia: Temple University Press, 2001).

16. R. Emerson Dobash, Russell P. Dobash, Kate Cavanagh, and Ruth Lewis, *Changing Violent Men* (Thousand Oaks, CA: Sage: 2000).

17. Anannya Bhattacharjee, *Whose Safety? Women of Color and the Violence of Law Enforcement* (Philadelphia, PA: American Friends Service Committee, Committee on Women, Population, and the Environment. 2001). Available full-text on line at www.afsc.org/JusticeVisions.htm

18. Kay Pranis, "Peacemaking Circles: Restorative Justice in Practice Allows Victims and Offenders to Begin Repairing the Harm," *Corrections Today* 59, no. 7 (December 1997), pp. 72ff; Howard Zehr, "A Restorative Lens" in *Changing Lenses* (Waterloo, Ontario: Herald Press, 1990), pp. 177–214.

19. Judith Lewis Herman, *Trauma and Recovery* (New York, Basic Books, 1992).

20. Herman cites several studies of rape victims in Trauma and Recovery, pp. 47–8. See also Catherine Cameron, *Resolving Childhood Trauma: A Long-Term Study of Abuse Survivors* (Thousand Oaks, CA: Sage, 2000).

21. Raymond Hernandez, "Children's Sexual Exploitation Underestimated, Study Finds," *New York Times on the Web* (September 10, 2001). http://www.nytimes.com/ 2001/01/10/national/10CHIL.html?todaysheadlines=&pagewanted=print9/10/01; Grant Peck, "Sex Trade Lures More Children, UN Says," *The Boston Globe* (Saturday December 8, 2001), p. A5; Marian Uhlman, "Sex Trade Targeting the Young Is Called Hidden Epidemic," *The Boston Globe* (Thursday September 11, 2001), p. A6.

22. Natasha Bita, "Sadly, the human scum also rises: Tsunamis swamp Asia," *The Weekend Australian*, January 8, 2005, Section: Features, Weekend Inquirer, p. 20.

23. For a look at debates about these alleged causes of violence, see Karin L. Swisher, Carol Wekesser, and William Barbour, eds., *Violence against Women* (San Diego, CA: Greenhaven Press, 1994).

24. Jeff Benedict, *Public Heroes, Private Felons: Athletes and Crimes against Women* (Boston: Northeastern University Press, 1997).

25. Bernard Lefkowitz, *Our Guys* (New York: Vintage Books, 1997), pp. 493–4.

26. Michael S. Kimmel, "Masculinity as Homophobia" (1994). For a range of essays on men and violence against women, children, and men, see Lee H. Bowker, ed., *Masculinities and Violence* (Thousand Oaks, CA: Sage, 1998).

27. For a discussion of these issues, see Walter D. Keseredy and Martin D. Schwartz, *Women Abuse on Campus: Results of the Canadian National Survey* (Thousand Oaks, CA: Sage, 1998); Nancy Worcester, "What Is the Battered Women's Movement Saying about Women Who Use Force?" *Wisconsin Coalition against Domestic Violence Newsletter* 20, no. 1 (Spring 2001), pp. 2–5, 16–17.

28. Ingeborg Breines, Robert Connell and Ingrid Eide, eds., *Male Roles, Masculinities and Violence: A Culture of Peace Perspective* (Paris: United Nations Educational, Scientific and Cultural Organization, 2000).

29. Øystein Gullvåg Holter, "Masculinities in Context: On Peace Issues and Patriarchal Orders," in Ingeborg Breines, Robert Connell, and Ingrid Eide, eds., *Male Roles, Masculinities and Violence: A Culture of Peace Perspective* (Paris: United Nations Educational, Scientific and Cultural Organization, 2000), pp. 61–83.

30. Paul Kivel, *Boys Will Be Men: Raising our Sons for Courage, Caring and Community* (Gabriola Island, B.C., Canada: New Society Publishers, 1999); Michael Kaufman, "Working with Men and Boys to Challenge Sexism and End Men's Violence," in Ingeborg Breines, Robert Connell, and Ingrid Eide, eds., *Male Roles, Masculinities and Violence: A Culture of Peace Perspective* (Paris: United Nations Educational, Scientific and Cultural Organization, 2000), pp. 213–22.

31. Chris Kraul, "Frustration Grows over Killings: In Juarez, victims' families complain that despite special prosecutor's work, answers are few and more women are dying," *Los Angeles Times* (February 1, 2005), part A, p. 3.

32. Cynthia Cockburn, *The Space between Us: Negotiating Gender and National Identities in Conflict* (New York: Zed Books, 1998).

54

WOMEN, VIOLENCE, AND RESISTANCE[1]

MELANIE KAYE/KANTROWITZ

Melanie Kaye/Kantrowitz was born in 1945 in Brooklyn, New York, and has worked in social change movements since the sixties. A graduate of the City College of New York, she earned her Ph.D. in Comparative Literature at the University of California at Berkeley. A writer, activist, and teacher, she lives in New York City. She is author of *My Jewish Face & Other Stories*, coeditor of *The Tribe of Dina: A Jewish Woman's Anthology*, and former editor and publisher of *Sinister Wisdom*, a lesbian/feminist journal.

Blocks to Resistance

Imagination: To Consider Violence

A woman raped by a landlord showing her an apartment remarks, "The only degrading thing I can recall about it is simply not being able to hit the guy. I just really wanted to sock him in the teeth."[2]

> Another woman, awakened and raped with a knife at her throat: . . .
> You never forget it and you're never the same. . . . It hits you where
> you're most vulnerable. . . . About six months to a year later some of
> the vulnerability disappeared. It was replaced by rage. Oh, I wish
> now I had hit him. Or killed him.[3]

Listen to women cheer at karate demonstrations simulating attack when the woman playing "victim" strikes back. Think about women's reaction to *Thelma & Louise*.[4] In response to violence, it's natural to consider violence.

Yet as a movement, we don't.

If a woman is abused and strikes back, we often work for her defense. We respond to her risk. But we do not ourselves shoulder it, even as a movement. Nor do we encourage women to avail ourselves of violence as a serious, perhaps effective option.

Why?

Obvious response #1: *Violence is wrong.*
Obvious response #2: *Violence won't work.*

Melanie Kaye/Kantrowitz, excerpt from "Women, Violence and Resistance" from *The Issue Is Power: Essays on Women, Jews, Violence and Resistance*. Reprinted with the permission of Aunt Lute Books.

What do we mean, *wrong?* What do we mean, *work?* When women are prepared to use violence, they are less likely to get raped, abused, and murdered.
Listen.

> . . . all of a sudden he got this crazy look in his eye and he said to
> me, "Now I'm going to kill you." Then I started saying my prayers.
> I knew there was nothing I could do. He started to hit me—I still
> wasn't sure if he wanted to rape me at this point—or just to kill me.
> He was hurting me, but hadn't yet gotten me into a strangle-hold
> because he was still drunk and off balance. Somehow we pushed
> into the kitchen where I kept looking at this big knife. But I didn't
> pick it up. Somehow no matter how much I hated him at that
> moment, I still couldn't imagine putting the knife in his flesh, and
> then I was afraid he would grab it and stick it into me. . . .[5]

I couldn't imagine.
I was afraid.

I couldn't imagine corresponds to *it's wrong.* Sticking the knife into his
flesh is unimaginable, too horrible.

This horror, this failure of imagination might have cost her life. Her life
against his, and she chooses his.

I was afraid corresponds to *it won't work.* Using the knife might make it
worse. But how much worse could it get? He's already threatened to kill her.

Is this in women's interest?

If we avoid the question of using violence because it makes us uncomfortable, many men have no such compunctions. They continue to rape, mutilate, beat and kill us. So we are not avoiding violence, only the guilt we associate with using it. Something about innocence is dangerous here. We are
innocent because helpless. As long as we insist on maintaining our innocence, we lock ourselves into helplessness. In this way we become complicit
with our oppression.

A few feminists have touched on the question. Phyllis Chesler, M. F.
Beal, Karen Haglund conclude similarly; in Chesler's words:

> Women, like men, must be capable of violence or self-defense
> before their refusal to use violence constitutes a free and moral
> choice rather than "making the best of a bad bargain."[6]

But how do we become capable? What if we are already capable? And
what if we don't refuse?

Let us begin to imagine putting the knife in his flesh. If we choose not to,
let the reason *not* be that we couldn't imagine doing it. The women who
wrote the excellent *Women's Gun Pamphlet* have an answer to the *violence is
wrong* voice:

> The only way I've figured out to try and eliminate the all-
> nurturing masochist in each of us is to remember that the man or

men who attack, rape, mutilate, and try to kill you, have done and will do the same to as many women as they can. While you defend yourself, bear in your mind all the women you love that you are fighting for, especially those you know who have been attacked.[7]

Violence and Power   Yes, I'm talking about violence. But the violence did not originate with us. If we submit, evade, fight back directly or indirectly — no matter what we do we are responding to a violence that already is. Janet Koenig has described how the oppressor's violence

> becomes routinized and ritualized. It becomes so part of the environment, of the school, factory, prison, and family that it is barely perceived consciously. Ideology distorts the perception of violence. The source of violence now appears to be not the system but those who rebel against it.[8]

And Assata Shakur succinctly remarks:

> Women have been raped throughout history, and now when we fight back, now that we have the consciousness to fight back — they call us violent.[9]

To avoid this conceptual error, Ti-Grace Atkinson would call responsive violence, the violence of rebellion, by another name:

> When "violence" appears *against* "oppression," it is a *negation of institutionalized* violence. "Violence," these opening blows are a positive humane act — under such circumstances. Such acts are *acts of bravery* . . . It is a betrayal of humanity, and of hope, to represent such acts as shameful, or regrettable.[10]

Not to deny the horror of violence. Or to invalidate or mock the part in us that does not want to harm. We have an honorable past on this subject. Often life has been preserved solely because of our efforts to feed, wash, clothe, and keep our families in health. We have been active in movements to stop slavery, wars, imperialism, lynching, and abuse of all kinds.

It's hard to transform such concerns into a willingness to cut down another woman's son.

Nor am I saying violence should be leapt to lightly. But the situation is hardly light. I am saying only that using violence should be thinkable. And that the grounds on which we decide whether or not to commit violence against men be *our* grounds: *is it in our interest?*

Violence is an aspect of power. In a conflictual society, where power imbalance exists, so does the possibility of physical force to meet physical threat. "Women," Karen Hagberg points out,

> are called violent (indeed, we actually consider ourselves violent) whenever we assert ourselves in the smallest ways. One woman recently described the verbal challenging of men on the streets as an act of violence.[11]

This is absurd or tragic. Yet the piece of embedded truth is that any woman's challenge to male power—from a calm "I'm not interested" to an assertive "please turn down your stereo"—may be perceived as aggressive and met with violence. Most of us know we risk danger in even a mild confrontation with a man. Every male-female interaction assumes: *in a physical fight he will win.* Every man assumes this about every woman. This is the assumption behind rape. As Ellen Willis remarked in 1968, *Men don't take us seriously because they're not physically afraid of us.*

An Analog: African American Liberation from Slavery   Recent scholarship about African Americans in the South during and after the Civil War sheds intriguing light on the relationship between violence and freedom. When the war began, the great abolitionist and former slave Frederick Douglass

> immediately called for the enlistment of slaves and free blacks into a "liberating army" that would carry the banner of emancipation through the South. Within thirty days, Douglass believed, 10,000 black soldiers could be assembled. "One black regiment alone would be, in such a war, the full equal of two white ones. The very fact of color in this case would be more terrible than powder and balls. The slaves would learn more as to the nature of the conflict from the presence of one such regiment, than from a thousand preachers."[12]

But Northern white men were not so sure. As they debated the question of arming Blacks—slaves or freedmen—three fears were repeated. They feared slave insurrections against slaveholders who, though the enemy, were, after all, white. They feared Black incompetence; no less a personage than President Lincoln speculated that, if Blacks were armed, "in a few weeks the arms would be in the hands of the rebels." But perhaps the deepest and most revealing fear was that Blacks would prove competent. As one Union congressman noted,

> If you make him the instrument by which your battles are fought, the means by which your victories are won, you must treat him as a victor is entitled to be treated, with all decent and becoming respect.[13]

In the South, the same debate was much more anxiety-laden: would armed slaves turn on their masters? (The transparency of the "happy slave" myth is evident in these musings.) What would happen if distinctions were levelled? "The day you make soldiers of them is the beginning of the end of the revolution," warned General Howell Cobb. "If slaves will make good soldiers, our whole theory of slavery is wrong."[14]

In fact, Black soldiers were crucial to the North, and their performance in the Union army, by all accounts courageous and impressive as Douglass had predicted, revealed that "the whole theory of slavery" was more resilient than General Cobb had imagined, surviving as it did the institution of slavery itself.

But whether violence is a tool, a back-up to power, a psychological release or an inevitable response to oppression,[15] *being able* to use violence may be a critical aspect of freedom. Listen to Felix Haywood, a former slave in Texas:

> If everymother's son of a black had thrown 'way his hoe and took up a gun to fight for his own freedom along with the Yankees, the war'd been over before it began. But we didn't do it. We couldn't help stick to our masters. We couldn't no more shoot 'em than we could fly. My father and me used to talk 'bout it. We decided we was too soft and freedom wasn't goin' to be much to our good even if we had an education.[16]

Couldn't shoot them. Soft. The definition of manliness that depends on murder may be the saddest comment on patriarchy anyone can dredge up. As W.E.B. Du Bois remarked with some disgust,

> How extraordinary, and what a tribute to ignorance and religious hypocrisy, is that fact that in the minds of most people, even those of liberals, only murder makes men. The slave pleaded; he was humble; he protected the women of the South, and the world ignored him. The slave killed white men; and behold, he was a man.[17]

What about the women? Slave women were vulnerable to sexual abuse by white and Black men alike, though solidarity between enslaved women and men appears to have been very strong.[18] Many women resisted, sometimes with violence. Rose Williams tells of taking a poker to the man chosen by her master for her to marry (i.e., breed with), and of capitulating only after her owner threatened her with a whipping.[19] Cherry Loguen used a stick to knock out a man armed with a knife who tried to rape her. Two women attacked by an overseer waited till he undressed and "pounced upon him, wrestled him to the ground, and then ran away."[20] It's likely that women were able to resist assaults and unwanted attention more forcefully from other slaves than from their owners, though Linda Brent's excruciating narrative of resistance to her owner's sexual demands demonstrates the lengths to which some women went to preserve their sexual integrity.[21]

Did women resist enslavement? During the Middle Passage, women, unlike men, were not chained or confined to the hold. While this freedom left them vulnerable to sexual abuse by the ship's crews, it also left them freer to rebel, and there are several reported instances of women inciting or assisting insurrections at sea.[22] On the plantations,

> Some murdered their masters, some were arsonists, and still others refused to be whipped. . . . Equipped with a whip and two healthy dogs, an Alabama overseer tied a woman named Crecie to a stump with intentions of beating her. To his pain and embarrassment, she jerked the stump out of the ground, grabbed the whip, and sent the overseer running.[23]

A Union official recorded several women entering the Union camp with marks of severe whipping. The whipper was caught and a male slave first lashed him twenty times, and then the women, one after another, gave him twenty lashes, according to the official, "to remind him that they were no longer his";[24] but maybe also because releasing rage where it belongs is one step towards healing.[25] There are also instances of women fighting against their men being taken away.[26]

The ability to defend oneself, one's people, one's dignity, to struggle for one's own liberation, is clearly a survival skill. As Robert Falls, former slave, summed it up: "If I had my life to live over, I would die fighting rather than be a slave again. . . ."[27]

Observations by Black and white, Southerners and Northerners indicate that the Black soldiery affected everyone strongly. Blacks felt pride. Whites felt fear. Both groups recognized that consciousness changed radically when the Black divisions marched through.

And not only consciousness. In New Orleans free Blacks formed two regiments for the Confederacy, in part to improve their status and esteem by learning firearms (though they were never called for combat duty).[28] We could argue the absurdity and tragedy of such a stance, not unlike the arguments that have swirled around Black police or military today. Yet Blacks understood that a Black soldiery might be fair, might protect them, would not automatically assume they were chattel and without rights. A Black soldiery gave Black—and white—people a vision of a differently ordered world: a hint that perhaps the whole theory of slavery was, indeed, wrong.

The analogy is suggestive. Women police officers, fire fighters, soldiers do challenge "the whole theory of slavery,"[29] as do women athletes and construction workers, as well as physicists. But particularly since physical domination so characterizes male-female relations under patriarchy, if women were to defend ourselves and other women, could avail ourselves of violence when needed; and if this potential for self-defense became an expectation, a norm, then patriarchal definitions of male and female would be shaken. Not only minds would change, but reality. Would men begin to wonder if *perhaps the whole theory of patriarchy is wrong?* Would women?

Fear of the Self/Fear of Our Power[30]

If in a patriarchal system violence is an aspect of power, if capacity for violence is a basis for resistance, it's obvious whose interests are served by *it won't work* and *it's wrong;* by the implied fear and horror.

Women often learn to see with the eyes of the dominant culture: male eyes. Especially middle-class heterosexual white women are taught to fear strong women, women with power, women with physical strength, angry women who express that anger forcefully. *It isn't ladylike. It isn't nice.* Even those of us who have long rejected these norms (or accepted our inability to live inside them) still may fear the explosiveness of anger—though this fear obscures the reason for our deep anger, which is our powerlessness. Instead of learning to cherish this rage and to direct it effectively, we often try to suppress it, in ourselves and in others. It's exactly as if we have an army we're afraid to mobilize, train, and use.

Yet we are not always victims. We can be violent. How have we managed to avoid noticing? The idea that men are inherently violent, women inherently non-violent, is dangerous, not only because it is a doctrine of biological superiority, and such doctrines have supported genocide.[31]

The idea that women are inherently non-violent is also dangerous because it's not true. Any doctrine that idealizes us as the non-violent sex idealizes our victimization and institutionalizes who men say we are: intrinsically nurturing, inherently gentle, intuitive, emotional. They think; we feel. They have power; we won't touch it with a ten-foot pole. Guns are for them; let's suffer in a special kind of womanly way.

Such an analysis dooms us to inappropriate kindness and passivity; overlooks both our capacity for and experience with violence; ignores in fact everything about us that we aren't sure we like, including how we sometimes abuse each other. Whatever we disapprove of, we call *theirs,* and then say, when women do these things—talk loud, use reason, fuck hard, act insensitive or competitive, ride motorcycles, carry weapons, explode with rage, fight—they are acting like men.[32]

But who defines "like men," "like women"? On what basis? Remember Sojourner Truth's challenge to restrictive definition: *ain't I a woman?* All women defined as deviant might well echo her words. We may be numerous enough to redefine the "norm." When we find many of us doing what only men are supposed to do, and nearly all of us expressing in some form what is supposed to be a male behavior, then maybe we need to enlarge our notion of who *we* are. The woman who is violent is not acting like a man. She may be announcing a host of contradictions: that her condition is intolerable; that she is or isn't afraid; that she feels entitled; that she has nothing to lose or something to protect; that she needs physical release; that she's a bully; that she has lost or given over or seeks control. But always, in addition, she announces that women are not who men say we are.

> TO SEE WOMEN'S VIOLENCE AS A FIELD INCLUDING:
> SLASHING YOUR WRISTS STANDING UP TO A THREATENING
> LANDLORD KILLING A RAPIST ATTACKING A WOMAN AT
> THE BARFIGHTING AN ABUSIVE HUSBAND PUNCHING
> YOUR LOVER PUNCHING A MAN WHO MOUTHS OFF AT
> YOU LEARNING KARATE KICKING A DOG SHOOTING UP
> WRESTLING FOR MONEY DRINKING TOO MUCH ALCOHOL
> WRESTLING FOR FUN BEATING YOUR CHILD KILLING
> ANOTHER WOMAN'S RAPIST

To see women's violence as a wide range of behavior which can serve, protect, endanger, or violate women and children—or be neutral.[33] To expose the taboo which clothes even our questions about violence. To admit that when we don't fight back against men's violence, it's not because we're passive, not even because we're good: but because we're afraid of what they'll do back.

And for good reason. Consider these words from two married women:

Sometimes I get so mad I wish I could hit him. I did once, but he hit me back, and he can hurt me more than I can hurt him.

When he's so much bigger and stronger, and you got four kids to take care of, what's a woman supposed to do?[34]

Consider the implications of the fact that in the late seventies a full 40% of the women imprisoned for homicide in Chicago's Cook County jail had killed men in response to physical abuse by these men.[35] Even though judges in some states have ruled to release women serving time on such convictions, many women still remain in prison.

The fact is, fighting back, even supporting women who fight back, can be dangerous. The wife who feigns sleep when her husband comes home drunk; the child who lies to avoid getting beaten; these are tactics based on experience. Sometimes evasion works better than confrontation. At least it has sometimes kept us alive.

We worry about making things worse. "If you do what I say, I won't hurt you," says the rapist, but the woman who trusts him forgets, in her desperation and terror, that he is, after all, a rapist: hardly a basis for trust. With the husband or mate, while appeasement may be plausible, it's hardly desirable as a way of life.

What happens to women who actively resist violence? The facts, especially about street violence, flatly contradict the usual police/male advice of "don't fight it." When a woman resists a rape *in any way*—saying NO like she means it, screaming, kicking, running, fighting—her chance of escaping ranges from 60–80%.[36]

Whereas *if she doesn't resist her chance of getting raped is 100%*.

Women and Guns

From my journal, 1978:

For three or four years I've dreamed about rape regularly. The can't run dreams. The can't scream ones. Dreams where I'm being attacked and I have a knife in my pocket but I can't get it, or I'm afraid to use it. The dream that keeps extending into more complication, more danger, until there he is again, "my" rapist. I even had a dream where I'm sitting by a lake and a man swims up, sticks his head out of the water, and says: "I'm your rapist."

In many of these dreams, I don't recognize the danger early enough to respond.

   Since I bought a gun and have learned to use it, my dreams
have changed. Whatever the situation, whatever the form of attack,
I simply whip out my gun. Sometimes I shoot. Sometimes I don't
even need to shoot, I just aim and he is suddenly harmless. The
man who called himself "my rapist " laughs at me when I draw
my gun; he says, "The hospital can suck those bullets out in no
time." But I know, and he doesn't, that it's a .38 I'm holding, and I
shoot, confident that the bullets will do the job.

If resistance alleviates abuse and increases dramatically our chances of
escape, how can we increase our ability to resist? The most certain way to refuse violation would be to keep a gun handy.
   Many women immediately reject this option. Some call guns "masculine." Many are simply terrified of guns' murderous power. But aside from
fears of legal repercussions or male retaliation, fears which are realistic and
need to be addressed — is a gun really more dangerous than, for example, a
car? Is owning a gun more dangerous than not owning one? Past the realistic fears is, I believe, a fear of our own selves.
   I've talked with many women about getting a gun and learning to shoot.

   R. tells me, "I'm afraid I'd kill my husband."
      Not to dismiss killings that happen in rage because a gun is
   handy (though how many of these killings are committed by
   women?) But to recognize that in her mind she's protected against
   killing her husband only because she lacks the means.

   K. says she's afraid she'd shoot the first man she saw acting like an
   asshole.
      I ask what she means by "an asshole." She says, "Like some
   man beating up on some woman." Again, she is protected (from
   her best impulses) only by her inability to act.

   N. says she's afraid she'd shoot her nose off.
      As if a woman who has learned to cook, play the recorder, ride
   the subway, drive a car, and change a diaper couldn't learn to shoot.

   H., B., C., E., many many women say, "I'm afraid if I have a gun
   it'll get used against me."

Of course this is exactly what men tell us. For example, in Boston in 1979,
after the sixth Black woman in as many weeks had been killed, police still
advised Black women against carrying weapons because they could be used
against them. Yet what alternatives did the police offer?
   In fact I've rarely heard of a real-life woman's weapon being used
against her, though I've seen it happen over and over again on TV and in the
movies. I've heard of a 14-year-old woman who shot her assailant with his
gun, a 17-year-old who sliced her attacker's jugular vein with his knife, a
mother who shot with his gun the policeman who threatened her child — she

killed him and wounded his partner.[37] Maybe it's men who shouldn't carry weapons. But no one tells them that.

I also discover among my friends women who aren't afraid of guns. L., who teaches me to shoot, grew up around guns in rural Oregon. P. learned to shoot in the army. F.'s father hunted. M.'s grandfather was a gangster. Against the dominant experience of women—which is to have little acquaintance with deadly weapons—an alternative perspective emerges: that of women who were taught to shoot as girls; country women who'd as soon live without a knife in the kitchen as a gun in the bedroom; women who recognize a gun as a tool: useful, dangerous but controllable, like a book of matches.

The first time L. took me shooting with a handgun, I tried a .22 pistol for a while, practiced aiming again and again till it came easy. Then I tried the .38. Fire leaped from the barrel, my hand jumped. TV and movies lie about the sound of guns: it is unbelievably loud. The noise, even with earplugs, shook me. After the first round I sat down, took a deep breath, and said, "I feel like I can't control it."

"It feels like that," L. said, "you just have to get used to how it feels."

After a few minutes, I got up to try again. I started to hit the target.

A learning experience, like a million others in a woman's life. Yet so many of us consider ourselves tiny children when it comes to guns. We're afraid a gun—a source of possible protection—will be turned against us. This fear deprives us of strength, lest our strength benefit them, not us. We're afraid what we'd do *if we could*—which, again, keeps us powerless, lest we use our power badly.

To fear ourselves is to use them as model:

> *they abuse their power, therefore we would too*

is to imagine only helplessness keeps us in line:

> *the more choices we have, the worse we'll be*

is to insist in some hidden corner of the body:

> *we need oppression*

Like, *you can't take the law into your own hands.*
But what better hands to take the law into?

Our fear of ourselves then is fear of ourselves empowered. As we worry about what we'd do if we could, we are undermined in our attempts to end our oppression. We are partly afraid we can't be trusted with freedom.

NOTES

1. I want to acknowledge general indebtedness to the work that preceded or has accompanied the writing of this essay. The first feminist speak-out on rape, in New York City in 1971, was documented in Noreen Connell and Cassandra Wilson, *Rape: The First Sourcebook for Women* (1974). Susan Griffin, *Rape: The Power of Consciousness*

(1979) includes her earlier essay, which is still one of the best discussions of the issue. Andrea Medea and Kathleen Thompson, *Against Rape* (1974) remains useful, as does Susan Brownmiller, *Against Our Will: Men, Women and Rape* (1975) — the classic, limited but essential. Early work on battering includes Erin Pizzey, *Scream Quietly or the Neighbors Will Hear You* (1974), Betsy Warrior, *Battered Lives* (1974) and Del Martin, *Battered Wives* (1976). Susan Schechter, *Women and Male Violence: The Visions and Struggles of the Battered Women's Movement* (1982) remains the best single text on battering to combine service-provider and activist consciousness. On incest, Florence Rush's early work is included in the Sourcebook noted above, and her book *The Best Kept Secret: Sexual Abuse of Children* (1980) contains the earliest discussion of how Freud suppressed information and revised his theory, based on his women patients' experience of incestuous abuse by male relatives, in favor of his oedipal theory that women fantasized this abuse. Sandra Butler, *Conspiracy of Silence: The Trauma of Incest* (1978) remains one of the clearest treatments built from women's experience, compassionate and politically savvy. Also, Judith Lewis Herman, with Lisa Hirschman, *Father-Daughter Incest* (1981). General books on violence against women: Andrea Dworkin's *Woman Hating* (1974) and *Our Blood* (1976); Kathleen Barry's *Female Sexual Slavery* (1979); and Frederique Delacorte and Felice Newman, eds., *Fight Back! Feminist Resistance to Male Violence* (1981). Pauline B. Bart and Patricia H. O'Brien, *Stopping Rape: Successful Survival Strategies* (1985), and Evelyn C. White, *Chain Chain Change: For Black Women Dealing with Physical and Emotional Abuse* (1985) are extremely useful.

I want also to acknowledge general indebtedness to numerous conversations in the late seventies with Paula King and Michaele Uccella, and to the many thinkers and activists with whom I worked in the Portland, Oregon movement to stop violence against women. Many women have read pieces of this essay over the years and shared their responses with me: Gloria Anzaldúa, Margaret Blanchard, Sandy Butler, Chrystos, Irena Klepfisz, Helena Lipstadt, Fabienne McPhail-Grant, Bernice Mennis, Maureen O'Neill, Linda Vance, and Judy Waterman, in addition, of course, to Joan Pinkvoss, my editor and publisher at Aunt Lute. I alone am responsible for its weaknesses.

2. *Sourcebook,* note 1, 49.

3. Brownmiller, note 1, 363.

4. Interesting that in patriarchal western culture, revenge is considered practically a sacred duty for men, Hamlet and Orestes being only two of the more obvious examples (both sons avenging their fathers in part against their mothers). But women are not even supposed to entertain vengeful feelings.

5. Griffin, *Consciousness,* note 1, 21.

6. Phyllis Chesler, *Women and Madness* (1973), 292; see also M. F. Beal, *S.A.F.E. House* (1976) and Karen Hagberg, "Why the Women's Movement Cannot Be Non-Violent," *Heresies 6: Women and Violence* (1979), 44, from Nadia Telsey and Linda Maslanko, with the help of the Women's Martial Art Union, Self-Defense for Women (1974).

7. *The Women's Gun Pamphlet by and for Women* (1975), 3.

8. Janet Koenig, "The Social Meaning of Violence," *Heresies 6,* note 6, 91.

9. Assata Shakur, from an interview in *Plexus* by Women Against Prison, quoted in Beal, note 7, 111.

10. Ti-Grace Atkinson, *Amazon Odyssey* (1974), ccxlix. The term *violence* she reserves to represent "a class function," available as a *tactic* only to the oppressor class (200).

11. Hagberg, note 6, 44.

12. Leon Litwack, *Been in the Storm So Long: The Aftermath of Slavery* (1980), 65–66.

13. Litwack, note 12, 66.

14. Litwack, note 12, 43. What is being said here? First, the "whole theory of slavery" boiled down to an assumption of African inferiority, less-than-humanness. Second, military prowess dominated patriarchal notions of humanness: only competent soldiers, i.e., men who could act like "real men," were equal human beings. Consider that slaves were not an unknown people but the very people who not only performed necessary physical labor, but also raised white Southern children and tended the white Southern sick; obviously, tenderness, intelligence, caring, etc. did not challenge "the whole theory of slavery." See Deborah Gray White, *Ar'n't I a Woman: Female Slaves in the Plantation South* (1985).

15. Frantz Fanon, *The Wretched of the Earth* (1963), discusses the political implications of the oppressed's psychological need to release rage.

16. Litwack, note 12, 46.

17. W.E.B. Du Bois, *Black Reconstruction* (1935), quoted in Litwack, note 12, 64.

18. See Angela Davis, "The Legacy of Slavery: Standards for a New Womanhood," in *Women, Race, and Class* (1981), 3–29, and Linda Brent, *Incidents in the Life of a Slave Girl* (1973; 1st pub. 1861), which depicts extreme sexual harassment and abuse suffered by enslaved Black women from white men, and solidarity among Black women and men, both enslaved and free. Of course Brent was writing an abolitionist document.

    It appears that women employed all the forms of resistance used by men, direct and indirect. But unlike the men, the women had no access to the military, no institutional focus through which to transform capacity for violence into organized strength. And if "manliness," as Du Bois caustically remarked, meant murder, "womanliness" translated into what Black women were deprived of, the right to be protected by their men, and to raise their own babies.

19. White, *Ar'n't I a Woman*, note 14, 102–3, citing B. A. Botkin, ed., *Lay My Burden Down: A Folk History of Slavery* (1945), 160–62.

20. White, note 14, 78.

21. Brent, note 18.

22. White, note 14, 63–64.

23. White, note 14, 77–78.

24. Litwack, note 12, 65.

25. Toni Morrison's *Beloved* (1987) and Sherley Anne William's *Dessa Rose* (1986) both imagine permutations of violence from enslaved women.

26. Litwack, note 12, 76, 114.

27. Litwack, note 12, 46.

28. Litwack, note 12, 42.

29. Susan Brownmiller argued in *Against Our Will* for the critical importance of integrating by gender the military and the police. Though we have seen some signal changes as some gender integration occurs, and though women police and soldiers may improve their individual status, challenge stereotypes, and offer better service or protection to women, it's no more an adequate solution to rape than Black soldiers were an adequate solution to racist violence. The missing link in Brownmiller's argument is the role of the army and police in the U.S., which is to safeguard the interests of the powerful at home and abroad. This means men. Until or unless male institutions truly serve our interest, we can't adequately fight for women through them. During the Civil War and Reconstruction the interests of northern capitalists uniquely coincided with the interests of the slaves.

30. An earlier version of part of this chapter appeared in *Fight Back*, note 1, co-authored by me and Michaele Uccella. The ideas emerged in our discussions; the actual writing was done by me.

31. Andrea Dworkin argued this in "Biological Superiority: The World's Most Dangerous and Deadly Idea," *Heresies 6,* note 6, 46.

32. "The belief that violence is somehow gender-linked is amazingly prevalent throughout all literature, even feminist literature. . . . Obviously it would be stupid and cruel to say that women are not brutally victimized, systematically, institutionally, across all age, class, and race barriers. Quite the contrary. But the assumption that women are inherently incapable of violence is something else. My own inquiry into the matter has shown me that this assumption is simply not true." Michaele Uccella, *Lesbian Violence,* presented at Goddard College and at the Montpelier (Vermont) Women's Center, September, 1978.

33. The theory that a woman's capacity for doing violence (however covert or unacceptable the expression) is also a capacity for resistance was developed by Michaele Uccella in *Lesbian Violence.*

34. Two women quoted in Lillian Rubin, *Worlds of Pain: Life in the Working Class Family* (1976), 117, 42.

35. C. McCormick, "Battered Women" (1977), cited by Schneider, Jordan, and Arguedas, "Representation of Women Who Defend Themselves," in *Heresies 6,* note 12, 100ff.

36. Police statistics from Portland, Oregon, 1976, indicated a 60% rate of escape for women who use some form of resistance. Considering that many women who get away don't bother to report to the police, the higher rate of 80% indicated by other studies seems plausible. (Of course many many women who don't escape also refuse to report to the police, perhaps as many as 90% of all women who get raped.) Bart, note 1, has compiled resistance strategies from women who escaped.

37. The first escape was recorded in the *Portland Oregonian* sometime in 1979; the second came from the *New York Post,* 1/31/79. Neither of these women was charged. Also note the following divine judgment: "An axwielding Portland youth was killed early Friday when he accidentally struck himself in the side of the neck while allegedly threatening two girls in the parking lot of a convenience market." *Oregon Journal,* 7/19/78.

55

THE ULTIMATE GROWTH INDUSTRY
Trafficking in Women and Girls

JAN GOODWIN

Jan Goodwin is the author of *Caught in the Crossfire* (1987) about Afghanistan and *Price of Honor: Muslim Women Lift the Veil of Silence on the Islamic World* (2003).

T he California travel agency brochure could not be more blunt: "Sex Tours to Thailand, Real Girls, Real Sex, Real Cheap," it reads. "These women are the most sexually available in the world. Did you know you can actually buy a virgin girl for as little as $200? You could fuck a different girl every night for the rest of your life." There is even a prize for the man that has sex with the most girls during the tour. As for AIDS, the brochure continues, "Thailand is safe. And all the places we visit are police protected."

What the ad copy doesn't say is that these "virgin girls" are frequently children who have been kidnapped or sold into brothels. Forced into prostitution, sometimes even chained to their beds, they lead lives that are brutal, and frequently short. Averaging 15 customers a day, they work all but two days a month. They must perform any act demanded by their customers, most of whom refuse to wear condoms. If they object, the brothel owners beat them into submission. According to human rights activists working in Thailand, a large percentage of the prostitutes there are under 15, and girls as young as eight are sold into the industry. Within six months of being sold into the sex trade, a girl is commonly HIV-infected.

But you don't have to travel to Asia; sexual servitude can be found here in the U.S. too, as an 18-month undercover investigation by the Global Survival Network discovered. For example, women from the former Soviet Union can be found in brothels in New York, Bethesda, Maryland, and Los Angeles. Fleeing a collapsing economy at home, these women pay up to $3,000 in "processing fees" for what they are promised will be good jobs abroad; instead, they are sold into sexual slavery. The industry is tightly controlled by the Russian mafia, whose contacts with their own government and immigration officials facilitate the acquisition of the necessary visas and passports. Women trying to escape have been murdered, and the threat that

Jan Goodwin, "The Ultimate Growth Industry: Trafficking in Women and Girls" from *On the Issues: The Progressive Woman's Quarterly* (Fall 1998). Reprinted with the permission of the author.

family members back home will be beaten to death is also used to keep women in line.

According to GSN, which is based in Washington, D.C., every year trafficking in women and girls puts billions of dollars into the coffers of criminal syndicates worldwide—an amount rivaling their incomes from drugs and guns. And there is another plus in trading in human flesh: dope and weapons can only be sold once; a woman or girl can be sold again and again.

As the disparities in the global economy widen, girl children and young women are increasingly seen as currency and quick profits. The United Nations estimates that, around the world, some 200 million people are forced to live as sexual or economic slaves, the latter often involving sexual exploitation as well. In Southeast Asia alone, a reported 60 to 70 million women and children have been sold in the sex industry in the last decade. "Slavery is one of the most undesirable consequences of globalization," says a UN spokesman, adding, "We regret that this is not considered a priority by any country at the moment."

Nor is trafficking in women and girls limited to prostitution; it is also used to supply the forced-marriage industry. In China today, for example, there are now three males for every two females in the population over the age of 15. This as a result of the government's "one child, one couple" policy, combined with the traditional, and still powerful, requirement for a son. If the first child is a girl, the fetus may be aborted, or the infant abandoned or even killed. As a consequence, young women and girls are being sold into marriage, in a revival of a once-standard feudal practice. According to Chinese government reports, in the first 10 months of 1990 alone, trafficking in brides increased by 60 percent over the previous year. Either kidnapped or sold by impoverished families, the young women are purchased by potential bridegrooms for up to $600. The government's Office for the Eradication of the Kidnapping and Sale of Women acknowleges some 50,000 such kidnappings per year (although human rights organizations believe the real numbers are much higher). And the profits are enormous. In a five-year period from 1991 to 1996, Chinese police freed 88,000 women and children who had been kidnapped for this purpose.

Particularly disturbing is the violence to which these forced brides are subjected. The abducted women, who can be as young as 13 or 14, are frequently gang-raped by the slave traders before being sold, a practice that is intended to terrify them into passivity, and is no doubt effective in many cases. Those who try to run from their new husbands are violently punished, even maimed, by the traffickers in ways that are too sickening to be printed here.

In some cases, sex tours from the U.S. to the Third World are offered as a means by which lonely men can find a mate. Norman Barabash, who runs Big Apple Oriental Tours out of Queens, New York, views his tours as a social development program. Until recently, $2,200 bought 10 days and 11 nights of "paradise" in the Philippines; since last year, when Big Apple was banned from doing business in that country, Barabash has been sending

American men to Thailand. Women in these countries have no jobs, and are dying to get American husbands, he says. "They are so set on landing one, they will do anything their conscience allows." According to Barabash, some 20 to 25 percent of his clients end up marrying women they meet on the tours.

Big Apple is only one of some 25 or 30 similar operations in the U.S. that ride on—and promote—the myth that "exotic oriental women are thrilled to meet American men, and know how to please and serve them," says Ken Franzblau, a lawyer for Equality Now, a human rights organization. Franzblau went underground for almost two years to investigate sex-tour companies in the U.S. "I posed as a shy man who felt insecure around women, and inquired about taking such a trip," he says. "I was told that all kinds of kinky sex would be available, and that the tour guides would negotiate prices for me with the pimps."

Franzblau points out that the operations demean women at both ends of their business. Reads one brochure: "Had enough of American bitches who won't give you the time of day, and are only interested in your bank account? In Asia you'll meet girls who will treat you with respect and appreciation, unlike their American counterparts." These operators insist that American women are unloving, feminist manhaters, he says. "At the destination end, sex tours create the ever-increasing demand to bring young women and girls into the sex industry."

In the Philippines and Thailand, prostitution is illegal. Here in the U.S., as well as in Germany, the Netherlands, Sweden, and Australia—all countries where sex tours originate—such "tourism" is likewise illegal, although in this country, the law applies only to traveling with the intent to engage in a sexual act with a juvenile, which is punishable for up to 10 years imprisonment. In the four years this law has been in force, however, there have been no prosecutions.

It is also illegal in virtually every state of America (including New York, where Big Apple operates) to promote prostitution, or knowingly profit from it. Yet sex-tour operators openly advertise in magazines and on the Internet, and the websites of many feature hardcore pornographic photographs of promised "delights." So, too, do the videos they send potential customers. An hour-long video sent to men interested in going on a Big Apple tour and viewed by *On the Issues* shows what is described as a wet T-shirt contest, but in reality is more a sex circus in which young women are stripped, and a mob of raucous overweight, aging American men suck on their nipples, perform oral sex, and otherwise explore their body cavities as they are passed around the crowd. The video also offers "daily introductions to the ladies of your choice who will be your companion for the night or around the clock." As two young women are shown cavorting naked in a jacuzzi, the voice-over cautions that if viewers don't take a tour, they will "miss an afternoon at a sex motel with two lovely ladies."

There is nothing subtle or obscure about the promotional video and its customer come-ons, but in a letter to Democratic Senator Catherine Abate last September, Queens County District Attorney Richard Brown wrote: "Our investigation [of Big Apple Oriental Tours], which has been quite extensive and included the use of undercover operatives as well as assistance provided by the FBI and the US Customs Service, has disclosed no provable violations of New York's criminal laws." At the time the decision not to pursue an indictment was made, the DA's office was in possession of the video.

After that ruling, Equality Now met with the DA, and offered additional evidence, including records of Franzblau's conversations with Big Apple's owner, and the reports of the two men who took the tours. The DA has subsequently reopened his investigation of the company.

Many other countries are also lax about cracking down on trafficking. The Japanese not only appear to condone the industry, they actively obstruct interference in it. Due to massive unemployment in the Philippines, even for those with college degrees, some 80,000 Filipinos work in Japan; 95 percent of them are women employed as "dance entertainers." Commonly, the passports of these "guest workers" are confiscated on arrival and their salaries withheld; according to Mizuho Matsuda, the director of HELP, the only shelter for abused migrant women workers in Tokyo, many are forced into prostitution. Japan's criminal syndicate, the Yazuka, is heavily involved in trafficking women for the country's sex-and-entertainment industry, and like their Russian counterpart, have contacts in the government, and therefore often enjoy its protection.

A grisly side of a grim industry is highlighted by the death of 22-year old Maricris Siosin, a graduate in modern dance. Five months after arriving in Tokyo, she was sent home in a closed coffin, with a death certificate stating she had died of hepatitis. When her family opened the coffin for the funeral, they discovered that she had been beaten and stabbed. An autopsy conducted by the Philippines National Bureau of Investigation and confirmed, at the request of Equality Now, by a leading pathologist in the U.S., showed that a double-edged sword had been thrust into her vagina.

In Japan, S&M has a long tradition, and extremely violent S&M comics are readily available. Many male commuters openly read them instead of newspapers as they travel to and from work. One theory is that Maricris was forced to participate in a "snuff" movie (a porno flick in which the woman is actually killed).

A Philippine government mission which was sent to Japan to investigate the murder was turned away by Japanese authorities. Similarly, Maricris' family has been denied access to medical documents and police records. Some 33 Filipino workers died in Japan the same year Maricris was killed. At least 12 of these deaths took place under "suspicious circumstances."

In other countries, local authorities facilitate sex trafficking. In the southern Thai town of Ranong, for example, brothels are surrounded by electrified barbed wire and armed guards to keep girls from escaping. The local police chief condones the practice, describing the brothels as an important part of the local economy. And while prostitution is illegal in Thailand, customers and owners alike have no fear of arrest. The police can be bought off, or accept payment in kind — free use of the brothels; a number of them also act as procurers for the traffickers.

The government periodically promises to crack down on the industry, but because of the amount of money it generates, invariably looks the other way. Of the five million annual visitors to Thailand on tourist visas, three out of four are men traveling alone, many of whom are from Europe, the Middle East, Japan, and the U.S. When raids are planned, the police often alert the brothels ahead of time. The only people arrested are the young prostitutes. Tragically, they are then frequently "recycled," often with the assistance of the local police, who resell them to agents of a different brothel. And so the tragic circle remains unbroken, until the girls become too sick to work, or die on the job, like the five young prostitutes on Phuket island, a popular vacation resort for foreigners in southern Thailand: When fire broke out in the brothel where they worked, they burned to death because they were chained to their beds and unable to escape.

Tourism in Thailand generates $3 billion annually, and the country's international image as a sexual paradise has made prostitution one of its most valuable economic subsectors. That international reputation is one even the U.S. Navy has recognized. The first port of call and liberty shore leave for much of the U.S. fleet after the Gulf War was Pattaya, a beach resort notorious as a center of Thailand's sex industry. This apparent reward for service was given despite the fact that at the time at least 50 percent of the prostitutes in the region were HIV-positive. Another major destination for sex traffickers is India, where an estimated 15 million women and girls, many of whom have been sold into it from impoverished Nepal, Bangladesh, and Pakistan, work in the sex industry.

"Women and girls are moved between a lot of different countries," says a spokesman for Human Rights Watch. Moreover, trafficking is not only a global phenomenon, it is a "hidden one." For example, the organization reported recently, the U.S. gives Thailand $4 million a year to control the traffic in narcotics, but no U.S. aid is aimed at curtailing sex trafficking there. It is imperative that the U.S. government "recognize the severity of the problem," says Human Rights Watch. "And the United Nations also needs to be very aggressive in fighting this modern form of slavery."

56

WHERE RACE AND GENDER MEET
Racism, Hate Crimes, and Pornography

HELEN ZIA

Helen Zia, the daughter of Chinese immigrants, grew up in the fifties when there were only 150,000 Chinese Americans in the entire country. An award-winning journalist, Zia has covered Asian American communities and social and political movements for more than twenty years. She lives in the San Francisco Bay Area.

There is a specific area where racism, hate crimes, and pornography intersect, and where current civil rights law fails: racially motivated, gender-based crimes against women of color. This area of bias-motivated sexual assault has been called "ethnorape"; I refer to it as "hate rape."

I started looking into this issue after years of organizing against hate killings of Asian Americans. After a while, I noticed that all the cases I could name concerned male victims. I wondered why. Perhaps it was because Asian-American men came into contact with perpetrator types more often or because they are more hated and therefore more often attacked by racists. But the subordination and vulnerability of Asian-American women, who are thought to be sexually exotic, subservient, and passive, argued against that interpretation. So where were the Asian-American women hate-crime victims?

Once I began looking, I found them, in random news clippings, in footnotes in books, through word of mouth. Let me share with you some examples I unearthed of bias-motivated attacks and sexual assaults:

- In February 1984, Ly Yung Cheung, a nineteen-year-old Chinese woman who was seven months pregnant, was pushed in front of a New York City subway train and decapitated. Her attacker, a white male high school teacher, claimed he suffered from "a phobia of Asian people" and was overcome with the urge to kill this woman. He successfully pleaded insanity. If this case had been investigated as a hate crime, there might have been more information about his so-called phobia and whether it was part of a pattern of racism. But it was not.

Helen Zia, "Where Race and Gender Meet: Racism, Hate Crimes, and Pornography" from *The Price We Pay: The Case Against Racist Speech, Hate Propaganda and Pornography,* edited by Laura Lederer and Richard Delgado (New York: Hill & Wang, 1995). Reprinted with the permission of Dr. Laura J. Lederer.

- On December 7, 1984, fifty-two-year-old Japanese American Helen Fukui disappeared in Denver, Colorado. Her decomposed body was found weeks later. Her disappearance on Pearl Harbor Day, when anti-Asian speech and incidents increase dramatically, was considered significant in the community. But the case was not investigated as a hate crime and no suspects were ever apprehended.
- In 1985 an eight-year-old Chinese girl named Jean Har-Kaw Fewel was found raped and lynched in Chapel Hill, North Carolina—two months after Penthouse featured pictures of Asian women in various poses of bondage and torture, including hanging bound from trees. Were epithets or pornography used during the attack? No one knows—her rape and killing were not investigated as a possible hate crime.
- Recently a serial rapist was convicted of kidnapping and raping a Japanese exchange student in Oregon. He had also assaulted a Japanese woman in Arizona, and another in San Francisco. He was sentenced to jail for these crimes, but they were never pursued as hate crimes, even though California has a hate statute. Was hate speech or race-specific pornography used? No one knows.
- At Ohio State University, two Asian women were gang raped by fraternity brothers in two separate incidents. One of the rapes was part of a racially targeted game called the "Ethnic Sex Challenge," in which the fraternity men followed an ethnic checklist indicating what kind of women to gang rape. Because the women feared humiliation and ostracism by their communities, neither reported the rapes. However, campus officials found out about the attacks, but did not take them up as hate crimes, or as anything else.

All of these incidents could have been investigated and prosecuted either as state hate crimes or as federal civil rights cases. But they were not. To have done so would have required one of two things: awareness and interest on the part of police investigators and prosecutors—who generally have a poor track record on race and gender issues—or awareness and support for civil rights charges by the Asian-American community—which is generally lacking on issues surrounding women, gender, sex, and sexual assault. The result is a double-silencing effect on the assaults and deaths of these women, who become invisible because of their gender and their race.

Although my research centers on hate crimes and Asian women, this silence and this failure to provide equal protection have parallels in all of the other classes protected by federal civil rights and hate statutes. That is, all other communities of color have a similar prosecution rate for hate crimes against the women in their communities—namely, zero. This dismal record is almost as bad in lesbian and gay antiviolence projects: the vast preponderance of hate crimes reported, tracked, and prosecuted concern gay men—very few concern lesbians. So where are all the women?

The answer to this question lies in the way our justice system was designed, and the way women are mere shadows in the existing civil rights framework. But in spite of this history, federal and state law do offer legal avenues for women to be heard. Federal civil rights prosecutions, for example, can be excellent platforms for high-visibility community education on the harmful impact of hate speech and behavior. When on June 19, 1982, two white auto workers in Detroit screamed racial epithets at Chinese-American Vincent Chin and said, "It's because of you motherfuckers that we're out of work," a public furor followed, raising the level of national discourse on what constitutes racism toward Asian Americans. Constitutional law professors, and members of the American Civil Liberties Union and the National Lawyers Guild had acted as if Asian Americans were not covered by civil rights law. Asian Americans emphatically corrected that misconception.

Hate crimes remedies can be used to force the criminal justice bureaucracy to adopt new attitudes. Patrick Purdy went to an elementary school in Stockton, California, in which 85 percent of the students came from Southeast Asia. When he selected that school as the place to open fire with his automatic weapon and killed five eight-year-olds and wounded thirty other children, the police and the media did not think it was a bias-motivated crime. Their denial reminds me of the response by the Montreal officials to the anti-feminist killings of fourteen women students there. But an outraged Asian-American community forced a state investigation into the Purdy incident and uncovered hate literature in the killer's effects. As a result, the community was validated, and, in addition, the criminal justice system and the media acquired a new level of understanding.

Imagine if a federal civil rights investigation had been launched in the case of the African-American student at St. John's University who was raped and sodomized by white members of the school lacrosse team, who were later acquitted. Investigators could have raised issues of those white men's attitudes toward the victim as a black woman, found out whether hate speech or race-specific pornography was present, investigated the overall racial climate on campus, and brought all of the silenced aspects of the incident to the public eye. Community discourse could have been raised to a high level.

Making these investigations happen will not be an easy road. Hate-crime efforts are generally expended on blatant cases, with high community consensus, not ones that bring up hard issues like gender-based violence. Yet these intersections of race and gender hatred are the very issues we must give voice to.

There is a serious difficulty with pushing for use of federal and state hate remedies. Some state statutes have been used against men of color: specifically, on behalf of white rape victims against African-American men. We know that the system, if left unchecked, will try to use antihate laws to enforce unequal justice. On the other hand, state hate statutes could be used to prosecute men of color who are believed to have assaulted women of color of another race—interminority assaults are increasing. Also, if violence against women generally were made into a hate crime, women of color could seek prosecutions against men in their own community for their gender-based violence—

even if this would make it harder to win the support of men in communities of color, and of women in those communities who would not want to be accused of dividing the community.

But at least within the Asian-American antiviolence community, this discourse is taking place now. Asian-American feminists in San Francisco have prepared a critique of the Asian movement against hate crimes and the men of that movement are listening. Other communities of color should also examine the nexus between race and gender for women of color, and by extension, for all women.

The legal system must expand the boundaries of existing law to include the most invisible women. There are hundreds of cases involving women of color waiting to be filed. Activists in the violence-against-women movement must reexamine current views on gender-based violence. Not all sexual assaults are the same. Racism in a sexual assault adds another dimension to the pain and harm inflicted. By taking women of color out of the legal shadows, out of invisibility, all women make gains toward full human dignity and human rights.

57

HOMOPHOBIA IN STRAIGHT MEN

TERRY A. KUPERS

Terry A. Kupers, M.D., a professor in the Graduate School of Psychology at The Wright Institute in Berkeley, California, practices psychiatry in Oakland. The author of *Public Therapy: The Practice of Psychotherapy in the Public Mental Health Clinic* (1981), and *Ending Therapy: The Meaning of Termination* (1988), he is married and has three young adult sons.

A few years ago I toured a high-security prison in the Midwest as an expert witness in litigation concerning the effects of prison conditions on prisoners' mental health. When I stepped into the main entry area of the prison, I saw a woman milling around with the men a short distance down one of the halls. She was blond, slim, very feminine—or so I thought on first glance. Actually, "she" was a young man, perhaps 21, dressed as a woman. Blond, blue-eyed, slight and sensuous, he played the part very well. He wore a flowing red gown that reached the floor, had a shawl draped across his chest in a way that did not permit one to assess the size of his breasts, wore make-up, and sported a very seductive female pose. I was surprised to see an attractive woman roaming around in a men's prison. One of the attorneys accompanying me on the tour told me with a wink that "she" was a he, and asked if I would like to talk to him.

The inmate told me he was not really gay, and certainly did not believe he would dress as a woman again after he was released, but on "the inside" it's the only way for him to survive unless he "locks up"; that is, asks for protective custody in a segregated section of the prison where inmates who do not feel safe on the "mainline" are housed, including those identified as "snitches" and child molesters. When this man arrived at the prison at 19 he was beat up and raped a number of times, and on several other occasions prison toughs fought with each other for the opportunity to use him sexually. He learned that it was safer to become the "woman" of a tough prisoner, that way he would not be beaten nor be the object of rivalries between prison toughs. He would become the passive sexual partner of one dominant man.

Later that day I met with a group of security officers. One mentioned the young man. I said I had met him. The officer asked if I'd like to hear the bit of advice he would have given that slight and fair young man if he had seen him when he entered the prison. Before I had a chance to answer, he blurted out:

> What you want to do is the first time you go out on the yard you
> break off a metal bed post and shove it down your trouser leg.
> Then, when a big guy comes up and pinches your ass or makes a
> lewd remark, you pull out the metal stick and smack him as hard
> as you can across the face. You'll both get thrown in the hole for
> ten days. Then, when you get out, everyone will respect you as a
> "crazy" and no one will hassle you for sex any more.

In prison, "butt-fucking" is the symbol of dominance. The strong do it, the weak must submit. Homosexual rape is a constant threat for those who cannot prove they are "man enough." According to Tom Cahill (1990), a survivor of prison rape: "We are victims of a system in which those who are dominated and humiliated come to dominate and humiliate others" (p. 33). Perhaps this explains why prisoners do so much body-building.

Free men do a lot of toughening, too. If it is not the physique it's the mind, or it's the reputation or the financial empire, but men are always building something that they believe will keep them off the bottom of the heap, out of range of those who would "shaft" them. This is not a complete explanation of men's competitiveness and defensiveness—competition is built into our social relations—but men's subjective dread of "being shafted" plays a part in sustaining those competitive social relations. The prison drama reverberates in the male psyche. It is as if men do not want to appear incapable of defending themselves against rape at any time. We stiffen our bodies when approached by other men who want to touch or hug and we keep men at a certain distance—where we can watch them and be certain that closeness and dependency will not make us too vulnerable.

58

STOPPING SEXUAL HARASSMENT
A Challenge for Community Education

ROBERT L. ALLEN

Robert L. Allen is a teacher, writer, and community activist who is deeply interested in men's issues. Since 1986 he has worked with the Oakland Men's Project, a community education organization that conducts workshops dealing with male violence, sexism, racism, and homophobia. At the University of California at Berkeley, he teaches African American and Ethnic Studies and a course called "Men of Color." Senior Editor of *The Black Scholar* journal, Allen is also coeditor of a recent book titled *Brotherman: The Odyssey of Black Men in America.* He is the father of a son, Casey.

There can be little doubt that an important outcome of the 1991 Senate Judiciary Committee hearings has been growing public recognition of sexual harassment as a major social problem. Virtually the entire nation has engaged in the public discourse around this issue, and this engagement is to be welcomed.

Like many men in the aftermath of Anita Hill's testimony, I found myself hearing harrowing reports of sexual harassment from women relatives and friends who had previously felt constrained to remain silent. They told me of awful things that had been said or done to them, on the job or in the streets, sometimes recently and sometimes years ago. They spoke of their anger and humiliation, of their shame and feelings of self-blame, of their fear of the consequences of speaking out or rebuking their harassers. They experienced sexual harassment—the imposition of unwanted sexual attention—as a violation of their human dignity.

I listened and shared their outrage—but I also found myself recalling things I had said or done to women in the recent or distant past, and the recollections were sometimes distinctly discomforting. I think an important value of these exchanges was the opportunity for men to learn from the personal testimony of women they love and respect how widespread sexual harassment is. At the same time, the self-reflection and discussions among men that were sometimes provoked by the women's stories offered an opportunity for men to recognize that harassing behavior is not simply an aberration, nor is it exclusively the province of macho males; on the contrary, harassing behavior is something that many of us men have engaged in at some point, if not on the job, then on the streets or on campus or even in our homes. We knew what we were doing, because we knew the women involved were made to feel uncomfortable or humiliated by our words or actions.

Why did we do it? Why do men harass women? Why, until recently, was such behavior generally acceptable in our culture—that is, acceptable to men? Aside from punishment, what can be done to stop harassing behavior?

In this essay I want to raise two points for consideration as part of the discourse on sexual harassment.

First, sexual harassment should not be dismissed as aberrant behavior, as the macho mentality gone wild, or as the result of male biology or uncontrollable sexual desire. Sexual harassment, like child abuse and domestic violence, is an outgrowth of socialization into male and female gender roles in a sexist society. It is learned behavior.

Second, if harassment, abuse, and violence are forms of learned behavior, they can also be unlearned. I therefore argue that in addition to legal or punitive approaches to sexual harassment, it is imperative to adopt a preventive approach through community education. We must create an environment, not only in the workplace but in our communities generally, in which harassment, abuse, and violence are no longer tolerated because men and women understand the damage such behavior does to all of us. That means adopting a social change perspective critical of the values of the dominant culture, a culture that is premised on inequality.

Gender roles are not foreordained by our biology or our genes. We learn gender roles as part of our socialization into the culture. When a child is born, the first question inevitably asked is "Boy or girl?" Our response to the child is then mediated by our knowledge of its genitals, and it is *our* actions that tell the child its gender identity and the behavior appropriate to that identity.

In California I work with an organization called the Oakland Men's Project (OMP). Formed in 1979, OMP is a nonprofit multiracial organization of men and women devoted to community education around issues of male violence, sexism, racism, and homophobia. Over the years we have worked with thousands of boys and men (and girls and women) in high schools, church groups, colleges, prisons, community groups, and rehabilitation programs. We conduct workshops that involve interactive role playing and discussions that allow men and women to examine gender roles and the social training we get in this culture.

In our workshops we ask young people what they think it means to be a man or a woman. It is remarkable how consistently they express the same set of expectations about appropriate male and female behavior. Men are expected to be in control, tough, aggressive, independent, competitive, and emotionally unexpressive (with the exception of anger and sexual desire, which are allowable emotions for men). Women, on the other hand, are expected to be polite, dependent, emotional, and sexy, to take care of others, and not to be too smart or pushy. In recent years we have noticed that sometimes girls will challenge these role expectations and occasionally even a boy will object, but for the most part they remain widely accepted. Paul Kivel, who has summed up the experience of the Oakland Men's Project in his *Men's Work: How to Stop the Violence That Tears Our Lives Apart,* refers to these as "core expectations" that we all have, especially men, regarding appropriate male and female behavior.

How do young men learn these expectations? At OMP, to illustrate the socialization process, we use what we call role plays that dramatize common situations most boys and men have experienced. One of these involves an interaction between a father and his ten-year-old son, both played by facilitators. The son is sitting at home watching television when the father comes in from work, orders the boy to turn off the TV, and berates him for the messiness of the room. When the boy tries to explain that he was going to clean up later, the father tells him to shut up and stop making excuses. Then he shoves the son's report card in his face and demands to know why he got a D in math. The boy says he did the best he could. The father shames the son, telling him that he is stupid and that D stands for "dummy." The boy says that's not fair and begins to stand up. The father shoves him down, saying, "Don't you dare get up in my face, I didn't say you could go anyplace!" The boy is visibly upset and begins to cry. The father gets even more angry: "Now what? You're crying? You little mama's boy! You sissy! You make me sick. When are you going to grow up and start acting like a man?" The father storms out of the room.

When we do this role play, it gets the undivided attention of everyone in the room, especially the boys. Almost every young person has had the experience of being scolded and shamed by an adult. Most boys have had the experience of being humiliated by an older male and being told that they are not acting like men.

When we stop the role play, we ask the boys how it made them feel to witness this scene between the father and son. There may be a moment of embarrassed silence, but then the boys speak up and say it made them mad, upset, sad, etc. Often this is the first time they have articulated the feelings brought up by such an encounter, which sadly often replicates their own experience. Indeed, the power of this role play is that it is so familiar.

We ask the boys what messages such encounters send. They say things like, "A man is tough. A man is in control. A man doesn't cry. It's okay for a man to yell at someone. A man can take it. A man is responsible. A man is competent. A man doesn't take crap from anyone else." As they speak, we write their comments on a blackboard. Then we draw a box around the comments and label it the "Act Like a Man" box. Most males in this culture are socialized to stay in the box. We learn this from our fathers, older brothers, guys on the street, television, sports, movies, and so on. We may also learn it from our mothers and grandmothers, or from the reactions of girls in school. The fact is that this notion of manhood is so pervasive in our culture that everyone knows the role and anyone can teach it to a boy.

We ask the boys what happens if you step out of the box, if you stop acting tough enough or man enough. They reply that you get called names: sissy, wimp, nerd, fag, queer, mama's boy, punk, girl, loser, fairy. And what is the point of the name calling? The boys say that it is a challenge and you're expected to fight to prove that you're not what they called you. In other words, if challenged, boys are expected to fight to prove that they're in the box—that they're tough and not gay or effeminate. Homophobia and fear of being identified with women in any way are strong messages boys receive from an early age.

We also ask about expectations of female behavior. The young people say things like, "A girl should be polite and clean, she shouldn't argue, she's pretty, she doesn't fight or act too smart, she helps others, she's emotional." We ask what happens when a girl refuses to be submissive and dependent, when she's assertive and smart and doesn't kowtow to the boys. Again the reply is that she will be called names: bitch, tomboy, dyke, whore, ballbreaker, cunt. And what is the point of the name calling? To tell the girl she'd better start "acting right." In other words, the name calling is like a slap in the face, reducing the girl to a despised sexual object, with the purpose of humiliating her and intimidating her into resuming "acceptable" behavior. If a girl fights when called names, she may emerge the victor, but her very success raises questions about her femininity.

Though our forays into junior highs and high schools hardly constitute systematic research, again and again we find the same core expectations of acceptable male and female behavior among young people. As I have said, there is a growing tendency to question these expectations, especially among young women, but the grip of traditional roles remains very strong.

Our work at OMP involves challenging role expectations by showing that male and female behaviors are neither biologically determined nor a function of "human nature" but are learned from our interactions with significant others and from the culture at large. Our workshops and role plays give boys and girls and men and women a way of analyzing social roles, not abstractly, but by drawing insights from their own experiences. Moreover, we show that social interactions involve making choices, and that we can break free of old roles by supporting each other in changing our choices.

An important component of our work is to look at structural relationships of power and inequality in our society. We ask workshop participants to think about their experiences with different social groups and to tell us which groups they think are more powerful and which are less powerful.

Most often this elicits statements to the effect that men as a group are more powerful than women as a group, whites more powerful than people of color, parents more powerful than children, teachers more powerful than pupils, the rich more powerful than the poor, straights more powerful than gays, bosses more powerful than workers, and so on. If we ask how these inequalities are maintained, we are told that it is done through laws, through rules and regulations, through discrimination and stereotypes, and ultimately through force and violence. Thus, despite our country's rhetoric of equality, experience teaches us that people are not treated equally, that we all have assigned places in the social hierarchy, and that violence is used to keep less powerful groups "in their place."

This violence takes many forms and is often legitimized through the process of blaming the victim. Consider the Rodney King case, in which the jury was told that the police officers thought he was dangerous because he was high on drugs and "out of control," and at the same time was persuaded that he was actually "in control," deliberately taunting and manipulating the officers. Either way, the message of this incredible argument was that Rodney King "deserved" the brutal beating he received and the policemen could be acquitted. Blaming victims for their own victimization is a widely employed means of justifying abuse and violence of all kinds.

Sexual harassment plays a part in reinforcing the power differential between men and women in our society, and that distinguishes it from flirtation or a simple mistake in judgment. For example, a man may harass a woman when she steps out of the role he expects her to play. In the workplace, "uppity" women who hold jobs traditionally held by men, or who are regarded as "too" assertive, competent, competitive, or emotionally reserved, are likely targets of harassment. Men may also harass women who are not "uppity" as a kind of ritual that confirms male dominance and female submissiveness. Thus, the female secretary or domestic worker may be "teased" or pinched or subjected to sexual remarks that serve to remind her of her low status and her vulnerability to men. She is expected to acquiesce in this treatment by laughing or otherwise acting as if the harassment is okay, thereby reaffirming the male's superior status and power. A woman worker may also be harassed by a male worker who is angry at the boss but fearful of the boss's power, and seeks to regain a sense of his own power by humiliating her.

Whether in the workplace or on the street, the purpose of sexual harassment is to reduce women to objects sexually vulnerable to men, and to reestablish the traditional power relationship between men and women. Indeed, women's sexual vulnerability to men is a key locus of male power, something men learn to expect. As boys we learn it from stories of sexual "conquest" we hear from older males; we learn it from films, magazines, pornography, advertising. We live in a capitalist culture that promises women's sexual availability as a reward to the male consumer of everything from cars to cigarettes. It is not surprising, then, that men come to believe that every woman should be sexually available to any man. Sexual harassment is both a manifestation and a reinforcement of an exploitive system in which men are socialized collectively and individually to expect to have power over women collectively and individually.

Moreover, of the thousands of women who experience sexual harassment every day, a great many of them are women of color and poor women employed in the jobs that racist and sexist discrimination forces them to take—as domestics, clerical workers, farm workers, sweatshop and factory workers. Not only are these women especially vulnerable to sexual harassment, they also have less access to the levers of power needed to seek redress. Often they do not report harassment because they fear revenge from their employers or know their complaints will be dismissed. They are doubly oppressed: subjected to abuse and then constrained to remain silent about it.

The nature of sexual harassment is such that it is particularly easy to blame the victims. Often there is a suggestion that the woman somehow provoked or invited the objectionable behavior by something she said or did, or simply the way she was dressed. And if she did not protest the behavior immediately, it is insinuated that she must have enjoyed it, and any subsequent protests are suspect. In any case, the female victim's character is called into question and the male harasser is conveniently let off the hook, again reinforcing male dominance.

Of course, all men don't engage in sexual harassment, but we must ask why men who witness it often fail to intervene. One reason is obvious: male bonding to maintain male dominance. Men who would not engage in harassing behavior themselves may condone it in others because they agree that women must be "kept in their place." A second reason is more hidden: men's fear of being shamed or even attacked by other men.

As boys, most men learn that other men are dangerous. How many of us were called names or beaten up by other males when we were young? How many of us were ridiculed and humiliated by fathers or older brothers or coaches or teachers? How many were sexually assaulted by another male? We protected ourselves in various ways. Some of us withdrew into the private world of our fantasies. Some of us became bullies. Some of us became alcoholics and addicts so we wouldn't have to feel the pain and fear. Most of us learned to camouflage ourselves: we took on the coloration of the men we feared, and we hoped that no one would challenge us. We never talked about our fear because that in itself was dangerous and could mark us as targets of ridicule or violence from other men.

Instead we learned to keep our fear inside, a secret. In fact, we learned to keep most of our emotions bottled up inside because any sincere expression of emotion in front of other men was risky business that set you up to be put down. Only one emotion was considered manly: anger. Some of us learned to take other feelings—pain, grief, sadness, shame, loneliness, depression, jealousy, helplessness, fearfulness—and translate them into anger, and then pass them on to someone weaker in the form of physical or psychological violence. The humiliation we experienced at work, the fear we experienced when hassled by cops, the grief we felt when a relationship ended, the helplessness we felt when we lost a job—we learned to take these feelings, roll them into a heavy fist of rage, and slam it into our wives, our children, our lovers, women on the job or on the streets, less powerful men.

Thus, women and children often live in fear of men, and men frequently live in fear of each other. Most of us men won't admit this, but deep inside we recognize that harassment, abuse, rape, and violence are not simply "women's issues"—they're our issues as well. We know, but seldom admit, that if we didn't constantly protect ourselves, other men would do to us what we all too often do to women and children—as men who have been imprisoned can attest. So those of us who are not abusers or harassers sometimes wear the camouflage suits; we try to be "one of the boys." We present a front of manly power and control no matter what we may be feeling inside. We jostle and joke and push and shove, we make cracks about women and boast of our conquests, and we haze any guy who is different. We go along with harassers so as not to expose our own vulnerability, our fear of being shamed by other men—the weak point in our male armor.

Nevertheless, men have a stake in challenging sexual harassment, abuse, violence, and the sexist role training that underpins these behaviors. In the first place, men are not unconnected to women. We form a community of men and women—and children—together. A woman who suffers harassment might be my mother, my sister, my niece. She might be your daughter or your sister or your wife. A woman who is harassed, abused, or raped is part of a community that includes male relatives, lovers, and friends who are also hurt by the injury done to her. Men have a stake in stopping the abuse because it is directed against women we love and cherish.

I would argue that men have a further stake in challenging sexual abuse and the sexism on which it is based. Men are also damaged by sexism. A system that requires us to act as though we are always in control and to repress our emotions takes a heavy toll. It undermines our sense of authenticity. It results in a loss of intimacy with women and children. It conceals but does not change our fear of other men. It produces stress that is hazardous to our health and shortens our life spans. It makes us sick in our souls and bodies, and it turns us into enemies of those we love and of ourselves.

Historically, Black men and women in America have been victims of especially brutal and systematic violence. In the past our community has been terrorized by the lynching (and castration) of thousands of Black men by white men, and the rape (and lynching) of thousands of Black women by white men. Today white mob violence and police brutality continue unabated. African American men know intimately the violent capabilities of other men. It is a tragedy that many of us have internalized the violence of this oppressive system and brought it into our communities and our homes. The injuries done by racism to Black men's self-esteem are sometimes devastating, but the expectations of manhood we have learned block us from revealing or acknowledging our pain. Instead, we too often transform it into rage and violence against those we love. This must stop. African American men, as frequent victims of white male violence, have a particular stake in standing with women and children against all forms of violence.

How can men of all races be brought into the struggle against harassment, abuse, and violence? That is the question we have been seeking to answer through our work at the Oakland Men's Project. We have learned that it is extremely important for men to begin talking with each other about these issues. In our experience we have seen that there are growing numbers of men who are critical of sexism. All too often, however, these men as individuals are isolated and fearful of raising their concerns with other men. It is time for men who want to stop the violence to reach out to other men and break through the barrier of fear that has silenced us.

This is not an easy task, but as we have learned at OMP, it can be done. The male sex role, with its insistence on emotional "coolness" and reserve, makes open and honest communication from the heart difficult between men. We can begin to break through this isolation by sharing the often painful and humiliating ways we were socialized into the male role as young boys. At OMP we have found that workshops using interactive role plays, like the father-son encounter described earlier, are an effective method of opening up communication between men. Such techniques enable us to examine how the male sex role often sets men up to be dominating, controlling, and abusive. In another role play we watch a bully harassing the new boy at school. We discuss what the bully gains or fails to gain by bullying. For example, the bully may be seeking to compel respect from the victim, but what the victim often feels is contempt. At the same time, the bully models abusive behavior for the victim. He fails to get what he wants, but he may teach the victim how to bully someone else.

Through role plays like these, we look at how men are trained to take the hurt that has been done to them, translate it into anger, and direct the anger at a weaker person in the form of violence. This is the cycle of violence. We see it, for example, in the fact that the great majority of child abusers were themselves abused as children.

Another role play we use recreates a high school dating scene in which a boy and his girlfriend are sitting in his car in a secluded spot at night. We recruit two students from the audience to play the roles. We tell them that the boy wants to have sex that night but the girl, although she likes him, does not. Then we ask them to play out the scene. Sometimes the two actors work out a resolution acceptable to both. Sometimes the girl gets out of the car and walks away. But often the tension simply builds as the boy attempts to dominate and get his way while the girl tries to be responsive without giving in to his demands. We stop the role play and talk with the actors about the pressures they felt to behave as they did in the situation. We relate these pressures to the male and female role expectations discussed earlier. We also talk about the risk of the situation escalating into violence and rape, and the need to recognize danger signs to prevent this from happening. (For other examples of role plays and antiviolence exercises for teens, see *Helping Teens Stop Violence,* by Allan Creighton and Paul Kivel.)

Interrupting the cycle of violence requires that we unlearn sex roles that set us up to be perpetrators and victims of abuse. I am not talking only about men who are harassers or batterers, or women who have been abused. I believe that in this culture most of us are at risk for abusive behavior because most of us have been socialized into traditional sex roles. The cycle of abuse and violence can be broken at its root by challenging those roles and the institutions that support them—that is, through a process of community education and social change.

It is important for men of all races to become involved in this process. Men can take responsibility for stopping the cycle of violence and offering alternatives to violence. Men working with boys can model supportive ways of interacting and constructive methods of using anger to bring about change. All of us constantly make choices about how we relate to others, and in the power of choice is the power of change, for we are not simply passive victims of our socialization. For African American men there is a special urgency to this work. Our sons are dying in record numbers, often at each other's hands in angry acts of violence whose goal is to prove their manhood. We need to be clear that anger itself is not the problem. In a racist society Black people and other people of color have good reason to be angry. The problem lies in how the anger is expressed. Turning the anger against ourselves or others in acts of abuse and violence is self-destructive. Using righteous anger to challenge racist and oppressive institutions empowers individuals and communities, creates the possibility of real change, and builds self-esteem. Black men's organizations such as Simba, the Omega Boys' Club, and 100 Black Men of America are helping to develop new models of manhood among teenage Black males. We need organizations like these in every city.

Equally important, men working together can model a new version of power—*power with* others to make change, as opposed to *power over* others to perpetuate domination. In our society power generally means the ability to control others directly, with violence as the ultimate means of control. Men are socialized to exercise this form of power in all their relationships. Women sometimes learn to do the same. But this kind of power necessarily sets up conflicts with others—those we seek to control—and is alienating and isolating for the individual power holder. Power *with* others breaks down the isolation we feel and makes it possible to relate as allies rather than as competitors or opponents. It allows us to recognize that we are a community of people—men, women, and children—who are interdependent.

All of us have had the experience of powerlessness, for all of us have been children. As children we learned what it meant to be controlled by others, and often we learned what it meant to be humiliated and shamed by others. Such experiences are painful, and we may prefer to forget them, but ironically, by "owning" them, we create the possibility of empowerment through establishing our connection with others who have had similar experiences. In this way it becomes possible for men to become allies of women and children, not out of guilt, but through insight into their own lives.

Harassment, abuse, and violence arise from a system of sexual and racial inequality. To stop them we must challenge the gender roles, institutions, and power structures upon which sexism and racism stand. This is a big task, but it is one each of us can undertake in small ways — in our homes, in our schools, in our communities. We can educate ourselves and offer our children new models of male and female behavior. We can support each other in finding healing responses to the pain and hurt we have suffered. We can insist that the schools educate young people about empowering ways to counter sexism and racism. We can confront institutionalized oppression and violence. We can support movements and organizations that work for progressive social change. In sum, working together with others as allies, we can build community responses to the system of inequality and the cycle of violence that blight our lives.

REFERENCES

Beneke, Timothy. *Men on Rape: What They Have to Say about Sexual Violence.* New York: St. Martin's Press, 1982.

Bravo, Ellen, and Ellen Cassedy. *The 9 to 5 Guide to Combatting Sexual Harassment.* New York: John Wiley and Sons, 1992.

Chrisman, Robert, and Robert L. Allen, eds. *Court of Appeal: The Black Community Speaks Out on the Racial and Sexual Politics of Thomas vs. Hill.* New York: Ballantine Books, 1992.

Creighton, Allan, with Paul Kivel. *Helping Teens Stop Violence: A Practical Guide for Parents, Counselors, and Educators.* Alameda, Calif.: Hunter House, 1992.

Hagan, Kay Leigh, ed. *Women Respond to the Men's Movement.* San Francisco: Harper-Collins, 1992.

Hemphill, Essex, ed. *Brother to Brother: New Writings by Black Gay Men.* Boston: Alyson Publications, 1991.

Jackson, Walter H. *Sporting the Right Attitude: Surviving Family Violence.* Los Angeles: Self Expansion, 1992.

Kaufman, Michael, ed. *Beyond Patriarchy: Essays by Men on Pleasure, Power, and Change.* New York: Oxford University Press, 1987.

Kimmel, Michael S., ed. *Men Confront Pornography.* New York: Meridian, 1990.

Kivel, Paul. *Men's Work: How to Stop the Violence That Tears Our Lives Apart.* Center City, Minn.: Hazelden, 1992.

Kunjufu, Jawanza. *Countering the Conspiracy to Destroy Black Boys.* Chicago: African American Images, 1985.

Lewis, Michael. *Shame: The Exposed Self.* New York: Free Press, 1992.

Madhubuti, Haki. *Black Men: Obsolete, Single, Dangerous?* Chicago: Third World Press, 1990.

Majors, Richard, and Janet Mancini Billson. *Cool Pose: The Dilemmas of Black Manhood in America.* New York: Lexington Books, 1992.

McGill, Michael E. *The McGill Report on Male Intimacy.* New York: Harper and Row, 1985.

Miedzian, Myriam. *Boys Will Be Boys: Breaking the Link between Masculinity and Violence.* New York: Doubleday, 1991.

Staples, Robert, ed. *The Black Family: Essays and Studies.* 4th ed. Belmont, Calif. Wadsworth, 1991.

Strauss, Susan, with Pamela Espeland. *Sexual Harassment and Teens: A Program for Positive Change.* Minneapolis: Free Spirit Publishing, 1992.

Wilkinson, Doris Y., and Ronald L. Taylor, eds. *The Black Male in America: Perspectives on His Status in Contemporary Society.* Chicago: Nelson-Hall, 1977.

59

HOW SAFE IS AMERICA?

DESIREE TAYLOR

Desiree Taylor was a student at the University of Massachusetts-Boston completing an individualized major in gender, religion, and the arts when she wrote this essay.

I saw a picture in a magazine in which a woman is walking away from the collapsed World Trade Center towers covered in orange dust from head to toe. Her face is twisted into a shocked and horrifying expression and she is turned around slightly looking back at the photographer as she walks away from the scene. What strikes me about this picture is that I have never seen another like it, such an elegant and stylish depiction of war. The woman is so immaculately dressed, her hair so stylishly cut, that the whole scene looks like a clever fashion spread from an upscale magazine. This just couldn't be real, but it is. Looking at this picture, I try to really see the woman in it. I try to feel the horror of her experience, but as I do I can also see that she is not from my America. She is from an America that before September 11 was in many ways safer and freer than mine before or after that day.

On September 12, the day after the attack on the United States, I watched the media coverage and a very middle-class looking woman interviewed on the street said she "no longer felt safe in America." I was born and have grown up in this country. As a mixed race, half Black, half white woman born into poverty, I have never felt safe here.

In America, life within one class is nothing at all like it is in another. On September 11 thousands of people died in the collapsed World Trade towers. They were not alone. Every day in this country people die from exploitation that originates right here at home. Some who toil and slave in service to a system of wealth and prestige, who don't even earn a living for their trouble, slit their wrists out of desperation and pain. Some die used up and exhausted, in hospital beds with two dollars and eighty-five cents in their purse, like my own mother. Some people work two or more jobs and try to fit some kind of life in between, maybe an education, which gets harder and harder as they lose out on more and more sleep. The amount of safety one can truly feel in America is directly related to how much money you have.

Safety Depends on Money

I think about these people who were and are anything but safe here. I think about those who sweat out unappreciated labor to make the American Dream seem so real, to make the consumer culture function. I wonder if the woman in the picture ever looked as closely at the people who are dying in the class war here at home as I do at her.

It enrages me to hear people saying they no longer feel safe here. The United States that is being attacked is the one the woman in the picture belongs to. It is the prosperous, comfortable United States. It is not my United States. But all of a sudden we are all in it together. The flags are brought out and everybody sings, "I'm proud to be an American."

But it's impossible for me to suddenly forget that the United States empire was built upon and is still maintained by abuses against the poor and minorities. I think about those who will fight and die in this war. I think about all the poor, and often Black, students from my high school who enlisted in the armed services to earn money for college. I think about all the students who wouldn't have been caught dead joining the armed forces, kids for whom the military was not one of their few options to move out of poverty. I think about how many low-income families are worrying right now about the lives of their enlisted children. I wonder what proportion of persons who will fight in this war will be those who are not sharing in the "American Dream." I believe that it will be disproportionally high.

Poor Invisible to Mainstream

The plight of low-income people in this country is invisible to mainstream America. This invisible other America, the poor, enters through side and back doors of hotels, through the servants' entrances. They live in segregated neighborhoods, and work jobs in which they are unseen even though they are in plain view.

For example, I went to Walgreens the other day and was handed a receipt that read at the top: "I'm Laqueeta [name changed]. I'm here to serve you." The message continued on the next line: "with our seven service basics." A middle-class person in this corporation decided that Laqueeta should hand this message out on every one of her receipts. What made someone earning a good salary think that this was a good idea? We're not even told what those seven service basics are, and they don't really matter. What matters is that the plantation-type American Dream is being acted out here. I, as a consumer, am for a moment in the seat of power with someone to serve me. This is meant to register with me, but the server is not. She doesn't matter. If she did, she would be able to survive doing this kind of work.

I decided to inquire about a cashier's job at Walgreens. The pay rate, I was told, is $6.75 an hour in Boston. When I worked hourly wage jobs in retail stores I learned that employers would keep employees just under 40 hours a week, so that officially they were not full-time and therefore not entitled by law to benefits. I do not know if Walgreens does this, but the practice is widespread. For 39 hours of work at $6.75 an hour, that is $263.25 a week before taxes and $758.16 per month after taxes. After subtracting $35 for a subway pass and at least $460 a month for rent and bills (and for rent this low that means living in a hovel with probably four other people she doesn't know), that leaves Laqueeta just $65.79 a week for food, clothing, savings, entertainment, household expenses, healthcare, and any other expense that might come up, including saving for college and a computer. I hope she doesn't have a child. How safe is Laqueeta in America? Does anybody care? The appearance of America's bounty is maintained by the exploitation of people right here at home who are in positions to be easily misused.

The United States feels very much to me like several countries made up of separate social/economic classes, who don't and perhaps won't take the time to really look at each other; they can't feel each other's pains, cannot relate, and largely live in separate worlds. Now that we're at war with outside forces, we are supposed to come together within the United States. We are all supposed to feel the same hurts and the same threats. We are all supposed to feel each other's pain. We are all supposed to defend justice and freedom. During the past few weeks we have heard over and over again that these acts of terrorism are not only attacks on the United States, but on everything the country stands for. They tell us these are attacks on freedom and justice itself. But how is this possible when here at home justice, freedom, and the American Dream are denied to so many?

60

WIELDING MASCULINITY INSIDE ABU GHRAIB:
Making Feminist Sense of an American Military Scandal

CYNTHIA ENLOE

Cynthia Enloe is Research Professor of International Development and Women's Studies at Clark University in Massachusetts. She teaches and writes about women, feminism and international politics. Her recent books include *Bananas, Beaches and Bases: Making Feminist Sense of International Politics* (2000) and *Maneuvers: The International Politics of Militarizing Women's Lives* (2000). Her newest book is *The Curious Feminist: Searching for Women in A New Age of Empire* (2004).

In April, 2004, a year after the US government launched its massive military invasion of Iraq, a series of shocking photographs of American soldiers abusing Iraqi prisoners began appearing on television news programs and the front pages of newspapers around the world. American male and female soldiers serving as prison guards in a prison called Abu Ghraib were shown deliberately humiliating and torturing scores of Iraqi men held in detention and under interrogation. The American soldiers were smiling broadly. They appeared to be taking enormous pleasure in humiliating their Iraqi charges.

Most people who saw these photographs—people in Seattle and Seoul, Miami and Madrid, Bangkok and Boston—can still describe the scenes. An American male soldier standing self-satisfied with his arms crossed and wearing surgical blue rubber gloves, while in front of him, an American woman soldier, smiling at the camera, is leaning on top of a pile of Iraqi naked men forced to contort themselves into a human pyramid. An American woman soldier, again smiling, holding an Iraqi male prisoner on a leash. An American woman soldier pointing to a naked Iraq man's genitals, apparently treating them as a joke. American male soldiers intimidating Iraqi naked male prisoners with snarling guard dogs. An Iraqi male prisoner

Cynthia Enloe, "Wielding Masculinity Inside Abu Ghraib: Making Feminist Sense of an American Military Scandal" from *Asian Journal of Women's Studies* 10, no. 3 (2004). Reprinted with the permission of the author.

standing alone on a box, his head hooded, electrical wires attached to different parts of his body. An Iraqi male prisoner forced to wear women's underwear. Not pictured, but substantiated, were Iraqi men forced to masturbate and to simulate oral sex with each other, as well as an Iraqi woman prisoner coerced by several American male soldiers into kissing them.

What does a feminist curiosity reveal about the causes and the implications of the American abuses of Iraqi prisoners at Abu Ghraib? Few of the US government's official investigators or the mainstream news commentators used feminist insights to make sense of what went on in the prison. The result, I think, is that we have not really gotten to the bottom of the Abu Ghraib story. One place to start employing a feminist set of tools is to explain why one American woman military guard in particular captured the attention of so many media editors and ordinary viewers and readers: the twenty-one year old enlisted army reservist Lynndie England.

What proved shocking to the millions of viewers of the prison clandestine photos were several things. First, the Abu Ghraib scenes suggested there existed a gaping chasm between, on the one hand, the US Bush administration's claim that its military invasion and overthrow of the brutal Saddam Hussein regime would bring a civilizing sort of "freedom" to the Iraqi people and, on the other hand, the seemingly barbaric treatment that American soldiers were willfully meting out to Iraqis held in captivity without trial. Second, it was shocking to witness such blatant abuse of imprisoned detainees by soldiers representing a government that had signed both the international Geneva Conventions against mistreatment of wartime combatants and the UN Convention Against Torture, as well as having passed its own anti-torture laws.

Yet there was a third source of shock that prompted scores of early media commentaries and intense conversations among ordinary viewers: seeing women engage in torture. Of the seven American soldiers, all low-ranking Army Reserve military police guards, whom the Pentagon court-martialed, three were women. Somehow, the American male soldier, the man in the blue surgical gloves (his name was Charles Graner), was not shocking to most viewers and so did not inspire much private consternation or a stream of op ed columns. Women, by conventional contrast, were expected to appear in wartime as mothers and wives of soldiers, occasionally as military nurses and truck mechanics, or most often as the victims of the wartime violence. Women were not—according to the conventional presumption—supposed to be the wielders of violence, certainly not the perpetrators of torture. When those deeply gendered presumptions were turned upside down, many people felt a sense of shock. "This is awful; how could this have happened?"

Private First Class Lynndie England, the young woman military guard photographed holding the man on a leash, thus became the source of intense public curiosity. The news photographers could not restrain themselves two months later, in early August, 2004, from showing England in her army camouflaged maternity uniform when she appeared at Fort Bragg for her pre-trial hearing. She had become pregnant as a result of her sexual liaison with another enlisted reservist while on duty in Abu Ghraib. Her sexual partner was Charles Graner. Yet Charles Graner's name was scarcely mentioned. He apparently was doing what men are expected to do in wartime: have sex and wield violence. The public's curiosity and its lack of curiosity thus matched its pattern of shock. All three were conventionally gendered. Using a feminist investigatory approach, one should find this lack of public and media curiosity about Charles Graner just as revealing as the public's and media's absorbing fascination with Lynndie England.

Responding to the torrent of Abu Ghraib stories coming out of Iraq during the spring and summer of 2004, President George W. Bush and his Secretary of Defense, Donald Rumsfeld, tried to reassure the public that the graphically abusive behavior inside the prison was not representative of America, nor did it reflect the Bush administration's own foreign policies. Rather, the Abu Ghraib abuses were the work of "rogue" soldiers, a "few bad apples." The "bad apple" explanation always goes like this: the institution is working fine, its values are appropriate, its internal dynamics are of a sort that sustain positive values and respectful, productive behavior. Thus, according to the "bad apple" explanation, nothing needs to be reassessed or reformed in the way the organization works; all that needs to happen to stop the abuse is to prosecute and remove those few individuals who refused to play by the established rules. Sometimes this may be true. Some listeners to the Bush administration's "bad apple" explanation, however, weren't reassured. They wondered if the Abu Ghraib abuses were not produced by just a few bad apples found in a solid, reliable barrel, but, instead, were produced by an essentially "bad barrel." They also wondered whether this "barrel" embraced not only the Abu Ghraib prison, but the larger US military, intelligence, and civilian command structures.

What makes a "barrel" go bad? That is, what turns an organization, an institution, or a whole system into one that at least ignores, perhaps even fosters abusive behavior by the individuals operating inside it? This question is relevant for every workplace, every political system, every international alliance. Here too, feminists have been working hard over the past three decades to develop a curiosity and a set of analytical tools with which we can all answer this important question. So many of us today live much of our lives within complex organizations, large and small — work places, local and national governments, health care systems, criminal justice systems, international organizations. Feminist researchers have revealed that virtually all organizations are gendered: that is, all organizations are shaped by the ideas about, and daily practices of masculinities and femininities. Ignoring the workings of gender, feminist investigators have found, makes it impossible for us to explain accurately what makes any organization "tick." That failure makes it impossible for us to hold an organization accountable. Yet most of the hundred-page long official reports into the Abu Ghraib abuse scandal were written by people who ignored these feminist lessons. They acted as if the dynamics of masculinity and femininity among low-level police and high level policy-makers made no difference. That assumption is very risky.

A series of US Senate hearings, along with a string of Defense Department investigations tried to explain what went wrong in Abu Ghraib and why. The most authoritative of the Defense Department reports were the "Taguba Report," the "Fay/Jones Report" (both named after generals who headed these investigations) and the "Schlesinger Report" (named after a civilian former Secretary of Defense who chaired this investigatory team). In addition, the CIA was conducting its own investigation, since its officials were deeply involved in interrogating—and often hiding in secret prisons— captured Afghans and Iraqis. Moreover, there were several human rights groups and journalists publishing their own findings during 2004. Together, they offered a host of valuable clues as to why this institutional "barrel" had gone bad. First was the discovery that lawyers inside the Defense and Justice Departments, as well as the White House, acting on instructions from their civilian superiors, produced interpretations of the Geneva Conventions and US law that deliberately shrank the definitions of "torture" down so far that American military and CIA personnel could order and conduct interrogations of Iraqis and Afghans in detention using techniques that otherwise would have been deemed violations of US and international law.

Second, investigators found that an American general, Geoffrey Miller, commander of the US prison at Guantanamo Bay, Cuba, was sent by Secretary Rumsfeld to Iraq in September, 2003, where he recommended that American commanders overseeing military prison operations in Iraq start employing the aggressive interrogation practices that were being used on Afghan and Arab male prisoners at Guantanamo. Somewhat surprisingly, General Miller later was named by the Pentagon to head the Abu Ghraib prison in the wake of the scandal. Third, investigators discovered that the intense, persistent pressure imposed on the military intelligence personnel by the Defense Department to generate information about who was launching insurgent assaults on the US occupying forces encouraged those military intelligence officers to put their own pressures on the military police guarding prisoners to "soften up" the men in their cell blocks, thus undercutting the military police men's and women's own chain of command (which led up to a female army general, Janice Karpinski, who claimed that her authority over her military police personnel had been undermined by intrusive military intelligence officers). This policy change, investigators concluded, dangerously blurred the valuable line between military policing and military interrogating. A fourth finding was that non-military personnel, including CIA operatives and outside contractors hired by the CIA and the Pentagon, were involved in the Abu Ghraib military interrogations in ways that may have fostered an assumption that the legal limitations on employing excessive force could be treated cavalierly: We're under threat, this is urgent, who can be bothered with the Geneva Conventions or legal niceties?

Did it matter where the women were inside the prison and up and down the larger American military and intelligence hierarchies—as low level police reservists, as a captain in the military intelligence unit, as a general advising the chief US commander in Iraq? Investigators apparently didn't ask. Did it matter what exactly Charles Graner's and the other male military policemen's daily relationships were to their female colleagues, who were in a numerical minority in the military police unit, in the military interrogation unit and in the CIA unit all stationed together at Abu Ghraib? The official investigators seemed not to think that asking this question would yield any insights. Was it significant that so many of the abuses perpetrated on the Iraqi prisoners were deliberately sexualized? Was hooding a male prisoner the same (in motivation and in result) as forcing him to simulate oral sex? No one seemed to judge these questions to be pertinent. Was it at all relevant that Charles Graner, the older and apparently most influential of the low-ranking guards charged, had been accused of physical intimidation by his former wife? No questions asked, no answers forthcoming. Among all the lawyers in the Defense and Justice Departments and in the White House who were ordered to draft guidelines to permit the US government's officials to sidestep the Geneva Conventions outlawing torture, were there any subtle pressures imposed on them to appear "manly" in a time of war? This question too seems to have been left on the investigative teams' shelves to gather dust.

Since the mid-1970s, feminists have been crafting skills to explain when and why organizations become arenas for sexist abuse. One of the great contributions of the work done by the "Second Wave" of the international women's movement has been to throw light on what breeds sex discrimination and sexual harassment inside organizations otherwise as dissimilar as a factory, a stock brokerage, a legislature, a university, a student movement, and a military. All of the Abu Ghraib reports' authors talked about a "climate", an "environment," or a "culture," having been created inside Abu Ghraib that fostered abusive acts. The conditions inside Abu Ghraib were portrayed as a climate of "confusion," of "chaos." It was feminists who gave us this innovative concept of organizational climate.

When trying to figure out why in some organizations women employees were subjected to sexist jokes, unwanted advances, and retribution for not going along with the jokes or not accepting those advances, feminist lawyers, advocates and scholars began to look beyond the formal policies and the written work rules. They explored something more amorphous but just as, maybe even more potent: that set of unofficial presumptions that shapes workplace interactions between men and men, and men and women. They followed the breadcrumbs to the casual, informal interactions between people up and down the organization's ladder. They investigated who drinks with whom after work, who sends sexist jokes to whom over office email, who pins up which sorts of pictures of women in their lockers or next to the coffee machine. And they looked into what those people in authority did not do. They discovered that *in*action is a form of action: "turning a blind eye" is itself a form of action. Inaction sends out signals to everyone in the organization about what is condoned. Feminists labeled these webs of presumptions, informal interactions, and deliberate inaction an organization's "climate." As feminists argued successfully in court, it is not sufficient for a stock brokerage or a college to include anti-sexual harassment guidelines in their official handbooks; employers have to take explicit steps to create a workplace climate in which women would be treated with fairness and respect.

By 2004, this feminist explanatory concept—organizational "climate"— had become so accepted by so many analysts that their debt to feminists had been forgotten. Generals Taguba, Jones and Fay, as well as former Defense Secretary Schlesinger, may never have taken a Women's Studies course, but when they were assigned the job of investigating Abu Ghraib they were drawing on the ideas and investigatory skills crafted for them by feminists.

However, more worrisome than their failure to acknowledge their intellectual and political debts was those journalists' and government investigators' ignoring the feminist lessons that go hand in hand with the concept of "climate." The first lesson: to make sense of any organization, we always must dig deep into the group's dominant presumptions about femininity and masculinity. The second lesson: we need to take seriously the experiences of women as they try to adapt to, or sometimes resist those dominant gendered presumptions—not because all women are angels, but because paying close attention to women's ideas and actions will shed light on why men with power act the way they do.

It is not as if the potency of ideas about masculinity and femininity had been totally absent from the US military's thinking. Between 1991 and 2004, there had been a string of military scandals that had compelled even those American senior officials who preferred to look the other way to face sexism straight on. The first stemmed from the September, 1991, gathering of American navy aircraft carrier pilots at a Hilton hotel in Las Vegas. Male pilots (all officers), fresh from their victory in the first Gulf War, lined a hotel corridor and physically assaulted every woman who stepped off the elevator. They made the "mistake" of assaulting a woman navy helicopter pilot who was serving as an aide to an admiral. Within months members of Congress and the media were telling the public about "Tailhook"—why it happened, who tried to cover it up. Close on the heels of the Navy's "Tailhook" scandal came the Army's Aberdeen training base sexual harassment scandal, followed by other revelations of military gay bashing, sexual harassment, and rapes by American male military personnel of their American female colleagues.

Then in September, 1995, the rape of a local school girl by two American male marines and a sailor in Okinawa sparked public demonstrations, new Okinawan women's organizing and more US Congressional investigations. At the start of the twenty-first century American media began to notice the patterns of international trafficking in Eastern European and Filipina women around American bases in South Korea, prompting official embarrassment in Washington (an embarrassment which had not been demonstrated earlier when American base commanders turned a classic "blind eye" toward a prostitution industry financed by their own male soldiers because it employed "just" local South Korean women). And in 2003, three new American military sexism scandals caught Washington policy-makers' attention: four American male soldiers returning from combat missions in Afghanistan murdered their female partners at Fort Bragg, North Carolina; a pattern of sexual harassment and rape by male cadets of female cadets—and superiors' refusal to treat these acts seriously—was revealed at the US Air Force Academy; and testimonies by at least sixty American women soldiers returning from tours of duty in Kuwait and Iraq described how they had been sexually assaulted by their male colleagues there—with, once again, senior officers choosing inaction, advising the American women soldiers to "get over it."

So it should have come as no surprise to American senior uniformed and civilian policy makers seeking to make sense of the abuses perpetrated in Abu Ghraib that a culture of sexism had come to permeate many sectors of US military life. If they had thought about what they had all learned in the last thirteen years—from Tailhook, Aberdeen, Fort Bragg, Okinawa, South Korea and the US Air Force Academy—they should have put the workings of masculinity and femininity at the top of their investigatory agendas. They should have made feminist curiosity one of their own principal tools. Perhaps Tillie Fowler did suggest to her colleagues that they think about these military sexual scandals when they began to delve into Abu Ghraib. A former Republican Congresswoman from Florida, Tillie Fowler, had been a principal investigator on the team that looked into the rapes (and their cover-ups) at the US Air Force Academy. Because of her leadership in that role Fowler was appointed to the commission headed by James Schlesinger investigating Abu Ghraib. Did she raise this comparison between the Air Force Academy case and Abu Ghraib? Did her male colleagues take her suggestion seriously?

Perhaps eventually the investigators did not make use of the feminist lessons and tools because they imagined that the lessons of Tailhook, the Air Force Academy and Okinawa were relevant only when all the perpetrators of sexualized abuse are men and all the victims are women. The presence of Lynndie England and the other women in Abu Ghraib's military police unit, they might have assumed, made the feminist tools sharpened in these earlier gendered military scandals inappropriate for their explorations. But the lesson of Tailhook, Okinawa and the most recent military scandals was *not* that the politics of masculinity and femininity matter only when men are the perpetrators and women are the victims. Instead, the deeper lesson of all these other military scandals is that we must always ask:

Has this organization (or this system of interlocking organizations) become masculinized in ways that privilege certain forms of masculinity, feminize its opposition and trivialize most forms of femininity?

With this core gender question in mind, we might uncover significant dynamics operating in Abu Ghraib and in the American military and civilian organizations that were supposed to be supervising the prison's personnel. First, American military police and their military and CIA intelligence colleagues might have been guided by their own masculinized fears of humiliation when they forced Iraqi men to go naked for days, to wear women's underwear and to masturbate in front of each other and American women guards. That is, belief in an allegedly "exotic," frail Iraqi masculinity, fraught with fears of nakedness and homosexuality, might not have been the chief motivator for the American police and intelligence personnel; it may have been their own home-grown American sense of masculinity's fragility — how easily manliness can be feminized — that prompted them to craft these prison humiliations. In this distorted masculinized scenario, the presence of women serving as military police might have proved especially useful. Choreographing the women guards' feminized roles so that they could act as ridiculing feminized spectators of male prisoners might have been imagined to intensify the masculinized demoralization. Dominant men trying to utilize at least some women to act in ways that undermine the masculinized self-esteem of rival men is not new.

What about the American women soldiers themselves? In the US military of 2004 women comprised 15% of active duty personnel, and 17% of all Reserves and National Guard (and a surprising 24% of the Army Reserves alone). From the very time these particular young women joined this military police unit, they, like their fellow male recruits, probably sought to fit into the group. If the reserve military police unit's evolving culture — perhaps fostered by their superiors for the sake of "morale" and "unit cohesion" — was one that privileged a certain form of masculinized humor, racism, and bravado, each woman would have had to decide how to deal with that. At least some of the women reservist recruits might have decided to join in, playing the roles assigned to them in order to gain the hoped-for reward of male acceptance. The facts that the Abu Ghraib prison was grossly understaffed during the fall of 2003 (too few guards for spiraling numbers of Iraqi detainees), that it was isolated from other military operations, and that its residents endured daily and nightly mortar attacks, would only serve to intensify the pressures on each soldier to gain acceptance from those unit members who seemed to represent the group's dominant masculinized culture. And Lynndie England's entering into a sexual liaison with Charles Graner? We need to treat this as more than merely a "lack of discipline." We need to ask what were the cause and effect dynamics between their sexual behaviors and the abuses of prisoners and staging of the photographs. Feminists have taught us never to brush off sexual relations as if they have nothing to do with organizational and political practices.

Then there is the masculinization of the military interrogators' organizational cultures, the masculinization of the CIA's field operatives and the workings of ideas about "manliness" shaping the entire US political system. Many men and women — as lawyers, as generals, as Cabinet officers, as elected officials — knew full well that aggressive interrogation techniques violated both the spirit and the language of the Geneva Conventions, the UN Convention Against Torture and the US federal law against torture. Yet during the months of waging wars in Afghanistan and Iraq most of these men and women kept silent. Feminists have taught us always to be curious about silence. Thus we need to ask: Did any of the American men involved in interrogations keep silent because they were afraid of being labeled "soft," or "weak," thereby jeopardizing their status as "manly" men. We need also to discover if any of the women who knew better kept silent because they were afraid that they would be labeled "feminine," thus risking being deemed by their colleagues untrustworthy, political outsiders.

We are not going to get to the bottom of the tortures perpetrated by Americans at Abu Ghraib unless we make use of a feminist curiosity and unless we revisit the feminist lessons derived from the scandals of Tailhook, Fort Bragg, Annapolis, Okinawa and the Air Force Academy. Those tools and lessons might shed a harsh light on an entire American military institutional culture and maybe even the climate of contemporary American political life. That institutional culture and that political climate together have profound implications not only for Americans. They are being held up as models to emulate in Korea, Japan, the Philippines, Afghanistan and Iraq. That, in turn, means that the insights offered by feminist analysts from those societies who have such intimate experiences with this US institutional culture and this political climate are likely to teach Americans a lot about themselves.

SOURCES AND FURTHER READING

Simon Bowers, "Merrill Lynch Accused of 'Institutional Sexism,'" *The Guardian*, (London), June 12, 2004.

Ximena Bunster-Burotto, "Surviving Beyond Fear: Women and Torture in Latin America," in June Nash and Helen Safa, editors, *Women and Change in Latin America*, South Hadley, MA, Bergin and Garvey Publishers, 1985, 297–325.

Cynthia Enloe, *Maneuvers: The International Politics of Militarizing Women's Lives*, Berkeley and London, University of California Press, 2000.

Barbara Ehrenreich, "All Together Now," Op. Ed., *New York Times*, July 15, 2004.

Seymour Hersh, "Annals of National Security: Torture at Abu Ghraib," *The New Yorker*, May 10, 2004, 42–47.

Seymour Hersh, "Annals of National Security: Chain of Command," *The New Yorker*, May 17, 2004, 38–43.

Seymour Hersh, "Annals of National Security: The Gray Zone," *The New Yorker*, May 24, 2004, 38–44.

Human Rights Watch, *The Road to Abu Ghraib*, New York, Human Rights Watch, 2004.

Douglas Jehl, "Some Abu Ghraib Abuses are Traced to Afghanistan," *The New York Times*, August 26, 2004.

Insook Kwon, "Militarization in My Heart," unpublished PhD Dissertation, Women's Studies Program, Clark University, Worcester, MA, USA, 1999.

Neil A. Lewis and Eric Schmitt, "Lawyers Decided Bans on Torture Didn't Bind Bush," *New York Times*, June 8, 2004.

Catherine Lutz and Jon Elliston, "Domestic Terror" [re: domestic violence against US army wives at Fort Bragg, North Carolina], in Elizabeth Castelli and Janet Jackson, editors, *Interventions: Activists and Academics Respond to Violence*, New York, Palgrave, 2004.

The Miles Foundation, "Brownback/Fitz Amendment to S. 2400" [re: sexual assaults of American women soldiers by American male soldiers], email correspondence, June 14, 2004, from Milesfdn@aol.com.

Miles Moffeit and Amy Herder, "Betrayal in the Ranks" [a series on domestic abuse inside the US military], *The Denver Post*, May, 2004. Available on the Web at: http//www.denverpost.com.

Office of the Inspector General, US Department of Defense, *The Tailhook Report*, New York, St. Martin's Press, 2003.

Yuko Ogasawara, *Office Ladies and Salaried Men: Power, Gender and Work in Japanese Companies*, Berkeley and London, University of California Press, 1998.

Eric Schmitt, "Abuse Panel Says Rules on Inmates Need Overhaul," *The New York Times*, August 25, 2004.

Marjorie A. Stockford, *The Bellwomen: The Story of the Landmark AT&T Sex Discrimination Case*, New Brunswick, NJ, Rutgers University Press, 2004.

Antonio Taguba, "Investigation of the 800th Military Police Brigade," Washington, D.C., US Department of Defense, April, 2004.

Sandra Whitworth, *Men, Militarism and UN Peacekeeping: A Gendered Analysis*, Boulder, CO, Lynne Rienner Publishers, 2004.

61

GENDER IN A TIME OF HOLY WAR
Fundamentalist Femiphobia
and Post-9/11 Masculinity

STEPHEN DUCAT

Stephen J. Ducat is a professor of psychology in the School of Humanities at New College of California, a licensed clinical psychologist in private practice, and a candidate at the Psychoanalytic Institute of Northern California. The author of *Taken In: American Gullibility and the Reagan Mythos,* he lives in the San Francisco Bay area.

"Soul" Brothers and Their Discontents

Christian-right crusaders Jerry Falwell and Pat Robertson agree with Osama bin Laden on one key theological point: America had it coming. "The pagans, and the abortionists, and the feminists, and the gays and lesbians . . . and the ACLU . . . helped make this happen," explained Mr. Falwell. Moreover, he warned shortly after the 9/11 terrorist attacks, "What we saw on Tuesday, as terrible as it is, could be minuscule if, in fact, God continues to lift the curtain and allow the enemies of America to give us probably what we deserve."[1]

Christian and Islamic fundamentalists, who are dramatically increasing their numbers across the globe, share more than a general distaste for the moral pollutants emanating from liberal Western culture and a dream of the apocalyptic violence that could cleanse the world of them. They are particularly aligned in their concern to discipline the feminine, whether it is women in social life or female identifications in the inner lives of men. Every variety of fundamentalism—ethnic, political, or religious—has as a key element an inability to tolerate ambiguity, and this has, in many places, wrought catastrophic devastation on bodies, cultures, and psyches. And the ambiguity these crusaders for certainty seem the least able to tolerate is that of gender. Thus, fundamentalists everywhere share a creed that includes the restoration of a fantasized golden age of unfettered patriarchal domination, harsh punishments for those who stray from their prescribed gender roles, a fascistic priggery mixed with terror regarding women's sexuality, and an absolute — and often murderous — intolerance of homosexuals. Of course, there are significant differences among various fundamental isms, and none can be reduced to only its gendered aspects. Nevertheless, it is not without significance that the zealous adherents of every form of tyrannical monomania tend to make policing the borders of masculinity and femininity central to their mission. These movements are, in other words, driven to a great extent by . . . anxious masculinity. The aim of this chapter is to shed light on the links between the external holy wars of fundamentalists and the internal wars of femiphobic men. It will also look at how the terrorist attacks in New York and Washington, and later the war in Iraq, catalyzed new configurations of masculinity in American culture and politics.

Misogyny in the Name of God

In the various media profiles of the 9/11 hijackers that appeared in the months following the terrorist attacks, many commentators struggled to make sense of these apostles of mass murder — perplexed not only by their nihilist vision of Islam, but also by the apparent paradoxes within their characters. For example, a number of reporters remarked on what they viewed as a contradiction between the antisexual fundamentalism of the jihadis, and their apparent enjoyment of lap dancing at the bon voyage strip-club bash prior to the suicide missions. Such behavior, however, should have come as no surprise, since numerous American fundamentalist preachers, such as Jim Bakker and Jimmy Swaggart, have demonstrated similar predilections. More importantly, what these journalists overlooked was that participation in a form of prostitution is quite consistent with that familiar theme of fundamentalist psychosexuality, the Madonna/whore split, whereby a dichotomy is constructed between good (veiled and private) and bad (unveiled and public) women . . . this split not only helps to keep women in their proper domestic place, but shores up the psychic quarantine of motherhood from sexuality.

Of course, the gothic horrors of fundamentalist misogyny are legion and go well beyond amusing peccadillos. In Pakistan the local governmental response to the trauma of a twenty-six-year-old female rape victim was to sentence her to death by stoning. Her crime consisted of violating a law against adultery, under which the issue of consent is irrelevant and an accusation of rape is regarded as a confession of forbidden sexual behavior. The man accused was set free, since the testimony of women in such courts is inadmissible.[2] According to human rights groups, 80 percent of all women in Pakistani jails are there for violating laws against extramarital sex.[3] It may be surprising for some to learn that the *hudood*, the legal code putatively based on the Koran, under which these women have been prosecuted, is not some ancient, time-honored tribal code. Rather, it was enacted only twenty-three years ago,[4] a fact that supports the assertion made by some scholars that fundamentalisms are not all centuries-old cultural and political systems, but (like Nazi Germany, which was also based on a fantasized past) are more like mutant forms of modernism, complete with their own Web sites and networks for purchasing and deploying exterminationist weaponry.

In Saudi Arabia, another U.S. ally against evildoers, religious police — otherwise known as the Commission for the Promotion of Virtue and Prevention of Vice — allowed fifteen young girls to be incinerated in a school fire in Mecca. Authorities stopped the men who tried to attempt a rescue because the girls were not wearing head scarves and *abayas,* traditional robes. As the would-be rescuers were "male strangers," argued officials, it would have been "sinful to approach" such inadequately attired females.[5] Apparently, a charred corpse is more virtuous than an uncovered female head.

Of course, the status of American women is in no way comparable to that of women who live under the iron fist of fundamentalist male domination in parts of Africa, the Middle East, and elsewhere. To make such an equation is to indulge in the sort of mindless relativism that some of the more naive postmodern leftists have embraced. At least women in the U.S. enjoy a significant measure of legal equality with men, including the right to receive an education, to vote or run for political office, to sign and enforce contracts, to take employment, to choose a spouse, and, for the moment anyway, to exercise reproductive choice. But these rights remain intact because Christian fundamentalists only *influence* the government, and have yet to actually constitute it.

America's Aspiring Ayatollahs

The selection of John Ashcroft for Attorney General — a man whose obdurate brand of Christianity would make Cotton Mather look like a depraved libertine — was a significant payback by George W. Bush to the Christian right, which provided generous donations of money and labor during the 2000 campaign. Mr. Ashcroft set the tone for his reign when early on he instructed aides to cover the naked breasts of Justice Department statuary.[6]

In 1996, then senator Ashcroft incorporated into the Welfare reform bill a "charitable choice" provision that allowed religious organizations, with minimal government oversight, to compete for federal funds to provide a variety of social services. Four years later, this desire among religious conservatives, in and out of power, to render the separation between church and state a more porous boundary found expression in the White House Office of Faith-Based and Community Initiatives. In addition to taking over government functions and receiving taxpayer dollars, participating religious institutions are free to engage in discriminatory hiring practices based on sexual orientation.

Even higher education has been subject to the surveillance and intervention of our fundamentalist Attorney General. In Texas, a biology professor posted an announcement on his Web site that students who wish to receive a letter of recommendation to science graduate programs had to honestly accept the scientific consensus on the origins of humanity, evolutionary theory. After having this heresy brought to their attention by a group of Christian lawyers, the Ashcroft Justice Department decided to launch an investigation.[7] Other prominent Republicans would doubtless applaud such federal actions, especially House majority leader Tom DeLay, who, following the school shootings at Columbine, said the carnage had happened "because our school systems teach our children that they are nothing but glorified apes who have evolutionized out of some primordial mud."[8]

Impeding the theocratic aims of the Christian right, along with those of their point man in the Bush administration, Attorney General Ashcroft, are certain legal constraints, as well as tensions with Bush administration social policy moderates such as Colin Powell. Ashcroft, nevertheless, continues to battle against an international women's rights treaty, the Convention on Elimination of All Forms of Discrimination Against Women (CEDAW), already ratified by 169 countries, which could help to prevent the kinds of institutionalized atrocities previously mentioned.[9] While the treaty contains no enforcement mechanism, CEDAW has already been cited as the basis for a variety of legislative efforts to protect women from domestic violence, to grant women inheritance rights equal to those enjoyed by men, and to establish laws against sexual harassment, in a number of countries that have ratified it. Nevertheless, Paul Bonicelle, a Bush appointee and a dean at Patrick Henry College—where courses in creationism are featured in the curriculum—regards the possibility of American ratification of CEDAW as "unthinkable" and "not something social conservatives can accept."[10] According to Janice Crouse, another Bush appointee, who is also a senior fellow at the Beverly La Haye Institute, a right-wing think tank, the treaty is part of a "frivolous and morally corrupt agenda designed to legalize prostitution, promote homosexuality, and abolish Mother's Day."[11] Needless to say, CEDAW mentions nothing about the latter two issues, and it calls on signatories to "suppress all forms of traffic in women and exploitation of prostitution of women."[12]

Strategic Spiritual Alliances

In spite of real differences, the parallels between Christian and Islamic fundamentalism are striking. This is not just my view; there are many among these otherwise divergent religious guardians of gender and sexual purity who view one another as essential allies. In early 2002, a large consortium of American Christian right organizations formally aligned itself with over fifty Islamic governments, including those of Iran, Libya, and Sudan, to prevent the adoption of measures at United Nations conferences that would expand civil rights for women and homosexuals. "We have realized that without countries like Sudan, abortion would have been recognized as a universal human right in a U.N. document," declared Austin Ruse, a conservative Catholic member of the American branch of the coalition.[13] Appreciation of this new partnership, and of the special affinity that binds it, was expressed on the Islamic side by Mokhtar Lamani, a Moroccan diplomat speaking for the fifty-three-nation Organization of Islamic Conferences: "The main issue that brings us together is defending the family values, the natural family. The Republican administration is so clear in defending the family values."[14] He went on to explain how offensive he found a proposed declaration at the June 2001 U.N. General Assembly on AIDS because it included, among other things, references to the need to protect "men who have sex with men" from becoming infected with the virus. Mr. Lamani seems to concur with his Christian fundamentalist comrades who insist that AIDS is God's punishment for homosexuality, and that no attempt should be made to save hell-bound sodomites from their just and divinely ordained fate. Summing up the official Bush administration position on this new Islamic-Christian alliance, a government spokesperson said, "We have tried to point out there are some areas of agreement between [us] and a lot of Islamic countries on these social issues."[15] Another zone of commonality was marked out at the 2002 World Summit on Sustainable Development, where the U.S., along with the Vatican and a group of Islamic countries, took a position opposing any agreement that included language portraying forced marriage, honor killings (murders of women whose sexual behavior has "dishonored" their families), and female genital mutilation as human rights violations.[16] Of course, there is a significant realpolitik motive behind the American government's conduct in these global forums; the administration wanted to cultivate support among Muslim nations for the global war on terrorism, and get them to at least look the other way when it invaded Iraq. Nevertheless, the fact that the U.S. does *not* resemble Saudi Arabia, Iran, or some other fundamentalist theocracy in its gender relations is a source of great consternation to many increasingly well organized Christian conservatives, and thus, not something those with feminist sensibilities can take for granted.

It is quite astonishing, however, the extent to which the prayers of the Christian right have been answered—not by any celestial being, but by the powerful mortal in the White House. A partial list of domestic and foreign policy positions adopted by the Bush administration makes clear the degree to which it functions as the political arm of Christian fundamentalism:

- *On Israel:* The White House has shown unconditional support for Prime Minister Sharon, whose strategy to handle conflict in the region consists of collective punishment of Palestinians, the expansion of West Bank settlements, and what appears to be the ultimate goal, the expulsion of the Palestinians. Not only have these policies increased terrorist attacks, but by doing so, and by increasing Israeli Jewish hegemony in the area, they seem to bring the Holy Land closer to fulfilling the Christian Right's reading of Biblical prophecy, their wishful fantasy of apocalypse, and their conviction that Jews who fail to convert when Jesus returns will perish in the horrors of the ensuing tribulation.

American fundamentalist Christians have not relied solely on their agents in the White House to realize their vision. Some groups have played a direct role in creating the preconditions for their "End Time" scenario by, for example, establishing privately funded social services to make it easier for Eastern European Jews to emigrate to Israel. On the surface, the explicit and ardent support the Christian right has expressed for the Sharon government in general, and for Jewish settlement in Palestinian areas in particular, may seem to contradict the affinity, described earlier, they have shown for some theocratic Arabs. These two stances are not mutually exclusive, however. The fundamentalist Christian concern with Israel is a spiritual one—doing what is necessary to fulfill prophecy. Their kinship with Islamic fundamentalists regimes has more to do with shared moral imperatives in this life—principally those related to gender and sexuality.

- *On the environment:* Many Christian fundamentalists are indifferent to the effects of Republican-initiated environmental deregulation, because they see in the ruination of the planet—whether by melting ice caps or dying coral reefs—yet one more harbinger of the much welcomed End Time when Christ will return.
- *On women's reproductive health:* The Bush administration has sought the restriction and, where possible, the prohibition of reproductive choice, whether in the form of abortion or contraception. It has pursued this fundamentalist goal not just in the U.S., but globally.
- *On human rights treaties:* As previously mentioned, the Republicans have addressed a key concern of femiphobic fundamentalists everywhere by opposing any international agreement that might promote gender equality or mitigate male domination.
- *On domestic civil rights legislation:* The GOP has been in perfect sync with the Christian right in its unflagging efforts to prevent American citizens from obtaining any legal protections against discrimination based on sexual orientation.
- *On education:* Republicans have acted in lockstep with their Christian fundamentalist constituents by supporting school vouchers, prayer in school, the elimination of sex education, the inclusion of Creationist fairy tales in science curricula, and the censorship of "unpatriotic" and "antireligious" textbooks.

Women Warriors for Patriarchy

Fundamentalist agendas, even those that seek to establish or extend male domination, are not the exclusive provinces of men. There are many conservative women who argue unapologetically and campaign *aggressively* in favor of female subordination. . . . [T]here is a significant minority of women who share the political views of right-wing men, although for different psychological, cultural, and political reasons. While these women do not constitute a homogenous group, they often share the antifeminist gender ideology of their male counterparts. In the U.S., one subgroup of neotraditional women has become especially visible in public life over the last decade. They constitute a growing brigade of carefully coiffed, stiletto-heeled conservative female pundits who identify with the phallic slash-and-burn style, as well as the politics, of their right-wing male counterparts.

In a monologue on his new program, *Real Time with Bill Maher*, Maher referred to Rush Limbaugh's prescription drug problem, and then noted, "This has been the toughest week for conservatives since Ann Coulter admitted she had a penis."[17] The audience got the joke because they intuitively understood that she is the paradigmatic right-wing phallic woman—combative, arrogant, impermeable to reason or attack, and reliant on femiphobic epithets like "girly-boy" and "panty-waist" to respond to her male critics.[18] Even the butch *National Review* tossed her out when she wrote of Islamic states, "We should invade their countries, kill their leaders and convert them to Christianity."[19]

With no discernible sense of irony, independent, wealthy, and highly educated upper-class women like Coulter, who relish leadership roles in business and politics, cynically praise the lives of domestic docility and deference led by their lower-middle-class Christian-right sisters. While they take a condescending I've-got-mine-thank-you attitude toward mothers who might need government services, and deride females who complain about sexual harassment, these conservative women save their greatest contempt for feminists, who are dismissed as an undifferentiated group of whiny victimology mongers. Insulated by class privilege, this subgroup of right-wing women is able to remain unmoved by the continuing global feminization of poverty, the extensive international slave trade in women, the remaining pay gap between the sexes, and the double shift of wage labor and unpaid housework most wives without domestic servants must perform. And then they accuse *feminists* of elitism. In addition, their historical amnesia apparently renders them unable to recall the debt they owe prior generations of women's rights activists, or the fact that there was a time when even money could not buy equality with men. These polished Republican spokeswomen have become so commonplace in the allegedly liberal media that most TV political talk shows would seem incomplete without at least one dominatrix of right-wing rectitude, like the relentless culture warrior Coulter, extending her pink lacquered talon to point out the liberal traitors in our midst.

Female crusaders for gender conservatism, of all classes and religions, can be found across the globe, from the United States to the Middle East. The late Beverly La Haye, founder of Concerned Women for America (and the person for whom the aforementioned right-wing think tank was named), was a politically outspoken and active woman who nevertheless insisted, "The woman who is truly spirit-filled will want to be totally submissive to her husband. . . . Submission is God's design for women."[20] The right-wing Christian men's organization Promise Keepers has held massive revival meetings across the country, which fill stadiums with tens of thousands of weepy reborn patriarchs who pledge to take back the familial throne. They are ardently supported in their efforts by a number of women's auxiliary groups. One of these, the Promise Reapers, sees itself as "born from the side of Promise Keepers, as Eve from Adam's side."[21] Another, the Heritage Keepers, instructs wives how to "let go of the reins" of marital authority. Their motto is "Submission is a place of honor."[22]

Echoing similar sentiments at religious schools in Pakistan and in Muslim towns and villages across the globe, many girls and women are devout practitioners of fundamentalist Islam, and firmly believe in social systems that deny women their most basic human rights. Some would fight to the death to support such systems. Wahida Kamily, a twenty-three-year-old, high-school educated Afghan woman explained, "We obey our husbands, and our husbands have more rights than us — that is our culture. If a wife doesn't listen to her husband, it's right for him to beat her."[23] Shafia Salaam, a sixteen-year-old Afghan girl living in Pakistan, was even more adamant. When discussing efforts of the American-led alliance to unseat the Taliban, she insisted, "I believe in Jihad. I will do whatever I can do. If I am provided the opportunity to get weapons, I will use them."[24]

The paradoxical point here is that women who happily, even fervidly, accommodate the demands of cultures and communities predicated on the political and sexual subjugation of women, and the privileging of all things male, do not necessarily do so from a position of passivity or as a result of coercion.

• • •

Flyboys and Action Figures: The Iconography of Gender in the New American Empire

By now, it is old news that the Bush administration had no postwar plans for American-occupied Iraq, that it shunned any advice that failed to comport with its fantasy of a "cakewalk," that there was no sound evidence that Saddam possessed weapons of mass destruction (the putative reason for the invasion), that it had nothing but contempt for the concerns of the majority of America's allies, and that the only scenario it prepared for was one that featured throngs of cheering and grateful Iraqi citizens. Of course, this sort of unilateralist arrogance and grandiose denial of our interdependence with the rest of the world did not begin with the current government.

In spite of the incalculable amount of tax dollars spent on global intelligence operations, a number of U.S. administrations have been oblivious to significant cultural and political developments in other countries. As a result, American officials, civil and military, have been repeatedly blindsided by upheavals around the world. A short list would have to include the surprise victory of the Vietnamese resistance to the American war there, the over-throw of the Shah of Iran, the implosion of the Soviet Union, the rise of Islamic fundamentalist terrorism, the attacks on the World Trade Center towers and the Pentagon, and now, of course, the situation in Iraq. Not that I'm complaining, but the United States seems to have become one of the most in-effectual imperial powers to ever lumber across the globe. And the Bush administration appears to have become the fullest expression of this blundering hubris and indifference to other cultures.

The fantasy that repudiating interdependence and multilateralism would make America stronger should have exploded along with the buildings on 9/11. And what remained should have dissolved in the face of our current bloody quagmire in Iraq. The behavior of the present Republican regime, however, suggests that nothing but spin and the choreography of photo opportunities have been affected by recent events. In sympathy with the manic triumphalism of the Bush administration after the initial military victory in Iraq, country singer Toby Keith recorded a song, "Courtesy of the Red, White and Blue," that quickly went to number one, and became a virtual anthem for the White House architects of permanent war. A few lines say it all: "You'll be sorry that you messed with the U.S. of A. 'Cuz we'll put a boot in your ass—It's the American way."[25] (I will leave it to the reader to ponder what body part the "boot" might be a downward displacement of.) This tune was also the perfect theme song for the president's most glorious, though later regretted, moment of image management, the famous Top Gun landing on the *USS Abraham Lincoln.*

Rarely in the history of political stagecraft has there been a more coherent spectacle, by which I mean a unity of phallic form with phallic content. The famous banner that proclaimed "Mission Accomplished" was a succinct denial of many aspects of reality: the enormity of the military, political, and cultural task that lay ahead for the American occupiers; the missing WMDs; and especially the *real* war on terror that got short shrift while Bush Jr. and company were taking care of some unfinished family business in Iraq. Corresponding to the phallic message on the banner was the flyboy himself. In addition to never having scuffed his snakeskin boots in combat, Bush Jr. appears, by current accounts, to have been AWOL during part of his Viet Nam–era service in the Texas Air National Guard.[26] While evidence may yet refute this widely held impression, many of the records of his service are missing as of this writing. Although the president's military drag performance was in obvious contrast to his history, Bush's photo opportunity became a phallic event primarily because it signified the boot-end of an unstoppable hypermasculine empire. He became, at least for a while, the principal iconic figure of resurrected American manhood. Those who find it improbable that this image of unilateralist swagger was interpreted in specifically phallic terms by the larger American public need only consider some examples of the pervasive media discourse that followed Bush's flight-suit promenade.

In an interview on Christopher Matthews' *Hardball* program, G. Gordon Liddy was not shy about expressing his admiration for the presidential pudenda: "And here comes George Bush. You know, he's in his flight suit, he's striding across the deck, and he's wearing his parachute harness, you know. And I've worn those because I parachute—and it makes the best of his manly characteristic. . . . You know, all those women who say size doesn't matter—they're all liars. Check that out . . . what a stud. . . ."[27] Both Salon.com's conservative commentator Andrew Sullivan[28] and leftist culture critic for the *Village Voice* Richard Goldstein[29] wrote articles regarding the authenticity of "Bush's basket." Unlike Sullivan, Goldstein was convinced the Commander of Chief had done a "sock job."[30]

By far the most compelling confirmation of the phallic meaning of the president's aircraft-carrier cakewalk was found on the hot-selling "George W. Bush Top Gun Action Figure" manufactured by Talking Presidents. I originally ordered one to use as part of the cover design for this book. The studly twelve-inch flyboy not only comes with a helmet and visor, goggles, and oxygen mask, but underneath his flight suit is a full "basket"—a genuine fake penis, apparently constructed with life-like silicone. This may not settle the debate between Sullivan and Goldstein, but it makes clear that at least one company realizes the extent to which American males need to know their president is not a Ken doll and is ready for action.

NOTES

1. Laurie Goodstein, "Falwell's Finger-Pointing Inappropriate, Bush Says," *New York Times*, September 15, 2001, A16.
2. Seth Mydans, "In Pakistan, Rape Victims Are the 'Criminals,'" *New York Times*, May 17, 2002, A3.
3. Ibid.
4. Ibid.
5. Maureen Dowd, "Father Knows Worst," *New York Times*, March 20, 2002, A27.
6. Vicki Haddock, "Son of a Preacher Man: How John Ashcroft's Religion Shapes His Public Service," *San Francisco Chronicle*, August 4, 2002, D6.
7. Nick Madigan, "Professor's Snub of Creationists Prompts U.S. Inquiry," *New York Times*, February 3, 2003, A11.
8. Paul Krugman, "Gotta Have Faith," *New York Times*, December 17, 2002, A35.
9. Nicholas D. Kristof, "Women's Rights: Why Not?" *New York Times*, June 18, 2002, A25.
10. Michelle Goldberg, "Yes to the Bible, No to the Treaty," Salon.com, June 22, 2002, http://www.salon.com/news/feature/2002/06/22/women/index_np.html.
11. Ibid.
12. Ibid.
13. Colum Lynch, "Islamic Bloc, Christian Right Team Up to Lobby U.N.," *The Washington Post*, June 17, 2002, A1.
14. Ibid.
15. Ibid.

16. Jennifer Block, "Christian Soldiers on the March," *The Nation,* February 3, 2003, 19.
17. Bill Maher, *Real Time,* HBO, January 23, 2004.
18. Charles Taylor, "When Right-Wing Fembots Attack," Salon.com, June 27, 2002, http://salon.com/books/feature/2002/06/27/coulter.
19. Ibid.
20. Caryl Rivers, "'Crazed Foes' of Women's Rights Are Advancing," *San Francisco Chronicle,* January 9, 1995, A25.
21. "The Promise Keepettes," *New York Times Magazine,* April 27, 1997, 15.
22. Ibid.
23. Nicholas D. Kristof, "The Veiled Resource," *New York Times,* December 11, 2001, A27.
24. Lynsey Addario, "Jihad's Women," *New York Times Magazine,* October 21, 2001, 40.
25. James MacKinnon, "Brand America," *New York Times,* January 27, 2003, B7.
26. David Corn, "Bush's Top Gun Photo-Op," Alternet.org, May 2, 2003, http://www.alternet.org/story.html?StoryID=15806.
27. G. Gordon Liddy, interviewed on *Hardball,* MSNBC, May 8, 2003.
28. Andrew Sullivan, "Idiocy of the Week," Salon.com, May 23, 2003, http://archive.salon.com/opinion/sullivan/2003/05/23/goldstein/index_np.html.
29. Richard Goldstein, "Bush's Basket: Why the President Had to Show His Balls," *The Village Voice,* http://www.villagevoice.com/issues/0321/goldstein.php.
30. Ibid.

PART X
Health and Illness

Women and men face different challenges related to health and illness. Gender-linked illnesses correlate with both genetic/biological differences between women and men and with socialized differences in the form of masculine and feminine behavior. Thus, women don't get testicular cancer, and the vast majority of lung cancer patients were men before women earned the right to smoke.[1] The structure of sex-segregated work and the widely shared assumption that men should engage in risky physical behavior put many women and men at different risks for various injuries and illnesses. These differences probably explain why women live longer than men in the United States.[2] They probably also explain why women are more likely than men to become addicted to prescription drugs and are more likely to report feeling depressed.[3]

Even when women and men suffer from the same diseases, the causes and experiences of the disease may differ. For example, alcoholic women tend to respond differently to their alcohol addiction than do alcoholic men in various ways. They are more likely to hide their addictions, to be diagnosed later than men, to feel depressed and suicidal in the midst of the disease, and to feel low levels of self-esteem since addiction and femininity are not ordinarily compatible.[4] Finally, they are more likely to be survivors of physical and sexual abuse than are male alcoholics.[5]

New research on the effects of environmental toxins on male and female reproductive systems suggests that these toxins create different kinds of illnesses in men than in women. For instance, Janet Raloff examined the impact of environmental toxins on men's reproductive health and concluded that toxins are linked to such reproductive issues as low sperm counts, testicles that fail to descend, and male urinary tract defects.[6]

Other factors, such as sexual orientation and race, intersect with gender to put different groups at higher or lower risk for illness and injury. The AIDS epidemic, for example, thus far has affected primarily men in the United States, in part because the majority of early victims of this epidemic were gay men and intravenous drug users (unlike in Africa, for example, where AIDS has primarily been a heterosexually transmitted disease). Few lesbians, on the other hand, have contracted AIDS.[7] The faces of people with HIV infection and AIDS are changing, however, as the epidemic spreads (see Campo, this part). Heterosexual women are now the fastest-growing group with AIDS in the United States.[8] Teenage girls, especially girls of color, are at particularly high risk; in some regions, they have higher rates of HIV infection than boys.[9]

Recent data suggest large discrepancies in the risk of contracting HIV/AIDS. About 64 percent of new HIV cases occur among African American women although they represent only 12 percent of the U.S. female population. About 18 percent of new cases occur among Latina women, although they represent only 13 percent of the U.S. female population.[10]

Race interacts with gender to create vast disparities in the health issues of Blacks and whites in the United States. African American women face higher rates of violence and childbirth-related illness and death than do white women.[11] Both Black and white men die from homicide at higher rates than Black and white women. Although both Black and white men die in automobile accidents at similar rates, Black men are more likely than white men to die in other kinds of accidents.[12] Among young men, Black men aged 15–24 are six times more likely than white men to die of homicide, and homicide is the principal cause of death for Black men in this age group.[13] Men are more likely than women to commit suicide, and among both women and men, whites are twice as likely as Blacks to do so.[14] The suicide gap between Black and white teens is narrowing, however, as more Black male teens commit suicide. White men are much more likely than men of color to contract testicular cancer.[15] Black men are twice as likely as white men to die of prostate cancer.[16]

The kinds of discrimination and oppression described throughout this book are present in the health care system as well. People who deviate from a Caucasian able-bodied, male norm are at higher risk for inadequate care. For example, the Institute of Medicine, an independent research institute that advises Congress, released a report in March 2002 that addressed racial disparities in health care. Unlike most prior studies, this one looked only at people who had health insurance, and concluded that racial discrepancies in quality of care persist even when people have similar insurance coverage. The report lists a wide array of suggestions, including increasing the number of underrepresented health care professionals along with better education of both professionals (especially) and consumers.[17] In addition to race and ethnicity, other factors affect health care. Women with disabilities, for example, are presumed by most doctors not to be sexual and not to want to be mothers.[18] Lesbians and gay men have health needs that many physicians fail to understand, including feeling uncomfortable with homophobic practitioners (and therefore avoiding health care) and protecting partners' rights in the face of illness or disability.[19] Disabled lesbians are hard pressed to find treatment facilities that can address their full array of medical needs when sexism, ableism, and homophobia intersect.[20] Trans liberationist Leslie Feinberg was ordered out of a hospital emergency room in the midst of a life-threatening illness when the physician discovered that although she appeared to be male, her body was female.[21] Fat women and men are frequently refused various kinds of treatment "until they lose weight," which is usually not feasible. The pressure on this group to take weight loss medication is high, with many women, especially, risking their health in order to try to get health care.[22]

Apart from differences in the kinds of health risks faced by various groups, the issue of access to health care is becoming increasingly serious in the United States. People who hold low-paying jobs without health insurance frequently cannot afford to buy it. Women are more likely than men to hold such jobs and are more likely than men to be the primary caretakers of children who need coverage.[23] A recent estimate put the number of uninsured people nationwide at 45 million.[24] Managed care is also interfering with health care in many cases, as doctors and patients must submit requests for treatment to third parties who do not know the individual patients involved. Without major structural reform of the health care system, this situation is very likely to worsen since individual and small collective efforts at empowerment cannot really change the system.

The privacy and autonomy of pregnant women continues to be an issue. Debates about abortion persist, as anti-choice advocates lobby for restricted access to abortion, and pro-choice advocates lobby to keep abortion easily accessible, safe, and legal. Ironically, it appears that states with the strongest restrictions on abortions are less likely to provide resources for children in need than do states with stronger abortion access.[25] The privacy rights of pregnant women have also come under attack in recent years, leading to the arrest of pregnant women for behavior perceived as threatening to their fetuses. The Supreme Court rendered some of this policing activity illegal in March 2001, as it struck down a South Carolina statute that required drug testing of pregnant women at a public hospital and the subsequent arrest of those found to be using drugs.[26] Advocates for children and women's health argue for supportive intervention and treatment when a fetus is allegedly placed at risk (for drug use, smoking, alcohol use, etc.), rather than arrest and incarceration.

The women's health movement has worked to address women's health concerns for the past 30 years. In the face of unresponsive health care systems, women have opened health clinics for women, have provided clandestine abortions when abortion was illegal, have lobbied for health-related legislation and research funding, and have written extensively about women's health. The success of the many editions of *Our Bodies Our Selves* since it was first published in 1970 attests to women's need for straightforward information about their bodies. Various editions of *Our Bodies Our Selves* have been translated into a total of 17 languages, and a recent version in Spanish (*Nuestos Cuerpos, Nuestras Vidas*) has not simply been translated but has also been revised to be more culturally appropriate for women in Latin America.[27] Organizations such as the National Women's Health Network (Washington, DC), the National Black Women's Health Project (Atlanta, GA), the National Black Women's Health Imperative (Washington, DC), the National Asian Women's Health Organization (San Francisco, CA), the National Latina Health Organization (Oakland, CA), and the Native American Women's Health Education Resource Center have all supported the movement for better health care for women via a wide range of health services, support, research, publications, education, and effective lobbying.

Women's health activism is illustrated by a recent article on hormone replacement therapy (HRT) by biologist and professor of Women's Studies

Nancy Worcester at the University of Wisconsin-Madison. Worcester discusses the importance of caution in prescribing drugs to large numbers of women without adequate long-term research. HRT is a case in point, and its frequent use to treat normal menopausal symptoms has been called into question. Six million women on HRT learned in July 2002 that the drugs they were taking could increase their risk of heart disease. Further investigation showed that HRT did not even improve the "quality of life" or women's memory. The National Women's Health Network had been questioning HRT for more than a decade. Worcester sets this example in the context of other medical treatments that turned out to be disastrous.[28] The lesson seems to be that when women's normal bodily functions are treated as fields for medical intervention, the results can be much more damaging than whatever negative effects the normal bodily functions seem to produce (e.g., hot flashes, miscarriages).

Organizations for men, such as the Prostate Cancer Action Network, have also lobbied for more attention to male-specific illnesses. Conflicting analyses over which gender has received more attention in health research has been the subject of much debate. Following an analysis of subjects in medical research published in a medical journal, the National Institutes of Health recently retracted a 1997 statement that "women were routinely excluded from medical research supported by NIH." Lobbying seems to have been effective in raising the number of women in clinical trials, and some critics argue that there was never a "gender gap."[29] Obviously, issues specific to both men and women (not to mention people who are gay, lesbian, or transgender) each need specific attention in order to ensure effective, humane, and accessible health care for everyone.

A growing literature on health and illness explores the links between illness or death and gender socialization, including the ways that various women and men cope with illness.[30] The readings in this part address several aspects of this large and growing field of study, focusing on men's health (Don Sabo), African American women's health and reproductive freedom (Evelyn L. Barbee and Marilyn Little), the importance of access to abortion for low-income women of color (Connie S. Chan), environmental toxins (Sandra Steingraber), AIDS (Rafael Campo), and health care for transgendered people (Kai Wright). The voices in this chapter make powerful pleas for decent health care for all people in a nontoxic world.

As you read these articles, you might want to think about your own health and that of people you know. Do all the people in your life have health insurance? Do the men you know seem to have masculinity-related illnesses? What do you think about the distinction between reproductive rights and reproductive freedom? Where do you stand on the debate about abortion? Have you ever thought about the potential toxicity of breast milk? What are your assumptions about the transmission of AIDS and who it affects? Do you know anyone who is transgendered? Do you know anyone who has experienced prejudice or discrimination in their search for health care—for whatever reason?

NOTES

1. Ingrid Waldron, "Contributions of Changing Gender Differences in Behavior and Social Roles to Changing Gender Differences in Mortality," in Donald Sabo and David Frederick Gordon, eds., *Men's Health and Illness: Gender, Power, and the Body* (Thousand Oaks, CA: Sage, 1995), p. 27; Robert Weissman, "Women and Tobacco," *The Network News* (National Women's Health Network) (March/April 2001), pp. 1, 4, 5.

2. Will H. Courtenay, "Behavioral Factors Associated with Disease, Injury, and Death among Men: Evidence and Implications for Prevention," *The Journal of Men's Studies* 9, no. 1 (Fall 2000), pp. 81ff; Judith M. Stillion, "Premature Death among Males: Extending the Bottom Line of Men's Health," in Sabo and Gordon, *Men's Health and Illness*, pp. 46–67.

3. Regarding addictions, see "Addictive Behaviors from the Women's Health Data Book," reprinted in Nancy Worcester and Marianne Whatley, eds., *Women's Health: Readings on Social, Economic, and Political Issues*, 2nd ed. (Dubuque, IA: Kendall/Hunt, 1994), pp. 153–57. Regarding depression, see Marian Murphy, "Women and Mental Health," reprinted in Worcester and Whatley, eds., *Women's Health*, pp. 127–32.

4. Rokelle Lerner, "What Does Female Have to Do with It?" *Professional Counselor* (August 1995), p. 20.

5. Willie Langeland and Christina Hartgers, "Child Sexual and Physical Abuse and Alcoholism: A Review," *Journal of Alcohol Studies* 59, no. 3 (May 1998), pp. 336–48.

6. Janet Raloff, "That Feminine Touch; Are Men Suffering from Prenatal or Childhood Exposures to 'Hormonal' Toxicants?" *Science News* 145 (January 22, 1994), pp. 56–8.

7. Ruth L. Schwartz, "New Alliances, Strange Bedfellows: Lesbians, Gay Men and AIDS," in Arlene Stein, ed., *Sisters, Sexperts, and Queers: Beyond the Lesbian Nation* (New York: Plume, 1993), pp. 230–44.

8. M. Wolfe, "Women and HIV/AIDS Education," paper prepared for the NEA Health Information Network, Atlanta, 1991. Cited in the American Association of University Women Educational Foundation, *How Schools Shortchange Girls* (New York: Marlowe, 1992), p. 137.

9. L. D'Angelo, et al., "HIV Infection in Adolescents: Can We Predict Who Is at Risk?," poster presentation at the Fifth International Conference on AIDS, June 1989. Data from Washington, DC, was reported. Cited in the American Association of University Women Educational Foundation, *How Schools Shortchange Girls*, p. 137.

10. DeAna Tucker, "The Feminization of HIV/AIDS: What Dick Cheney Needs to Know," *The Women's Health Activist* 30, no. 1 (January/February 2005), p. 3.

11. Paul Simao, "Pregnancy Death Highest for Black Women, US Study Shows," *The Boston Globe* (Friday May 11, 2002), p. A27; Evelyn L. Barbee and Marilyn Little, "Health, Social Class, and African-American Women," in Stanlie M. James and Abena P. A. Buscia, eds., *Theorizing Black Feminisms: The Visionary Pragmatism of Black Women* (New York: Routledge, 1993).

12. Stillion, "Premature Death among Males," p. 52.

13. Jewell Taylor Gibbs, "Anger in Young Black Males: Victims or Victimizers?" in Richard G. Majors & Jacob U. Gordon, eds., *The American Black Male: His Status and His Future* (Chicago: Nelson-Hall, 1994), p. 128.

14. Stillion, "Premature Death among Males," p. 53.

15. David Frederick Gordon, "Testicular Cancer and Masculinity," in Sabo and Gordon, *Men's Health and Illness*.

16. National Cancer Institute, *Cancer among Blacks and Other Minorities: Statistical Profiles* (Washington, DC: U.S. Department of Health and Human Services, NIH Publication #86-2785, 1986), p. 10.

17. Brian D. Smedley, Adrienne Y. Stith, & Alan R. Nelson, eds. *Unequal Treatment: Confronting Racial and Ethnic Disparities in Health Care.* (Washington, DC: Institute of Medicine, 2002).

18. Carol J. Gill, "Editorial: When Is a Woman Not a Woman?" *Sexuality and Disability* 12, no. 2 (1994), pp. 117–9; Carrie Killoran, "Women with Disabilities Having Children: It's Our Right Too," *Sexuality and Disability* 12, no. 2 (1994), pp. 121–26.

19. Ann Pollinger Haas, "Lesbian Health Issues: An Overview," in Alice J. Dan, ed., *Reframing Women's Health: Multidisciplinary Research and Practice* (Thousand Oaks, CA: Sage Publications, 1994), pp. 339–56.

20. Corbett Joan O'Toole, "Disabled Lesbians: Challenging Monocultural Constructs," *Sexuality and Disability* 14, no. 3 (1996), pp. 221–36.

21. Leslie Feinberg, *Trans Liberation: Beyond Pink or Blue* (Boston: Beacon Press, 1998), p. 2.

22. Pat Lyons, "The Great Weight Debate: Where Have All the Feminists Gone?" *The Network News* 23, no. 5 (September/October, 1998), pp. 1ff.

23. I recently saw an advertisement in Boston offering health insurance for children. Parents had the option to insure their children when they could not afford to insure the whole family.

24. U.S. Chamber of Commerce, "Number of Uninsured Americans Rises" August 31, 2004. http://www.uschamber.com/publications/weekly/update/040831.htm.

25. Jean Reith Schroedel, *Is the Fetus a Person? A Comparison of Policies across the Fifty States* (Ithaca, NY: Cornell University Press, 2000).

26. Lynn P. Paltrow, "South Carolina: Where Pregnancy Is a Crime" *The Network News* (National Women's Health Network) (July/August 2000), pp. 3–4; Jean Reith Schroedel, *Is the Fetus a Person?*; Lyle Denniston, "Drug Test Ruling Backs Pregnant Women's Privacy," *The Boston Globe* (Thursday March 22, 2001), p. A3.

27. For the most recent edition in English, see Boston Women's Health Book Collective, *Our Bodies Our Selves: A New Edition for a New Era* (New York: Simon & Schuster, 2005). In Spanish: La Colectiva del Libro de Salud de las Mujeres de Boston, *Nuestos Cuerpos, Nuestras Vidas: La Guía Definitive para la Salud de la Mujer Latina* (Nueva York/New York: Siete Cuentos Editorial/Seven Stories Press, 2000). For an example of an early groundbreaking book in the women's health movement that was important enough to be republished 25 years later, see Barbara Seaman, *The Doctor's Case against the Pill, 25th Anniversary Edition* (Alameda, CA: Hunter House, 1995).

28. Nancy Worcester, "Hormone Replacement Therapy (HRT): Getting to the Heart of Politics and Women's Health" *NWSA Journal* Vol. 16, no. 3 (Fall 2004), pp. 56–69.

29. Cathy Young, "It's Time to End the Gender Gap in Health Care," *The Boston Globe* (Wednesday November 15, 2000), p. A27.

30. For more information on women's and men's health, see Sabo and Gordon, *Men's Health and Illness* (Thousand Oaks, CA: Sage Publications, 1995); Worcester and Whatley, eds., *Women's Health* (Dubuque, Iowa: Kendall-Hunt, 1994); Evelyn C. White, ed., *The Black Women's Health Book* (Seattle: Seal Press, 1990).

62

MASCULINITIES AND MEN'S HEALTH
Moving toward Post–
Superman Era Prevention

DON SABO

Don Sabo, Ph.D., is professor of sociology at D'Youville College in Buffalo, New York. His latest books include (with Leslie Heywood, Kathleen Miller and Merrill Melnick) *Her Life Depends on It: Sport, Physical Activity, and the Health and Well-being of American Girls;* (with Michael Messner) *Sex, Violence & Power in Sport;* and (with Dave Gordon) *Men's Health & Illness: Gender, Power, & the Body.* He directed the nationwide Women's Sports Foundation study *Sport and Teen Pregnancy* (1998).

M y grandfather used to smile and say, "Find out where you're going to die and stay the hell away from there." Grandpa had never studied epidemiology (the study of variations in health and illness in society), but he understood that certain behaviors, attitudes, and cultural practices can put individuals at risk for accidents, illness, or death. This chapter presents an overview of men's health that proceeds from the basic assumption that aspects of traditional masculinity can be dangerous to men's health (Sabo & Gordon, 1995; Harrison, Chin, & Ficarrotto, 1992). First, I identify some gender differences in relation to morbidity (sickness) and mortality (death). Next, I examine how the risk for illness varies from one male group to another. I then discuss an array of men's health issues and a preventative strategy for enhancing men's health.

Gender Differences in Health and Illness

When British sociologist Ashley Montagu put forth the thesis in 1953 that women were biologically superior to men, he shook up the prevailing chauvinistic beliefs that men were stronger, smarter, and better than women. His

Don Sabo, "Masculinities and Men's Health." Portions of this selection previously appeared in *Nursing Care in the Community,* second edition, edited by J. Cookfair (St. Louis, Missouri: Mosby-Year Book, 1996). Reprinted by permission.

argument was partly based on epidemiological data that show males are more vulnerable to mortality than females from before birth and throughout the life span.

Mortality

From the time of conception, men are more likely to succumb to prenatal and neonatal death than females. Men's chances of dying during the prenatal stage of development are about 12% greater than those of females and, during the neonatal (newborn) stage, 130% greater than those of females. A number of neonatal disorders are common to males but not females, such as bacterial infections, respiratory illness, digestive diseases, and some circulatory disorders of the aorta and pulmonary artery. Table 1 compares male and female infant mortality rates across historical time. Though the infant mortality rate decreases over time, the persistence of the higher rates for males than females suggests that biological factors may be operating. Data also show that males have higher mortality rates than females in every age category, from "under one year" through "over 85" (National Center for Health Statistics, 1992). In fact, men are more likely to die in 9 out of the 10 leading causes of death in the United States. (See Table 2.)

Females have greater life expectancy than males in the United States, Canada, and postindustrial societies (Verbrugge and Wingard, 1987; Waldron, 1986). This fact suggests a female biological advantage, but a closer analysis of changing trends in the gap between women's and men's life expectancy indicates that social and cultural factors related to lifestyle, gender identity, and behavior are operating as well. Life expectancy among American females is about 78.3 years but 71.3 years for males (National Center for Health Statistics, 1990). As Waldron's (1995) analysis of shifting mortality patterns between the sexes during the 20th century shows, however, women's relative advantage in life expectancy over men was rather small at the beginning of the 20th century. During the mid-20th century, female mortality declined more rapidly than

TABLE 1   Infant Mortality Rate

Year	Both Sexes	Males	Females
1940	47.0	52.5	41.3
1950	29.2	32.8	25.5
1960	26.0	29.3	22.6
1970	20.0	22.4	17.5
1980	12.6	13.9	11.2
1989	9.8	10.8	8.8

Note: Rates are for infant (under 1 year) deaths per 1,000 live births for all races.
Sources: Adapted from *Monthly Vital Statistics Report,* Vol. 40, No. 8. Supplement 2, January 7, 1992, p. 41.

TABLE 2   Death Rates by Sex and 10 Leading Causes: 1989

Cause of Death	Age-Adjusted Death Rate Per 100,000 Population			
	Total	Male	Female	Sex Differential
Diseases of the heart	155.9	210.2	112.3	1.87
Malignant neoplasms	133.0	163.4	111.7	1.45
Accidents and adverse effects	33.8	49.5	18.9	2.62
Cerebrovascular disease	28.0	30.4	26.2	1.16
Chronic liver disease, cirrhosis	8.9	12.8	5.5	2.33
Diabetes	11.5	2.0	11.0	1.09
Suicide	11.3	18.6	4.5	4.13
Homicide and legal intervention	9.4	14.7	4.1	3.59

Sources: Adapted from the *U.S. Bureau of the Census: Statistical Abstracts of the United States: 1992* (112th ed., p. 84), Washington, DC.

male mortality, thereby increasing the gender gap in life expectancy. Whereas women benefited from decreased maternal mortality, the midcentury trend toward a lowering of men's life expectancy was slowed by increasing mortality from coronary heart disease and lung cancer that were, in turn, mainly due to higher rates of cigarette smoking among males.

The most recent trends show that differences between women's and men's mortality decreased during the 1980s; that is, female life expectancy was 7.9 years greater than that of males in 1979 and 6.9 years in 1989 (National Center for Health Statistics, 1992). Waldron explains that some changes in behavioral patterns between the sexes, such as increased smoking among women, have narrowed the gap between men's formerly higher mortality rates from lung cancer, chronic obstructive pulmonary disease, and ischemic heart disease. In summary, it appears that both biological and sociocultural factors are involved with shaping patterns of men's and women's mortality. In fact, Waldron (1976) suggests that gender-related behaviors rather than strictly biogenic factors account for about three-quarters of the variation in men's early mortality.

Morbidity

Whereas females generally outlive males, females report higher morbidity rates, even after controlling for maternity. National health surveys show that females experience acute illnesses such as respiratory conditions, infective and parasitic conditions, and digestive system disorders at higher rates than males do; however, males sustain more injuries (Givens, 1979; Cypress, 1981; Dawson & Adams, 1987). Men's higher injury rates are partly owed to gender differences in socialization and lifestyle, such as learning to prove manhood through recklessness, involvement in contact sports, and working in risky blue-collar occupations.

Females are generally more likely than males to experience chronic conditions such as anemia, chronic enteritis and colitis, migraine headaches, arthritis, diabetes, and thyroid disease. However, males are more prone to develop chronic illnesses such as coronary heart disease, emphysema, and gout. Although chronic conditions do not ordinarily cause death, they often limit activity or cause disability.

After noting gender differences in morbidity, Cockerham (1995) asks whether women really do experience more illness than men—or could it be that women are more sensitive to bodily sensations than men, or that men are not as prone as women to report symptoms and seek medical care? He concludes, "The best evidence indicates that the overall differences in morbidity are real" and, further, that they are due to a mixture of biological, psychological, and social influences (p. 42).

Masculinities and Men's Health

There is no such thing as masculinity; there are only masculinities (Sabo & Gordon, 1995). A limitation of early gender theory was its treatment of "all men" as a single, large category in relation to "all women" (Connell, 1987). The fact is, however, that all men are not alike, nor do all male groups share the same stakes in the gender order. At any given historical moment, there are competing masculinities—some dominant, some marginalized, and some stigmatized—each with its respective structural, psychosocial, and cultural moorings. There are substantial differences between the health options of homeless men, working-class men, lower-class men, gay men, men with AIDS, prison inmates, men of color, and their comparatively advantaged middle- and upper-class, white, professional male counterparts. Similarly, a wide range of individual differences exists between the ways that men and women act out "femininity" and "masculinity" in their everyday lives. A health profile of several male groups is discussed below.

Adolescent Males

Pleck, Sonenstein, and Ku (1992) applied critical feminist perspectives to their research on problem behaviors and health among adolescent males. A national sampling of adolescent, never-married males aged 15–19 were interviewed in 1980 and 1988. Hypothesis tests were geared to assessing whether "masculine ideology" (which measured the presence of traditional male role attitudes) put boys at risk for an array of problem behaviors. The researchers found a significant, independent association with seven of ten problem behaviors. Specifically, traditionally masculine attitudes were associated with being suspended from school, drinking and use of street drugs, frequency of being picked up by the police, being sexually active, the number of heterosexual partners in the last year, and tricking or forcing someone to have sex. These kinds of behaviors, which are in part expressions of the pursuit of traditional masculinity, elevate boys' risk for sexually transmitted diseases, HIV transmission, and early death by accident or homicide. At the same time, however, these same behaviors can also encourage victimization of women through men's violence, sexual assault, unwanted teenage pregnancy, and sexually transmitted diseases.

Adolescence is a phase of accelerated physiological development, and good nutrition during this period is important to future health. Obesity puts adults at risk for a variety of diseases such as coronary heart disease, diabetes mellitus, joint disease, and certain cancers. Obese adolescents are also apt to become obese adults, thus elevating long-term risk for illness. National Health and Nutrition Examination Surveys show that obesity among adolescents increased by 6% during 1976–80 and 1988–91. During 1988–91, 22% of females of 12–18 years were overweight, and 20% of males in this age group were as well (*Morbidity and Mortality Weekly Report*, 1994a).

Males form a majority of the estimated 1.3 million teenagers who run away from home each year in the United States. For both boys and girls, living on the streets raises the risk of poor nutrition, homicide, alcoholism, drug abuse, and AIDS. Young adults in their 20s comprise about 20% of new AIDS cases and, when you calculate the lengthy latency period, it is evident that they are being infected in their teenage years. Runaways are also more likely to be victims of crime and sexual exploitation (Hull, 1994).

Clearly, adolescent males face a spectrum of potential health problems — some that threaten their present well-being, and others that could take their toll in the future.

Men of Color

Patterns of health and illness among men of color can be partly understood against the historical and social context of economic inequality. Generally, because African Americans, Hispanics, and Native Americans are disproportionately poor, they are more apt to work in low-paying and dangerous occupations, reside in polluted environments, be exposed to toxic substances, experience the threat and reality of crime, and worry about meeting basic needs. Cultural barriers can also complicate their access to available health care. Poverty is correlated with lower educational attainment, which, in turn, mitigates against adoption of preventative health behaviors.

The neglect of public health in the United States is particularly pronounced in relation to African Americans (Polych & Sabo, 1996). For example, in Harlem, where 96% of the inhabitants are African American and 41% live below the poverty line, the survival curve beyond the age of 40 for men is lower than that of men living in Bangladesh (McCord & Freeman, 1990). Even though African American men have higher rates of alcoholism, infectious diseases, and drug-related conditions, for example, they are less apt to receive health care, and when they do, they are more apt to receive inferior care

(Bullard, 1992; Staples, 1995). Statistics like the following led Gibbs (1988) to describe young African American males as an "endangered species":

- The number of young African American male homicide victims in 1977 (5,734) was higher than the number killed in the Vietnam War during 1963–72 (5,640) (Gibbs, 1988:258).
- Homicide is the leading cause of death among young African American males. The probability of a black man dying from homicide is about the same as that of a white male dying from an accident (Reed, 1991).
- More than 36% of urban African American males are drug and alcohol abusers (Staples, 1995).
- In 1993 the rate of contracting AIDS for African American males aged 13 and older was almost 5 times higher than the rate for white males (*Morbidity and Mortality Weekly Report*, 1994b).

The health profile of Native Americans and Native Canadians is also poor. For example, alcohol is the number-one killer of Native Americans between the ages of 14 and 44 (May, 1986), and 42% of Native American male adolescents are problem drinkers, compared to 34% of same-age white males (Lamarine, 1988). Native Americans (10–18 years of age) comprise 34% of inpatient admissions to adolescent detoxification programs (Moore, 1988). Compared to the "all race" population, Native American youth exhibit more serious problems in the areas of depression, suicide, anxiety, substance use, and general health status (Blum et al., 1992). The rates of morbidity, mortality from injury, and contracting AIDS are also higher (Sugarman et al., 1993; Metler et al., 1991).

Like those of many other racial and ethnic groups, the health problems facing American and Canadian natives correlate with the effects of poverty and social marginalization, such as dropping out of school, a sense of hopelessness, the experience of prejudice, poor nutrition, and lack of regular health care. Those who care about men's health, therefore, need to be attuned to the potential interplay between gender, race/ethnicity, cultural differences, and economic conditions when working with racial and ethnic minorities.

Gay and Bisexual Men

Gay and bisexual men are estimated to constitute 5% to 10% of the male population. In the past, gay men have been viewed as evil, sinful, sick, emotionally immature, and socially undesirable. Many health professionals and the wider public have harbored mixed feelings and homophobic attitudes toward gay and bisexual men. Gay men's identity, their lifestyles, and the social responses to homosexuality can impact the health of gay and bisexual men. Stigmatization and marginalization, for example, may lead to emotional confusion and suicide among gay male adolescents. For gay and bisexual men who are "in the closet," anxiety and stress can tax emotional and physical health. When seeking medical services, gay and bisexual men must often cope with the homophobia of health care workers or deal with the threat of losing health care insurance if their sexual orientation is made known.

Whether they are straight or gay, men tend to have more sexual contacts than women do, which heightens men's risk for contracting sexually trans-mitted diseases (STDs). Men's sexual attitudes and behaviors are closely tied to the way masculinity has been socially constructed. For example, real men are taught to suppress their emotions, which can lead to a separation of sex from feeling. Traditionally, men are also encouraged to be daring, which can lead to risky sexual decisions. In addition, contrary to common myths about gay male effeminacy, masculinity also plays a powerful role in shaping gay and bisexual men's identity and behavior. To the extent that traditional mas-culinity informs sexual activity of men, masculinity can be a barrier to safer sexual behavior among men. This insight leads Kimmel and Levine (1989) to assert that "to educate men about safe sex, then, means to confront the issues of masculinity" (p. 352). In addition to practicing abstinence and safer sex as preventive strategies, therefore, they argue that traditional beliefs about masculinity be challenged as a form of risk reduction.

Men who have sex with men remain the largest risk group for HIV trans-mission. For gay and bisexual men who are infected by the HIV virus, the personal burden of living with an AIDS diagnosis is made heavier by the stigma associated with homosexuality. The cultural meanings associated with AIDS can also filter into gender and sexual identities. Tewksbury's (1995) interviews with 45 HIV positive gay men showed how masculinity, sexuality, stigmatization, and interpersonal commitment mesh in decision making related to risky sexual behavior. Most of the men practiced celibacy in order to prevent others from contracting the disease; others practiced safe sex, and a few went on having unprotected sex.

Prison Inmates

There are 1.3 million men imprisoned in American jails and prisons (Nadel-mann & Wenner, 1994). The United States has the highest rate of incarceration of any nation in the world, 426 prisoners for every 100,000 people (American College of Physicians, 1992), followed by South Africa and the former Soviet Union (Mauer, 1992). Racial and ethnic minorities are overrepresented among those behind bars. Black and Hispanic males, for example, comprise 85% of prisoners in the New York State prison system (Green, 1991).

The prison system acts as a pocket of risk, within which men already at high risk of having a preexisting AIDS infection are exposed to conditions that further heighten the risk of contracting HIV (Toepell, 1992) or other in-fections such as tuberculosis (Bellin, Fletcher, & Safyer, 1993) or hepatitis. The corrections system is part of an institutional chain that facilitates trans-mission of HIV and other infections in certain North American populations, particularly among poor, inner-city, minority males. Prisoners are burdened not only by social disadvantage but also by high rates of physical illness, mental disorder, and substance abuse that jeopardize their health (Editor, *Lancet*, 1991).

AIDS prevalence is markedly higher among state and federal inmates than in the general U.S. population, with a known aggregate rate in 1992 of 202 per 100,000 population (Brewer & Derrickson, 1992) compared to a total population prevalence of 14.65 in 100,000 (American College of Physicians, 1992). The cumulative total of American prisoners with AIDS in 1989 was estimated to be 5,411, a 72% increase over the previous year (Belbot & del Carmen, 1991). The total number of AIDS cases reported in U.S. corrections as of 1993 was 11,565 (a minimum estimate of the true cumulative incidence among U.S. inmates) (Hammett; cited in Expert Committee on AIDS and Prisons, 1994). In New York State, at least 10,000 of the state's 55,000 prisoners are believed to be infected (Prisoners with AIDS/HIV Support Action Network, 1992). In Canadian federal penitentiaries, it is believed that 1 in 20 inmates is HIV infected (Hankins; cited in Expert Committee on AIDS and Prison, 1994).

The HIV virus is primarily transmitted between adults by unprotected penetrative sex or by needle sharing, without bleaching, with an infected partner. Sexual contacts between prisoners occur mainly through consensual unions and secondarily though sexual assault and rape (Vaid; cited in Expert Committee on AIDS and Prisons, 1994). The amount of IV drug use behind prison walls is unknown, although it is known to be prevalent and the scarcity of needles often leads to sharing of needles and sharps (Prisoners with AIDS/HIV Support Action Network, 1992).

The failure to provide comprehensive health education and treatment interventions in prisons not only puts more inmates at risk for HIV infection, but also threatens the public at large. Prisons are not hermetically sealed enclaves set apart from the community but an integral part of society (Editor, *Lancet*, 1991). Prisoners regularly move in and out of the prison system. In 1989, prisons in the United States admitted 467,227 persons and discharged 386,228 (American College of Physicians, 1992). The average age of inmates admitted to prison in 1989 was 29.6, with 75% between 18 and 34 years; 94.3% were male. These former inmates return to their communities after having served an average of 18 months inside (Dubler & Sidel, 1989). Within three years, 62.5% will be rearrested and jailed. Recidivism is highest among poor black and Hispanic men. The extent to which the drug-related social practices and sexual activities of released or paroled inmates who are HIV positive are putting others at risk upon return to their communities is unresearched and unknown.

Male Athletes

Injury is everywhere in sport. It is evident in the lives and bodies of athletes who regularly experience bruises, torn ligaments, broken bones, aches, lacerations, muscle tears, and so forth. For example, about 300,000 football-related injuries per year require treatment in hospital emergency rooms

(Miedzian, 1991). Critics of violent contact sports claim that athletes are paying too high a physical price for their participation. George D. Lundberg (1994), editor of the *Journal of the American Medical Association*, has called for a ban on boxing in the Olympics and in the U.S. military. His editorial entreaty, though based on clinical evidence for neurological harm from boxing, is also couched in a wider critique of the exploitative economics of the sport.

Injuries are basically unavoidable in sports, but, in traditional men's sports, there has been a tendency to glorify pain and injury, to inflict injury on others, and to sacrifice one's body in order to "win at all costs." The "no pain, no gain"philosophy, which is rooted in traditional cultural equations between masculinity and sports, can jeopardize the health of athletes who conform to its ethos (Sabo, 1994).

The connections between sport, masculinity, and health are evidenced in Klein's (1993) study of how bodybuilders use anabolic steroids, overtrain, and engage in extreme dietary practices. He spent years as an ethnographic researcher in the muscled world of the bodybuilding subculture, where masculinity is equated to maximum muscularity and men's striving for bigness and physical strength hides emotional insecurity and low self-esteem.

A nationwide survey of American male high school seniors found that 6.6% used or had used anabolic steroids. About two-thirds of this group were athletes (Buckley et al., 1988). Anabolic steroid use has been linked to health risks such as liver disease, kidney problems, atrophy of the testicles, elevated risk of injury, and premature skeletal maturation.

Klein lays bare a tragic irony in American subculture—the powerful male athlete, a symbol of strength and health, has often sacrificed his health in pursuit of ideal masculinity (Messner & Sabo, 1994).

Men's Health Issues

Advocates of men's health have identified a variety of issues that impact directly on men's lives. Some of these issues may concern you or men you care about.

Testicular Cancer

The epidemiological data on testicular cancer are sobering. Though relatively rare in the general population, it is the fourth most common cause of death among males of 15–35 years, accounting for 14% of all cancer deaths for this age group. It is the most common form of cancer affecting males of 20–34 years. The incidence of testicular cancer is increasing, and about 6,100 new U.S. cases were diagnosed in 1991 (American Cancer Society, 1991). If detected early, the cure rate is high, whereas delayed diagnosis is life threatening. Regular testicular self-examination (TSE), therefore, is a potentially effective means for ensuring early detection and successful treatment. Regrettably, however, most physicians do not teach TSE techniques (Rudolf & Quinn, 1988).

Denial may influence men's perceptions of testicular cancer and TSE (Blesch, 1986). Studies show that most males are not aware of testicular cancer, and even among those who are aware, many are reluctant to examine their testicles as a preventive measure. Even when symptoms are recognized, men sometimes postpone seeking treatment. Moreover, men who are taught TSE are often initially receptive, but their practice of TSE decreases over time. Men's resistance to TSE has been linked to awkwardness about touching themselves, associating touching genitals with homosexuality or masturbation, or the idea that TSE is not a manly behavior. And finally, men's individual reluctance to discuss testicular cancer partly derives from the widespread cultural silence that envelops it. The penis is a cultural symbol of male power, authority, and sexual domination. Its symbolic efficacy in traditional, male-dominated gender relations, therefore, would be eroded or neutralized by the realities of testicular cancer.

Disease of the Prostate

Middle-aged and elderly men are likely to develop medical problems with the prostate gland. Some men may experience benign prostatic hyperplasia, an enlargement of the prostate gland that is associated with symptoms such as dribbling after urination, frequent urination, or incontinence. Others may develop infections (prostatitis) or malignant prostatic hyperplasia (prostate cancer). Prostate cancer is the third leading cause of death from cancer in men, accounting for 15.7 deaths per 100,000 population in 1989. Prostate cancer is now more common than lung cancer (Martin, 1990). One in 10 men will develop this cancer by age 85, with African American males showing a higher prevalence rate than whites (Greco & Blank, 1993).

Treatments for prostate problems depend on the specific diagnosis and may range from medication to radiation and surgery. As is the case with testicular cancer, survival from prostate cancer is enhanced by early detection. Raising men's awareness about the health risks associated with the prostate gland, therefore, may prevent unnecessary morbidity and mortality. Unfortunately, the more invasive surgical treatments for prostate cancer can produce incontinence and impotence, and there has been no systematic research on men's psychosocial reactions and adjustment to sexual dysfunction associated with treatments for prostate cancer.

Alcohol Abuse

Although social and medical problems stemming from alcohol abuse involve both sexes, males comprise the largest segment of alcohol abusers. Some researchers have begun exploring the connections between the influence of the traditional male role on alcohol abuse. Isenhart and Silversmith (1994) show how, in a variety of occupational contexts, expectations surrounding masculinity encourage heavy drinking while working or socializing during after-work or off-duty hours. Some predominantly male occupational groups, such as longshoremen (Hitz, 1973), salesmen (Cosper, 1979), and members of the military (Pursch, 1976), are known to engage in high rates of alcohol consumption. Mass media play a role in sensationalizing links between booze and male bravado. Postman, Nystrom, Strate, and Weingartner (1987) studied the thematic content of 40 beer commercials and identified a variety of stereotypical portrayals of the male role that were used to promote beer drinking: reward for a job well done; manly activities that feature strength, risk, and daring; male friendship and esprit de corps; romantic success with women. The researchers estimate that, between the ages of 2 and 18, children view about 100,000 beer commercials.

Findings from a Harvard School of Public Health (1994) survey of 17,600 students at 140 colleges found that 44% engaged in "binge drinking," defined as drinking five drinks in rapid succession for males and four drinks for females. Males were more apt to report binge drinking during the past two weeks than females: 50% and 39% respectively. Sixty percent of the males who binged three or more times in the past two weeks reported driving after drinking, compared to 49% of their female counterparts, thus increasing the risk for accident, injury, and death. Compared to non–binge drinkers, binge drinkers were seven times more likely to engage in unprotected sex, thus elevating the risk for unwanted pregnancy and sexually transmitted disease. Alcohol-related automobile accidents are the top cause of death among 16- to 24-year-olds, especially among males (Henderson & Anderson, 1989). For all males, the age-adjusted death rate from automobile accidents in 1991 was 26.2 per 100,000 for African American males and 24.2 per 100,000 for white males, 2.5 and 3.0 times higher than for white and African American females respectively (*Morbidity and Mortality Weekly Report,* 1994d). The number of automobile fatalities among male adolescents that results from a mixture of alcohol abuse and masculine daring is unknown.

Men and AIDS

Human immunodeficiency virus (HIV) infection became a leading cause of death among males in the 1980s. Among men aged 25–44 in 1990, HIV infection was the second leading cause of death, compared to the sixth leading cause of death among same-age women (*Morbidity and Mortality Weekly Report,* 1993a). Among reported cases of acquired immunodeficiency syndrome (AIDS) for adolescent and adult men in 1992, 60% were men who had sex with other men, 21% were intravenous drug users, 4% were exposed through heterosexual sexual contact, 6% were men who had sex with men and injected drugs, and 1% were transfusion recipients. Among the cases of AIDS among adolescent and adult women in 1992, 45% were intravenous drug users, 39% were infected through heterosexual contact, and 4% were transfusion recipients (*Morbidity and Mortality Weekly Report,* 1993a).

Because most AIDS cases have been among men who have sex with other men, perceptions of the epidemic and its victims have been tinctured by sexual attitudes. In North American cultures, the stigma associated with AIDS is fused with the stigma linked to homosexuality. Feelings about men with AIDS can be mixed and complicated by homophobia.

Thoughts and feelings about men with AIDS are also influenced by attitudes toward race, ethnicity, drug abuse, and social marginality. Centers for Disease Control data show, for example, that men of color aged 13 and older constituted 51% (45,039) of the 89,165 AIDS cases reported in 1993. Women of color made up 71% of the cases reported among females aged 13 and older (*Morbidity and Mortality Weekly Report,* 1994b). The high rate of AIDS among racial and ethnic minorities has kindled racial prejudices in some minds, and AIDS is sometimes seen as a "minority disease." Although African American or Hispanic males may be at a greater risk of contracting HIV/AIDS, just as yellow fingers do not cause lung disease, it is not race or ethnicity that confers risk, but the behaviors they engage in and the social circumstances of their lives.

Perceptions of HIV/AIDS can also be influenced by attitudes toward poverty and poor people. HIV infection is linked to economic problems that include community disintegration, unemployment, homelessness, eroding urban tax bases, mental illness, substance abuse, and criminalization (Wallace, 1991). For example, males comprise the majority of homeless persons. Poverty and homelessness overlap with drug addiction, which, in turn, is linked to HIV infection. Of persons hospitalized with HIV in New York City, 9–18% have been found to be homeless (Torres et al, 1990). Of homeless men tested for HIV at a New York City shelter, 62% of those who took the test were seropositive (Ron & Rogers, 1989). Among runaway or homeless youth in New York City, 7% tested positive, and this rate rose to 15% among the 19- and 20-year-olds. Of homeless men in Baltimore, 85% admitted to substance use problems (Weinreb & Bassuk, 1990).

Suicide

The suicide rates for both African American and white males increased between 1970 and 1989, whereas female rates decreased. Indeed, males are more likely than females to commit suicide from middle childhood until old age (Stillion, 1985, 1995). Compared to females, males typically deploy more violent means of attempting suicide (e.g., guns or hanging rather than pills) and are more likely to complete that act. Men's selection of more violent methods to kill themselves is consistent with traditionally masculine behavior (Stillion, White, McDowell, & Edwards, 1989).

Canetto (1995) interviewed male survivors of suicide attempts in order to better understand sex differences in suicidal behavior. Although she recognizes that men's psychosocial reactions and adjustments to nonfatal suicide vary by race/ethnicity, socioeconomic status, and age, she also finds that gender identity is an important factor in men's experiences. Suicide data show that men attempt suicide less often than women but are more likely to die than women. Canetto indicates that men's comparative "success" rate points toward a tragic irony that, consistent with gender stereotypes, men's failure even at suicide undercuts the cultural mandate that men are supposed to succeed at everything. A lack of embroilment in traditionally masculine expectations, she suggests, may actually increase the likelihood of surviving a suicide attempt for some men.

Elderly males in North America commit suicide significantly more often than elderly females. Whereas white women's lethal suicide rate peaks at age 50, white men age 60 and older have the highest rate of lethal suicide, even surpassing that rate for younger males (Manton et al., 1987). Canetto (1992) argues that elderly men's higher suicide mortality is chiefly owed to gender differences in coping. She writes,

> Older women may have more flexible and diverse ways of coping than older men. Compared to older men, older women may be more willing and capable of adopting different coping strategies — "passive" or "active," "connected" or "independent" — depending on the situation (p. 92).

She attributes men's limited coping abilities to gender socialization and development.

Erectile Disorders

Men often joke about their penises or tease one another about penis size and erectile potency ("not getting it up"). In contrast, they rarely discuss their concerns about impotence in a serious way. Men's silences in this regard are regrettable in that many men, both young and old, experience recurrent or periodic difficulties getting or maintaining an erection. Estimates of the number of American men with erectile disorders range from 10 million to 30 million (Krane, Goldstein, & Saenz de Tejada, 1989; National Institutes of Health, 1993). The Massachusetts Male Aging Study of the general population of noninstitutionalized, healthy American men between ages 40 and 70 years found that 52% reported minimal, moderate, or complete impotence (Feldman et al., 1994). The prevalence of erectile disorders increased with age, and 9.6% of the men were afflicted by complete impotence.

During the 1960s and 1970s, erectile disorders were largely thought to stem from psychological problems such as depression, financial worries, or work-related stress. Masculine stereotypes about male sexual prowess, phallic power, or being in charge of lovemaking were also said to put too much pressure to perform on some males (Zilbergeld, 1993). In contrast, physiological explanations of erectile disorders and medical treatments have been increasingly emphasized since the 1980s. Today diagnosis and treatment of erectile disorders should combine psychological and medical assessment (Ackerman & Carey, 1995).

Men's Violence

Men's violence is a major public health problem. The traditional masculine stereotype calls on males to be aggressive and tough. Anger is a by-product of aggression and toughness and, ultimately, part of the inner terrain of traditional masculinity (Sabo, 1993). Images of angry young men are compelling vehicles used by some males to separate themselves from women and to measure their status with respect to other males. Men's anger and violence derive, in part, from sex inequality. Men use the threat or application of violence to maintain their political and economic advantage over women and lower-status men. Male socialization reflects and reinforces these larger patterns of domination.

Homicide is the second leading cause of death among 15- to 19-year-old males. Males aged 15–34 years made up almost half (49%, or 13,122) of homicide victims in the United States in 1991. The homicide rate for this age group increased by 50% from 1985 to 1991 (*Morbidity and Mortality Weekly Report*, 1994c).

Women are especially victimized by men's anger and violence in the form of rape, date rape, wife beating, assault, sexual harassment on the job, and verbal harassment (Thorne-Finch, 1992). That the reality and potential of men's violence impact women's mental and physical health can be surely assumed. However, men's violence also exacts a toll on men themselves in the forms of fighting, gang clashes, hazing, gay-bashing, intentional infliction of injury, homicide, suicide, and organized warfare.

Summary

It is ironic that two of the best-known actors who portrayed Superman have met with disaster. George Reeves, who starred in the original black-and-white television show, committed suicide, and Christopher Reeve, who portrayed the "man of steel" in recent film versions, was paralyzed by an accident during a high-risk equestrian event. Perhaps one lesson to be learned here is that, behind the cultural facade of mythic masculinity, men are vulnerable. Indeed, as we have seen in this chapter, some of the cultural messages sewn into the cloak of masculinity can put men at risk for illness and early death. A sensible preventive health strategy for the 1990s calls upon men to critically evaluate the Superman legacy, that is, to challenge the negative aspects of traditional masculinity that endanger their health, while hanging on to the positive aspects of masculinity and men's lifestyles that heighten men's physical vitality.

The promotion of men's health also requires a sharper recognition that the sources of men's risks for many diseases do not strictly reside in men's psyches, gender identities, or the roles that they enact in daily life. Men's roles, routines, and relations with others are fixed in the historical and structural relations that constitute the larger gender order. As we have seen, not all men or male groups share the same access to social resources, educational attainment, and opportunity that, in turn, can influence their health options. Yes, men need to pursue personal change in order to enhance their health, but without changing the political, economic, and ideological structures of the gender order, the subjective gains and insights forged within individuals can easily erode and fade away. If men are going to pursue self-healing, therefore, they need to create an overall preventive strategy that at once seeks to change potentially harmful aspects of traditional masculinity and meets the health needs of lower-status men.

REFERENCES

Ackerman, M. D., & Carey, P. C. (1995). *Journal of Counseling & Clinical Psychology, 63*(6), 862–876.

American Cancer Society (1991). Cancer Facts and Figures—1991. Atlanta, GA: American Cancer Society.

American College of Physicians. (1992). The crisis in correctional health care: The impact of the national drug control strategy on correctional health services. *Annals of Internal Medicine, 117*(1), 71–77.

Belbot, B. A., & del Carmen, R. B. (1991). AIDS in prison: Legal issues. *Crime and Delinquency, 31*(1), 135–153.

Bellin, E. Y., Fletcher, D. D., & Safyer, S. M. (1993). Association of tuberculosis infection with increased time in or admission to the New York City jail system. *Journal of the American Medical Association, 269*(17), 2228–2231.

Blesch, K. (1986). Health beliefs about testicular cancer and self-examination among professional men. *Oncology Nursing Forum, 13*(1), 29–33.

Blum, R., Harman, B., Harris, L., Bergeissen, L., & Restrick, M. (1992). American Indian–Alaska native youth health. *Journal of American Medical Association, 267*(12), 1637–1644.

Brewer, T. F., & Derrickson, J. (1992). AIDS in prison: A review of epidemiology and preventive policy. *AIDS, 6*(7), 623–628.

Buckley, W. E., Yesalis, C. E., Friedl, K. E., Anderson, W. A., Steit, A. L., & Wright, J. E. (1988). Estimated prevalence of anabolic steroid use among male high school seniors. *Journal of the American Medical Association, 260*(23), 3441–3446.

Bullard, R. D., (1992). Urban infrastructure: Social, environmental, and health risks to African Americans. In B. J. Tidwell (Ed.), *The State of Black America* (pp. 183–196). New York: National Urban League.

Canetto, S. S. (1995). Men who survive a suicidal act: Successful coping or failed masculinity? In D. Sabo & D. Gordon (Eds.), *Men's health and illness* (pp. 292–304). Newbury Park, CA: Sage.

Canetto, S. S. (1992). Gender and suicide in the elderly. *Suicide and Life-Threatening Behavior, 22*(1), 80–97.

Cockerham, W. C. (1995). *Medical sociology.* Englewood Cliffs, NJ: Prentice Hall.

Connell, R. W. (1987). *Gender and power.* Stanford: Stanford University Press.

Cosper, R. (1979). Drinking as conformity: A critique of sociological literature on occupational differences in drinking. *Journal of Studies on Alcoholism, 40,* 868–891.

Cypress, B. (1981). Patients' reasons for visiting physicians: National ambulatory medical care survey, U.S. 1977–78. DHHS Publication No. (PHS) 82-1717, Series 13, No. 56. Hyattsville, MD: National Center for Health Statistics, December, 1981a.

Dawson, D. A., & Adams, P. F. (1987). Current estimates from the national health interview survey: U.S. 1986. Vital Health Statistics Series, Series 10, No. 164. DHHS

Publication No. (PHS) 87-1592, Public Health Service. Washington, DC: U.S. Government Printing Office.

Dubler, N. N., & Sidel, V. W. (1989). On research on HIV infection and AIDS in correctional institutions. *The Milbank Quarterly, 67*(1–2), 81–94.

Editor. (1991, March 16). Health care for prisoners: Implications of "Kalk's refusal." *Lancet, 337,* 647–648.

Expert Committee on AIDS and Prison. (1994). *HIV/AIDS in prisons: Summary report and recommendations to the Expert Committee on AIDS and Prisons* (Ministry of Supply and Services Canada Catalogue No. JS82-68/2-1994). Ottawa, Ontario, Canada: Correctional Service of Canada.

Feldman, H. A., Goldstein, I., Hatzichristou, D. G., Krane, R. J., & McKinlay, J. B. (1994). Impotence and its medical and psychosocial correlates: Results of the Massachusetts Male Aging Study. *Journal of Urology, 151,* 54–61.

Gibbs, J. T. (Ed.) (1988). *Young, black, and male in America: An endangered species.* Dover, MA: Auburn House.

Givens, J. (1979). Current estimates from the health interview survey: U.S. 1978. DHHS Publications No. (PHS) 80-1551, Series 10, No. 130. Hyattsville, MD: Office of Health Research Statistics, November 1979.

Greco, K. E., & Blank, B. (1993). Prostate-specific antigen: The new early detection test for prostate cancer. *Nurse Practitioner, 18*(5), 30–38.

Green, A. P. (1991). Blacks unheard. *Update* (Winter), New York State Coalition for Criminal Justice, 6–7.

Harrison, J., Chin, J., & Ficarrotto, T. (1992). Warning: Masculinity may be dangerous to your health. In M. S. Kimmel & M. A. Messner (Eds.), *Men's lives* (pp. 271–285). New York: Macmillian.

Harvard School of Public Health. Study reported by Wechsler, H., Davenport, A., Dowdall, G., Moeykens, B., & Castillo, S. (1994). Health and behavioral consequences of binge drinking in college: A national survery of students at 140 campuses. *Journal of the American Medical Association, 272*(21), 1672–1677.

Henderson, D. C., & Anderson, S. C. (1989). Adolescents and chemical dependency. *Social Work in Health Care, 14*(1), 87–105.

Hitz, D. (1973). Drunken sailors and others: Drinking problems in specific occupations. *Quarterly Journal of Studies on Alcohol, 34,* 496–505.

Hull, J. D. (1994, November 21). Running scared. *Time, 144*(2), 93–99.

Isenhart, C. E., & Silversmith, D. J. (1994). The influence of the traditional male role on alcohol abuse and the therapeutic process. *Journal of Men's Studies, 3*(2), 127–135.

Kimmel, M. S., and Levine, M. P. (1989). Men and AIDS. In M. S. Kimmel & M. A. Messner (Eds.), *Men's lives* (pp. 344–354). New York: Macmillian.

Klein, A. (1993). Little big men: Bodybuilding subculture and gender construction. Albany, NY: SUNY Press.

Krane, R. J., Goldstein, I., Saentz de Tejada, I. (1989). Impotence. *New England Journal of Medicine, 321,* 1648–1659.

Lamarine, R. (1988). Alcohol abuse among Native Americans. *Journal of Community Health, 13*(3), 143–153.

Lundberg, G. D. (1994, June 8). Let's stop boxing in the Olympics and the United States military. *Journal of the American Medical Association, 271*(22), 1990.

Manton, K. G., Blazer, D. G., & Woodbury, M. A. (1987). Suicide in middle age and later life: Sex and race specific life table and cohort analysis. *Journal of Gerontology, 42,* 219–227.

Martin, J. (1990). Male cancer awareness: Impact of an employee education program. *Oncology Nursing Forum, 17*(1), 59–64.

Mauer, M. (1992). Men in American prisons: Trends, causes, and issues. *Men's Studies Review, 9*(1), 10–12. A special issue on men in prison, edited by Don Sabo and Willie London.

May, P. (1986). Alcohol and drug misuse prevention programs for American Indians: Needs and opportunities. *Journal of Studies of Alcohol, 47*(3), 187–195.

McCord, C., & Freeman, H. P. (1990). Excess mortality in Harlem. *New England Journal of Medicine, 322*(22), 1606–1607.

Messner, M. A., & Sabo, D. (1994). *Sex, violence, and power in sports: Rethinking masculinity.* Freedom. CA: Crossing Press.

Metler, R., Conway, G. & Stehr-Green, J. (1991). AIDS surveillance among American Indians and Alaskan natives. *American Journal of Public Health, 81*(11), 1469–1471.

Miedzian, M. (1991). *Boys will be boys: Breaking the link between masculinity and violence.* New York: Doubleday.

Montagu, A. (1953). *The natural superiority of women.* New York: Macmillian.

Moore, D. (1988). Reducing alcohol and other drug use among Native American youth. *Alcohol Drug Abuse and Mental Health, 15*(6), 2–3.

Morbidity and Mortality Weekly Report. (1993a). Update: Mortality attributable to HIV infection/AIDS among persons aged 25–44 years—United States, 1990–91. *42*(25), 481–486.

Morbidity and Mortality Weekly Report. (1994a). Prevalence of overweight among adolescents—United States, 1988–91, *43*(44), 818–819.

Morbidity and Mortality Weekly Report. (1994b). AIDS among racial/ethnic minorities—United States, 1993, *43*(35), 644–651.

Morbidity and Mortality Weekly Report. (1994c). Homicides among 15–19-year-old males—United States, *43*(40), 725–728.

Morbidity and Mortality Weekly Report. (1994d). Deaths resulting from firearm- and motor-vehicle-related injuries—United States, 1968–1991. *43*(3), 37–42.

Nadelmann, P., & Wenner, L. (1994, May 5). Toward a sane national drug policy [Editorial]. *Rolling Stone,* 24–26.

National Center for Health Statistics. (1990). *Health, United States, 1989.* Hyattsville, MD: Public Health Service.

National Center for Health Statistics. (1992). Advance report of final mortality statistics, 1989. *Monthly Vital Statistics Report, 40* (Suppl. 2) (DHHS Publication No. [PHS] 92-1120).

National Institutes of Health. (1993). Consensus development panel on impotence. *Journal of the American Medical Association, 270,* 83–90.

Pleck, J., Sonenstein, F. L., & Ku, L. C. (1992). In R. Ketterlinus, & M. E. Lamb (Eds.), *Adolescent problem behaviors.* Hillsdale, NJ: Larwence Erlbaum Associates.

Polych, C., & Sabo, D. (1996). Gender politics, pain, and illness: The AIDS epidemic in North American prisons. In D. Sabo & D. Gordon (Eds.), *Men's health and illness* (pp. 139–157), Newbury Park, CA: Sage.

Postman, N., Nystrom, C., Strate, L., & Weingartner, C. (1987). *Myths, men and beer: An analysis of beer commercials on broadcast television,* 1987. Falls Church, VA: Foundation for Traffic Safety.

Prisoners with AIDS/HIV Support Action Network. (1992). *HIV/AIDS in prison systems: A comprehensive strategy* (Brief to the Minister of Correctional Services and the Minister of Health). Toronto: Prisoners with AIDS/HIV Support Action Network.

Pursch, J. A. (1976). From quonset hut to naval hospital: The story of an alcoholism rehabilitation service. *Journal of Studies on Alcohol, 37,* 1655–1666.

Reed, W. L. (1991). Trends in homicide among African Americans. *Trotter Institute Review, 5,* 11–16.

Ron, A., & Rogers, D. E. (1989). AIDS in New York City: The role of intravenous drug users. *Bulletin of the New York Academy of Medicine, 65*(7), 787–800.

Rudolf, V., & Quinn, K. (1988). The practice of TSE among college men: Effectiveness of an educational program. *Oncology Nursing Forum, 15*(1), 45–48.

Sabo, D., & Gordon, D. (1995). *Men's health and illness: Gender, power, and the body.* Newbury Park, CA: Sage.

Sabo, D. (1994). The body politics of sports injury: Culture, power, and the pain principle. A paper presented at the annual meeting of the National Athletic Trainers Association, Dallas, TX, June 6, 1994.

Sabo, D. (1993). Understanding men. In Kimball G. (Ed.), *Everything you need to know to succeed after college*, (pp. 71–93), Chico, CA: Equality Press.

Staples, R. (1995). *Health and illness among African-American males.* In D. Sabo and D. Gordon (Eds.), *Men's health and illness*, (pp. 121–138), Newbury Park, CA: Sage.

Stillion, J. (1985). *Death and the sexes: An examination of differential longevity, attitudes, behaviors, and coping skills.* New York: Hemisphere.

Stillion, J. (1995). Premature death among males: Rethinking links between masculinity and health. In D. Sabo and D. Gordon (Eds.), *Men's health and illness*, (pp. 46–67), Newbury Park, CA: Sage.

Stillion, J., White, H., McDowell, E. E., & Edwards, P. (1989). Ageism and sexism in suicide attitudes. *Death Studies, 13,* 247–261.

Sugarman, J., Soderberg, R., Gordon, J., & Rivera, F. (1993). Racial misclassifications of American Indians: Its effects on injury rates in Oregon, 1989–1990. *American Journal of Public Health, 83*(5), 681–684.

Tewksbury, R. (1995). Sexual adaptation among gay men with HIV. In D. Sabo and D. Gordon (Eds.), *Men's health and illness* (pp. 222–245), Newbury Park, CA: Sage.

Thorne-Finch, R. (1992). *Ending the silence: The origins and treatment of male violence against women.* Toronto: University or Toronto Press.

Toepell, A. R. (1992). *Prisoners and AIDS: AIDS education needs assessment.* Toronto: John Howard Society of Metropolitan Toronto.

Torres, R. A., Mani, S., Altholz, J., & Brickner, P. W. (1990). HIV infection among homeless men in a New York City shelter. *Archives of Internal Medicine, 150,* 2030–2036.

Verbrugge, L. M., & Wingard, D. L. (1987). Sex differentials in health and mortality. *Women's Health, 12,* 103–145.

Waldron, I. (1995). Contributions of changing gender differences in mortality. In D. Sabo and D. Gordon (Eds.), *Men's health and illness* (pp. 22–45), Newbury Park, CA: Sage.

Waldron, I. (1986). What do we know about sex differences in mortality? *Population Bulletin of the U.N., No. 18-1985,* 59–76.

Waldron, I. (1976). Why do women live longer than men? *Journal of Human Stress, 2,* 1–13.

Wallace, R. (1991). Traveling waves of HIV infection on a low dimensional "sociogeographic" network. *Social Science Medicine, 32*(7), 847–852.

Weinreb, L. F., & Bassuk, E. L. (1990). Substance abuse: A growing problem among homeless families. *Families and Community Health, 13*(1), 55–64.

Zilbergeld, B. (1993). *The new male sexuality.* New York: Bantam.

63

HEALTH, SOCIAL CLASS AND AFRICAN-AMERICAN WOMEN

EVELYN L. BARBEE • MARILYN LITTLE

Evelyn L. Barbee is a Black feminist nurse anthropologist who was educated at Teachers College, Columbia University and at the University of Washington. Her writings are published in anthropology and nursing journals. Her current research interests are cultural strategies used by women of color to deal with dysphoria, and violence against women of color. She is currently at the School of Nursing at Boston College.

Marilyn Little earned a Ph.D. at the University of Minnesota and is currently at the Centre for Ecology and Spirituality in Ontario, Canada. A medical geographer by specialization, her research is primarily concerned with the political ecology of malnutrition. A recent publication is "Charity versus Justice: The New World Order and the Old Problem of World Hunger," in *Eliminating Hunger in Africa* (eds. Newman and Griffith).

T he litany of health problems which plague African-American women at rates disproportionate to their percentage of the US population is familiar: hypertension, lupus, diabetes, maternal mortality, cervical cancer, etc. Of these problems, the success rate in terms of maintenance (in cases of chronic diseases) and cure (in cases of episodic illnesses) is affected by the constant circumscribing effect of being an African-American female in a white, patriarchal, racist society. This chapter asserts that being African-American and female constitutes a unique position in American society. The position of African-American women in American society is unique because the same ideology used during slavery to justify the roles of Black women underlies the external, controlling images of contemporary African-American women (Collins, 1990). As a result, the multiple jeopardies (King, 1988) and externally imposed images of African-American women interact in ways that serve to compromise their health status.

Consequently, the health needs of the African-American woman cannot be met by reformulation or "reform" of racist health policies or sexist health policies; rather her needs will only be addressed by looking at the point where the two sets of policies converge and form a barrier to her mental, emotional and physical well-being. Although we agree with King's (1988) conclusion that scholarly descriptions that concentrate on our multiple oppressions "have confounded our ability to discover and appreciate the ways in which African-American women are not victims," one area that has not been adequately explored, an area in which African-American women currently and historically have been victimized, is the "health care" arena.

In 1988 an estimated 30.3 million African-Americans represented more than 12 percent of the population (US Bureau of the Census, 1989a). More than 52 percent of these 30.3 million people were female. Within the African-American population the ratio of women to men is 110 to 100. The respective Euro-American sex ratio is 104 females for every 100 males. Although African-American males outnumber females up until the age of 20 years, after the age of 20 years the number of African-American women to men increases to the extent that the ratio at ages 65 years and over is 149:100 (US Bureau of the Census, 1989a).

In terms of family structure, 51 percent of African-American families were married couples; 43 percent were female householders, no husband present; and 6 percent were male householders, no wife present (US Bureau of the Census, 1989b). The respective median incomes for these households were: $27,182, $9,710 and $17,455. Among families that included children under 18 years of age, those households headed by women were four times more likely to be poor than those of two-parent families (US Bureau of the Census, 1988).

The Position of African-American Women

Contemporary efforts to explain the position of African-American women in the USA were built upon the notion of "double jeopardy" (Beale, 1970). Beale's idea recognized that African-American women faced double discrimination because of their race and sex. Lewis's (1977) exploration of the structural position of African-American women was premised on "double jeopardy." "While inequality is *manifested* in the exclusion of a group from public life, it is actually *generated* in the group's unequal access to power and resources in a hierarchically arranged social order" (Lewis, 1977:343). Because African-American women have membership in two subordinate groups, African-American and women, they lack access to authority and resources in society and are in structural opposition with the dominant racial/ethnic group (Euro-American) and the dominant sexual group (male) (Lewis, 1977).

In her critique of the concepts of double jeopardy and triple jeopardy (racism, sexism and classism), King (1988) noted that because each conceptualization presumes direct independent effect on status, neither was able to deal with the interactive effects of sexism, racism and classism. African-American women are subjected to several, simultaneous oppressions which involve multiplicative relationships. The importance of any one factor in explaining African-American women's circumstances varies and is dependent upon the particular aspect of life under consideration and the reference group to whom African-American women are being compared (King, 1988). In regard to health, the multifaceted influences of race, gender and often social class interact in ways that render African-American women less healthy and more vulnerable to sickness than Euro-American women. Furthermore, they have to contend with their illness at the same time that they seek care from the racist, sexist and class-based system of American medicine.

While African-American women may be invisible in many spheres of life (hooks, 1981), their visibility vis-à-vis the medical establishment appears to be dependent upon procedures that need to be practiced (e.g., hysterectomies) and drugs that need to be tested (e.g., birth control). Elsewhere Barbee (1992) argued that the externally produced images of African-American women profoundly influence how medical and social professionals treat African-American women when these women are victims of violence. Here it is argued that these same images influence the kind of medical care or treatment given or not given to African-American women.

Images of African-American Women

Because of the interactions among racism, sexism and often classism, African-American women occupy a structural position in which they are viewed as subordinate to all other women and men in this society. Beliefs, myths and stereotypes about African-American women have served to intensify their status as "other." This view of the African-American woman as an object encourages the deployment of externally applied images and makes it particularly difficult to be viewed as a person, let alone an individual, by medical practitioners. As Christensen (1988: 191) noted: "No other woman has suffered physical and mental abuse, degradation, and exploitation on North American shores comparable to that experienced by the Black female."

In pointing out that race, class and gender oppression depend on powerful ideological justification for their existence, Collins (1990) identifies four externally defined, socially constructed, controlling images that are applied to African-American women. These images are mammy, the faithful, obedient domestic servant; the matriarch; the welfare mother, and the Jezebel. The prevailing images of mammy, matriarch, welfare mother, and Jezebel provide the ideological justification for racial oppression, gender subordination and economic exploitation (Collins, 1990). Each of these images contributes to society's and consequently medicine's view of African-American women.

The mammy image, the faithful, obedient servant, was created to justify the economic exploitation of Black women during slavery. As a social construction, its persistence is due to a need to rationalize the long-standing restriction of Black women to domestic service (Collins, 1990). In general, medical workers are not receptive to questions from clients and patients. Those who subscribe to the mammy image are even less receptive to questions from African-American women. An additional danger is that those African-American women who internalize the mammy image may consciously and unconsciously sustain gender and racial exploitation in a number of ways. One of the more dangerous consequences may be a tendency to agree voluntarily to medical procedures because they believe in obeying the doctor.

Matriarchs are considered to be overly aggressive, emasculating, strong, independent, unfeminine women. The matriarch image implies the actuality of a social order in which women exercise social and political power. This image is central to the interlocking systems of race, class and gender oppression. The matriarch image allows the dominant group to blame African-American women for the success or failure of their children (Collins, 1990). An additional effect of this image is that it allows "helping" professionals to ignore African-American women when they need assistance. It is difficult to acknowledge that an African-American woman needs medical assistance when she is constantly referred to as being "strong."

Equally damaging is the welfare mother image. This is essentially an updated version of the breeder image that was created during slavery (Collins, 1990). Welfare mothers are viewed as being too lazy to work and thus are content to sit around and collect their welfare checks. This current objectification of African-American women as welfare mothers serves to label their fertility as unnecessary and dangerous. The welfare mother image provides Euro-Americans (and some African-Americans who have embraced these images without understanding their underlying ideology) with ideological justification for restricting the fertility of some African-American women because they are producing too many economically non-productive children (Davis, 1983).

The Jezebel image is one of a whore or a sexually aggressive woman (Collins, 1990). As Collins (1990) notes, the whore image is a central link in the Euro-American elite male's images of African-American women because attempts to control African-American women's sexuality lie at the heart of African-American women's oppression. Historically, the sexually promiscuous stereotype was used to contrast African-American women with the "virtuous" Euro-American woman. It also provided the rationale that justified the sexual assaults on Black women by Euro-American men (Collins, 1990; hooks, 1981). In contemporary times the Jezebel image is used as reason both for the sexual denigration of African-American women and for ignoring or minimizing such sexual abuse. The repercussions of these images on African-American women are most clearly seen in health statistics. While these "facts" are in and of themselves tragic enough, the real tragedy lies in how they have been used in an attempt to undermine the self-esteem of African-American women.

Health Statistics and the Right to Privacy

One of the first things a poor person loses is the right to privacy. She must surrender information about her private life in exchange for a modicum of basic needs which the state grudgingly provides. The fact that the information extracted often goes beyond what is required for service is of little use to her. She is powerless and in need. *They* have the ability to determine her ineligible and consequently to affect her physical survival.

The vulnerability of the poor is ruthlessly exploited in the name of science. Countless graduate students in the health sciences have benefited from this vulnerability. Innumerable theses and dissertations have been written based on data collected from the poor. The informants were usually corralled at points of defenselessness: while waiting for WIC tickets (a nutritional supplement program for poor women and children), for emergency medical care, etc. Many of these women probably had no idea that it was unnecessary to submit to the questions. Some may have been given an option but believed compliance would improve their future service.

The data collected are never returned to the informants in a way that is useful. The original reports are written for the intellectual elite. The final dissemination of the data is through the mass media and only then if the results are newsworthy (i.e., sensational). Results are deemed newsworthy when they support the prevailing myths of our system. The master myth relevant to health is the inherent (i.e., genetic) instability of African-Americans' minds, bodies and "culture."

The right to privacy is predicated by income and mediated by race. The vast numbers of poor whites have not been an issue of interest for the intellectual elite. There has been historically a conscious choice to analyze health data by race, not by income. The impact of this decision is manifested by our present inability to relieve the health problems of many Americans as we remain the only industrialized society outside of South Africa not to have a national health insurance plan. It is unquestionable that the same obstacles as in South Africa exist in the USA: the unwillingness to provide adequate health care to all regardless of color or income.

Public health statistics support the resistance to a national health insurance as they imply an inequity in health problems. When they suggest that only certain segments of the population suffer from certain diseases, and then are used to promote interventions for another segment of the population, health statistics are used as instruments of oppression. For example, although health statistics clearly indicate that coronary heart disease (CHD) is and has been a very serious problem for African-American women, public intervention programs imply that it is primarily a problem for Euro-American males. African-American women's death rate from CHD exceeds that of Euro-American women (Myers, 1986). Although there are different types of heart disease, the different types share common risk factors. For African-American women these risk factors include cigarette smoking, hypertension, obesity and diabetes. The social and structural risk factors include higher life stresses (Harburg *et al.*, 1973), truncated medical care access and lower-quality care (Yellin *et al.*, 1983).

A comparison of other CHD impact variables attributable to smoking (deaths, related lost years of life, cases, related hospital days, related days of restricted activity and related medical expenditures) between African-American and Euro-American women concluded that there were no "racial" differences (Kumanyika and Savage, 1986: 243). However, these comparisons did not take into account the fact that a large number of African-American women are heads of households and often responsible for young children. The sociocultural impact of CHD on African-American women is much greater for them and their families than it is for Euro-American women.

The prevalence of hypertension in African-American women increases with age and is 1.7 to 3 times higher in African-American women than Euro-American women in every age group (Kumanyika and Savage, 1986). In addition to being a risk factor for heart disease and heart failure, hypertension leads to pathological changes which can cause kidney disease or stroke. Demographically the highest levels of blood pressure for African-American women are in the South and the West. A major structural risk factor for hypertension is stress. Urban women's blood pressures are lower than those of rural women (Kumanyika and Savage, 1986). The aetiology for these demographic differences is unknown. Hypertension is often associated with another health problem of African-American women, obesity.

Obesity, an excess of body fat, can range from mild (120 percent) to severe (more than 200 percent) of the desirable or ideal body weight (Moore, 1990). Overweight, a weight in excess of the desirable body weight (Moore, 1990), is often confused with obesity. Because the prevalence of overweight in African-American women is higher than that of comparable groups of Euro-American women (Gillum, 1987), fat is a feminist issue that affects large numbers of African-American women.

Research-identified variables that make it more difficult for African-American women to lose weight are: (1) education below college level, (2) marriage and (3) low family income (Kahn *et al.*, 1991). Narratives from African-American women reveal entirely different factors:

> I work for General Electric making batteries, and from the stuff
> they suit me up in, I know it's killing me. My home life is not
> working. My old man is an alcoholic. My kids got babies. Things
> are not well with me. And the one thing I know I can do when I
> come home is to cook me a pot of food and sit down in front of the
> TV and eat it. And you can't take that away from me until you're
> ready to give me something in its place. (Avery, 1990: 7)

What confounds the issue in regard to weight and African-American women are Eurocentric notions about attractiveness, biomedical determinations about health and African-American cultural ideas about beauty. Many of the negative traits associated with obesity, lack of control, unattractiveness and slovenliness, have long been associated with African-Americans as a "race." On the one hand, Eurocentric ideas about obesity tend to equate fat with unattractiveness. Consequently, those African-American women who subscribe to Euro-American standards of beauty are placed in a double bind in which one culturally evaluated trait (obesity) reinforces this society's negative view of their physical appearance. On the other hand, in African-American communities, a certain level of obesity is considered attractive. Historically, African-Americans have associated degrees of overweight with well-being. To be thin was to be "poor." The African-American community's preference for "healthy" women has resulted in much lower rates of anorexia and bulimia for African-American women. However, the close relationship between adult onset diabetes and obesity requires that African-American women closely monitor their weight.

Diabetes is a disease that has particularly severe consequences for African-American women. Data from the 1981 National Health Interviews demonstrated that African-American women's diabetes rate was 38.2 per 1,000. One of the ten leading causes of death in 1988 was diabetes mellitus, and African-American women's death rate from this was 27.3 versus 17.6 for Euro-American women (National Center for Health Statistics, 1990). An additional problem for African-American women is that the associations among obesity, diabetes and hypertension increase the risk for heart disease.

Comparison health statistics between African-American and Euro-American women that illustrate less, little or no difference in incidence between them for a specific disease sometimes serve to mask the enormity of certain problems for African-American women. Breast cancer statistics are a case in point. For years the focus on the lower incidence of breast cancer in African-American versus Euro-American women effectively served to mask the fact that African-American women have a higher death rate from breast cancer than Euro-American women. Although the breast cancer rate for African-American women is less than that for Euro-American women, their mortality rate for this disease exceeds that of any other group of women (National Center for Health Statistics, 1990). Some of the reasons given for this disparity in mortality rates are socioeconomic status (SES), later stage at diagnosis and delay in detection and treatment, treatment differences, and biological/constitutional factors (Report of the Secretary's Task Force, 1986). Since biological/constitutional factors are neither defined nor discussed in the report, they can be dismissed as factors. SES, later stage at diagnosis and delay in treatment are related to problems of access. Poverty is a major factor in both later diagnosis and delay in treatment. The poor have not benefited from the various advances in cancer prevention, detection and treatment (American Cancer Society, 1990). However, poverty is not the only factor. McWhorter and Mayer (1987) found that when age, stage of cancer and histology were adjusted, African-American women received less aggressive surgical treatment, were less likely to be treated surgically and were more likely to be treated nonsurgically than Euro-American women.

Human Immunodeficiency Virus (HIV)/Autoimmunodeficiency Disease (AIDS)

AIDS is a national problem that is wreaking devastation in the African-American community. It is one of the ten leading causes of death for the African-American population (National Center for Health Statistics, 1990). African-Americans accounted for 25 percent of the AIDS deaths in 1988 (National Center for Health Statistics, 1990). HIV affects African-American women in a number of ways. First, African-American women and their children are part of the fastest-growing population of AIDS victims. Second, if diagnosed with AIDS, in addition to being concerned about herself, the woman has to be concerned with the effect of her death on her children. Third, the case definition of AIDS is based upon a male profile. As a result the profile does not take into account gynecological manifestations of HIV. As Anastos and Marte note: "If women's disease manifests with the same infections as it does in men, it may be recognized and reported as AIDS; if the infections, still HIV related, are different, the women are not considered to have AIDS" (1989: 6). Since eligibility for Supplemental Security Income (SSI) is based upon a diagnosis of AIDS, many women with AIDS are deemed ineligible for SSI benefits. Fourth, if a woman is pregnant and HIV positive, she is concerned with transmitting the disease to her newborn. Fifth, if she is diagnosed as HIV positive, her chances of contracting AIDS are higher and she will die sooner than her Euro-American sister. This disparity is usually accounted for by the mode of transmission. Many African-American women are exposed to HIV through intravenous drug use. As a result, the virus reaches their bloodstream much faster than it does when the virus is transmitted through sexual contact. Sixth, if someone in a woman's family, i.e., her child or partner, contracts the disease, in all likelihood she will be responsible for taking care of them.

Mental Health

In 1979, African-American women reported a lower level of well-being than African-American males, white females and white males (Institute for Urban Affairs and Research, 1981). One third of the women surveyed reported a level of distress comparable with that of an independent sample of mental health patients (Institute for Urban Affairs and Research, 1981). Although the research on depression in African-American women reports high rates of depressive symptomatology and depression (Carrington, 1980; Dressler, 1987; Dressler and Badger, 1985; Gary *et al.*, 1985), African-American women are less likely to be medically diagnosed as depressive than Euro-American females (Smith, 1981).

Among African-Americans the highest rates of depression occur in women under 45 years of age; the lowest rates are in African-Americans aged 45 years and older. At all ages and income levels, women's depressive symptomatology is greater than men's (Gary *et al.*, 1985). Factors that increase the risk of depression in younger African-American women are: being poor, being between 18 and 45 years of age, being unemployed, high school education or less, the presence of minor children in the household, and being divorced or separated (Brown, 1990).

There is some evidence that suggests that support networks as traditionally viewed are not as useful to African-American women when they are depressed. In an examination of the relationships among economic stressors, extended kin support, active coping and depressive symptoms in a sample of 285 African-American households in a southern community, Dressler (1987) found a positive relationship between extended kin support and depressive symptoms. Women who reported higher active coping strategies reported fewer depressive symptoms. In addition to the previously discussed medical conditions two other conditions that disproportionally affect the health of African-American women are reproductive rights and violence.

Reproductive Rights versus Reproductive Freedom

We take issue with the notion of reproductive rights, particularly as it concerns African-American women. The national debate on reproductive rights is one that almost totally eclipses the interest and needs of African-American women. The debate, from its intellectual framework to its proposed goals, does not address the serious health problems of marginalized groups. The philosophical boundaries of the debate are seriously compromised. To talk in terms of "reproductive rights" is an intellectual abdication to a legal system primarily concerned with property rights, *not* human rights. The phrase is an oxymoron. Human reproduction is not a right; it is a biological possibility. The two major opponents in the debate have chosen or accepted the media terms of "pro choice" and "right to life." The right to life seems to presume the "right" begins with conception, is most vibrant during gestation and ends at birth. The success of neither of the two will significantly improve the plight of Black females who have historically suffered disproportionally from the institutionalized attack on the Black family and "Third World" rates of infant mortality.

Tervalon (1988) notes that there are three interconnected aspects of reproductive rights: access to abortion, infant mortality and forced sterilization. Rather than talking about reproductive rights, it would be more accurate to speak of reproductive freedom. Reproductive freedom is defined here as unrestrained access to the medical knowledge (information) available in one's society that is necessary for the optimum maintenance of one's reproductive health. In addition to the aspects referred to by Tervalon, reproductive freedom would include safe, effective, affordable forms of birth control, family planning, sexual education, freedom from forced sterilization

(Ditzion and Golden, 1984), the right of consenting adults to conduct their sex lives as they choose, reduction in African-American infant and maternal mortality rates, and affordable access to diagnosis and treatment of sexually transmitted diseases (STDs).

The lack of reproductive freedom has resulted in disastrous consequences for African-American women. These consequences include being three times more likely than Euro-American women to die of causes associated with pregnancy, childbirth and the puerperium (the period during and immediately after childbirth), an infant mortality rate of 17.6 (National Center for Health Statistics, 1990) and sterilization. Sterilization of African-American women encompasses a broad range of issues: (1) the right of African-American women to give informed consent to surgical procedures; (2) the racism that underlies the actions of physicians and surgeons who treat African-American women; and (3) the need for African-American women to be informed about a broad range of gynecological problems which may lead to hysterectomies or other sterilizing procedures (Black Women's Community Development Foundation, 1974). Data on sterilization in the USA demonstrate that a higher percentage of African-American women are sterilized and that the rate of sterilization of African-American women is increasing (Mosher and Pratt, 1990). The respective figures for African-American and Euro-American women's sterilization in 1982 and 1988 were 38.1 percent versus 26.1 percent and 30 percent versus 22.1 percent (Mosher and Pratt, 1990).

This high rate of sterilization underscores African-American women's lack of basic human rights. It sends a clear message about the links between African-American women's sexuality, fertility and roles within the political economy (Collins, 1990). Under slavery Black women were reproducers of human capital; slave women who reproduced often were rewarded (Giddings, 1984). Over time, changes in the political economy have transformed African-American women's fertility from a necessity for an economy in need of cheap labor to a costly threat to political and economic stability (Collins, 1990). As a result, the fertility of African-American women, particularly those who carry the image of welfare mothers, must be controlled. Additional issues of sterilization include: the relationship of African-American women to the pro- and anti-abortion movements, the role that African-American women should play in policy-making around these issues, the genocide issue, and the effort of African-American women to balance their right not to have unwanted children with their fears of genocidal national and international policies (Black Women's Community Development Foundation, 1974).

The year 1990 was to have been the target date for the completion of the "second public health revolution" (US Department of Health, Education and Welfare, 1979: vii). Goals were set to improve the health conditions of all ages of the US populace. A primary goal was to reduce the national infant mortality rate to 9 deaths per 1,000 live births. The ability of the USA as a nation to execute a second revolution was in doubt from the beginning. Joseph A. Califano in the foreword of the report which listed the goals wrote: "What is in doubt is whether we have the personal discipline and political will to solve these problems" (US Department of Health, Education and Welfare, 1979: viii). Some communities in the USA have reached the goal of "9 by 90." Other communities, poor, marginalized and dark in hue, have infant mortality rates exceeding 30 per 1,000. When the debate over reproductive rights is over, the debate that begins at the birth of each African-American child will still rage: can s/he survive? Will this child be allowed to thrive?

Violence

Although violence in African-American communities is disproportional in its effects upon women, the continued focus has been on the African-American male homicide rate. This exclusive focus on males serves to mask the violence to which African-American women are constantly exposed. For African-American women crime statistics are also health statistics. Homicide is one of the ten leading causes of death for African-American women. The reported rape rate for African-American women is almost three times that of Euro-American women (US Department of Justice, 1991). Once raped, African-American women have a harder time getting police and medical professionals to believe them.

In popular African-American magazines rape, a crime of violence usually perpetrated against women, is explained by African-American male authorities as being caused by male frustration. Although one would like to believe that African-American male physicians might bring more sensitivity and awareness to the problems of African-American women, often male physicians are unwilling or unable to recognize either their own sexism or their own inability to understand that sexual violence transcends race. Thus in an article about rape in *Ebony* magazine, Alvin Poussaint, an African-American male psychiatrist, concluded that the high rate of rape of African-American women was due to the "feelings of rejection" of African-American males and to their need to bolster their self-esteem (Norment, 1991: 96).

Poussaint's apologist stance comes dangerously close to the rationale used historically by Euro-American males to justify their sexual abuse of African-American women. He joins the long line of African-American males who do not believe that Black males should be held responsible for their violence against African-American women (Lorde, 1990). Most rapes are planned (Amir, 1971), which suggests premeditation and hence responsibility. African-American male psychiatrists are not the only ones to beg the issue on the subject of rape in African-American communities. Ironically, Davis (1983) in an entire chapter on rape, in a book about women, while appropriately criticizing Euro-American women's treatises about the African-American male rapist, ignores the high rape rate of African-American women in African-American communities.

In addition to the high rape rate, there is also a high prevalence of sexual abuse. According to the empirical literature, African-American women are more frequently victims of sexual abuse than Euro-American women (Katz and Mazur, 1979). Furthermore, African-American women are at risk of rape and child sexual abuse across all age groups (Amir, 1971; Peters, 1976; Kercher and McShane, 1984). Wyatt (1985) found that African-American pre-teens were most likely to experience abuse in their homes from male nuclear or extended family members. African-American women reported more incidence of sexual abuse involving stepfathers, mothers' boyfriends, foster fathers, male cousins and other relatives than did Euro-American women (Wyatt, 1985).

Although battering is a strong concern of African-American women, Coley and Beckett (1988) in a twenty-year (1967–87) review of the empirical literature in counseling, psychology, social work and sociology, found only two sources on battering and African-American women. In addition to being physically battered, African-American women are also psychologically battered through music. The lyrics in some rap songs or hip hop music are especially violent toward and degrading of women. In an interesting combination of blaming the victim, transforming violence to sexism and holding women accountable for male behavior, a hip hop expert writes:

> As I once told a sister, hip hop lyrics are, among other things, what
> a lot of Black men say about Black women when Black women
> aren't around. In this sense the music is no more or less sexist than
> your fathers, brothers, husbands, friends and lovers and in many
> cases more upfront. As an unerringly precise reflection of the
> community, hip hop's sexist thinking will change when the
> community changes. Because women are the ones best able to
> define sexism, they will have to challenge the music—tell it how to
> change and make it change—if change is to come. (Allen, 1989: 117)

If males are creating and perpetuating violent, sexist lyrics, why is it women's responsibility to change them? Another question is why would African-American women take part in such music? African-American women who participate in and create women-abusing rap lyrics, have essentially embraced the external controlling images and are participating in their own oppression.

Hospitals Are Dangerous

In addition to having to deal with the danger in the communities, African-American women are exposed to added dangers when they seek medical care. The vulnerability of African-American women is only too apparent. Dr. Norma Goodwin (1990: 12) in her analysis of why African-Americans die six to seven years earlier than their white counterparts listed two factors central to the dilemma of black females: "the lack of culturally sensitive health information" and "decreased access to high quality care." These factors are excruciatingly sensitive to the economic status of the individual. The African-American woman all too often finds herself on Medicaid (health insurance for the poor), not Medicare (health insurance for the elderly). The reluctance of private physicians to accept Medicaid is not even apologetic. Even so, those individuals are better off than the estimated 35 million Americans without any form of health insurance (Edelman, 1987).

The absence of a national health insurance means that many African-American women receive their basic health care from public health clinics and county hospitals. The other historical source of health care is the university research hospital. Most of the major university hospitals in the country are located in economically distressed areas. For centuries marginalized groups have served the medical establishment as disease models, guinea pigs and cadavers. The ever-present vulnerability of African-American women was brought back to our memories with the exposé of medical research at Cook County Hospital in Chicago in 1988.

More than 200 pregnant women were given a drug, Dilantin, without their knowledge. Fortunately, to date, the drug, used normally to treat epilepsy, has not caused damage to the resulting offspring or their mothers. The fact that such blatant abuses of human rights can occur in a publicly monitored setting only indicates the probability of what is occurring in private practices. According to the Public Citizen Health Research Group, the trend is for clinical trials to be conducted in doctors' offices (1990b: 1). That African-American women will continue to be guinea pigs sacrificed to the US medical establishment is a foregone conclusion. In 1989, the Food and Drug Administration found that there were irregularities in the informed consent forms in 75 percent of the investigations of drug trials conducted in doctors' offices, outpatient clinics and hospitals (Public Citizen Health Research Group, 1990b: 1). Those same factors elucidated by Goodwin suggest who is most likely to participate in experimental drug trials.

Summary

Lewis suggested in 1977 that the structural position of African-American women would cause them to become more responsive to feminist issues. One area in which Lewis's prophecy has materialized is in the area of African-American women's health. One of the first conferences exclusively devoted to African-American women's health was sponsored by the Black Women's Community Development Foundation. As B. Smith pointed out: "The health of Black women is a subject of major importance for those of us who are committed to learning, teaching, and writing about our sisters" (1982: 103).

Although there is a greater awareness of African-American women's health problems, the massive budget cuts for social and health programs under the Reagan-Bush administrations have only served to undermine the progress of and place pressure on local African-American women's health initiatives. At the state level, redefinition of the eligibility requirements for Medicaid have reduced or eliminated medical coverage for large numbers of African-American women and their children. At a time when we should be concentrating on thriving, we are still concerned with survival. However, as Collins (1990: 92) noted: "Resisting by doing something that 'is not expected' could not have occurred without Black women's long-standing rejection of mammies, matriarchs, and other controlling images." The development of the National Black Women's Health Project and the organization of the First National Conference on Black Women's Health exemplifies doing the "unexpected." The Black Women's Health Project's first conference on Black women's health received an overwhelming response. In addition the Black Women's Health Project has developed regional networks that provide an environment that encourages African-American women to define and respond to their own health problems.

At the First National Conference on Black Women's Health Issues, Christmas, an African-American woman physician, made the following points about African-American women's health: (1) we must not accept the blame for our condition; (2) we must be responsible for ourselves and at the same time hold the medical community and community agencies accountable, and (3) we must demand affordable, accessible, responsive facilities and medical providers (Butler, 1984). The life we want is one in which basic health care is assured. African-American women need and have a right to health. The state must try to provide safe living and workplace conditions, a safe environment, primary health care and adequate nutrition throughout life to its citizens. These rights which the state could guarantee are not on the table for debate.

REFERENCES

Allen, H. (1989) "Rap Is Our Music!" *Essence* 20 (12): 78–80, 114, 117, 119.

American Cancer Society (1990) *Cancer and the Poor: A Report to the Nation,* Atlanta, GA: American Cancer Society.

Amir, M. (1971) *Patterns of Forcible Rape,* Chicago: University of Chicago Press.

Anastos, K. and Marte, K. (1989) "Women—The Missing Persons in the AIDS Epidemic," *Health/PAC Bulletin* 19 (4): 6–11.

Avery, B. Y. (1990) "Breathing Life into Ourselves: The Evolution of the Black Women's Health Project," in E. White (ed.) *The Black Women's Health Book: Speaking for Ourselves,* Seattle: Seal Press: 4–10.

Barbee, E. L. (1992) "Ethnicity and Woman Abuse in the United States," in C. Sampselle (ed.) *Violence Against Women: Nursing Research, Practice and Education Issues,* Washington, DC: Hemisphere: 153–66.

Beale, F. (1970) "Double Jeopardy: To Be Black and Female," in T. Cade (ed.) *The Black Female,* New York: New American Library: 90–100.

Black Women's Community Development Foundation (1974) *Miniconsultation on the Mental and Physical Health Problem of Black Women,* Washington, DC: Black Women's Community Development Foundation.

Brown, D. R. (1990) "Depression Among Blacks," in D. S. Ruiz (ed.) *Handbook of Mental Health and Mental Disorder Among Black Americans,* New York: Greenwood Press: 71–93.

Butler, E. (1984) "The First National Conference on Black Women's Health Issues," in N. Worcester and M. H. Whatley (eds.) *Women's Health: Readings in Social, Economic & Political Issues,* Dubuque, IA: Kendall/Hunt: 37–42.

Carrington, C. H. (1980) "Depression in Black Women: A Theoretical Appraisal," in L. F. Rodgers-Rose (ed.) *The Black Woman,* Beverly Hills, CA: Sage: 265–71.

Christensen, C. P. (1988) "Issues in Sex Therapy with Ethnic and Racial Minority Women," *Women & Therapy* 7: 187–205.

Coley, S. M. and Beckett, J. O. (1988) "Black Battered Women: A Review of the Literature," *Journal of Counseling and Development* 66: 266–70.

Collins, P. H. (1990) *Black Feminist Thought: Knowledge, Consciousness, and the Politics of Empowerment,* Boston, Mass.: Unwin Hyman.

Davis, A. Y. (1983) *Women, Race and Class,* New York: Vintage Books.

Ditzion, J. and Golden, J. (1984) "Introduction," in Boston Women's Health Book Collective, *The New Our Bodies Ourselves,* New York: Simon & Schuster: 201–2.

Dressler, W. W. (1987) "The Stress Process in a Southern Black Community: Implications for Prevention Research," *Human Organization* 46: 211–20.

Dressler, W. W. and Badger, L. W. (1985) "Epidemiology of Depressive Symptoms in Black Communities," *Journal of Nervous and Mental Disease* 173: 212–20.

Edelman, M. W. (1987) *Families in Peril,* Cambridge, Mass.: Harvard University Press.

Gary, L. E., Brown, D. R., Milburn, N. G., Thomas, V. G. and Lockley, D. S. (1985) *Pathways: A Study of Black Informal Support Networks,* Washington, DC: Institute for Urban Affairs and Research, Howard University.

Giddings, P. (1984) *When and Where I Enter . . . : The Impact of Black Women on Race and Sex in America,* Toronto: Bantam Books.

Gillum, R. F. (1987) "Overweight and Obesity in Black Women: A Review of Published Data from the National Center for Health Statistics," *Journal of the National Medical Association* 79: 865–71.

Goodwin, N. J. (1990) "Health and the African-American Community," *Crisis* 97 (8): 12 and 50.

Harburg, E., Erfurt, J. C., Chape, L. S., Hauestein, L. S., Schull, W. J. and Schork, M. A. (1973) "Socioecological Stress Areas and Black-White Blood Pressure: Detroit," *Journal of Chronic Diseases* 26: 595–611.

hooks, bell (1981) *Ain't I a Woman: Black Women and Feminism;* Boston, Mass.: South End Press.

Institute for Urban Affairs and Research. (1981) *Statistical Profile of the Black Female,* Washington, DC: Howard University 7 (1): 1–4.

Kahn, H. S., Williamson, D. F. and Stevens, J. A. (1991) "Race and Weight Change in US Women: The Roles of Socioeconomic and Marital Status," *American Journal of Public Health* 81: 319–23.

Katz, S. and Mazur, M. (1979) *Understanding the Rape Victim: A Synthesis of Research Findings,* New York: Wiley.

Kercher, G. and McShane, M. (1984) "The Prevalence of Child Sexual Abuse Victimization in an Adult Sample of Texas Residents," *Child Abuse and Neglect* 8: 495–502.

King, D. K. (1988) "Multiple Jeopardy, Multiple Consciousness: The Context of a Black Feminist Ideology," *Signs: Journal of Women in Culture and Society* 14 (1) (August): 42–72.

Kumanyika, S. and Savage, D. D. (1986) "Ischemic Heart Disease Risk Factors in Black Americans," in Report of the Secretary's Task Force on Black & Minority Health, Vol. IV, *Cardiovascular and Cerebrovascular Disease, Part 2,* US Department of Health and Human Services, Washington, DC: US Government Printing Office: 229–90.

Lewis, D. (1977) "A Response to Inequality: Black Women, Racism and Sexism," *Signs: Journal of Women in Culture and Society* 3: 339–405.

Lorde, A. (1990) *Need: a Chorale for Black Woman Voices,* Latham, NY: Kitchen Table Press.

McWhorter, W. P. and Mayer, W. J. (1987) "Black/White Differences in Type of Initial Breast Cancer Treatment and Implications for Survival," *American Journal of Public Health* 77: 1515–17.

Moore, M. C. (1990) "Nutritional Alterations," in P. G. Beare and J. L. Myers (eds.) *Principles and Practices of Adult Health Nursing,* St. Louis, MO: Mosby: 343–84.

Mosher, W. D. and Pratt, W. F. (1990) *Contraceptive Use in the United States, 1973–88, Advance data from vital and health statistics;* no. 182, Hyattsville, MD: National Center for Health Statistics.

Myers, H. F. (1986) "Coronary Heart Disease in Black Populations: Current Research, Treatment and Prevention Needs," in Report of the Secretary's Task Force on Black & Minority Health, Vol. IV, *Cardiovascular and Cerebrovascular Disease, Part 2,* US Department of Health and Human Services, Washington, DC: US Government Printing Office: 303–44.

National Center for Health Statistics (1990) *Advance Report of Final Mortality Statistics, 1988,* Monthly Vital Statistics report; Vol. 39, no. 7, supplement, Hyattsville, MD: Public Health Service.

Norment, L. (1991) "What's Behind the Dramatic Rise in Rapes?" *Ebony* 46 (11) (September): 92, 94, 96–8.

Peters, J. J. (1976) "Children Who Are Victims of Sexual Assault and the Psychology of Offenders," *American Journal of Psychotherapy* 30: 393–421.

Public Citizen Health Research Group (1990a) *Health Letter* 6 (8).

——— (1990b) *Health Letter* 6 (11).

Report of the Secretary's Task Force on Black & Minority Health (1986) Vol. III, *Cancer* US Department of Health and Human Services, Washington, DC: US Government Printing Office.

Smith, B. (1982) "Black Women's Health: Notes for a Course," in G. T. Hull, P. Bell-Scott and B. Smith (eds.) *All the Women Are White, All the Blacks Are Men, But Some of Us Are Brave,* Old Westbury, NY: Feminist Press: 103–14.

Smith, E. J. (1981) "Mental Health and Service Delivery Systems for Black Women," *Journal of Black Studies* 17: 126–41.

Tervalon, M. (1988) "Black Women's Reproductive Rights," in N. Worcester and M. H. Whatley (eds.) *Women's Health: Readings in Social, Economic & Political Issues,* Dubuque, IA: Kendall/Hunt: 136–7.

US Bureau of the Census Current Population Reports (1988) series P-60, no. 161, *Money, Income and Poverty Status in the United States: 1987,* Washington, DC: US Government Printing Office: August.

US Bureau of the Census Current Population Reports (1989a) series P-25, no. 1018, *Projection of the Population of the United States by Age, Sex and Race: 1988 to 2080,* Washington, DC: US Government Printing Office: January.

US Bureau of the Census Current Population Reports (1989b) series P-20, no. 433, *Marital Status and Living Arrangements: March, 1988,* Washington, DC: US Government Printing Office: January.

US Department of Health, Education and Welfare (1979) *Healthy People,* Washington, DC: US Government Printing Office.

US Department of Justice, Office of Justice Programs, Bureau of Justice Statistics (1991) *Criminal Victimization in the United States: 1973–88 Trends,* Washington, DC: US Government Printing Office: July.

Wyatt, G. E. (1985) "The Sexual Abuse of Afro-American and White Women in Childhood," *Child Abuse and Neglect* 9: 507–19.

Yellin, E. H., Kramer, I. S. and Epstein, W. V. (1983) "Is Health Care Use Equivalent Across Social Groups? A Diagnosis-Based Study," *American Journal of Public Health* 73: 563–71.

64

REPRODUCTIVE ISSUES ARE ESSENTIAL SURVIVAL ISSUES FOR THE ASIAN-AMERICAN COMMUNITIES

CONNIE S. CHAN

Connie S. Chan was born in Hong Kong, grew up in Hawaii, and now lives in Boston, Massachusetts. Bilingual and bicultural in her upbringing, she has experienced the world from a multicultural perspective. She is Professor of Human Services at the University of Massachusetts Boston. Her research and publications focus on the intersection of gender, culture, and sexuality issues in Asian American women. She continues to work within Asian American communities to provide access to culturally appropriate health services.

When the Asian-American communities in the United States list their priorities for political action and organizing, several issues concerning basic survival are usually included: access to bilingual education, housing, health care, and child care, among others. Yet the essential survival issue of access to reproductive counseling, education, and abortions is frequently missing from the agenda of Asian-American community organizations. Why is the reproductive issue perceived as unimportant to the Asian-American communities? I think there are several reasons—ignorance, classism, sexism, and language barriers. Of course, these issues are interrelated, and I'll try to make the connections between them.

First, let me state that I am not an "expert" on the topic of reproductive issues in the Asian-American communities, but I do have first-hand experiences which have given me some insight into the problems. Several years ago, I was a staff psychologist at a local community health center serving the greater Boston Asian population. Most of our patients were recent immigrants from China, Vietnam, Cambodia, Laos, and Hong Kong. Almost all of these new immigrants understood little or no English. With few resources (financial or otherwise), many newcomers struggled to make sense of life in the United States and to survive in whatever fashion they could.

Connie S. Chan, "Reproductive Issues Are Essential Survival Issues for the Asian-American Communities" from *From Abortion to Reproductive Freedom,* edited by Marlene Gerber Fried. Reprinted with the permission of South End Press.

At the health center, the staff tried to help by providing information and advocacy in getting through our confusing system. I thought we did a pretty good job until I found out that neither our health education department nor our obgyn department provided *any* counseling or information about birth control or abortion services. The medical department had interpreted our federal funding regulations as prohibiting not only the performance of abortions on-site, but also the dissemination of information which might lead to, or help patients to obtain, an abortion.

Needless to say, as a feminist and as an activist, I was horrified. When I found out that pregnant women who inquired about abortions were given only a name of a white, English-speaking ob-gyn doctor and sent out alone, it seemed a morally and ethically neglectful practice. One of the nurse-midwives agreed with me and suggested that I could serve as an interpreter/advocate for pregnant women who needed to have abortions, or at least wanted to discuss the option with the English-speaking ob-gyn doctor. The only catch was that I would have to do it on my own time, I could not claim any affiliation with the health center, and I could not suggest follow-up care at the health center.

Not fully knowing the nature of what I was volunteering for, I agreed to interpret and advocate for Cantonese-speaking pregnant women at their appointments with the obstetrician. It turned out that over the course of three years I interpreted during at least a hundred abortions for Asian immigrant women who spoke no English. After the first few abortions, the obstetrician realized how essential it was to have an interpreter present, and began to require that all non-English-speaking women have an interpreter during the abortion procedure.

As a middle-class, educated, bilingual Asian-American woman, I was aware of the importance of having the choice to have an abortion, and the necessity of fighting for the right to choose for myself. I had been unaware of how the right to have an abortion is also a right to survival in this country if you are a poor, uneducated, non-English-speaking immigrant.

The women I interpreted for were, for the most part, not young. Nor were they single. They ranged in age from 25 to 45, with a majority in their late twenties and early thirties. Almost all were married and had two or more children. Some had as many as five or six children. They needed to have abortions because they had been unlucky enough to have gotten pregnant after arriving in this country. Their families were barely surviving on the low wages that many new immigrant workers earned as restaurant workers, garment factory workers, or domestic help. Almost all of the women worked full-time: the ones who had young children left them with older, retired family members or did piece-work at home; those with older children worked in the factories or hotels. Without fail each woman would tell me that she needed to have an abortion because their family could not afford another mouth to feed, that the family could not afford to lose her salary contribution, not even for a few months, to care for an infant. In some ways, one could not even say that these women were choosing to have abortions. The choice had already been made for them, and it was a choice of basic survival.

Kai Ling was one of the women for whom I interpreted. A 35-year-old mother of four children, ages 2 to 7, she and her husband emigrated to the United States from Vietnam. They had no choice; in their emigration, they were refugees whose village had been destroyed and felt fortunate to escape with their lives and all four of their children. Life in the United States was difficult, but they were scraping by, living with another family in a small apartment where their entire family slept in one room. Their hope was that their children would receive an education and "make it" in American society; they lived with the deferred dream for the next generation.

When Kai Ling found out that she was pregnant, she felt desperate. Because she and her husband love children and live for their children, they wanted desperately to keep this child, this one who would be born in America and be an American citizen from birth. Yet they sadly realized that they could not afford another child, they could not survive on just one salary, they could not feed another one. Their commitment was to the children they already had, and to keeping their family together.

When I accompanied Kai Ling to her abortion, she was saddened but resigned to what she had to do. The $300 that she brought to the clinic represented almost a month of wages for her; she had borrowed the money from family and friends. She would pay it back, she said, by working weekends for the next ten weeks. Their major regret was that she would not be able to buy any new clothes for her children this year because of this unexpected expense.

Kai Ling spoke very little English. She did not understand why she had to go to a white American doctor for her abortion instead of receiving services from her Asian doctor at the health center. She had no real understanding of reproductive rights issues, of *Roe v. Wade*, or of why there were demonstrators waving pictures of fetuses and yelling at her as we entered the clinic. Mercifully, she did not understand the questions they shouted at her in English, and she did not ask me what they had said, remarking only that the protesters seemed very angry at someone. She felt sure, I think, that they were not angry at her. She had done nothing to provoke anyone's anger. She was merely trying to survive in this country under this country's rules.

It is a crime and an injustice that Kai Ling could not receive counseling in her language and services from her doctors at the Asian neighborhood health center. It is a crime that she had to borrow $300 to pay for her own abortion, that her Medicaid benefits did not pay for it. It is a grave injustice that she had to have me, a stranger, interpreting for her during her abortion because her own doctor could not perform the procedure at her clinic. It was not a matter of choice for her to abort her pregnancy, but a matter of basic survival.

Kai Ling speaks no English. Kai Ling will probably never attend a march or a rally for choice. She will not sign any petitions. She might not even vote. But it is for her and the countless thousands of immigrant women like her that we need to continue to struggle for reproductive rights. Within the

Asian-American communities, the immigrant women who are most affected by the lack of access to abortions have the least power. They do not speak English; they do not demand equal access to health care; their needs are easily overlooked.

Thus, it is up to those of us who are bilingual, who can speak English, and who can speak to these issues, to do so. We need to ensure that the issue of reproductive rights is an essential item on the Asian-American political agenda. It is not a women's issue; it is a community issue.

We must speak for the Kai Lings, for their children, for their right to survive as a family. We must, as activists, make the connections between the issues of oppression based upon gender, race, national origin, sexual orientation, class, or language. We can and must lead the Asian-American communities to recognize the importance of the essential issue of reproductive rights for the survival of these communities.

65

WHY THE PRECAUTIONARY PRINCIPLE?
A Meditation on Polyvinyl Chloride (PVC) and the Breasts of Mothers*

SANDRA STEINGRABER

Sandra Steingraber, Ph.D., is currently on the faculty at Cornell University's Center for the Environment in Ithaca, New York. She is the author of *Living Downstream: An Ecologist Looks at Cancer and the Environment* and *Having Faith: An Ecologist's Journey to Motherhood.*

Those of you who know me know that when I talk on these topics I usually speak out of two identities: biologist and cancer activist. My diagnosis with bladder cancer at age 20 makes more urgent my scientific research. Conversely, my Ph.D. in ecology informs my understanding of

Sandra Steingraber, "Why the Precautionary Principle? A Meditation on Polyvinyl Chloride (PVC) and the Breasts of Mothers" from *Protecting Public Health and the Environment: Implementing the Precautionary Principle,* edited by Carolyn Raffensperger and Joel Tickner. Copyright © 1999 by Island Press. Reprinted with the permission of the publishers.

*Remarks delivered at the Lowell Center for Sustainable Production's workshop, Building Materials into the Coming Millennium, Boston, November 1998.

how and why I became a cancer patient in the first place: bladder cancer is considered a quintessential environmental disease. Links between environment and public health became the topic of my third book, *Living Downstream*, but since I have been given the task of speaking about the effect of toxic materials on future generations, I'm going to speak out of another one of my identities — that of a mother.

I'm a very new mother. I gave birth in September 1998 to my daughter and first child. So, I'm going to speak very intimately and in the present tense. You know it's a very powerful thing for a person with a cancer history to have a child. It's a very long commitment for those of us unaccustomed to looking far into the future. My daughter's name is Faith.

I'm also learning what all parents must learn, which is a new kind of love. It's a love that's more than an emotion or a feeling. It's a deep physical craving like hunger or thirst. It's the realization that you would lay down your life for this eight-pound person without a second thought. You would pick up arms for them. You would empty your bank account. It's love without boundaries and were this kind of love directed at another adult, it would be considered totally inappropriate. A kind of fatal attraction. Maybe, when directed at babies, we should call this "natal attraction."

I say this to remind us all what is at stake. If we would die or kill for our children, wouldn't we do anything within our power to keep toxics out of their food supply? Especially if we knew, in fact, there were alternatives to these toxics?

Of all human food, breast milk is now the most contaminated. Because it is one rung up on the food chain higher than the foods we adults eat, the trace amounts of toxic residues carried into mothers' bodies become even more concentrated in the milk their breasts produce. To be specific, it's about 10 to 100 times more contaminated with dioxins than the next highest level of stuff on the human food chain, which are animal-derived fats in dairy, meat, eggs, and fish. This is why a breast-fed infant receives its so-called "safe" lifetime limit of dioxin in the first six months of drinking breast milk. Study after study also shows that the concentration of carcinogens in human breast milk declines steadily as nursing continues. Thus the protective effect of breast feeding on the mother appears to be a direct result of downloading a lifelong burden of carcinogens from her breasts into the tiny body of her infant.

When it comes to the production, use, and disposal of PVC (polyvinyl chloride), the breasts of breast-feeding mothers are the tailpipe. Representatives from the vinyl industry emphasize how common a material PVC is, and they are correct. It is found in medical products, toys, food packaging, and vinyl siding. What they don't say is that sooner or later all of these products are tossed into the trash, and here in New England, we tend to shovel our trash into incinerators. Incinerators are de facto laboratories for dioxin manufacturer, and PVC is the main ingredient in this process. The dioxin created by the burning of PVC drifts from the stacks of these incinerators, attaches to dust particles in the atmosphere, and eventually sifts down to

Earth as either dry deposition or in rain drops. This deposition then coats crops and other plants, which are eaten by cows, chickens and hogs. Or, alternatively, it's rained into rivers and lakes and insinuates itself into the flesh of fish. As a breast-feeding mother, I take these molecules into my body and distill them in my breast tissue. This is done through a process through which fat globules from throughout my whole body are mobilized and carried into the breast lobes, where, under the direction of a pituitary hormone called prolactin, they are made into human milk. Then, under the direction of another pituitary hormone called oxytocin, this milk springs from the grape-like lobes and flows down long tubules into the nipple, which is a kind of sieve, and into the back of the throat of the breast-feeding infant. My daughter.

So, this, then, is the connection. This milk, my milk, contains dioxins from old vinyl siding, discarded window blinds, junked toys, and used I.V. bags. Plastic parts of buildings that were burned down accidentally are also housed in my breasts. These are indisputable facts. They are facts that we scientists are not arguing about. What we do spend a lot of time debating is what exactly are the health effects on the generation of children that my daughter belongs to. We don't know with certainty because these kids have not reached the age at which a lot of diseases possibly linked to dioxin exposure would manifest themselves. Unlike mice and rats, we have long generational times. We do know with certainty that childhood cancers are on the rise, and indeed they are rising faster than adult cancers. We don't have any official explanation for that yet.

Let me tell you something else I've learned about breast feeding. It's an ecstatic experience. The same hormone (oxytocin) that allows milk to flow from the back of the chest wall into the nipple also controls female orgasm. This so-called let-down reflex makes the breast feel very warm and full and fizzy, as if it were a shaken-up Coke bottle. That's not unpleasant. Moreover, the mouths of infants—their gums, tongues, and palates—are perfectly designed to receive this milk. A newborn's mouth and a woman's nipple are like partners in a tango. The most expensive breast pump—and I have a $500 one—can only extract about half of the volume that a newborn baby can because such machines cannot possibly imitate the intimate and exquisite tonguing, sucking, and gumming motion that infants use to extract milk from the nipple, which is not unpleasant either.

Through this ecstatic dance, the breast-fed infant receives not just calories, but antibodies. Indeed the immune system is developed through the process of breast feeding, which is why breast-fed infants have fewer bouts of infectious diseases than bottle-fed babies. In fact, the milk produced in the first few days after birth is almost all immunological in function. This early milk is not white at all but clear and sticky and is called colostrum. Then, from colostrum you move to what's called transitional milk, which is very fatty and looks like liquid butter. Presumably then, transitional milk is even more contaminated than mature milk, which comes in at about two weeks post-partum. Interestingly, breast milk is so completely digested that the feces of breast-fed babies doesn't even smell bad. It has the odor of warm yogurt and the color of French mustard. By contrast, the excretions of babies fed on formula are notoriously unpleasant.

What is the price for the many benefits of breast milk? We don't yet know. However, one recent Dutch study found that schoolchildren who were breast fed as babies had three times the level of PCBs* in their blood as compared to children who had been exclusively formula fed. PCBs are probably carcinogens. Why should there be any price for breast feeding? It should be a zero-risk activity.

If there was ever a need to invoke the Precautionary Principle—the idea that we must protect human life from possible toxic danger well in advance of scientific proof about that danger—it is here, deep inside the chest walls of nursing mothers where capillaries carry fat globules into the milk-producing lobes of the mammary gland. Not only do we know little about the long-term health effects of dioxin and PCB exposure in newborns, we haven't even identified all the thousands of constituent elements in breast milk that these contaminants might act on. For example, in 1997 researchers described 130 different sugars unique to human milk. Called oligosaccharides, these sugars are not digested but function instead to protect the infant from infection by binding tightly to intestinal pathogens. Additionally, they appear to serve as a source of sialic acid, which is essential to brain development.

So, this is my conclusion. Breast feeding is a sacred act. It is a holy thing. To talk about breast feeding versus bottle feeding, to weigh the known risks of infectious diseases against the possible risks of childhood or adult cancers is an obscene argument. Those of us who are advocates for women and children and those of us who are parents of any kind need to become advocates for uncontaminated breast milk. A woman's body is the first environment. If there are toxic materials from PVC in the breasts of women, then it becomes our moral imperative to solve the problem. If alternatives to PVC exist, then it becomes morally imperative that we embrace the alternatives and make them a reality.

---

*Editor's Note: 1.5 billion pounds of PCBs (Polychlorinated Biphenyls) were manufactured in the United States prior to being banned by the Environmental Protection Agency in 1977 due to their toxicity. They were used in many aspects of manufacturing including in electrical equipment, plastics, paint, rubber, carbonless paper, etc. They persist in the environment—and in our bodies—due to their longevity and stability and are defined by the EPA as "probable human carcinogens" based on animal studies and studies of workers exposed to PCBs. (www.epa.gov/opptintr/pcb/)

66

DOES SILENCIO = MUERTE?
Notes on Translating the AIDS Epidemic

DR. RAFAEL CAMPO

Dr. Rafael Campo teaches and practices internal medicine at Harvard Medical School and Beth Israel Deaconess Medical Center in Boston. He is the award-winning author of several books, including "The Poetry of Healing" (W. W. Norton, 1997) and the collection of poems "Diva" (Duke University Press, 1999).

Palomita chatters in one of my clinic exam rooms in Boston, her strongly accented voice filling the chilly institutional chrome-and-vinyl space with Puerto Rican warmth. She's off on another dramatic monologue, telling me about her new boyfriend.

"Edgar, he loves me, you know, he call me *mamacita*. He want me to be the mother of his children someday, OK? I ain't no slut. *Mira,* I don't need to use no condom with him."

Even the way she dresses is a form of urgent communication—the plunging neckline of her tropically patterned blouse, whose tails knotted above her waist also expose her flat stomach, the skin-tight denim jeans, the gold, four-inch hoop earrings, and the necklace with her name spelled out in cursive with tiny sparkling stones. Her black hair is pulled back tightly, except for a small squiggle greased flat against her forehead in the shape of an upside-down question mark.

"People think bad of him 'cause they say he dealing drugs. I tell them, 'No way, you shut your stupid mouths. He good to me and beside, he cleaner than you is.' Sure, he got his other girls now and then, but he pick them out *bien* carefully, you know what I mean. That his right as man of the house. No way he gonna give me *la SIDA.* We too smart for none of that shit. We trust each other. We communicate. We gonna buy us a house somewhere *bien bonita.* Someday we gonna make it."

She is seventeen years old, hasn't finished high school, and cannot read English. I have just diagnosed her with herpes, and I am trying to talk to her

Rafael Campo, "Does Silencio = Muerte? Notes on Translating the AIDS Epidemic" from *The Progressive* 63 (10). Reprinted with the permission of *The Progressive* magazine, 409 East Main Street, Madison, WI 53703.

about AIDS and "safer sex."Her Edgar, who is also a patient of mine, tested HIV-positive last week. It's clear they have not discussed it.

Latinos are dying at an alarming rate from AIDS. And for all our glorious presence on the world's stage—in music, literature, art, from MacArthur grants to MTV to *Sports Illustrated*—this is one superlative no one can really boast about. Few Latinos dare even to mention the epidemic. The frenetic beat of salsa in our dance clubs seems to drown out the terrifying statistics, while the bright murals in our barrios cover up the ugly blood-red graffiti, and that "magical realism" of our fictions imagines a world where we can lose our accents and live in Vermont, where secret family recipes conjure up idealized heterosexual love in an ultimately just universe unblemished by plague.

Here, loud and clear, for once, are some of the more stark, sobering facts: In the U.S., Latinos accounted for one-fifth of all AIDS cases reported to the Centers for Disease Control last year, while making up only one-tenth of the U.S. population; AIDS has been the leading cause of death since 1991 for young Latino men in this country; in areas with especially high numbers of Latinos, such as Fort Lauderdale, Miami, Los Angeles, and New York, AIDS deaths among Latina women were four times the national average since 1995. While the infection rate among whites continues to decline, today, and every day, 100 people of color are newly diagnosed with HIV infection. Behold our isolated and desperate substance users, the most marginalized of the marginalized, our forsaken impoverished, and our irreplaceable young people.

I do not have to wonder at the reasons for the silence among Latinos about the burgeoning AIDS epidemic that is decimating us. Though I stare into its face every day in the clinic where I work, there are times when even I want to forget, to pretend it is not happening, to believe my people are invincible and can never be put down again. I want to believe Palomita is HIV-negative, that Edgar will stop shooting drugs and someday return to get on the right triple combination of anti-viral medications. I fervently hope that César, a twenty-year-old Colombian man who keeps missing his appointments, is taking his protease inhibitors so that his viral load remains undetectable. I do not really know who pays for his drugs, since he is uninsured, but my thoughts do not dwell on it. In the end, I want to go home and rest after a long day in the clinic, to make love to my partner of fourteen years and feel that I'll never have to confront another epidemic. I want to look into his dark, Puerto Rican eyes and never have to speak of AIDS again.

But I know better. I know we must speak out—about the ongoing disenfranchisement of Latinos despite our much-touted successes, about the vicious homophobia of a *machista,* about Latino culture that especially fears and hates gay people whom it believes "deserve" AIDS, about the antipathy of the Catholic Church so many Latinos pray to for guidance they don't receive, about the unfulfilled dream of total and untainted assimilation for so many Mexicans, Dominicans, Cubans, and Puerto Ricans who came to America with nothing.

To break any of these silences is especially tempting, since together they allow me to blame most of the usual targets of my rage and frustration. Others are more difficult to penetrate, such as the persistent lack of access in Latino communities to lifesaving information about AIDS. Still others make almost no sense to me at all. Rosa, another patient of mine, tells me she knows she should not have sex without condoms, but continues to do so anyway because she is afraid her drug-dealing boyfriend would think she no longer loves him. Yet she hardly imagines that he might be using drugs, or wonders whether he has other sexual partners.

Our silence, in all its forms, is killing us. I wince at the familiar ring of this realization. I can't help but remember my patient Ernesto in his hospital bed with his partner Jesús sitting quietly at his side, a tiny statue of the Virgin of Guadalupe keeping its mute vigil, no other family or friends around. Ernesto died years ago of AIDS. It is not passé or trite or irrelevant to ask why we remain silent. It is absolutely imperative. We must understand the causes of our *silencio*.

Most of the Spanish-speaking patients who come to my clinic do not much resemble Ricky Martin or Daisy Fuentes or Antonio Sabato Jr. They are "the working poor," janitors or delivery boys or hotel laundry workers or high school dropouts or dishwashers—people with jobs that pay subsistence wages and provide no health benefits. Still, they consider themselves fortunate because so many have no jobs at all.

Many of them are illiterate, and many more speak no English. They have come to Boston mostly from Puerto Rico, but some are from Cuba, the Dominican Republic, Mexico, Colombia, Guatemala, El Salvador, and Nicaragua. Some sleep on park benches when the weather is warm enough and in shelters during the winter. Some live in crowded apartments. Some are undocumented immigrants. Some have lost their welfare benefits, some are trying to apply for temporary assistance, and almost none have enough to feed themselves and their families.

Older couples too often have lost children to drugs, street violence, and AIDS. Young people too often blame their parents and their teachers for their problems. Some know very little about AIDS and fault homosexuals, injection drug users, and prostitutes for poisoning the community. Some view *la SIDA* with resignation and see it as inevitable, part of the price some must pay for a chance at a better life.

But the vast majority of Latinos in the U.S. remain shortchanged, despite the glittering success of a few. For every Federico Peña, many more anonymous "illegals" are deported to Mexico each day, never given the chance to contribute to our society at all. For every Sammy Sosa, a makeshift boat full of Dominicans is lost at sea. And even more noxious than the large-scale efforts to dismantle affirmative action or to deny basic social services (including health care) to undocumented immigrants are the daily insults and obstacles that prevent Latinos from sharing fully in our nation's life. Lack of economic opportunities pushes Latinos toward criminal activities as a means to survive.

Discrimination and rejection breed the kind of despair that drug use and unsafe sex only temporarily ameliorate. The despair and the apathy, heightened by what the very few who are successful have achieved, numb the soul.

It's a common litany, yet I can't help but see how this imposed demoralization is manifest in the behavior of so many of my patients. Why leave an abusive relationship, they say, when all that awaits is the cold streets? Why insist on a condom when it's so much easier not to and the reasons to go on living are not so clear anyway? It doesn't seem farfetched to me that this cumulative hopelessness is fueling the AIDS epidemic.

But these causes, the subject of so many lefty social work dissertations, do not get at the entire problem. We remain ourselves a culture in which men treat women as icons—or as powerless objects of our legendary sexual passions. Our wives must be as pure as we believe our own mothers to be, and yet we pursue our mistresses with the zeal of matadors about to make the kill. Brute force is excused as a necessary means by which Latino men must exert control over weak-willed women, and it is by no means secret that in the shadow of the AIDS epidemic lurks another senseless killer, the domestic violence that too often goes unreported.

Could Palomita and Rosa fear more then just losing the financial support of their boyfriends? For Yolanda, another patient of mine with HIV infection, it was the beatings from her husband that finally drove her onto the streets, where prostitution soon became her only means of making a living. Now she is dying.

Sexism's virulent *hermano* is homophobia. AIDS has long been considered a disease exclusively of homosexuals—especially in Spanish-speaking communities, where not only is HIV strongly associated with gayness, it is further stigmatized as having been imported from the decadent white world. Since we cannot speak calmly and rationally of homosexuality, we certainly cannot bring up AIDS, perhaps the only affliction that could be worse.

Latinos are allowed to be gay only outside the confines of their families and old neighborhoods. Indeed, many Latino men who have sex with men would never even consider themselves "gay" at all, a derogatory term that they would apply only to those whom they consider to be their "passive" partners. Even those who take pride in their homosexuality are not immune to this hatred. I have many gay Latino friends whose parents will not allow their partners to visit during holidays, friends who go to great lengths to (literally) "straighten out" their homes when family is coming to visit by creating fictitious separate bedrooms and removing anything suggestive of homosexuality (which can get difficult, when one gets down to the joint Andy Garcia fan club application, the Frida Kahlo shrine, or the autographed and framed Gigi Fernandez poster).

Hand in hand with both sexism and homophobia goes Catholicism. Latinos are overwhelmingly Catholic, and the Catholic hierarchy remains overwhelmingly not only anti-gay, but also opposed to the use of condoms as a means to prevent HIV transmission. (The only time I have ever heard

AIDS mentioned in a Catholic church was at a wedding service, when it was invoked as a reminder of what punishments lay in store for the fornicators and homosexuals who scorned marriage.) While on the one hand preaching about the sanctity of life, our religious leaders have abetted the deaths of countless Latinos by refusing to endorse the use of condoms as a means to prevent AIDS transmission.

No one disagrees with the monotonous message that abstinence is the safest sex of all. Yet in today's ascendant moment, when young Latinos must party—we drink our Cuba libres followed by café con leche, dance the merengue provocatively with shiny crucifixes dangling around our necks, and later engage in sultry, unsafe sex, even if always (supposedly) with partners of the opposite sex—such teaching is utterly impractical.

Then there are the people like me, the Cuban doctors and Chicano lawyers, the Nuyorican politicians and the displaced Argentine activists—those who mean well but who have allowed the silence to engulf us, too. The thick warm blanket of our insularity and relative power comforts us. We are a small, tightly knit group; we work hard and hope to send our children to Harvard or Stanford or Yale, praying that they stay out of trouble. We increasingly vote Republican, elated that George W. Bush tosses out a few words in a halting Spanish, and fearing that a liberal government might take away too much of what we have struggled to make for ourselves—and might allow too many others in for a share of our pie. We would hardly acknowledge Palomita and Edgar if we passed them in the street, and we might even regret their very existence, the way they bring all of us down by their ignorance and poverty. Full of our quiet self-righteousness, gripping our briefcases just a bit more tightly, we might not even feel sorry for them if we knew they were being afflicted with AIDS.

Mario Cooper, a former deputy chief of staff for the Democratic National Committee, knows first-hand about a community's indifference to AIDS. Black, gay, and HIV-positive, he spearheaded an initiative sponsored by the Harvard AIDS Institute called Leading for Life. The summit brought together prominent members of the African American community to talk frankly about their own AIDS epidemic—just as uncontrolled, just as deadly, and until last year's summit, just as silent as the one ravaging Latinos.

"The key is to make people understand this is about all of us," Cooper says, as we brainstorm a list of possible invitees to another meeting, to be called *Unidos para la Vida*. Inspired by his past success in Boston, where the likes of Marian Wright Edelman, Henry Louis Gates Jr., and Dr. Alvin Poussaint eventually heeded his call to action, Cooper is now intent on tackling the same issue for Latinos.

"What came out of the Leading for Life meeting was incredible," he says. "Suddenly, everyone was paying attention, and things started happening for young African Americans. They started to learn more about AIDS." He is beaming, and we add Oscar de la Renta, Cristina, and Edward James Olmos to the list. "We have the chance to do the same thing here."

But after a few weeks of working on the project with him and others at the Harvard AIDS Institute, it became clear to us that we might be facing even greater obstacles than those he encountered in the black community. We had hardly even gotten started when conflicts over terminology almost sank the entire effort. "Latino" competed with "Hispanic," while all of us felt that neither term fully articulated the rich diversity and numerous points of origin of those who undeniably formed some kind of a community. Some of us secretly questioned whether a shared vulnerability to AIDS was itself enough to try to unify us. Was a Puerto Rican injection drug user in Hartford, Connecticut, really facing the same issues as a Salvadoran undocumented immigrant selling sex in El Paso, Texas? Was loyalty to the Venezuelan community, or Nicaraguan community, imperiled by joining this larger group? At times, we saw evidence of the kind of pecking-order mentality (in which certain nationalities consider themselves superior to others) that has since the days of Bolívar interfered with efforts to unify Spain's colonies in the New World.

If these mostly suppressed internal divisions were not enough to surmount, we also battled the general lack of interest in AIDS—yesterday's news, no matter how loudly we shouted the latest statistics, no matter how emphatically we pointed out the lack of access for Latinos to the new treatments.

"Don't they have a cure for that now?" remarked one person I called, exemplifying precisely the sort of misinformation we were working to correct, her breathy laugh further revealing both the kind of distancing from—and absence of comfort with—the entire issue that surely reinforced her lack of knowledge.

Others were simply fatalistic. "You can't change the way these kids think and behave," said one person who declined the invitation to attend the summit, "so why bother?"

"Tell them to stop having sex," came one memorably blunt response, before the phone crashed down on the other end.

"I pray for them," said another pious woman. "I pray that they will renounce their wicked ways and find peace in Christ." She then regretted to inform me that she would be unable to attend the summit.

The special insight I thought I could bring to the effort, as a gay Latino poet doctor who writes both poems and prescriptions, seemed to be of less and less use, as more and more "no" answers, accompanied by their usually polite excuses, filtered back to us. Weeks later, when the situation grew bleakest, Cooper only urged us to redouble our efforts. "We're dealing with a situation that is almost unfathomable to most of these people," he said. "It's an epidemic no one wants to believe exists. Latinos are supposed to be the rising stars of the next millennium, not the carriers of a disease that could wipe out humanity." What was on one level a glaring public health crisis had to be understood more radically. "We have to ask ourselves why this message isn't getting out. We're kidding ourselves if we think we're the magic solution. In fact, we may be part of the problem."

The work of Walt Odets, the Berkeley psychologist who shook up the safer sex establishment, immediately came to mind. Odets observed young gay men at the height of the AIDS epidemic in San Francisco, noting a pervasive hopelessness in the face of a belief that infection with HIV was inevitable. Behind the apathy and denial, might not the same thing exist in this second-wave epidemic among inner-city Latinos? The stupidity of our early efforts at sloganeering, which tried to encapsulate a myriad of complex issues under a single bright banner, suddenly became utterly apparent to me. What faced us was not simply a matter of speaking out, of breaking a silence so many Latinos already living with HIV had already renounced. What we had to do was learn to speak their language, to incorporate in our every effort an entirely new mode of expression.

I knew right then that we had a lot more work to do.

Palomita's mood is decidedly less cheerful today. She is three-and-a-half-months pregnant, but that's not why she starts to cry. It's the end of January, and my office is just as cold as ever. A thin crust of ice is gradually forming on everything outside. Last week, while Palomita's HIV test was being run, a storm knocked out power to most of New England. My heart feels as empty and dark as one of the houses caught in the blackout now that I've read out her result.

"I don't believe you. You mean, I'm gonna die of AIDS?" A leaden moment passes before the inevitable next question. "And what about my baby?"

Looking at Palomita, I wonder again at how AIDS does not get prevented, how it seems to have a terrible life of its own. I want to answer her questions, explain to her that AZT lowers the risk of maternal fetal transmission, that the new triple combination anti-retroviral regimens, if she takes them exactly as prescribed, could buy her many years with her child. But I can't. Instead I keep thinking about her name, which means "little dove," and trying to imagine the innocence her parents must have seen in her tiny face when they named her, trying to feel that boundless joy at the earliest moment of a new life. I am looking at Palomita as she cries, framed by a window from which she cannot fly. I am imagining peace. In her beautiful brown face, mirror of a million souls, I try to envision us all in a world without AIDS.

67

TO BE POOR AND TRANSGENDER

KAI WRIGHT

Kai Wright is a freelance writer based in Washington, D.C. More of his work is available at *www.kaiwright.com.* He can be contacted at wright_kai@hotmail.com.

Sharmus has been a sex worker for about five years. She started after breaking up with a boyfriend who was supporting her while she was out of work. It was quick money, and, as with many of her transgender friends, she didn't believe there were many other jobs out there for her.

"You have your good nights, and your bad nights," says Sharmus, thirty-five. "There are no fringe benefits. Summer time is the best time; the winter is hard," she explains, casually ticking off the pros and cons of being a prostitute. "It's just hard getting a job. Nobody really wants to hire you, and when they do hire you they give you a hard time."

Sex work was not in her plans back when she transitioned from male to female at age twenty-one. "Sometimes I regret it," she sighs. "My lifetime goal was to be a schoolteacher."

Her uncertainty is to be expected. Our culture depicts people whose discomfort with gender norms goes beyond being tomboys or feminine men as mere curiosity items for trash TV ("Your woman is really a man!" episodes of *Jerry Springer*). This collective ignorance leaves people like Sharmus without much guidance. Many go through puberty and into adulthood without meeting people like themselves. The resulting high rates of depression, drug use, violence, and suicidal thoughts are unsurprising.

"One of the greatest agonies one can experience is gender dysphoria," says transgender activist Jessica Xavier. "When your anatomy doesn't match who you are inside, it's the worst feeling in the world."

Sharmus and Xavier are part of a group whose existence challenges normative gender. They include drag performers, heterosexual cross-dressers, and people from all walks of life who live permanently in a gender other than that assigned at birth. They range from individuals who have had thousands of dollars worth of reconstructive surgery to people who simply style themselves in a way that feels comfortable.

Kai Wright, "To Be Poor and Transgender" from *The Progressive*, 65 (10). Reprinted with the permission of *The Progressive* magazine, 409 East Main Street, Madison, WI 53703.

Around the nation, a growing cadre of activists is working to build bridges between all of these populations and to encourage the formation of an umbrella community called "transgender." What the members of this latest American identity group share is a far more practical understanding of gender politics than that of the ethereal, academic world to which it is often relegated. From employment to health services, transgender folks, particularly those in low-income environments, face enormous barriers when navigating even the most basic aspects of life—all because of their gender transgressions.

"We continue to be one of the most stigmatized populations on the planet," says Xavier, the former director of a national coalition of transgender political groups called It's Time!—America. Xavier recently cajoled the local health department into financing a survey of around 250 transgender people in D.C. Forty percent of respondents had not finished high school, and another 40 percent were unemployed. Almost half had no health insurance and reported not seeing a physician regularly. A quarter reported being HIV-positive, and another 35 percent reported having seriously considered suicide.

Xavier's was the latest in a series of such studies done in cities where relatively emboldened trans activists have pushed local officials to begin considering public policy solutions to their health care concerns. Across the board, they have found largely the same thing: higher rates of just about every indicator of social and economic distress. "And all because of the stigma," Xavier concludes.

One problem that stands out, Xavier and others say, is the need for accessible counseling and medical supervision for those who are in the process of gender transitioning. Most medical professionals require certain steps, outlined in a set of protocols dubbed the "Benjamin Standards of Care." First, a therapist must diagnose you with "Gender Identity Disorder," which the American Psychiatric Association established in 1979. In adults, the diagnosis essentially confirms that your "gender dysphoria" is profound enough that the drastic step of making physiological alterations to God's plan is an acceptable treatment.

The diagnosis clears you for reconstructive surgery and hormone therapy. Hormone use for gender transitioning is strictly off-label, but select doctors will nevertheless prescribe a particular hormone and simply file paperwork for one of its approved usages. While there is disagreement within the trans community about how this process should be altered, most unite around frustration with the gatekeeping nature of it all—the notion that one must first ask permission, then be declared insane, before being allowed to violate our gender rules.

For Angela (a pseudonym), this means choosing between the career she's spent ten years building and her recent decision to live as a male. Angela, twenty-eight, gained security clearance while serving in the Marines. Despite having climbed to officer rank, she fled the forces when it became clear they were going to throw her out for being a lesbian.

As a civilian, her clearance allowed her to land a well-paying job at an aerospace engineering firm. The position has afforded her partner of four years a comfortable life, and even occasionally helps support her partner's budding acting career. But all of that will be jeopardized once a gender-identity-disorder diagnosis is placed in Angela's medical records. Technically, it's a mental health problem, and that would likely prompt the revocation of her clearance when it next comes up for review. So Angela and her partner are again searching for new ways she can use her skills.

Middle class professionals like Angela have options. The barriers to a legal and safe gender transition are surmountable, if profound. But for people like Sharmus, the whole discussion is absurd.

Sharmus has never had "body work" done, but she's taken some hormones in the past. In her world, spending thousands of dollars on therapy, surgery, and hormone treatments is impossible, but a hyper-feminine appearance is still highly valued — not only for personal aesthetics, but also for professional development. So a thriving black market has developed. In D.C., for $200 to $300, you can have silicone injected into your chest to create breasts. Thirty bucks will get you around 100 hormone pills, though injections are usually cheaper.

"When I was taking the hormone shots, my girlfriend was shooting me," Sharmus explains. "You get a knot in the breasts first, then your skin gets soft. After about two months, my breasts started forming."

With hormones, often someone who has taken them before supplies and mentors a curious friend. Similar arrangements develop with silicone, but just as often there's a dealer in town who also injects clients. The silicone is not encased, as it would be with an implant, but rather injected with large syringes directly into varying body parts. In some cases, the materials injected are not even silicone, but substitutes made from more readily available things such as dishwashing liquid or floor wax. Similarly, some men wanting estrogen will simply take birth-control pills. Testosterone is harder to improvise, but even the real thing can irreparably damage internal organs when taken improperly. All of this can result in fatalities.

"I have known several people that passed," Sharmus sighs. She steers clear of silicone and stopped taking unsupervised hormones. A couple of years ago, she started working with an organization called Helping Individual Prostitutes Survive, or HIPS. She conducts outreach for HIPS, offering information on how to protect against HIV and other sexually transmitted diseases, and encouraging colleagues to leave the silicone alone.

Omar Reyes, whose drag persona is former Miss Gay America, works for La Clinica del Pueblo, a D.C. clinic serving the city's ballooning Latino community. Reyes uses his male birth name and male pronouns but considers himself transgender because of his drag work and his discomfort with male gender "norms." In his monthly transgender support group and in conversations with other *dragas* he meets at his weekly show, Reyes harps on the *malas noticias* about silicone. But he recognizes why it's attractive: It's cheap, and it's fast.

"They put silicone in their face and their bodies and, in just a very short period, they can look like a woman," he says. This is particularly important for drag performers and sex workers, whose income may depend on how exaggeratedly feminine they look. "We have to deal with the fact that they want to look like a woman, and this is the short-term way to do it."

Reyes and Xavier want to see someone in D.C. start a low-cost clinic devoted to counseling and treatment for people who are transitioning. Gay health centers in Boston, Los Angeles, New York City, San Francisco, and Seattle all have such clinics already and are developing their own sets of protocols for how the process should work. Earlier this year, San Francisco became the first jurisdiction in the United States to include sex reassignment surgery and related treatments in its health plan for civil servants. This is the kind of thing Xavier says we need to see more of.

But even if the services were there, getting people into them would take work. Most transgender people tell horrifying stories of the treatment they have experienced in health care settings. In one of the most high-profile cases nationally, a trans woman named Tyra Hunter died in 1995 when D.C. paramedics refused to treat her wounds from a car accident. After removing her clothes at the scene of the accident and discovering her male genitals, a paramedic allegedly ceased treating Hunter and began shouting taunts. She died at the hospital later. Following a lengthy court battle, Hunter's family won a suit against the city.

There are many less prominent examples. From the hospital nurse who gawks when helping a trans woman into her dressing gown to the gynecologist who responds with disbelief when a trans man comes in for a checkup, the small indignities act as perhaps the greatest barriers to health care.

"They feel like when you go for services, people are going to give attitude," Reyes says. "Therefore, you find that they don't even think about going for help when they really need it."

Tanika Walker, who goes by Lucky, is your standard eighteen-year-old hard ass: short-sighted, stubborn-headed, determined to be the toughest guy in the room. Born and raised in rough-and-tumble southeast Washington, D.C., Lucky has a mop of dreadlocks, light mustache, tattoos, and brands—including the name of a deceased sibling spelled out in cigarette burns. These all send one message: I'm the wrong dude to mess with.

Like Angela, Lucky is in the process of transitioning genders to become a young man. It's an emotional journey she began when she was fourteen years old. Along the way, she's been yanked out of school and tossed out of her home. She's also been involved in a lot of disastrous relationships, marred by violence, often her own.

"I know that I'm homosexual, that I'm a lesbian," Lucky says, groping to explain her feelings. "But at the same time, it's like, I look so much like a boy. I act so much like a boy. I want to be a boy."

So far, however, Lucky's transition is primarily stylistic. She still uses her birth name and answers to female pronouns, but she describes her gender as "not anything." She uses only the men's bathroom because she's had too many fights with women who thought she was a Peeping Tom in the ladies' room. And she'd much rather her friends call her "dawg" than "girlfriend." Among African American lesbians, Lucky fits into a category of women often dubbed "doms," short for dominant.

"I never had chests," Lucky brags. "Never. Around the time you're supposed to start getting chests, I didn't get any. So I was like, am I made to be like this? I was the little girl all of the other little girls couldn't play with 'cause I was too boyish."

The dyke jokes started early, sometime in middle school. She settled on a violent response to the taunting just as early. Her fighting became routine enough that by her sophomore year the school suggested counseling for her "identity crisis." She balked and, instead, came out to her mom, who promptly threw her out of the house. "I was like, how am I having an identity crisis? I know what I am," Lucky remembers. "My mom said I had to go."

Lucky enrolled herself in the Job Corps and by the time she was seventeen had her GED. She came back to D.C., moved in with her godsister, and began dating a thirty-two-year-old woman.

But the relationship quickly turned violent, and the godsister put Lucky out as well. She turned to one of her brothers and started dating someone her own age. But it was a stormy relationship, and Lucky battered her partner. After one of their more brutal fights, the young woman called the police and Lucky wound up in jail for a month for aggravated assault. That was this April. In May, she started dating another young woman, and she believes this relationship will work out. She's also started hanging out at the Sexual Minority Youth Assistance League (SMYAL).

One urgent lesson she's trying to learn is that violence isn't her only option when conflict arises. But she dismisses the severity of her problem. "I would be, like, 'Go away and leave me alone,'" she says, describing how the fights started. "And she would just keep hitting me in the arm or something. But it didn't really affect me; it would just be real irritating. She used to do stupid stuff like that to aggravate me. So I just hit her. And when I hit her, I blacked her eye out or something."

She sums up her life in a gigantic understatement, saying, "It's just some things I've been through that a normal eighteen-year-old female wouldn't have been through."

Twenty-year-old Vassar College senior Kiana Moore began transitioning at seventeen. She is articulate and engaging, has never been in trouble, and is studying to become a clinical psychologist. As the only transgender person on her campus, she comes out to the entire first-year class every term during one of the school's diversity programs. She spent this summer interning at SMYAL, counseling Lucky and fifteen to twenty other mainly black transgender youth. What these young folks need, she says, are more role models.

"I am here at SMYAL working as an intern, but where else can you go around this country and see a trans intern? Where can you see a trans person who's in college?" Moore asks. "And so you don't really have anyone to connect to or know about. So if they are at high risk [for social problems], that's why. Because there's nothing there for them at all."

Moore has what Xavier calls "passing privilege." She's a beautiful and confident black woman most people would never assume is transgender. That's something usually achieved only by those with significant resources.

And once trans people have found they can pass — usually middle class whites living in the suburbs — they don't want to ruin it by becoming an activist or a role model.

"You lose something if you help, because then you put yourself in the spotlight. And if you are a pretty, passable female, you don't want to do that," Moore explains. "We don't want to be advocates, because then we're Kiana the transsexual instead of Kiana the new neighbor."

And thus the activists trying to build a transgender community and social movement face much the same battle gay activists confronted for years: Those with the resources to help have too much to lose.

But Moore sees promise in the youth she spent the summer with. "Every time I talk to them I always give them a big hug before, during, and after the session, because that's the only way I can say I'm here and I think you're stronger than me," she says. "They deal with their problems, and they come in here, and they smile, every day. And they take care of each other."

PART XI
A World That Is Truly Human

In the introduction to this book, Gerda Lerner calls for " . . . a world free of dominance and hierarchy, a world that is truly human." A democratic society depends on equal access to the rights and benefits of the social order. It requires a system in which people born tied down by ropes of oppression are given the means to untie themselves and are offered equal opportunities once they are free. In a truly human world, the ropes would not exist. Our social, political, and economic systems do not provide such opportunities, so individuals, groups, and communities are left on their own to devise empowerment strategies.

As many authors in this book have said or implied, altering the gender system, entrenched as it is in many structural arrangements, requires change at many levels—in individuals, in relationships, in families, in communities, in all social institutions, in national alliances, through legal reform, and through global policy and action. Recall Elizabeth Janeway's conclusion, reported in the introduction to this book, that disempowered people can become empowered only after we question the truth of the ideas of those in power. Janeway argues that disbelief, the first stage of empowerment, needs to be followed by action, both individual and collective.

A current strategy used to address gender injustice is to call for the treatment of women's rights as human rights. As mentioned in the introduction, this call harks back to an early women's movement definition of feminism: feminism is the radical notion that women are human. Human rights activist and scholar Charlotte Bunch, director of the Center for Women's Global Leadership at Rutgers University, argues that gender-related abuse "offers the greatest challenge to the field of human rights today."[1] She reports that women and girls are subjected to a wide range of abuse not perpetrated on men and boys, such as abortion of female fetuses, restricted nutrition, women's and girls' lack of control over their bodies (as reflected in high death rates from illegal abortions and female genital mutilation), and overt violence against them of the types described earlier in this book by Melanie Kaye/Kantrowitz, Jan Goodwin, Helen Zia, and others. Bunch concludes, "Female subordination runs so deep that it is still viewed as inevitable or natural, rather than seen as a politically constructed reality maintained by patriarchal interests, ideology, and institutions."[2]

Bunch recommends four approaches to alleviating these injustices. Attention to *political and civil rights* would focus, for example, on the sexual abuse of female political prisoners and female refugees. Attention to *socioeconomic rights* would address the right to food, shelter, health care, and employment. Attention to *legal rights* would protect women against sex discrimination. And finally, a *feminist transformation of human rights* designed to explicitly focus on violations in women's lives would address other ways in which women are oppressed such as battering, rape, forced marriage, lack of reproductive rights, compulsory heterosexuality, and genital mutilation.[3] Rita Arditti (this part) lays out a clear case for addressing women's rights as human rights. In fact, most of the issues addressed in this book are human rights issues.

A new approach to peace — the "culture of peace" perspective — addresses gender in the context of violence. Analyzing the gendered nature of war and warriors, critics of world violence have dissected masculinity with the goal of changing how masculine identities and behaviors are developed and expressed, both at the microlevel in interpersonal relationships and at the international level as expressed in wars.[4] They have also examined women's roles and their potential for helping to create a more peaceful world.[5] Although many women have struggled to actively intervene in the interest of peace (see for example Svirsky, this part), political scientist Cynthia Enloe believes that we have a long way to go before women can make a serious impact on moving the world away from militarization and toward peace: "At the opening of the new century, militarization continues to rely on women located in different social, economic, ideological, and cultural locations remaining uninformed about, unconnected to, or even hostile toward one another. The experiences of fragmentation have provided an incentive for some current feminists to expend more intellectual and organizing energy in understanding those differences and reducing the hostilities they can foment."[6]

Given the power of gender oppression and the other oppressions addressed in this book, there is no way to create a humane world unless many women and men are able to work within and across groups to fight for change that will benefit the largest number of people. Educators Rita Hardiman and Bailey Jackson have proposed a theory of stages of social identity development that helps me to think about this issue at both a personal and a collective level.[7] They argue that in order to struggle against oppression, people first need to have a critical analysis of oppressive aspects of the social order. Next, they need to gather with members of their own groups to solidify their identities independent of the systems of oppression. For people with privilege — who Hardiman and Jackson call agents — this means identifying their privilege and understanding how it contributes to the oppression of others. For people without privilege — who Hardiman and Jackson call targets — this means understanding how oppression has affected them, both externally and internally as internalized subordination. Given that most people experience a mix of privilege and oppression, and are therefore a combination of both targets and agents, the development of one's identity is a complex process.

Ultimately, Hardiman and Jackson suggest that once people have gained enough confidence in their awareness of their identities, having embraced both the privileged and the oppressed aspects of themselves, they will be ready to work for social justice across the boundaries of identity and special interests. Instead of focusing only on the needs of their own group(s), they will be able to begin working in broad-based movements for social justice, understanding how others are oppressed, and building coalitions that have political clout. Oppression against anyone contributes to an unequal world. The writers in this book would ask us to use our sociological imaginations to understand the dimensions of oppression, work on our identities, become clear about using our privileges in ways designed to share the privilege, root out our internalized oppression, solidify our sense of pride and empowerment, and go about working creatively with other women and men to create peace in a world that is truly human.

In the preceding readings, we have heard from many people working for change in specific areas. In this final section, we hear from several people working toward a more human world across various differences and at various levels including organizational policies (National Organization for Men Against Sexism); women's movement politics (Gloria Anzaldúa and M. Annette Jaimes with Theresa Halsey); the effects of prison growth on African American communities (Geoff Ward and Manning Marable); international peace activism (Gila Svirsky); and women's rights as human rights (Rita Arditti).

In relation to this final set of readings, I suggest that you consider these questions: What, if anything, do you personally think should be done about the array of challenges presented in this book? Do the authors in this section offer any suggestions or approaches that make sense to you? Finally, as you think about the array of issues you have encountered in here, consider this question: If a human rights framework were to inform our approach to gender inequality, and if policy, law, and disciplinary action were brought to bear on violators of human rights, which of the gender inequalities addressed in this book might diminish or even disappear?

NOTES

1. Charlotte Bunch, "Women's Rights as Human Rights: Toward a Re Vision of Human Rights," in Charlotte Bunch and Roxanna Carrillo, *Gender Violence: A Development and Human Rights Issue* (New Brunswick, NJ: Center for Women's Global Leadership, 1991), p. 3.
2. Bunch, "Women's Rights," p. 7.
3. Bunch, "Women's Rights," pp. 10–13.
4. Ingeborg Breines, Robert Connell, & Ingrid Eide, eds., *Male Roles, Masculinities and Violence: A Culture of Peace Perspective* (Paris: UNESCO, 2000).
5. Ingeborg Breines, Dorota Gierycz and Betty Reardon, eds., *Towards a Women's Agenda for a Culture of Peace* (Paris: UNESCO Publishing, 1999).
6. Cynthia Enloe, *Maneuvers: The International Politics of Militarizing Women's Lives* (Berkeley, CA: University of California Press, 2000), p. 295.
7. Rita Hardiman and Bailey Jackson, "Conceptual Foundations for Social Justice Courses," in Maurianne Adams, Lee Ann Bell, and Pat Griffin, eds., *Teaching for Diversity and Social Justice: A Sourcebook* (New York: Routledge, 1997).

68

STATEMENT OF PRINCIPLES

NATIONAL ORGANIZATION FOR MEN AGAINST SEXISM

National Organization for Men Against Sexism www.nomas.org.

The National Organization for Men Against Sexism is an activist organization of men and women supporting positive changes for men. NOMAS advocates a perspective that is pro-feminist, gay-affirmative, and committed to justice on a broad range of social issues including race, class, age, religion, and physical abilities. We affirm that working to make this nation's ideals of equality substantive is the finest expression of what it means to be men.

We believe that the new opportunities becoming available to women and men will be beneficial to both. Men can live as happier and more fulfilled human beings by challenging the old-fashioned rules of masculinity that embody the assumption of male superiority.

Traditional masculinity includes many positive characteristics in which we take pride and find strength, but it also contains qualities that have limited and harmed us. We are deeply supportive of men who are struggling with the issues of traditional masculinity. As an organization for changing men, we care about men and are especially concerned with men's problems, as well as the difficult issues in most men's lives.

As an organization for changing men, we strongly support the continuing struggle of women for full equality. We applaud and support the insights and positive social changes that feminism has stimulated for both women and men. We oppose such injustices to women as economic and legal discrimination, rape, domestic violence, sexual harassment, and many others. Women and men can and do work together as allies to change the injustices that have so often made them see one another as enemies.

One of the strongest and deepest anxieties of most American men is their fear of homosexuality. This homophobia contributes directly to the many injustices experienced by gay, lesbian, and bisexual persons, and is a debilitating restriction for heterosexual men. We call for an end to all forms of discrimination based on sexual–affectional orientation, and for the creation of a gay-affirmative society.

We also acknowledge that many people are oppressed today because of their race, class, age, religion, and physical condition. We believe that such injustices are vitally connected to sexism, with its fundamental premise of unequal distribution of power.

Our goal is to change not just ourselves and other men, but also the institutions that create inequality. We welcome any person who agrees in substance with these principles to membership in the National Organization for Men Against Sexism.

69

THE BLOW-UP . . .
A CLASH OF REALITIES

GLORIA E. ANZALDÚA

Gloria E. Anzaldúa was a tejana patlache (queer) nepantlera spiritual activist. Her book *Borderlands/La frontera: The New Mestiza* was chosen as one of the one hundred Best Books of the Century by both Hungry Mind Review and by Utne Reader. She was the author of *Interviews/Entrevistas* (edited by AnaLouise Keating); two bilingual children's books, *Friends from the Other Side/Amigos del otro lado* and *Prietita and the Ghost Woman/Prietita y la Llorona;* editor of *Making Face, Making Soul/Haciendo caras: Creative and Critical Perspectives by Feminists-of-Color;* and co-editor of *This Bridge Called My Back: Writings by Radical Women of Color.* Gloria played a pivotal role in redefining U.S. feminisms, culture studies, Chicano/a issues, U.S. American literature, ethnic studies, queer theory, and postcolonial theory. She died in 2004.

New knowledge occurs through tension, difficulties, mistakes and chaos.
— RISA D'ANGELES

You fly in from another speaking gig on the East Coast, arriving at the feminist academic conference late. Hayas un desmadre. A racist incident has unleashed flames of anger held in check for decades. In postures of defiance, enraged women of color protest their exclusion from the

Gloria E. Anzaldúa, "The Blow Up . . . A Clash of Realities" from *This Bridge We Call Home: Radical Visions for Transformation,* edited by Gloria Anzaldúa and AnaLouise Keating. Copyright © 2002 by Gloria Anzaldúa and Analouise Keating. Reprinted with the permission of Routledge/Taylor & Francis Books, Inc.

woman's organization decision-making processes; "white" middle-class women stand, arms crossed, refusing to alter its policies. When they continue conducting business as usual las mujeres de color walk out.

The urgency compelling every woman to give testimony to her views is so thick you can almost taste it. Caras reflejan angustia and blanched looks of shock; eyes glint with hostility; feelings of disgust, bitterness, disillusionment, and betrayal clash, spatter, and scatter in all directions. These emotions flare through your body as you turn from one group to another like a weathervane. You lose yourself in the maelstrom, no longer able to find the calm place within as everything collapses into unresolvable conflict. You know that in the heart of the conflagration lies its solution, but your own anguish clouds true perception. Catching your co-presenter's eye, you both grimace in recognition. Though for years you've felt the tectonic bedrock of feminism shifting under your feet, you never imagined the seismic crack would be so devastating, the blow-out so scorching. El mar de coraje (anger) se te viene encima — you recoil from its heat. Trying to be objective, you distance yourself until you feel as though you're in an airplane observing safely from above.

Like most feminist conferences, this one begins as a bridge, a place of mutual access where thousands crisscross, network, share ideas, and struggle together to resolve women's issues. After fifteen years of struggle, of putting their trust on this common space, of waiting for the organization to deal with racism as it's promised, the women of color and some Jewish, working-class, and progressive white allies feel betrayed by their white middle-class sisters. Seething in frustration, they cancel their panels and workshops, quejandose que las feministas anglas do not allow their intellectual, emotional, and spiritual realities into this academic setting. They're tired of being treated as outsiders. They feel that whites still view issues of racism as the concern of women of color alone, anti-Semitism the concern only of Jewish women, homophobia the concern of lesbians, and class the concern of working-class and poor women. They accuse whites of reinscribing the imperialist tradition of dominance and call them on their white privilege.

White women accuse women of color and their allies of emotionalism — after all, this is the academy. Feeling unjustly attacked, they adamantly proclaim they're not racist but just following the organization's policies. Though their intentions — making "common ground" — are good, they don't realize que su base de acuerdo may be different or too narrow from el terreno comunal de otras mujeres and not really common at all. They ignore the input of mujeres de color in defining common ground.

You view most white women's racism as covert and always cloaked. An insidious desconocimiento, it refuses to allow emotional awareness and its threat into their consciousness. They deny their recognition of the situation, then forget having denied this recognition. This forgetting of having forgotten their denial (repression) is at the core of desconocimiento. Though most white feminists intellectually acknowledge racism, they distance themselves from personal responsibility, often acting as though their reality and ways of knowing are universal, not culturally determined. They assume that feminist racialized "others" share their same values and goals. Some view gender and race oppression as interchangable. As members of a colonized gender, they believe they're experts on oppression and can define all its forms; thus they don't have to listen/learn from racial others. They herd women of color under the banner of their brand of feminism and impose their experiences and interpretations of reality, especially of academic life, on them—all racist acts.

The refusal to think about race (itself a form of racism) is a "white" privilege. The white women who do think about race rarely delve beyond the surface: they allude to the category, cite a few women-of-color texts, tack on a token book to their syllabi, and assume they've dealt with race. Though many understand the racism perpetrated by white individuals, most do not understand the racism inherent in their identities, in their cultures' stories. They can't see that racism harms them as well as people of color, itself a racially superior attitude. Those who see don't feel prepared to deal with race, though they do "feel bad" about it, suffering the monkey on their backs—survivor guilt, the guilt of privilege that, unacknowledged, breeds greater guilt.

When their racism is exposed they claim they're the victims of attacks and are outraged at being "mauled" by these pit-bullish others. They use white privilege to coax women of color to toe the line. When that doesn't work they pull rank. They fail to meet the women of color halfway, don't bother negotiating the give-and-take between "majority" culture and "minority." Though they may pay lip service to diversity issues, most don't shift from positions of power. The privilege of whiteness allows them to evade questions of complicity with those in power; it gives leave to disrespect other peoples' realities and types of knowledge—race and soul remain four-letter words. Their socialization does not allow women-of-color consciousness to transform their thinking. Afraid of losing material and psychological privilege, they drown others' voices with white noise.

Con nudo en la garganta, you look at your hermanas de color, challenged warriors, who try to stop being victims only to fall into the trap of claiming moral higher ground, using skin color as license for judging a whole category of people. They're forced to belabor the point because most white women won't listen. Leading with their wounds focuses their energy on the role of victim: oh, poor me, I'm so oppressed. Though inadvertently at times you too assume this attitude, you have little sympathy for it. Buying into victimhood forces you/them to compete for the coveted prize of the walking wounded. Many are driven to use the truth of their ill treatment as a stick to beat whites into waking up; they are the experts on oppression and thus don't have to listen/learn from whites. Some women of color—las meras meras—strut around with macha in-your-face aggressiveness. Hiding their vulnerabilities behind clenched fists and a "que se chinguen" attitude, they overlook the wounds bonding them to the other and instead focus on las heridas (wounds) that divide. As a writer one of your tasks is to expose the dualistic nature of the debate between whites and people of color, the false idealized pictures and other desconocimientos each group has but would rather ignore, and promote a more holistic perspective.

Seeing women from both camps throw words at each other like stones gives you stomach cramps. Apedradas (pelted with stones), each woman tries to regain her ground. Weaving her experience into a storyline where she's the one put-upon, she incites her allies to torch the bridge with inflammatory rhetoric. Pitting herself against the other (the enemy), she feeds las llamas her energy and repressed shadow parts, turning the conference into a militarized zone where desconocimiento runs rampant. In full-frontal attack, each camp adopts an "us-versus-them" model that assumes a winner and loser, a wrong and right—the prevailing conflict resolution paradigm of our times, one we continue using despite the recognition that confrontational tactics rarely settle disputes for the long run.

You watch some women react to psychological violence in instinctive knee-jerk ways or in ways they've programmed themselves or have been programmed to respond. The usual tactics for dealing with conflict and threat are fighting, fleeing, freezing, or submitting. Those fighting or fleeing shut their ears and assume a hypervigilant guard mode to help them attack or escape. Those freezing separate their awareness from the reality of what's happening—they dissociate. Those submitting surrender their ground to more aggressive forces. All struggle to burrow back into their past histories, former skins, familiar racial and class enclaves even though these may be rife with discomfort and disillusionment and no longer feel like "home."

Caught in the middle of the power struggle, you're forced to take sides, forced to negotiate another identity crisis. Being coerced to turn your back on one group/person and favor the other feels like a knife to the heart. It reminds you of the seventies when other lesbians reprimanded you and urged you to abandon your friendships with men. Women of color will brand you disloyal if you don't walk out with them. Nationalistic fence-maintainers will label you malinchista; lesbians will think you not queer enough. You retreat from your feelings, take refuge in your head, priding yourself on equanimity, an objectivity detached from the biases of personal fear, anger, anxiety. As you observe others, pitying their misguided actions, you catch yourself feeling superior because you don't let your emotions take over. Not you, you've achieved spiritual and emotional equilibrium. You'd like to believe that detachment is always a strength, that remaining emotionally distant allows you to bring a sense of balance to conflicted situations. But instead of attaining spiritual non-attachment, you've withdrawn from painful feelings—a detachment that cuts you from your body and its feelings.

What takes a bashing is not so much you but the idea/picture of who you think you are, an illusion you're hell-bent on protecting and preserving at all costs. You overlook the fact that your self-image and history (autohistoria) are not carved in stone but drawn on sand and subject to the winds. A threat to your identifications and interpretations of reality enrages your shadow-beast, who views the new knowledge as an attack to your bodily integrity. And it is a death threat—to the belief that posits the self as local and limited to a physical body, a body perceived as a container separating the self from other people and other forms of knowledge. New conocimientos (insights) threaten your sense of what's "real" when it's up against what's "real" to the other. But it's precisely this threat that triggers transformation.

You think you've made progress, gained a new awareness, found a new version of reality, created a workable story, fulfilled an obligation, and followed your own conscience. But when you cast to the world what you've created and put your ideals into action, the contradictions explode in your face. Your story fails the reality test. But is the failure due to flaws in your story—based on the tenuous nature of relationship between you and the whole—or is it due to all-too-human and therefore imperfect members of the community?

The bridge buckles under the weight of these feminist factions, and as in the Russian "Tale of Two Goats on the Bridge" (MacDonald), the different groups butt each other off. With other in-betweeners (nepantleras) from both sides of the divide you navigate entre tres aguas trying to sustain some sort of dialogue among the groups. Pronto llegas a un crucero—you have to decide whether to walk off or remain on the bridge and try to facilitate passage. Though you've always been a bridge, not a separatist, es difícil decidir. From the eye of the storm you choose to hold fast to the bridge and witness for all camps. With only half the participants present at the roundtable, you use the forum to discuss the causes of the blow-up and possible strategies to resolve the conflict.

Often in the following days you and other nepantleras feel frustrated, tempted to walk out as the bridge undergoes more tremors. Negotiating cuesta trabajo. Las nepantleras must alter their mode of interaction—make it more inclusive, open. In a to-and-fro motion they shift from their customary position to the reality of first one group then the other. Though tempted to retreat behind racial lines and hide behind simplistic walls of identity, las nepantleras know their work lies in positioning themselves—exposed and raw—in the crack between these worlds, and in revealing current categories as unworkable. Saben que las heridas that separate and those that bond arise from the same source. Besides fighting, fleeing, freezing, or submitting las nepantleras usan otra media—they employ a fifth tactic.

Recognizing that the basic human hunger to be heard, understood, and accepted is not being met, las nepantleras listen to members of both camps. By attending to what the other is not saying, what she's not doing, what isn't happening, and by looking for the opposite, unacknowledged emotion—the opposite of anger is fear, of self-righteousness is guilt, of hate is love—las nepantleras attempt to see through the other's situation to her underlying unconscious desire. Accepting doubts and ambiguity, they reframe the conflict and shift the point of view. Sitting face-to-face with all parties, they identify common bonds, name reciprocities and connections, and finally draft a mutually agreeable contract.

When perpetual conflict erodes a sense of connectedness and wholeness la nepantlera calls on the "connectionist"[1] faculty to show the deep common ground and interwoven kinship among all things and people. This faculty, one of less-structured thoughts, less-rigid categorizations, and thinner boundaries, allows us to picture—via reverie, dreaming, and artistic creativity—similarities instead of solid divisions. In gatherings where people luxuriate in their power to prevent change instead of using it to cause transformation, where they spew verbal abuse in a war of words and do not leave space for others to save face, where feelings are easily bruised or too intense to be controlled by will alone—la nepantlera proposes individual and group rituals to contain volatile feelings and channel them into acts of conocimiento.

In gatherings where people feel powerless la nepantlera offers rituals to say good-bye to old ways of relating; prayers to thank life for making us face loss, anger, guilt, fear, and separation; rezos to acknowledge our individual wounds; and commitments to not give up on others just because they hurt us. In gatherings where we've forgotten that the aim of conflict is peace, la nepantlera proposes spiritual techniques (mindfulness, openess, receptivity) along with activist tactics. Where before we saw only separateness, differences, and polarities, our connectionist sense of spirit recognizes nurturance and reciprocity and encourages alliances among groups working to transform communities. In gatherings where we feel our dreams have been sucked out of us, la nepantlera leads us in celebrating la comunidad soñada, reminding us that spirit connects the irreconcilable warring parts para que todo el mundo se haga un país, so that the whole world may become un pueblo.

NOTES

Quiero darle las gracias a mis "comadres in writing" por sus comentarios: a Carmen Morones, Randy Conner, Irene Reti, Liliana Wilson Grez, Kit Quan, and, most especially, AnaLouise Keating for her numerous, generous readings, right-on suggestions, and co-creation of this essay—les agradesco por animarme cuando me desanimaba. Thanks also to Bonnie Bentson and my graduate students in the Public Intellectuals Program at Florida Atlantic University.

1. I borrow this term from the "connectionist nets," the neural net consisting of billions of neurons in the human cortex. Connections are made in all states of consciousness, the most broad in artistic reverie and in dreaming, not in focused logical waking thought. The power of the imaginary must be utilized in conflict resolution.

REFERENCES

MacDonald, Margaret Read. "Tale of Two Goats on the Bridge." In *Peace Tales: World Folktales to Talk About.* North Haven, CT: Linnet Books, 1992.

70

AMERICAN INDIAN WOMEN
At the Center of Indigenous Resistance in Contemporary North America

M. ANNETTE JAIMES WITH THERESA HALSEY

M. Annette Jaimes has changed her name to Mariana Jaimes-Guerrero. She is an enrolled Juañeno/Yaqui and has been a writer and researcher for Women of All Red Nations (WARN), supporter of the Indigenous Women's Network, and a board member of the American Indian Anti-Defamation Council. A former instructor with the Center for Studies of Ethnicity and Race in America at the University of Colorado, she was instrumental in developing the American Indian Studies Program on that campus. In addition to her many published articles on indigenous people, she is editor of and contributor to *The State of Native North America* (South End Press), which was awarded a Gustavus Myers International Human Rights Award, and is author of *Native Womanism: Blueprint for a Global Revolution* (South End Press). Jaimes-Guerrero recently established the Center for Indigenous Global Studies.

Theresa Halsey (Standing Rock Sioux) is a long-time community activist, mostly focusing on educational issues. She is currently director of the Title V American Indian Education Program with the Boulder Valley (Colorado) School District.

> *A people is not defeated until the hearts of its women are on the ground.*
> TRADITIONAL CHEYENNE SAYING

> *The United States has not shown me the terms of my Surrender.*
> MARIE LEGO, PIT RIVER NATION, 1970

The two brief quotations forming the epigraph of this chapter were selected to represent a constant pattern of reality within Native North American life from the earliest times. This is that women have always formed the backbone of indigenous nations on this continent. Contrary to those images of meekness, docility, and subordination to males with which we women typically have been portrayed by the dominant culture's books

M. Annette Jaimes with Theresa Halsey, "American Indian Women: At the Center of Indigenous Resistance in Contemporary North America" from *The State of Native America: Genocide, Colonization, and Resistance,* edited by M. Annette Jaimes. Reprinted with the permission of South End Press.

and movies, anthropology, and political ideologues of both rightist and left-ist persuasions, it is women who have formed the very core of indigenous resistance to genocide and colonization since the first moment of conflict be-tween Indians and invaders. In contemporary terms, this heritage has in-formed and guided generations of native women such as the elder Marie Lego, who provided crucial leadership to the Pit River Nation's land claims struggle in northern California during the 1970s.[1]

In Washington state, women such as Janet McCloud (Tulalip) and Ra-mona Bennett (Puyallup) had already assumed leading roles in the fishing rights struggles of the '60s, efforts which, probably more than any other phe-nomena, set in motion the "hard-line" Indian liberation movements of the modern day. These were not political organizing campaigns of the ballot and petition sort. Rather, they were, and continue to be, conflicts involving the disappearance of entire peoples. As Bennett has explained the nature of the fishing rights confrontations:

> At this time, our people were fighting to preserve their last treaty
> right—the right to fish. We lost our land base. There was no game
> in the area. . . . We're dependent not just economically but
> culturally on the right to fish. Fishing is part of our art forms and
> religion and diet, and the entire culture is based around it. And so
> when we talk about [Euroamerica's] ripping off the right to fish,
> we're talking about cultural genocide.[2]

The fish-ins . . . were initially pursued within a framework of "civil dis-obedience" and "principled nonviolence," which went nowhere other than to incur massive official and quasi-official violence in response. "They [the police] came right on the reservation with a force of three hundred people," Bennett recounts. "They gassed us, they clubbed people around, they laid $125,000 bail on us. At that time I was a member of the Puyallup Tribal Council, and I was spokesman for the camp [of local fishing rights activists]. And I told them what our policy was: that we were there to protect our In-dian fishermen. And because I used a voice-gun, I'm being charged with in-citing a riot. I'm faced with an eight year sentence."[3] It was an elder Nisqually woman who pushed the fishing rights movement in western Washington to adopt the policy of armed self-defense, which ultimately proved successful (the struggle in eastern Washington took a somewhat dif-ferent course to the same position and results):

> Finally, one of the boys went down to the river to fish, and his
> mother went up on the bank. And she said: "This boy is nineteen
> years old and we've been fighting on this river for as many years
> as he's been alive. And no one is going to pound my son around,
> no one is going to arrest him. No one is going to touch my son or
> I'm going to shoot them. " And she had a rifle. . . . Then we had an
> armed camp in the city of Tacoma.[4]

The same sort of dynamic was involved in South Dakota during the early 1970s, when elder Oglala Lakota women such as Ellen Moves Camp and Gladys Bissonette assumed the leadership in establishing what was called the Oglala Sioux Civil Rights Organization (OSCRO) on the Pine Ridge Reservation. According to Bissonette, "Every time us women gathered to protest or demonstrate, they [federal authorities] always aimed machine guns at us women and children."[5] In response, she became a major advocate of armed self-defense at the reservation hamlet of Wounded Knee in 1973, remained within the defensive perimeter for the entire 71 days the U.S. government besieged the Indians inside, and became a primary negotiator for what was called the "Independent Oglala Nation."[6] Both women remained quite visible in the Oglala resistance to U.S. domination despite a virtual counterinsurgency war waged by the government on Pine Ridge during the three years following Wounded Knee.[7]

At Big Mountain, in the former "Navajo-Hopi Joint Use Area" in Arizona, where the federal government is even now attempting to forcibly relocate more than 10,000 traditional Diné (Navajos) in order to open the way for corporate exploitation of the rich coal reserves underlying their land, it is again elder women who have stood at the forefront of resistance, refusing to leave the homes of their ancestors. One of them, Pauline Whitesinger, was the first to physically confront government personnel attempting to fence off her land. Another, Katherine Smith, was the first to do so with a rifle.[8] Such women have constituted a literal physical barrier blocking consummation of the government's relocation/mining effort for more than a decade.[9] Many similar stories, all of them accruing from the past quarter-century, might be told in order to demonstrate the extent to which women have galvanized and centered contemporary native resistance.

The costs of such uncompromising (and uncompromised) activism have often been high. To quote Ada Deer, who, along with Lucille Chapman, became an essential spokesperson for the Menominee restoration movement in Wisconsin during the late 1960s and early '70s: "I wanted to get involved. People said I was too young, too naïve — you can't fight the system. I dropped out of law school. That was the price I had to pay to be involved."[10] Gladys Bissonette lost a son, Pedro, and a daughter, Jeanette, murdered by federal surrogates on Pine Ridge in the aftermath of Wounded Knee.[11] Other native women, such as American Indian Movement (AIM) members Tina Trudell and Anna Mae Pictou Aquash, have paid with their own and sometimes their children's lives for their prominent defiance of their colonizers.[12] Yet, it stands as a testament to the strength of American Indian women that such grim sacrifices have served, not to deter them from standing up for the rights of native people, but as an inspiration to do so. Mohawk activist and scholar Shirley Hill Witt recalls the burial of Aquash after her execution-style murder on Pine Ridge:

> Some women had driven from Pine Ridge the night before — a very dangerous act — "to do what needed to be done." Young women

dug the grave. A ceremonial tipi was set up. . . . A woman seven months pregnant gathered sage and cedar to be burned in the tipi. Young AIM members were pallbearers: they laid her on pine boughs while spiritual leaders spoke the sacred words and performed the ancient duties. People brought presents for Anna Mae to take with her to the spirit world. They also brought presents for her two sisters to carry back to Nova Scotia with them to give to her orphaned daughters. . . . The executioners of Anna Mae did not snuff out a meddlesome woman. They exalted a Brave Hearted Woman for all time.[13]

The motivations of indigenous women in undertaking such risks are un-equivocal. As Maria Sanchez, a leading member of the Northern Cheyenne re-sistance to corporate "development" of their reservation, puts it: "I am the mother of nine children. My concern is for their future, for their children, and for future generations. As a woman, I draw strength from the traditional spiri-tual people . . . from my nation. The oil and gas companies are building a huge gas chamber for the Northern Cheyennes."[14] Pauline Whitesinger has stated, "I think there is no way we can survive if we are moved to some other land away from ours. We are just going to waste away. People tell me to move, but I've got no place to go. I am not moving anywhere, that is certain."[15] Roberta Blackgoat, another leader of the Big Mountain resistance, concurs: "If this land dies, the people die with it. We are a nation. We will fight anyone who tries to push us off our land."[16] All across North America, the message from native women is the same.[17] The explicitly nationalist content of indigenous women's activism has been addressed by Lorelei DeCora Means, a Minneconjou Lakota AIM member and one of the founders of Women of All Red Nations (WARN):

We are *American Indian* women, in that order. We are oppressed, first and foremost, as American Indians, as peoples colonized by the United States of America, *not* as women. As Indians, we can never forget that. Our survival, the survival of every one of us—man, woman and child—*as Indians* depends on it. Decolonization is the agenda, the whole agenda, and until it is accomplished, it is the *only* agenda that counts for American Indians. It will take every one of us—every single one of us—to get the job done. We haven't got the time, energy or resources for anything else while our lands are being destroyed and our children are dying of avoidable diseases and malnutrition. So we tend to view those who come to us wanting to form alliances on the basis of "new" and "different" or "broader" and "more important" issues to be a little less than friends, especially since most of them come from the Euroamerican population which benefits most directly from our ongoing colonization.[18]

As Janet McCloud sees it:

Most of these "progressive" non-Indian ideas like "class struggle" would at the present time divert us into participating as "equals" in our own colonization. Or, like "women's liberation," would divide us among ourselves in such a way as to leave us colonized in the name of "gender equity." Some of us can't help but think maybe a lot of these "better ideas" offered by non-Indians claiming to be our "allies" are intended to accomplish exactly these sorts of diversion and disunity within our movement. So, let me toss out a different sort of "progression" to all you marxists and socialists and feminists out there. *You* join *us* in liberating *our* land and lives. Lose the privilege *you* acquire at *our* expense by occupying *our* land. Make *that* your first priority for as long as it takes to make it happen. *Then* we'll join you in fixing up whatever's left of the class and gender problems in your society, and our own, if need be. *But,* if you're not willing to do that, then don't presume to tell *us* how we should go about our liberation, what priorities and values we should have. Since you're standing on our land, we've got to view you as just another oppressor trying to hang on to what's ours. And that doesn't leave us a whole lot to talk about, now does it?[19]

• • •

The Road Ahead

Interestingly, women of other nonwhite sectors of the North American population have shared many native women's criticisms of the Euroamerican feminist phenomenon. African American women in particular have been outspoken in this regard. As Gloria Joseph argues:

> The White women's movement has had its own explicit forms of racism in the way it has given high priority to certain aspects of struggles and neglected others . . . because of the inherently racist assumptions and perspectives brought to bear in the first articulations by the White women's movement. . . . The Black movement scorns feminism partially on the basis of misinformation, and partially due to a valid perception of the White middle class nature of the movement. An additional reason is due to the myopic ways that white feminists have generalized their sexual-political analysis and have confirmed their racism in the forms their feminism has assumed.[20]

The "self-righteous indignation" and defensiveness that Joseph discerns as experienced by most Euroamerican feminists when confronted with such critiques is elsewhere explained by bell hooks as a response resting in the vested interest of those who feel it:

> Feminist emphasis on "common oppression" in the United States was less a strategy for politicization than an appropriation by conservative and liberal women of a radical political vocabulary

that masked the extent to which they shaped the movement so that it addressed and promoted their class interests. . . . White women who dominate feminist discourse, who for the most part make and articulate feminist theory, have little or no understanding of white supremacy as a racial politic, of the psychological impact of class, of their [own] political status within a racist, sexist, capitalist state."[21]

"I was struck," hooks says in her book, *Ain't I a Woman,* "by the fact that the ideology of feminism, with its emphasis on transforming and changing the social structure of the U.S., in no way resembled the reality of American feminism. Largely because [white] feminists themselves, as they attempted to take feminism beyond the realm of radical rhetoric into the sphere of American life, revealed that they remained imprisoned in the very structures they hoped to change. Consequently, the sisterhood we all talked about has not become a reality."[22] It is time to "talk back" to white feminists, hooks argues, "spoiling their celebration, their 'sisterhood,' their 'togetherness.'"[23] This must be done because in adhering to feminism in its present form

> we learn to look to those empowered by the very systems of domination that wound and hurt us for some understanding of who we are that will be liberating and we never find that. It is necessary for [women of color] to do the work ourselves if we want to know more about our experience, if we want to see that experience from perspectives not shaped by domination.[24]

Asian American women, Chicanas, and Latinas have agreed in substantial part with such assessments.[25] Women of color in general tend not to favor the notion of a "politics" which would divide and weaken their communities by defining "male energy" as "the enemy." It is not for nothing that no community of color in North America has ever produced a counterpart to white feminism's SCUM (Society for Cutting Up Men). Women's liberation, in the view of most "minority" women in the United States and Canada, cannot occur in any context other than the wider liberation, from Euroamerican colonial domination, of the peoples of which women of color are a part. Our sense of priorities is therefore radically—and irrevocably—different from those espoused by the "mainstream" women's movement.

Within this alienation from feminism lies the potential for the sorts of alliances which may in the end prove most truly beneficial to American Indian people. By forging links to organizations composed of other women of color, founded not merely to fight gender oppression, but also to struggle against racial and cultural oppression, native women can prove instrumental in creating an alternative movement of women in North America, one which is mutually respectful of the rights, needs, cultural particularities, and historical divergences of each sector of its membership, and which is therefore free of the adherence to white supremacist hegemony previously marring feminist thinking and practice. Any such movement of women—including those

Euroamerican women who see its thrust as corresponding to their own values and interests as human beings — cannot help but be of crucial importance within the liberation struggles waged by peoples of color to dismantle the apparatus of Eurocentric power in every area of the continent. The greater the extent to which these struggles succeed, the closer the core agenda of Native North America — recovery of land and resources, reassertion of self-determining forms of government, and reconstitution of traditional social relations within our nations — will come to realization.

NOTES

1. For further information on Marie Lego and the context of her struggle, see Jaimes, M. Annette, "The Pit River Indian Land Claims Dispute in Northern California," *Journal of Ethnic Studies,* Vol. 4, No. 4, Winter 1987.
2. Quoted in Katz, Jane B., *I Am the Fire of Time: The Voices of Native American Women,* E. P. Dutton Publisher, New York 1977, p. 146.
3. Quoted in ibid., p. 147. Bennett was eventually acquitted after being shot, while seven months pregnant, and wounded by white vigilantes.
4. Ibid.
5. Quoted in ibid., p. 141.
6. The best account of the roles of Gladys Bissonette and Ellen Moves Camp during the siege may be found in Editors, *Voices from Wounded Knee, 1973, Akwesasne Notes,* Mohawk Nation via Rooseveltown, NY, 1974.
7. Churchill, Ward, and Tim Van der Wall. *The COINTELPRO Papers: Documents on the FBI's Secret Wars Against Dissent in the United States,* South End Press, Boston, 1990, pp. 231–302. Also see Matthiessen, Peter, *In the Spirit of Crazy Horse,* Viking Press, New York (2nd edition) 1991.
8. Kammer, Jerry, *The Second Long Walk: The Navajo-Hopi Land Dispute,* University of New Mexico Press, Albuquerque, 1980, pp. 1–2, 209.
9. For further information on Big Mountain, see Parlow, Anita, *Cry, Sacred Land: Big Mountain, USA,* Christic Institute, Washington. D.C., 1988.
10. Quoted in Katz. op. cit., p. 151. For further background on Ada Deer, see her autobiography (Deer, Ada, with R. E. Simon, Jr., *Speaking Out,* Children's Press, Chicago, 1970).
11. On the murders of Pedro and Jeanette Bissonette, see Churchill, Ward, and Jim Vander Wall, *Agents of Repression: The FBI's Secret Wars Against the Black Panther Party and the American Indian Movement,* South End Press, Boston, 1988, pp. 187, 200–3.
12. Concerning the murders of Tina Manning Trudell, her three children (Ricarda Star, age five; Sunshine Karma, three; and Eli Changing Sun, one), and her mother, Leah Hicks Manning, see ibid., pp. 361–4. On Aquash, see Brand, Johanna, *The Life and Death of Anna Mae Aquash,* James Lorimax Publishers, Toronto, 1978.
13. Hill Witt, Shirley, "The Brave-Hearted Women: The Struggle at Wounded Knee," *Akwesasne Notes,* Vol. 8, No. 2, 1976, p. 16.
14. Quoted in Katz, op. cit., pp. 145–6.
15. Quoted in Kammer, op. cit., p. 18.
16. From a talk delivered during International Women's Week, the University of Colorado at Boulder, April 1984 (tape on file).

17. Such sentiments are hardly unique to the United States. For articulation by Canadian Indian women, see Silman, Janet, *Enough Is Enough: Aboriginal Women Speak Out*, The Women's Press, Toronto, 1987.

18. From a talk delivered during International Women's Week, the University of Colorado at Boulder, April 1985 (tape on file).

19. From a talk delivered during International Women's Week, University of Colorado at Boulder, April 1984 (tape on file).

20. Joseph, Gloria I., and Jill Lewis, *Common Differences: Conflicts in Black and White Feminist Perspectives*, South End Press, Boston, 1981, pp. 4–6.

21. hooks, bell, *Feminist Theory: From Margin to Center*, South End Press, Boston, 1984, pp. 4–8.

22. hooks, bell, *Ain't I a Woman: Black Women and Feminism*, South End Press, Boston, 1981, p. 190.

23. hooks, bell, *Talking Back: Thinking Feminist, Thinking Black*, South End Press, Boston, 1989, p. 149.

24. Ibid., pp. 150–1.

25. For a sample of these perspectives, see Moraga, Cherríe, and Gloria Anzaldúa, eds., *This Bridge Called My Back: Writings by Radical Women of Color*, Kitchen Table Press, New York, 1983.

71

TOWARD A NEW CIVIC LEADERSHIP:
The Africana Criminal Justice Project

GEOFF K. WARD AND MANNING MARABLE

Geoff K. Ward is currently the Andrew W. Mellon Foundation Postdoctoral Fellow on Race, Crime, and Justice at the Vera Institute of Justice, where he is studying how African-American professionals and organizations worked to improve services to children and youth in Harlem between 1910 and 1960. Ward is also a Visiting Scholar at the Institute for Research in African-American Studies at Columbia University (1200 Amsterdam Avenue, New York, NY 10027; e-mail: Gkw2001@ columbia.edu), where he is teaching and helping to coordinate the Africana Criminal Justice Project.

Manning Marable is professor and director of the Institute for Research in African-American Studies at Columbia University (e-mail: marable1@manningmarable.net), and specializes in African-American history. He is the editor of the journal *SOULS*, and the author of many books, including *What Black America Thinks: Race, Ideology, and Political Power* (1998), *Black Liberation in Conservative America* (1997), *Speaking Truth to Power: Essays on Race, Radicalism and Resistance* (1996), *Beyond Black and White* (1995), and *Race, Reform, and Rebellion: The Second Reconstruction in Black America, 1945–1990* (1991).

Introduction

The extraordinary growth and carceral thrust of United States criminal justice policy and procedure over the past quarter century has led observers to label this a "prison nation" (see Abramsky, 2002; Wacquant, 2001). There is hardly a more fitting description for how the prison in particular, and criminal justice system in general, have emerged as dominant fixtures on our cultural, economic, and political landscape. Our leaders offer mass criminalization and incarceration as surrogate responses to persistent poverty and unemployment, drug abuse, violence, mental health problems, failing public schools, and other American dilemmas. Its beneficiaries notwithstanding, the ascendance of a fundamentally inhumane, fiscally absurd, and socially

Geoff K. Ward and Manning Marable, "Toward a New Civic Leadership: The Africana Criminal Justice Project," *Social Justice* 30, no. 2 (2003). Copyright © 2003 by *Social Justice*. Reprinted with the permission of the publisher.

dysfunctional criminal justice apparatus signals the failure of societal leadership, and a call to civic action.

In this essay, we briefly consider how mass criminalization and incarceration have affected African-American individuals, families, and communities, particularly in terms of civic capacity and participation. We follow this discussion with an overview of the Africana Criminal Justice Project, a research, education, and organizing initiative aiming to help identify and eradicate dimensions of racialized social and political exclusion that are generated, reproduced, and intensified by past and present U.S. criminal justice policy. Through this work, the Africana Criminal Justice Project seeks to reframe academic and policy debates on issues of race and criminal justice, and help to mobilize initiatives to address the crisis of racialized mass incarceration. Critical research and education initiatives within Africana Studies can contribute to this effort, but especially important will be organizing civic leadership among former prisoners themselves, and within communities facing the staggering collateral consequences of the overdevelopment of the prison.

Birth of a Prison Nation: A Brief Overview

The ascent of our prison nation is apparent wherever one turns, and equally daunting in its quantitative and qualitative proportions. Researchers have documented that more than two million adults are currently incarcerated in this country, a result of over two decades of continually increasing rates and terms of incarceration. In 1972, 93 of every 100,000 adults in this country were incarcerated. By 1998, the rate had more than quadrupled to 452 per 100,000, with many prisoners facing longer mandatory sentences (Zimring, 2001: 161–162).

To house this inmate population, there are now over 1,000 state and federal prisons, an average of more than 20 facilities per state. Many of these are new facilities. Between 1817 and 1981 for example, New York opened 33 state prisons. Then, in the relatively few years between 1982 and 1999, New York built 38 more prisons. Nationally, approximately 700 new prisons have been built in the past 20 years alone, most of which are located in rural communities, many miles from the urban centers where most prisoners and their loved ones dwell. The prison has become a sort of backward frontier in a land of ever-diminishing opportunity, a destination drawing busloads each day. Since 1998, about 600,000 people have returned from prisons to their communities each year (Sentencing Project, 2002).

This growing population of prisoners is hardly a societal cross-section. Rather, the U.S. prison and jail population is disproportionately comprised of young, poorly educated, under- and unemployed people of color. Nearly two-thirds of all state prisoners in 1991 had less than a high school education, and one-third of all prisoners were unemployed at the time of their arrest. About one-half of all prisoners are African-American. The rate of incarceration among African-Americans was so high in 1989 that it surpassed even that of blacks living under the apartheid regime of South Africa.

Mass criminalization and incarceration increasingly affect women of color. From 1980 to 2000, the female inmate population in the U.S. increased by more than 500% and the rate of incarceration for black women has increased more than that of black men. In addition to the particular hardships experienced by incarcerated women themselves, the growing number of women in prison has introduced tremendous strains on children, extended families, and child welfare resources. In 1993, there were 1.5 million children in this country with incarcerated mothers, a statistic that has undoubtedly increased in the decade since (Bloom and Steinhart, 1993). Eighty percent of all imprisoned women have children, and of those women, 70% are single mothers. Like their male counterparts, the majority of women prisoners were either unemployed or earning under $15,000 in annual income in the year before their arrest and conviction. In excess of three-fourths of all women who are incarcerated have been convicted of nonviolent crimes.

The incredible increase in rates of incarceration in the United States over the past three decades is well documented, as is its disproportionate impact on poor men and women of color. Far less is known about the broader and enduring political, economic, and social consequences of these trends. The depth and consequences of our social investment in the prison is likely most evident outside the walls and beyond the statistics, permeating the layers of our cultural fabric, and the lived experiences of the individuals, families, and communities that occupy the old ground zeroes of our "wars" on drugs and crime.

Developments in public education offer a case in point. In several states, dollar-for-dollar divestment in public education has funded the construction of jails and prisons. Further, penal "zero-tolerance" policies and policing strategies have been adopted in urban public school management, effectively criminalizing student misbehavior in otherwise severely under-resourced schools. Divestment in education and the criminalization of school misconduct, combined with the disruption of social ties and mechanisms of informal social control through high levels of incarceration, likely result in a direct pipeline from failing public school systems to hopeless prisons, a conveyor almost exclusive to black and Latino/a communities. To be sure, our devolution into a prison nation is only first apparent in the outward indicators of facilities and their inmates, and most profound in its broader and more complex implications for the web of social and political relations.

It is welcome news that rates of incarceration have finally slowed, but even if the prisons were miraculously emptied tomorrow, our need to understand how decades of mass incarceration have affected U.S. society would remain. It is critical that we interrogate precisely how the rise of the prison as a dominant social institution has adversely affected other cultural and institutional spheres, and what we can do to address these developments. A growing number of activists, scholars, and other stakeholders is committing itself to this work, recognizing the fundamental contradictions and challenges mass criminalization and incarceration pose for the ideal of an open and democratic society, especially considering the racial dynamics in these mechanisms of exclusion (see Mauer and Chesney-Lind, 2002; Wacquant, 2001).

Criminal Injustice and Civic Alienation: Sketches of the Black Experience

At an accelerated pace over the past 25 years, millions of Americans have been subject to criminal sanctions that revoke or substantially limit fundamental rights of citizenship and the capacity to function as civic actors. Through this continuum of punishments, an individual who has been convicted of a crime, served a term of incarceration, and completed parole continues to be punished at every turn. Scholars and policy advocates have used terms such as "civil disability" and "civil death" to descibe these sanctions, and particularly the barriers they impose on those seeking to live, work, and participate in civil society free of discrimination.

Forms of civic alienation and exclusion deriving from criminal justice administration are found in multiple institutional contexts, including housing, education, employment, and governance. The disqualification of felons and prisoners from federal Pell Grant and other student aid program eligibility, the removal of educational programs from correctional institutions, the liberalization of access to juvenile delinquency records, and the disqualification of those with felony drug convictions from welfare support and access to public housing are all examples of criminal justice policies that severely diminish civic capacity and participation. However, short of outright deportation, the most striking representation of civil death in U.S. criminal justice policy, and one that may serve to reinforce all others over time, is the issue of felon disfranchisement, the temporary or permanent disqualification of voting rights for current and former felons.

Despite its relative invisibility in public discourse on U.S. criminal justice policy, felon disfranchisement is not an unusual occurrence. In 48 of the 50 states, adults incarcerated in state correctional facilities are not allowed to vote. Most states maintain voting restrictions for varying periods for people formerly incarcerated for felony convictions. In more than a dozen states, ex-felons are prohibited from voting for the remainder of their lives, barring their completion of a cumbersome and often costly voting-right restoration process. Overall, 4.3 million citizens—including 1.4 million black Americans—have lost the right to vote for life (Fellner and Mauer, 1998).

As of 1999, approximately 13% of all black male adults were disqualified from voting due to criminal convictions. In the state of Florida alone, over 250,000 African-Americans cannot vote because of felon disfranchisement. In Mississippi, Alabama, South Carolina, Texas, and other states, between one-quarter and one-fifth of *all voting age black residents* have either permanently or temporarily been stripped of their access to the ballot (*Ibid.*). As revealed in the most recent presidential election, there can be very substantial and long-term consequences to these patterns of political exclusion (see Uggen and Manza, 2000). Looking forward, we should be concerned that because of a felony conviction, juveniles can lose access to the ballot, for life in some states, even before they possess it.

Compounding the problem of felon disfranchisement is the enumeration of prisoners as residents of prison towns in the U.S. census and the use of these counts to form legislative districts. This practice has the dual effect of diluting the voting power of individuals in the prisoner's home district, usually urban ghettoes, while inflating the influence of voters in the typically rural districts where prisons are based. Many of these voting residents will have policy interests rather distinct and often in opposition to those prisoners and urban dwellers whose voting power they assume (Wagner, 2002). Here, then, is another means by which current and former prisoners, along with their dependents and political allies, experience systematic alienation and exclusion in democratic processes of civic engagement. The intersection of race (as well as gender and class), mass incarceration, and residential segregation in our society concentrates this powerlessness, now and into the future, thus intensifying the marginalization of black and brown communities.

Curtailed access to education compliments disfranchisement in the scenario of civil death and must be addressed in efforts to promote and enhance the civic capacity and participation of current and former prisoners. Despite clear evidence that educational achievement in correctional institutions greatly decreases rates of recidivism, current criminal justice policies provide fewer and fewer resources and incentives for educational development in the adult and juvenile justice systems. Beyond their implications for recidivism and labor market participation, however, exclusionary educational policies curtail civic capacity by disabling individuals who could otherwise exercise a more informed voice in appointive processes of representative government, in debates on public policy, and in local community leadership. Here lies another contour to the problem of the "imprisoned intellectual," where mass incarceration involves formal denial of opportunities for developing the human mind.

It is important to stress that although these sanctions are directed at individual offenders, they have an aggregate social and historical consequence, an impact concentrated in the highly segregated and poor African-American and Latino/a communities from which prisoners disproportionately come, and to which the vast majority return. Felon disfranchisement illustrates how this impact can reach beyond the individual convicted of a crime to the detriment of those individuals, families, and communities with whom their lives are intertwined. Disfranchisement not only limits the civic capacity of a substantial constituency of former prisoners but, by extension, also the capacity of their dependants, their political allies, and their advocates. In the aggregate, whole communities can lose the capacity to participate in representative governance, and thus to influence a wide range of policies related to education, health care, criminal justice, employment, and other matters bearing upon individual and collective life chances. Skeptics will counter that prisoners are not inclined to vote anyway, but this ignores the generally low U.S. voter participation rate, and more important, makes the error of valuing civil rights according to how often they are used.

Research has not begun to truly map out the ecological and political dimensions of civic incapacitation through criminal justice sanctions, but the communities marked by this hyper-marginalization are likely rather distinct. In 1992, nearly 80% of inmates at New York's Rikers Island Prison resided in only 10 New York City communities. Although New York's felon disfranchisement laws are less onerous than others are, these data likely reflect a common pattern of concentrated criminalization and incarceration in residential areas. In states with severe civil disqualifications, this concentration can effectively remove a community with large numbers of current and former prisoners, along with their dependents and allies, from processes of representative governance. Indeed, there is a point at which civil death becomes civil genocide, or, the effective "whipping out" of a particular public within the body politic.

Toward a New Civic Leadership: The Africana Criminal Justice Project

The African-American experience is burdened by a long history of disfranchisement that—from emancipation through the 21st century—has largely been facilitated through criminal justice sanctions. Ever since the collapse of the first Reconstruction, racialized criminal justice policies and procedures have substantially weakened the ability of otherwise marginalized African-American communities to participate in democratic processes of civic engagement. This includes appointive processes of local, state, and federal government, as well as more movement in public space, access to education and employment, the ability to sit on juries, and to otherwise participate in civil life and leadership.

African-American civic capacity and participation have been truncated over the years by a variety of criminal justice mechanisms, from the nebulous "Black Codes" of the Jim Crow era, the systematic exclusion of black children and youth from juvenile rehabilitative institutions and programs, the brutality of the convict lease and chain gang systems, police complicity with mob violence and other forms of corruption, exclusion from the ranks of justice workers and professionals, to disparate applications of the death penalty and much more. The potentially severe and long-term impact of criminal injustice systems for black civic capacity is also evident in covert government efforts to neutralize or destroy popular black political movements and in the continuing ordeal of black political prisoners. These imprisoned intellectuals and organizers have been removed from their communities for decades now, and might otherwise be playing integral roles in the civic leadership so needed in many of these communities today.

Paired with contemporary manifestations, the long history of racialized disfranchisement through criminal justice sanctions suggests for some the futility of efforts to promote black civic capacity and participation through research, education, and organizing initiatives. It has been suggested, for example, that civil society in the U.S. exists in fundamental opposition to black people, that is, by their formal and informal exclusion. By this logic, there is an irresolvable contradiction in the very term African-American, and no possibility for a meaningful black civic capacity or participation in U.S. civil society.

Without denying that ideological and institutional expressions of white supremacy permeate U.S. and other Western societies, and recognizing the profound marginality of the black civic actor, the dismissal of black civic capacity and participation outright is a historically inaccurate and fatalistic concession to the scope and power of structural racism. Oppressive regimes from chattel slavery to Jim Crow teach us that, even at the sites of greatest oppression, civil death is never complete. African-Americans and their allies have in this past century and before made important strides in redefining our individual and collective circumstance in this nation's legal, political, and social milieu. It has been a long, often slow and nonlinear progression. However, actors as diverse as Nat Turner, Frederick Douglass, Sojourner Truth, Ida B. Wells-Barnett, W.E.B. DuBois, Marcus Garvey, Fannie Lou Hamer, and Malcolm X have demonstrated that expertise in the very meaning of civil society, and especially our distance from it, can be drawn from a lived experience in the crucible of oppression and used to transform society.

Several of the most prominent African-American civic leaders and political commentators of our era — Malcolm X, George Jackson, and Mumia Abu-Jamal — generated incisive analyses and an enhanced leadership capacity within the context of the prison, reflecting not only that prisoners can survive incarceration, but also that some will manage to grow spiritually and intellectually in this most stifling of contexts. This is not at all to romanticize the horrors of this peculiar institution. The dynamic described here is evident across each of the regimes that have sought to stamp out the humanity and civic capacity of African-American people. Yet the particular barriers faced by generations of black civic actors have been oppressive, but also enabling and generative, especially for developing insight into how exclusionary systems operate and how one can escape, disrupt, and uproot them. Among the possible outcomes of oppression, in other words, is a thickening of the analytic lens and a resolve to act on its findings.

This dynamic points to the importance of engaging and further developing black intellectual work on crime and justice, especially by those who have experienced the alienation of criminalization and incarceration. In the African-American context, critical works begin to appear in the form slave narratives, continuing through the writings of black scholars, literary and political figures, and the prolific political prisoners of the post-Civil Rights period. If the heftiest lens forms at the proverbial bottom of the well, it will be critical to tap the contemporary intellectual work of current and former prisoners, their families, and supporters. Who better to address the problems of mass incarceration than those who have borne the brunt of its destructive and exclusionary force?

The challenge of gathering these insights has been taken up recently by a group of scholars, justice practitioners, students, and community activists working on the *Africana Criminal Justice Project,* an initiative based at Columbia University's Center for Contemporary Black History. We begin with the position that as an interdisciplinary field of research and education, Africana Studies has fostered innovative and effective approaches to the study of African-Americans and the Black Diaspora communities, especially in terms of social interaction, inequality, and change. Indeed, Africana Studies is further distinguished by its forthright commitment to the pursuit of social and racial justice, or rather, its determination to be relevant and useful to its communities of interest. Though not often recognized for contributions to the study of crime and justice, a long line of black scholars and public intellectuals has developed such analyses from various disciplinary and ideological perspectives, contributing to what is distinguishable today as a literature of Africana criminology and criminal justice. These streams of knowledge — from current and former black prisoners, public intellectuals, activists, artists, and scholars — might offer valuable intellectual frameworks for understanding problems of crime and justice, and particular guidance on ways to abolish what one early 20th-century black community leader aptly termed, "the slavery of our inequitous criminal justice system" (Washington, 1918).

Through the *Africana Criminal Justice Project,* we hope to further develop and stimulate engagement with this intellectual tradition in black studies, to identify its contributions to the analysis of the contemporary crisis of racialized mass incarceration, and to support initiatives seeking to address this crisis, especially through the promotion of black civic capacity and leadership. The project is meant to compliment and expand the important work of a growing community of activists, scholars, practitioners, and community leaders, who have undertaken to steer this nation off its destructive course of mass imprisonment and to address the collateral damages resulting from decades of commitment to this failure of social policy. Ultimately, we hope these efforts will help to inform and sustain a growing civic movement that seeks to dismantle the barriers of structural racism presently enforced by mass criminalization and incarceration, and that ultimately undermine the possibility of a truly open and democratic society.

REFERENCES

Abramsky, Sasha. 2002. *Hard Time Blues: How Politics Built a Prison Nation.* New York: St. Martins Press.

Bloom, Barbara and David Steinhart. 1993. *Why Punish Children.* San Francisco: National Council on Crime and Delinquency.

Fellner, Jamie and Marc Mauer. 1998. *Losing the Vote: The Impact of Felony Disenfranchisement Laws in the United States.* Washington, D.C.: Human Rights Watch and The Sentencing Project.

Mauer, Marc and Meda Chesney-Lind (eds.). 2002. *Invisible Punishment: The Collateral Consequences of Mass Imprisonment*. New York: The New Press.

Sentencing Project. 2002. "Prisoners Re-entering the Community." *Fact Sheet #1036*. Washington, D.C.: The Sentencing Project.

Uggen, Christopher and Jeff Manza. 2000. "The Political Consequences of Felon Disenfranchisement Laws in the United States." Paper presented at the annual meeting of the American Sociological Association, Washington, D.C., August 16, 2000.

Wacquant, Loïc. 2001. "Deadly Symbiosis: When Ghetto and Prison Meet and Merge." *Punishment & Society* 3,1: 95–134.

Wagner, Peter. 2002. "Importing Constituents: Prisoners and Political Clout in New York." Springfield, MA: Prison Policy Initiative.

Washington, Josephine T. 1918. "Child Saving in Alabama." *Colored American Magazine* 14: 48–51.

Zimring, Franklin. 2001. "Imprisonment Rates and the New Politics of Criminal Punishment." *Punishment & Society* 3,1 (January): 161–166.

72

ORGANIZING FOR PEACE IN ISRAEL:
Why Israeli Women Want a Peace Movement of Their Own

GILA SVIRSKY

Gila Svirsky is a veteran peace and human rights activist in Israel, and has headed some of the major peace and human rights organizations in Israel—the New Israel Fund, Bat Shalom, and B'Tselem. She has been a member of Women in Black since its inception, and co-founded the Coalition of Women for Peace, which brings together nine Israeli women's peace organizations and engages in some dramatic acts of resistance to end Israel's occupation of the Palestinian territories. Svirsky has also addressed the UN Security Council (in 2002) about the role of women in negotiations for peace. She writes extensively about political issues in the Middle East, and is the recipient of several peace prizes.

On Sunday, February 4, 2001, 500 women gathered on the road opposite Israel's ministry of defense in Tel Aviv. We dressed in black and donned sandwich boards with the word "closure" painted across them in Hebrew, Arabic, and English. At a signal, a small group of us slowly moved into the road and sat down, forming a line clear across it and completely blocking all passage of cars. Within moments, another group of women joined us and stood with their placards facing the cars. We formed a solid block of "closure" signs that completely stopped traffic in both directions. This, we felt, might help the generals understand what a "closure" feels like—what it's like to be prevented from entering or leaving your city or village, a tactic frequently imposed on Palestinian towns. Within minutes, policemen roared up on motorcycles shrieking with sirens. They plowed in and grabbed women, with considerable force, and threw us into police vans. Other women replaced the first group on the road, until they were arrested, too. Seventeen of us spent the night in jail.

This action, carried out by the Coalition of Women for Peace, launched a dramatic and often daring series of direct-action events. Until the "closure" demonstration, the women's peace movement in Israel had mostly used vigils, dialogue, and joint activities with Palestinian women. Now it had added nonviolent resistance to its repertoire. In this article, I will look at the diverse strategies and ideological underpinnings of the women's peace movement in Israel. I believe that this analysis will make evident why we feel that we need "a peace movement of our own."

The Coalition of Women for Peace is composed of 9 different women's peace organizations in Israel, each with its own strategy and target audience (see sidebar #1). The Coalition speaks for the women's peace movement as a whole and has its own range of activities: It conducts mass rallies and outreach programs to Israeli populations who do not generally share our political views; it organizes bus tours of the occupied territories, urgent-action e-mail lists, and trilingual websites to mobilize international opinion; and participates in direct action in the Occupied Territories. Much of the Coalition's nonviolent resistance has included acts declared illegal by the authorities, such as blocking the entrance to the ministry of defense. Some actions are carried out together with mixed-gender peace organizations, such as rebuilding Palestinian homes that the Israeli Defense Force (IDF) demolished or removing blockades and filling in trenches intended to enforce the closure. Women have blocked bulldozers with their bodies, chained themselves to olive trees, and confronted soldiers in efforts to prevent further destruction of Palestinian homes and property. Much joint work has also been done with Palestinian women to prevent construction of the so-called security wall. Some of the Coalition's actions have ended in arrests, and many ended in injury to protesters by security forces. (See Sidebar #2 for the Coalition's principles.)

The women's peace movement has also engaged in humanitarian aid as a political statement: helping Palestinian families with the olive harvest; providing school supplies, infant food, sanitary napkins, and other needs. Astonishingly, we generally have to struggle with the IDF to allow aid to enter the Palestinian areas.

The Coalition has also held some dramatic public actions within Israel. Three months after the current Intifadah began in fall 2000, 5,000 Israeli and

Palestinian women marched together from the Israeli to the Palestinian side of Jerusalem under the banner "We Refuse to be Enemies." We held a concert for peace, featuring Israeli and Palestinian women performing works that express our longing for peace. We organized a cavalcade of cars that drove through Israel bearing signs like, "The Price of the Occupation is Too High!" We staged a mass "die-in" in Tel Aviv: 1,000 women dressed in black lying flat out on the hot summer pavement under the banner "The Occupation is Killing Us All." Most recently, we have held "walking exhibitions," holding blown-up photos of the carnage in Gaza and standing opposite the lines of people waiting to buy tickets for theater or concert performances in the heartland of cultured Israel. As the violence continues, we wrack our brains to come up with new ways of waking up other Israelis.

Women constitute the majority of participants even in the mixed-gender peace movement, though they rarely become the decision-makers in these groups. Women are also the initiators and main actors in the organization Black Laundry: Lesbians and Gay Men Against the Occupation. I would be remiss if I did not also mention that lesbians are disproportionately represented throughout the peace and human rights community.

Ideologically, the Coalition of Women for Peace has a broader social vision than that of the mixed-gender peace organizations. We view the conflict as integrally related to social, economic, and gender issues. Indeed, the conflict with the Palestinians directly affects both gender inequality and oppression of the poor. Regarding gender inequality, in a society at war—where it is predominantly the men who are risking their lives in army service and making military and political decisions—men and their views become valued and privileged over women and our views. This entrenches inequality for women, leaving us at a disadvantage in competing for jobs, political office, and social status. The conflict also deepens poverty, as Israel sinks vast resources into security at the expense of housing, education, health care for the elderly, and other social needs. And since few women are capital holders but rather are likely to find themselves among the poor, women become the first victims of unemployment and recession, both of which currently plague the Israeli economy.

While ending the conflict is important for its own sake—to protect men and women on both sides—it is also important for the sake of the equality of women and the enfranchisement of the poor.

The most successful peace movement ever in Israel was a women's organization—the Four Mothers Movement. This group, founded in 1997 by four women whose sons served in the Israeli occupation of southern Lebanon, sought to mobilize the Israeli public to demand that Israel withdraw its troops from Lebanon, on the grounds that Israel's prolonged presence there served no security purpose and jeopardized the lives of soldiers. The movement was initially met with scorn from senior military officers. "What do women know about security?" they mocked. Indeed, at the heart of the Four Mothers' strategy was the leveraging of their status as mothers.

This was effective in a society that may disrespect professional women but honors its mothers. The Four Mothers Movement never used civil disobedience but rather held small demonstrations and vigils that highlighted the sincerity of their plea as law-abiding women, not activists or politicians. Their status as mothers who had sons serving in combat units gave them the right, in the eyes of the public, to challenge Israeli policy in Lebanon. They demanded—and were accorded—meetings with the highest government officials, whose inadequate answers were then magnified through the well-run media work of this group. The mother-oriented nature of this movement, and its dissociation from partisan politics, struck an empathetic nerve among the Israeli public. The deaths of Israeli soldiers were on the increase in Lebanon, and the message of the Four Mothers fell on attentive ears, feeding public dismay over the seemingly endless body bags. When some generals weighed in on the mothers' side, the tide was reversed. Within three years of the start of the movement, the Israeli army withdrew from Lebanon.

The Four Mothers Movement disbanded in 2000 upon the Israeli evacuation of its troops from Lebanon. Avowedly non-feminist and non-radical, the women in this movement successfully exploited the traditional role of motherhood to buttress their emotional appeal. And yet, scratching the surface reveals that a large proportion of the activists were themselves feminists, progressives, and professional women—and highly skilled at using the media. The apparent success of this movement deserves a careful analysis: The peace movement may have paid a high price for exalting women as mothers rather than thinkers and doers. Is it possible that women, a group that often includes people particularly skilled at bridge-building, will continue to be kept away from the peace negotiation tables around the world because we nurture our maternal image?

The women's peace movement in Israel has consistently articulated progressive positions—well before the mixed-gender peace movement adopted them. Women advocated a two-state solution, sharing Jerusalem, and returning to Israel's 1967 border long before other peace movements reached these conclusions. These views are today rapidly approaching consensus within Israel, but when we first uttered them, we were branded "pariahs"—the title of the only article in an Israeli newspaper that ever featured our movement.

The women's peace movement continues to assume unpopular positions: encouraging young people to refuse to serve in an army of occupation, labeling as "war crimes" some military actions, advocating against the so-called "security fence," refusing to go along with the prevalent military culture. Our actions are often imaginative and original in a relentless (though often futile) effort to arouse media interest and win public sympathy. Women have also proven to be steadfast peace activists, maintaining the Women in Black vigil every single week for almost 17 years.

Above all, women in both Israel and Palestine have crossed the great divide, forging a peace agreement decades before the Rabin-Arafat talks and maintaining their links with each other despite the Palestinian suicide-bombings, the Israeli invasions, and all the lives lost and destroyed. The feminist principles of an egalitarian world and the nonviolent resolution of conflict have been at the core of our commitment, enabling Israeli and Palestinian women to sustain our alliance for peace despite the bitter reality outside and the pressures within our own societies.

SIDEBAR #1

The Coalition of Women for Peace includes nine different women's organizations in Israel, each using a different strategy, all with the goal of promoting peace with our Arab neighbors, particularly the Palestinians. These organizations include a mix of Jewish and Palestinian women, all citizens of Israel. The member organizations and their strategies:

- *Bat Shalom* is the Israeli sister organization to the Palestinian *Jerusalem Center for Women,* both of which are joined as *The Jerusalem Link.* Members hammer out political accords with Palestinian women, conduct dialogue groups, document the history of women in conflict, and conduct actions on the ground.
- *The Fifth Mother* is the re-grouped Four Mothers Movement, which was instrumental in ending the Israeli occupation of Lebanon. The Fifth Mother does outreach to centrist women with a "soft" (not "radical") political message, such as "war is not my language."
- The women of *MachsomWatch* seek to reduce the physical abuse and humiliation of Palestinians that often takes place at checkpoints (*machsomim*) erected to enforce closures. The presence of these women watching and reporting is sometimes enough to prevent problems. A MachsomWatch woman once stopped a soldier from firing at a child by deflecting his gun, leading to her arrest for "interfering with the IDF" (the Israeli Defense Force).
- *Neled* women, living near the old border with Palestine, run co-existence programs for women on both sides of the border.
- *New Profile* broke new ground in Israel by raising awareness about the heightened militarism in Israeli society, which is often invisible because of its very pervasiveness. New Profile supports men and women who refuse to do military service, and encourages other formats of "refusal": "We refuse to raise our children for war, to ignore war crimes committed in our name, to continue our normal lives while others are suffering because of us."
- *Noga* is a feminist journal that publishes news and analysis of issues in Israel and abroad from a feminist perspective.

(continued on next page)

(continued)

- *TANDI: Movement of Democratic Women for Israel* is the oldest of the groups, founded in 1948, when Israel was founded. It runs workshops and programs to empower and mobilize disadvantaged Palestinian women who are citizens of Israel.
- *WILPF* is the Israeli chapter of the Women's International League for Peace and Freedom, and maintains our connection with this important international network.
- Last, and best known, *Women in Black* refers to groups of women (and the men who join us) who hold one-hour vigils on busy crossroads in Israel every Friday, dressed in black and calling for an end to the occupation. The international movement of Women in Black, which began in Jerusalem, has twice been nominated for the Nobel Peace Prize.

SIDEBAR #2

The principles of the Coalition of Women for Peace were formulated at a meeting on November 8, 2000:

- An end to the occupation.
- The full involvement of women in negotiations for peace.
- Establishment of the state of Palestinian side-by-side with the state of Israel based on the 1967 borders.
- The recognition of Jerusalem as the shared capital of two states.
- Israel must recognize its share of responsibility for the results of the 1948 war and cooperate in finding a just solution for the Palestinian refugees.
- Opposition to the militarism that permeates Israeli society.
- Equal rights for women and all residents of Israel.
- Social and economic justice for Israel's citizens and integration in the region.

73

WOMEN'S HUMAN RIGHTS:
It's about Time!

RITA ARDITTI

Rita Arditti is a member of the faculty of the Graduate College of the Union Institute and University. She was born and grew up in Argentina and lives in the United States. She has been active in the women's movement since the late sixties and learned about Human Rights doing support work for the Argentine Human Rights movement in the eighties. She is the author of *Searching for Life: The Grandmothers of the Plaza de Mayo and the Disappeared Children of Argentina* (University of California Press, 1999).

> *The advancement of women and the achievement of equality between women and men are a matter of human rights and a condition for social justice and should not be seen in isolation as a women's issue. They are the only way to build a sustainable, just and developed society. Empowerment of women and equality between women and men are prerequisites for achieving political, social, economic, cultural and environmental security among all peoples.*
>
> PLATFORM FOR ACTION, ARTICLE 41,
> FOURTH WORLD CONFERENCE ON WOMEN, BEIJING, 1995.

At the first meeting of a five-day seminar on Women and Human Rights that I was leading for doctoral students, one of the two men attending expressed deep skepticism about the need to discuss Human Rights through the lens of women's experiences. Didn't the Universal Declaration of Human Rights apply to everybody? Didn't Article 1 of the Declaration state that "All human beings are born free and equal in dignity and rights?" So, what was the fuss all about? Why was Women and Human Rights even a topic worthy of exploration? As far as he was concerned, we would be wasting our time.

When I recovered from my surprise at his attitude I offered a "yes, but . . ." answer that got me more or less intact through that first session. For the rest of the seminar, however, his questions stayed with me, forcing me to clarify, expand, examine, and connect in new ways each topic discussed. By the end of the seminar, I was happy to hear that he had changed his mind. He found the

Rita Arditti, "Women's Human Rights: It's about Time!" Reprinted with the permission of the author.

seminar to be a mind expanding experience and expressed his appreciation for the new insights he gathered. I believe that the shock I experienced because of his bluntness at the beginning of the seminar forced me to dig deeper and do a better job. For that, I thank him.

I hope that this article will be useful to others who, like him, have questions about the relevance of the topic and to those who already believe that women's rights must be an integral part of the human rights paradigm and want to convince others to join them in this belief.

The Universal Declaration of Human Rights

The Universal Declaration of Human Rights, adopted in 1948 by the United Nations starts by asserting that freedom, justice, and peace in the world depend upon the recognition of human dignity and the rights of all members of the human family.[1] It then goes on to spell out a variety of political, civic, social, cultural and economic rights in its 30 articles. Political and civic rights have received most of the attention in the West, while economic, social, and cultural rights have been seen with suspicion, as if not fully qualifying as human rights. For people in the global South, however, this distinction does not make sense and it is because of their unrelenting insistence that now official UN circles have started more and more to pay attention to those rights.

According to the Declaration, all human beings have "inherent dignity," are "born free and equal," are "endowed with reason and conscience," and are " entitled to all the rights and freedoms set forth in this Declaration." Rights are not earned or conferred; they are part and parcel of the human condition. We have those rights by the very fact of our existence, simply because we are born, and the respect for those rights is considered essential to create a free, just, and peaceful world. Moreover, human rights are seen as indivisible and interdependent—they constitute a whole where each right is linked to the others and necessary for the full realization of the principles embodied in the Declaration.

Yes, my learner was right, the Declaration (and later UN documents since 1948) in its final written form, applies to all human beings. However, since its inception, the Declaration has struggled with the issue of women and its inclusion in the human rights framework.[2] Language was one of the first important issues that needed to be addressed. Originally article 1 read *"All men are brothers . . ."* Hansa Mehta, a legislator from India and a member of the Human Rights commission working on the Declaration, fought against the use of exclusionary language and warned the commission that the wording in article 1 would be construed so as to exclude women.[3] She eventually convinced her colleagues and in 1948, at the last meeting of the Commission, *"All human beings"* was the term accepted, though strangely enough the rest of the Declaration remains written in non-inclusive language ("man," "brotherhood," "his," "him").

Indeed, a brief history of the rights of women in the United Nations reveals that though equality between the sexes was asserted in the basic human rights documents, in practice women's rights were marginalized and not considered part of the human rights paradigm.[4] It was not until 1979, when the United Nations adopted the Convention on the Elimination of All Forms of Discrimination Against Women (CEDAW), that the rights of women were finally enshrined in the transnational human rights perspective.

Feminists from around the world were of course interested in the human rights conversation at the international level and participated and followed it attentively from its beginning. There is now a vast literature on women and human rights from legal and activist perspectives at the international and local levels. In this article I can simply mention a few of the many contributions that I have found especially useful because of the clarity with which they express the author's viewpoints and because they seem representative of many of the discussions held through the years.

Are Human Rights Only for Men?

When feminists started to question the lack of attention to women's rights in the human rights paradigm and asserted that women's rights were not those of a "special" interest group but belonged at the center of the human rights conversation, they identified at least three themes that threw some light on this critical issue. One was the separation between public and private life which is considered "normal" in most societies; the second was the hidden issues associated with the power differential that permeate the relations between men and women in the great majority of cultures; and the third was the gap between the ideals of the UN documents[5] and its practical implementation by a largely male establishment.

The separation of the public and private spheres is a given in patriarchal societies and ensures the control of women by men within different groups and at all levels. The male, as head of the household rules home life and the individual *right to privacy*, an important human right, is often interpreted as if in the familial sphere there should **not be** governmental or community interference. The *right to privacy*, which includes the right to choose with whom one associates and deals with all reproductive decisions, becomes instead the right of men to control their "private" families. In other words, the human rights of women are not protected in the home with the result that the intimate relations between men and women follow a rigid hierarchical pattern and are left out of the human rights framework.[6] As for the public sphere, civil and political rights, which are concerned with the right to life, seem primarily directed at the protection of men in public life. As such they do not address the many life-threatening situations that women encounter all over the world, like infanticide, malnutrition, reproductive health hazards, illegal abortion, less access to health care, trafficking, forced prostitution and many other forms of violence.[7]

The second theme, that of the power differential between men and women, manifests itself in the persistent discrimination against women in practically all spheres of life, in the violence aimed at maintaining women in a subordinate role, and in the dismissal of that pattern as a private or cultural matter. Charlotte Bunch, among others, saw violence against women as a political issue which resulted from the ". . . structural relationships of power, domination and privilege between women and men in society" (491). Bunch located women's bodies as the physical territory of this political struggle, as demonstrated by the resistance to allow control of women's bodies to women and the plethora of laws and regulations that ensure the physical subjugation of women to men.[8]

And on the topic of implementation of women's human rights by the international law-making institutions that developed and support the traditional human rights framework, feminists pointed out that these institutions are very male-dominated "rendering suspect the claim of the objectivity and universality of international human rights law" (103).[9] For instance, the International Court of Justice, (also known as the World Court) in The Hague, the principal judicial organ of the UN, with 15 elected judges, has only one woman member as of 2004. And the International Law Commission, established by the UN General Assembly in 1947 to promote the progressive development of international law and its codification, with 34 members, elected its very first woman member only in 2001. As for the UN Secretariat, which carries on the day-to-day work of the organization, women hold 32.7 percent of the positions at the senior level. All in all, there is an over-representation of men, which extends also to the committees that monitor the implementation of human rights treaties.[10] Implementation is an especially important issue in order to make declarations and treaties truly effective in the lives of women.

Recognizing that women's rights are human rights is an ongoing and arduous process and an agenda for struggle. New themes and areas of activism continue to arise as a result of this awareness and contribute to deepen and widen the human rights conversation in the near and far future. In the next section I address some of the activism that has both propelled and emerged from the women's human rights agenda.

Women's Transnational Organizing

For the past 25 years women activists from all over the world, but particularly from the global South, have played an increasingly important role in the recognition of the rights of women as part of the human rights framework. The *First United Nations Decade for Women* which took place in 1976–1985 marked an explicit commitment to women's issues and in the midpoint of the decade, in 1979, the General Assembly adopted the *Convention for the Elimination of All Forms of Discrimination Against Women* (CEDAW).[11] This Convention expressly addresses violations of the human rights of women and it represents a truly major step in the struggle for the recognition of women's rights as human rights. Its preamble and 30 articles are widely and rightly seen as an international bill of rights for women. Its first article sets the tone of the document by defining discrimination against women as

> "any distinction, exclusion, or restriction made on the basis of sex, which has the effect or purpose of impairing or nullifying the recognition, enjoyment or exercise by women, irrespective of their marital status, on a basis of equality of men and women, of human rights and fundamental freedom in the political, economic, social, cultural, civil, or any other field."

From this first article flows the rest of the document, specifying concrete steps to end discrimination against women and requiring action in all fields to advance women's human rights. Significantly, the Convention is the "only human rights treaty which affirms the reproductive rights of women and targets culture and tradition as influential forces shaping gender roles and family relations."[12] Just to give an idea of some of its salient points: CEDAW requires the end of traffic in women and the exploitation of prostitutes; mandates equal rights of women and men regarding their nationality and that of their children; demands equal access for women to family benefits, credit, bank loans, sports and cultural life; focuses on the problems of rural women; guarantees equality before the law and equal access to administer property; requires steps to ensure equality in marriage and family relations, etc. CEDAW should be read in its entirety to fully appreciate its comprehensiveness. CEDAW has been ratified by 179 countries as of October 2004.[13]

Since the 1975 UN World Conference on Women in Mexico City, marking International Women's Year, women activists from all over the planet have converged not only at the UN Women's conferences in Copenhagen (1980), Nairobi (1985), and Beijing (1995), but also at the UN World conferences on Environment and Development (Rio de Janeiro, 1992), Human Rights (Vienna, 1993) and Population and Development (Cairo, 1994), pressing for the recognition of women's rights as human rights in all spheres of life. Many voices have convincingly argued that thanks to the persistent work of these activists, the UN global conferences have successfully incorporated gender analysis into areas previously considered "gender-neutral" and that this "gendering the agenda"[14] has greatly contributed to the recognition of women's rights. In other words, gender has now become part and parcel of the important global conversations in all spheres of life, such as war, peace, health, development, militarism, security, globalization, etc.

In 1995, twenty years after the first Women's conference, 3,000 women participated in the official UN Fourth World Conference on Women in Beijing, China, and over 30,000 attended the parallel NGO (non-governmental organizations) forum. Out of this conference emerged another significant document, the Platform for Action (PfA), which acknowledges the continual barriers to women's empowerment and calls on governments, NGOs and the private sector to take action. It highlights 12 critical areas of concern which are interrelated, interdependent, and considered "high priority."[15] They are worth listing because they present a succinct summary of the main issues that impede the incorporation of women as full members of society all over the world and provide a map that helps inspire us and remind us of what still needs to be done. They are:

- The persistent and increasing burden of poverty on women
- Inequalities and inadequacies in and unequal access to education and training
- Inequalities and inadequacies in and unequal access to health care and related services
- Violence against women
- The effects of armed or other kinds of conflict on women, including those living under foreign occupation
- Inequality in economic structures and policies, in all forms of productive activities and in access to resources
- Inequality between men and women in the sharing of power and decision-making at all levels
- Insufficient mechanisms at all levels to promote the advancement of women
- Lack of respect for and inadequate promotion and protection of the human rights of women
- Stereotyping of women and inequality in women's access to and participation in all communication systems, especially in the media
- Gender inequalities in the management of natural resources and in the safeguarding of the environment
- Persistent discrimination against and violation of the rights of the girl child.

The Beijing conference was also the scenario of the emerging backlash that the success of the transnational women's movement has generated. Well organized conservative right-wing groups from various countries (including the United States) framed women's rights as threats to family, nation, and God.[16] This countermovement objected to issues such as reproductive rights and LGBT rights, and engaged in a vigorous defense of traditional marriage and family arrangements. Women's rights were portrayed as an attempt to discount and take over national and religious values. In spite of this backlash, the conference managed to produce the PfA, which was signed by more than 180 governments although several countries expressed reservations about language that seemed to support abortion or alternative family structures.

Furthermore, in addition to this backlash, globalization and the huge influence of the United States in the international scene have allowed for direct impact on the lives of women all over the world, making more necessary than ever the transnational organizing for women's rights. Consider for instance, the Global Gag Rule. President Bush's first action when he took power in 2001 was to stop all United States financing to the United Nations Population Fund (UNPF) allegedly because the Fund "promotes" abortion. This was undoubtedly an attempt to impose conservative U.S. policies on the rest of the world and is in direct violation of women's reproductive and sexual health as explicitly addressed in the UN Conference on Population and Development in Cairo in 1994. The Global Gag Rule "denies health organizations in countries that receive US family planning monies the right to use their own, non–U.S. funds to perform abortions (even where legal), provide abortion counseling or referrals or advocate to change abortion laws."[17] This has had huge consequences for the health and lives of women in the poorest parts of the world and has prompted a solidarity campaign started by two women in the United States, Lois Abraham and Jane Roberts, to raise $34 million, one dollar at a time, to make up the funds that have been denied to the UNPF.[18]

One encouraging example of women's transnational organizing has been the case of the International Criminal Court (ICC) based in The Hague. The Rome Statute, the creating document for the ICC, raised the standards of responding to crimes against women by recognizing rape, sexual slavery, enforced prostitution, forced pregnancy, enforced sterilization and sexual violence as war crimes and crimes against humanity. Of the 18 judges elected last year, seven are women. This is an unprecedented proportion in international law circles and reflects the successful work of the Women's Caucus for Gender Justice whose mission is "strengthening advocacy in Women's Human Rights and international justice."[19]

Women's Rights and Cultural Relativism

The debates about the universality versus relativism of human rights have been going on since the UN started to work on the Declaration. Are human rights truly universal or are they relative to culture/religion/or nation? In fact, even before the Universal Declaration of Human Rights had been adopted by the UN, the American Anthropological Association wrote to the Human Rights Commission expressing concern about the limitations of a "statement of rights conceived only in terms of the values prevalent in the countries of Western Europe and America."[20] Much work has taken place around this issue with contributions by historians, philosophers, activists, and public intellectuals from many different cultural and religious backgrounds.

However, the central themes of the Declaration, based on the dignity and common humanity of all people, have generally held strong while allowing for differences in implementation and emphasis. This has been reinforced by the 1993 UN Vienna Declaration on Human Rights which states that human rights "must be considered in the context of a dynamic and evolving process of international norm-setting, bearing in mind the significance of national and regional particularities and various historical, cultural and religious backgrounds."[21] At the same time, the Vienna conference became the focus for organizing the worldwide Global Campaign for Women's Human Rights which brought to the international scene the idea that "women's rights are human rights." As a result, the *Vienna Declaration and Programme of Action* states that "The human rights of women and of the girl-child are an inalienable, integral and indivisible part of universal human rights."[22]

It seems though that in practice, over and over again the universality of human rights is particularly challenged when applied to women. The resistance to women's rights often takes the form of adopting a cultural relativism viewpoint and claiming that women's position in the private sphere leaves women outside the human rights framework. Specific abuses of women such as sexual slavery, genital mutilation,[23] forced marriage, systematic rape, violence in the home, discrimination at many levels, etc., continue unabated worldwide.

Many factors come into play in the discussion of universality and relativism particularly because of the history of Western colonialism, national resistance movements, and the role of women in transmitting culture. Women are seen in most societies as the bearers and reproducers of culture and as such they carry a special weight in terms of maintaining tradition and group identity. Equating women with culture often manifests itself in traditional legal systems (sometimes referred as "customary laws") that discriminate against women in family life—i.e. divorce, inheritance, marriage, child custody, property ownership, etc. How to deal with the tension between women's rights as articulated in CEDAW and various cultural and religious systems can be a frustrating matter and as such it has been the focus of intense discussions. One thing that has emerged from these conversations is the need to avoid the "arrogant gaze" of the outsider (i.e. the West) and be extremely aware of the strategies used when trying to modify or eradicate cultural practices that harm women.[24]

I will illustrate the complexity of the issue by looking at a particular situation that was useful to me because it allowed me to think and learn about these issues in a concrete fashion. In March 2002, Amina Lawal, a poor Muslim woman in her early thirties was sentenced to death by stoning by a lower Shari'a court in the Katsina state of northern Nigeria, allegedly because of adultery. Married at age 14, she was divorced and at a later stage she became pregnant and had a baby daughter.[25] This case attracted considerable international attention. Petitions to the president of Nigeria, Olusegun Obasanjo, and the Minister of Justice, Kanu Godwin Agabi, were circulated and gathered millions of signatures asking that the death penalty be suspended. I signed several of these petitions and encouraged others to do so.

However, on May of 2003, BAOBAB for Women's Human Rights in Nigeria (a HR organization working on the case in Nigeria) posted a letter on the Internet asking people to stop the international Amina Lawal protest letter campaigns. The reasons for this request were many and varied, including the fact that many of the letters in circulation were inaccurate and could even damage Amina Lawal's situation because of the backlash they could create. They pointed out that in a similar case some time ago, a sentence of flogging was carried out illegally and with no notice, deliberately to defy international pressure. A clear example of letters being inaccurate was a letter stating that Amina Lawal was set to be stoned on a certain date, August 27, 2003, (which was the date of her appeal) and that the Nigerian Supreme Court had upheld her sentence. BAOBAB clarified that the Amina Lawal case was still being appealed at the State Shari'a Court of Appeal and that if the appeal was not successful she would appeal to the Federal Shari'a Court and if that was also unsuccessful it would go to the Supreme Court of Nigeria. In other words, there was no imminent threat of executing the sentence and the appeal process had not been exhausted. Moreover, BAOBAB pointed out that they had never lost an appeal process and that it is the lower courts that are the most conservative and repressive in Nigeria. They explained that when petitions with inaccurate information are circulated, they damage the credibility of the local activists because everyone assumes that they have provided the information to the international networks. Furthermore they pointed out that the strategy they were pursuing through an appeal strengthens the local groups, sends the message that people have a right to appeal and challenge injustices successfully, and makes clear that the conviction should not have been made in the first place. They also argued that a successful appeal is more powerful than a pardon because a pardon means that the person was guilty but the state is willing to forgive them.

Another problem with some of the letters was/is that often the international media presents Islam as being incompatible with human rights and this helps foster racism and support right-wing and conservative elements in the West. The petitions may be seen as fostering those attitudes also. Condemning a whole faith because of the behavior of some extremist factions does not help local progressive movements and gives license to these factions which can seriously threaten the life and safety of the victims and those who support them. Vigilante groups are a real problem in Nigeria and can act quickly when they have an excuse to do so and Western criticism may provide such an excuse. BAOBAB and other local groups asked for international solidarity and respect for the wishes of the local activists involved with the issues on the ground and that those interested in supporting cases like the Amina Lawal case get in touch with them to discuss strategies of solidarity and support. They welcomed resources, in terms of expertise, exchanges of information, knowledge of similar situations and money to support the victims and to pay for the expenses of the appeal process. Eventually Amina Lawal's sentence was overturned by the Shari'a Federal Court and the charges against her dropped.[26]

This experience was an eye-opener for me and an opportunity to increase my sensitivity to and understanding of how to work on international issues and be able to offer support from a more informed position. As a result I now feel that caution and in-depth research about local activism will be my first concern before I leap into action when I learn about situations in countries and cultures with which I am unfamiliar. In the Amina Lawal case, I stopped signing petitions and instead sent money to BAOBAB to support their work. In retrospect I marvel about my own naivete. Thanks to the Internet, I regularly read news about Argentina both in the Argentine and U.S. media, which keeps me in touch with my country of origin. I know all too well how differently news is portrayed in each country and how the lack of historical and cultural perspectives distorts the news, even in the case of well intentioned observers. The distortions range from egregious errors over simple facts to cultural assumptions and generalizations which are frequently laughable.

Clearly, cultural beliefs, attitudes, and values have often been used to justify the oppression of women. Justifications such as "this is how we do things, this is part of our culture," negate the fact that cultures are dynamic entities, that what is acceptable today is different from what was acceptable 100 years ago (i.e., slavery, foot-binding, widow-burning, etc.). Resistance to cultural change is hard to overcome but we cannot give up and accept practices that deny women basic human rights. Furthermore, extremist positions often present themselves as the "true" bearers of culture in spite of the fact that there are different ideologies and deep contradictions within the cultures themselves. Supporting local activists to engage in "internal dialogue," since women do not speak with only one voice, followed by external dialogue with the transnational women's movement, seems a prudent strategy, though at times admittedly a slow and frustrating one, in furthering the recognition of women's rights.

Bringing Beijing to the U.S.

What about the U.S. and women's human rights? The concept of human rights is still foreign to the majority of the population in this country and a poll in 1997 showed that 92 percent of people interviewed had never heard of the Universal Declaration of Human Rights.[27] Many people think that violations of women's human rights take place only abroad and discount the necessary and continuous work that hundreds of organizations perform locally everyday to uphold women's human rights in the United States. As Loretta Ross, founder of the Atlanta-based National Center for Human Rights Education has perceptively said:

"Most people still think of Human Rights as letter-writing campaigns to help free political prisoners. Few people realize that women's movements, the anti-war and anti-poverty movements, disability rights and even the environmental justice movement have supporting language in the Universal Declaration of Human Rights."[28]

In the United States, violence against women takes place in both private and public spheres and is compounded by other factors such as race, ethnicity, class, sexual orientation, disability, and age. Violence against women manifests itself in sexual harassment in school and workplace, sexual abuse, forced prostitution, battering, marital rape, and domestic violence. Domestic violence has gained some attention because of the work of committed activists who have brought the issue into the open.[29] But is domestic violence the only form of violence we should worry about? If we focus exclusively on that issue and do not look also at the social context it is easy to forget that domestic violence takes place in a society that systematically discriminates against women economically, legally, and culturally.

Clearly, in the United States as in the rest of the world, we must look at all the aspects in the culture that erode women's human rights. So, when we talk about women and violence we need to remember the violence against women in prison in the form of rape, sexual assault, groping during body searches, shackling during childbirth and general medical neglect.[30] We need to be aware of the control of women's sexuality and reproductive choice, which affects particularly poor women, and of the increased vulnerability of women to the AIDS epidemic because of the refusal of men to wear condoms. And most glaringly, we need to examine the total impunity for the perpetrators of these actions. In fact, often, the reactions to many of these abuses is to "blame the victim" and to ostracize and shame those who have the courage to speak up about the abuses that they have suffered.

Introducing the human rights framework in the United States will allow us to have an integrated perspective within which any violation of women's human rights will be seen as part of the larger denial of humanity to women. Such a perspective will end the fragmentation and separation of the various types of human rights abuses. It will take us out of the "single-issue" focus and enable coalitions and multi layered campaigns to emerge, zeroing in on the denial of women's dignity in its many manifestations, and fostering transnational connections and a better understanding of the global forces that affect women's rights in the United States.[31]

In the case of women's reproductive and sexual health rights, for instance, it is becoming increasingly clear how these rights, locally and internationally, are connected to economic justice and that they must be linked to grassroots organizing and a campaign to end poverty. Otherwise they remain abstract and unattainable.[32] Another prime example which powerfully illustrates the intersection of various forms of human rights violations in the United States is that of women on welfare, where gender, race, and poverty come together to ensure that poor single mothers of color are blamed and punished for their situations. In 1996, under President Clinton, the PRWORA (Personal Responsibility Work Opportunity Reconciliation Act) known as "welfare reform" was passed and the welfare system known as Temporary Assistance for Needy Families (TANF) was established. Practically all the critical areas listed in the Beijing Platform for Action are violated by this "welfare reform."

The majority of people currently on welfare are poor mothers of color. Study after study shows that family homelessness and hunger have continued to increase and that the low-wage work available for women with limited education leaves them in an extremely vulnerable situation.[33] The act punishes young single mothers, is based on a patriarchal view of the family which promotes marriage as the solution, and contains especially harsh measures against legal immigrants. As Gwendolyn Mink points out, TANF fosters women's dependency on individual men ". . . by sanctioning mothers with mandatory work outside the home if they remain single. Mothers who are married do not have to work outside the home, even though they receive welfare, for labor market work by only one parent in a two parent family satisfies TANF's work requirements."[34] TANF requires mothers to "reveal the identity of her child's father and must pursue a child support order against him." It also pressures women to open their families to biological fathers and promotes their involvement, regardless of poor mothers' understanding and judgement of what is best for themselves and their children. TANF also lets states who have "family cap" policies withhold benefits from children born to mothers on welfare. By dismissing women's caregiving work, forcing women into the labor market and increasing their dependence on men, TANF reduces poor mothers on welfare to creatures who are denied any opportunity for growth or nourishment that would help them on their path to strength, freedom, and independence.

Not surprisingly, the movement for the recognition of economic rights as human rights continues to grow in the United States and organizations like the Kensington Welfare Rights Union in Philadelphia, founded in 1991, have received well deserved national and international attention for their organizing efforts. The inspired leadership of their founder, Cheri Honkala, has taken their case to the Organization of American States and to the UN accusing the U.S. government of human rights violation on the issues of welfare, health care, and housing. They have used for their education campaigns: articles 23, (right to desirable work and to join trade unions), article 25 (right to an adequate living standard) and article 26 (right to education) from the Universal Declaration to shift the attention from scarcity to greed: "We say that scarcity is not the issue — greed is."[35]

Finally, and furthermore, the United States has an extremely poor record in terms of ratification of the international treaties that provide the legal framework for the application of the rights articulated in the Universal Declaration. The United States has voted against the creation of the International Criminal Court (ICC), and has not ratified the Covenant on Economic, Social and Cultural Rights (ICESCR), or the Convention on the Elimination of All Forms of Discrimination Against Women (CEDAW), or the Convention on the Rights of the Child (CRC) as well as other important treaties. As a result of this inertia, social activists have started pursuing the possibility of local treaty implementation, bypassing the mammoth federal bureaucracy and harsh resistance of archaic legislators, who keep yawning at the mention of treaty ratification. The city of San Francisco adopted CEDAW in 1998 and codified it into law raising the eyebrows of the political establishment nationwide. In 2003, San Francisco finished its five-year implementation plan and one of its accomplishments has been a "gender analysis" of selected city departments and legislation turning the Commission on the Status of Women into a permanent city department. Obstacles remain regarding implementation, compliance, and analysis of the intersectionality of gender with other forms of discrimination, due to race and class. But there is a general sense that the local understanding of human rights has increased and the creation of a five-year Action Plan in 2003 calls for establishing an anti-discrimination committee reporting directly to the local authorities, advocating for resources and acting as liaison with similar efforts elsewhere.[36]

Inspired by the San Francisco experience, the Human Rights Initiative was born in New York City in 2002 attempting to obtain local ratification for CEDAW and for CERD (Convention on the Elimination of All Forms of Racial Discrimination). A broad coalition of progressive groups is at the heart of the coalition and the hope is to introduce legislation by 2005. When passed, the Initiative is expected to counteract discrimination against women of color, the most marginalized population in the city. And yet another local effort has recently been started in Massachusetts, the Mass CEDAW Project.[37]

Much remains to be done. Education about human rights in the United States is at the beginning stages. The resistance to the application of the human rights framework to problems in the United States, (sometimes called "U.S. exceptionalism") has been hard to overcome, but there are hopeful signs on the horizon. A plethora of groups has emerged in the last ten years or so, trying to connect the local with the global, understanding that fragmentation and isolation are convenient tools for the maintenance of privilege and injustice.[38]

Local initiatives for ratification of treaties, human rights education in schools and universities, and a growing interest from activist groups to integrate the human rights framework in their work give me reasons for optimism. One of the women responsible for the introduction of the city ordinance in San Francisco, Krishanti Dharmaraj, who is also one of the founders of the Women's Institute for Leadership Development for Human Rights, has said: "I do not know how else to do social change in this complex world but to do human rights."[39] Her phrase summarizes well the hope and promise of the human rights framework. It simply reasserts the original and powerful insights first articulated in the Universal Declaration. It continually reminds us of the indivisibility and interdependence of human rights so that truly ALL women will be included in the struggles against discrimination, exploitation, and violence. Linking the local to the global will strengthen our movement for justice for all and put human dignity at the forefront of the struggle.

Like the quote at the beginning of this article from the Beijing Platform of Action states, the advancement of women and the full recognition of our humanity is the only way to build a sustainable, just and developed society. So, let's get to work!

NOTES

1. The work of Eleanor Roosevelt, as chair of the Human Rights committee which drafted the Declaration, was instrumental for its adoption by the UN General Assembly. See Glendon, Mary Ann. 2001. *A World Made New: Eleanor Roosevelt and the Universal Declaration of Human Rights.* Random House: New York. The book includes various drafts of the Declaration and the final version.

2. Ibid. See pages 90–93; 111–112; 153–154; 162; 164; 177.

3. Ibid. See page 90.

4. Reanda, Laura. Spring 1981. "Human Rights and Women's Rights: The United Nations Approach." *Human Rights Quarterly* 3, No. 2: 11–31.

5. The Universal Declaration is simply that, a declaration, and it is not legally binding. Two UN Covenants were eventually drafted to implement the principles of the Declaration: the Covenant on Civil and Political Rights and the Covenant on Economic, Social and Cultural Rights. Nations that ratify these covenants are legally bound to enforce the implementation of the human rights listed in the covenants.

6. Eisler, Riane. Spring 1987. "Human Rights: Toward an Integrated Theory for Action." *Human Rights Quarterly.* 25–46. See also Gerda Lerner. 1986. *The Creation of Patriarchy.* Oxford University Press: New York, NY.

7. Charlesworth, Hilary. 1995. "Human Rights as Men's Rights." In *Women's Rights, Human Rights: International Feminist Perspectives,* edited by Julie Peters and Andrea Wolper. 103-113. Routledge, New York, NY. Women, though, have also taken leadership roles in the movement for the protection of civic and political rights worldwide. See for instance, Bouvard, Marguerite Guzman. 1996. *Women Reshaping Human Rights: How Extraordinary Activists Are Changing the World and Revolutionizing Motherhood: The Mothers of the Plaza de Mayo.* 1994. Both published by Scholarly Resources, Wilmington, Delaware; Arditti, Rita. 1999. *Searching for Life: The Grandmothers of the Plaza de Mayo and the Disappeared Children of Argentina.* 1999. Berkeley: University of California Press; Clements, Alan. 1997. *The Voice of Hope: Conversations with Aung San Suu Kyi.* New York: Seven Stories Press; and many others.

8. Bunch, Charlotte. 1990. "Women's Rights as Human Rights: Toward a Re-Vision of Human Rights." *Human Rights Quarterly* 12, No. 4: 486–498.

9. See note 7, p 103.

10. Charlesworth, Hilary. 2002. "The Hidden Gender of International Law." *16 Temp.Int'l & Comp. L.J. 93.*

11. In 1976, the United Nations Development Fund for Women (UNIFEM) was created to provide financial support for innovative projects mainly directed at rural and poor urban women in developing countries. For CEDAW, see Tinker, Catherine. Spring 1981. "Human Rights for Women: The UN Convention on the Elimination of All forms of Discrimination Against Women" *Human Rights Quarterly* 3, No. 2: 32–43.

12. www.un.org/womenwatch/daw/cedaw/cedaw/htm.

13. Many states that have ratified the Convention have done so with "reservations," some of which are quite substantial and compromise the integrity of the convention. For more on this important point see Cook, Rebecca, "Reservations to the Convention on the Elimination of All Forms of Discrimination Against Women," 1990. *Va.J. Int'l L.* 30: 643–716.

    An interesting addition to CEDAW is the "Optional Protocol," a separate treaty which countries that have ratified CEDAW can also sign. It allows a woman whose rights have been violated to bring her claims to the U.N. and her government will have to answer her claim at the international level. 39 countries have signed on to the Optional Protocol.

14. Friedman, Elizabeth Jay. 2003. "Gendering the Agenda: The Impact of the Transnational Women's Rights Movement at the UN conferences of the 1990s". *Women's Studies International Forum* 26, No. 4: 313–331.

15. www.un.org/womenwatch/daw/beijing/platform

16. See note 14 and Butler, Jennifer. 2002. "New Sheriff in Town: The Christian Right Shapes U.S. Agenda at the United Nations." *The Public Eye.* XVI, No. 2: 14–22.

17. Petchesky, Rosalind. 2004, June. www.radiofeminista.net./junio04/notas/cairo +10-ing3.htm. Washington, Joi. "The U.S., Rowing Against the Tide." *National Women's Health Network.* 29, Issue 3: 3.

18. www.34millionfriends.org

19. The Women's Caucus for Gender Justice has changed its name to "Women's Initiatives for Gender Justice" and their web address is: www.iccwomen.org. For more info on the ICC go to: www.icc-cpi.int and www.iccnow.org.

20. American Anthropological Association, "Statement on Human Rights," 49 *American Anthropologist* 539 (1947). Quoted in Glendon, Mary Ann, see note 1, p. 222.

21. Quoted in Steiner, Henry J. and Philip Alston. 1996. *International Human Rights in Context: Law, Politics, Morals.* New York: Oxford University Press. 235.

22. Ibid. 928.

23. The term "genital mutilation" covers a wide range of practices which vary in extent and severity involving women's genitals. Other terms used are "female circumcision," "female genital cutting," and "female genital surgery." Some Western feminists's views on the issue gave rise to a public debate raising issues of colonialism, racism, and simplistic constructions regarding women in the countries where these practices are carried on. See *Genital Cutting and Transnational Sisterhood: Disputing U.S. Polemics.* 2002. Edited by Stanlie M. James and Claire C. Robertson. Urbana and Chicago: University of Illinois Press. Note especially the Prologue, a "Position paper on Clitoridectomy and Infibulation" drafted by the Women's Caucus of the African Studies Association (first appeared in 1983) and Cheryl Chase's essay " 'Cultural Practice' or 'Reconstructive Surgery'? Genital Cutting, the Intersex Movement and Medical Double Standards." See also Nahid Toubia's work, *Female Genital Mutilation: A Call for Global Action.* 1993. Women Ink, and visit www.rainbo.org, the webpage of Research, Action and Information for the Bodily Integrity of Women, an African led international non-governmental organization.

24. Coomaraswamy, Radhika, 2002. "Are Women's Rights Universal? Re-engaging the Local." *Meridians: feminism, race, transnationalism.* 3, No. 1, 1–18. Abdullahi Ahmed An-Na'im. 1994. "State Responsibility Under International Human Rights To Change Religious and Customary Laws" in *Human Rights of Women: National and International Perspectives,* edited by Rebecca J. Cook. Philadelphia: University of Pennsylvania Press.

25. Currently in some states in Northern Nigeria new Shari'a-based penal codes, which apply only to Muslims, have been introduced. According to these laws, pregnancy out of marriage amounts to adultery. The man supposedly responsible for the pregnancy denied having sex with Amina and charges against him were dropped.

26. For a more detailed discussion of this case see "Please Stop the International Amina Lawal Protest Letter Campaigns" at www.whrnet.org/docs/action-03-05-07.html. Arditti, Rita. *Amina Lawal-To Sign or Not To Sign.* www.umb.edu/

human_rights/issues/index. September 25, 2003. Also visit the webpage of Women Living Under Muslin Laws, an international solidarity network: www. wluml.org

27. Hart Survey on Attitudes and Knowledge of Human Rights/Adults. 1997. At www.hrusa.org/features.shtm

28. *Close to Home: Case Studies of Human Rights Work in the United States.* 2004. A Ford Foundation Report. Also at: www.fordfound.org/publication/recent_articles.

29. U.S. Department of Justice, Office of Justice Programs, 2000. "Extent, Nature, and Consequences of Intimate Partner Violence: Findings from the National Violence Against Women Survey." Battered Mothers' Testimony Project at the Wellesley Centers for Women. November 2002. *Battered Mothers Speak Out: A Human Rights Report on Domestic Violence and Child Custody in the Massachusetts Family Courts.*

30. Davis, Angela Y. and Cassandra Shaylor. 2001. "Race, Gender, and the Prison Industrial Complex: California and Beyond" in *Time to Rise: US Women of Color — Issues and Strategies. A Report for the UN World Conference Against Racism, Racial Discrimination, Xenophobia, and Related Intolerance.* Edited by Maylei Blackwell, Linda Burnham, and Jung Hee Choi. Women of Color Resource Center. Berkeley, CA.

31. Mallika Dutt. 1994. *With Liberty and Justice for All: Women's Human Rights in the United States.* Center for Women's Global Leadership. Douglass College, New Brunswick. NJ.

32. Petchesky, Rosalind Pollack. 2000. "Human Rights, Reproductive Health and Economic Justice—Why they are Indivisible." *Reproductive Health Matters,* 8, No. 15. Also at http://urban.hunter.cuny.edu/~respet/RHMedit00.htm.

33. Burnham, Linda. 2002. "Welfare Reform, Family Hardship, and Women of Color" in *Lost Ground: Welfare Reform, Poverty, and Beyond* edited by Randy Albelda and Ann Withorn. Boston: South End Press.

34. Mink, Gwendolyn. 2002. "Violating Women: Rights Abuses in the Welfare Police State" in *Lost Ground,* see note above.

35. see note 28.

36. Ibid.

37. For information on the NYC Human Rights Initiative contact cedawcerdnyc@yahoo.com; for information on the Mass CEDAW Project contact MassCEDAW@yahoo.com.

38. *Something Inside so Strong: A Resource Guide on Human Rights in the United States.* Distributed by the U.S. Human Rights Network. www.ushrnetwork.org. This resource guide was drawn from the Second Leadership Summit on Human Rights in the United States held in July 2002.

39. see note 28.

NAME INDEX

SUBJECT INDEX